JEAN BOUCHET

for Richard

 JEAN BOUCHET

JENNIFER BRITNELL

Published by Edinburgh University Press for the
UNIVERSITY OF DURHAM

© Jennifer Britnell 1986
Edinburgh University Press
22 George Square, Edinburgh
Set in Linotronic Palatino by
Speedspools, Edinburgh, and
printed in Great Britain by
Redwood Burn Limited,
Trowbridge, Wilts
British Library Cataloguing
    in Publication Data
Britnell, Jennifer
Jean Bouchet
1. Bouchet, Jean—
    Criticism and interpretation
I. Title
841'.3   PQ1605.B75
ISBN 0 85224 533 5

Contents

Contents

Acknowledgements

I am grateful to many scholars who have advised me during the preparation of this book, and first and foremost to Dr M. A. Screech and to the late Professor D. P. Walker. They guided the work for my thesis, and continued to be sources of information and inspiration. The annual Renaissance Colloquium meeting at University College London under their aegis was a testing ground for several parts of this book, and I should like to thank its members for their comments and encouragement. My thanks are due to Mr G. Bonner, Dr Cecily Boulding, Professor M. M. McGowan, Miss E. M. Rutson, Dr D. J. Shaw and Madam Jeanne Veyrin-Forrer, all of whom responded most helpfully to my queries; to Professor R. E. Asher, who gave me permission to quote from his thesis; to Mademoiselle Suzanne Bagoly, who has allowed me to benefit from her recent research on Bouchet. My research has been assisted on several occasions by grants from the Staff Travel Fund of the University of Durham, and I am indebted to many librarians, particularly in the British Library, the Bibliothèque Nationale and the Bibliothèque Municipale de Poitiers. Among my colleagues in the University of Durham I am particularly grateful to Professor D. B. Wilson of the French Department, Dr M. M. Harvey of the History Department and Dr A. I. Doyle and Miss E. M. Rainey of the University Library. My special thanks go to Dr Ann Moss and Dr Richard Britnell for reading the manuscript and for patiently providing criticism and advice which has been invaluable.

Introduction

JEAN BOUCHET is well known to students of Renaissance France as the longest surviving *rhétoriqueur* poet. He has found a place in many specialised studies, but no general study of his work has been undertaken since Auguste Hamon's biography in 1901.[1] Hamon's book, although still very useful as an account of Bouchet's life, is by now, after eighty years' work on the French Renaissance, inadequate as an introduction to Bouchet's work. Bouchet, poet, historian, moralist and religious writer, composing works between 1496 and 1557, is recognised to be a significant figure from many different points of view. First of all, although he spent most of his life in Poitiers, he met or corresponded with a large number of important people and is sometimes a unique source of information about them. He appears to have had considerable influence on the development of the production of mystery plays throughout his region of France. From a literary point of view, we can see him as a poet adapting a taste formed before 1500 as he reacts to the changed aesthetics of a different age. In the course of his long life he saw both the early percolation of humanism into France and the first flowering of the French Renaissance, and we find in his work a curious blending of encouragement and resistance to the renewal of classical influence. Finally, the subject matter of most of his work is of interest because it summarises the fruits of his own wide reading and was intended to benefit those who knew no Latin.

Herein lies Bouchet's major importance as a writer. It was his books of information and instruction that won him his widest readership among his contemporaries. He was a populariser of knowledge; legal, moral, historical and theological. He is a determinedly Christian writer in one of the most confused periods of the Church's history, and his success in appealing to readers of religious literature justifies a close consideration of the stance he adopted. He is at once an eloquent critic of the shortcomings of the Church and one of the very earliest writers in French attempting to combat Lutheranism by providing alternative instruction in French. Bouchet intends his instruction to be a summary of the Catholic Church's teaching and his readers accepted it as such; he can therefore be seen as representing in 1530 a body of moderate lay Catholic opinion and thus providing a standard of orthodoxy other than the theologians of the Sorbonne with which to compare writers like Marot, Marguerite de Navarre and his friend, Rabelais.

This study concentrates chiefly on Bouchet's writing. The first chapter summarises what is known of his life, his contacts with other writers, the local nobility and the court, and his activities with regard to royal entries and mystery plays. Thereafter chapters 2, 3 and 4 are devoted to three major areas of his writing: poetry, moral writing and history. In these chapters I discuss his approach and methods in these various types of writing, concentrating on the forms he chooses and the way that his sources are used.

The last three chapters deal with his religious writing and, as a preliminary, with his treatment of religious controversy. Exactly half-way through Bouchet's life Luther nailed his ninety-five theses to the church door at Wittenberg; a few years later Luther had been excommunicated, many of his propositions had been condemned by the Sorbonne, and in France measures began to be taken to repress heresy. Bouchet had already shown a lively interest in Church reform and religious writing before the threat of heresy. In his later career he emerges as an active opponent of heresy while still remaining an outspoken critic of the Church. Chapter 5 is devoted to his treatment of controversial subjects like the need for reform in the Church, Gallicanism, conciliarism and eventually the spread of heresy and the development of evangelical groups in France. This involves examining passages from various types of writing, moral, historical and polemical. Finally, chapters 6 and 7 deal with his religious works, before and after the spread of heresy, attempting to show their significance by setting them in a context of comparable literature and of contemporary controversy.

The earlier chapters thus concentrate on form more than content, whereas the later ones, on religious writing, analyse this important area of his subject matter. In discussing both his moral and his historical writing it has been necessary to leave unexplored many subjects on which the substance of what he says would also repay study. Although in some *rhétoriqueur* poetry the substance cannot be analysed with very great profit because the subject is slight, deliberately conventional, dictated by the expectations of whatever genre is used as by the courtly audience which the writer served, and obviously secondary in interest to the form, Bouchet's case is quite different. He was not a court-based *rhétoriqueur* poet but a provincial *procureur* writing a variety of books that convey information. He wrote in many cases the sort of books that would be useful for his colleagues or his children. His didactic aims permeate all his writing, including his poetry, which, as we shall see, tends to adopt forms consistent with the clear communication of substance. Given

that he was a popular instructive writer, the views he puts forward
in his works represent both an influence on and a reflection of the
climate of opinion at the time. This is not, of course, to suggest that
his subject matter was original; on the contrary, he writes always
with the expressed intention of being conventional and basing himself on sound authority. He also writes in forms of which the contemporary reader did indeed have predictable expectations. Any
useful assessment of what he has to say must therefore proceed
from a consideration of his form and of his sources, and from
comparison with similar works by other writers.

Bouchet himself reveals a sharp sense of difference and even
conflict between form and substance, perhaps induced by the fact
that what he was often trying to do—communicate instruction—
and the art which he cultivated—*la seconde rhétorique*—were not
wholly compatible. Some of his writing is extremely utilitarian,
consciously rejecting the blandishments of elaborate form. And yet
Bouchet's work did not always have the enlightenment of his in-
feriors as its main aim; he had patrons to cultivate and he would
have become a court poet if he could. Thus he appears deeply
concerned with form in verse and prose; he presents himself as
captivated by the Muses, and many a time expresses regret that his
profession prevented him from cultivating poetry more intensively.
No critic who has written on Bouchet has found much good to say
about his verse and I shall make no attempt to reverse their judgements. But it is worth noting that his weakness, apart from prolixity,
lies primarily in an extremely pedestrian use of language, which
bedevils poems that are metrically inventive and interesting in their
overall conception. He writes in a wide variety of carefully calculated forms and has a precise, sometimes very literal, sense of
genre. Judging by the number of times that he defends his occupation of writing, he seems to have had scruples about the legitimacy
of diverting his energies from his profession in reponse to the
seductions of the Muse. The fact that his writing was so obviously
useful to other people no doubt helped to allay these qualms.
Moreover, Christian duty certainly required him to edify his neighbour, and nobody could read Bouchet's works without forming the
impression that the writer was a pious man.

When he mentions the substance of his writing he always dis-
claims any personal element in his subject matter; on the contrary,
he asserts that the value of what he says resides in the fact that he
has taken all his material from good authorities. Very frequently he
makes a statement to the effect that 'il n'y a rien du mien fors
l'invencion',[2] by which he means principally the imaginative framework within which the instruction drawn from authoritative sources
is presented. Always his avowed intention is to present the truth as
found in the sanctified vessels of tradition.

With regard to his use of authorities it should therefore be noted at the outset that, like other vernacular prose authors who write to inform at this period, he looks to the modern eye like a plagiarist. His prose is often a patchwork of quotation from his authorities, usually an abridged translation of someone else's Latin, occasionally French. Exactly the same technique is used by Jean Lemaire de Belges in some of his prose works. In fact the author's role involves keeping a firm hand on the matter and paraphrasing and adapting where necessary, making additions to suit his own purpose and welding together material from different authorities. The finished work is uniquely the author's own when this process is accomplished with skill as it is by Lemaire and by Bouchet, even though any given passage is likely to be condensed translation from another author. In verse, the autonomy of the author is clearer. Here Bouchet less frequently follows other authors closely, but his ideas are still taken from suitable authorities, which are often acknowledged or quoted in a marginal note.

I have concluded this study with two appendixes: one giving notes on Bouchet's friends and acquaintances as recorded particularly in the *Epîtres familières* and in a series of *Epitaphes* in the *Généalogies*, together with some who figure in liminary material in other works; the other deals with the chronology of the *Epîtres familières*. The former is intended to give an impression of his wide acquaintance and also to gather together some of the information about his contemporaries that can be gleaned from his writing. The latter attempts to provide chronological data that may be necessary for using that information.

Throughout this study in quoting from fifteenth- and sixteenth-century texts I have differentiated between i and j, u and v, placed accents on final é, ée, és, ées and à, après, dès, où, etc., supplied cedillas and apostrophes, expanded abbreviations and modernised the punctuation.

The following short titles for Bouchet's works are employed throughout; numbers refer to sections in the bibliography, part one.

Amoureux transi
　　1, *L'Amoureux transy sans espoir* . . . [1503–7?]
Anciennes et modernes
　　13, *Les anciennes et modernes genealogies des Roys de France*, 1528
Angoisses
　　16, *Les Angoysses et remedes d'amour*, 1537
Annales
　　10, *Les Annales d'Acquitaine*, first edition 1524; all references are to the 1557 edition unless otherwise stated

Cantiques
> 9 and 21, *Cantiques et oraisons contemplatives de l'ame penitente*, [MS c.1524]

Chapelet
> 6, *Le Chappellet des princes*, 1517

Déploration
> 3, *La Deploration de l'eglise militante*, 1512

Epître de Marie
> 6, *Epistre de la royne Marie*, 1517

Epître d'Henri
> 4, *Epistre envoyée des Champs Elisées au roy Henry d'Engleterre*, [1512]

Epîtres, élégies
> 15, *Epistres, elegies, epigrammes et epitaphes*, 1535

Epîtres familières, Ep. Fam., Epîtres morales, Ep. Mor.
> 19, *Epistres morales et familieres du Traverseur*, 1545

Forme et ordre
> 18, *Forme et ordre de plaidoirie*, 1542

Généalogies
> 13, The 1545 edition of the *Anciennes et modernes,* which includes several other works

Gén. Ep.
> An *épitaphe* from the series in the *Généalogies*

Histoire de Clotaire
> 7, *L'Histoire et cronicque de Clotaire*, 1518

Jugement
> 17, *Le Jugement poetic de l'honneur femenin*, 1538

Labyrinthe
> 8, *Le Labirynth de Fortune*, 1522

Opuscules
> 11, *Opusculles du Traverseur*, 1525

Panégyrique
> 12, *Le Panegyric du Chevallier sans reproche*, 1527

Renards
> 2, *Les Regnars traversant . . .* [1503–4]

Temple
> 5, *Le Temple de Bonne Renommée*, 1517

Triomphes
> 14, *Les Triumphes de la noble et amoureuse dame*, 1530

Triomphes du roi
> 20, *Triomphes du tres Chrestien . . . roy de France, François premier de ce nom*, 1549

Other abbreviations:

Hamon = A. Hamon, *Un Grand Rhétoriqueur poitevin* . . ., 1901

BN = Bibliothèque Nationale

BL = British Library

PL = *Patrologia Latina*, ed. Migne

BHR = *Bibliothèque d'Humanisme et Renaissance*

RHLF = *Revue d'histoire littéraire de la France*

BSAO = *Bulletin de la Société des Antiquaires de l'Ouest*

MSAO = *Mémoires de la Société des Antiquaires de l'Ouest*

NOTES

1. Auguste Hamon, *Un Grand Rhétoriqueur poitevin, Jean Bouchet, 1476-1557?*, Paris, 1901. Before Hamon's work Bouchet had been included in the collections of authors described by La Croix du Maine, Du Verdier, Colletet, Niceron, Goujet and Dreux du Radier, and he was the subject of a perceptive little study by M. H. Ouvré. Hamon's work has remained the standard authority, together with the inevitably depressing but informative chapter in Henry Guy, *L'Ecole des rhétoriqueurs*, Paris, 1910. But several aspects of Bouchet's work have been covered by modern scholars who have either included him in their treatment of a wider theme (for example, R. E. Asher on early French legendary history, P. M. Smith on the anti-courtier trend, F. Joukovsky on memorial writing and certain mythological themes), or else have examined small sections of his writing (M. Holban on verse from the *Triomphes*, S. Cigada on the *Temple*, my own article on the *Cantiques*). Such detailed studies on precise questions have begun to give a clearer picture of Bouchet's methods of work and of his artistic and didactic aims than was previously discernible from the patronising critics of the early twentieth century. Most recently Paul Zumthor has made some stimulating and illuminating comments on Bouchet in his re-evaluation of the *rhétoriqueurs, Le Masque et la lumière*, Paris, 1978.

2. *Triomphes*, +3 ro; cf. *Ep. Fam.* 41, f.xxxiii ro, col.1.

Bouchet's Life

1
Career[1]

Jean Bouchet was born in Poitiers on 30 January 1476, the son of
Pierre Bouchet, *procureur en court laye à Poitiers*. His father had the
misfortune to die in 1480 from poison intended for somebody else.[2]
Bouchet studied at the Collège de Puygareau, which was attached
to the Faculty of Arts at the University of Poitiers. It is difficult to
establish how far his studies went, but it is likely that he was at least
bachelier ès arts, the basic university grade.[3] At some time in his life
before 1532 he received the tonsure, and this was probably in his
youth.[4]

According to his later views on the matter, he fell prey to the
temptation of the World in adolescence,[5] and went off to the court
hoping to find a royal patron for his poetry. We hear of him accompanying a deputation from Poitiers to the court of Charles VIII at
Lyons in April 1496.[6] He presented some poems to Charles VIII and
was graciously referred to the patronage of Florimond Robertet.[7]
But lack of money soon drove him to Paris to study law by becoming
a clerk to a *procureur*: he was thus a member of the Basoche in Paris.[8]
He seems to have gone to Paris by about 1497, and was certainly
there, with occasional visits to Poitiers, until at least 1503.[9] His first
printed work appeared in Paris in 1503–04. He was back in Poitiers
as a *procureur* by 1507 at the latest, and he remained settled there
exercising this profession for the rest of his life.[10]

As a fully-fledged *procureur*, he was an attorney-at-law: he was
attached to the Law courts at Poitiers and would look after cases for
his clients, supplying the *avocat* with the necessary material and
acting for his client in all transactions concerning a case. He would
also act for a client in matters other than litigation.[11] In a passage of
good advice to his colleagues, Bouchet says that the *procureur* need
only be learned in French.[12] It was a relatively low grade in the legal
profession, certainly requiring no university study of law. Bouchet
must have been much better read than many of his colleagues. The
procureur did, however, need to be well versed in procedure, and

Bouchet concentrates on this aspect of his profession in his one work devoted to a legal subject, the *Forme et ordre de plaidoirie en toutes les cours royalles et subalternes de ce royaulme,* 1542. He revised this work for publication after the ordinance of Villers-Cotterets in 1539, by which styles of procedure had been fixed. It was printed in small format, with roman type and, unusual in Bouchet's works, page rather than folio numbering: it has a clear table of contents and is in short the perfect manual. His stated intention is 'à ce qu'on puisse plus facilement trouver en ung petit volume ce qui est en plusieurs'.[13] His most important clients were Louis de La Trémoille and his family, who also became his principal literary patrons. The Chapter at Chauvigny was another major client.[14]

Materially he prospered. His marriage with Françoise Bonnyot probably took place soon after his return to Poitiers. His wife came from a well-to-do family in Chauvigny and seems to have brought him a fair amount of property.[15] Bouchet eventually owned a country house in the Chauvigny district to which he took his family when there was plague in Poitiers, a frequent occurrence in the 1520s and early 1530s. He also owned a house in the centre of Poitiers. He was a *bourgeois* member of the town council, the *mois et cent*.[16] He is found representing Poitiers in a deputation to the King in 1522, and as a member of a commission examining new bylaws in 1537;[17] he was clearly a man of some importance in the community. He had at least eight children. Three daughters married, one became a nun. His eldest son Gabriel followed his father's profession, beginning to take over his duties with the Chauvigny chapter from 1537. Another son, Joseph, had literary aspirations.[18] The date of Bouchet's death is not known. He was still writing to the Chauvigny chapter in 1554 and the last revised edition of the *Annales d'Acquitaine* came in 1557. His death can probably be placed somewhere between 1557 and 1559, when he was in his eighties.[19] Apart from his work as a *procureur* and the reputation acquired by his writing, he had also achieved local and wider prominence by directing mystery plays in Poitiers. This brought him several requests to do the same elsewhere, although he refused in each case.

2

Works[20]

Although obviously busily employed as a *procureur*, his writing was an enduring interest; he says that he spent at least an hour every day on it, and longer when the plague drove him out of Poitiers to the country.[21] By this he probably meant not only writing but also finding out the material, for Bouchet slowly but surely became a very well-informed man, and perhaps his principal importance as a writer is as a populariser in a variety of fields for the vernacular reader. He began as a *rhétoriqueur* poet. His earliest poems are those

contained in the *Amoureux transy sans espoir*: this motley collection
begins with the love poem that gives the collection its title and goes
on with other pieces including a *Remedium amoris* and two poems
about Charles VIII. One of these supports the King's Italian policy
and is perhaps one of those presented to Charles in 1496; the other
is an epitaph. His first major work was *Les Regnars traversant les
perilleuses voyes des folles fiances du monde*; it was from this title that he
took the name with which he signed his later works, 'le Traverseur
des voies perilleuses'.[22] Leaning heavily on Chartier, Bouchet
tackles the prime moral genre of the *rhétoriqueur*, the review of the
vices of each estate of society, using a mixture of verse and prose.
Under the aegis of Jean d'Auton he entered the field of Gallican and
conciliarist controversy with two poems composed during the war
between Louis XII and Pope Julius II, 1511–13. By this time he was
back in Poitiers and the connection with the La Trémoille family
opened up new opportunities. *Le Chappellet des Princes*, a collection
of moral *ballades* and *rondeaux* was written for the young son of La
Trémoille's heir, the Prince de Talmont, and the *Temple de Bonne
Renommée*, 1517, is a poem in memory of the Prince after his death
from wounds sustained at Marignano.

None of these works of the first part of Bouchet's life distinguishes
him from any other *rhétoriqueur* in search of a patron. But now began
the series of works in which Bouchet's studies started to bear fruit
and he became an important populariser. One after another appeared the historico-hagiographical *Histoire et Cronicque du roi Clotaire* (1518), the philosophical *Labirynth de Fortune* (1522), a collection
of prayers (*c.*1524) and the first edition of his great work, which was
the fruit of many years of labour, the *Annales d'Acquitaine* (1524).
This latter above all assured his reputation; evidence suggests that
he began work on it in about 1514. His two other major works
followed shortly, the enormously successful *Anciennes et modernes
genealogies des rois de France* (1528), in which a portrait of each king is
accompanied by a rhymed history of his reign, and, in 1530, the
Triumphes de la noble et amoureuse dame, a manual of religious instruction taking the form of an allegory of the progress of the soul. This
in its own field is comparable in size and scope to the *Annales*.

At the same time he produced in 1527 a tribute to yet another
dead patron, Louis de La Trémoille, in *Le Panegyric du Chevalier sans
reproche*; perhaps indicative of his historical interests at this time,
the work takes the form of a biography of La Trémoille, largely in
prose but with some verse ornament. The next phase of his production consisted of a number of collections of poetry, none of them
successful on the scale of his popularising works but interesting in
that they chart the evolution of his poetic taste. Some evidence of
this is apparent in the *Opuscules du Traverseur* of 1525, three-quarters
of which consists of reworkings of earlier moral poems. But in the

Epistres, Elegies, Epigrammes et Epitaphes commemorating Renée de Bourbon (1535), *Les Angoysses et remedes d'amour* (1537) and *Le Jugement poetic de l'honneur femenin* (1538) he began to experiment with the new genres of elegy and epigram, and also reworked some of his very early poetry. In the early 1530s he wrote a great deal, some of which was not published until much later. The *Forme et ordre de plaidoirie* of 1542 is another example of popularising, this time for the benefit of his own profession. The *Epistres morales et familières* in 1545 gather together *épîtres* written throughout his life, although most of the *Epîtres morales* were written between 1525 and 1534. In this collection too, change in poetic taste and in style of moralising is evident; a comparison with the *Renards* makes the changes particularly striking. Content too is much richer; fruit of Bouchet's long reading is to be found in these *Epîtres*, which are in their way very learned poems.

Most of Bouchet's works were published in whole or in part more than once by the author, and in most cases he made revisions. The major revisions to his verse were caused by changes in metrical practice after about 1515, but in many cases he went on tinkering even with revised versions. Some poems were revised because he wished to alter the sense. Variants of both form and sense are of great interest, reflecting his reactions to changing tastes and events. In 1545, he seems to have sought to issue definitive editions of the major part of his work. Nearly all his *épîtres* are gathered in the volume just mentioned, and a large proportion of his other poetry is added to the *Anciennes et modernes genealogies* to form the handsome folio volume entitled *Les Genealogies, effigies et epitaphes des roys de France*; this offers the third printed version of some of his poems. In the same year the *Annales*, already corrected and augmented in 1526, 1532 and 1535, received a new edition with further corrections and additions. Bouchet says in an introduction to the *Généalogies* that it is the third of five projected volumes.[23] However, the other two never appeared. The *Triumphes de la noble et amoureuse dame* might have been one of the works that he intended to reissue, but it was readily available in Paris editions. Moreover, having had it carefully checked by theologians before it was published, Bouchet never subsequently altered it in any way.

Apart from a final revision of the *Annales* in 1557 his last work was the *Triomphes du très Chrestien Roy de France* (1549), a long poem inspired by the death of François Ier, which met with little success.

Bouchet published his early works in Paris, but 1518 saw the beginning of a long association with succeeding generations of the Poitiers printers and booksellers de Marnef and Bouchet (not apparently related to the poet).[24] From then all first editions were printed in Poitiers, but other Paris printers continued to print most of his works, particularly those of the 1520s, and between 1536 and 1541 in particular his three major works, the *Annales*, the *Triomphes* and the *Généalogies*, went through several editions in Paris. Thereafter the popularity there of his works ends abruptly, with the exception of the *Triomphes*, which had further editions in 1542, 1545 and 1555. No Paris printer reproduced the poetry collections of the 1530s although, much to Bouchet's annoyance,[25] Denis Janot printed several collections of verse taken from longer works like the *Panégyrique* and the *Triomphes*.

Altogether the evidence from the number of editions of his works shows that Bouchet was a relatively popular writer in various fields, and a very popular historical and religious writer. As a poet he lived long enough to become old-fashioned twice. When Du Bellay includes *Le Traverseur* as one of those who should be 'renvoyés à la Table ronde', it is worth noting that all the other poets in the list are from a later generation than Bouchet's.[26] Bouchet, who learned his trade under Charles VIII, had already changed his poetic style in imitation of the court poets of Louis XII, and modified it further under François Ier. The *Quintil Horatian*'s riposte to Du Bellay is typical, however, of those who praise Bouchet:

> Le traverseur Bouchet pour son temps a esté loué, & est encore, comme chaste & chrestien scripteur, non lascif & paganisant, comme ceux du jourd'huy, & si a fait & poursuivy grands & continuels œuvres, non pas petites sonneries.[27]

The neo-latin poet Hubert Sussanneau praised Bouchet's virtue;[28] in 1533 Pierre Grognet referred to him as 'homme sçavant';[29] in 1589 he was mentioned as 'le docte Bouchet' and remembered particularly for the *Triomphes*.[30] Bouchet's main popularity was in the genres in which he appeared supremely 'docte' and 'chrestien'—his works of instruction.

All the best examples of other people's comments on him are to be found among the *Epîtres Familières*. Although obviously not unbiased evidence of the esteem in which Bouchet was held, these have the great value of providing a picture of the wide contacts which Bouchet's reputation brought him. These *épîtres*, combined with dedications and prefaces in his other works, enable us to reconstruct a life with a range of acquaintances and influence far wider than a provincial *procureur* could normally have expected.

3
Patrons, Friends and Literary Contacts[31]

We have noted that Bouchet visited the court of Charles VIII at Lyons with a contingent from Poitiers in 1496, but for some reason was not able to enter the service of Florimond Robertet in spite of the King's directive. Bouchet is not known to have had any more contact with the court until Louis de La Trémoille took him to the court of Louis XII. Bouchet tells us in the *Panégyrique* that he worked for La Trémoille for fifteen years, which suggests that he entered his service in about 1510.[32] Whether or not under the auspices of La Trémoille, he was present in Tours when the King held a council of the Gallican Church there in 1510;[33] more definite evidence of his presence at court is found when he records hearing Louis xii speaking to La Trémoille about the plays of the Basoche.[34] He also addresses Louis xii in 2 *Ep. Mor.* 1 on kings, saying that he writes at the request of the King; later he said that he was asked by the King to write this *épître* about a year before Louis died, 'Que commençois avoir à luy accès'.[35] Once again he had nearly managed to establish himself as a court poet. In this *épître* too he claims Jean d'Auton as his mentor. Jean d'Auton, historiographer to the King and court poet, was made abbot of Angle-sur-Anglin in Poitou by Louis xii and seems to have retired there after the King's death, by which time Bouchet's relations with him were well established. Bouchet is writing under his aegis with the *Déploration* and the *Epître d'Henry* of 1512 which imitate works by d'Auton and appear to be attempts to win royal favour. With the accession of François 1er, d'Auton withdrew from the court, but the La Trémoille family remained a contact for Bouchet, and he dedicated *L'Histoire de Clotaire* to Queen Claude in 1517. He was employed in some capacity by Marguerite d'Alençon during the period between 1519 and 1521 when she held land at Fontenay.[36] He also cultivated the widow of Artus Gouffier, another local nobleman who had been the King's tutor and his *grand-maître*: this suggests earlier contact with Gouffier, who died in 1519. Bouchet's desire for contacts with the court of François 1er is best represented by a series of dedications to members of the royal family: the *Labyrinthe* of 1522 to Marguerite d'Alençon; the *Anciennes et modernes généalogies*, 1528, to the Dauphin; the *Triomphes*, 1530/1, to the new Queen Eleanor; the *Jugement*, 1538, to the King; and the *Triomphes du roi*, 1549, to the new King Henri ii.[37] These, together with his commemorative works on deceased members of the royal family (particularly Louise de Savoie, the Dauphin and François 1er)[38] only suggest that he wanted royal patronage, not that he had obtained it. Sometimes he was able to present his works to a member of the royal family travelling near Poitiers.[39] But it is clear from the *Epîtres Familières* that during the 1530s some of Bouchet's works were presented at court by Louis de Ronsard, seigneur de la Possonière, related by marriage to the La Trémoille family, father of the poet, Pierre de Ronsard, and for many years faithful servant of the Crown. Ronsard was a friend of long standing. In about 1515 he had called Bouchet to Paris and had instructed him in certain metrical rules. In 1530 Bouchet asked him to present the *Triomphes* to Queen Eleanor and he recorded that later Ronsard had presented the *Jugement* to the King. It was also at Ronsard's request that the King, the Dauphin and Marguerite de Navarre all wrote letters asking the abbess Louise de Bourbon to admit Bouchet's youngest daughter, Marie, to the convent of Sainte-Croix without a dowry. Clearly then, through the good offices of this friend, Bouchet was not completely bereft of royal notice.

Local noblemen were nevertheless more accessible patrons, and the La Trémoille connection in particular was invaluable. Bouchet was one of several *procureurs* employed on the La Trémoille estates,[40] but he had particularly close connections with the wife of Louis II de La Trémoille, Gabrielle de Bourbon. Gabrielle herself wrote devotional works; Bouchet arranged for some of them to be bound and illuminated.[41] He was obviously a frequent visitor at their château at Thouars, discussing literature both with Gabrielle and with her only son, Charles de La Trémoille, Prince de Talmont, who is also said to have presented some of Bouchet's writing at court. Charles inspired three of Bouchet's works: he commissioned *L'Epistre de la royne Marie*, and the *Chapelet des princes* was written for his young son. After Charles' death at Marignano in 1515 Bouchet wrote the *Temple de Bonne Renommée* in his memory. Gabrielle lived for less than a year after her son's death. Bouchet continued to receive the favour of Louis de La Trémoille and certainly derived from him information about Louis' own life and military activities; these bore fruit in the account of the early part of the reign of François Ier in the *Annales* and above all in the *Panégyrique*, the biography of Louis II de La Trémoille, written after his death at the battle of Pavia in 1525.

Bouchet retained contact with the family when Louis' less illustrious grandson came into the title, and the connection figures to a certain extent in his writing,[42] but he also cultivated other noble houses of the region. As well as his addresses to Hélène de Hangest, widow of Artus Gouffier, the *Epîtres Familières* and the series of epitaphs in the *Généalogies* reveal his connections with François du Fou, André de Vivonne, Antoinette d'Illiers, Madame de Montreuil-Bonnin. Such contacts with the local nobility also meant more connections at court. In addition, during the 1530s, he cultivated another branch of the Bourbon family in Renée de Bourbon, abbess of Fontevrault, and her niece Louise, abbess of Sainte-Croix in Poitiers. Thus his writing undoubtedly gave him an entrée into local aristocratic circles and beyond.

The *Epîtres* give even better insight into Bouchet's specifically literary contacts. His devotion to poetry was an early one and, as a schoolboy in Poitiers, he formed friendships with others who wanted to write (Pierre Rivière, Pierre Gervaise, Pierre Blanchet). His friendship with Jean d'Auton, begun well before 1511, lasted until d'Auton's death in 1528. Throughout the 1520s in particular Bouchet had a network of literary acquaintances in the Poitiers region, and was regarded by them as an important literary figure.

One main centre was the Augustinian house of Fontaine-le-Comte, just outside Poitiers, presided over by the abbot Antoine Ardillon—the 'noble Ardillon' of *Pantagruel* ch.5. Much attention has rightly been centred on the group of scholars and writers who met here and who eventually welcomed Rabelais into their midst during his time as a Benedictine.[43] Rabelais' patron at this period was Geoffroy d'Estissac, bishop of Maillezais, whose monastery at Ligugé was also to become a venue for the group.

Bouchet met Ardillon as early as 1514, but in Bouchet's works we first meet the abbot in 1522 as the author of a Latin liminary epistle in praise of the *Labyrinthe*. It may be assumed that the group was forming by this date. Ardillon is addressed in the introductory poem to the *Annales* in 1524, and in a series of *Epîtres familières* dating from about 1525 to 1536. In *Ep*. 30, the second of the series, we are told that at Fontaine-le-Comte Bouchet would meet

> Ce Rabellay, sans oublier Quentin,
> Troian, Petit, tous divers en vesture,
> Et d'ung vouloir en humaine escripture,
> Desquelz par foiz quelques motz je soubstraitz
> Qu'à mon vulgaire et maternel j'atraiz
> Tout en ce point que je les puis comprendre
> Selon mon sens et mon petit entendre   (*Ep. Fam.* 30)

Rabelais was probably the most recent arrival in the group. Although it is not impossible that he had had some contact with the Poitiers humanists while still at Fontenay-le-Comte—André Tiraqueau, for example, was a learned friend of Rabelais from Fontenay, whom Bouchet had met by 1514 and to whom he addressed *epîtres*—it is probable that Rabelais' visits to Fontaine-le-Comte were all roughly in the period 1525 to 1527 while he was a Benedictine. By then Nicolas Petit, a lawyer and a neo-Latin poet, had already come to Poitiers from Paris; he died young in 1532 having published two volumes of neo-Latin poetry and several liminary poems to works by Bouchet. 'Quentin' is the Quintinus Heduus who wrote a long Latin liminary epistle in praise of the *Annales*; he was later to become a celebrated teacher of Canon Law in Paris. Quintin provides more evidence of the links between various members of the group: in 1524, the year of the *Annales*, he delivered two orations in Poitiers, one in the Cathedral and one in the church of Saint-Hilaire. The latter was given in the presence of the Bishop of Maillezais, Geoffroy d'Estissac; it was on the subject of St Hilary, and in the course of it Quintin praised Bouchet's historical work. These two orations were subsequently printed, and the editor of the volume included a dedicatory letter to Ardillon in which he praised both Bouchet and Nicolas Petit.[44] This occasion may have helped to bring about Bouchet's personal contacts with d'Estissac and his nephew, Louis; in his *epître* to Rabelais he is congratulating himself on the gracious reception they had accorded him. They were to become additional contacts for him at Court—although, as Ardillon is told in *Ep.* 73, Louis d'Estissac brought Bouchet the bad news that the *procureur* was considered much too fond of criticising his betters.

No doubt many other learned men from the region joined the gatherings. Trojan, whom Bouchet mentions, was a young Franciscan who in 1525 checked the theology of the *Epître de Justice*. We may add with fair certainty a lawyer from Dauphiné, Gaspar Romanèche, who must be the 'Solon daulphinois' at the banquet described in *Ep.* 34. At the same banquet 'un qui portoit le blanc' is presumably a Cistercian, perhaps the abbot of Valence, Ponce de La Grève.[45]

It may readily be supposed that history was one of the subjects of common interest, and several others can be postulated. Clearly Bouchet regarded Fontaine-le-Comte as a place of great learning, a centre for 'lettres latines'. In the heading of Rabelais' *épître* to Bouchet Rabelais is described as 'homme de grans lettres Grecques et Latines'. It is noticeable that in his *épître* to Ardillon, Petit and Rabelais, Bouchet frequently adopts a mythological style, peopling the woods with dryads and naiads who join them in their gatherings; this style he must have thought suitable for a circle of scholars and neo-Latin poets. Poetry was no doubt one of the subjects the group discussed; if Nicolas Petit was the leading light as far as neo-Latin poetry was concerned, Bouchet himself was the expert in vernacular verse. It is worth noting that Rabelais' *épître* to Bouchet is one of his longest pieces of French verse and it is a reasonable supposition that Bouchet gave him some instruction in the art.[46]

Law must have been a favourite topic. Romanèche, Petit, Quintin, Ponce de La Grève all had qualifications in law; Bouchet was a practising *procureur*; d'Estissac is praised by Bouchet for his learning, including 'en canonique'. Trojan was given the *Epître de Justice* to check, which suggests some competence in the subject. Rabelais' interest in law is well known. Other lawyers no doubt joined their gatherings; the University of Poitiers was a major centre for the teaching of law and Bouchet reveals friendships with many other lawyers from the University and the courts at Poitiers (for example Robert Irland, Germain Emery, François Thibault). Thus it is not surprising that in the midst of the legal comedy of the *Tiers Livre*, Frère Jan remembers that while he was at Fontaine-le-Comte under Ardillon he met Perrin Dendin, the man who was so successful at settling cases (ch.43).

Astronomy and astrology interested many of these men, and notably Rabelais. In this period Bouchet was much concerned with the problems surrounding first and second causes and planetary influences. The subject is treated at length in the *Labyrinthe*, and by 1525 in the revised version of the *Déploration* he was denouncing

magic, divination and astrology as both dangerous and on the
increase. Gaspar Romanèche is said in *Ep.* 20 to have written a book
about 'the flood which may come about because of men's sins'—this
must have been a work on the predictions of floods for 1524 because
of the planetary conjunctions due to take place in that year. It seems
likely that Bouchet's depiction of astrology as a growing menace in
1525 was an aftermath of this flood scare. Other small indications
suggest nevertheless a respect for astronomy kept properly in its
place; *rhétoriqueur* poets often use periphrases to suggest what sign
the sun is in and thus what season the poem is set in, but in some
épîtres to members of this group Bouchet makes more precise references to the relative positions of sun and moon—as if, like the
well-educated Gargantua, he was accustomed to go out in the even-
ing to check the position of the celestial bodies.[47]

In some ways the most intriguing topic is theology. In *Ep.* 34
Bouchet makes clear that theology was the subject under discussion
at the banquet. This was the decade during which Bouchet became
alarmed at the spread of Lutheranism and at the end of which he
produced his manual of religious instruction, the *Triomphes*. There
is plenty of evidence of his friendship with theologians, monastics
and secular clergy in and around Poitiers (for example Antoine
d'Asnières, Jacques Prévost, Louis Bastard, Guy de Bourdeilles,
Jean d'Auton, Jacques Godart). But among the group definitely
known to have been meeting at Fontaine-le-Comte were a number
whose views on theology were evolving rapidly in the later 1520s.
Apart from Rabelais himself, Quintin may perhaps have held
dangerously trenchant views on reform at this time, and Trojan
almost certainly went over to the Reformation, along with Ponce de
La Grève's successor at Valence.[48] The possible influence of theological discussions at Fontaine-le-Comte in this period is a factor
that must be taken into account when considering the *Triomphes*.

It is hardly surprising that Bouchet should express so much pleasure at the prospect of visiting Fontaine-le-Comte and Ligugé. There
he met a group of scholars open to the new learning who no doubt
influenced him considerably. Older than most of them, and more
famous than any of them at the time, he must have been a respected
and valued member of the group, and one whose wide reading
made his contributions to discussion far from negligible.

As time went on he developed contacts with more distant groups
of writers: Jean Mary de Ruffec, Michel Desarpens, Germain Colin
Bucher. Established poets visited him (Mellin de Saint-Gelais) or
exchanged letters with him (Jean Parmentier). Later in the 1530s,
Thomas Le Prévost, Jacques Le Lieur and Baptiste Le Chandelier, a
group of poets from Rouen, exchanged *épîtres* with him. Several of
these letters relate to the art of poetry and the role of the poet, but
they also broach religious questions. It was apparently through this

Rouen correspondence that Bouchet became involved in the controversy between Marot and Sagon: he appears almost to invite an
approach from Sagon but then firmly refuses to write against Marot.
There is no trace of personal acquaintance with Marot himself,
although Bouchet had another set of literary contacts in Lyons with
members of a group of neo-Latin writers whom Marot knew well:
Claude Cottereau, whom Bouchet met when he came to Poitiers to
study, and Hubert Sussanneau.

It is of course possible to form an unusually clear picture of his
contacts because of the evidence of the *Epîtres Familières*; no doubt
Bouchet liked collecting important recipients and, even better, con-
tributors to this collection. The picture given is one of a writer
widely known and well thought of by other poets, by writers who
themselves wrote in Latin and cultivated the new learning, and by
vernacular writers involved in the major centre for French religious
poetry at the time, Rouen.

By the mid-1530s, thanks to the *Triomphes,* Bouchet had the reputation of being an opponent of heresy. But, as we have seen, in the
1520s he had several contacts with men who wished to see changes
in the Church. In the *Epîtres* he preserves correspondence with
some friends whose orthodoxy was in doubt or who had actually
gone over to the Reform by the time the *Epîtres* were published in
1545.[49]

4

Royal Entries and Mystery Plays

One major aspect of Bouchet's activities, which will receive little
attention in the study of his literary works, is his contribution to the
organisation of royal entries and the production of mystery plays in
Poitiers. Yet this activity must have brought him into great prominence in his home town.

There have been several accounts of his involvement with royal
entries and mystery plays, notably by Hamon and Clouzot.[50] Most
recently, in his study of theatre in the round, Rey-Flaud has invest-
ed the subject with a new significance by showing that Bouchet was
responsible for a technique of presenting mysteries in a circular
theatre that became popular all over the area of the Loire and the
West. The technique is even evident in a royal entry with which he
was involved.[51]

This must then be considered an extremely important aspect of
Bouchet's life: unfortunately the information is uneven and tantalis-
ing, deriving mostly from his own writings, the *Annales* and the
Epîtres Familières. Where external evidence is available, it shows that
Bouchet was far more important than his own account would
suggest.[52] To take first the case of royal entries, Bouchet himself
never mentions that he had any part in organising one. He gives a

detailed account of the three tableaux, complete with verse inscriptions, which celebrated the entry of François Ier into Poitiers in January 1520, but gives no hint of who was responsible for organising the entry.[53] However, we must conclude, as all previous scholars have done, that he had himself directed it.[54] This can be deduced from the example provided by another occasion, the entry of the Queen and the Dauphin into Nantes in 1532. Bouchet makes only a brief mention of this entry in the *Annales*, but other records survive that give a most unexpected picture of Bouchet's expertise and reputation in such matters.[55]

On 7 June 1532, the town council of Nantes decided to send to Bouchet for his advice on the 'joyeulsetés et feinctes'[56] for the forthcoming entries. He sent them various 'memoires et articles', but on 30 June they resolved to ask him to come to Nantes in person. He must have refused, for on 12 July they again sent the original representative, Gilles Kernela, to try to persuade him to come. Kernela was back in Nantes on 22 July, without Bouchet, but having at least obtained 'le devys des mysteres queulx seront faicts par les carrefours ès entrées de la royne et monseigneur le daulphin, que a composés Bouschet'. Gilles Kernela was chosen to be one of the two directors of the production; a statement of his expenses shows that he had had to persuade Bouchet to stay three days in Poitiers at a time when Bouchet wanted to get out of town away from the plague. Presumably Bouchet had instructed him in how to set about organising the displays, which duly took place on 14 and 18 August.

A description of the tableaux at Nantes survives, although unfortunately not the verse that would help to explain them. There were four points in the town where stages were erected, so eight tableaux were needed for the two entries. There are some points of similarity between the scenes at Nantes and those at Poitiers in 1520, also with Bouchet's descriptions of allegorical persons in works like the *Labyrinthe de Fortune* and the *Triomphes de la noble et amoureuse dame*. At Nantes the series for Queen Eleanor employs personifications in three out of the four scenes: for example *Humaine Providence* leads in chains *Bonheur* and *Malheur* (personifications who hold a *débat* in the *Labyrinthe*). The series for the Dauphin is more varied: the first tableau uses heraldic material, uniting the ermine, the fleur-de-lys and the dolphin—at Poitiers in 1520 there had been a gigantic lily slowly revolving, flanked by a salamander and an ermine. Another represents the Dauphin with Time and an astrologer, together reminiscent of the figure of Time depicted in the *Triomphes*.[57]

In 1539 the Emperor Charles v entered Poitiers. Bouchet speaks of the magnificence of the Emperor's journey through France, but does not describe the entry.[58] The surviving descriptions reveal some similarities with the 1520 entry—both employed for instance a fountain running with wine.[59] But the later entry is far more classical in inspiration, and all the verse is in Latin. It is unlikely that Bouchet was in charge of this entry, but it is just as unlikely that he had no hand in it. One of the tableaux in 1520 had featured a man representing Poitiers. In 1539, the origin of the Poitevins was represented by medallions showing Hercules and Agathyrsus. This legendary ancestry is recorded in the 1532 and later editions of the *Annales*.[60]

The evidence for Bouchet's involvement with mystery plays demonstrates a similar widespread reputation and a similar reluctance to move more than a step from his home town whatever the inducements offered. He first records having watched a mystery of the passion in Poitiers in 1486 when he was only ten.[61] He makes no mention of a production in 1508, but the records in Poitiers show not only that the Mystery of the Passion was presented in August of that year, but also that 'd'icelluy mistaire estoient entrepreneurs maistres Jehan Maignen et Jehan Bouschet'.[62] Jean Maignen was certainly a friend of Bouchet's; in 1532 Bouchet addresses his *Epître de vieillesse* to Maignen after 37 years of friendship—but he does not mention their common interest in mystery plays. There is evidence that Bouchet had been involved with the theatre of the Basoche in Paris, which may help to explain how he came to be one of the organisers of the great theatrical event in Poitiers in 1508.[63]

In July 1534 the Mystery of the Passion was again produced in Poitiers. This time Bouchet has rather more to say in the *Annales* and in an *Epître* to the actors.[64] Other *épîtres* concerning productions in other towns bring additional information. Bouchet was the director of the production, which lasted for eleven days and depicted the events from the Incarnation to the sending of the Holy Spirit. It was performed in a circular theatre constructed in the Marché-Vieil. Another source reveals that this theatre was not nearly big enough for the thousands of would-be spectators.[65] Perhaps because of an alteration in the date there was not enough time to prepare the scenery properly.[66] Bouchet writes regretfully to his actors about some of these shortcomings:

S'il y a heu es fainctes des deffaulx
Et à couvrir le parc et eschauffaulx
Tous faict en rond, en fault faire les plainctes
Contre ung tendeur, et le faiseur des fainctes
Painctres aussi (sans faire d'eulx contemps)
Car ilz n'ont heu l'espace ne le temps.
Dieu l'a permis, affin que folle gloire
N'aneantist euvre tant meritoire.[67]

He was able to see better scenery at Saumur where the Passion was performed three weeks later in the remains of a Roman theatre.[68] The director here was Thomas Le Prévost, a poet summoned from Rouen to direct the mystery for the town. Bouchet and he had exchanged civil *épîtres* earlier in the year.[69] But Bouchet was unreservedly pleased with his actors in Poitiers, and in his *épître* speaks of the usefulness of the enterprise, which must lead to meditation and imitation of the life of Christ. A year later he composed an epitaph for the actor who had taken the part of Christ.[70]

Bouchet's fame in the region was established. Other towns began to wish for the prestige and profit that could come from the production of a mystery. Later in 1534 the people of Issoudun tried to persuade Bouchet to direct a Passion for them; he refused to come himself but gave them much practical advice and sent his papers.[71] This may indeed have been the main point of the request, made in a verse *épître* by the man whom Bouchet assumes will in fact be the director of the production. We can see from Bouchet's reply why poets like Bouchet and Le Prévost were called upon to direct mysteries; an important part of their role was to update an older text:

> Du moule ay prins ce que j'ay bon trouvé
> Et ce qui est par l'eglise approuvé,
> Car il y a on moule aulcuns passages
> Qui n'ont passé par l'escolle des sages,
> Dont par conseil j'ay fait rescision
> Et en ces lieux mis quelque addition.
> Vous supploirez les deffaulx d'escripture
> Lors que d'iceulx on fera la lecture.[72]

It is assumed that Bouchet had revised the Passion of either Jean Michel or the Greban brothers.[73]

Bouchet said in *Ep. Fam.* 90 to his actors that he had now seen the Passion three times and prayed that he might see the Acts of the Apostles before he died. However he missed a chance that soon presented itself. Two years later he is writing to Jean Chaponneau, an Augustinian (soon to go over to the Reform) who was directing the Acts at Bourges. He apologises not only for not being able to come and see the mystery, but also for having been forced to refuse to come to Bourges

> Pour visiter les livres et papiers
> De ce jeu sainct[74]

This *épître* implies that he had been offered considerable inducements to go to Bourges and that his refusal (because of illness and pressure of legal work) had caused offence.[75]

There can be no doubt of Bouchet's great reputation as both author/adaptor and as 'metteur-en-scene' of entries and mystery plays. Part of their importance in his eyes was their magnificence. 'Triomphes', 'triomphant' are words that recur in his descriptions of both forms of display. The glory of God, the glory of the crown, the glory of Poitiers are all at issue. Although he exhorts the people of Issoudun to choose suitable costumes and not to dress the Pharisees as richly as Herod or Pilate, the richness of the apparel is a factor that he regularly comments on with reference to both types of spectacle. But mystery plays can also be seen to accord with the more mundanely pious interests revealed in so many of his major writings: the fostering of devotional feeling and religious knowledge among simple people.

NOTES

1. Bouchet's life and career are quite well documented, principally from what he tells us himself, above all in the *Ep. Mor.*, the *Ep. Fam.* and the *Annales*. Hamon's account, although diffuse, is full, including material from the La Trémoille archives and archives at Poitiers. It can be supplemented on some points by Alfred Richard's article *Notes biographiques sur les Bouchet, imprimeurs et procureurs à Poitiers au XVIe siècle*, Poitiers, 1912. The summary that follows draws on these two authors but the notes give references to the original source when this is in Bouchet's own work.

2. For his birth see *Annales*, f.159 vo: the date given is 'ladicte année mil quatre cents soixante et quinze, le penultime jour de janvier'—Bouchet takes note of both the usage of Aquitaine whereby the year began on Lady Day, 25 March, and that of Paris which began the year at Easter (*Annales*, f.181 vo). For Pierre Bouchet, see appendix A.

3. See *Gén. Ep.* 46 on his teacher, Julien Tortereau. Bouchet evokes the recreations of his college days in *Ep. Fam.* 23. In 2 *Ep. Mor.* 11, f.48 ro, writing in 1534, he comments that the expansion of printing has now made it possible for less wealthy students to follow law courses at university; he remembers a time when a faulty manuscript of a law course would have cost 150 *écus*, and poorer students had to be content to study arts and perhaps theology. On the University of Poitiers at this period see R. Favreau, 'Aspects de l'université de Poitiers au XVe siècle', *BSAO*, 4e série, v, 1959-60, pp.31-71, also *Histoire de l'université de Poitiers. Passé et présent (1432-1932)*, ed. P. Boissonnade, Poitiers, 1932.

4. He describes himself as 'simple clerc tonsuré' in 1 *Ep. Mor.* 1, f.1 ro, col.1. Minor orders requiring the tonsure but not the vow of celibacy (e.g. acolytes, readers) could be conferred on quite young boys, certainly under the age of 14 (cf. Council of Trent, Sessio XXIII, *De Reformatione*, cap.vi).

5. See for example I *Ep. Mor.* 14, f.34 vo, col.2 and *Ep. Fam.* 61, f.xli vo, col.2.

6. *Annales*, f.181 vo. As Easter fell on 3 April in 1496 and on 26 March in 1497, 1496 is certainly meant.

7. *Panégyrique*, 1527: in a dedicatory letter to Florimond Robertet he refers to Charles VIII

> par le commandement duquel (en faveur d'aucunes legieres fantasies rithmées que mon ignorante jeunesse peu de temps avant son decès luy presenta) fuz à mon importunée instance et priere à vostre service destiné, ce que ne voulut, à mon grant regret et perte, fortune. (+2 ro).

8. The Basoche was originally the society of law clerks in Paris; similar societies grew up in most of those provincial towns which had a *parlement*. As well as their importance as a professional organisation, they were famous for their dramatic presentations, particularly satirical plays. See H. G. Harvey, *The Theatre of the Basoche*, Harvard, 1941. See 2 *Ep. Mor.* 5, f.28 ro-vo, *Ep. Fam.* 2 and 42.

9. Hamon (p.14) notes that in the *Temple* (1517) Bouchet says that 20 years ago he saw Jean Vacquerie (d.1497) preside over the Parlement de Paris. In the *Annales* Bouchet notes, with the phrase 'comme je vy', certain events at which he was present in Paris: f.(183)/[182] ro, 2 July 1498; f.186 vo, 25 November 1501; f.187 vo, the events following the crime of a heretic committed on 25 August 1503. *Ep. Fam.* 2 shows that he travelled from Paris to Poitiers in August 1501; he was in Poitiers on 23 December 1501 (*Annales*, f.186 vo).

10. Richard, *Notes*, p.12, shows that Bouchet was *procureur* to the Chapter at Chauvigny by 29 March 1507. See the bibliography for a discussion of the dating of his two earliest publications.

11. Bouchet describes the strictly legal duties of a *procureur* in 2 *Ep. Mor.* 5, f.27 ro-28 ro, and in chapter 8 of *Forme et ordre* (pp.34-43). Surviving correspondence shows that he undertook a variety of other transactions for his clients. On *procureurs* in the period see B. Guenée, *Tribunaux et gens de justice dans le bailliage de Senlis à la fin du Moyen Age (vers 1380-vers 1550)*, Paris, 1963, pp.202-12.

12. 2 *Ep. Mor.* 5, f.27 ro, col.2.

13. *Forme et ordre*, ā2 ro.

14. See Richard, *Notes*, pp.12-15.

15. *Ibid.*, pp.12-14; Hamon p.31 (especially n.2).

16. Hamon pp.138-9, 165. Bouchet records his attendance at a meeting c.1549, *Annales*, f.325 vo.

17. B. Ledain, 'Les maires de Poitiers', *MSAO*, 2e série, xx, 1897, pp.215-774; see pp.509 and 529.

18. For Gabriel, Joseph and Marie see appendix A. For the references to his other children see particularly *Ep. Fam.* 95, f.lxiv vo, col.2. See Hamon, p.31 n.2 and p.137, for a document no later than 1524 naming two sons-in-law. For examples of affectionate references to his wife and children see especially *Ep. Fam.* 67 and 77.

19. See Hamon, pp.165-6.

20. For details of the editions, see the bibliography.

21. For example in 1 *Ep. Mor.* 14, f.38 vo, col.2, *Ep. Fam.* 23, 41, 104. In 23 he says that his writing never earned him enough to keep his family for two months.

22. Used for the first time in the *Déploration* of 1512. As well as this pen-name he adopted two *devises*, which he used for the first time in the *Labyrinthe de Fortune*: the anagram *Ha bien touché* and the motto *Spe labor levis*. (A variant of the latter, *Spe labor iocundus*, had already appeared in the *Chapelet* of 1517 and the *Histoire de Clotaire* of 1518).

23. *Généalogies*, aa6 vo.

24. Richard, *Notes*, pp.11-12. The de Marnef brothers were also booksellers in Paris and sold their editions of Bouchet's works there as well as in Poitiers.

25. *Ep. Mor.*, liminary f.[6] ro.
26. *Deffence et Illustration*, ed. H. Chamard, Paris, 1948, p.177.
27. *Ibid.*, n.5.
28. In the epigram *Ad Joseph. Buchetum, Ludorum libri*, Paris, 1538, f.42, which concludes:
    Virtutum ratio non est aliunde petenda
    Si vis exemplum sumere, sume domi.
    On Sussanneau, see appendix A.
29. In the *Louange des bons facteurs* from *Le second volume des Mots dorez du grant Cathon*, reproduced in A. de Montaiglon, *Recueil de poésies françoises des XVe et XVIe siècles*, Paris, 1855-78, vol.VII, see p.8.
30. Robert Le Roquez, *Le Miroir de l'eternité*, Caen, 1585 (but composed in about 1560):
    Et en Poictiers le docte Jean Bouchet,
    Lequel a peinct de sa plume dorée
    Le vray discours de l'âme incorporée.
    Quoted by M. de Grève, *L'Interprétation de Rabelais au XVIe siècle*, Geneva, 1961, p.161, n.57.
31. Details concerning the people mentioned in this section will be found in appendix A.
32. *Panégyrique*, [f.3] ro.
33. *Annales*, f.189 ro.
34. *Annales*, f.193 vo-194 ro; see also 1 *Ep. Mor.* 13, f.32 vo, col.2; 2 *Ep. Mor.* 1, f.3 ro, col.1 (where he says 'Un jour à Bloys en vostre chambre estois . . .').
35. 2 *Ep. Mor.* 3, f.17 ro, col.1.
36. See P. Jourda, *Répertoire analytique et chronologique de la correspondance de Marguerite d'Angoulême*, Paris, 1930, p.5, no.6 ([1520] 8 Avril, A Guillaume Vernade, à Fontenay-le-Comte: Ordre de payer à J. Bouchet à Poitiers, la somme de 28 écus en remerciements des besognes dont elle l'a chargé).
37. It should be noted that several works have two dedications, one to a member of the royal family and one to someone less illustrious who presumably might also be expected to reward the author. See the bibliography.
38. Respectively the *Jugement*, the *Déploration du Dauphin* in the *Généalogies* (ff.68-70) and the *Triomphes du roi*.
39. In 2 *Ep. Mor.* 11, f.47 vo, col.2, he says that he presented the *Anciennes et modernes généalogies* to the Dauphin at Bonnivet, and that the *Triomphes* were presented to Queen Eleanor when she passed near Poitiers. In the latter case he either used as an intermediary, or was introduced by, Louis de Ronsard.
40. Hamon, p.39 n.3, quotes from Thibaudeau, *Histoire du Poitou*, vol.2, Niort, 1840, pp.263-5, a document of 1534 that gives an account of the publication of the *coutume* of Poitou in 1514. Among those present at the *couvent des frères mineurs* in Poitiers were Louis Rideau, designated *procureur* of Louis de La Trémoille, and Jean Bouchet, described as 'procureur de messire Louis de Bourbon, chevalier, prince de la Roche-sur-Yon'. It is worth noting some others who were present: Ponce de La Grève, Ardillon, André de Vivonne, Pierre Régnier, André Tiraqueau (for all of these, see appendix A).

41. Hamon, pp.57-8.
42. *Le Jugement* has a dedication to Anne de Laval, wife of François de La Trémoille; otherwise there are merely a few mentions of their children in the *Ep. Fam.*, and in the *Gén. Eps*, and a *Déploration* on the death of François (*Généalogies*, ff.86-90). However, in his function of *procureur*, Bouchet was extensively employed by François (Hamon, p.68), and considerable business correspondence between them survives in the Chartrier de Thouars.
43. Hamon, pp.76-97; A. Lefranc, 'Sur quelques amis de Rabelais', *Revue des études rabelaisiennes*, 5, 1907, pp.52-6 and 'Rabelais secrétaire de G. d'Estissac', *Revue des études rabelaisiennes*, 7, 1909, pp.411-13; J. Plattard, *L'Adolescence de Rabelais en Poitou*, Paris, 1923.
44. For details see appendix A under Quintin.
45. The banquet had not taken place at Fontaine-le-Comte, but Bouchet writes to tell Ardillon that those present intend to meet there on the following Thursday to continue their debate. Also mentioned is 'ung Phoronée'. Phoroneus is the name of the brother of Io; the adjective is sometimes used in Latin in the general sense 'Argive'. Bouchet may mean someone with strong Greek connections—perhaps very learned in Greek? Quintin, who in his later works shows considerable knowledge of Greek might be the man in question, but this is mere guesswork. This *épître* has several elusive and allusive expressions; it gives the impression of being rather private to the group of people for whom it is intended.
46. See J. Plattard, 'Rabelais réputé poète par quelques écrivains de son temps', *Revue des études rabelaisiennes*, 10, 1912, pp.291-304; R. Lebègue, 'Rabelais et les grands rhétoriqueurs', *Les Lettres romanes*, 12, 1958, pp.5-18.
47. See appendix B, introduction and notes on 34 and 49. To those slight indications we may add that in *Ep.* 48 Rabelais refers briefly to the stars and their courses (lines 13-16) and that *Ep.* 35 to Ardillon is dated rather unexpectedly
    Escript ce jour que Jesus tint l'Empire
    Sur mer et vens, à quoy l'Eglise aspire . . .
This may simply be a way of dating the poem the second Sunday in Epiphany, when the portion of Gospel to be read at Mass recounts Christ's stilling of the storm; on the other hand it may be a means of evoking the group's current discussions of the flood predictions.
48. Discussed in appendix A.
49. In addition to those already mentioned, see appendix A for Chaponneau and Germain Colin.
50. Hamon, pp.107-31; H. Clouzot, *L'Ancien théâtre en Poitou*, Niort, 1901, pp.27-44.
51. H. Rey-Flaud, *Le Cercle magique: Essai sur le théâtre en rond à la fin du Moyen Age*, Gallimard, 1973, pp.137-43. On the circular stage erected for an entry, see p.139 and p.43.
52. On mysteries, the evidence from Bouchet's works is in the *Annales*, ff.168 ro-vo and 267 vo, *Ep. Fam.* 22, 23, 88, 89, 90, 91, 92, 101 and *Gén. Ep.* 52 and 76. Hamon and Clouzot cite in addition documents from Poitiers relating to the 1508 and 1534 produc-

tions, together with references in Le Riche, *Journal* and G. Bouchet, *Sérées*. On entries, Bouchet describes that of Poitiers 1520 in
some detail, *Annales*, ff.203 vo-205 ro, and he records many
others, for instance Charles VIII, Poitiers 1486, f.168 vo; Louis
XII, Paris 1498, f.(183)/[182] ro (noting that he himself saw it);
Philip, Archduke of Austria, Paris and Poitiers 1501, f.186 vo
(noting that he saw them); several during the reign of François
Ier and particularly those of Queen Eleanor, 1531 and 1532, Paris,
ff.261 vo-263 ro (citing the account of G. Bouchetel), Rouen f.264
vo, Nantes f.265 ro; the Emperor Charles V, Poitiers 1539, ff.283
vo-284 ro. He does not describe this last entry, saying that many
saw and have recorded the Emperor's reception in France, but he
says that he has seen entries of Charles VIII, Louis XII and
François Ier and has read of the 'entrées et triomphes' of previous
kings, but knows of no King of France who has received so great
a triumph as François arranged for the Emperor. These references amply demonstrate his interest in entries, but proof that he
himself was involved in arranging any comes only from archive
material in Nantes on the entry of 1532, used by both Hamon and
Clouzot.

53.   *Annales*, ff.203 vo-204 vo.
54.   See the arguments of Hamon, p.127 n.1.
55.   *Annales*, f.265 ro. The documents at Nantes are described briefly
      in the *Inventaire sommaire des archives communales antérieures à
      1790: Ville de Nantes*, ed. S. de la Nicollière-Teijeiro, vol.1,
      Nantes, 1888, p.26 (AA.30) and pp.126-7 (CC.112). They were
      used by Dugast-Matifeux in 'Une fête à Nantes au XVIe siècle:
      Jean Bouchet de Poitiers', *Revue des provinces de l'Ouest*, année 3,
      1855, pp.537-49. The following account and quotations are taken
      from this article. See also Hamon, pp.127-31.
56.   For *feintes*, meaning in this context *représentation*, see B. Guenée
      and F. Lehoux, *Les Entrées royales françaises de 1328 à 1515*, Paris,
      1968, pp.25-9. These performances became an increasingly im-
      portant feature of entries in the course of the fifteenth century.
57.   At Nantes the Astrologer was dressed in antique fashion, Time
      had a purple robe covered in gold stars, peacock wings, white
      wig and beard and a white hat. In the *Triomphes*, f.iiii ro, Time
      has a robe of many colours, stars on his face, a crown of nine
      turning circles, a sun on his forehead and a moon on the back of
      his head, long white hair and beard, wings on his arms and legs,
      and he carries a whip.
58.   *Annales*, f.284 ro.
59.   I have used an Italian account, *La solenne et triomphante entrata de
      la Cesarea Maesta nella Franza*, BL 1318.c.7(5); see [f.4] ro.
60.   See M-R. Jung, *Hercule dans la littérature française du XVIe siècle*,
      Geneva, 1966, p.64.
61.   *Annales*, f.168 ro-vo.
62.   See Hamon, p.110, Clouzot, *L'Ancien théâtre*, p.327; R. Favreau,
      La Ville de Poitiers à la fin du moyen âge, Poitiers, 1978, p.555 n.635.
63.   In *Ep. Fam.* 42 he replies to the *Roi de la Basoche* at Bordeaux who
      had apparently asked him for a play; he declines to write one,
      while describing himself as 'cestuy là qui puis trente ans mous-
      chet / A la bazoche à Paris'. Clouzot (pp.52-3). assumes that

Bouchet wrote satirical plays for the Basoche, and older critics have attributed particular plays to him, but *Ep. Fam.* 42, although admittedly ambivalent, would seem to deny it; on balance I accept Hamon's rejection of such attributions (pp.107-8, 412).

64. *Annales*, f.267 vo; *Ep. Fam.* 90.

65. Guillaume Le Riche, *Journal*, ed. A. D. de la Fontenelle de Vaudoré, Saint-Maixent, 1846, pp.2-3.

66. Hamon and Clouzot both assume that the performance, which took place in July, had been planned for August but had been brought forward; they suppose that the reason was to make it coincide better with military musters held in June and early July. However, the assumption that August was the date originally planned rests on the tacit hypothesis that *Ep. Fam.* 23 (to Pierre Gervaise) should be dated 1534. See appendix B for evidence suggesting that *Ep. Fam.* 22 and 23 refer to a performance planned for an earlier year between 1529 and 1532.

67. *Ep. Fam.* 90, f.lx ro, col.1. See Rey-Flaud, *Cercle magique*, p.68 n.2 for the sense of *feintes* (here *décors*); pp.79-82 for *parc*; p.68-9 for *échafaud*.

68. *Annales*, f.267 vo; Clouzot, *L'Ancien théâtre*, p.40.

69. *Ep. Fam.* 88, 89. It is not clear what, if any, co-operation there was between the two productions. Critics usually assume that the same actors were involved (Hamon, p.117), but it is then difficult to understand the role of Le Prévost. The assumption rests on some lines in *Ep. Fam.* 89: Bouchet is busy, he says, with trivial things:

> Viles je dy par l'estimation
> De ceulx, lesquelz joueront la passion
> Tant à Poictiers qu'à Saulmur ceste année.

Clouzot takes these lines to prove that Bouchet expected the same actors to be involved (p.39). Bouchet nowhere else suggests that the same actors were in the two productions, and it does not seem impossible to understand these lines as referring to two sets of people.

70. *Gén. Ep.* 76 (Jean Orneau). Hamon and Clouzot also assume that the subject of *épitaphe* 52, Jean Formond, was a member of the cast. Guillaume Le Riche was an actor ('Le 19, j'ai commencé à jouer la Passion à Poitiers', *Journal*, p.2); Bouchet tells Pierre Gervaise that:

> Nous pourrons veoir jouer mainte personne
> De noz amys . . . (*Ep. Fam.* 23, f.xxv ro, col.2)

71. *Ep. Fam.* 91, 92. See Rey-Flaud, *Cercle magique*, pp.140-1, on the production at Issoudun.

72. *Ep. Fam.* 92, f.lxii ro, col.2.

73. Discussed by Clouzot, *L'Ancien théâtre*, p.34.

74. *Ep. Fam.* 101, f.lxvii ro, col.1.

75. For Jean Chaponneau and the production at Bourges, see E. Picot, *Notice sur Jehan Chaponneau*, Paris, 1879, and R. Lebègue, *Le Mystère des Actes des Apôtres*, Paris, 1929.

Bouchet's Poetry

1
Introduction

Bouchet is always classified as a *grand rhétoriqueur*. His avowed early
models were late medieval poets, Burgundian and French; he claims
to have imitated Jean de Meung, Alain Chartier, Georges Chastellain, Jean Castel, Jean Meschinot, Octavien de Saint-Gelais, Jacques
Millet and the Greban brothers, Arnoul and Simon.[1] His earliest
poetry was written in the reign of Charles VIII, before 1498, and his
last published verse appeared in 1549. So if he is classified among
the last group of *rhétoriqueur* poets who flourished under Louis XII,
he is doomed to appear for the final half of his career as a survival
from an earlier age. Lemaire, Cretin, de La Vigne, Jean Marot,
d'Auton were all dead before 1530.

In fact Bouchet's poetry as it develops differs increasingly from
these writers. Bouchet himself more than once in his career announced that he had brought his verse up to date.[2] Yet his poetry
does not greatly resemble that of Marot and his disciples, who were
his contemporaries just as much as were the *rhétoriqueurs*. The
account of his poetry that follows will attempt to show how his
poetry changed in the course of fifty years, and which characteristics
of successive fashions in poetry he was to adopt.

His very earliest work was the product of imitation of models at a
distance. Later he describes himself in his youth in the following
terms:

> je, qui avois commencé escripre en vers et prose certains opus-
> cules, suyvans la phrase d'aulcuns anciens orateurs françois,
> qui ont escript plusieurs traictez si tresbons en matiere que rien
> plus, toutesfois en style ung peu barbare, durans les regnes de
> Charles huytiesme et Loys douziesme, derriers Roys de France
> . . .[3]

Thus, as a young man in Poitiers enamoured of poetry, he modelled
himself on the work of well-known poets that he had read.

But what a *rhétoriqueur* poet needed above all was a patron.
Ideally he needed a place at Court. There is every reason to suppose

that some of the verses in the *Amoureux transi*, his earliest collection, were among those that Bouchet tells us he presented to Charles VIII; the prose and verse political allegory entitled *Comment ledict Amoureux transy sans espoir se complaint des estatz sur le voyage et guerre de Naples* seems deliberately designed to please the King.[4] As we have seen, Bouchet nearly succeeded in winning a place at Court, but the plans fell through, and instead he became for all his life a provincial *procureur*.

The *rhétoriqueur*'s need for a place at Court was not just a material one but artistic as well. As Zumthor has cogently argued,[5] in its most characteristic form the *rhétoriqueur*'s art is a public one, an art of pomp, parade and eulogy. Its subject is never solely private; it needs some grander theme. Ideally it needs the King. Cut off from any hope of public display the solitary poet might write love poetry or moral poetry, but he would not produce the elaborate, highly decorated set pieces that are the bookish equivalent of the triumphal arches and allegorical tableaux of a royal entry. Such a book needs a patron to whom it can be presented, it is an artefact intended to beautify a court.

Bouchet was not of course in an entirely solitary position, having gained the patronage of the La Trémoille family. They fulfilled the dual functions of patrons to be celebrated in their own right, and possible intermediaries for reaching the Court. Throughout his career he retained some sort of contact with Court circles, without ever penetrating to the magic circle of the true Court poet. This uncertain position, which meant that there was no point in aiming his work at an exclusively courtly audience, was doubtless an important factor in the development of his didactic poetry. On the other hand those contacts which he had gave him the opportunity of keeping up with the fashions in Court poetry. First of all Jean d'Auton, chronicler at the Court of Louis XII. Bouchet refers to him as his 'maistre et enseigneur', 'qui me as cest art voulu aprendre'.[6] When supporting royal policy during the war between Louis XII and the Pope, Bouchet first imitates the form of one of d'Auton's poems on the crisis, then adopts the framework used in an exchange of *épîtres* between d'Auton and Lemaire.[7] Next, the courtier Louis de Ronsard instructed Bouchet in certain metrical matters, in part, as we shall see, reflecting the use of Court poets influenced by Lemaire. Bouchet's contacts with the Court of François Ier are less easy to determine, and probably less important. But Ronsard, who was presenting Bouchet's works at Court in the 1530s, continued to be a potential source of information. We know too that Mellin de Saint-Gelais visited Bouchet in 1536.

Also mitigating the effects of provincial isolation were his contacts with practising poets in centres other than the Court. His correspondence with the Normandy poets, of which the earliest record is the exchange with Parmentier, c.1528, was quite extensive, judging from the examples of it preserved in the *Epîtres Familières*.[8] Of the younger poets who wrote to him, Germain Colin Bucher was a particularly lively and stimulating correspondent.[9] Contacts with the neo-Latin poets at Lyons appear more nebulous and perhaps resulted primarily from meetings with people studying in Poitiers. But this in itself was an extraordinarily important means of extending his horizons, since so many writers and humanists did visit Poitiers in the sixteenth century. The circle meeting at Fontaine-le-Comte and Ligugé belies any idea of provincial stagnation.

This network of contacts with fellow poets and writers, at Court and elsewhere, must help to explain why, although never really sounding 'up-to-date' in his verse, Bouchet, as we shall see, adopted certain 'up-to-date' developments with surprising rapidity.

It is clear, however, that while hoping for royal notice Bouchet did not have a primarily courtly audience, and on the whole his works are aimed at a wider readership, including the latinless whom he claims to instruct. Many aspects of *rhétoriqueur* poetics are not compatible with successful instruction because they devalue and transcend meaning.[10] Accordingly we shall find Bouchet at various times choosing to write in prose because it conveys the substance better,[11] deciding not to adopt a metrical rule on the grounds that it will interfere with his sense,[12] and making increasingly sparing use of those verbal ornaments that are now thought of as *rhétoriqueur* acrobatics. That such restraint involved some sacrifice of his inclinations is suggested by the passage in which he says of his work generally:

Car je l'ay prins du latin sans doubtance
Où j'ay tasché garder tousjours substance
Voire trop mieulx que l'art de rethoricque
Dont je sçay peu, car peu je m'y applicque.
Et toutesfois le treuve savoureux
Tant et si fort que j'en suis amoureux.[13]

This statement of the primacy of substance over form, followed so rapidly by the mounting enthusiasm of his avowal of love for rhetoric, suggests a conflict. This was ultimately resolved by adopting a very plain form for didactic works in verse. Increasingly he confined himself to the decasyllabic couplet and forms that lend themselves to this unvaried metre, the *épître* and the *épitaphe*. The best examples of learned instructive works in verse are the *Anciennes et modernes généalogies des roys de France* and the *Epîtres morales*. Religious poetry also provides striking examples of simplicity of form and stress on usefulness. Bouchet writes to the Rouennais Jacques Le Lieur in about 1536:

Parquoy, seigneur, te plaira m'excuser
Si je ne veulx en ton pays user

De chants royaulx, car ce ne'est ma pratique.
Rien je n'entends en celle theorique.[14]

For many *rhétoriqueurs* the *chant royal* in praise of the Virgin submitted to the *Puy* was a central genre. Bouchet never attempted it. His
one religious poem that can be compared to *Puy* poetry is simpler in
form than a *chant royal*; it has eleven 12-line stanzas, which allow for
the development of more material, and the manner is more direct,
less allusive than most *Puy* poetry.[15] Otherwise Bouchet's religious
poetry is restricted to *épîtres* and some *dizains*, together with the
collections of prayers composed probably between 1520 and 1523,
the *Cantiques et oraisons contemplatives de l'âme pénitente*. In the dedicatory letter the usefulness of this collection is stressed; the prayers
are for use by the latinless, and the short ones in particular seem
aimed at very simple people. Here the use of 'vers et metres' is
justified 'parce qu'ilz sont plus faciles à retenir que la prose'—it is
difficult to imagine a more utilitarian reason. Moreover, the composition is in very undecorated verse—'en vers et metres plains et
vulgaires'.[16] There are examples in the *Annales* and the *Généalogies* of
similar simple little verses, designed to make memorable one single
fact or moral.[17]

However, at the same time Bouchet continued to compose works
in which we are able to see the development of his aesthetic tastes.
One important group of poems has a partly didactic content but is
aimed at a more sophisticated audience. This is memorial verse. It
has already been said that ideally the *rhétoriqueur* art is one of public
pomp, and that the poet without Court connections is deprived of
his subject. But commemorative verse is one highly ornamented
genre that could be cultivated by any poet who had just lost his
patron or whose patron was bereaved. Verse of this type presents
Bouchet with a frame of reference comparable to that of the Court
poet, which the *rhétoriqueur* had ideally been. Commemorative
verse is by no means exclusively funereal; although consisting in
part of lamentations, the fictions associated with it are often decidedly pretty. This is particularly the case when the dead person is
associated with some imaginary place or building, which gives the
opportunity for ornamental description.[18] Bouchet composed five
major works of this type, which span his career: the *Temple de bonne
renommée*, 1517; the *Labyrinthe*, 1522; the *Epîtres, élégies*, 1535; the
Jugement, 1538; and the *Triomphes du roi*, 1549. These works, intended to show off the poet's art in the grand manner, allow us to see
clearly how his poetic practice changed.

Two other sets of verse are also more obviously literary in inspiration and do not have instruction as their main purpose, however
edifying they may in fact be. First, love poetry. About this Bouchet
had the severest scruples, and the *Angoisses et remèdes d'amour* is
really a *remedium amoris*, but as a rewriting in the 1530s of the early

Amoureux transi it presents many very interesting developments. The only other love poetry appears in occasional artificial *épîtres* in the *Epîtres familières*.[19] This collection as a whole offers a second example of the development of his poetic practice, particularly in the group of *épîtres poétiques*, in which poetic fictions are employed, often for humorous effect.

It is on these works that I shall concentrate when examining the different aspects of Bouchet's poetic practice. The aspects to be studied reflect Bouchet's own perception of the poet's art. Bouchet had an exalted concept of poetry. He knew well Boccaccio's defence of poetry at the end of the *Genealogia deorum gentilium* and used its arguments in defence of *l'art de metrificature* in his *Temple*.[20] But when he defends poetry he concentrates on what Sebillet was to call the 'nue escorce', that is to say, metrics and rhetoric, the 'art' of poetry which 'couvre artificiélement . . . son ame naturélement divine'.[21] Certainly Bouchet describes poetry as 'science infuse', 'par grace diffuse'; later he uses the term 'sacré poete', and often speaks of the inspiration of the Muses, Mercury or Apollo.[22] But his most prestigious defences of poetry concern metrics: poetry 'measures', as God measured when creating the world; verse is used in the Old Testament, in psalms and hymns. The rhetoric of poetry requires knowledge and learning and promotes virtue, in the same way as its prose counterpart.[23] The subject matter of poetry may be extremely elevated; some Christian poets are said to write 'pure theologie', Dante and Petrarch, for example; he himself modestly denies being one of 'ces grans orateurs / Qui des secretz divins sont scrutateurs'.[24] But we shall see that he accords mythological 'fictions poétiques' no spiritual significance and does not seem to take them very seriously. The language and measure of poetry are a 'science' worth cultivating—and yet they cannot just be learned; 'doulx et fluent langage' is a gift of nature.[25] Again here, as he formulates this common-place deriving from Horace, *Ars poetica* lines 408–11, he concentrates on the language in which poetry is expressed. Thus Bouchet has a concept of poetry that is coloured by humanist and classical ideas and vocabulary—he is well acquainted, for instance, with the term 'fureur poétique'.[26] But the poetry that he praises so highly remains essentially the 'art de seconde rhétorique'.

Thus when we examine the terminology that he uses, we find that Bouchet often calls writing verse the 'art des orateurs' and 'rhétorique'.[27] The main art of the poet is to write in metre, 'en vers', 'en mètres', 'en rithme'.[28] The term 'rhétorique' means the arranging of words in metre, together with the wider sense of the choice, arrangement and expression of the subject matter in suitable language, applicable in verse as in prose.[29] When Bouchet uses the term 'poésie' and its derivatives, like other *rhétoriqueurs* he tends to use it to refer to the invention of fictions, particularly mythological—

thus the title *épître poétique* means that the poem contains such fictions.[30]

I shall therefore examine in turn his metrical practice, his language and his use of poetic fictions. In the case of poetic fiction the interplay between medieval and classical material is important; the growing classical influence on his poetry will be examined in a final section on his use of the classical genres of elegy and epigram.

2

Metre

In his first collection of verse, the *Amoureux transi*, Bouchet tries his hand at a variety of metrical patterns. The title poem is written in stanzas, $10^a10^a10^a4^b$ $10^b10^b10^b4^c$, etc., and octosyllabic ababbcbc. Decasyllabic couplets are used for the narrative passages. One *complainte* and two *épîtres* are in decasyllabic couplets, then a further *complainte* alternates decasyllabic and octosyllabic stanzas, both with the rhyme scheme aabaabbbabba. The *Complainte sur la guerre de Naples* employs five different types of stanza.[31] There are various types of *rondeaux* and *ballades*[32] and a prayer to the Virgin in decasyllabic couplets.

Rhymes are mostly *riches*, and frequently *équivoques*. As an enrichment at the beginning of a passage in elevated tone he often employs a string of rhymes based on long adjectives ending in the same suffix, e.g. 'herculeicque', 'mortificque', 'mundificque', 'umbrificque'.[33] But the device is rarely sustained; the most striking ingenuity in rhyme is a passage of *rimes batelées* extending over thirty stanzas.[34]

Already we can perceive a preference for the decasyllable. The only other line-length used at all frequently is the octosyllable. But there is a very respectable variety of stanza patterns, mostly isometric.[35] The verse of the *Renards* shows a similar picture, with some slight experiment with six- and seven-syllable lines.[36]

As we have seen, Bouchet had learnt his art by imitating the works of the fifteenth-century masters. Perhaps he used an *art de rhétorique* to help him with the intricacies of rhymes and rhyme schemes.[37] At this stage in his career, metre and rhyme are the most prominent features of his art in writing verse. It is therefore not surprising that his earliest, most clear-cut and most self-conscious change of practice came in this field.

There are three rules that Bouchet adopted between 1515 and 1519. Later, in 1530, he asserted that Louis de Ronsard had invited him to Paris in about 1515 and had instructed him in all three.[38] His original practice was thus corrected by a courtier with up-to-date knowledge of Court poetry. In one case at least the result was that he reacted very quickly indeed to a change of practice among poets at Court.

The case in question concerns the cesura in the decasyllabic line.[39] In the *Amoureux transi* Bouchet had made free use of both the epic and the lyric cesura. That is to say that he allowed himself the licence of having a mute e uncounted at the cesura, as though it were at the end of a line (the epic cesura):

Noble princesse, | royne de tous les cieulx

But he also allows mute e to be counted as the fourth syllable immediately before the cesura (the lyric cesura):

Saincte eglise | vous en donne la gloire[40]

The epic cesura is the product of a strongly marked cesura. The lyric cesura runs counter to this tendency; although less metrically shocking it does more violence to the rhythm of the line. Poets at the Court of Louis XII allowed themselves both these licences, although they tended to prefer one or the other. André de La Vigne favoured the epic, while Octavien de Saint-Gelais and Gringore in his early writings inclined to the lyric.[41] Bouchet himself hardly used the epic cesura in his two poems of 1512, but he continued to use the lyric freely. The usage of some poets has been studied thoroughly: Robertet for instance frequently used the lyric cesura, but Jean Marot in his earlier non-lyric works preferred the epic, as did Cretin.[42]

I think that it is possible to be more precise in one respect than Kastner in his study of the epic cesura, and to show that several poets with court connections changed their practice more or less together in a period of a very few years at the end of the reign of Louis XII and the beginning of that of François Ier.[43] We know from Clément Marot's *Adolescence Clémentine* of 1532 that in his earliest poems he had used the epic cesura, but that he had been corrected by Jean Lemaire de Belges. This must have been c.1514.[44] Some Burgundian poets had already abandoned the epic cesura,[45] and Lemaire had come from Burgundy to settle at the Court of France by 1512. His influence must have been very powerful, and somehow the rejection of the epic cesura extends to the lyric cesura, which Lemaire had used, albeit sparingly.[46] By 1516 Bouchet abandoned both the epic and the lyric cesura; what is more, he began to rewrite some of his earlier works in order to eliminate these licences.[47] In the preface to the *Chapelet*, published in 1517 but written before September 1515, he cites Lemaire as the source of both rules:

Et ay gardé une reigle qui veult en rithme de dix piedz la premiere partie de la ligne, si elle est de rithme imparfaicte, estre de cinq piedz, et sinalimphée avec le surplus. Ce que j'ay veu seullement observer et garder à Maistre Jehan le Maire, indiciaire et orateur moderne, et non à Maistre Alain Charretier, aux Grebans, Georges, Castel, Meschinot, Millet, Maistre Octavyan de Sainct Gelaiz, ne à plusieurs aultres bons orateurs en rithme, les euvres desquelz j'ay tousjours veu bien extimer. Jaçoit ce que ceste reigle, que je trouve rigoureuse, doibve estre observée pour la perfection du mettre, en ensuyvant les reigles latines.[48]

Bouchet here sounds rather resentful at feeling obliged to adopt such a rule. The reason he gives for it—Latin prosody—is obscure; the point is probably that in Latin pentameters, and usually in the hexameter, the cesura falls after a long syllable.[49] But in adopting the rule he is abreast of fashionable change. Many poets with Court connections seem to have changed their practice at much the same time. Gringore modified his practice after 1512, keeping the rule with very few exceptions from 1516 onwards.[50] Jean d'Auton observed it in his later work.[51] Jean Marot cut down his use of the epic cesura drastically from at least 1514, and hardly used the lyric cesura at all after 1511.[52] Cretin abandoned the lyric cesura in his later poems, although he was fairly tenacious of the epic cesura.[53] The case of Clément Marot has already been mentioned.[54] Bouchet's statement of the rule is one of the earliest, the other very early formulation being in the announcement of the Rouen *Puy* of 1516: this stated that the lines of the prize-winning *chant royal* should have no *coupes féminines* that were not elided.[55] Subsequently, in 1521, Fabri formulated the rule, again with reference to the *chant royal*, and it appears as a general rule in an anonymous *art de rhétorique* of perhaps about 1525.[56] It is a rule first observed by highly professional poets with Court connections. Bouchet is with them from the very beginning, and formulates the rule for a wider public. Other provincials catch up slowly. Eustorg de Beaulieu published a collection of poems in Bordeaux in 1529 that abounds in epic cesuras, but there are none in a collection that he published in 1537.[57] Michel d'Amboise is just as bad in 1530, but by 1532 he has seen the light. He talks about the 'abisme d'erreurs commise par mon inscience', particularly as regards the 'quadratures' (the term used for the first four syllables of a decasyllabic line); but now he has steeped himself 'en . . . œuvres Cretiennes, Marotiennes et Bouchetiques'.[58] So in 1532 Bouchet ranks with Cretin and Marot as a model for at least one poet. If we can take the *Epîtres familières* at face value, Bouchet instructed another young poet in this rule.[59]

Clearly the rule did need to be pointed out to the aspiring poet; two poets at Court who conspicuously failed to adopt this change of practice were François 1er and Marguerite de Navarre.[60] The case of Marguerite is quite clear: she favoured the lyric cesura, and did not cut down on it until after 1532 when, Marichal suggests, Marot may have instructed her in the matter. Many of the variants in the *Miroir de l'âme pécheresse* are brought about by corrections to the cesura.[61] Bouchet's first formulation of the rule would lead one to believe that he had simply observed it in the works of Lemaire, but the later *épître* to Ronsard shows that he had been instructed in it. Clearly, however, he regarded Lemaire and other Burgundian poets as the source of the rule.[62]

Another rule, which he says Ronsard taught him, was the alternation of masculine and feminine rhymes.[63] Looking back on his early errors in 1536 he says:

> En rithme plate (qu'on appelle Leonyne) ne ordonnois ne entrelaissois les masculins et femenins vers, comme a communement fait monseigneur Octavian de S. Gelaiz, evesque d'Engoulesme, en ses Epistres d'Ovide et Eneides de Virgille par luy de latin en françois traduictes.[64]

Bouchet was not quite so swift to abide by this rule. He ignores it in the passages of decasyllabic couplets in the *Temple* of 1517, while keeping the rule about the cesura. In the same year he published the *Epître de Marie*, probably composed early in 1515, which also ignores it. But his next work containing decasyllabic couplets observes the rule fairly rigorously; this is the *Labyrinthe* published in 1522 and probably begun 1519–20. The first *Epître familière* to abide by the rule is one in which the *Labyrinthe* is mentioned (*Ep.* 15). Thereafter he formulates the rule for other poets (*Ep.* 72; 107, in which he says that he likes to see alternation observed in *vers croisez* as well as couplets; and 67, in which he shows Germain Colin Bucher that alternation can be observed in *rime florentine*, i.e. *terza rima*). All his later verse keeps the rule, although he does not undertake the radical revisions necessary to make his earlier work conform.

In observing this rule from at least 1522 he is almost alone. Cretin observed alternation in some of his works, particularly in his *Chroniques*, but Clément Marot did not feel obliged to abide by it.[65] Few of Bouchet's correspondents in the *Epîtres familières* keep the rule. It was not generally accepted until the Pléiade, and then for reasons said to be connected with music.[66] But for Bouchet, who liked ingenious metrical complications, it was invaluable, since it provided one of the few formal devices available in the series of decasyllabic couplets which he was increasingly to employ.

The last rule concerns the *rondeau*. Here Bouchet was at first actually resistant, and his reason is most significant. In the *Chapelet* of 1517, a series of fifty *rondeaux* and five *ballades* on moral themes, he says, in the introduction that we have already quoted concerning the cesura:

> Combien que ung rondeau bien acomply doibve selon l'opinion d'aulcuns clorre et rentrer, toutesvoyes n'ay peu observer ceste rigueur en si grant nombre de rondeaulx, doubtant pour telle observance laisser la substance de ma matiere, mais à l'exemple d'aulcuns orateurs bien extimez, qui ont maintenu ung rondeau estre parfaict ou rentrement seullement, me suys contenté de faire rentrer partie desditz rondeaulx, et l'aultre partie clorre et rentrer.[67]

Rentrer simply means the double repetition of the opening words of the *rondeau* to form a refrain—this the most characteristic mark of a *rondeau*. But *clore* means that the *rondeau* should be so constructed that it makes sense not only with the refrain, but also without it.[68] The devastating effect of this rule can best be seen by comparing one of the 1517 *rondeaux*, which does not keep the rule, with a revised version first published in 1525 in which the rule is kept:

> *Chapelet*
> Legiereté est tousjours reprouchable
> Car de folie est par trop approuchable
> On doibt avoir tousjours son sens racis
> Et le tenir soubz une pierre assis
> Sans l'eventer, car trop il est muable,
>   L'oppinion de toy soit immuable
> Et par conseil la tiens constant et stable
> En evitant comme ou droit est precis
>   Legiereté.
> Il est vilain à prince redoubtable
> Et à ung juge ou autre homme notable
> Quant ung cas est par luy soudain decis
> Et que l'on dict en des lieux plus de six
> 'Mal a jugé'. Fuys donc comme le diable
>   Legiereté.

> *Opuscules*
> En toutes gens est tousjours reprochable
> Legiereté de folie approchable
> On doit avoir le sens ferme et racis
> Et le tenir soubz une pierre assis
> Sans l'eventer, car il est trop muable,
>   L'oppinion ne soit pour ce immuable
> Mais pour conseil ferme, constante et stable
> A la raison soit ung dire precis
>   En toutes gens.
> Il est vilain à prince redoubtab[l]e
> Et à ung juge, ou aultre homme notable
> Quant ung cas est soudain par luy decis
> Et que l'on dict en des lieux plus de six
> 'Mal a jugé': La chose n'est louable
>   En toutes gens.[69]

The rule is a trivialising one. It means that it is very difficult to use the subject or object of the main verb in the refrain; in practice adverbial phrases are nearly always chosen. The possibility of having a keyword chiming through the *rondeau*, as in the first version here, is thus greatly reduced. The reason for Bouchet's initial rejection of the rule is not, however, aesthetic. He fears damage to the substance, the meaning of this moral verse.

In fact, as so often, he is in a quandary, demonstrated by the fact that when he republished these *rondeaux* in the *Opuscules* of 1525 he rewrote all those in which he had not kept the rule. His sense of a hoop, through which he would like to be able to jump, ultimately won. With all these three rules, Bouchet is accepting additional technical difficulties that actually cut out possible areas of stylistic effect. It is interesting that Cretin continued to use the epic cesura to some small degree, and Gratien du Pont defended it, saying that 'la composition n'en seroit si fluyde ne liberalle, qu'est une chose tres requise et louable en la dicte science'.[70] Marot would have no truck with the mechanical alternation of masculine and feminine rhymes, keeping instead the possibility of manipulating the different effects of the two types of rhyme. The *rondeau* was simply ousted by other short forms—the *dizain* and ultimately the sonnet—that placed fewer constraints on the development of meaning, metaphor and wit. But Bouchet loved metrical difficulties; it is in such technical problems that the appealing difficulty of poetry lies. And so ultimately he espouses all these rules.

Nevertheless, as we have seen, such rules, attractive as he found them, were in conflict with his paramount aim of being useful in his poetry. Some developments in his verse after 1520 can be explained by his attempts to resolve this problem. In moral and other instructive works he abandons strophic forms in favour of decasyllabic couplets, and thus chooses forms that lend themselves to isometric couplets, notably the *épître* and the *épitaphe*. Here, apart from the rhyme itself, which continues to be mostly *riche* or *équivoque*,[71] the sole metrical ornament is the alternation of masculine and feminine rhyme. This could not hinder his meaning seriously, although it probably made him more long-winded as he laboured to express every particle of his substance. The overwhelming preponderance of the decasyllable in Bouchet's work is thus partly explained. But an examination of his more ornate poems shows that this tendency was not confined to didactic writing.

If we now examine the distribution of different metres in his five memorial works, it is possible to trace a very clear development.

The *Temple* has a fair right to be considered the height of Bouchet's achievement as a *rhétoriqueur*. Its ornaments are those of *rhétoriqueur* metrics, sharpened by his new consciousness of the cesura rule and enriched by a use of poetic fictions probably inspired by Lemaire.[72] In order to appreciate the metrical patterns we must take note of the structure of the poem. An *acteur* provides the framework narration, while a different projection of the author, *Le Traverseur*, is the protagonist who laments the death of Charles de La Trémoille. *Le Traverseur* seeks for his lost master, and is introduced by Cybele to the *Champ de Vertus*, among whose twelve tabernacles he finds the *Temple de Bonne Renommée* and witnesses the ceremony at which an

image of Charles is placed in the temple. A very large part of the
work is in decasyllabic couplets: the narrative of the *acteur* and the
long description of the twelve tabernacles, which is full of historical
exempla and moral and satirical reflections. But elsewhere there is
metrical complexity, for it is by metre that speakers are to some
extent differentiated. This device is standard among *rhétoriqueurs*.[73]
Le Traverseur speaks in several different strophic forms: in his initial
lament a 13-line stanza rhyming aabaabbccdccd is alternated with
stanzas all with a different pattern of line lengths. Most are heterometric, as for example:

> Zephirus musse ta verdure
> Affin qu'on temps que le ver dure
> Dessus le dure
> Ne puisse avoir resjouissance.
> Boreas, remply de froidure,
> Prepare moy toute laidure
> Tant que je endure
> Tousjours par dure desplaisance.
> Je dy fy de toute plaisance
> Et aisance,
> Pour plorer la desconfiture
> De celuy qui eut la puissance
> De me donner bonne aventure.[74]

Here the rhyme is a prominent ornament, all at least *riches*, several
équivoques.

Later *Le Traverseur* speaks in a decasyllabic 10-line stanza and
Cybele is given a decasyllabic 8-line stanza rhyming abaabbcc; the
same metre is later used for epitaphs. *Bonne renommée* has a 9-line
decasyllabic scheme, aabaabbcc. The greatest complexity is reserved
for the Virtues in a *Chant et oraison sur le corps du trespassé*; this
consists of six 7-line stanzas rhyming ababbcc. There is a further
decoration here, in that the eighteen rhymes spell out a verse of the
liturgy.[75]

Thus metrical variety is used to heighten lyrical passages and to
characterise the different actors in the narrative, a technique regularly used by Bouchet's models. But he has rather diluted the effectiveness of the device by the long central passage of decasyllabic
couplets that is really the heart of the book. Even in this highly
ornamented work the provision of information, however interesting, is at war with technique.

The *Labyrinthe* of 1522 in one respect improves on the *rhétoriqueur*
technique of the *Temple*. The story of the *Labyrinthe* allegory is much
more complicated and there are far more personifications. For the
initial lament and for the narration he uses decasyllabic couplets,
now alternating masculine and feminine rhymes. But for the speech
of the various personifications he uses stanzas of 5, 7, 8, 9, 10, 11, 12

and 13 lines. There is now a significance in the way these stanzas are distributed. *Humaine Discipline* speaks in 8-line stanzas, but the superior *Veritable Doctrine* speaks in 10-line stanzas: since decasyllables are used, this makes a perfect square, 10 by 10. The three Theological Virtues in the second part discourse at length, each with her own stanza pattern. Faith has 12 lines, doubtless representing the twelve articles of faith, Hope has 7, Charity has 9. Another technical feature of the first part is the appearance of two debates. *Le Conflit d'Eur et de Malheur* is a series of 194 5-line stanzas (aabba) giving contradictory historical examples of fortune and misfortune. Later comes a series of *rondeaux* (all made to both 'clore et rentrer') forming a debate between *Humaine Discipline* and *Veritable Doctrine*.

But in another respect the *Labyrinthe* represents a development away from *rhétoriqueur* diversity, a development that may be regarded as an impoverishment. Bouchet now uses the decasyllable exclusively. Heterometric stanzas, an attractive feature of the *Temple*, disappear completely, never to return. Even the series of *rondeaux* was the last new set that Bouchet was to write: subsequently he practically abandoned the form.

A heavy preference for the decasyllable, although not necessarily arranged in couplets, is thus characteristic of all Bouchet's work after 1520, and not merely the didactic. We have seen that this in fact merely exaggerates a tendency already present in his work. Preference for isometric forms is equally evident in Marot and his followers; apart from *chansons* and related forms the heterometric stanzas of the *rhétoriqueurs* practically disappear. The preference for the decasyllable over any other metre is also accentuated in most writers of this period. If, as seems likely, the growing fixity of the structure of French made the slightly longer line desirable,[76] this would be from the start of his career a pressing reason for Bouchet to prefer it, given his concern with providing information. The alexandrine, however, must have seemed too unfamiliar to him in spite of various examples in his predecessors; he only uses it once, in an epitaph for La Trémoille.[77]

After the *Labyrinthe* Bouchet detached himself still further from *rhétoriqueur* practices. He writes for the most part in the inevitable decasyllabic couplet and in newly favoured short forms. *Ballades* disappear along with *rondeaux*, and the use of varied stanza patterns begins to decline. The *Angoisses et remèdes d'amour*, contains two new poems written in stanza form, aabaabbbcc and aabaabbccdccd. One interesting point about the latter scheme is that metre in this poem is made to reflect the sense of the poem in a way that exploits his recently adopted constraint of alternation. In the first six stanzas of *La Dame se complaignant de son desloyal ami* the a and c rhymes are masculine and the b and d feminine. This pattern is reversed in stanza seven, which is a turning point in the narrative, when the girl begins to tell how she became pregnant and was deserted by her lover. The pattern is reversed again in the last two stanzas, where narrative is replaced by imprecation against her fate.[78]

As well as these there are passages in the two memorial works of the 1530s, the *Epîtres, élégies* and the *Jugement*, that use stanza forms. But in the same works he experiments with short isometric forms, among which he particularly favours the *douzain*. In the 1520s and 1530s the *dizain* was gaining popularity, but Bouchet presumably liked a little more room for manoeuvre. He had occasionally used short forms in his early work for epitaphs, and he used them now for the associated form of the epigram.[79] The *Epîtres, élégies* and the *Jugement* are for the greater part made up of decasyllabic couplets and epigrams of various lengths. The same is true of the small amount of new verse printed in the *Généalogies* in 1545.[80] And finally, in the *Triomphes du roi*, his last work in the grand manner, a monumental piece similar in some ways to the *Labyrinthe*, rich in poetic fictions, the dominant metre is decasyllabic couplets; fictional speakers are sometimes characterised by distinctive stanza forms as they were in the earlier work, but they are also allowed to speak in couplets. And in the second part, which features the Theological Virtues, only decasyllabic couplets are used.[81]

Bouchet had never employed the most intricate *rhétoriqueur* forms, and metrical diversity was always restricted to a fairly small part of his writing. But it is clear that, having adopted the technical difficulties of the cesura rule, which made for a better-sounding line, and alternation, which gave more pattern to decasyllabic couplets, he increasingly ignored the opportunities for technical flamboyance and for diversity that the *Arts de Rhétorique* had offered. He moves with the times in gradually restricting himself to decasyllabic couplets and short isometric forms. In this development we can see the requirements of his subject matter and the dictates of fashion working together.

3

Language

The language of Bouchet's poetry reveals less clear-cut change than the metrics. But it is possible to discern a development in those works that require an elevated style, a development that may perhaps reflect his admiration for the style cultivated by Clément Marot and other younger writers.

In the *Amoureux transi* he exhibits many of the rhetorical ornamentations favoured by his contemporaries. His favourite rhetorical figures are accumulation, particularly of names and exempla from mythology and history, personification, the use of sentences or proverbs at the end of a stanza (*epiphonema*), repetition, antithesis, exclamation, apostrophe, alliteration.[82] But of the more complex

and ingenious verbal devices particularly characteristic of *rhétoriqueur* poets we find just a few examples; in one stanza alliteration is
extended to what was called *rime senée*:

Faulse fortune, fragile, fantasticque,
Folle, fumeuse, folliant, follaticque,
Favorisant follastres follement . . .[83]

There is one puzzle verse that can be read both forwards and
backwards; if the words are read in reverse order the sense is the
opposite of the words read in normal order:

Poictevins sont loyaulx, non caulx,
Feables, non voulans meffaire,
Begnins non rudes, bons non faulx . . .[84]

And one can find just a few examples of punning *double-entendre*:

Paris fut juge et si les visita
Et pour Venus sentence intergeta
Quant tous leurs cas furent par luy congneuz.[85]

In the prose accompanying verse passages the vocabulary is latinate, he employs accumulation, particularly of adjectives, and his
sentence structure multiplies subordinate clauses:

> (Melancolie) feit de cruelz et divers exploitz en la re-
> gion de mon pouvre entendement, et tellement qu'elle
> greva les quatre vertuz sensitives enracinées en ma de-
> bille corporance, qui sont sensitive, estimative, ymagina-
> tive et memoire, au moyen de quoy ma fragille sensua-
> lité, pressée des choses susdictes, fut contrainte pour
> contenter mon naturel appetit (environ l'aube du jour
> que Phebus nous rappelle aux mondains abuz) prendre
> quelque repos ou leger somme.[86]

His verbis
utitur
Virgilius
in Eneid.

Bouchet thus associates a concentration of verbal figures and
latinate vocabulary with the high style in both verse and prose, but
he does not use the more flamboyant figures in either very great
concentration or over very extended passages.

If we pass to a work of his maturity as a *rhétoriqueur*, the *Temple*,
the main technique of the central passage describing the twelve
tabernacles is accumulation of examples. In the more highly ornamented passages which, as we have already seen, are distinguished
by metrical variety, there is a greater density of verbal device. We
have noted that Bouchet distinguishes the voice of the *acteur* from
that of the *Traverseur* by a difference in metre. At the beginning of
the *Traverseur's* lament the tone of the language is also raised:

Plorez, mes yeulx, plorez sans fin et cesse,
Magnifestez par larmes ma tristesse,
Veillez tousjours sans plus prendre repos.
Ma pauvre langue, helas, prenez adresse
De prononcer, si povez, ma tristesse
Et ne tenez jamais aultre propos . . .[87]

Here he uses apostrophe, repetition of structure, alliteration, and enumeration of all the parts of his body that are to express his grief. The short line passages lend themselves to an intensification of such devices, with the rhyme much more prominent:

O mort mordente
Sanguinolente
Qui tout abas;
Mort extuente,
Dure et cruente
En tes combas,
As tu au bas
Mon maistre mis?
As tu soubmis
Dessoubz ta darde
L'homme promis
A ses amys
Pour seure garde?[88]

But towards the end of the lament it would be difficult to distinguish the language from that of the narrative passages:

De sa maison c'estoit la perle ou rose;
De sa beaulté chose vraie propose
Qu'il estoit grant, bien formé par nature,
Et si n'eust sceu Foulquet en sa paincture
Homme pourtraire aussi beau qu'il estoit.
Long nez avoit, yeulx vers, blanche taincture,
Barbe assez forte et cheveux par mesure,
Et en son port gravement se portoit.[89]

Another illustration of the relative simplicity of his language is a passage that should be the lyrical climax, when the Virtues chant a prayer around the bier. Metrical complexity is at its height here, as the rhymes of each stanza spell out a versicle and response from the appropriate part of the liturgy of the Mass for the Dead, 'A porta / inferi / erue / domine / animam / eius':

O Dieu puissant, du quel le monde estre
Et dont chascun a tous les jours sup-   A
Veuillez ouyr l'oraison qu'on fer-
Pour le proffit et salutaire   Port
De cestuy-là, duquel tres bon rap-
Nous vous faisons, car le mort suport-   A
Patiemment, dont honneur rapport-[90]

In this first stanza it will be noted that in spite of the constraints of the rhyme the meaning is perfectly clear. It will also be noted that the tone of the language is extremely prosaic given the circumstances; the opening invocation deteriorates into an end-of-term report.

It can be seen that where Bouchet aims at a grand manner he uses rhetorical devices of a mainly verbal kind. His excursions into metaphor are simple and conventional ('la darde de la mort', 'la perle ou rose de sa maison'). But in using verbal devices he appears relatively diffuse and unable or unwilling to sustain the density of figure that one finds, for example, in Molinet.[91] Nevertheless, verbal device remains his main means of decorating his verse; he does not experiment with language that appeals in a different way. This can be demonstrated in a passage from the *Temple* in which Bouchet is drawing on material used by Lemaire. As *Le Traverseur* wonders where to find Charles de La Trémoille, his meditations on nymphs derive from Boccaccio via Lemaire's *Illustrations*:[92]

> Seroit-il point chassant par les fourestz
> Acompaigné des tresbeles driades?
> Car il amoit de chasse les apprestz
> Et y faisoit courses et grans estrades.
> Seroit-il point avec les oreades,
> Lievres courant par les lieux montueux?
> Seroit-il point es fluves fluctueux
> Acompaigné des tresdoulces nayades?
> Seroit-il point soubz arbres fructueux,
> Cuyllant du fruict avec amadriades?
>
> Seroit-il point avecques les hymnydes
> Par my les prez sur les belles floretes,
> Ou au jardin des sades Hesperides
> En divisant plaisamment de amouretes?
> Seroit-il point es fontaines très nectes
> Et rutillans que gardent les nappées?
> Non, pour certain, telles nymphes ou phées
> Ne poursuyvoit, car ce ne sont que fables;
> Mais desiroit marcialles trophées
> Semblablement toutes choses louables.[93]

This mythological material is attractive and a decoration in itself. But we may compare these stanzas with Lemaire's treatment of the nymphs in the *Temple de Venus*:

> Nymphes aussi, diligentes et prestes,
> A la deësse ont offert leur service,
> Tout à l'entour faisans danses et festes.
>
> Les nappéës exerçans leur office
> Font bouillonner fontaines argentines,
> Creans ung bruit à sommeil très propice.
>
> Puis à dresser les tentes celestines
> Ont mis leur soing les mygnonnes dryades,
> Faisans de bois ombrageuses courtines . . .[94]

Lemaire's adjectives in particular are more emotive and visually

appealing—'diligentes et prestes, argentines, celestines, mygnon-
nes'—in comparison with Bouchet's 'tresbeles, tresdoulces, belles,
tresnectes, rutillans'. Bouchet's most carefully chosen adjectives
serve quite a different purpose, the alliterative and etymological
play of 'lieux montueux, fluves fluctueux' and 'fructueux / fruit'.
Such verbal ornamentation is not dense; the main rhetorical devices
of the stanzas are repetition of structure, 'Seroit-il point . . .' and
enumeration. The names of the various types of nymph, all at the
rhyme, are a decorative feature in themselves in Bouchet's verse,
whereas Lemaire has gone beyond this to exploit their plastic possibilities.

The *Temple* is a good example of Bouchet's *rhétoriqueur* style at its
height. We have seen that from the metrical point of view Bouchet
changed his practice considerably in the later part of his career and,
like Marot and his imitators, tended to restrict himself to decasyllabic couplets and isometric short forms. Such differences as we find
in the language of his later poetry seem to be the result of the
influence of the style made fashionable particularly by Marot. Clément Marot used the verbal figures of the *rhétoriqueur* not for independent showy and ingenious ornamentation, but, less obtrusively,
as persuasive devices in rhetorical discourse. Bouchet had never
cultivated a great density of such techniques, and he was very
concerned with communicating his substance. One might therefore
expect the newer style to suit him, as it makes the language of
poetry that of elegant discourse, manipulating the verbal devices of
rhetoric with apparent ease and naturalness. But such a style must
be employed with very great skill if it is not to fall flat. Bouchet's
comments on his own and other people's style in the *Epîtres* suggest
that he well appreciated the qualities of the new style. The adjectives
that he applies to it are 'doux', 'poly', 'eloquent', 'plaisant', 'facile'.
His description of Marot is particularly revealing:

> . . . Nature
> Le rend plaisant en la sienne escripture,
> Et a l'esprit si grant et si gentil
> Qu'en tous ses vers il est doulx et facil;
> Impossible est de veoir rime plus doulce
> En ce où l'esprit par nature le poulse.[95]

Elsewhere he calls Marot a 'vray poète né'.[96] 'Nature' and 'naturel'
are terms that recur in connection with the new style, whereas the
older poets were praised for their excellent 'artifice'. This reflects
Horace's dictum on the relative importance of nature and art:

> Natura fieret laudabile carmen an arte
> Quesitum est: ego nec studium sine divite vena
> Nec rude quid possit video ingenium   (*Ars poetica* 408–10)

Sagon, by contrast with Marot, is said to be 'orateur bien apprins',
but to lack the 'doulceur du langage' of his opponent.[97]

Certainly then Bouchet appreciated the new style and in some circumstances he tried his best to imitate it. He openly imitates well-known poems by Marot; for example, in the *Triomphes du roi*:

L'un ne peut rien fors d'amoureuse rithme,
L'autre en rithmant sur amours il s'enrithme.[98]

And in the *Généalogies* he addresses the *maistre des requestes ordinaire du roy*, Lazare de Baïf, asking to be let off some tax:

'Si fauldra il payer, ou qu'on vous livre'
(Dist le sergent par grand affection)
'Sur tous voz biens briefve execution'.
'Je le veux bien, non sur ma librairie,
(Dis-je au sergent) ne sur ma rymairie;
Car je m'attends en faire au Roy present . . .'[99]

Both these examples come from very late works, but the change in his language is perceptible well before this. It can be seen particularly clearly in the *Angoisses*, 1537, where two poems composed in about 1500 are juxtaposed with two new ones that are completely different. We have already noted that Bouchet retained his earlier manner to the extent of writing his two new elegies in stanza form, but the verbal decoration is dramatically lighter than in his early poetry. Devices like alliteration, repetition and balancing are still used, but discreetly rather than showily. There is no use of personification, a prominent device in the original poem entitled *L'Amoureux transi*; instead he uses direct narrative and description of the lover's psychological state:

Las il me vint courtoisement tenter
Par doulx regars et honneste acointer,
Me promectant que seroys son espouse.
Par chascun jour me venoit tourmenter
De longs propos, et non sans se venter,
A celle fin qu'à son vouloir m'expouse.
Longtemps je fuz, que de toute la chose
Qu'il me disoit, compte je ne tenois,
Et rudement vers luy me maintenois
En mesprisant sa tant folle entreprise;
Ses argumens très bien je destournois
Et à vertuz du tout me retournois.
De faire ainsi fuz en jeunesse apprise.[100]

These last lines are rather a nice evocation of the girl's self-righteousness before her fall. This is the poem in which Bouchet marks the turning-points in the narrative with a change in the pattern of *alternance des rimes*. In the final stanza he contrives, with rather obvious effort, to place a key word at the very end of the poem:

[Folle amour] Sous faulx semblant elle mect en ruyne
Saiges et folz, pauvres et indigens,
Princes et roys, monarches et regens,

Preux chevalliers et gens plus droictz que sierges,
Moynes cloistriers, et docteurs refulgens,
Theologiens en vertuz emergens,
Femmes d'honneur, mariées et vierges.[101]

In short, he now looks for devices that harmonise with the sense of his verse. He rarely now accumulates verbal devices for their own sake.

The modification of his style can be perceived in his treatment of motifs from classical poets. Like many *rhétoriqueurs* Bouchet imitates certain well-known figures from the Latin poets, and particularly when introducing a narrative with meteorological and astrological references. One of his favourite passages from Virgil is used very differently in 1522 and 1549:

Jamque rubescebat stellis aurora fugatis. Vergi. Enei ii

Aurora interea miseris mortalibus animam, Extullerat lucem refferens opera atque labores. Verg. Ene. xi.

Postera vix summos spargebat lumine montes, Orta dies cum primum alto se gurgite tollunt, Solis equi lucemque elatis naribus efflant. Virg. Enei. xii.

Lors que Aurora du ciel eut les estelles
Quant à nos yeulx abscond par façons telles
Qu'on povoit veoir Titan treslumineux
Chassant de nuyt l'umbre caligineux
Et appellant de toutes pars les hommes
A labeur prendre, et supporter les sommes
De cestuy monde et les journelz travaulx,
Et que ses prompts et allegres chevaulx
Passoient roufflans, mieulx que ne fit Pegase
Dessus le mont de Orient, dit Caucase
Qui de ses rais begnins et siderez
Eut abbatu par moiens moderez
De son amye Aurora la rouzée,
Dont elle avoit mainte terre arrousée . . .
                                    (*Labyrinthe*)[102]

Et quand Aurore eut l'Oceane mer
Habandonnée, et qu'elle vint ramer
Les blancs chevaulx du char qui Phebus porte,
Et qu'au labeur tous humains elle exhorte,
En repellant les ombres de la nuyt
Et le dormir, trop long, qui souvent nuyct . . .
                                    (*Triomphes du roi*)[103]

The second version has not been developed by amplification, it uses simpler vocabulary, simpler rhymes and simpler word order.

Simplicity, however, does not guarantee success. Bouchet's prolixity militates against elegance, and it cannot be denied that he often sounds flatly prosaic. He had always used *enjambement* very freely, and this tendency becomes even more noticeable. In the *Epîtres morales* it seems to be a deliberate feature of his style to combine *enjambement* with chains of subordinate and co-ordinate clauses:

Et si doit plus desirer le bon pere,
Qui a desir que son enfant prospere,

Despendre argent pour science acquerir
A son enfant, que grands biens luy querir.
Car les grands biens pourra soubdain despendre,
Et le sçavoir demeure, qui pretendre
Fera l'enfant d'avoir biens et honneurs
Plus que son pere, et en plus grands valeurs.[104]

The effect of an endless chain of sense is enhanced here by repetition of vocabulary. In this discursive poetry he seems to wish to imitate the manner of argument in prose; he may even wish to give to his verse something of the flavour of Latin.[105] There is no reason to suppose that this effect is not deliberate, for when experimenting with short isometric forms he contrives in one series at least to achieve a density appropriate to such a form; here the repetition of vocabulary has a completely different effect:

Par le peché d'Adam la mort j'attends,
Par Jesuchrist en mourant j'attends vie,
Et par la loy à damnation tends,
Foy par espoir à salut me convie:
La loy me damne et la foy y obvie,
Car je n'ay faict ce que la loy me dit.
Si par la loy damné suis et mauldict,
D'autant que n'ay la saincte loy tenue,
A ce Jesus par la foy contredit,
Qui ha pour nous en croix mort soubtenue.[106]

This is reminiscent of Marguerite de Navarre's elaborate interlacing and repetition of key concepts in some passages of *Le Miroir de l'Ame pécheresse*, a work that Bouchet admired and of which there are echoes elsewhere in his verse.[107]

It is worth asking why in the early part of his career Bouchet fails to employ the density of verbal devices paraded by some of his models, and why in the latter part his style is often so aggressively flat. Lack of talent is one obvious answer. But while this may explain the halting rhythm of his decasyllables, it really does not explain his relatively light use of verbal figures, because he is patently capable of employing the flamboyant high style when he so chooses. It is true that his *clausulae humilitatis* normally take the form of apologies for deficiencies in language[108] and, more significantly, he says of his style in 1522:

Et si je n'ay doulx et fluent langage
Je n'ay pas eu de nature ce gage
Plus advenant est ung don naturel
Que le sçavoir d'homme artificiel.[109]

This might indicate that he did not feel his talents as a writer lay in the manipulation of language. But it is difficult to know how precise an interpretation may be placed on these lines because of their echo of Horace's stress on natural gifts—it is another *clausula humilitatis*

to deny natural ability. We must also note that in the *Annales* he
makes a virtue of writing 'en gros langaige et non pas curial' because
he goes on to complain that some historians are more interested in
eloquence than truth.[110] In 1522 he says to the theologian Jacques
Prévost:

> Et si par les orateurs en mon absence et vous present j'estoys
> reprins d'avoir aucunesfois usé de langaige contrainct, vous
> plaise aussi . . . me excuser et leur remonstrer que ce a esté pour
> garder la substance des matieres difficilles où impossible est de
> equivoquer de termes sans se mettre en dangier d'erreur.[111]

Concern for the true record, concern for his substance, dictate their
own style. And let us note that at the end of the lament of the
Traverseur in the *Temple*, which was quoted as an example of prosiness, he introduced a description of his patron with the phrase
'chose vraie propose'. Inasmuch as the flatness of his language is
due to a lack of verbal ornament it must be considered a deliberate
choice of plain idiom in the interests of clarity and truthfulness.

The language of Marot pruned of the flamboyance of the *rhétoriqueurs* is still a poetic language, which might conflict with truth.
When Bouchet is trying to vie with the Court poets in the *Jugement*
and actually addresses the King, he produces a strange mixture of
sycophancy and self-respect verging on tactlessness. Intermittently
he adopts the role of honest, plain-speaking man who has something worth saying and does not mind too much how he says it:

> Je suis certain que ma phrase n'est telle
> Comme de ceulx lesquelz sont soubz vostre aelle,
> Mais voux sçavez combien est different
> Le stille dur (toutesfoiz apparent)
> Des beaux traictez qu'en matiere feconde
> A faict Seneque, à la doulce faconde
> De Cicero, Saluste et aultres maints
> Qui en ung temps ont escript des Rommains;
> Et toutesfois on tient chers ses ouvrages
> Tant sont moraulx, et mesmement les sages.[112]

It is not unduly humble to compare oneself with Seneca. In the
narrative of the *Jugement* itself there are some striking passages of
unvarnished fact at variance with the grand eulogistic tone adopted
for this memorial for the King's mother. He reflects that it was
unfair that Louise should have died so young, given her sensible
mode of life:

> Car de viande aulcune ne prenoit
> Qu'elle ne sceust que sayne on la tenoit.[113]

He also seems to wish to indicate that Louise, although no doubt
bound for eternal glory, may well at present be in Purgatory.[114]
Such prosiness and apparent ineptness are probably a deliberate
parade of 'truth-telling'.

Thus throughout his career Bouchet's style is affected by his concern for the true presentation of his subject matter. But it is also clear that in the latter part of his career tastes changed, and that for this reason too he made a more discreet use of verbal figures and abandoned the more elaborate devices that he had toyed with at the beginning of his career.

Yet in the 1530s and 1540s he was still writing works that would seem to require some sort of elevated style—notably the *Jugement*, and the *Triomphes du roi* which commemorates François 1er. He would no longer rely on metrical diversity or verbal pomp to provide him with a suitable style. What seems to replace them is the dignity of the classics, in two ways. First, the elaboration of poetic fictions drawn from classical mythology, secondly the label of classical genre applied to poems that for the most part have little else classical about them.

4

Poetic Fictions

Poetic fictions concern not the form but the subject matter of poetry. They are thus not confined to verse; they can just as well be used to decorate prose, and are used for this purpose by Lemaire in the *Illustrations* and by Bouchet in the *Panégyrique*. But in spite of this they remain the distinguishing mark of the poet. M-R. Jung has shown how the vernacular terms cognate with *poetria* came to refer specifically to the aspects of poetry that dealt with mythological fiction.[115] Although Fabri says that 'poète', 'orateur' and 'rhétoricien' are used indiscriminately in French,[116] some poets at the beginning of the sixteenth century regularly use the terms 'poétique', etc., to mean 'using mythological fictions'.[117] In the course of the century 'poète' and 'poétique' come to embrace all aspects of poetry, including what an earlier generation would usually have styled 'rhétorique'.[118] But throughout his career Bouchet continues to associate these terms most commonly with fictions.

A narrative using such fictions is the poet's 'invention'; they are associated with fantasy and imagination.[119] There seems no reason why the term 'fictions poétiques' should be confined to mythological fictions, for the poet who uses personifications like *Dame Rhétorique*, *Raison*, etc., may be doing much the same thing as one who is using the Muses and Minerva.[120] In fact Bouchet describes an *épître* by a friend of his that contains such personifications as 'faicte en fictions poeticques'.[121] Certainly he more commonly has mythology in mind when using the term, but we must consider narratives using personifications under this heading too, partly because they are in some ways so similar, but partly as well because of the interplay between mythology and personification found in many works.

The trouble with poetic fictions is that they are not true. At the very beginning of his career Bouchet says of *poeterie*:

> Pour les subtilles invencions et choses admirables en elle contenue est reputée plus fabulatoire que veridique. Nam miranda canunt, sed non credenda poethe—Les poetes chantent choses de admiration, mais non pas à croire. Toutesfois ne sont point leurs dictz tous fabulatoires, mais tresvrays historiques moraulx.[122]

Much the same point is made thirty years later:

> Si nous parlons de ficte poesie
> Quand elle est bien par gens prudens choisie
> Peult prouffiter en la moralisant
> Mais aultrement à mal est induysant[123]

Poetic fictions are untrue and dangerous—unless interpreted in some moral sense that will render them useful and true. Mythological fiction then is useful for the moral lessons it can appealingly impart. It is sugar on a moral pill—as Bouchet is still saying of the *Triomphes du roi*:

> Lequel petit œuvre j'ay mis en vers, au moien de quelques fictions Poétiques appliquées à l'histoire, pour l'enrichir à l'exemple d'Homere, et pour adoulcir le moral.[124]

However, it is important that such interpretations of mythology should remain on the moral plane and should not impinge on the spiritual. Again, at the very beginning of his career, Bouchet underlines the theological errors of pagan poets and implies that he rejects theological interpretations of Ovid and Virgil:

> Des poethes pareillement,
> Choses nouvelles composans,
> Dit Aristote expressement
> Que iceulx furent antiquement
> Les premiers theologisans
> Dieux et deesses baptisans
> A plaisir par fais auctentiques
> Dont vindrent plusieurs heretiques
> Qui tresfollement se fioient
> En telz dieux et les adoroient
> Reputans Ovide et Virgille
> Vray dire comme l'evangille
> Avecques la probacion
> De philosophie inutile
> Fourrée en ceste ambicion[125]

He himself, when using mythological fictions in memorial works to represent the renown of prominent people after their death or the glory obtainable in this life, always draws a clear distinction between the moral plane and the spiritual; such glory is a just reward for virtue but it is not the same as salvation. So when in the *Temple*

Charles de La Trémoille is judged by Cybele's daughter Renown to be worthy of a place in one of her tabernacles, or when the effigy of Louise de Savoie in the *Jugement* is borne off by Mercury to the underworld and she is judged by Rhadamanthus and the other judges worthy of a place in the *Palais des claires dames*, there is in each case a careful explanation that this fiction only expresses the renown that they have earned in life and that will continue after death; it has nothing to do with salvation.[126] And when he wishes to commemorate a distinguished and saintly abbess, Renée de Bourbon, even when expressing the same idea of her continuing renown on earth, he considers that mythological fictions would be unsuitable for a woman whom he thinks of as a potential saint:

> Plus amplement de la dame eusse escript
> Et de sa mort selon mon rude esprit
> Mais de appliquer fiction Poeticque
> A tel deces je y trouverois replicque
> Parce qui'il est question de louher
> Une qui s'est voulu toute vouher
> A Dieu puissant, et à chose divine
> Et d'en parler Poesie n'est digne
> Et davantaige il n'est en mon povoir
> D'y appliquer le Poetic sçavoir.[127]

It is clearly mythological fiction that troubles him in such a context, for in the event he invents a fiction of his own. He has a vision of stars from which emerge the head and shoulders of women crowned with flowers. Arranged in three rows, they represent holy women, other Christian women of good renown and wise pagan women; Renée is welcomed into the first row.[128]

When he wishes to treat theological subjects within the framework of a fictional narrative he always uses personifications: in both the *Labyrinthe* and the *Triomphes du roi*, which deal with aspects of life on this earth, fortune and the pursuit of nobility, he moves in the second part of the book to consider human life from a spiritual rather than a purely moral point of view, and he has in each case a vision of three ladies, who turn out to be Faith, Hope and Charity. As well as using personifications for all theological concepts he also continues in varying degrees to use them, interspersed with mythological figures, in his moral works.

That he should mix the two types of figure is hardly surprising given his main source for mythological material, which is Boccaccio's *Genealogia deorum*. Sergio Cigada has demonstrated Bouchet's enormous debt to Boccaccio in the *Temple*.[129] Bouchet already knew the *Genealogia deorum* in 1503—he was quoting from the first book when he said that Aristotle called poets the first theologians[130]—but he does not exploit the source extensively before the *Temple*. As well as offering information about the gods, demi-gods, heroes and heroines of mythology, Boccaccio offers a range of interpretations: historical and euhemeristic, which equate pagan deities with human kings or with notable inventors; physical, which consider them as expressions of the nature of the earth, the skies and astrological influences; finally the moral, which sees them as depicting virtues or vices, or their stories as exemplifying some moral conflict. Boccaccio discusses several figures that can be regarded as personifications—*Fama, Gratia, Metus*, etc. Bouchet takes many different types of information from Boccaccio; characters, descriptions, interpretations, exempla. So in the *Temple* he takes from the *Genealogia* the descriptions of Somnus, Cybele, and the *Enfer poétique*, the enumeration and description of mythological figures in the *Investigation poétique* (when the *Traverseur* is wondering with which god his master is to be found) and quite a lot of information concerning characters to be found in the various tabernacles.[131] He also takes most of his arguments in defence of poetry from Boccaccio.[132] The *Genealogia* remains a source of material for fictions concerning Muses and nymphs, and for some of the mythological figures in the *Jugement*, particularly *Fame, Mercure* and the Underworld; but the other work with a really massive debt to Boccaccio is the *Triomphes du roi* of 1549, Bouchet's last work. Here *Poésie* gives an account of the plurality of the ancient gods, and then provides explanations of what is meant by them. Chapter 2, on 'La Pluralité des Dieux, selon les Gentilz', draws on Boccaccio's account of the genealogy of the gods beginning with Chaos and Demogorgon. The explanations given in chapter 4 also draw on Boccaccio's physical and moral interpretations, for example:

> Par Jupiter le feu est entendu:
> Sa seur Juno le clair air represente.
> Il l'espousa, dont sens nous est rendu,
> Que l'air et feu sont conjoinctz en temps deu:
> Et qu'il convient que l'air du feu se sente.[133]

The Muses are described and then explained in moral terms, which Boccaccio took from Fulgentius:

> Ou aultrement Clio c'est le desir
> De conquerir science et bon sçavoir.
> En ce desir Euterpé prend plaisir:
> Melpomené par ce s'en veult saisir,
> Et Thalia d'esprit se veult pourvoir.
> Polymnia faict la memoire avoir:
> Puis Erato invente à sa lucerne.
> Terpsicoré l'invention discerne,
>   Urania par sa nature elit;
> Tout cela fait Caliopé profere:
> Voyla comment les Poètes on lit,
> Les fictions ainsi l'on embelit.[134]

Finally the idea that noble men were treated by the poets as gods provides a distinguished background for the concept of nobility, which Bouchet then proceeds to examine.

When Bouchet first used Boccaccio so extensively in 1516 he appears to have been relatively original. Sergio Cigada points out that so far not a great deal of concrete evidence of direct imitation of the *Genealogia deorum* has been found in *rhétoriqueur* writers, in spite of the diffusion of manuscripts and translations of the work; the *Temple* is thus an important example of the assimilation of Boccaccio's generation of Italian humanist learning.[135] Cigada also shows that, in a passage describing various types of nymph, Bouchet is admittedly using material from Boccaccio, but with one eye on how Lemaire had used it before him in the first book of the *Illustrations de Gaule*.[136] It seems to me very likely that Bouchet was imitating Lemaire in this lavish use of material from Boccaccio. I do not mean that Bouchet got to know the *Genealogia deorum* via Lemaire: it is plain from the *Renards* that he already knew the work. Nor do I mean that Lemaire was unique in using mythological material, moralising it and letting it co-exist with personifications. But the fact remains that Lemaire in the *Illustrations* used such material on an unprecedented scale. With so recent an example available of a monumental work by an author whom Bouchet admired and imitated in other ways, it seems likely that the *Temple* bears witness to Bouchet's realisation on reading the *Illustrations* of the possibilities offered by mythological material from Boccaccio: erudite decoration, ways of approaching moral concepts other than by the usual personification of abstractions, the rich picturesqueness of the stories and characters of classical mythology. All these things are there for the taking in the *Genealogia deorum*, and in exploiting this source Bouchet was in all probability reacting quite swiftly to a new emphasis in Lemaire's very successful work.[137]

If so we must certainly see the treatment of mythology in the *Temple* as evidence of Bouchet's wish to adopt a modernising, 'humanist' approach. This is borne out in the enthusiastic tone of the work, in which the tabernacle of arts and sciences is described at greatest length, where the inventor of printing is singled out for special praise[138] and which incorporates a defence of poetry in general and of French poetry in particular. Bouchet's use of mythological fiction continues to have such connotations. In the *Epîtres familières* those letters that he addresses to the humanist group meeting at Fontaine-le-Comte are particularly liable to allude to literary composition in terms of fictions featuring Muses and nymphs. The *Jugement*, by means of which he was trying to gain the favour of François Ier and vie with the reigning Court poets, employs a narrative framework using mainly mythological characters and places. When he brings the *Amoureux transi* up to date as the

Angoisses et remèdes, he turns *Raison* into *Pallas.* Of course, as time wore on, and Bouchet continued to use his material in exactly the same way, as suggested by *Genealogia deorum,* he looked more and more old-fashioned; the full-blooded Boccaccian treatment of the gods in the *Triomphes du roi* is something of an anachronism in 1549, by which time such rigorously applied historical, physical and moral interpretations were losing popularity.[139]

We must now examine for what purpose and to what effect Bouchet employs mythological fiction. The first purpose is undoubtedly for grandeur, for the glorification of his subject. This is its function in the memorial works, which, as we have seen, in the earlier part of his career are also highly decorated by means of metre and language. The *Temple* is presented from the outset as an inspired work:

> Les dictes Muses, de Apolo et l'eloquent Mercure acompaignées, estoient venus presenter à mon esprit diverses invencions et fantasies avec toutes les especes de rithme pour d'icelles prendre ce que bon me sembleroit.[140]

Everything is designed to give consequence to Charles de La Trémoille: the *Traverseur* is visited by Cybele, who tells him that his master lives on with her daughter, *Bonne Renommée;* all the pagan gods in turn are judged unworthy of the company of Charles, since they all exhibit some failing to which he was not subject; the Virtues argue about which of their tabernacles Charles should be placed in, since they all have a claim on him. The fictions permit a series of rich and intriguing descriptions, which further ornament the work (*Cybele, Bonne Renommée,* the *Temple* itself): from this point of view mythological figures and personifications and symbolic buildings function in the same way. All these are signals that the *Temple* is a very grand work. It is interesting therefore to discover that there were those who did not consider that Charles de La Trémoille was quite grand enough to support this edifice. A few years later Bouchet complained that envious persons had criticised the *Temple,* saying that 'je use de adulation, en exaltant soubz umbre de deploration ung bien amé chevalier oultre et pardessus les Roys'.[141] The last words are particularly revealing. We are reminded again that the *rhétoriqueurs'* art is a very public art, and only the status of the subject publicly recognised prevents fictions of this type being ridiculous. Perhaps in his eagerness to honour his patron and show off his ability Bouchet neglected to recognise that the status of his subject was not quite up to the poetic treatment bestowed upon him.

Subsequently Bouchet reserved such very grandiose treatment for royalty, Louise de Savoie and François 1er. His next memorial work, the *Labyrinthe de Fortune* of 1522, in memory of Artus Gouffier, avoids the problem: he laments Gouffier at the beginning, but then

lets the fiction of the *Labyrinthe* arise from the meditations on life
that this death has provoked. The Labyrinth is not erected to the
honour of Gouffier, instead it represents human life on this earth.
The fiction employs personifications almost exclusively, and the
classical myth of Daedalus' Labyrinth is used to introduce a view of
life governed by Fortune, as *Humaine Discipline* teaches. Thus here
the mythological element serves the different purpose of introducing us to classical philosophies, which must be corrected by
Véritable Doctrine, Christian theology. In the *Panégyrique* of 1527,
writing a eulogy of Louis de La Trémoille, Bouchet chooses a historical genre, the panegyric in prose. He does, however, permit himself
some poetic fictions for the glory of his patron; in his youth Louis
has a vision of Mars, another of Venus and her band, later he sees
Minerva.[142] In 1538 in the *Jugement* for Louise de Savoie, extensive
fictions again give consequence to the subject. Mercury is busying
himself on behalf of Louise, fetching her effigy from St Denis and
producing the witnesses (the 'nymphs' Nature, Fortune and Grace)
who will vouch for her worthiness. Minos, Rhadamanthus and
Eacus find unanimously in her favour. If Bouchet was very sincere
in his overpraise of Charles de La Trémoille he perhaps had difficulties in the other direction here. He makes Eacus decide that no
notice should be taken of the murmurings of *Bruyct commun* and
L'Inconstance du peuple. (It is not really surprising that Bouchet never
became a court poet.)[143] But the splendour of the setting—the flight
over the Acheron and the vision of the underworld—is not in
question. In the *Triomphes du roi*, 1549, François Ier gets the grandest
treatment of all. After the concept of nobility has been given the
magnificent ancestry of the plurality of pagan gods, the Muse Erato
escorts Bouchet to watch the young Prince make his way through
the dangerous paths that lead to the *Séjour de Noblesse*. Venus appears before François as she did before La Trémoille; so does Minerva, and they prepare to fight a battle over him; Venus enlists help
from the underworld but Minerva goes to seek aid from the celestial
bodies, which permits Bouchet to evoke the mountains of the classical world, the nine heavens and the music of the spheres. This is the
most ambitious use of classical material Bouchet ever attempted.

Another way in which Bouchet frequently uses mythological
material is to express the pursuit of poetry, particularly in some
locus amœnus. The Muses appear, dancing, singing and playing
instruments—often rather rustic ones. 'Cornemuse', no doubt originally induced by the rhyme, nevertheless suggests a cheerful,
bucolic gathering. Joukovsky has discussed these passages and
shows that Bouchet is one of the earliest vernacular writers to
associate the Muses with the countryside rather than the allegorical
landscape in which they more commonly appear in the early sixteenth century:

J. Bouchet a donc le mérite de conduire les neuf sœurs dans une campagne verdoyante, où l'accompagnent certains collègues.[144]

This is particularly true of *Ep.* 23, addressed to his childhood friend Pierre Gervaise, in which he remembers their youthful literary efforts. It is interesting to note that the *épître* by Gervaise, which it answers, recounts a vision of *Rhétorique* and *Beau Parler*, whereas Bouchet prefers mythological evocations of the literary art. These two *épîtres* date from about 1529,[145] by which time Bouchet had described Apollo and the Muses several times. An early example is addressed to Nicolas Petit as a response to a Latin Ode: it contains the following passage:

Il m'a semblé qu'estois en paradis
Des orateurs, où l'on va par abditz
Et secretz lieux des Muses sicilides
Armonisans es umbres Castalides
Et que voyois Apole chevelu
Citharisant dessoulz son chief velu
A ton honneur une Ode morpheique
Et te bailloit la couronne orpheique
Comme à celuy qui bien le meritoit.[146]

Others are addressed to Ardillon (30, 34); in 78 the Muses instruct Bouchet to tell Ardillon of the death of Nicolas Petit.

Bouchet is particularly apt to adopt this mythological expression of the literary art, together with its allied subject, a pleasant place peopled with nymphs, when he is writing to his humanist friends who gathered at Fontaine-le-Comte. His *épître* to Rabelais describes Ligugé in similar terms.[147] There were neo-Latin poets in this group, not least among them Nicolas Petit himself, who had produced a volume of *Sylvae* employing poetic fictions.[148] It is probable that such contact with neo-Latin poetry in this period reinforced the taste he had acquired from Lemaire for scenery and gatherings decorated by mythological characters. It is worth noting that one of Nicolas Petit's liminary pieces for Bouchet's works, a Latin poem in the *Panégyrique*, takes as its subject 'the apparition of Virtue and Pleasure before Louis de La Trémoille'—in other words, he chooses a poetic fiction similar to the one with which Bouchet had decorated his own work.[149]

In Bouchet's *épître* to Petit the evocation of the Muses and Apollo has the effect of glorifying his friend. But we have noticed that Muses also appear in less ceremonial guise. This brings us to the third way in which Bouchet uses mythological material, which is for familiar and even comic effect. This is one of his most agreeable veins, and one in which he proves himself inventive within the conventions of his mythological material. He uses it in the early 1520s to sweeten requests. In *Ep.* 25 François du Fou receives a

delightfully learned fiction reviewing the forests of the ancient
world and their denizens: this ends up as a request for a present of
game for a relative's wedding feast, the exact date of which is
casually mentioned. Fictions make for good flattery too: the pro-
spective mayor of Poitiers receives a letter from his dead wife in the
Elysian fields, assuring him that all the gods are making the necessary preparations for his inaugural banquet, right down to Deverra
who is organising the sweeping and Myagrus who will get rid of
intruding flies.[150] Mercury, the god of eloquence, under whose
influence Bouchet claims to have been born,[151] frequently features
in such humorous fictions. One particularly ingenious fantasy appears as an introduction to the *Annales*. *Dame Aquitanicque* is sad
because no one has written her history; down flies Mercury to tell
Bouchet he must undertake the job, and fanning out the wings on
his feet tells Bouchet to choose a quill. In the accompanying woodcut, the author has apparently just plucked his feather from the
wing on Mercury's left foot.[152] Mercury appears in another request
poem; in *Ep.* 24 Bouchet has involved himself in a bad deal over the
cutting of some La Trémoille woods and wants his patroness to help
him. He represents himself wandering miserably through a wood
as night falls, and being terrified by Silvanus and his gang of satyrs,
etc. But later he comes across Mercury and the Muses:

Si me congneut Mercure de bien loing
Et si me feit sortir d'un petit coing
Où m'estois mis oyant leurs cornemuses,
Puis me mena devant toutes les muses
Où fuz contrainct tout au long reciter
Le mal lequel me faisoit contrister,
Dont chascun d'eux se print tresfort à rire.[153]

Very often, as here, the humour arises from a comic presentation
of the authorial *persona*. This is not by any means confined to
mythological narrative: in the *Temple* the *acteur* gets worried when
Le Traverseur falls down insensible and fears he will be arrested for
murder; in the *Labyrinthe* he gets discouraged on the way to the
Séjour d'Honneur and sits down at the roadside with 'un dur chillou
de regret amoureux' stuck in his foot.[154] But the device is even more
pleasingly incongruous when he is faced with the majesty of pagan
deities. Play on grand classical concepts produces the same effect;
in a context dealing with poetic composition, the ready-made expression 'car ma vielle ay mis dessous le banc' becomes an amusing
variant on 'hanging up one's lyre'.[155] Perhaps his best joke comes in
the *Triomphes du roi* when he has been listening to *Poésie* expatiating
on the plurality of pagan gods, and he expresses his disapproval.
Whereupon *Poésie* gets very cross indeed:

Lors commença la fureur Poetique
De Poesie à me faire replique.

She crossly explains what is meant by the plurality of the gods and
marches off in high dudgeon:

> Incontinant, Poesie sacrée
> En sa fureur print chemin par la prée

followed by a crestfallen and tongue-tied *Traverseur*

> Mais je n'ausois aulcun mot plus luy dire,
> Doubtant rejet et la response d'ire.[156]

This travesty of poetic fury was even a rather topical joke in 1549.

Such levity suggests again that he did not really think mythology
a matter to be taken too seriously; it can be justified on moral
grounds but giving pleasure is its real function. The fourth and last
use of mythological fiction is its pictorial value. Here yet again the
same applies to any fiction, mythological or otherwise. If anything
Bouchet shows a surer hand in the description of personifications,
which have the two-fold appeal of visual attractiveness and ingenious moral significance. Here for instance is *Humaine Discipline*, an
attractive but unsatisfactory lady from the *Labyrinthe*:

> D'ars liberaulx estoit faicte et nourrie
> Face monstrant de femme non marrie
> Elle portoit une cocte d'argent
> A lettres d'ors lassées par art gent
> Qui dès le temps que au monde fut yssue
> Dame Grammaire avoit ainsi tissue . . .
> La robbe estoit de couleur aerée
> De poincts de chiffre en fin or figurée
> Que Arismeticque avoit faict de ses mains
> Plaisante à voir à plusieurs des humains . . .
> Dessus son chief, portoit riche chappeau
> D'or esmaillé, d'artifice nouveau
> Où dessus l'or en lieu de pierres fines
> En bosse estoient les planetes et signes . . .[157]

Such figures could be, and were in fact, brought to life in *tableaux* for
royal entries. Bouchet went on inventing such figures throughout
his career. The accoutrements of mythological figures lack the immediately accessible symbolic sense to be found in personifications,
and so these sometimes have to be laboriously explained, but they
have an exotic visual appeal of their own. Here for example is Pan,
point for point as he appears in the *Genealogia Deorum* Book 1
chapter 4:

> Ce Pan avoit deux cornes sur le front
> Tendans au ciel, sur ung visage ront
> De couleur rouge, et la barbe tres grande,
> Vestu de peau faict en façon de bande,
> Laquelle estoit de diverses couleurs,
> Monstrant à tous ses forces et valeurs,
> Avec sa verge et fluste septenaire

De chalumeaux, pour plaisir ordinaire.
Ses membres bas il avoit tous veluz
Et piedz de chevre en corne resoluz.[158]

In the last section we saw that Bouchet did not use language in such a way as to make his nymphs so visually and emotionally appealing as those of Lemaire; he makes little attempt to play on his reader's senses. But he does give an itemised description, which would make it possible for an artist to draw the figure. Some of Bouchet's books actually contain woodcut illustrations that very accurately represent the accompanying text. As well as a woodcut in the *Annales* depicting Mercury and the author in the *Jardin de France,* and one of the unhappy lovers with Pallas in the *Angoisses,*[159] there is a remarkable series done for the *Jugement,* depicting Mercury and the judges of the underworld as well as the *Palais des claires dames.* The picture, showing Mercury flying over the Acheron with the effigy of Louise in his hand and Bouchet sitting on his shoulder, attests both the pictorial and comic value of mythological fictions.[160] It looks very much as if Bouchet intended a series of such illustrations to accompany the *Triomphes du roi,* but there are none; the pubisher presumably jibbed at the expense.[161] We are thus sadly deprived of a visual impression of Poetry in a fury or of François Ier rejecting Venus in favour of Minerva.

5

The Use of Classical Genres: Epigrams and Elegies

The clearest new development in Bouchet's poetry of the latter part of his career is the use of the names of classical genres. In 1532, for the first time he calls one of his poems an 'epigramme'; he entitles his little book on Renée de Bourbon in 1535 *Epistres, elegies, epigrammes et epitaphes* and the *Angoisses* of 1537 and the *Jugement* of 1538 contain respectively elegies and epigrams.

The case of the epigram is the more straightforward.[162] Bouchet suddenly became very eager to call poems epigrams. The first example appears in the 1532 edition of the *Annales.* It is one of the earliest French poems to be referred to as 'ung petit epigramme':

Cy dessoubz gist dame Claude de France,
Fille de roy, de roy femme et espouse,
Qui surmonta de tous vices l'oultrance
Et triumpha par vertuz, où se expouse
L'ame est en ciel, le corps icy repouse;
On n'a poinct sceu que offense fist mortelle,
Et deceda, laissant lignée belle,
On moys juillet mil cinq cens vingt et quatre.
Prions tous Dieu que la sienne sequelle
Puisse tousjours ses ennemys combatre.[163]

This poem is indistinguishable from a whole series that Bouchet had

previously called *épitaphes*. But in the same volume he records the
death of Louise de Savoie and says 'Dont j'ay faict ung petit traicté
à sa louange, intitulé le Palais et Epigrammes des cleres Dames'.[164]
This must be the work that eventually, six years later, was printed
as the *Jugement*. After his first epigram/epitaph for Queen Claude
he always uses 'epigram' in a more precise sense: it is an inscription.
In the *Temple* the Virtues had placed tablets bearing epitaphs around
the tomb of Charles.[165] This is the type of *épitaphe* that now regularly
becomes an *épigramme*. The Virtues place nine *épigrammes* for Renée
on tablets round her tomb. In the *Jugement* the *épigrammes* are inscriptions carved in the *Palais des claires dames*. A series for the
Dauphin François first printed in the *Généalogies* of 1545 are all once
again inscribed on tablets round his tomb.[166] So important is the
fictional narrative that turns epitaphs into inscriptions and thus into
epigrams that when he reproduces the nine epigrams for Renée in
the *Généalogies* all by themselves, without the narrative framework,
he simply includes them among the other *épitaphes*.[167]

For Bouchet then, an epigram is an inscription. It is also relatively
short. He refers in the *Jugement* to 'ces tant briefz et abstrainctz
épigrammes'.[168] Those of the *Jugement* are mostly *douzains*, though
some have one or more additional couplets inserted into the basic
pattern aba abb ccd ccd.[169] The style of the epigrams for Renée is
more decorated as Bouchet lets each Virtue praise her; here we get
some suggestion at least of witty ingenuity, but hardly classical in
inspiration:

> *Epigrame de Foy . . .*
> Ci gist Renée où la Foy reposa,
> Qui repos a, car elle fut fidelle,
> Fidellement à Dieu se disposa
> Et disposée, à amour se exposa,
> En s'exposant eut l'amour eternelle.
> L'eternité celeste essencielle
> Et une essence a creu en Trinité
> Triple personne aussi en unité.[170]

In the *Jugement*, however, the point of the epigrams is to record
what is noteworthy about the lady in question and the style is
therefore plainer, not to say flat:

> *Epigramme de Rebecca femme du Patriarche Isaac.*
> Je monstray bien (qui suys Rebecca dicte)
> Au serviteur d'Abraham ma doulceur:
> Quand luy donnay voluntiers sans redicte
> De mon eau clere en ma buye petite,
> Dont il estoit benin intercesseur.
> Qui cause fut dont de cœur franc et seur
> Femme je fuz d'Isaac le patriarche,
> Et que je fuz en son pais et marche,

Où ung beau filz Jacob luy enfantay,
Auquel (voyant d'Esau la demarche)
Je feiz donner d'aisneesse la marche
De par Isaac, où caulte me monstray.[171]

Sebillet in his *Art poétique* of 1548, when making his opening
remarks concerning the epigram, speaks precisely of its origin as an
inscription and its resultant brevity.[172] Bouchet's concept of the
epigram seems to derive solely from such etymological considerations. The word *épigramme* already existed in French in the sense of
'inscription' as well as that of 'short Latin poem'.[173] Bouchet certainly makes no attempt to imitate any Latin poem called an epigram.
Instead, like Sebillet later, he seems to assume that the Latin genres
already have equivalents in existing French forms. The only distinction to be drawn between Bouchet's *épigrammes* and *épitaphes* is that
more of the *épigrammes* are short, and his cultivation of them accompanies the tendency in his later works to use the short isometric
forms that had become popular.

The case of the elegy is a little more complicated. We are first
promised an elegy in the *Epîtres, élégies* for Renée. Bouchet is not the
sole author of this slight work. The *procureur général* of the Order,
Conrad de Lommeau, is announced as joint author, the first piece
being an *épître* addressed by him to Bouchet.[174] The authorship of
the other pieces is not always made clear. The *épigrammes* are
labelled as such, but none of the other poems is entitled *élégie*. Some
controversy has arisen among scholars who have studied the elegy
as to whether there really is one at all, and if so, which poem it is.[175]
One of the poems, however, is called a *Déploration*.[176] In Latin
poetry the elegy was used much more commonly for love poetry
than for poetry on death, but the term does at least suggest a
mournful poem, and Sebillet later conceded that *complaintes* and
déplorations might be classified as *élégies*.[177] Bouchet himself in his
Epître aux écoliers, in which he discusses various classical genres,
describes the genre in the following terms:

Semblablement ilz usoient d'élégie
Que les Romains appellerent Nenie
Pour deplorer la fortune ou la mort
Des gens de nom, ou ceulx que Venus mord
D'amour trop grant, par amoureuses plainctes,
Par grans regrectz, et par doulces complainctes.
Les vers en sont plaisans et familiers,
Graves assez, propres et singuliers.
Calymachus en acquist la louange
Premier en Grèce, à luy depuis se range
Entre latins Properce et Tibullus,
Ovide aussi, poètes bien vouluz.[178]

Thus Bouchet is perfectly well informed about the classical elegy and knows that its proper subjects are death, misfortune or love. Clark is quite reasonably inclined to dismiss the use of the term *élégies* in the title as vague and mainly for alliterative effect, but I think that, given Bouchet's cultivation of *épigrammes* at the same time, we may assume that he used the word deliberately, and that, with the same combination of etymological sense and assumption that many French and Latin genres are the same, he may use it because the collection contains one or more *Déplorations*. But certainly there is nothing in the poems themselves to suggest that they have been composed with the classical elegy in mind.

The *élégies* of the *Angoisses* are a different case. Bouchet now applies the term very deliberately to four poems of unhappy love, two written right at the beginning of his career and served up now with corrected cesuras and the new label *élégie*; the other two are new poems. In this new label we may perhaps see the influence of Marot's success in writing love poems that are called *élégies*.[179] But the influence does not go very far. As we have seen, these new poems show some changes in language and technique, which might be put down to the influence of Marot, but not particularly that of Marot's elegies, and these changes are not evident only in Bouchet's elegies. Most of Marot's elegies are *épîtres*, Bouchet's are not; they imitate nothing of Marot's elegies beyond perhaps the use of the term. Bouchet in fact puts all his fictional love letters into the *Epîtres familières*.[180] The new *élégies* are laments in the first person, an elderly man who has fallen in love and the fallen maiden whose laments we have already discussed.[181] There is some little influence of the *Heroides* in the latter poem, and a slight Ovidian and classical flavour is imparted to the *Remèdes d'amour*; in 1500 this had been the *Livret de raison*, but it is now spoken by Pallas and occasionally refers to Ovid's *Remedium*.[182] So such influences as there are seem marginally classical rather than anything else.

With the possible exception of these love elegies, it is difficult to see any influence of contemporary French poetry on Bouchet's sudden and very early adoption of these names of classical genres for his poetry. When Marot actually applied the title *épigrammes* to his poems in 1538 it seems to have been under the influence of neo-Latin poets in Lyons who were producing collections of *Epigrammata* in the 1530s.[183] Bouchet had some connections with these Lyons poets, but if anything his interest in epigrams rather predates theirs.

It certainly seems likely that we should look to neo-Latin poetry to explain Bouchet's sudden adoption of classical labels, but we need not look as far as Lyons. As we have seen, there were plenty of opportunities for Bouchet to meet neo-Latin poets in and around Poitiers. And above all, Nicolas Petit. Petit died aged 35 in October 1532; most of the information that we have about him comes from

Bouchet's *Ep. Fam.* 78 recording his death. Born in Normandy, brought up in Paris, he studied law at Poitiers and became a *recteur* at the university. Bouchet praises him as a *grant orateur*; he was one of the group that met at Fontaine-le-Comte. He published two collections of Latin verse and an edition of a work by Mantuanus, and he also contributed liminary verse to several of Bouchet's works. The first are four brief verses in the *Annales* of 1524,[184] but more significant are those that appear in the *Panégyrique* of 1527. Here we find an *Epigramma de apparitione virtutis et voluptatis facta Ludovico Trimollio* and several other pieces, including a *carmen elegum* on the death of Louis de La Trémoille.[185] Petit and other friends writing neo-Latin verse might well, when writing in Latin, have styled Bouchet's existing deplorations and short epitaphs as *carmina elega* and *epigrammata*. It therefore seems likely that the influence of this group in Poitiers explains Bouchet's adoption of the terms. Once having adopted them he was conscious of their novelty and used them in works directed at the Court in which he wished to appear learned and modish. But Court poetry cannot be his original inspiration for using the genres.[186]

NOTES

1. See for example *Chapelet*, f.xxxiiii ro, *Angoisses*, [A2] vo.
2. *Chapelet*, f.xxxiiii ro; *Angoisses*, [A2] vo; *Généalogies*, aa6 vo, in which he says, writing in 1545:

   > J'ay reveu, corrigé et amendé, sćelon les modernes Orateurs, aulcuns de mes opuscules, et iceulx remis en leur ordre au plus près qu'il m'a esté possible du style que les Orateurs de ce regne gardent et observent.

3. *Généalogies*, aa6 vo.
4. *Amoureux transi*, h5 ro-m5 ro. The political propaganda is strongly royalist; the *Prince de Noblesse* is given the last word over both *Église* and *Peuple*. In later works Bouchet is much more respectful of the rights of the Church: see chapter 5.
5. *Masque*, particularly chapter 3, *Le Jeu de la cour*.
6. See the *épître* addressed to d'Auton in the *Labyrinthe*, 1524 ed., xl ro-vo.
7. See chapter 5.
8. Parmentier was from Dieppe but was a regular competitor at the Rouen *Puy*. The other poets were centred in Rouen. See *Ep. Fam.* 43, 44, 88, 89, 98, 99, 106, 107, 108, 109, 110, 114, 121.
9. *Ep. Fam.* 64-7; see appendix. Colin addresses Bouchet in an *épître poétique*, (see *infra*, n.23) and, in another, experiments with *terza rima*.
10. For example the devices described by Zumthor, *Masque*, ch.15, *Les Jongleurs de syllabes*, pp.244-66; also much of their use of rhyme. *Ibid.*, p.239:

    > La rime signifie globalement la prééminence des mots sur les choses; et si nos vieux rhétoriqueurs ont tenté une aventure, c'est de donner à la rime la liberté qui lui revient.

11. *Renards*, a4 vo. See chapter 3.
12. *Chapelet*, f.xxxiiii ro. See *infra*.
13. *Temple*, f.lxiiii ro.
14. *Ep. Fam.* 98, f.lxv vo, col.2. See also *Ep. Fam.* 121.
15. A prayer to the Virgin, surviving only in MS, published by K. Chesney in *BHR* 1, 1941, pp.196-202. See the bibliography. The use of the lyric cesura in any case indicates a date of composition before 1515: see *infra*.
16. BN MS N.A.F.11555, f.1 ro-vo. See chapter 6.
17. Quatrains containing the dates of important events appear throughout the *Annales*; several are reprinted in the *Généalogies*, f.161 ro. See *ibid.*, f.162 vo for

    patrons scelon l'ordre de A.B.C. commençant par toutes les lettres latines elementaires, une après l'aultre, pour les filles qui veulent apprendre à escripre, et instructifz à bonnes meurs.

18. See F. Joukovsky, *La Gloire dans la poésie française et néolatine du XVIe siècle*, Geneva, 1969, pp.517-42; Guy, *Rhétoriqueurs*, §205; Zumthor, *Masque*, pp.188, 191-2. Lemaire's *Temple d'honneur et de vertus*, commemorating Pierre de Bourbon, 1503/4, is particularly appealing in plastic terms and, with its partially classical inspiration, gives a new impetus to the genre (ed. H. Hornik, Geneva and Paris, 1957).
19. The following *Ep. Fam.* are love poems, rejections of love or have love as one of their themes: 2-4 (reworked from the *Amoureux transi*), 5, 7, 12, 13, 19, 26, 32, 55, 62, 63, 75, 76, 92, 94.
20. See *infra*, section 4.
21. Sebillet, *Art poétique*, ed. F. Gaiffe, Paris, 1932, p.10 lines 14-16.
22. See *Temple*, lix vo; for 'sacré poète' see for example *Ep. Fam.* 98; for the Muses etc. see *infra*.
23. *Temple*, lxiiii ro.
24. *Temple*, f.lxii vo; *Triomphes*, a2 vo.
25. *Labyrinthe*, v7 vo; see *infra*.
26. *Triomphes du roi*; see *infra*.
27. There are many good examples of these and other terms in the section of the *Temple* beginning f.lviii vo, 'Le tabernacle des ars et sciences'. See f.lix ro for 'orateurs', f.lxi ro for 'rhetorique'. He uses the term 'rhetoriciens', f.lx vo, but 'rithmeurs' is a term of abuse, f.lix vo, lxiii ro.
28. *Ibid.*, numerous examples ff.lix ro-lxiiii ro. On 'rithme', 'rime', both used by Bouchet, see Zumthor, *Masque*, p.233.
29. 'Rhétorique' has the wider sense in *Temple*, f.lix vo, lxiiii ro.
30. Thus in the *Temple* the 'Investigation poétique' involves searching among the famous figures of mythology, the 'enfer poétique' is the classical underworld. See M-R. Jung, 'Poetria', *Vox Romanica*, 30, 1971, pp.44-64, especially pp.58-60. Fictions can decorate prose as well as poetry, and Bouchet uses them in the *Panégyrique*, but the term is usually restricted to compositions in verse. Cf. *Temple*, f.lix ro:

    Semblablement je vy par fantasie
    Les inventeurs de l'art de poesie
    Et les aucteurs qui se voulurent mectre
    A composer premierement en metre.

All the examples that follow these lines are of poets. See *infra*, section 4.

31.   One stanza is octosyllabic (used for the discourse of *Peuple*), aabaabbabba; the rest (for the *Prince* and *Eglise*) are decasyllabic: aabaabbbcc, abaabbcc, aabaabbbccdccd, aabaabbcc. As well as these 11, 10, 8, 14 and 9-line stanzas, he employs in the *Complaincte de Chrestienté* (o1 ro) a 13-line decasyllabic stanza, aabaabbccdccd.

32.   Two *ballades* are octosyllabic, the rest decasyllabic. Two rhyme schemes are used, ababbcbc and ababbccdcd. A *ballade double croisée* has the 'scheme aabaabbbabba (*envoi* bbabba). He writes one *rondeau simple*, abbaabAabbaA, one *double*, aabbaaabAaabbaA (both decasyllabic).

33.   o5 vo.

34.   k1 ro-k6 ro. The stanza form is abaabbcc; the rhymes at the cesura occur in lines 2, 4, 5, 6 and 7. This passage is spoken by *Eglise*.

35.   There are also six epitaphs using five different rhyme schemes; four have 9 lines, one 15, one 17.

36.   Among the *exhortations* that conclude the chapters of the *Renards* three are heterometric and one hexasyllabic (c6 ro). In the second treatise on *Folles fiances* the main metre is the octosyllable; there is one five-line passage of heptasyllables (16 vo).

37.   On such *arts*, see E. Langlois, *Recueil d'arts de seconde rhétorique*, Paris, 1902.

38.   Par le moyen de quoy je corrig[e]ay
             Le Chapellet des Princes, que erigeay
             A la rigueur de toute quadrature
             Et du rentrer et clore en l'ouverture
             En tous mes vers de epistres leonyns
             Je entremeslay depuis de femenins
             Et masculins, deux à deux . . .   (*Triomphes* a3 ro)

39.   On this question see especially L. E. Kastner, 'Les Grands rhétoriqueurs et l'abolition de la coupe féminine', *Revue des langues romanes*, 45, 1903, pp.289-97. See also Hamon, p.326 and Langlois, *Recueil*, pp.lxxxv-lxxxvii.

40.   *Amoureux transi*, n4 vo and n1 ro.

41.   Based on an examination of La Vigne's *Vergier d'Honneur*, (Paris, [1520?], BL C.107.e.l.) Saint-Gelais, *Le Sejour d'honneur*, ed. J. A. James, Chapel Hill, 1977 and those poems by Gringore that appear in volume I of *Œuvres complètes*, ed. d'Héricault and Montaiglon, Paris, 1858.

42.   Robertet, *Œuvres poétiques*, ed. M. Zsuppán, Geneva–Paris, 1970, pp.58-9; E. M. Rutson, *The Life and Works of Jean Marot*, thesis deposited at the Bodleian Library, Oxford, 1961, pp.236, 238; Cretin, *Œuvres poétiques*, ed. K. Chesney, Paris, 1932, pp.LII-LVI.

43.   Kastner, *art. cit.*, argues that Lemaire was by no means the first to refrain from using epic cesuras, and that for some time after him there were two opposing camps on the question until Marot's example finally banished both the epic and the lyric cesura. He does, however, note that subsequent protests about the rule came mostly from the provinces (p.294).

44. C. Marot, *Les Epîtres*, ed. C. A. Mayer, London, 1958, p.96. See J. Frappier, 'Sur quelques emprunts de Clément Marot à Jean Lemaire de Belges', *Mélanges de philologie et d'histoire littéraire offerts à E. Huguet*, Paris, 1940, pp.161-76.

45. Kastner, *art. cit.*, p.290. Bouchet in 1536 acknowledges the example of other 'orateurs Belgiques', although his first discussion of the rule, cited *infra*, refers only to Lemaire. (*Angoisses*, [A2] vo: quoted by Kastner, p.291.)

46. Kastner, p.296, uses this evidence to suggest that Clément Marot was not influenced by Lemaire in rejecting the lyric cesura, but that he was following his own sense of rhythm, helped on by the weakening of the e in pronunciation, or that he was perhaps imitating Cretin. It is clear, however, that several Court poets abandoned the lyric cesura at about the same time. Lemaire's use of the lyric cesura is very slight (see J. Frappier's editions of *Les Epîtres de l'amant vert*, Lille-Geneva, 1948, p.xlv n.2; *La Concorde des deux langages*, Paris, 1947, p.lxi). Discussions among Court poets about the epic cesura would no doubt have embraced the lyric cesura as well.

47. Already in the *Chapelet* in 1517 some *ballades* from the *Amoureux transi* and the *Renards* are published in a corrected form. It is therefore impossible to know whether the *Epître de Marie* was originally written with epic or lyric cesuras in 1515: if so, he would have corrected them for the first printing in the *Chapelet* volume. Other verse from the *Amoureux transi* is published in corrected form in the *Angoisses* and the *Epîtres familières*. The verse in the *Renards* is corrected in the manuscript revision. The *Déploration* was corrected in the *Opuscules* of 1525, and the *Epître d'Henri* existed in a corrected form some time before it was reprinted in the *Epîtres familières* (see the bibliography). Thus Bouchet eventually corrected nearly all his early work.

48. *Chapelet*, f.xxxiii ro-vo. 'Rithme imparfaicte' means 'ending with a mute e'. 'Estre de cinq piedz' means that the mute e must not come at the fourth syllable (lyric cesura). 'Sinalimphée avec le surplus' means that it must be elided with a following vowel (cutting out the epic cesura).

49. Sebillet when alluding to the cesura rule in the decasyllable also makes a comparison with 'les héroiques Latins' (*Art poétique françoys*, ed. F. Gaiffe, Paris, 1932, p.125). Bouchet compares the alternation of masculine and feminine couplets to Virgil's pentameters and hexameters (*Ep. Fam.* 72). In the *Temple* he apparently suggests that in French verse poets should abide by the rules of Latin prosody:

> Voire y convient user de rethoricque
> Comme en latin, et garder par praticque
> Le long et brief   (f.lxi ro).

But this can be explained by a passage from *Ep. Fam.* 107:

> Voire doit on, sans que les vers on griefve,
> Avoir esgard à la longue et la briefve
> Qu'on congnoistra par le parler commun
> Sur la voyelle, où ne pense chascun.
> En bon françois ce mot cy 'advertisse'
> Est long sur 'i', et brief ce mot 'notice'.

Cf. Hamon, p.315. Thus Bouchet is certainly not advocating 'vers mesurés à l'antique'; he simply wants writers in French to take note of the length of pronunciation of French vowels, just as Latin writers had to consider quantity. But it is clear that he wishes to find analogies between the existing metric practice of French and that of Latin; this is analogous to his treatment of classical genres: see *infra*.

50. *Les Abuz du monde*, 1509, and the polemical pieces of 1510-12 use many lyric and some epic cesuras. But there are hardly any in the *Fantasies de Mère Sotte*, 1516, the *Menus Propos* of 1521 or the *Heures de Nostre Dame*, 1525. Approximate figures for the *Espoir de Paix*, 1511 are 76 lyric and 6 epic in only 360 lines; for the whole of the *Fantasies de Mère Sotte*, 8 lyric and 3 epic.

51. The verse written while he was still at Court uses the epic cesura occasionally, the lyric cesura freely (e.g. the verse in his *Chroniques*, up to 1507, and the two poems of 1511 imitated by Bouchet). But he uses neither in his *épîtres* to Bouchet in the *Labyrinthe* and the *Panégyrique*. In this case though, as no work between 1511 and 1522 survives, it can be argued that he followed Bouchet in adopting the rule.

52. See E. M. Rutson, *Jean Marot*, pp.236-8.

53. *Œuvres*, ed. Chesney, pp.LII-LVI.

54. See note 44. Guillaume Michel de Tours also appears to keep the rule from his first published work, *La Forest de conscience*, Paris, 1516. Not a great deal is known of Michel's life: see E. Armstrong ('Notes on the works of Guillaume Michel, dit de Tours', *BHR*, 31, 1969, pp.257-81).

55. Quoted by A. Héron, in his edition of Pierre Fabri's *Grand et vrai art de pleine rhétorique*, Rouen, 1889-90, vol.3, p.63.

56. For Fabri, see *ibid.*, vol.2, p.97; also Langlois, *Recueil*, p.LXXXVI. For the anonymous *art* see *Recueil*, p.268; for its date (1524-5) see pp.LXXIII-IV. It may have been composed before 1524, since the *terminus a quo* is the death of Lemaire.

57. *Les Gestes des solliciteurs*, Bordeaux, 1529; *Les Divers rapportz*, Lyon, 1537.

58. *La Penthaire de l'esclave fortuné*, Paris, 1530 (BL 1073.e.1); *Les Epistres veneriennes de l'esclave fortuné*, Paris, 1536 (BL 241.g.33): see the introduction, dated 1532, A1 vo.

59. Michel Desarpens, *Ep. Fam.* 72.

60. See François Ier, *Œuvres poétiques*, ed. J. E. Kane, Geneva, 1984, p.61. For comments on Marguerite's practice, see *La Coche*, ed. R. Marichal, Geneva, 1971, pp.58-61.

61. *La Coche*, p.59.

62. Cf. n.45, also *Ep. Fam.* 72.

63. Quoted in n.38. See Hamon, p.54; Langlois, *Recueil*, pp.LXXVII-LXXXV; L. E. Kastner, 'L'Alternance des rimes depuis Octavien de Saint-Gelais jusqu'à Ronsard', *Revue des Langues Romanes*, 47, 1904, pp.336-47.

64. *Angoisses*, [A2] vo. See Langlois and Kastner on Octavien de Saint-Gelais' use of *alternance*. It seems reasonable to suppose that Ronsard had cited Saint-Gelais as an exponent of the rule when he suggested to Bouchet that he should adopt it.

65. See Cretin, *Œuvres*, ed. Chesney, pp.LVIII-LIX; Marot, *Les Epîtres*, ed. Mayer, p.49.

66. See H. Chamard, *Histoire de la Pléiade*, Paris, 1939-40, vol.4, pp.128-33, but also Brian Jeffery, 'The idea of music in Ronsard's poetry', in *Ronsard the Poet*, ed. T. Cave, London, 1973, pp.209-39, especially pp.212-17.

67. f.xxxiiii ro.

68. The rule is formulated in the 1525 *Art* (Langlois, *Recueil*, p.287) and by Gratien du Pont, *Art et science de rhetoricque metriffiée*, Toulouse, 1539, f.xxv ro-vo. Fabri also discusses it, but using the terms 'clos' and 'ouvert' (ed. Héron, vol.2, pp.63-7). The rule seems to be a survival from the older type of *rondeau* with a longer refrain. See my article ' "Clore et rentrer": the decline of the *rondeau*', *French Studies*, 37, 1983, pp.285-95.

69. *Chapelet*, f.xlviii vo, *Opuscules*, 1526, f8 vo-g1 ro.

70. Cretin, *Œuvres*, ed. Chesney, pp.LII-LIV; Gratien du Pont, *Art et Science*, f.ix ro-vo; see Kastner *art. cit.*, pp.294-5.

71. I use these terms for convenience in the sense that modern scholarship normally gives them; contemporary terminology varies from one *art de rhétorique* to another. As can be seen by the passage from the *Angoisses* at n.64 Bouchet uses *leonyne* to mean couplets. (Cf. Fabri, *Grand et vrai art*, vol.2, p.29). There are a few *Ep. Fam.* written entirely in *rimes équivoques*; those by Bouchet himself are nos 5 and 63, also 21, which is said to be 'en synonimes', a deep *équivoque* rhyme; cf. Fabri, *ibid.*, p.21.

72. See *infra*, p.47.

73. Two examples: Molinet's *Ressource du petit peuple*, reproduced by Zumthor, *Masque*, pp.282-98; J. Marot, *Le Voyage de Gênes*, ed. G. Trisolini, Geneva, 1974.

74. f.iiii ro-vo.

75. See *infra*, p.36.

76. See Ch. Camproux, 'Langue et métrique: à propos du décasyllabe des "Epîtres" de Marot', *Le français moderne*, 32, 1964, pp.194-205.

77. *Panégyrique*, f.cxciiii ro-cxciv vo; also appears as *Gen. Ep.* 36. One of the most notable examples of the use of the alexandrine by the *rhétoriqueurs* was Lemaire's *Temple de Minerve* in the *Concorde des deux langages*.

78. *Angoisses*, pp.xlv-l, d7 ro-e1 ro. There are twelve stanzas in all. Cf. *infra*.

79. *Infra*.

80. The new verse includes many of the *épitaphes*, the *Déploration* of the Dauphin and of François de La Trémoille, *Dizains moraulx* and *Aultres dizains*. The *Patrons pour les filles* (see n.17) are a series of quatrains. A few of the *épitaphes* are octosyllabic; *Ep. Fam.* 124 is unusual in being octosyllabic, but it was written in response to an octosyllabic *épître* by Cottereau (123).

81. Erato, Genius, Venus and Minerva all speak in different chapters in both stanza forms and couplets.

82. For example: accumulation e1 vo, etc., e2 vo, e3 ro-vo; personification a5 vo, etc.; epiphonema f4 vo, etc. (*Le Livret de raison*); repetition g1 ro; antithesis l3 vo, etc.; exclamation e5 vo-e6; alliteration e2 vo-e3 ro; apostrophe e1 ro, etc.

83. e3 ro. See Zumthor, *Masque*, p.249.

84. o6 ro. See Zumthor, *Masque*, pp.273-4. There are two more ex-
     amples of little verses of this type in Bouchet's work, first printed
     in 1525 at the end of the *Epître de Justice* in the *Opuscules*: see 2 *Ep.*
     Mor. 5, f.30 ro, col.1.
85. e3 vo. See Zumthor, *Masque*, pp.137-41; for 'cas' meaning sexual
     organs see *ibid.*, p.169, also *Gargantua*, xxxiii, line 19.
86. h6 vo-i1 ro. The reference to the *Aeneid* is to Book xi lines 182-3:
     'Aurora interea miseris mortalibus almam / extulerat lucem refer-
     ens opera atque labores.' It will be noted how little Bouchet's
     vocabulary reflects his classical source.
87. *Temple*, f.iii vo.
88. f.v ro.
89. f.ix vo-x ro.
90. f.lxxix vo. The rhyme scheme is ababbcc; here a = A, b = port
     and c = A. In all but one of the other stanzas the a and c rhymes
     are different. The additional device of *support-* and *raport-* chim-
     ing with the rhyme *port* is not repeated in the other stanzas.
91. Compare for instance the *Traverseur's* lament in the *Temple* with
     Molinet's *Bergier sans solas* (*Faictz et dictz*, ed. N. Dupire, s.a.t.f.,
     Paris, 1936-39, vol.1, pp.209-24). In Molinet's poem the alternate
     decasyllabic stanzas employ *rime batelée* throughout, and all
     through the poem Molinet cultivates rich vocabulary and pun-
     ning and alliterative devices.
92. See *infra*, p.47.
93. f.xiiii ro.
94. *Concorde des deux langages*, ed. Frappier, p.11.
95. *Ep. Fam.* 107, f.lxxi vo-lxxii ro. It will be noticed that, as was
     mentioned earlier, Bouchet is thinking solely in terms of the
     language, metre and rhyme of poetry. Marot's 'grant esprit'
     makes for eloquence.
96. *Ep. Fam.* 114, f.lxxvi ro, col.2.
97. *Ep. Fam.* 107, f.lxxii ro, col.1.
98. *Triomphes du roi*, f.xcvi ro; cf. Marot, *Epîtres*, no.i, lines 1-2.
99. *Généalogies*, f.142 vo; cf. Marot, *Epîtres*, no.xi and no.xxxvi,
     lines 127-34.
100. *Angoisses*, p.xlv-vi.
101. e1 vo (p.1).
102. *Labyrinthe*, A1 ro; references to *Aeneid* 3 (*sic*), 521; 11, 182-3; 12,
     113-15.
103. *Triomphes du roi*, f.xiii vo. Principal reminiscence is *Aeneid* 11,
     182-3. Cf. *supra* n.102, and also 86. Cf. also *Angoisses*, A3 vo-A4
     ro.
104. 1 *Ep. Mor.* 8, f.24 vo, col.2.
105. See *infra*, chapter 3. Cf. also the passage from the *Jugement* quoted
     at note 112.
106. *Généalogies*, f.136 vo-137 ro (from *Douze dizains de la convenance de
     la loy avec la foy*).
107. See for example *Le Miroir de l'âme pécheresse*, ed. J. L. Allaire,
     Munich, 1972, lines 881-90. Cf. also lines 881, 901, etc. and
     Bouchet's *Triomphès du roi*, f.cxxviii ro:
     > Amour, amour, tu faiz ouvrir les cieux,
     > Tu ferme et cloz les Enfers furieux.
     > O doulce loy, laquelle est accomplie
     > Par cest amour, qui par Foy multiplie.

Marguerite for her part seems to have drawn some of her inspiration for the *Miroir* from Bouchet's *Triomphes*; see chapter 7.

108. *Renards*, a4 vo; *Histoire de Clotaire*, a8 ro; *Labyrinthe*, A3 ro; *Triomphes du roi*, f.vi vo. On *clausulae humilitatis* see Zumthor, *Masque*, pp.17-18.

109. *Labyrinthe*, 1524 ed., u7 vo.

110. *Annales*,)(3 ro. 'Curial' here means 'courtly'; cf. *Labyrinthe*, 1524, xl vo; d'Auton is praised for 'le parler curial' of his *Chronique*.

111. *Labyrinthe*, quoted from the edition of P. Le Noir, Bodleian Douce BB.507, GG1 ro.

112. *Jugement*, A7 ro-vo. Cf. chapter 3.

113. f.5 vo.

114. ff.5 vo-6 ro.

115. See n.30.

116. *Grand et vrai art*, ed. Héron, vol.1, p.11.

117. Apart from the examples of *épîtres poétiques* in Bouchet's *Ep. Fam.*, we can cite Jean Robertet's *Ballade poétique*, also referred to as *Dictier poetical*, *Œuvres*, ed. Zsuppán, p.95. Cf. Molinet's *Traictié soubz obscure poetrie*, *Faictz et dictz*, ed. Dupire, vol.2, pp.704-8.

118. So for example Sebillet and his *Art poétique*.

119. In the *Temple* Bouchet says that the Muses came 'presenter à mon esprit diverses invencions et fantasies avec toutes les especes de rithme' (see n.140). In the *Epîtres*, *élégies* he has a vision of starwomen and virtues, after which he says, 'Tout cecy veu, je dy par fantasie, . . . Reprins mon sens' (e4 vo). In the *Triomphes du roi*, *Dame Imaginative* peoples his mind (f.ii ro). On *invention*, cf. G. Castor, *Pléiade Poetics*, Cambridge, 1964, especially pp.107-10.

120. A point made by F. Rigolot, *Poétique et onomastique*, Geneva, 1977, pp.52-3.

121. *Ep. Fam.* 22.

122. *Renards*, h2 ro.

123. 1 *Ep. Mor.* 13, f.32 vo, col.1. It must be borne in mind that both these disapproving statements about poetry appear in moral works in which Bouchet is reviewing the vanity of *all* human pursuits.

124. *Triomphes du roi*, liminary [f.2] ro.

125. *Renards*, g4 vo, col.2. The reference to Aristotle on poets comes from the first book of Boccaccio's *Genealogia deorum* (see *infra*, n.130). The references to Ovid and Virgil suggest that Bouchet disapproved of reading spiritual allegories into the works of Virgil and Ovid. The vernacular version of the *Metamorphoses*, *La Bible des poètes* (first printed 1484) used such interpretations liberally. This version of Ovid's work abruptly lost its popularity after 1532, when a revision omitting all the allegorizations was published. See Ann Moss, *Ovid in Renaissance France*, London, 1982, p.38.

126. See *Temple*, f.lxxxi ro-vo, xvii ro; *Jugement*, f.v vo-vi ro and f.xi ro.

127. *Epîtres*, *élégies*, 1535, f1 ro.

128. *Ibid.*, c3 vo.

129. 'La "Genealogia Deorum Gentilium" del Boccaccio e il "Temple de Bonne Renommee" di Jean Bouchet', in *Il Boccaccio nella cultura*

francese, ed. C. Pellegrini, Florence, 1971, pp.521-56. Cigada gives evidence to show that Bouchet was using a Latin version rather than a French translation (p.525 n.7); this would correspond with his normal practice.

130. See *Genealogie deorum gentilium libri*, ed. V. Romano, 2 vols, Bari, 1951, vol.1, p.10.
131. See Cigada, *art. cit.*
132. *Ibid.*, pp.544-9. Bouchet did not, however, find in Boccaccio his first argument, which is that there is something divine in 'metrificature' because God observed 'mesure' in creating the world (*Temple*, f.lix vo). Cf. Sebillet, *Art poétique*, ed. Gaiffe, p.10, lines 2-8.
133. f.ix ro. Cf. *Genealogia*, Book 9, ch.1, p.437.
134. f.ix vo-x ro. Cf. *Genealogia*, Book 11, ch.2, vol.2, pp.540-1.
135. *Art. cit.*, pp.553-4.
136. *Ibid.*, pp.542-3. We have already examined part of Bouchet's treatment of nymphs, together with Lemaire's treatment of the same material in the *Concorde*. The passage from the *Illustrations* is in Book I, ch.24; see *Œuvres*, ed. Stecher, vol.1, pp.172-3.
137. It is worth noting that Lemaire's friend Petrus Lavinius began a commentary on the *Metamorphoses* (1510) in which he draws heavily on Boccaccio. See Ann Moss, *Ovid*, pp.31-6.
138. See *Temple*, f.lxvi vo. Bouchet attributes the discovery to 'Petrus Alemanus', probably Peter Schoeffer, Gutenberg's assistant: 'cause il est de la grant ouverture / De tout sçavoir qui gist en escripture'.
139. This subject is discussed by Ann Moss, *Poetry and Fable*, Cambridge, 1984, pp.41-9.
140. Liminary f.[4] ro.
141. *Labyrinthe*, 1524, A2 vo. He insists on the truthfulness of his praise of Charles again in the *Panégyrique* ch.27, once more complaining of envious detractors.
142. In the description of Venus, *Panégyrique* ff.xix ro-xxi ro, the influence of Lemaire's *Illustrations* is obvious.
143. For the judgement of Eacus, see E2 ro-E4 ro. Even the three witnesses are rather cautious in their praise of Louise; *Nature* praises her for her beauty, noble birth and splendid children; *Fortune* for her great temporal possessions and for her prudence in prosperity and adversity alike; *Grace* for her eloquence, moderation, deportment, for the good upbringing of her children and for prudence in government. (*Grace*, although said to be a 'don de Dieu', is not to be confused with *Grace divine*. Instead she is a quality that 'faict bien parler et prescher'; she cannot rate very highly in moral terms. Boccaccio admits that the figure may be somewhat ambiguous; see *Genealogia* Book 1, ch.16, vol.1, p.47-8). This eulogy seems rather silent about any important virtue other than prudence. Bouchet probably could not forgive Louise for her role in the affair of Charles de Bourbon (see chapter 4).
144. *Poésie et mythologie au XVIᵉ siècle*, Paris, 1969, p.79. See also pp.50-1, 76-80, 105-6. See also Alice Hulubei, *L'Eglogue en France au XVIᵉ siècle*, Paris, 1938, pp.245-8.
145. See appendix B.

146. *Ep. Fam.* 21, f.xxii vo, col.1. Interestingly this *épître* dating probably from the early 1520s combines poetic fictions calculated to please his neo-Latin poet friend with a complex rhyme scheme, *synonymes*; cf. n.71.
147. *Ep. Fam.* 49. He enumerates the nymphs of the surrounding countryside.
148. *Sylvae,* Paris, *c.*1522. See for example the complicated fictions concerning Arion, (B1-H2). See Joukovsky, *Poésie et mythologie,* p.16 n.13, p.29, p.91 n.59. Petit published two other volumes of Christian neo-Latin poetry, *Elegiae de redemptione humana* with Jean Fossier, Paris, 1517, and an edition of *De sacris diebus* by Mantuanus, Poitiers, 1526.
149. *Panégyrique,* [f.3] vo.
150. *Ep. Fam.* 59. Myiagrus occurs in Pliny, *Natural History* 10, xxviii, as a god who disposes of plague-bearing flies. Bouchet no doubt knew that Deverra figures in the *City of God,* Book 6, ch.9, as an example of the ridiculous pagan practice of assigning lowly offices to gods (*verrere* = to sweep). Cf. the account of a banquet of the planets before La Trémoille's second marriage, *Panégyrique,* ff.clxvii ro-clxx ro.
151. See for instance *Jugement,* B7 vo.
152. *Annales,* title page vo. The woodcut appears in all the Poitiers editions of Bouchet's lifetime. It is reproduced by Robert Brun in *Le Livre français illustré de la Renaissance,* Paris, 1969, plate xxviii.
153. *Ep. Fam.* 24, f.xxv vo, col.2.
154. *Temple,* f.x ro; *Labyrinthe,* 1524, M8 vo.
155. *Ep. Fam.* 61, f.xli vo, col.2. Cf. Villon, *Testament,* line 717.
156. *Triomphes du roi,* 1549, f.viii ro and xiii vo.
157. *Labyrinthe,* 1524, B3 ro-vo.
158. *Triomphes du roi,* f.ii vo. Cf. *Genealogia deorum,* vol.1, p.21-2:
    Is ante alia fronti habet infixa cornua in celum tendentia, barbam prolixam et in pectus pendulam, et loco pallii pellem distinctam maculis, quam nebridem vocavere prisci, sic et manu virgam atque septem calamorum fistulam. Preterea inferioribus membris yrsutum atque hyspidum dicit, et pedes habere capreos et, ut addit Virgilius, purpuream faciem.
159. Woodcut at [A4] vo, illustrating the narrrative of the very end of the book. See Brun, *Le Livre illustré,* p.141. Reproduced in *Généalogies,* f.143 ro.
160. See B7 ro. Brun, *Le Livre illustré,* p.142.
161. The *Triomphes du roi* sold very badly; La Bouralière shows that the original printing was issued again with a new title-page and liminary ff. in 1565 and 1574. (*L'Imprimerie et la libraire à Poitiers pendant le XVIe siècle,* Paris, 1900, p.135.)
162. Bouchet's epigrams in the *Jugement* are discussed by P. M. Smith and C. A. Mayer in 'La Première Épigramme française: Clément Marot, Jean Bouchet et Michel d'Amboise. Définition, sources, antériorité', *BHR* 32, 1970, p.579-602. They are concerned with poems that fulfil their criteria of either having been imitated directly or indirectly from the Greek Anthology, Martial or other Latin poets who wrote epigrams, or else reproducing in some way the manner of classical epigrams. While these criteria are

valid for the subsequent history of the epigram, they do not permit the authors to see the interest and significance of Bouchet's early adoption of the term.

163. *Annales*, 1 March 1531 o.s., f.clxxiii vo.
164. *Ibid.*, f.ccxiii vo. A further example of Bouchet's sudden enthusiasm for the term is found in *Ep. Fam.* 69 and 70; Michel Desarpens sends Bouchet an *épitaphe* on the death of Jacques Prévost (d. December 1530), and Bouchet writes back to praise 'l'invention de ce doulx epigramme', f.xlviii ro, col.2.
165. *Temple*, ff.lxxxi vo-lxxxix ro.
166. *Epîtres, élégies*, e2 vo, etc., *Généalogies* ff.69 vo-70 vo.
167. *Généalogies*, ff.81 vo-82 ro.
168. f.xxxi ro.
169. C. A. Mayer suggested that the fifteen 14-line epigrams should be regarded as sonnets ('Le premier sonnet français: Marot, Mellin de Saint-Gelais et Jean Bouchet', *RHLF*, 1967, pp.481-93). But Y. Giraud pointed out that the 14-line pattern was merely arrived at by inserting a couplet into the middle of a *douzain* pattern (*RHLF*, 1968, pp.875-6). The structure of the four epigrams with 16 lines, one with 13 and one with 22 is arrived at in the same way. The remaining 105 poems are all *douzains* of the same pattern, abaabbccdccd. The 14-line poems are in no way distinguished from the others, and there is no reason at all to suppose that Bouchet thought of them as sonnets.
170. *Epîtres, élégies*, e3 ro. This device is called *rime annexée*; see Fabri, *Grand et vrai art*, ed. Héron, vol.2, p.44.
171. *Jugement*, f.xxxiii ro.
172. *Art poétique*, ed. Gaiffe, p.103:
> Poème de tant peu de vers qu'en requiert le titre ou super-scription d'œuvre que ce soit, comme porte l'étymologie du mot, et l'usage premier de l'épigramme, qui fut en Gréce et Italie premiérement approprié aus bastimens et edifices ...

Sebillet mentions the *douzain* as the longest form chosen by good French poets (p.104).
173. The word is first attested in French with the sense 'inscription' in the late fourteenth century (Jean Lefèvre, *La Vieille*; see Godefroy, *Complément*). It gradually lost this sense as French epigrams were written and it was increasingly associated with short, witty poems. When Ronsard used the word in the sense of 'epitaph' Muret took the trouble to explain that 'épigramme en grec signifie toute inscription' (see *Œuvres*, ed. Laumonier, IV, p.55 and P. Laurent, 'Contribution à l'histoire du lexique français', *Romania*, LXV, 1939, p.174). Cotgrave still offers 'inscription' as one sense of 'épigramme', but in 1690 Furetière only mentions inscriptions when tracing the origin of the word, and the *Dictionnaire de l'Académie* in 1694 makes no reference at all to inscriptions.
174. See the bibliography.
175. C. N. Scollen, *The Birth of the Elegy in France, 1500-1550*, Geneva, 1967, pp.58-61; J. E. Clark, *Elégie: the Fortunes of a Classical Genre in Sixteenth-Century France*, The Hague–Paris, 1975, p.39 n.50. Scollen assumes that the main piece by Bouchet, c2 ro-f1 vo, is an elegy; this takes the form of an *épître* to Lommeau but it includes the fiction of the star-women and the epigrams of the Virtues.

Clark wrongly assumes that Scollen is talking about an earlier piece, *Déploration de virginité, religion et clousture* (b3 ro-b4 vo; this piece is by Lommeau: it does not alternate masculine and feminine rhymes). But in either case his point is that none of the poems bears the title *élégie*: 'We prefer the plural word *élégies* in the title of the collection to be just another example of the vague use of the word during the 1530s: the alliteration of the title is no doubt the only *raison d'être* for its inclusion there'. He also points out that Bouchet includes the word 'élégie' in lists of poems he had written before 1530, for example in the preface to the *Triomphes* (1530). It is very true that Bouchet quite often gives such lists whose terms are difficult to fit to his surviving works, and Clark may well be correct in his interpretation. But it can also be argued that these lists reflect Bouchet's belief that classical genres already had French equivalents: thus he might have referred to any of his *déplorations* as *élégies*.

176. The piece by Lommeau just mentioned. There is also a suggestion that Bouchet's *élégie* of commemoration might be considered a *déploration*. Bouchet sees the star-women after regretting that he has no adequate language 'Pour deplorer Dame tant bonne et sage' (c3 ro).

177. *Art poétique*, p.178:
Complaintes et deplorations sembleroient estre comprises soubz l'élégie, qui ne les sonderoit au vif. Car l'élégie proprement veut dire complainte. Mais les usages et différentes sortes d'icelles me contraignent t'en faire traité particulier.

178. 1 *Ep. Mor.* 13, f.33 ro, col.1.

179. See Scollen, *Birth of the Elegy*, pp.61-71. She concludes that in writing both love elegies and one on death Bouchet was following the example of Marot in applying the name 'elegy' to a poem in French—Marot first published a group of twenty-one elegies in the *Suite de l'Adolescence Clementine*, 1533. She also notes, however, that Marot had not at this stage written an elegy on death. Clark, *Elégie*, pp.39-43, does not speculate on Bouchet's reason for using the term, but notes that there is no trace of Marot's influence beyond the general theme of love.

180. Discussed briefly by Scollen, *Birth of the Elegy*, pp.31-2; see *supra* n.19.

181. See Clark, *Elégie*, p.43.

182. Cf. Scollen, *Birth of the Elegy*, pp.69-71.

183. Marot first applies the term to his poems in 1538, although many of his earlier poems were later called *épigrammes*. The neo-Latin epigram was particularly popular in Lyons from about 1536. See J. Hutton, *The Greek Anthology in France*, Ithaca, 1946, pp.301-3, especially n.6.

184. These appear on the title page of the 1557 *Annales*. See also a Latin epigram concerning the origin of the Poitevins, f.4 vo; this appeared for the first time in the 1532 edition—the one that first includes the *épigramme* on Queen Claude. In that edition too there was a *carmen elegum* by Petit, but this disappears in all later editions. The *Anciennes et modernes généalogies* of 1528 contains some of his verse.

185. *Panégyrique*, f.[3] vo, ff.cxciv vo-cxcvi vo.

186. We may note here that Bouchet's only excursion into another
     new genre, the *blason*, appears among the epitaphs in the *Géné-*
     alogies, 82, *Epitaphe contenant le blason d'un bon cheval*. See Alison
     Saunders, *The Sixteenth-Century Blason Poétique*, University of
     Durham Publications, 1981, p.45 n.53.

Bouchet's Moral Writing

1
Introduction

a) *Definitions of Moral Writing*
The first point to be made about moral writing is that it is different
from theological writing. We saw in the last chapter that, when
employing poetic fictions, Bouchet restricts their significance to the
moral plane, and that when writing memorial works he is careful to
distinguish between continuing renown in this world and life eternal in the next. The moral plane concerns life as it is lived on this
earth and man's relations with other men. The spiritual plane deals
with man's hopes of salvation and his relation with God. The moral
plane is typically governed by the four cardinal (or moral) virtues:
prudence, justice, temperance and fortitude. The spiritual plane
deals with the three theological virtues, faith, hope and charity.[1]
The two planes are of course linked; in moral theology the true end
of all human action is the pursuit of God, and living a good life on
earth is both symptomatic and the natural result of this pursuit.
Charity links the two planes because it consists of love of man as
well as love of God. Thus some of the instruction under the heading
of charity in theological writing is indistinguishable from the precepts of moral writing. But the planes are nevertheless different.
This no doubt explains why Zumthor finds in the *Epîtres morales* a
lack of theology, describing them as 'énonçant les règles idéales
d'un comportement vertueux, sans jamais renvoyer explicitement
aux structures doctrinales sous-jacentes'.[2] In fact, as we shall see,
there is an unusually extensive treatment of theological matters in
the *Epîtres morales*, but Bouchet does not explain the theology of
salvation there or elsewhere in his moral works. This is because the
underlying Christianity is not in doubt; it is simply assumed that in
all estates man's aim is salvation, and it would be out of place to
discuss the spiritual relation between the individual and God in
moral writing, which is more concerned with groups of men and
their actions in this world. But one has only to turn to one of his
treatments of the theological virtues in other works to find the
dogmas clearly formulated.

It is worth noting that so clear a division between the moral and the spiritual precludes the treatment of subjects that we regard as central themes of moral writing in the great seventeenth-century *moralistes*. For a writer like Bouchet, working in the medieval Christian tradition, moral writing deals with men's behaviour, particularly in relationship to each other in society, but Man as Man can only be defined by his relation to God; 'Human nature' is thus a theological rather than a moral subject. The treatment of Man without reference to theology develops in the Renaissance with the assimilation of classical philosophers, moralists and satirists, but Bouchet shows no sign of any such development. All his moral works treat men in society, and most typically they deal with the estates.

Even when this distinction between theological and moral writing has been made, it is still not immediately obvious just which of Bouchet's works should be classified as specifically 'moral'. Nearly all his works incorporate some moral writing, because he always has the intention of edifying the reader. Thus historical writing is morally useful because it provides examples of evil to be shunned:

    A ce que ceulx qui lisent telz exemples
    Ayent vouloir (de plus n'abuser) amples.[3]
It also offers models of goodness to be imitated:
    Affin de induire aucuns jeunes hommes du temps present, qui
    vivent assez ou trop selon leur desordonné appetit, à y prendre
    exemple, en sorte qu'ilz puissent par augmentation et accrois-
    sement de vertuz servir la chose publicque.[4]
In the *Panégyrique* not only is La Trémoille an example to be followed, he is instructed at length on how to govern by Juno, who calls herself *Puissance Regnative*.[5]

The memorial poems examined in the last chapter offer particularly tricky problems of definition. They contain a great deal of moral instruction and *exempla*, but their main interest is that they exalt Virtue, employing a number of classical concepts, and they thus force Bouchet to grapple with the problem of what spiritual value should be attached to good moral behaviour. This for him is a theological problem, and by examining it we can see clearly how Bouchet regards the relationship between the moral and the spiritual plane.

The problem of the value of virtue exercised the minds of many of Bouchet's contemporaries, particularly those most impressed by the virtuous pagans of the classical world. Like many other writers of the time Bouchet deals in these memorial works with classical concepts of renown, glory and honour, which are difficult to integrate into the Christian view of fallen human nature. In her study of the treatment of *gloire* by Renaissance poets, Joukovsky notes that in his later works Bouchet is strikingly pessimistic about the possibility of man achieving just renown through virtue.[6] This pessimism arises from his theological preoccupations. From the moral point of view he sees as valuable the pursuit of nobility, which signals a man out among his fellows, and the pursuit of renown, which may provide man with a sort of immortality in this world. Bouchet always insists that the best type of nobility and renown, and the only durable one, is derived from virtue:

> La noblesse de vertuz, qui excede en extimacion commune la noblesse de lignaige . . .[7]

> Et de ces biens on ne doit faire compte
> Fors de vertuz, qui les aultres surmonte . . .
> Brief il convient fors vertuz que tout meure.[8]

But however noble, renowned or indeed virtuous a man may have been, he was still a sinner and dependent upon God's grace for eternal life. In his later works particularly, this theological doctrine is never far from Bouchet's thoughts. So in the *Triomphes du roi* his intentions are unambiguously explained in his dedication to Henri II:

> J'ay par ma Poesie escript l'histoire [de François Ier]. Et en ce faisant donne à congnoistre l'origine de Noblesse: qui sont les vraiz Nobles, et qui meritent avoir et tenir Sceptre Royal, et ce qu'on doit faire pour heureusement regner, et vivre en ce monde noblement en tous estatz.[9]

But Bouchet's work is divided into two parts, which, he admonishes Henri II, should not be read the one without the other:

> Et encores evidemment monstrer, qu'après y avoir vescu morallement, le tout n'est que vanité, c'est à dire chose momentanée, transitoire et de petite durée, et que par ceste seule Noblesse on ne peut parvenir à la gloire eternelle, sans avoir la Noblesse Evangelique et Spirituelle.[10]

In the first part François achieves the nobility of virtue. But in the second, after his death, the poet's vision of the 'parc de noblesse' crumbles, and the *Traverseur* must learn the 'noblesse evangelique' that comes from faith, hope and charity. Nowhere does Bouchet express more clearly the limitations of earthly glory, honour and good works.

This attitude is not restricted to his later writing, it is implicit at least in all the memorial works. He always makes clear that the renown that men win for their virtue cannot be compared with salvation. Even in the *Temple,* the most optimistic in tone, the point arises in an unexpected way which shows how superficial was Bouchet's assimilation of classical concepts of renown and glory. He makes *Bonne Renommée* explain that there are three modes of life available to humans: life on earth, renown after death, and eternal life. The second type is won by virtue cultivated during life on earth.

The third type also requires men to cultivate virtue and at this stage, before his theological studies occasioned by the spread of Lutheranism, Bouchet does not specifically mention the role of faith or divine grace. But a passing reference to the pagans shows clearly that virtue alone does not win salvation:

Quant aux paiens qui les vertuz amerent,
Par bon renom les remunere Dieu:
Les biensfaiz sont paiez en quelque lieu.[11]

It is important to appreciate the background of this idea. It derives from a well-known passage in the *City of God*, where Augustine, who took the view that the pagan pursuit of virtue stemmed from a sinful desire for honour, ironically assures us that since the virtuous Romans are honoured all over the world, 'they have no reason to complain of God's justice; they have their reward'.[12] Augustine assumes that they are all damned. Bouchet's lines therefore suggest that the virtuous pagans' only reward for virtue is renown, and by implication that they are in hell. Certainly his description of limbo in the *Triomphes* does not admit any pagans, although the development of the doctrine of limbo had allowed some thinkers to envisage a better fate than hell for the virtuous pagans; by the time Bouchet was writing some were prepared, by means of the doctrine of limbo, to envisage even the salvation of some virtuous pagans who had believed in one God.[13] It appears that Bouchet has no truck with any such idea. On the other hand he appears to follow theologians later than Augustine in accepting that for all its limitations the moral virtue of the pagans was genuine, and this too accords with the later theology of the *Triomphes*.[14]

Here we are on the fringes of theological questions central to the Lutheran reformation, and when Bouchet treats contemporary religious controversy he formulates over and over again doctrines involving salvation, grace, faith, charity and good works. It can be seen that he was already interested in aspects of these problems before they became a matter of Lutheran controversy. To this extent he resembles humanists who wanted to encourage Christians to imitate pagan virtues. But Joukovsky is surely right to underline his relative lack of optimism about human virtue; he is much too concerned with theological problems to fail to make the limitations of man's virtue explicit.

So paradoxically it is in some of the memorial works employing potentially pagan concepts[15] that Bouchet combines moral *exempla* with theological exposition of doctrines concerning salvation and the importance of faith and works. His moral and satirical works proper are more pervasively Christian but less theological. It is accepted without theological explanation that anyone wishing to be saved should cultivate virtue and eschew vice. And in fact no theological problem really arises, because the moral works are more concerned with sin and its avoidance than with the glorious cultivation of virtue.

The group of works that can be regarded as essentially moral works and that will be discussed here comprises the *Renards* of 1503, the *Déploration* of 1512, the *Chapelet*, 1517, and the *Epîtres morales*, mostly written between 1525 and 1535 but published in 1545. To these can be added two small collections of *rondeaux, ballades morales* and *dizains moraulx*.[16] The underlying homogeneity of the moral teaching of this group is striking; so too is the contrasting diversity of forms employed. At first sight these works have little in common, but in fact they are all variations on the favourite late medieval approach to considering man in society, that is, the division into estates.[17] Where the subject matter of these different works overlaps it is in many respects remarkably consistent throughout his career. When we come to examine them, we shall show how this material is cast in a variety of different moulds with different effects.

b) *Purposes and Problems*

Moral writing of the type found in the works just listed makes up a large proportion of *rhétoriqueur* output. Zumthor has noted that its structure comprises two modes, 'affirmation élogieuse ou dénonciation'.[18] The writer may praise an estate and describe how its members should ideally behave, or he may denounce the abuses to which it is prone. It is presented by its authors as morally edifying to the individual and socially useful, because it praises virtue and holds vice up to opprobrium.

One is inevitably led to doubt whether these works had much real instructive or corrective value. In the first place it is often a confirmative and comfortable type of writing; the reader had innumerable books that instructed him in the same moral commonplaces and denounced the same vices. We shall see later that twice Bouchet's works were published in collections that gathered together treatises of similar tone and subject. The uniformity of material no doubt helps to explain the great variety of forms that Bouchet and other writers sought to employ. It is also a socially conservative form of writing; the use of the estates for the structure of the work enshrines and sanctifies this perception of the structure of society.

In the second place, many factors blunt the critical effectiveness of these works. Writers who primarily criticise abuse can be viewed as writing satire, and it has often been said that *rhétoriqueur* satire is very anodyne, for two reasons: first because it remains generalised and does not name names; secondly because criticism is usually offset in some way, either by praise of the same estate or by further criticism of a different estate. So Guy could speak of 'ces pièces innocemment agressives' and 'ces critiques dont personne ne s'offense parce qu'elles enveloppent tout le monde'.[19]

But however justified these doubts may be on the whole, one should not too lightly dismiss the impact of critical writing. We may in the first place underestimate the effect of apparently generalised criticisms. Bouchet very often discusses the difficulties attendant on praising and blaming individuals or groups. In the dedication to the *Temple*, he says that it is dangerous to praise or blame, for if one praises one is accused of flattery by the envious, and if one criticises 'vices publicques' some guilty person will say that it has been done deliberately to offend him.[20] We have seen that he says in the *Labyrinthe* that he was accused of disproportionate flattery in the *Temple*; in an *épître* to Ardillon he concedes that he has often praised people 'oultre mesure'.[21] On the other hand he includes in the *Epîtres familières* an *épître* addressed to him by Germain Emery which appears to accuse him of speaking ill of other people. In his reply Bouchet defends himself—'oncq' ne le feis'. He claims that he has named dead perpetrators of crimes in his histories, but otherwise his criticism of evil behaviour has always been restricted to blatant abuse, 'crime public', and couched in general terms.[22] This is indeed the avowed principle of his moral writing; already in 1503 he claims to

> reprimer en general les vices qui ont à present cours, non voulant y comprendre aucun particulierement, mais ramentevoir à chascun ce qu'il luy touche, et dont il se sent coulpable.[23]

While this is to a certain extent literary commonplace reflecting the type of satire written by Horace,[24] it does correspond to his practice in moral works. However, such generalised criticism may be perceived, correctly or falsely, as having a precise target. This happened with Bouchet's criticisms. Some people said that he was responsible for the reformation imposed upon the convent of Sainte-Croix in 1519 because of what he had said about its original foundation and the accompanying moral reflections in the *Histoire de Clotaire*.[25] On another occasion he was informed that he was unpopular at court; in a fit of depression he writes to Ardillon

> Pour vous narrer que je suis presque à sac
> (Comme m'a dit le seigneur de Scissac)
> En la grant court, où j'ay acquis reproche
> De trop reprendre, et que trop près j'aproche
> De verité, comme si je sçavois
> Tout ce qu'on faict, telle me fut sa voix.[26]

This was written probably in about 1530 and was no doubt the result of the *Panégyrique*, which eulogises Louis de La Trémoille and attacks courtiers. Confessing that he has sometimes been excessive in praise he concludes that this is the source of his unpopularity: 'En louant un, à l'autre je desplais'.[27] This is more exactly true than it sounds, for Bouchet does sometimes employ a technique of criticism

by implication through the praise of something different. It is difficult to read the *épître morale* on kings, which takes the form of a
personal address to Louis xii but was not printed until 1545, without wondering whether the way in which Louis is praised does not
imply criticism of his successor (his willingness to hear criticism, his
prudence, his chastity).[28]

However, it is not surprising if courtiers took offence at his criticism, for some of his bitterest attacks were directed at them. Pauline
Smith, who has studied anti-courtier literature in the sixteenth
century, concludes that in the first part of the century Bouchet was
'the most implacable, prolific and consistent opponent of courtiers'.[29] The *épître* to Ardillon lends support to this conclusion, and it
shows that generalised criticism was not felt to be anodyne by
members of the groups under attack.

The other way in which criticism may be blunted is by juxtaposing
criticism of a group either with praise of the same group or with
more criticism of other groups. Here it is simply worth noting how
very eager Bouchet is to achieve such an effect and not to appear to
single out one particular group for criticism. It is implicit in the
method of reviewing the faults of the various estates that all the
estates are mutually dependent, that all have their own shortcomings and all must look to their own amendment. Bouchet strives
to make this point explicit. In his earliest moral work, the *Renards*,
his approach is wholly critical, and a balance of criticism is only
achieved by the juxtaposition of blame of different estates. And so
he concludes his preface:

> en priant ceulx qui liront ce livre, que je nomme 'Les Renars du
> monde', qu'ilz ne lisent une partie sans l'autre, car ilz trouve-
> ront finablement que l'iniquité de tous les estas est reciprocque
> et cause c'estassavoir l'une du mal de l'autre, et par ce que leur
> union et bonne aliance seroit et pourroit estre le moyen de leur
> felicité mondaine, et en fain de beatitude eternelle.[30]

When he revised the work he made the point in a more pessimistic
way, more suitable to the tone of the book; he beseeches his readers:

> qu'ilz ne lisent ung chappitre sans l'autre, car en ce faisant,
> congnoistront que le maulvaiz Regnar d'un estat est cause de la
> perdicion et destruction de l'autre.[31]

In the other work in which he undertakes a review of the whole of
society, the *Epîtres morales*, his approach is altered. Here he seeks to
achieve a balanced view not only by juxtaposing the vices of each
estate, but also by including in each *épître* a statement of the dignity,
the rights and the duties of an estate as well as the criticism of
abuses. This is pointed out in an introductory verse, in which he still
feels it necessary to make an appeal to the reader not to be selective:

L'argument des Epistres Morales
Si vous lisez ces morales Epistres,

Considerez le motif de l'Acteur,
Qui à chascun rend ses honneurs et tiltres,
Voulant garder la reigle d'Orateur;
Et si par foiz il est declamateur,
Blasme et reprend d'aucuns estatz les vices,
Il se reduit par après aux offices
Et aux vertuz que chascun doit avoir
En son estat, au cours du temps propices,
Et ne veuillez l'une sans l'autre veoir.[32]

Bouchet is pointing out the rhetorical difficulties inherent in moral writing, and seems indeed to express some of the shortcomings of *pro et contra* argument that Rabelais explores in the *Tiers Livre*. His early method, used in the *Renards traversans*, employs a series of speeches *contra*, leaving the reader to sort out the balance of blame. The *Epîtres morales* within the ambit of the individual *épître* juxtapose the case for each estate with the case against, as well as juxtaposing the various estates in the whole collection of *épîtres*. But still truth lies only in the totality of these procedures and the writer relies on the reader not to be swept away by one side of the argument; he depends on the reader to draw the two sides together and to compare one estate with all the rest. Hence the admonition not to look at one side of the case without the other.[33]

c) *The Use of Classical Sources*

Charges of presumption in criticising and advising other people could be met by Bouchet's usual defence that only the *invention* was his own and that all the substance came from good authorities. The manipulation of authorities is of great importance in his moral writing and in the case of each work we shall discuss the various ways in which his authorities are used. Among the references that he gives, the largest number are to the Bible; these and other Christian sources predominate. But it is not surprising to find classical authors also prominent in his moral writing.

Although Bouchet sometimes paraphrases a sentence from an authority without drawing attention to the fact, on the whole he advertises his sources by citing the author, sometimes complete with a quotation. From the *Déploration* of 1512 until the *Opuscules* of 1525 he uses a technique of heavy marginal annotation in which author and quotation in Latin appear. This technique fell out of fashion, no doubt partly because printers found it awkward and expensive; in the *Epîtres* there are references to sources but no quotations. In some cases references merely add weight to the French text, sometimes the sentence is paraphrased in the French; sometimes a reference indicates a passage that is adapted or imitated at some length.

Among the classical sources used in these various ways, Cicero predominates. Bouchet's favourite text is the *De Officiis*; this is hardly surprising, for this treatise on man's duties to his fellows had for centuries influenced Christian moral theology.[34] Many sentences are quoted from the *De Officiis* to support points made in the verse. Cicero's work also provides the best example of a classical text exploited at some length; his *De Senectute* is used for 1 *Ep. Mor.* 14 on old age; we shall see that Bouchet imitates the framework, borrows several arguments and to some small degree imitates the rhetoric.

Another important source is Seneca, although on the occasion on which he is cited most extensively Bouchet is referring to a work believed to be by Seneca but which is actually by a sixth-century Christian writer.[35] It is significant that of these two major sources for moral commonplace, Seneca was believed at the time Bouchet was writing to have become a Christian[36] and Cicero's work was traditionally well-integrated into Christian moral writing. I have little doubt that he had these two writers in mind as models when he published his collection of letters under the title of *Epîtres morales et familières*.

Classical writers are often exploited as sources of *exempla*; Bouchet particularly favours the *Facta et dicta memorabilia* of Valerius Maximus.[37] The richest text by far from the point of view of diverse classical allusion is the *Labyrinthe de Fortune*, a hybrid work, philosophical, moral and theological, learned rather than popular, in which Bouchet first depicts a classical world-picture where Fortune governs all, only subsequently to correct the errors of *Humaine Discipline* with the true theological picture as presented by *Veritable Doctrine*. The classical texts of the *Labyrinthe* thus tend to be illustrative rather than authoritative. Apart from historians, who provide examples of good and bad fortune, the main classical authorities cited in the first part are Virgil, Ovid and Valerius Maximus, followed by Aristotle, then Horace, Seneca, Cicero and Juvenal; there are also one or two references each to Pliny, Persius, Terence, Lucan, Apuleius and Sophocles. But in the longer second part there are only about a third as many references to classical authors and now Cicero is the most frequent, followed by Valerius Maximus and Aristotle; Sallust, Seneca and Juvenal appear two or three times each, but Virgil, Ovid and Horace only once.[38] This pattern of the second, Christian, part is much more typical of the use of classical authorities in his moral works proper except that Aristotle is more prominent in the *Labyrinthe* than in the less philosophical moral writings. Thus the classical influence on his moral writings is in practice mainly restricted to historical exempla and to those classical authors who were particularly well integrated into Christian tradition.

Most of Bouchet's moral writing is in verse, so one might reason-

ably expect him to look to the Latin satirical poets, especially by the
time that he was writing the *Epîtres morales*. There are certainly
references to both Horace and Juvenal and paraphrases of odd
sentences from them, but not in very great force.[39] More interesting
than his actual use of the classical satirists are the passages in which
he discusses satire.[40] The first of these comes in the *Temple* in the
section on the inventors of arts:

Près des susdictz vy Menipus servus,
Semblablement Demetrius Tarsus,
Premiers aucteurs (comme on dit) de satire,
Lesquelz donnoient à plusieurs gens martire
Par leurs blasons, car les gens ilz nommoient
Et leurs pechez publicquement disoient,
Dont il advinst que soubz ceste licence
On medisoit de chascun sans silence,
Parquoy fut lors satire defendue.
Mais depuis fut aultrement estendue [*sic*],
C'estassavoir par ung Lucilius,
Par Pertius, Flacus Horatius
Et Juvenal, qui les vices et maulx
Ont fort repris en termes generaulx.[41]

This account doubtless reflects the views of commentators in
editions of the Latin satirical poets—first the older type of satire,
which gave rise to scandal because it named names and criticised
vice with too much licence, and was therefore suppressed by law;
then the newer type making only general criticisms, whose exponents were the great Latin satirists.[42]

It is odd that he does not here make the connection that he
regularly makes later between satire and the theatre. Nearly all the
commentators on Latin satirists suggest that satire was a dramatic
form in antiquity,[43] and in later passages by Bouchet this element is
very prominent in his description of satire. Following his usual
practice of equating classical genres and modern French ones, he
claims that the *sotie* is the contemporary equivalent of satire.

Since it is difficult to regard *sotie* as the heir of Lucilius, Horace,
Juvenal and Persius one would assume that he is thinking of the
older type of satire described by the commentators, the type that
was scandalous and had to be banned. But in fact he never makes
such a distinction very clear and the equation between *sotie* and
satire seems to colour his presentation of satire in general.

One would certainly expect Bouchet to think of himself as writing
in the Latin tradition of corrective moral writing, just as the Latin
translator of the *Narrenschiff* claims Brant as a satirist in the wake of
Lucilius and the others;[44] the purpose of the writing and its general
approach are sufficient grounds for a comparison to be made without any imitation of style or language. But rather than claiming to

write satire himself, Bouchet has some harsh things to say about the genre. In his *Epître aux écoliers,* which gives some of the earliest descriptions of classical genres in French, he describes first tragedy and comedy, then satire:

Et tiercement aultres poetes sont
Satyres dictz, qui tous leurs metres font
Reprehensifz de tous pechez publiques,
Les reprenans par leurs vers satyriques,
Qui sont picquans, voire jusques au sang,
Ne craignans rien, mais de tout parlent franc,
Louans vertuz, et detestans tout vice,
Sans espargner par crainte aulcun convice.[45]

Here he speaks in forceful language of the acerbity of a satirist's criticism. He goes on to acknowledge its usefulness and its respectable Latin ancestors, which are full of *sententiae* worth quoting:

Lesquelz peuent bien jeunes gens eriger
A bonnes meurs, & vertuz eriger,
Et à laisser les maulvaises coustumes
Des vitieux remplies d'apostumes.
    Horatius, Perse & aussi Juvenal,
Furent aucteurs de ce jeu Satyral
Entre Latins, comme on veoit par leurs livres,
Lesquelz ne sont de sentences delivres.[46]

One would think from *jeu satyral* that these authors were play-wrights.[47] He goes on to say that satire is not always so respectable:

Mais par autant que de detraction
Usent souvent, par folle affection,
Nommans aucuns, et faisans du scandalle,
On dit Satyre estre une chose malle.
En France elle a de sotie le nom.[48]

In fact the way in which he goes on to describe the *sotie* suggests that it is not wholly bad:

Par ce que sotz des gens de grand renom
Et des petitz jouent les grands follies
Sur eschaffaulx en parolles polies,
Qui est permis par les princes & Roys
A celle fin qu'ilz sachent les derroys
De leur conseil, qu'on ne leur ause dire,
Desquelz ilz sont advertiz par Satyre.
Le roy Loys douziesme desiroit
Qu'on les jouast à Paris, et disoit
Que par telz jeux il sçavoit maintes faultes
Qu'on luy celoit par surprinses trop caultes.[49]

This anecdote about Louis XII turns up elsewhere in Bouchet's writing.[50] It is difficult to know just what significance should be placed on this description of dramatic satire, particularly considering Bouchet's known but undefined connections with the Basoche in Paris under Louis XII. In an *épître* to the *Roi de la Bazoche* at Bordeaux refusing to write a play for the group, he insists that although writers should endeavour to correct vice and promote virtue, one should use 'motz non trop picquans'; people should not be tormented.

> Par fors rappors ne par aigres satyres,
> Car pleines sont de discors et martires.[51]

It seems that stage satire too readily indulges in defamation and scandalous vituperation. Moreover, he continues, it is always unwise to irritate great lords.

The things of which he appears to disapprove in stage satire, particularly the naming of names, would not apply to Horatian satire. Without these dubious dramatic connections Bouchet might have been more eager to call himself a satirist. But as with the epigram and the elegy, the basis for such a comparison would not be imitation of the satirical poets. As I have said, Latin prose writers seem to inspire the naming of his *épître* collection; there is no very marked influence from either Horace's *Epistles* or from his *Satires*.

2
The Moral Works

In the studies of Bouchet's moral works that follow, more is said about the form than about the substance of his moral writing. This is not because his subject matter is so uniform or conventional as to be featureless; on the contrary, within the framework of fairly standard material he expresses many distinctive points of view. Every subject he treats could be studied to show how he uses commonplace and what brand of teaching is ultimately produced. Scholars have already examined his treatment of some topics, notably his attack on courtiers and some aspects of his treatment of marriage.[52] In a later chapter I shall examine the substance of his discussion of the Church and churchmen. But by concentrating here on the ways in which Bouchet tackles his material, I hope in particular to demonstrate the hazards of taking out of context passages in which Bouchet criticises or condemns something. The context in which he does so very often attentuates the criticism; occasionally however it makes it more severe. It is thus vital to take the context into account when using Bouchet as an example of any particular point of view.

a) *Les Renards Traversans*
The first of Bouchet's works to be printed, this is an odd work, published in odd circumstances that are not wholly explained. It was printed by Antoine Vérard in late 1503 or early 1504, and its full title appears on the title page as: *Les regnars traversant les perilleuses voyes des folles fiances du monde. Composées par Sebastien Brand, lequel*

composa la nef des folz derrenierement imprimée à Paris. Et autres plusieurs choses composées par autres facteurs.

By falsely attributing this work to Brant, Antoine Vérard was cashing in on the enormous popularity of Brant's *Narrenschiff* which, having come out in German in 1494, had already been translated into Latin and had appeared in three different French versions.[53] Vérard had had a special set of ten woodcuts made to illustrate Bouchet's work; no doubt he was eager to ensure good sales.[54] After the *Renards* itself came a hotch-potch of other moral and comminatory works, one probably by Bouchet, several definitely not.[55] Bouchet says later that Vérard had cut down his prose, added works not by him, given the work a title of his own invention and attributed the work to Brant; for this Bouchet had successfully taken him to court and received compensation.[56] We know of this only from Bouchet himself, but records show that Michel Le Noir's edition, which copied Vérard's in 1504, was the subject of a law suit.[57] The book was thus surrounded by a surprising amount of chicanery.

Vérard's attribution of the work to Brant is not entirely gratuitous, for Bouchet is inspired by one of Brant's works and quotes a passage from it by way of introduction. Much as he admired the *Narrenschiff*—he had intended to translate it himself but gave up the project when he found that his friend Pierre Rivière had undertaken a translation[58]—he does not imitate it here. Instead the *Renards* is inspired by a short poem of Brant's entitled *Von dem Fuchshatz*. Originally written in German, it was printed, together with a large woodcut illustration, in 1497. Brant rendered the poem into Latin verse and included it in his *Varia carmina* of 1498 under the title *De spectaculo conflictuque vulpium Alopekiomachia*. It has no accompanying woodcut in the *Varia carmina*, but it is possible that a Latin version of the original broadsheet was printed.[59]

Bouchet owes far more to this poem than has been realised. The most striking feature of the *Renards*, the bizarre activities of the foxes which are illustrated in the woodcuts, draw their inspiration from Brant. Brant's poem first describes the fox, which is presented as the type of cunning and deceit and a symbol of contemporary man. This description is the part of the poem which is reproduced in the *Renards*.[60] Brant then goes on to describe the scene illustrated in his woodcut, in which foxes are represented in a variety of activities. Some are being chased, some are acting as hounds with their leash held by a lynx. Tails figure prominently (the German for fox's tail, 'Fuchsschwanz', has derivatives 'Fuchsschwänzen' and 'Fuchsschwänzer' meaning 'to flatter' and 'sycophant'). So one fox has a basket full of tails, one has no tail, one has two, one has a burning torch for a tail, etc. These variations are picked out in the verse, which is a series of allusive references to dangers besetting the Emperor Maximilian. In the later part of the poem the Emperor is

advised to beware of foxes, but also to imitate them to the extent of
being too cunning to be deceived.

Bouchet's work consists of thirteen chapters, ten of which begin
with a vision of foxes or other beasts illustrated in a woodcut.
Bouchet first quotes Brant's description of the fox and goes on to
write a chapter in verse expanding the theme, *La complexion du renart
avec la significacion d'icelle selon maistre Sebastien Brand.*[61] Thereafter
the foxes appear in the visions afforded to the *acteur*. Four of these
are inspired directly from the Brant woodcut and poem: foxes sow-
ing tails, a fox polluting a badger's lair, a fox carrying a flaming
torch, and a vision featuring a lynx, a lion, a bear and dragon.[62] Two
others have some element suggested by Brant: the fox who tries to
put off hounds with his stench, and the hens that feature in a vision
of foxes dressed as lawyers.[63] The four remaining visions are conventional and do not derive from Brant: foxes dressed as noblemen,
foxes dressed as hermits (representing hypocrisy), foxes knocking
down a church and foxes dressed as shepherds (representing the
clergy).[64] It can be seen that the more striking and mysterious
figures derive from Brant, whereas Bouchet himself has created
only emblems whose sense is obvious.

Bouchet does not owe a great deal to Brant in his interpretation of
these figures. Brant indeed often only offers hints as to what they
might mean: Bouchet takes and elaborates some of these hints, but
is himself responsible for all the detail of the interpretation.[65] He
also enriches the figures by accompanying them with Biblical texts.
The figures in Brant's woodcut are captioned with couplets of enig-
matic verse, but in Bouchet's woodcuts they bear one or more texts
from the Bible, which are expounded in the prose. The debt to Brant
then is limited to the imaginative framework, but this is a considerable debt because of its picturesque and intriguing nature.

Most of the *Renards* is in prose, as Bouchet explains:

> Lequel livret j'ay composé en prose, par ce qu'elle est de plus
> facil engin, et que par icelle on peut mieulx au long escripre ce
> que le sens ordonne.[66]

This stress on the importance of his sense is immediately reflected
in the sombre tone of the work. Everything is designed to impress
the reader with the seriousness of the subject. The biblical texts that
accompany the woodcuts are mostly lamenting or minatory texts
taken from the prophets.[67] They are quoted, translated and their
import developed. The mood is set with the first text from the
Lamentations of Jeremiah, 'O vos omnes qui transitis per viam,
attendite et videte si est dolor sicut dolor meus' (Lam. 1 v.12).[68] The
first chapter in verse reviews the evil of 'le temps qui court' and
introduces the vision of the foxes. In the second, 'Declaracion du
motif de l'acteur', he develops similar themes in prose, introducing
the verse 'Magis laudavi mortuos quam vivos' (Ecclesiastes 4 v.2).

He seeks to create a sense of urgency about the evils of the present day; introducing a conventional complaint about lack of charity, injustice, etc., he relates it to contemporary reality by alluding to the long absences from the kingdom of Charles VIII and the spread of new diseases.[69]

The ten visions do not form a methodical attack on the estates. Instead, after describing each vision, the *acteur* gives the interpretation that has come to him after long meditation and this in some cases involves one class of people—chapter 4 is on the murmurs and blasphemy of the common people, chapter 5 is the nobility, chapter 11 the clergy—but others represent vices that cut across estates: chapter 6 deals with 'folz esperans' of various kinds; chapter 8 covers the envious, usurers and 'folz amoureux', all of which are suggested by the figure of the fox who pollutes the badger's den and thus drives the badger away. The last chapter, with its figure of lynx, lion, bear and dragon, deals with the punishments and wrath of God.

Throughout the work Bouchet adopts a declamatory, admonitory and portentous tone, heavy with apostrophe, rhetorical questions and imperatives:

O gens aveuglez et plains de petite constance et muable couraige, peuple aisé à contemption et legier à estre par le dyable seduit qui ne povez paix endurer, murmurez vous contre Dieu . . . ?[70]

O gens qui vous nommez nobles de lignée, pensez en vous mesmes que vous avez davantaige sur ung povre laboureur, et que vous a donné nature ou vostre père plus avant fors ce que Dieu a mis par privilege de grace en vous ou voz predecesseurs.[71]

The alarming tone of the work is achieved by imitating the manner of his main source, Alain Chartier. Bouchet names no sources other than Brant, although he claims to write 'après la revolucion de plusieurs livres approuvez desquelz je me suis aydé'.[72] But in fact he borrows heavily from Chartier. His borrowings from *Le Curial* in chapter 6, *Des folz esperans*, have been well demonstrated by Pauline Smith.[73] He also uses *Le Livre d'Espérance*; chapters 5, 6, 9, 10, 11, 12 and 13 all owe something to this treatise and in some cases the borrowings are extensive.[74]

Chartier was writing *Le Livre d'Espérance* in an apparently despairing mood towards the end of the Hundred Years' War. He reflects on the wickedness of France and God's heavy temporal punishments. The book is incomplete, but he was working towards consolation of the *acteur* by means of the theological virtues. *Foy* and *Espérance* in turn address *Entendement*. Into their mouths are put bitter criticisms, particularly of abuses in the Church.

Bouchet has no consolatory purpose in the *Renards*; he is only

interested in wickedness and God's punishments. He takes from
Chartier material concerning the government of Kings, the corruption of the clergy, what is meant by the wrath of God and the
punishments of God. Thus some of his most outspoken criticism of
the powers in the land comes from Chartier, and in some cases he
attenuates the boldness of its substance—for example, on the subject of the compulsory celibacy of the clergy.[75] But sometimes he
takes a point further than Chartier does, and in any case the effect is
altered by the difference in the mode of address. In Chartier the
estates are apostrophised and criticised by the authoritative voices
of *Foy* and *Espérance*, whereas in Bouchet the merely authorial voice
of the *acteur* harangues his fellow Frenchmen. It is a personal voice,
explicitly that of a young man working as a *procureur* in Paris. The
effect is bolder and more presumptuous.

Some of Bouchet's most impressive eloquence comes to him from
Chartier. The manner of direct address, rhetorical question, imperative, is derived from him.[76] But the material from Chartier is
thoroughly worked over: rearranged, usually abridged, amplified
by other material, reworded.

We may take as an example a passage from chapter 10, *Des
violateurs de l'eglise*. This is addressed to noblemen, and it precedes
a chapter on *La dissolucion des gens d'Eglise*. In Chartier the subjects
are treated in reverse order: the violation of the church is seen as
stemming from the dissolution of the clergy, and *Foy* berates Christians generally for failing to honour the Church. In comparison with
Chartier, then, Bouchet is gentler on churchmen and harder on the
nobility. In the following section, Bouchet speaks of payments due
to the Church:

₡ Des sensives, oblacions et offertes de l'eglise

₡ Vous desrobez, ou malicieusement retenez, les *censives, obla-
    tions et offertes ecclesiaulx, qui est le vray patrimoine du crucifix, qu'il
    acquist de son precieux sang* en l'arbre de la croix. Pensez-vous
    qu'il vous en laisse impunys, et ceulx qui le tollerent et per-
    mettent? Cuydez-vous que l'orreur de vostre peché et la gran-
    deur de vostre *offense damnable, qui forclot toute grace de bien faire,*
    ne cause pas vengeance trescruelle sur vous? *Regardez la pro-
    phetie de Daniel, qui designe la venue de l'antecrist et le temps de
    persecucion pour l'abhominacion du temple et detraction du quotidien
    sacrifice*. Et si voulez fonder excuse sur la multitude des grans
    biens que possede l'eglise, pourtant vous, qui ne les avez don-
    nez, ne les devez ne pouez oster.[77]

This passage contains parts of the following sentences from Chartier, but sets them in a different context:

Et lors Costentin, meu au bien et relevement de l'Eglise, lui
donna les possesions terriennez qu'elle tient, qui depuis s'est
augmentee dez dismez et oblations courans avecquez les

sensives et offertes ecclesiaulx, qui est le droit patrimoine du crucefix, qu'il acquist de son precieux sang par sa tres douloureuse passion.[78]

[Ceste seulle offence suffist] . . . pour le pechié d'un fayre ses consors maleureux. Car *l'offence* est si *damnable* qu'elle *forclot toute grace de bien faire,* et tout eur de prouffiter en vertu.[79]

Maiz la *prophecie de Daniel* reste advenir, *qui designe la venue d'Anticrist et le temps de persecution pour les abhominations du temple et distration du cotidien sacrifice.*[80]

This example shows how pervasive is the text of Chartier, which provides nearly half the words of this passage even though Bouchet is developing an independent argument. The presence of the material from Chartier is partly to be explained by the need for authority; the voice of Bouchet's illustrious forbear would be recognised by his most alert readers. The source is also invaluable for creating the context in which the *Renards* should be read. The use of the Antichrist prophecy from Daniel just quoted from both works is most significant. With its emblematic animal figures, its doom-laden texts from the Old Testament prophets, its harping on the theme of God's punishments in *this* world as well as damnation in the next, its list of portentous events that have occurred very recently, the *Renards* is cast in a prophetic mould. When Bouchet says at the beginning, 'Je n'entendz point icy prophetiser',[81] he is in fact acknowledging the mode of his writing. It is not actual prophecy like Lichtenberger's *Pronosticatio* or Aytinger's commentary on the *Revelations* of Methodius,[82] but it is a type of moral writing that criticises vice in the perspective of threatened divine punishment in this world, seeking to capture the tone of the Old Testament prophets. Chartier's *Livre d'Espérance* is of a similar nature, and its prophetic qualities were recognised by Lemaire, who quoted from it as a vernacular explanation of a series of alarming prophecies in Latin.[83] Bouchet quotes from the same passage in the *Renards.*[84]

In both Chartier's and Bouchet's work the *acteur* is sunk in melancholy and fears for the state of the world. Seeing the foxes:

je congnoissoye visiblement le monde estre pire qu'i[l] ne fut oncques et ruyne prouchaine nous en advenir et [sic] remede n'y estoit de brief donné[85]

Within this prophetic mode and alongside his debts to Chartier, Bouchet makes some very pointed criticisms. In the passage on church offerings just quoted he considers two ways in which the Church may be deprived of her due, either by direct robbery or by failure to pay church taxes. He introduces and refutes what was no doubt an argument commonly used to defend such practices. In the section on the murmurings of the common people his complaints against them—their love of litigation, their over-rich dress, their use of blasphemy—are described with detail and vigour, always creat-

ing the impression that Bouchet speaks from everyday experience:
J'ay veu l'enfant de dix ans jurer sans honte à l'exemple de son
pere 'le sang et la vertu de Dieu' publiquement: esse pas hor-
reur et chose trop espoventable?[86]

The language in which the legal profession is criticised is particularly violent and appeals constantly to personal experience:

Après les delaiz ordinaires ilz font les nouvelles productions
qui rien ne servent à la matiere, pour plus faire durer la mau-
vaise cause qu'ilz soustiennent contre Dieu et leur conscience,
en extorquant tousjours argent de leurs parties, voire et tous
ceulx-là qui mieulx y sçavent faire quelque tromperie sont les
mieulx prisez. Je n'en dy plus pour mon honneur et par autant
que je suis du mestier. Mais je y ay tant veu faire d'abus et
tromperies que je ne puis ma parolle retenir.[87]

In addition there is a series of references to very recent portentous
events: the execution of a heretic, the prodigy of red crosses seen at
Liège and so on.[88] In short, Bouchet succeeds in giving the book a
tone of immediacy and urgency, utterly appropriate to the prophetic
mode and rather uncomfortable for the reader.

The book's impact may be traced through its subsequent history,
which was in some respects as peculiar as the circumstances of its
original publication. Vérard soon reprinted it in a different format
and Michel Le Noir issued an edition in 1504, which caused more
litigation. Initially then the book did quite well, no doubt helped by
the name of Brant and the woodcuts. Somebody made a manuscript
that copied the printed edition. Thereafter the work disappeared,
but surfaced again with Paris editions in 1522 and 1531.[89] None of
these printed editions bears Bouchet's name on the title page, although they all contain the acrostic verse that reveals it. Bouchet
himself laid claim to the work by calling himself the 'Traverseur des
voies perilleuses' in his subsequent publications, and later he included the book in lists of his works and referred several times to
Vérard's iniquities with regard to the case.

Of considerable interest, however, is reaction to the work among
people who had no idea of its provenance. The *Renards* was printed
in Dutch translation in 1517, and from Dutch was translated into
German and printed in 1546 and 1585.[90] The first German editor
points out that the date of composition, which he believed to have
been before 1515, precludes the possibility of the author being a
Lutheran.[91] The second, obviously himself a Protestant, refutes the
idea that the book might actually have been written by Luther; he
too thinks it was written in Dutch in 1495. But he is sure that the
author was a God-fearing, learned and well-read man, wise in the
ways of the world, writing with great earnestness and zeal.[92] Coming back to France, we find parts of the *Renards* and of a French
translation of the *Narrenschiff* interwoven and presented as a *Cinqui-*

esme livre des faictz et dictz du noble Pantagruel in 1549.[93] Thus, read
later in the century, the book's mordant criticisms looked just the
sort of thing that a protestant or an evangelical opponent of the
contemporary Church might have written.[94] Certainly it is much
more violent in tone than Bouchet's later treatment of substantially
the same material. It is surprising how much of the substance of
what is said in the *Renards* reappears in the *Epîtres morales*. But it
would appear that Bouchet was not entirely happy with his youthful
ferocity, for he rewrote the *Renards*. A manuscript survives, which
was made in 1531.[95] Bouchet had probably reworked the original
text rather earlier. Among the alterations, he muted the immediacy
of the tone, cutting out some of the references to events which in
any case were now long past, but also modifying the use of apostrophe.[96] The revised version is more sedate. The *Renards* is certainly the only one of Bouchet's works which can at all be described as
rabble-rousing; it is worth noting that the horrendous tone of the
original was not lost on Vérard, who accompanied Bouchet's work
with several poems by other authors that represent the laments of
sinners in hell: the customer could thus buy an agreeable package
of fire and brimstone.[97] There is also included another work, which
is probably by Bouchet, although he never bothered to reissue it.[98]
It is introduced as follows:

> Comment l'acteur si veult monstrer
> Des renars la folle fiance,
> Disant que nul glorifier
> Ne se doit point en sa science.[99]

This work contributes the *folles fiances* to the title of the book as a
whole. A brief authorial preface presents it as a sequel to the *Renards*. Mostly in verse, the tone here is more reminiscent of Brant's
Narrenschiff as the *acteur* considers the folly of trusting in earthly
things, treating first the gifts of nature, particularly corporeal
beauty, and secondly, the sciences (theology, astrology, geometry,
arithmetic, music, poetry, grammar, logic); here he attacks not the
arts themselves but the folly and abuse to which their practitioners
are prone; thirdly a whole series of mechanical arts (agriculture,
wool working, building, medicine, foundry work, 'architetho-
nique',[100] soldiering, navigation); fourthly the inventors of arts and
sciences. This is followed by a set of seven *ballades* and other verse
development on the deadly sins, and finally a series of verses on
the 'estatz du monde' (church, monasticism, aspects of temporal
powers, justice, married people, maidens, minstrels). The notion of
'folles fiances' runs through the treatment of all sections. Some of
these are very interesting in the light they shed on contemporary
practices; we have quoted from the section *poeterie* in the last chapter.[101] This, however, is a good example of material that must be
treated with caution because of the rhetorical nature of the exercise.

All activities are treated as potential 'folles fiances' and there is no balancing defence of the activity. Taken out of context each individual section sounds far more damning than it does when accompanied by criticisms of so many other qualities and pursuits. The tone of the work is in fact blander than that of the *Renards* proper; all things are vanity: thus the work shelters under the aegis of the Wisdom literature of the Bible rather than that of the prophets of doom.

b) *La Déploration de l'Eglise*
The full title of this little work of 1512 shows that it is to some degree polemical: *La Deploration de l'eglise militante sur ses persecutions interiores et exteriores et imploration de aide en ses adversitez par elle soustenues en l'an mil cinq cens dix et cinq cens unze: que presidoit en la chaire monseigneur sainct Pierre Julius Secundus.*

I shall discuss in a later chapter the propagandist content of this work, which imitates d'Auton's *Epître élégiaque par l'église militante* and figures among the group of works produced to support Louis XII in his war against Pope Julius II. However, Bouchet's poem has a broader theme than the conflict of the moment; the greater part of the poem deals with the internal problems of the Church: simony, avarice, ambition and immorality. Unlike most of the other works written during the crisis, these criticisms of the Church do not seem to be there merely to add fuel to anti-papal propaganda; on the contrary, Bouchet gives the impression that the troubles of 1510 and 1511 are a pretext for talking about the need for reformation. Here at its most acute we see the contrast between the ideal of what the clerical estate should be and the abuse to which it is subject. The poem belongs to the moral tradition of dealing with the estates of society, concentrating on just one estate, the Church. Certainly Bouchet felt that the validity of his poem outlived the war with Julius II; adapting the topical material but leaving the complaints about abuse virtually unchanged, he included a version of the *Déploration* in the collection of moral works published as the *Opuscules du traverseur* in 1525.

The main stylistic interest of the poem is the way in which he treats authorities. The poem has a brief fictional framework introducing a vision of the Church, and for the most part consists of the lament of the Church couched in eighty-four 13-line stanzas. In the margin beside almost every one of these stanzas is one or more sentences in Latin, complete with source reference. This is a technique that Bouchet could have seen in one of the works by other authors in the *Renards*;[102] among his contemporaries Gringore employed it in his moral works *Les Folles Entreprises* and *Les Abuz du monde.*[103]

The largest number of these quotations is drawn from the Bible.

Bouchet enhances the tone of lamentation at the beginning with a series of quotations from the Book of Lamentations:

| Quomodo sedet sola civitas plena populo. Treni primo. | Or suis je bien seule en adversité
Moy l'eglise, dicte de Dieu cité . . .[104] |

The *Déploration* imparts a sense of fear of impending doom similar to that of the *Renards*; some of the prophetic texts reappear and there are references to judgements and punishments to come:

| Deus iudex iustus fortis et patiens etc. psal. vii. | Dieu seuffre tout, qui est lassus es cieulx,
Mais de ces maulx si tresinjurieux
Se vengera, voire bien briefvement.[105] |

Biblical texts are invaluable for setting the seal of authority on what is said, and he makes particularly effective use of a number of New Testament verses of very clear sense and direct expression: 'Qui maior est vestrum fiat sicut minister' (Mat. 20 v.26, paraphrased), set beside a stanza on the duties of a bishop, and repeated when the Pope is addressed; 'Beati pacifici quoniam filii Dei vocabuntur' (Mat. 5 v.9), beside lines about the Pope going to war; 'Domus mea domus orationis vocabitur, vos autem fecistis illam speluncam latronum' (Mat. 21 v.13), at the beginning of the passage on simony.[106]

Of his other sources a mere handful are classical, mostly from Cicero's *De Officiis*.[107] But the longest quotations are taken from Christian writers, notably St Bernard and more especially from Canon Law. The quotation of passages from Canon Law is a remarkably effective way of justifying criticism of clerical abuse. His first stanza against simony is accompanied by the following quotation:

> Fertur symoniaca heresis (que prima contra Dei ecclesiam dyabolica supplantatione surrepsit: et in ipso ortu suo zelo apostolice ultionis percussa atque damnata est) in regni vestri finibus dominari, i.q.i.c. Fertur; quod dirigitur a Gregorio, Theodorico et Theodoberto regibus francorum.[108]

Here we see a Pope addressing kings in gravest terms about simony, describing it as a heresy of diabolical inspiration. A reader who knew his Canon Law would know that the passage goes on to say that simoniacal priests can be of no help to their flocks.

In several cases he summarises a law in his own Latin and then gives references to it; thus, beside a complaint about absent bishops, he states:

> Omne beneficium quantumcumque minimum requirit residentiam de iure communi. Ca. quia nonnulli; ca. quia in tantum, et fere per totum de. cle. non. resi.[109]

Here there is a bald statement of the principle together with an impressive number of references.

This technique enables Bouchet to construct a formidable indictment of the churchmen of his day by setting their shortcomings against the principles they were supposed to follow. But it also reflects a fundamentally conservative attitude towards possible reformation. The *Déploration* is less radical than the *Renards* because of this weight of authority. In the first place it establishes firmly that abuse alone needs to be reformed; the statutes of the Church are by implication right and just, if only they could be enforced. Secondly, although the complaints in the French verse are outspoken enough, they are very much more weighty when backed up by the authorities. But these of course can only be understood by those who read Latin, so a grave and disquieting level of sense is available only to the educated. In the *Renards* Bouchet quoted his biblical texts in Latin and then translated them. Here much of the Latin is in effect translated in the verse, but it is much less obvious to the latinless reader exactly what idea is being backed up by authority, nor would it be clear what the authority was. It is probable too that the more educated the reader, the more he would read into the accompanying Latin text. It can in fact be understood by anyone who reads Latin, because sentences are quoted as well as references being given, but a reader who recognised the references and knew the text would perceive a further layer of suggestion just from the texts chosen. For instance, he would recognise that in citing the terms of the Pragmatic Sanction against a verse critical of university graduates, Bouchet was using the Sorbonne's favourite Gallican weapon against itself.[110] Although there is no evidence in this text of hidden senses suggested in this way, it is a technique that makes it possible to make allusions to dangerous ideas for the sole benefit of those sufficiently learned to understand the references and therefore presumably also sufficiently well educated not to be put at any risk by such ideas.[111] The technique of course also has the advantage of parading the author's learning. So although the criticisms levelled against the Church are extremely serious and, as will be seen in chapter 5, in some cases go beyond the commonplace of this type of literature, they are presented as the criticisms of a loyal son of the Church. Making the figure of the Church herself voice the complaints is an important measure in achieving this effect, and just to make sure five stanzas are devoted to expounding the dignity of priests, 'et comment on ne doit surprendre sur eulx et leur auctorité'.[112]

c) *Le Chapelet des Princes*, 1517

This collection of *rondeaux* and *ballades* is utterly different from the two works discussed so far. Yet it has in common with them the treatment of the estates of society, like the *Déploration* examining one estate only, the prince.

Like the *Renards*, it appears as one work among several in a moral compilation, and again the printer has gathered works with a similar theme. The volume in which the *Chapelet* appears was sold under the title of Georges Chastellain's *Temple de Jehan Bocace*. This little treatise is addressed to the unhappy queen of Henry VI of England and contains instruction on how to face evil fortune and on the requisite virtues. This is followed by a prose *Instruction du jeune prince*. Thus the unifying theme of the volume, and the tradition into which the *Chapelet* fits, is the instruction of princes.

The prince whom Bouchet seeks to instruct is the young François de La Trémoille, son of the Prince de Talmont; the collection must have been put together shortly before the latter's death after Marignano in September 1515. The social situation of the *acteur* of the *Renards* was that of the young clerk railing against the iniquities of his superiors; now he is the *rhétoriqueur* poet laying a gift before his patron. The *Chapelet* is remarkable for its craftsmanship.

The idea of the *Chapelet* suggests a coronet. It is so used by Molinet in his *Chapelet des Dames* for Mary of Burgundy, which is a coronet of flowers representing virtues and spelling out the name MARIE.[113] The connection with Mary is apt because the word is used with reference to the Virgin's coronet and it also means the rosary, the series of prayers consisting of fifty Ave Marias interspersed with five Paternosters, which can be represented by a string of beads. All these ideas are exploited by Bouchet in the form of his work: notions of richness and royalty implicit in the coronet, the circularity of both coronet and string of beads, the disposition of prayers in the rosary, the repetition of formulae implied by these prayers.

Beginning with a *ballade*, which gives in acrostic the names 'Charles de La Trémoille' and 'Jehan Bouchet', the work thereafter comprises fifty *rondeaux* and five *ballades*, disposed like the beads of a rosary. *Ballade* form suggests circularity with its repeated final lines and its *envoi*, which in each case begins with the word 'Prince'. The subjects of the five *ballades*, are, in the first, 'l'estre et naissance de seigneurie', thereafter one by one the four cardinal virtues. These regularly appearing *ballades* give a powerful sense of structure to the work, particularly once the cycle of cardinal virtues has begun.

The *Ave Marias* are represented by *rondeaux*, each introduced by an explanatory title and a sentence in Latin from an authority. Thus there are in each case three modes of conveying sense, which will be examined in turn. First, the title, which is always brief, after the first three taking the form 'Le prince (ne) doibt estre/faire (quelque chose)'. Here then is a precept, the moral lesson in its most condensed form and at its most imperative—but a dignified imperative, the verb 'devoir' pointing to the duties of an estate that also has privileges. The recurrence of the formula suggests the repetition of a rosary.

Next comes the Latin sentence, the value of which Bouchet underlines in his preface to Charles de la Trémoille:

> Et affin qu'il plaise à mondict seigneur vostre filz adjouxter à mes rondeaulx meilleure foy, les ay voulu prouver par auctoritez moralles sur iceulx rondeaulx inserées.[114]

One effect is to afford to the latinate reader a layer of sense not available to the latinless. The sources of the sentences are nearly equally divided between biblical and classical. There are twelve different sources in all, but in each group two predominate: from the Bible, Proverbs (9) and Ecclesiasticus (9); classical (or apparently so) Cicero, *De Officiis* (13) and the pseudo-Senecan *De formula honestae vitae* (9).[115] Among the Biblical texts three more come from the Book of Wisdom. These sources indicate the mode of writing just as they did in the *Renards*, but here it is a different one. The work is placed under the auspices of the Wisdom literature of the Bible— proverbial truths, lessons in life and virtue in their most prestigious formulation. The universality of the truth is underlined by the complementary set of classical texts: Cicero on man's duties (*devoir*) to his fellows, a classical text which treats the four cardinal virtues; 'Seneca' on how to live well, in a text which was also known as *De Quatuor virtutibus*.

The sense of the title and the sense of the sentence, although always complementary, are not identical. For instance, *rondeau* 41 beginning 'Legiereté' quoted in the last chapter is introduced as follows:

¢ Le prince ne doibt estre trop soudain
¢ Cogitatio tua stabilis et firma sit: sive deliberet:
   sive queret: sive contempletur.
   Se. de for. ho. vi.[116]

The *rondeau* brings together the themes of rashness and changeableness. Similarly *rondeau* 39 deals both with envy and with delight in an enemy's misfortunes:

¢ Le prince ne doibt estre envieux.
¢ Cum ceciderit inimicus tuus ne gaudeas et in ruina eius non exultet cor tuum; ne forte videat Dominus et displiceat ei: et auferat ab eo iram suam. Proverb xxiiii.

Si monter veulx par haulx faictz à honneur,
N'aies jamais d'autruy gloire doleur,
Car Dieu souvent par sa grant providence
A telles gens prepare decadence,
Et tous leurs faictz il tourne à deshonneur.

Ne t'esjouys si tu voys en langueur
Ton ennemy, ne use plus de rigueur
Quant nuyre puis par superintendance
   Si monter veulx.

Dieu est des biens de ce monde donneur;
Tout vient de luy, soit vertuz ou bon eur,
Si donc en donne à autruy n'est prudence
De t'en marrir, penses sans diffidence
Que de ta part il fault prendre labeur,
   Si monter veulx.[117]

The latinless reader is not losing the moral lesson, but he is losing
the pithy formulation of part of that lesson together with any associations that the Latin text might have if he recognised its context.[118]

  Given that Bouchet is often combining two slightly different precepts in his *rondeau*, a great deal of matter has to be packed into a
form which had traditionally been used more commonly for light
and erotic subjects. He uses exclusively the now popular *rondeau
double*, which has thirteen lines not counting the short refrains. The
rondeau form helps to suggest circularity with its twice repeated
refrain, and the intricate artistry demanded by the fixed form com-
plements the notion of the rich coronet. Jean Marot also offered a
rondeau cycle of moral advice to the great with his *Doctrinal des
Princesses*.[119]

  The *Chapelet* is thus courtly in conception, and it shares with the
memorial works a wider range of *rhétoriqueur* poetic techniques than
those used in the other moral works. And yet this conception is to
some degree at odds with the import of the work. Bouchet is very
concerned with his moral lessons; this after all is the work in which
he refuses to adopt the rule that the *rondeau* must 'clore'; the large
amount of substance that he was trying to handle no doubt added
to his reluctance to submit to any further metrical difficulty. Moreover, when the lessons of the *Chapelet* are examined, it soon emerges
that they are by no means equally divided between the four cardinal
virtues. Prudence predominates. All the sentences from the pseudo-
Seneca are taken from the section on Prudence, although Bouchet
groups most of them round the *ballade* on Justice. No doubt Prudence is a virtue that lends itself to being taught in a *doctrinal*, but it
is also a virtue most likely to appeal to a bourgeois in his overlord.
There is nothing very courtly about the way *rondeau* 29 expounds its
precept and sentence:

  ¢ Le prince se doibt garder de desplaire à ses subgectz
  ¢ Illud quidem natura non patitur ut aliorum spoliis nostras facul-
    tates copias et opes augeamus. Tuli. de offi. libro tertio.

  Pour estre aymé par grace universelle
  Et pour regner en gloyre et en haulte helle,
  De ses subgectz fault le bien pourchasser,
  Ce qu'on ne faict, comme croy, pour chasser
  Par vignes, champs et blez à grant sequelle.

L'on abat tout par façon Dieu scet quelle;
Le blé se pert, la vigne n'est si belle
Comme seroit, dont on se doibt passer
    Pour estre aymé.

Si les subgectz ont chien, cheval, bas, celle,
Ou aultre bien, il convient qu'on les celle,
Car mains seigneurs ne font que cabasser,
Et par procès veulent tout embrasser
Ce n'est à eulx procedé de bon zelle,
    Pour estre aymé.[120]

This is a particularly striking example of a tension often evident in instructions to Princes between lordly pursuits and the interests of subjects. *L'Instruction du jeune prince* printed in the same volume as the *Chapelet* strives in its seventh chapter to advocate economy as a protection of 'magnificence'.[121] The homeliness of the tone runs contrary to the ornateness of the framework of the *Chapelet* and underlines Bouchet's very didactic intentions even in this courtly work. The analogy of the rosary, the biblical texts and a number of religious precepts among the lessons confirm the piety of the approach. The very large number of *rondeaux*[122] allows him to give a wide range of advice to the prince, both about the cultivation of virtue at a personal level and about the practicalities of ruling. The lessons of the *Chapelet* will be repeated in the *Epître aux rois*.

d) *Epîtres morales*

The first *épître morale* to be printed appeared in the *Opuscules du Traverseur* of 1525. One might underrate this small book with its apparently lightweight title, but the volume is presented with great solemnity. It consists of four works, three of which are corrected versions of earlier moral works, the *Déploration*, the *Chapelet* and the other moral *ballades* and *rondeaux* which had been printed with the *Chapelet*. These are preceded by a new work, the *Epître de Justice*. Thus the collection as a whole contains works addressed to the three major estates: the Church, kings and princes, the law. In the new work on his own estate, Bouchet inaugurates a new way of addressing the estates, and he assembles an impressive introduction. On the first page the Franciscan Jean Trojan addresses a long laudatory epistle in Latin to Bouchet, who had asked him to examine the *Epître de Justice* from a theological point of view.[123] A verse *épître* by Bouchet to the *avocat* Germain Emery is answered with another Latin epistle praising the *Opuscules* as a whole.[124] Both of his friends stress the clarity, elegance and usefulness of his work. Both affect a humanist style in their Latin. Trojan was one of the group who met at Fontaine-le-Comte. Clearly the term *opuscules* is important as much for its latinity as for its sense. Bouchet's moral works are now being set in a more classical context.

He was obviously pleased with his experiment of using a long verse épître for a moral work, and went on writing them, particularly during the period in the early 1530s when he had to stay in the country because of the plague in Poitiers. The collection was probably complete ten years before it was published as two books of Epîtres morales in 1545.

It is worth speculating why Bouchet finally chose the épître as a vehicle for his most ambitious moral work. The choice might be explained by the growing popularity of the genre, but Bouchet had no obvious models among his contemporaries for using it for extensive moral discussion as early as 1525. Of the forms he had used before, the rondeau and ballade were plainly unsuitable for further development. The technique of the Déploration makes it difficult to handle many different estates, and it is also too rhetorical for the balance of praise and blame that Bouchet was increasingly to seek. The interpretation of figures like the foxes in a moral sense no longer appeals either, being probably too limited for his discursive approach. The épître is a non-declamatory way of addressing the estates, it is open to any structure the author cares to impose on it, and it employs a personal authorial voice which can be adapted to a range of respectful or accusing tones.

It seems likely that the main literary influence on Bouchet when he chose the épître for his moral writing was classical. In particular, he may have had in mind Seneca's Epistulae morales. Seneca's prestige as a supposed correspondent of St Paul would encourage his use as a model.[125] There are very occasional references to Seneca in the Epîtres but there is no evidence of sustained imitation.[126] The device of supposing an objection being raised by his recipient and then refuting it is used frequently by Seneca in these letters and is also used extensively by Bouchet, although I would hesitate to maintain that Seneca was his source for such a common device. It will however be remembered that in the preface to the Jugement Bouchet likened his work to that of Seneca, whose style was 'dur' in comparison to that of Cicero. There is no real similarity between the distinctively epigrammatic prose style of Seneca and that of Bouchet's verse; the comparison no doubt arose because Quintilian, who always praises the style of Cicero, makes criticisms of that of Seneca.[127] But the comparison may be significant if Bouchet was conscious of having imitated Seneca in choosing letters as a vehicle for moral works.

In spite of a fair sprinkling of brief references to Seneca, Horace, Juvenal and other classical writers there is little extensive imitation of classical moralists and satirists. The reason is obviously that Bouchet's analysis of society made such borrowings very difficult. Classical moral writers do not use the medieval concept of the hierarchy of estates. Even when subject matter does overlap Bouchet is too concerned with the detail of contemporary reality to adapt descriptions of the classical world.[128] Moreover, his classical models often treat subjects that Bouchet could only have discussed in a theological context; Seneca's letters, for example, are a major source for Stoic philosophy. And yet Bouchet does seem to some small degree to suggest comparison with classical writers, although not particularly poets. We can point to the title *Epîtres morales*, and to the accompanying collection of *Epîtres familières*.[129] Collections consisting solely of *épîtres* are unusual among *rhétoriqueurs* although they become very popular in the middle of the century; there are however many examples of classical collections of letters: Horace and Cicero as well as Seneca. In the *épîtres morales* Bouchet abandons any fictional or allegorical narrative, instead his authorial voice is markedly personal, as is the voice of the classical writer of epistles. The best evidence is provided by the one example of extended use of a classical text. This is the *Epître de vieillesse*, 1 *Ep. Mor.* 14, which adopts the framework and some of the arguments of Cicero's *De Senectute*. The source is noted in several marginal references. Again we must note that it is classical prose, not verse, that is evoked. Cicero's treatise imagines Cato discussing his own old age with friends; Bouchet, representing himself on the brink of old age, addresses a friend of 39 years' standing. He takes from Cicero four reasons that make old age appear wretched, many of the opposing arguments and also ideas on the pleasures available to the old. There is some imitation of Cicero's figures, as with an extended simile concerning the pilot of a ship; a number of classical examples of active old men come from Cicero. Bouchet describes his own experience of life rather in the way that Cato does. Cato is made to state his beliefs about death and the afterlife; Bouchet very deliberately substitutes a profession of faith and hope of salvation. Although these borrowings are intermittent and do not even account for half the substance of Bouchet's *épître*, Cicero is obviously his inspiration and starting point here, his partial model for themes and to a very much lesser extent for his rhetoric.

None of the classical texts exploited by Bouchet are unusual or in any way new to the Renaissance. But it does seem that his own moral writing, in a rather similar way to his poetry, exhibits an awareness of the increasing fashionableness of classical material and an adoption of the trend, but only in rather superficial ways. For, as we shall see, the underlying orthodox medieval Christian foundations of his writing are untouched.

Learned these poems certainly are, if not with a primarily classical learning. By the time that Bouchet composed most of the *Epîtres* he had written both the *Annales* and the *Triomphes*. The fruit of his wide reading enriches all the *Epîtres*. In 1525 the *Epître de Justice* has heavy marginal annotation like that of the *Déploration*. Bouchet notes in his letter to Emery that he has placed quotations in Latin beside his French verse and he asks Emery to add some more quotations if he can.[130] He uses a wide variety of authorities; more historical texts are referred to, and Civil Law takes its place beside Canon Law. Particularly when he turns his attention to the different grades of the legal profession Civil Law becomes almost the only authority, partly because his advice and criticism are so detailed that only a specialised authority provides relevant material, partly too no doubt in order to pursue the policy of quoting a profession's own texts against it.

Even in the *Epître de Justice*, however, the reference without a quotation is beginning to take over from the long quotations that we saw in the *Déploration*. In 1545 virtually no quotations survive, and there are even some *épîtres* with no marginal references at all. The fashion for margins black with Latin had passed. Thus Bouchet's erudition is not paraded so obviously although he is still employing many different authorities. The significance of the references that are given varies from a confirmation text to an indication of a text that is imitated at length. A reference to St Bernard in the section on the Pope indicates a long borrowing from *De Consideratione*.[131] He gives no reference at all to a text by Aeneas Sylvius Piccolomini, which he imitates when addressing courtiers.[132] It becomes much harder to assess the import of his references; they must now be followed up by the reader unless he is learned enough to recognise the point from the reference alone; thus the marginalia appeal to a more exclusively learned audience than the earlier texts, which offered something at least to anyone who could read Latin.

The picture of society enshrined in the *Epîtres morales* is very conservative. In the volume finally published in 1545 there are twenty-five *épîtres* of various lengths, organised into two books, which treat the concept of 'estate' in two different ways. The hierarchies of the first book are those of what may be called spiritual society. Beginning with the ministers of the Church, he proceeds to the related groups of monks, preachers, nuns, Knights of St John of Jerusalem. All these estates are celibate. By a line of thought that assesses the spiritual status of different types of non-celibacy he next addresses widows, then married people. This leads him to consider men as part of a family group and at different stages in life, and so the book continues with parents, children (male), maidens, servants, masters, scholars and old age. The second book has the more obvious theme of hierarchies and callings of lay society: kings, courtiers, noblemen, soldiers, the law, subjects, tax collectors, doctors and related professions, merchants, artisans, printers. Within each *épître* the approach is not identical, but particularly in the major ones to the great estates he begins by showing the divine institution and the biblical and later history of the estate. In comparison with a work like the *Renards*, such a preliminary account of the origin of the estate puts a different complexion on even very grave criticisms made later. And once set among the rest of the *Epîtres morales*, the estate appears yet more clearly as part of an immutable structure that no abuse, however serious, could undermine. The vertiginous prophetic prospect of the *Renards* yields to the monumental solidity of the historically based *Epîtres*.

In the *Argument des Epîtres Morales*, Bouchet claims to balance his criticisms with the duties and virtues of each estate. He is indeed quite successful in solving the problems he perceives in balancing one group against another and the praise and blame of any particular group. The major *epîtres* begin with eulogy and pass on to criticism and advice; this is the basic pattern of each *epître* which, combined with the balancing effect of one *epître* juxtaposed with another, helps to achieve a broad view not at all reminiscent of *pro* and *contra* argument. The two different ways of categorising the estates of men are also of value in representing the complexity of the world, as is a considerable variety of approach within the basic pattern of the *epître*.

The two longest *epîtres* are addressed to two very important estates, the Church and the Law. When Bouchet originally wrote the *Epître de Justice* he established the method of the *epître morale* in its most developed form. Both these *epîtres* begin with a theological account of the origin of the estate, thus providing the estate with an unquestionably dignified background. The first ten chapters of the *Epître de Justice*, 2 *Ep. Mor.* 5, deal with the first law of nature governing creation, the second law prescribing love of God and love of man which governed Adam and Eve and then, tracing the concept of law through biblical history, the subsequent laws of the ten commandments, of grace and of Canon Law. He explains that law is the earthly remedy for the Fall. In the *Epître* to the Church, 1 *Ep. Mor.* 1, he devotes three chapters to the superiority of the clergy over kings, the development of priestly functions in the Old Testament and, with paraphrase from the Gospels, Peter's confession of faith and the institution of the Christian priesthood, stressing the unique functions of the priest: consecration of the host and absolution.

In both cases he has made a magnificent assertion of the dignity of the estate. In each case comes a turning-point marked by the word *aussi*.[133] Those who have the highest office must also therefore bear the heaviest burdens. In the *Epître de Justice* he now works down the hierarchy of justice, from kings and emperors to counsellors, judges, and so on right down to the hangman.[134] Each grade is offered advice, warning and criticism. In the *epître* to the Church the structure is slightly different. In seven chapters on the duties of a

. priest he lists the qualities that they should possess ('vous debvez
. . .'); in each case the section proceeds from exhortation to criticism.
The criticism is not fierce; he seems concerned to offer good advice
to help the ordinary parish priest to fulfil his obligations. The section
on chastity is particularly developed as he defends the institution of
compulsory celibacy of the clergy. He uses the method of imagining
excuses put to him by a priest and disposing of the argument. He
maintains that it is better to live in married chastity than to be an
unchaste celibate priest, so urges care in receiving men into the
priesthood and warns of situations liable to give rise to temptation.
Thereafter, he turns to consider the higher levels of the hierarchy of
the Church: Pope, cardinals, archbishops and bishops, all who hold
benefices. These are the sections in which the severest criticisms
occur; the higher échelons are addressed with stern gravity, and are
represented as being responsible for the shortcomings of the lower
orders of clergy. In the section on the Pope he adopts a respectful
attitude, while suggesting serious sins that might afflict the papacy.
Marginal references to Canon Law here are to conciliar texts that
suggest the possibility of deposing an unworthy Pope.[135]

Both these *épîtres* treat subjects that figure in the *Renards*. The
Epître de Justice is presented as an answer to those who attack
lawyers without regard for the dignity of the profession. It might
even be regarded as an answer to Bouchet's own attacks in the
Renards, which were passionate denunciations of the way the poor
were treated by lawyers. A greater number of particular abuses are
referred to in the course of the *Epître*, but the effect is quite different
because he instructs rather than denounces:

Les advocatz bons, loyaulx et directz
Se gardent bien que par tours indirectz
Delayent trop bonne ou maulvaise cause,
Ne d'inventer soubz umbre d'une clause
Quelque moien d'obscurer un cler droict;
Dampné seroit qui faire le vouldroit.[136]

cf.   Erigez voz aureilles et escoutez les grans exclamacions que
contre vous font les povres; lesquelz par vostre inique et damné
conseil avez mys au greffre de brouillerie et procès dont ne
peuent avoir yssue sans leur destruction et confusion vituper-
able. Leurs plaintes vous procurent gouttes de sang et ven-
geance cruelle ainsi que dit Iheremie. Leurs maledictions vous
preparent la voye d'enfer si vous n'y remediez. Le remede si est
de restituer.[137]

In the *épître* to the clergy he uses various texts and themes that had
already appeared in the *Renards*. In the sections addressed to the
clergy as a whole the effect is again so muted as to be quite different,
particularly as he affects to disbelieve the graver abuses. But in the
section addressed to bishops, in which he suggests all the abuses

the bishops ought to put a stop to, the language takes on a vigour
much more reminiscent of the *Renards*:

> Vous les verrez en nopces et banquetz,
> Danser, saulter et porter les bouquetz,
> Baiser, taster et faire actes scurrilles,
> Oultrepassans follies puerilles.
> Vous les verrez yvroigner, taverner,
> Jouer à jeux dissolutz, galerner,
> Et faire pis qu'avanturiers de guerre;
> Le ciel en put, et lasse en est la terre.[138]

It is entirely characteristic of the different scope and atmosphere of
the *Epîtres* that he should offer a token apology for such language,
but the apology turns into a lively defence:

> Le doys-je escrire, attendu le canon
> Qui le defend? Il sembleroit que non,
> Mais je suis clerc tonsuré, qui m'hardie
> En charité d'en faire tragedie,
> Veu que chascun du peuple a interest
> En tout cecy, veu le mal tel qu'il est,
> Car qui se taist consentir on presume
> A un delict, comme la loy resume.[139]

This apology shows one of the ways in which Bouchet uses the
authorial voice in these *épîtres*. Throughout the voice is very much
that of Bouchet himself, a man in his later middle age, *procureur*,
writer, husband, father. In these *épîtres* to the great and powerful
estates he adopts a tone of respect, humility up to a point, but
combined with fearless truth-telling. A similar approach to that
of the two *épîtres* we have been discussing, is adopted in those addressed to the nobility (2,3), to scholars (1,13), and to a certain
extent to monks (1,2) and to preachers (1,3). In all those dealing
with the Church he had of course by this time to take into account
criticisms coming from Lutheran heretics; this particularly colours
the *épître* addressed to monks, which although very critical is also
defensive.

The treatment of less powerful estates is rather different. In three
cases Bouchet writes with a particular recipient in mind; this was
the case with nuns (1,4) and with widows (1,6); these *épîtres* are
kindly, a little unctuous, comforting, much more laudatory than
critical. The *épître* addressed to the Knights of St John of Jerusalem
(1,5) is also addressed to a friend, Florent Guyvereau, commander
of the order; this is a short *épître* which does little more than praise
the order; the critical part of the moral exercise is achieved by listing
sins that the brothers do not commit. The *épîtres* addressed to still
lowlier estates are more patronising in their advice and warnings
but also less stern and mordant than those addressed to the great.
The *épître* to parents (1,8) very soon turns into a catalogue of good

advice for pregnancy and onwards from the experienced father of eight children. The whole group of *épîtres* broadly concerned with family life, 1 *Ep. Mor.* 7–12, are interesting for the dignity given even to these lower levels of anybody's hierarchy. None of them is at all satirical. The *épître* to masters (1,12), who have the power, has some stern criticism, but to servants Bouchet says:

Ce que j'en diz n'est de haulte science,
Mais je le sçay par vraye experience,
Car j'ay servy, non sans peine et soulcy,
Et servy suis à present, Dieu mercy.[140]

The intention to comfort the lower orders seems obvious. The *épître* on marriage (1,7), particularly in the light of its setting after the celibate religious estates, appears as a sympathetic defence of marriage. Underlining that matrimony is a holy estate, instituted of God, he says that to speak evil of the other sex is to blaspheme the work of God. He depicts the chaste pleasures of the marriage bed, stressing the 'douceur' and comfort of married love:

Soulas n'est tel que d'homme et femme ensemble
En lict d'honneur couchez, comme il me semble.
 Il n'est plaisir si doulx et asseuré
Que d'homme et femme en lict bien mesuré
De chaste amour, qui est ornée et paincte
De doulx plaisirs, sans danger et sans craincte.
Il n'est doulceur plus grand que ceste cy;
En la prenant on n'a peur ne soulcy
D'offenser Dieu, mais souvent on merite
Et les haux cieulx de quelque ame on herite.[141]

He goes on to repeat the teaching on marital intercourse, which he had originally taken from a sermon by Raulin and used in the *Triomphes*, showing to what extent venial sin may be involved and where mortal sin starts.[142] Within the tradition of moral theology that he follows he is liberal and sympathetic to women. And the fact that he speaks as a married layman removes his comments from the usual context of the celibate condescending to weaker brethren. Indeed, his treatment of the possible sinfulness of intercourse seems designed to reassure troubled consciences.

There remains a group of *épîtres*, particularly in the second book, where Bouchet is treating professions whose honourableness is open to question. Here the tone is different again; more argument is needed to defend the estate and the warning tone of the advice that follows is more pessimistic. Soldiers (2,4), are defended vigorously; he begins the *épître* by explaining the concept of the just war, using traditional arguments that derive from Cicero and Augustine. Tax-gatherers (2,7), although worthy, have unfortunate biblical precedents; in this *épître* Bouchet demonstrates his professional expertise by showing in detail the sort of abuses that tax-gatherers could perpetrate. He takes a traditional view of merchants (2,9), and even as he argues for the merits of their estate exposes the difficulty of being saved when one is involved in such a profession; his advice is centred on how the merchant can avoid offending God. Worst of all is the *épître* to courtiers (2,2). He can find hardly any good to say of the estate; from the beginning it is described as dangerous:

> . . . vos estatz, qui sont tres dangereux,
> Et s'ilz sont beaux, toutesfois onereux[143]

Moreover Bouchet speaks throughout the *épître* as someone who had some experience of the estate. In fact the picturesque description of the wretched life of a courtier paraphrases Piccolomini's *De Curialium Miseriis Epistola*, as Pauline Smith has shown.[144] This is followed by a passage of advice, which has no direct source but is equally condemnatory, using the technique of demolishing the excuses that courtiers might offer, and he concludes:

> Je n'en dy plus, car le trop long parler
> De ce propos engendreroit par l'aer
> Murmure et cry contre moy et ma plume,
> Vous suppliant que mieulx on se remplume
> D'amour divin, que de l'amour mondain.[145]

This *épître* is exceptional in its unrelieved criticism, and so supports Smith's contention that Bouchet should be regarded as a major anti-courtier writer of the period.

There is one exception to the general rule that the more powerful the estate the sterner the criticism, and that is the *Epître aux rois*, the first of the second book. It owes a lot to the formulations of the *Chapelet* ('les roys et princes doyvent estre sçavans', etc.) and deals primarily in precepts and *exempla*. Although the King is told not to do certain things the critical aspects are muted; instead the theme throughout is that the King's duty is to be more virtuous than his subjects. Kings were originally set up for their singular virtue, for their beneficence to the nation, for the proper execution of justice and for the defence of the state. Although above the law, the King should observe the law.

This *épître* is set apart from the others in that it purports to have been written much earlier and takes the form of a personal address to Louis XII. There is no reason to disbelieve Bouchet's explicit assertion that Louis had instructed him to write such an *épître*,[146] but it is also clear that if this *épître* was writen before 1515 it was the subject of considerable revision. The rhymes alternate masculine and feminine, and Bouchet did not normally revise his early work to make it abide by this rule. As I have already said, this *épître* appears to me to achieve some critical effects through praising the virtues of François Ier's predecessor, who had been called 'le père du peuple'. It should certainly be read in conjunction with the one addressed to subjects (2,6) where Bouchet is writing in 1535 in the reign of François 1er and speaks of fifteen troubled years. Certainly subjects are offered an array of biblical arguments to show that kingship comes from God and that subjects have a duty of reverence to their lords and must not murmur against them. But reading the two *épîtres* together it might well appear that subjects had more to murmur about under some kings than others.[147]

The *Epîtres morales* form a long work weighty with substance. They are the fruits of Bouchet's long labours and the most authoritative and comprehensive of his moral writings; indeed it would be difficult to find their parallel in the *rhétoriqueur* tradition out of which they grew.

Although critical of abuse and often detailed in these criticisms, the critical and satirical aspect of moral writing is less prominent in the *Epîtres* than it was in his very early writings. This is partly the result of a different way of casting his material, but it is also reasonable to assume that the older and established Bouchet was more mellow, more understanding of the difficulties of the establishment and less sympathetic to trouble-makers. He prefers his criticism to take the form of advising people what they should do as opposed to denouncing what at worst they do.

The *Epîtres* give a highly conservative view of society because of the theological and historical approach to each estate. However sharp subsequent criticism may be, it operates only in the context of a fundamentally unchangeable social order. Bouchet's perception of society is religious in its assumptions and he appears old-fashioned partly because the influence on him of the classical thought which was to transform moral writing is necessarily superficial. I said at the beginning of this chapter that theological writing and moral writing are distinct. In fact Bouchet uses a great deal of theological material in these *épîtres*; he does not explain man's individual relation to God or expound the doctrines concerning salvation, but he uses references to creation, the fall and freewill to set estates in their proper context. He also uses theological concepts when the risk of damnation is a real concern; he speaks of venial and mortal sin. But he was conscious in doing this of bringing an unusual dimension to a moral work; in the *Opuscules* he says to Emery:

> Et parautant que je n'ay seulement
> Parlé des loix, mais theologallement,
> Voire cocté du latin mon vulgaire,
> A ce qu'il soit tousjours plus salutaire
> Je l'ay fait veoir à ung theologien.[148]

This demonstrates that Bouchet was well aware of a difference between moral and theological writing; in the *Epîtres* he nevertheless brings in those theological doctrines that have the advantage first of making his depiction of the estates all the more authoritative, secondly of making his teaching more useful, not for the abstract cultivation of remarkable virtue but for the avoidance of those things that might jeopardise salvation.

NOTES

1. In the *Triomphes* the Soul in Book 1 receives her moral education from the four cardinal virtues. In Book 2, after her fall and repentance, she is instructed by the three theological virtues.
2. *Masque*, p.73.
3. *Ep. Fam.* 41, f.xxxii vo, col.1.
4. *Temple*, liminary [f.4] ro. See also *infra*, chapter 4.
5. *Panégyrique*, ff.xci ro-cxxv vo.
6. *Gloire*, p.187.
7. *Chapelet*, f.xxxiiii ro.
8. *Temple*, ff.lxxx vo-lxxxi ro.
9. *Triomphes du roi*, liminary [f.2] ro.
10. *Ibid*. Cf. *supra*, chapter 2, on his use of poetic fictions.
11. *Temple*, f.lxxxii ro.
12. *City of God*, 5, 15; reference to Mat. 6 v.2.
13. In the *Triomphes* Bouchet speaks of the limbo of unbaptised infants and the limbo of the fathers, which he describes as 'le lymbe des saincts peres et aultres circunciz . . .' (f.cli vo). Dante depicts Virgil, Homer and other poets of antiquity in Limbo, *Inferno*, canto ɪv. Ficino is an example of a thinker who would allow certain pagan philosophers into the limbo of the Fathers and thence to salvation: see Raymond Marcel, *Marsile Ficin (1433-1499)*, Paris, 1958, p.636.
14. See for instance St Thomas Aquinas, *Summa Theologica*, Prima secundae, q.lxv, art.2. For the question of virtuous actions done without faith, see *Triomphes*, f.cvi ro, and *infra*, chapter 7.
15. The *Labyrinthe*, with its discussion of Fortune, culminates in an exposition of faith, hope and charity.
16. The *Chapelet* is followed by further *rondeaux* and *ballades* which continued to be printed with it; the *Généalogies* of 1545 contains *Dizains moraulx sur les Apophthegmes . . . des sept sages de Grece*, together with further *dizains* on the seven deadly sins, the Beatitudes, the concordance of the Law and Faith, the abuses of the world, etc. (ff.129 ro-142 ro).
17. See Ruth Mohl, *The Three Estates in Medieval and Renaissance Literature*, New York, 1933. In the *Ep. Mor.* Bouchet uses more elaborate classifications than the simple division into nobles, clergy and common people; the tripartite pattern is completely abandoned. But his approach reveals the traits discerned by Mohl as typical of this literature (see especially pp.6-7, where she lists four characteristic topics: enumeration of the estates; lamentation over their shortcomings; philosophical reflections on the divine ordination of each estate and its importance to the state; remedies for the defections of the estates).
18. *Masque*, p.121.
19. *Ecole des rhétoriqueurs*, p.69.
20. *Temple*, liminary [f.4] vo.

21. *Ep. Fam.* 73, f.xlix ro, col.2.
22. *Ep. Fam.* 40 and 41, written probably in the late 1520s. Emery was an *avocat* who provided a liminary epistle for the *Opuscules* of 1525. His *épître* advises Bouchet in a general way never to speak ill of other people. It does sound as if Emery thought Bouchet had slandered him behind his back, but the two *épîtres* may just as well be a literary fiction allowing both writers to discuss this moral question. They occur in a cluster of *Ep. Fam.* which all refer in some way to the *Opuscules* or discuss satire: 36, 38, 39, 40, 41, 42.
23. *Renards*, a4 vo. col.1.
24. The earlier satirist Lucilius had named particular victims, but Horace's criticisms are much more generalised; see E. Fraenkel, *Horace*, Oxford, 1957, reprint 1980, especially p.80. Juvenal notes the dangers of naming names as Lucilius had done (*Satire* 1, 153-7).
25. *Annales*, f.205 ro. Bouchet denies that his work could have had any such effect.
26. *Ep. Fam.* 73, f.xlix ro, col.1. He is referring to Louis d'Estissac.
27. *Ibid.*, col.2.
28. 2 *Ep. Mor.* 1. See *infra*.
29. *The Anti-Courtier Trend in Sixteenth-Century French Literature*, Geneva, 1966, p.97.
30. a4 vo, col.1.
31. Ms, f.2 ro.
32. Title page vo.
33. See M. A. Screech, *The Rabelaisian Marriage*, London, 1958, for a discussion of the problem in the context of the *querelle des femmes*, and particularly pp.9-10 on Bouchet.
34. See N. E. Nelson, 'Cicero's "De Officiis" in Christian Thought 300-1300', University of Michigan Publications, *Language and Literature*, 10, 1933, pp.59-160.
35. In the *Chapelet* he refers to *De formula honestae vitae*, a work actually by St Martin of Braga; see *infra*, n.115.
36. Because of his supposed correspondence with St Paul, the authenticity of which was only just beginning to be questioned.
37. Examples in the *Déploration*, the *Chapelet*, the *Labyrinthe*. The work is a handbook of illustrative examples for rhetoricians.
38. The satirists feature in the second part in those passages in which Bouchet criticises people who fail to cultivate the theological virtues.
39. There are references to Juvenal in the *Labyrinthe* and the *Ep. Mor.*, and to Horace (particularly the *Ars poetica*) in the *Labyrinthe* and the *Ep. Fam.*—although in the latter case the references take the form of sentences imitated without the author being named: there are hardly any marginal references in the *Ep. Fam.*
40. For an analysis of Bouchet's concept of satire as revealed in the *Epîtres* see D. J. Shaw, 'More about the "Dramatic *Satyre*"', *BHR*, 30, 1968, pp.301-25, particularly pp.310-13.
41. *Temple*, f.lxiiii vo. This description is earlier than that in 1 *Ep. Mor.* 13, which was the earliest by a French poet known to O. Trtnik-Rossettini, *Les Influences anciennes et italiennes sur la satire en France au XVIe siècle*, Florence, 1958, pp.43-4. There are brief

descriptions of satire in French translations of the *Stultifera navis,*
based on Locher's prologue; see for example the translation
attributed to P. Rivière, Paris, 1497, a2 vo, also *La grant nef des
folz,* Paris, 1499, a2 vo, col.2 (see *infra,* nn.44 and 53).

42. See, for example, Bartholomeus Fontius in a *Vita Persii*: he says
     that one type of satire was nearly the same as Old Comedy; first
     it praised good men but afterwards it criticised bad ones by
     name. As more and more licence was used, a law was passed to
     ban this type of poem. New comedy arose, which resembled the
     older type in criticising vices but not in naming names. Both
     Greeks and Latins cultivated the new satire; Lucilius was the
     first among the Latins to excel in it . . . (See the edition of the
     works of Juvenal and Persius published in Venice by Baptista de
     Tortis, 1482, BL IB.32443, e4 ro.)
     See also excerpts from commentators quoted by Shaw, 'Dram-
     atic *Satyre*': Merula mentions both Menippus and a Demetrius in
     his account of satire among the Greeks (p.304).

43. Shaw, 'Dramatic *Satyre*', pp.303-8.

44. *Stultifera navis,* tr. J. Locher, Basle, Olpe, 1497. See *Prologus,* ff.vii
     vo-viii ro.

45. 1 *Ep. Mor.* 13, f.32 vo, col.2.

46. *Ibid.*

47. Cf. Shaw, 'Dramatic *Satyre*', p.311, n.31.

48. 1 *Ep. Mor.* 13, f.32 vo, col.2.

49. *Ibid.*

50. See *supra,* chapter 1, n.34.

51. *Ep. Fam.* 42, f.xxxiiii vo, col.1. Cf. Shaw, 'Dramatic *Satyre*', pp.
     312-13.

52. Smith, *Anti-Courtier Trend*; Screech, *Rabelaisian Marriage.*

53. The translation into Latin by J. Locher had several editions in
     1497. The French verse translation believed to be by P. Rivière
     was printed in Paris in 1497 (BL IB.40534). Prose versions were
     printed in Lyons (G. Balsarin, 1498, BN Rés Yh.2) and Paris (G.
     de Marnef, 1499 (o.s.) BL IB.40230).

54. E. Picot and A. Piaget, 'Une supercherie d'Antoine Vérard, "Les
     Regnars traversans" de Jehan Bouchet', *Romania,* 22, 1893, pp.
     244-60; J. Macfarlane, *Antoine Vérard,* London, 1900, pp.xxvii-
     xxviii, also nos 149 and 182 (wrongly dated).

55. See Picot, *art. cit.,* pp.246-50.

56. *Angoisses,* [A2] ro-vo, and the *ép.* to printers, 2 *Ep. Mor.* 11, f.47
     vo. He also gives some account in the preface to the revised M s
     version (*infra,* n.95); see the bibliography.

57. Picot, *art. cit.,* p.253.

58. *Gén. Ep.* 49. On the translation believed to be by Pierre Rivière,
     see E. Du Bruck, 'Sebastian Brant in France: A "Ship of Fools" by
     Pierre Rivière (1497)', *Revue de littérature comparée,* 48, 1974, pp.
     248-56.

59. For a reproduction of the German broadsheet see *Flugblätter des
     Sebastian Brant,* ed. P. Heitz, Strasburg, 1915, no.18. In a post-
     script, p.xiii, F. Schultz suggests that there was a Latin broad-
     sheet version. The *Alopekiomachia* is dedicated to Maximilian and
     appears in the *Varia Carmina,* Basle, Olpe, 1498, h1 vo-h3 vo. It
     was mentioned as being Bouchet's source by C. Schmidt, *Histoire*

littéraire de l'Alsace à la fin du XVe et au commencement du XVIe siècle,
2 vols, Paris, 1879, vol.1, p.261-2 (note); see also Picot, *art. cit.*
p.244.

60. *Renards*, a1 vo; cf. *Varia Carmina*, h2 ro. lines 5-16, 19-30. The first
four lines quoted by Bouchet appear later in the poem, h2 vo.

61. Chapter 3, a4 vo.

62. Chapters 4, 8, 9 and 13.

63. Chapters 6 and 12.

64. Chapters 5, 7, 10 and 11.

65. For example:

> Est que distribuit caudas sine fine nocentes
> Spargit, et in partes dividit omnigenas
> Has agitant bine quas foedera ficta ligarunt
> At nihil efficient: preda cupita fugit. (h2 vo)

Bouchet interprets this figure as suggesting the murmurs and
blasphemy of the people, thus picking out only the notions of
harm and division.

66. a4 vo, col.1.

67. For example, Jeremiah 2 v.19, 6 v.28, 12 v.9, 22 v.13; Ezekiel 22
v.26, 34 v.2; Zephaniah 3 v.3, 3 v.8; Isaiah 50 v.11; Lamentations
1 v.12 and the very appropriate 5 v.18 (Disperiit mons Syon;
vulpes ambulaverunt in eo). There are 19 texts in all.

68. Among his other crimes Vérard had falsified the title of this
work; it should have been called *Les Renars du monde* and the
acteur should figure as the *traverseur des voyes perilleuses* suggested
by this verse (a4 vo, col.1). Bouchet thereafter adopted 'le Traverseur des voyes perilleuses' or simply 'Le Traverseur' as a pen-
name.

69. a4 ro, col.2.

70. a6 vo, col.1.

71. b3 ro, col.1.

72. a4 vo, col.1.

73. *Anti-Courtier Trend*, pp.65-7.

74. *Le Livre de l'Espérance*, ed. François Rouy, (thèse), Brest, 1967.
There were at least two incunabula editions of Chartier's *Fais*;
see ed. Rouy, pp.XLVI-XLIX.

75. See *infra*, chapter 5.

76. For a study of Chartier's style in this treatise, see F. Rouy,
L'Esthétique du traité moral d'après les œuvres d'Alain Chartier, Geneva, 1980, particularly pp.166-248.

77. d3 ro, cols 1-2. Reference to Daniel 9 v.27.

78. *Le Livre de l'Espérance*, ed. Rouy, Prose VIII, lines 211-17.

79. Prose VIII, lines 312-16.

80. Prose XVI, lines 194-7.

81. a3 vo, col.1.

82. On contemporary prophetic writing see Marjorie Reeves, *The
Influence of Prophecy in the Later Middle Ages*, Oxford, 1969.

83. See my article, 'Jean Lemaire de Belges and Prophecy', *Journal of
the Warburg and Courtauld Institutes*, 42, 1979, pp.144-66, especially pp.165-6.

84. On the compulsory celibacy of the clergy, d5 vo-d6 ro; *Le Livre de
l'Espérance*, ed. Rouy, Prose XVI, lines 135-60. See *infra*, chapter 5.

85. a4 ro, col.1.

86. b1 vo, col.2.
87. e4 ro, col.1.
88. e6 ro.
89. For details of these editions and the M S, see the bibliography.
90. See the bibliography, and Richter, 'Von den losen Füchsen dieser
     Welt, nur eine Übersetzung aus dem Französischen des Jean
     Bouchet', *Zeitschrift für neufranzösische Sprache und Litteratur*, 9,
     1887, pp.326-33.
91. *Von den losen Füchsen dieser Welt*, Frankfurt, 1546; see title and
     glosses at v2'ro and vo.
92. *Von den losen Füchsen* . . . 1585, B2 ro: 'Doch mus derselbe
     Schribent gewiss ein frommer, Gottsfürchtiger, gelerther und
     belesener Mann, auch der Welt Hendel kündig und erfahren
     gewest sein'.
93. A. Lefranc, 'Un prétendu V^e livre de Rabelais', *Revue des études
     rabelaisiennes*, 1, 1903, pp.29-54, 122-42; M. de Grève, *Interpréta-
     tion de Rabelais* p.82-3. The writer chooses particularly material on
     abuses in the Church.
94. We can compare this with the treatment of Lemaire's *Traicté des
     schismes*, translated into English in 1539 and into Latin by German
     Protestants in 1566.
95. Bibliothèque municipale de Poitiers, M S 440. I am most grateful
     to the Librarian for supplying me with a microfilm of this manu-
     script. It was owned by the archivist Alfred Richard, who de-
     scribes it in *Notes*, pp.15-20. He suggests that the date 'mil v^cxxx
     et ung', which is crossed out in the colophon, is the date when
     the copyist completed the manuscript (p.16). He gives it as his
     opinion that the hand of the copy is not that of Bouchet, but that
     the corrections are (pp.18-19).
96. In the last chapter, 'Des pugnicions de Dieu et des adversitez des
     bons', the red crosses at Liège are said to have appeared 'puis dix
     ans' [z8 vo], which would suggest that he was writing in about
     1511. However the corrections in the verse suggest revisions in
     1515 or later, and the pestilence 'qui a de present cours' in the
     printed text also occurs 'puis dix ans' in the M S [aa1 ro]. Some of
     the prodigies are removed from this chapter (e.g. the heretic
     priest). 'Françoys' sometimes becomes the more general 'pech-
     eurs', e.g. [z8 vo].
97. A poem beginning 'Gens endormis en pechez tant infaitz', f3 ro,
     which appears in a M S made for François Ier and is the work of a
     poet calling himself 'Le Douloureux'; [*La Complainte douloureuse
     de l'ame damnée*] and a [*Petit dialogue entre Dieu et le Diable*], m1 ro,
     m5 vo, which are both found in fifteenth-century collections;
     [Ung enseignement moult piteux], m6 vo, a long work originally
     composed in 1366 by Jehan de Remin. See Picot, *art. cit.*
98. Some of the *ballades* are reproduced in the collection that follows
     the *Chapelet*.
99. f5 vo, col.1.
100. Understood oddly as foundry work; it seems to follow on from
     the preceding section.
101. The whole section, together with the section on music, is repro-
     duced by K. Chesney in *Fleurs de rhétorique*, Oxford, 1950, pp.58-
     63.

102. The work by Jehan de Remin: see *supra*, n.97.

103. *Les Abuz du monde*, Paris, P. Le Dru, 1509, BL 11474.a.24; *Les Folles Entreprises*, Paris, P. Le Dru, 1505, BN Rés. Ye.1321, published in *Œuvres complètes*, vol.1, pp.11-144, with the marginal annotation moved to footnotes. Gringore gives just the name of an author and a sentence in Latin, without reference to the work from which it comes.

104. A3 vo; Lamentations 1 v.1.

105. A6 ro; Psalm 7 v.11. The text from Daniel 9 appears again, C2 ro, as the Church threatens the Pope with some terrible persecution that will be caused by the abuses.

106. B3 ro and C1 vo; C3 ro, A5 ro.

107. Five from Cicero, one from Horace, one from Aristotle, three from Valerius Maximus.

108. A4 vo. Decreti secunda pars, c.1 q.1 cap.xxviii *Fertur*.

109. B4 ro. Dec. Greg. Lib III tit. IV is entitled *De clericis non residentibus in ecclesia vel praebenda*. He singles out cap.3, *quia nonnulli*, and from tit.v (*De praebendis et dignitatibus*) cap.5, *quia in tantum*.

110. B2 ro-vo. The passage from the Pragmatic Sanction which he quotes is from *De collationibus*, § *Dum autem*. See *infra*, chapter 5, n.22.

111. In the theological passages of the *Labyrinthe* there are references to heresy available only in the marginal notes; in the *Epîtres morales* a reference he gives suggests that the Pope may be deposed, but this is not implied in the French text. See *infra*, chapter 5, n.89, and chapter 6.

112. B8 ro-C1 vo.

113. *Faictz et dictz*, ed. Dupire, vol. 1, pp.100-26.

114. f.xxxiiii vo. In later editions these are relegated to smaller print in the margins, but in the first they have equal prominence with the title and the *rondeau*.

115. This short treatise, also called *De quattuor virtutibus*, was composed by St Martin of Braga in the sixth century; it imitates Seneca's manner and was believed to be by him. It treats the four cardinal virtues and then maintains that they should be exercised with moderation. There were many editions of the work available, both by itself and with other works by Seneca. If Bouchet had used the very recent edition of Seneca's works issued by Erasmus in Basle, 1515 (BL 524.i.7), he would have seen that Erasmus briefly questions the authenticity of the tract on the grounds of its style (title page vo). In the same way Erasmus questions the authenticity of the correspondence between Seneca and St Paul. This would in no way have deterred Bouchet from using the tract: cf. chapter 4 at n.106. Rabelais includes the text among those read to Gargantua by Jobelin Bridé (*Gargantua* ch.13/14).

116. f.xlviii vo. Sentence taken from the section on Prudence in *De formula honestae vitae*. Text in *PL* 72, cols 21-8; see col.24.

117. f.xlvii vo; Proverbs 24 v.17-18. The reading 'providence' in line 3 is taken from the *Opuscules*: in the *Chapelet* it reads 'prudence', which does not scan and is no doubt a misprint.

118. For example *Rondeau* 7, f.xxxvii ro, Le prince doibt craindre Dieu, is accompanied by Daniel 4 v.22: 'Septem tempora mutabuntur

super te, donec scias quod dominetur excelsus in regno homi-
num et cuicunque voluerit, det illud.' This is more impressive if
recognised as Daniel's interpretation of the prophetic dream of
divine punishment about to overtake King Nebuchadnezzar,
who is to dwell with beasts of the field for seven years.

119.   Edited by G. Trisolini in *Le Lexique de Jehan Marot dans 'Le Doctrinal
des Princesses et nobles Dames'*, Ravenna, 1978, pp.87-101. The
cycle consists of 24 *rondeaux*, each with a brief title: e.g. D'estre
bon exemple aux autres; De bien faire durant la vie. Marot uses
the *rondeau double*. Unfortunately the *Doctrinal* cannot be dated
exactly, so it is impossible to know who was influencing whom
(see *Lexique*, pp.7-17). If the dates allowed it, I would expect that
Bouchet took the idea of his *rondeau* cycle from Marot.

120.   f.xliiii ro. Sentence from Cicero, *De Officiis*, 3, 5(22).

121.   f.xxviii ro. The *Instruction* is the work of Ghillebert de Lannoy,
d.1462.

122.   Jean Marot's *Doctrinal* has only 24.

123.   I have used the edition of 1526. Trojan's letter appears [f.1]
vo-[f.2] ro. See appendix A for Trojan.

124.   [f.2] vo-[f.4] ro. See *supra*, n.22, on Emery.

125.   Cf. *supra*, n.115.

126.   There are marginal references in 1,12 (*Seneca epistola 48*); 2,1
(*Seneca epistola 37* and *Seneca 8*: i.e. *Thyestes*, 213); 2,3 (*Seneca in
for. fut.?*).

127.   Quintilian, *Institutio Oratoria*, x, 1, 125-31.

128.   For example, in his *ép.* to masters of servants (1,12) he makes one
reference to Seneca's epistle on slaves, 47 (*sic*): he translates the
precept 'Sic cum inferiore vivas, quemadmodum tecum superi-
orem velis vivere'. But he makes no effort to adapt any other
themes from the epistle.

129.   The *Argument des Epistres familieres*, title page vo, points out that
the collection contains letters by people 'Au Grec, Latin plusque
au françois dispos', thus underlining his connections with humanist writers.

130.   *Opuscules*, 1526, [f.2] vo, [f.3] ro; see *infra* at n.148.

131.   St Bernard's *Epistola ad dominum Papam Eugenium*, known as *De
Consideratione* (*PL* 182, cols 727-808) was famous as a solemn
reminder to Popes of their grave duties. Bouchet borrows a
passage from Book 2, asking the Pope to consider what he is and
offering a series of impressive titles reminding him of his duties.

132.   See Smith, *Anti-Courtier Trend*, pp.74-5. The text is Aeneas Sylvius Piccolomini, *De Curialium Miseriis Epistola*; see *ibid.*, pp.20,
22-4.

133.   1 *Ep. Mor.* 1, f.3 ro, col.1; 2 *Ep. Mor.* 5, f.24 ro, col.1.

134.   This caused a jocular exchange of letters between Bouchet and
the *Huissiers* and *Sergents royaulx* of Paris, who were not pleased
at finding themselves grouped with hangmen (*Ep. Fam.* 38 and
39).

135.   See *infra*, chapter 5, n.89.

136.   2 *Ep. Mor.* 5, f.27 ro, cols 1-2. Accompanied by a marginal note:
1. properandum. c. de iudi. 3. q. i. c. decernimus (i.e. *Codex*,
lib.3, 1, *De iudiciis*, 13, Properandum nobis visum est . . .).

137.   *Renards*, e3 vo, cols 1-2.

138. f.7 vo, col.2.
139. *Ibid*.
140. 1 *Ep. Mor*. 11, f.30 ro, col.1.
141. 1 *Ep. Mor*. 7, f.23 ro, col.1.
142. f.23 ro, col.2. See *infra*, chapter 7, n.61. Cf. the account of theologians' treatment of sex and the married penitent given by Thomas N. Tentler, *Sin and Confession on the Eve of the Reformation*, Princeton, 1977, pp.162-232. Both in this *ép*. and in the *Triomphes* Bouchet appears liberal.
143. 2 *Ep. Mor*. 2, f.8 vo, col.1.
144. *Anti-Courtier Trend*, pp.74-5, 91-2.
145. f.11 vo, col.2.
146. In the first section of the *épître*, f.1 ro, col.1, and also in 2 *Ep. Mor*. 3, f.17 ro, col.1, when he says that the King asked him to write it a year before he died (*c*.1513-14). He never claims actually to have presented the work to the King.
147. Cf. *infra*, chapter 4, section 4.
148. [f.2] vo.

Bouchet as a Historian

1
The Historical Writings: Aims, Methods and Sources

It was arguably as a historian that Bouchet made his greatest reputation. His historical studies date from the very beginning of his career, when he was asked by Charles VIII to write a life of St Radegonde, Queen of France. It seems to have been towards the end of the reign of Louis XII that he conceived the great plan that was to result in a history of the kings of France and of his own province, Aquitaine.

History was an integral part of the *rhétoriqueur* tradition, for many *rhétoriqueur* poets (for example, Chastellain, Molinet, d'Auton, Lemaire) were employed by their patrons as official chroniclers; this was no doubt a factor in raising the status of history written in French. The early sixteenth century was a period when many influences were at work on all types of historical writing. On the one hand humanists were attempting to write histories of France that were not only more accurate but also more elegant, that is to say, in good classical Latin. Robert Gaguin published his *De origine et gestis Francorum perquam utile compendium* in 1497, and Paolo Emilio was commissioned by Charles VIII to compose a new history of France in a style comparable to that of classical historians.[1] On the other hand printing gave a massive impetus to trends already discernible in late medieval France: the use of history for the glorification of the French monarchy and its use for specific propaganda purposes. Champier and Seyssel wrote on the genealogies of the French kings and in praise of monarchy; Lemaire's *Illustrations* provided the French monarchy with still more illustrious forebears.[2] All these writers also used historical material to support the policies of Louis XII, for example during his war with Venice.[3] Bouchet himself was using history in this way in order to attack the English in his *Epître d'Henri*.

Bouchet published all his four main historical works in the decade 1518–28:

1) *L'Histoire et cronicque de Clotaire, premier de ce nom . . . et de sa*

tresillustre espouse madame saincte Radegonde, 1517 (o.s.). This is a
prose history of the reign of the sixth-century king Clotaire, used as
a framework for the life of his wife, St Radegonde, one of Poitiers'
most notable saints. The book is therefore a combination of chronicle and saint's life, embellished with moral reflections and elegant
speeches. It is divided into four books, following the stages of St
Radegonde's life as a girl, a wife, a nun, and finally her death and
the miracles which followed. But throughout the book biography is
interwoven with a detailed account of the activities of the Frankish
kings. Bouchet tells us that Charles v i i i had directed him to translate the legend of St Radegonde, but that in the light of his later
reading he was thoroughly dissatisfied with his youthful work and
rewrote it.[4] The result is a most unusual blending of hagiography
with history, all the more appropriate in that its main subject was,
albeit briefly, Queen of France.

2) *Les Annales d'Aquitaine, faictz et gestes en sommaire des Roys de
France, d'Angleterre et des pays de Naples et de Milan,* first published in
1524. This is Bouchet's major historical work, a prose chronicle of
his province and its rulers from its origins. As Aquitaine's ruler was
for the greater part of its history the king of France, the work is to a
large extent a national chronicle. Since the English kings also held
parts of Aquitaine for long periods, they too are included. It is
divided into four books, the first dealing with the origins of Aquitaine and Poitiers up to the end of the Roman occupation; the
second from the rule of the Visigoths up to the reign of Charles the
Bald when Aquitaine became a duchy; the third from Charles the
Bald to Louis v i i i; the fourth from Louis i x, under whom the duchy
of Aquitaine was divided up, until about 1520. This last part is, even
in the first edition, longer than all the rest put together, and it grew
still longer as Bouchet brought his chronicle up to date in a series of
new editions up to 1557.[5]

3) *Les Anciennes et modernes genealogies des roys de France et mesmement
du roy Pharamond avec leurs Epitaphes et Effigies.* By 1518 Bouchet had
already almost completed a historical work entitled *Les Annales et
epitaphes des roys de France,* but wishing to say more about his native
region he divided his material between two works, the *Annales
d'Aquitaine,* which concern his province, and these *Généalogies,* printed a few years later in 1528, which glorify his nation.[6] Beginning
with a prose account of the Frankish kings before Pharamond,
Bouchet thereafter devotes to each king a woodcut portrait, a prose
synopsis of the reign, and a verse epitaph in which each king
reviews his deeds. Factual as the account of each king's reign is, and
unembellished as is the verse of the epitaphs, this work clearly
combines the chronicle mode with the glorification of the French
monarchy. The specially-made portraits of every French king from
Pharamond no doubt clinched the success of this book, which

enjoyed considerable popularity for some ten years after its first appearance.

4) *Le Panegyric du Chevallier sans reproche*, 1527. This work on the other hand had only one sixteenth-century edition. It is the life of Bouchet's patron Louis de La Trémoille, who had been killed at Pavia. The prose account is decorated with intermittent verse and with fictions, the appearance of Venus, Mars and Minerva to the young Louis. It also includes a long moral development on government. Only in this one instance does Bouchet adopt this more decorated type of history, analogous with Lemaire's practice in the *Illustrations*. For he is functioning here like a courtier-*rhétoriqueur* and glorifying his patron.

As far as the genre of these works is concerned, the first point to be made is that they are entitled with a precision that clearly indicates the genre and the style that the reader should expect. The distinction between *annales* and *historia* had been well established since classical times. *Annales* record the events of each year; their merits, according to Cicero, are merely clarity and brevity. *Historia* on the other hand is a truly literary genre requiring elegant diction, eloquence, the ability to weigh events and to explain their causes and results.[7] Thus, in calling his history of Aquitaine *Annales*, Bouchet was disclaiming a high rhetorical mode,[8] and indeed his work is for the most part a chronicle, recording events in chronological order and, as will be seen from quotations later in this chapter, in a very plain style. Bouchet apologises for writing so plainly and in the vernacular:

> Vous suppliant . . . excuser et supporter l'imperfection du langage vulgaire, à l'ornement et acoustrement duquel je n'ay prins peine ne labeur, mais seulement à la verité de l'histoire.[9]

Nevertheless, his aims in the *Annales* are not quite so humble as the title suggests, as his reference here to 'la vérité de l'histoire' shows. Similarly he will complain in 1545 that Parisian printers have made additions to the *Annales* comprising 'choses triviales, non sentans l'histoire'.[10] From the rhetorical point of view his work may not rank as *historia*, but the pains that he has taken to sort out truth from error require no apology; in this sense the value of his work is indeed that of *historia*. But the rhetorical distinction is also the one that appears to dictate the title *Histoire et chronique du roi Clotaire*, for the work is, as its title suggests, a mixed genre. We may perceive it as 'chronique' inasmuch as it recounts the events of the Frankish kingdom, but 'histoire' as it draws a laudatory portrait of St Radegonde; it is accordingly written in a variety of prose styles, sometimes the plain style of the *Annales*, but in places heavily ornamented with rhetorical figures, and unlike the *Annales* it is decorated with invented speeches. The *panegyricus* is a high rhetorical genre, a eulogy that had its literary origins in the *laudatio funebris*. It was also considered extremely instructive.[11] Bouchet reserves this title for the biography of his late patron, highly decorated both with mythological fictions and with invented speeches, highly edifying to Louis's great-grand-children, to servants of the monarchy, even to the King himself, all of whom should seek to imitate the military, governmental and personal virtues of the 'Chevalier sans reproche'.[12]

Finally the title of the *Anciennes et modernes genealogies, effigies et epitaphes des roys de France* spells out the exact contents of the book: the essay on kings before Pharamond, followed by a numbered entry for each of the subsequent kings comprising a brief genealogy and chronicle, a portrait and a verse epitaph. This particular blend of contents brings together a variety of different ways of glorifying the monarchy. The style of both prose and verse is plain; it is the combination of elements that achieves the encomiastic effect. Although more transitory, the success of this book was for a time greater even than that of the *Annales*. The portraits were no doubt partly responsible for this success. One shameless plagiarist, Bar-thélemy de Chasseneuz, who without any acknowledgement ac-companied his own brief Latin verses with Bouchet's verse epitaphs and copies of the woodcuts, claimed that the woodcuts were copied from statues in the Palais Royal in Paris.[13] True or not, this claim suggests a frame of reference. The series of statues of the kings of France from Pharamond stood in the Grand' Salle of the Palais de Justice until destroyed by fire in 1618. Begun in the early fourteenth century, they are an example of the growth of late medieval nationalism centering on the figure of the king.[14] Bouchet would have seen them, for Basoche plays were performed on the great marble table in the Grand' Salle. It seems impossible to discover whether there is any basis in Chasseneuz's claim that Bouchet's artist had based the effigies on these statues; even if Bouchet got the initial idea for his book from seeing this line of kings in stone, he did not give the same list of kings as the one used in the Palais but worked out his own.[15] However, Bouchet is taking the idea of the visual representation of the king's predecessors—an element that was of increasing importance in royal entries from the second half of the fifteenth century[16]—and incorporating it into the historical genre of genealogy and chronicle. He actually refers to his work as an 'art de memoire', suggesting the mnemonic value of numerically ordered images.[17] His book must surely have been an influential factor in the subsequent popularity both of the enumeration of French kings and of their portraiture. Just as by 1550 all 57 of Henri II's predecessors are represented in his entry into Rouen,[18] so later in the century printed collections of royal portraits abound, some series being actually copied from the effigies in Bouchet's book.[19] He had helped to create a new way of glorifying the monarchy by means of the printed book.

Traditionally the aims of history had been defined as edification and the true record of events. In the course of the sixteenth century, in spite of all the conflicting aims of edification, elegance, glorification and propaganda, very substantial progress was to be made in sorting out myth from history, falsehood from truth. In part this came about because expertise from other areas, notably philology and law, was brought to bear upon historical problems.[20] But even in the early sixteenth century, when formal histories were still largely concerned with simply chronicling dates and events, it came to seem increasingly important that of those dates and events it should be a true chronicle.[21]

Such was certainly Bouchet's view. His stated aims in his histories always stress the search for truth. As we have seen, inasmuch as he asserts that the *Annales* are valuable, he does so on the grounds that he has sought for truth rather than for elegance of style. Before examining how he tried to achieve this we should consider his other possible aims. A claim that he frequently makes is the traditional one that his work is edifying. He repeatedly asserts that by contemplating virtuous deeds performed in the past men acquire both a desire to emulate them and vicarious experience by means of which they can conduct their own affairs prudently:

> Narration et estude de hystoires et exemples est une chose qui excite les hommes et femmes à honnestement vivre autant ou plus que les loix et statuz.[22]

In the *Panégyrique*:

> Le fruict de lire les histoires (par le tesmoignage de Flavius Albinus) est acquerir une desireuse emulacion d'honneur et ung vouloir de suyvir et ressembler en meurs et gestes ceulx desquelz on oyt bien dire . . . la congnoissance des choses gerées excite les humains courages à prudence, magnanimité, droicture, modestie et aultres vertuz tendans à souveraine felicité et esloigner du contraire.[23]

In the *Généalogies*:

> Par telle estude (i.e. les livres des historiographes hebrieux, grecz et latins) les jeunes auroient l'experience approchant de celle par laquelle les vieilz et anciens hommes sont prudens estimez, et seroient les entreprinses de guerres plus rares, et mieulx considerées, les batailles par plus grand vertu et moins cruellement conduictes, et plus facilement par paix dirimées.[24]

Sometimes it is appropriate to reinforce the moral lessons to be gained; in the *Histoire de Clotaire* he claims to have provided additional edification

> en decorant l'histoire pour la doctrine des dames d'aucunes moralles sentences, persuasions et remonstrances, et de plusieurs aultres petites choses curieuses.[25]

It is partly because history is so edifying that it finds its place to such a marked degree in Bouchet's moral and memorial works as well as the works we are considering here.

Hand in hand with edification goes the glorification of the subject. This is obvious in the *Panégyrique*, in the account of St Radegonde's life, in the enumeration of the kings of France. Where possible the subject is to be treated as an *exemplum*, to the edification of the reader and the greater glory of the subject. This too is true of history as it is found in moral and memorial works where he gives the history of an institution or offers historical parallels revealing virtues similar to those of his subject. In the *Annales d'Aquitaine* Bouchet tells us of his desire to do honour to his province and also to his native town, 'pour la decoration de la cité, eglise et université de Poictiers'; 'en escripvant la cronique d'Acquitaine j'ay une particuliere affection de parler des antiquitez de Poictiers où j'ay prins ma nativité'.[26]

Like other writers Bouchet had also turned to history for arguments in polemic. Clearly then one of his problems as a historian must have been that the desire to edify, to praise and to drum up support could come into conflict with the demands of truth. In examining his historical method we should look separately at his treatment of past and contemporary history, since they pose rather different problems, both in the finding of information and in the maintenance of impartiality.

As far as past history is concerned, the *Histoire de Clotaire*, the *Généalogies* and the earlier parts of the *Annales*, all in draft at least by 1518, must have resulted from the same period of intensive work finding and evaluating sources. Bouchet stresses the pains he has taken to read authorities, find old documents and sort out chronological difficulties. Of the *Annales* he says:

> me suis . . . curieusement enquis par toutes les histoires, croniques, pancartes, lettres autentiques, epitaphes et autres tesmoignages dont j'ay peu finer.[27]

Of the life of St Radegonde as told in the *Histoire de Clotaire* he claims

> De laquelle je n'ay parlé par adulation mendatieuse, ne adjouxté quant au faict de l'histoire aucune chose non veritable ou supersticieuse, mais me suis entierement fondé sur ce qui a esté escript par sainct Gregoire, arcevesque de Tours, qui fut celuy qui feit ses obseques et funerailles, par sainct Fortune evesque de Poictiers qui fut grant amy et familier en Dieu de ladicte saincte, par Baudoyne sa servante, par les croniques Sigiberti, Annonnii Monachi, Vincentii Belvacensis, Landulphi de Columpna, Roberti Gaguini et autres historiens qui ont escript de ladicte saincte, l'ung d'une chose et l'autre d'une autre.[28]

From these two statements emerge two features of his method. First of all his search in local houses, churches and monasteries for old documents. We shall see that he frequently cites such sources in the *Histoire de Clotaire* and in the *Annales*, usually saying where he found the document in question; he also mentions having visited the library of Saint-Denis.[29] Secondly can be seen his firm grasp of the principle that a contemporary record is likely to be the most valuable, and a record written fairly close to the event likely to be more reliable than one written much later—this latter point seems implicit in the fact that he lists his sources in chronological order. This principle does not by any means always preserve him from error, as for instance on one of the many occasions when he re-proves Gaguin, for presuming to disagree with a supposedly con-temporary writer.[30] But in itself it is a valuable principle, and one all the more necessary when the material available had become so much more plentiful because of the beginnings of printing. The nature of the chronicler's task was altered by the large number of historical works that appeared in the early years of printing; it was now much easier for writers to compare sources and so gradually to evolve a more critical method when trying to resolve discrepancies. Bouchet refers to, and had clearly in most cases actually consulted, a large number of printed chronicles and other texts. He may have been led to some of them by Lemaire, who gives a list of his authorities in each of the three books of the *Illustrations*. These texts, together with local manuscript material, provided him with plenty of problems and discrepancies to solve in his search for truth.

His dominant principle is that, wherever possible, sources should be reconciled. The passage from the *Histoire de Clotaire* just quoted continues:

> que j'ay accumulées et accordées avecques les temps et dates au mieulx qu'il m'a esté possible, et non sans grant labeur.[31]

There are numerous examples in his works of his efforts to render conflicting accounts compatible. In the *Généalogies*, after mentioning various views on the origin of the name Frank, he concludes:

> Toutesfoys je m'esvertueray, Dieu aydant, de monstrer en la deduction de ce petit œuvre, sans aultre epilogation, que es oppinions cy dessus recitées n'y a si grand contrarieté qu'on pourroit de prime face juger, et qu'icelles bien entendues peu-vent estre vrayes.[32]

In the *Annales*, discussing the baptism of the Emperor Constantine, he says that the usual explanation, that Constantine decided to be baptised after his victory against Maxentius, is not necessarily in conflict with the story in the legend of St Silvester that it was because the Pope had cured him of leprosy—'il peult estre que ce fut pour ces deux causes',[33] But he rejects as an error introduced by copyists the statement in St Jerome's *Chronicon* that Constantine was baptised at the end of his reign by an Arian bishop called Eusebius.[34] In general however he harmonises his sources wherever possible, and this principle, combined with his search for original documents, can, as we shall see, lead him into dramatic error.

Difficulties arising over dates are particularly stressed by Bouchet in the sentence just quoted. This betrays a view of history primarily concerned with cataloguing events year by year—the work precisely of the annalist—and of getting them in the right year. The same preoccupation not surprisingly is revealed in the introductory poem of the *Annales*:

> Où j'ay prins peine en diverses années
> Et plusieurs nuicts du dormir condamnées
> Pour calculer les faultes et erreurs
> Des ans et jours, venans des imprimeurs
> Comme je croy, et souvent par la faulte
> Des orateurs, lesquels en chose haulte
> Et style beau mettent plus leurs esprits
> Qu'en verité, dont souvent sont repris.[35]

Although printers as so often are made the scapegoats for error here, Bouchet is also raising the question of the possible conflict between decoration and truth in *historia*. This is a commonplace even among more rhetorical writers; Cicero insists that the historian's main preoccupation must be truth, and a rhetorician who lets his style deform his matter is clearly blameworthy.[36] But we have already seen that Bouchet consistently adopts the plainest of styles in chronicles, and even in the more laudatory genre he claims not to have sacrificed truthfulness. Hence his insistence that he has added nothing 'non veritable ou superstitieuse' to the history of Radegonde, nor spoken of her 'par adulation mendatieuse'. As we have seen, he admits to a certain amount of moral decoration by way of additional instruction. In practice this means that he permits himself, for example, to compose a speech on 'dying well' for Radegonde to deliver to her husband Clotaire as they lie in bed together. But he will not accept the fifteenth-century story that Radegonde, although married, remained a virgin.

Contemporary or nearly contemporary history presented him with different methodological problems. The result also needs to be assessed rather differently both from the point of view of its usefulness to his contemporaries and of its value now. On the history of eras before his own, his work has no interest as a primary source except inasmuch as he may testify to the existence of documents and monuments in Poitou.[37] On his own period however he remains indisputably valuable as a local historian, having been a witness of many events in Poitiers itself, and also as the biographer of Louis de La Trémoille—the *Panégyrique*, although decried by historians for its style and excessive kindness to its subject, has nevertheless been reprinted several times and provides information not otherwise available, some of it gleaned by Bouchet in conversa-

tions with La Trémoille.[38] But although some passages of the contemporary portions of the *Annales* do have first-hand information,
on the whole the account of the great events of his own times is
inevitably second-hand. Thus once again its main interest is how it
ranked as a source of information for Bouchet's original readers.
The importance of more modern history was marked from the first
edition of the *Annales*. The four parts of the work are of very unequal
length; the first three, which cover the period up to 1227, fill 72
leaves and the fourth, from 1227 to 1519, fills 78. This disproportion
increased with successive editions. The corrected edition of 1526
added little, but the chronicle was brought up to date in the editions
of 1532, 1535, 1545 and 1557. By 1557 Part Four contains 283 leaves,
against 95 for the first three parts, and more than 200 of these 283
relate to Bouchet's own lifetime. For all the period from at least the
invasions of Italy he is writing of events of which he had some
experience. Since the date when the duchy of Aquitaine had fallen
definitively to the French crown Bouchet's chronicle is predomin-
antly a national chronicle, while still including anything of special
interest to his region. This has not always been realised by scholars
writing on historiography who have been led by its title to believe
that it was of mainly local interest.

As a national chronicle it was one among several vernacular
chronicles that not only treated France's remoter past but also
brought events up to date in successive editions. Notable among
these are Nicole Gille's *Annales et Chronique,* which its author ended
with the death of Louis xi but which was brought up to date in a
whole series of editions throughout the century from 1525; Alain
Bouchard's *Grandes Chroniques de Bretagne,* first published in 1514,
and covering the period up to the death of François ii of Brittany in
1488: continuations appeared in editions of 1518, 1531, 1532 and
1541; finally *La Mer des croniques,* a title that from 1518 was applied
to a chronicle comprising Desrey's translation of Gaguin's *Compendium,* complete with Desrey's continuation up to 1515, and anonymous continuations in successive editions between 1518 and 1536.
In none of these three cases is the original author responsible for the
continuations. Hauser concluded that there was little of value to be
got from these apparently independent accounts of contemporary
history because they were all copying each other.[39] For the reigns of
Charles viii and Louis xii he found the dominant text to be that of
Gaguin-Desrey. In Bouchet's case, however, this text is not simply
copied but abridged, and supplemented with additional information:

> En somme, l'annaliste poitevin est plus original, et surtout plus
> probe que la plupart de ses confrères. Il s'est inspiré de ses
> prédécesseurs; il ne les a pas plagiés. Par contre, il a été plagié.[40]

This is so true that one can say that there are only two accounts of these two reigns: Desrey's, as appearing in the *Mer des croniques* and copied in one version of the continuations to Bouchard, and Bouchet's, which, while it uses Desrey, is recognisably different, and is copied in the continuation to Gilles and in the other continuation to Bouchard. For history between 1519 and 1530 Bouchet is largely independent while the others seem to be related; his additions in 1531–35 are again copied by the 1541 continuation to Bouchard.[41] We also find one amateur historian copying out passages from Bouchet's *Annales*.[42]

These borrowings suggest that Bouchet's chronicle of recent history appeared useful to his contemporaries and certainly the extent of his coverage compares very well with the other accounts. The *Mer des croniques* is particularly scrappy: even in 1536 only 15 folios out of 256 are devoted to the reign of François 1er. The better continuation of Bouchard only gives 17 out of 262; Bouchet by contrast, uses 68 out of 265 for the reign up to 1532.

After 1515 he no longer had any continuous narrative source to follow, and it would seem that he kept a record from year to year collecting documents where possible. His main sources are as follows:

a) *Official publications.* He often gives part of the text of royal ordinances,[43] and he reproduces the text of treaties—e.g. the marriage treaty with Spain in 1516, the Treaty of Madrid (which he says he heard published in Poitiers on 14 February 1527), the treaty with England 1527, ('les articles dudit accord estoyent tels, si ce que j'en vy par escript contenoit verité'),[44] the *Paix des Dames*.[45]

b) *Plaquettes.* These news leaflets are sometimes semi-official publicity for some important event, sometimes an independent testimony.[46] Bouchet, like several other writers, uses a *plaquette* concerning the procession in Paris and the King's speech of January 1535 against the *Placard* heretics.[47] Other examples are his accounts of the Diets of Augsburg and Ratisbon, which depend heavily on *plaquettes*.[48] In fact whenever Bouchet suddenly goes into great detail on some subject he is usually reproducing an official publication or some other *plaquette*, usually with a certain amount of omission or précis.

c) *Information received privately.* This is more difficult to detect. The terms of his reference to the Anglo-French treaty of 1527 make it possible that he has a private source. He sometimes mentions a correspondent, and there is complementary evidence from the *Epîtres Familières* of people sending him information. Germain Colin Bucher sent him news about the Knights of St John of Jerusalem; the Seigneur de Mihervé sent him some details about fighting the Emperor's troops in Northern France. Up to 1525 at least the La Trémoille connection was an important source of information.[49]

d) *Other published histories.* The additions of 1531 and 1535 do not seem to exploit any source of this type, but in the 1557 edition he draws to a certain extent on Guillaume Paradin's *Histoire de Nostre Temps*.[50] There may be more borrowings of this sort that I have not found.

Bouchet appears then to have been a conscientious gatherer of information, although for the most part not to have had access to sources that would enable him to give any view of events behind their obvious façade. He nevertheless gave one of the best accounts of the current reign available to contemporaries, and he has often been read since without being recognised, via his plagiarists.[51]

Bouchet's historical writing can be seen as one of his major contributions to popularising knowledge. He was offering to his contemporaries an account in French of past and recent history, which in some respects, notably hagiography and modern history, was very superior to similar works in French. Its strength rests not in popularising intentions but in scholarly ones. Although not always successfully, Bouchet was trying hard to solve historical problems. This was recognised by some scholarly contemporaries, who suggest that what he was writing was a type of history more often to be found in Latin. His friend Quintin praises him for writing in French. He says that the French should praise their own race as they properly deserve and they should do so in French: 'sua—id est optima—lingua'. Lemaire was a shining example, and now Bouchet is much to be praised for his patient researches. He has made many things plain—for instance the dispute between the French and the English over Aquitaine, '(dissidium) nulli antea satis cognitum, nunc tam in plano positum est, ut vel trimus infans diiudicet'.[52] Robert Ceneau, however, regrets his choice of language:

> Cui nimirum Bocheto si suam de re Gallica enarrationem accuratissime contextam, et magna fide fultam, adhibitis in suam rem certissimis ad faciendam fidem indiciis ac testimoniis, venusto quodam latinae elocutionis ornatu vestire et expolire contingisset, adiecta insuper Galliae topographia: vix aptius quicquam atque absolutius gens ipsa Gallica in suo aere (quod ad rem de qua agitur pertinet) consequi potuisset.[53]

Nevertheless he praises Bouchet handsomely:

> Bochetus (vir certe in eorum statuendus numero, qui cum lectione multa, clarissimi etiam argutiam iudicii coniunxerunt) author est, a primaeva nominis Gallici memoria, Aquitaniam regii honoris diademate expolitam fuisse, et magnifice decoratam.[54]

Quintin was ultimately to be proved right; the explosion of historical writing in the later part of the century made the vernacular more than respectable. Kelley says of these historians, so often, like Bouchet himself, lawyers, that they were engaged in 'a new voca-

tion best described as public enlightenment'.[55] Although his actual
achievement was to be judged more harshly as time went by and
standards of historical scholarship were raised,[56] Bouchet anticipates some of the aims of these later writers, just as he was to
anticipate the aims of the Counter-Reformation in providing religious instruction in French. For both past and contemporary history
Bouchet read widely and worked diligently, applying certain sound
and excellent principles to problems. His credulity, combined with
lack of adequate data, very often produced the wrong answer, but
not always.

In order to demonstrate the strengths and weaknesses of his
achievement it is necessary to select specific topics, and I propose to
examine his treatment of three areas that present particularly tricky
problems. First his treatment of the early history of France, in which
the search for truth comes up against patriotic myth. Secondly,
hagiographical material, which provides a large proportion of his
source material in the early period and which may bring truth into
conflict with piety. Finally his treatment of certain aspects of contemporary history, where truth may conflict with politics; here
relations between Church and State provide a particularly interesting topic, as patriotism and piety may pull in opposite directions.

2
Mythical History

In dealing with the very early history of his province and his country, Bouchet had plentiful examples of writers who offered him
fascinating material with which to fill the gaps left by classical
historians.[57] The legend of the Trojan origin of the Franks had been
current throughout the Middle Ages and had received a recent
revitalisation in Lemaire's *Illustrations de Gaule*. According to this
legend, the wandering Trojans had founded the city of Sicambria;
they became known as 'Franks' and had subsequently settled on the
banks of the Rhine.

To this medieval legendary history of France had been added
material from two brand-new forgeries. Annius of Viterbo had
provided invaluable information about affairs in Gaul before the
arrival of the Franks. In his *Antiquities* of 1498, he published supposed fragments of ancient authors including Berosus and Man-
etho, whose chronicles tell of the re-peopling of the world in the
aftermath of the Flood until the founding of Troy.[58] This provided a
history of the origins of the Celts, complete with the founding of the
order of Druids and of Bards. Thus the Gauls were provided with an
illustrious ancestry. Lemaire used this information extensively in
the *Illustrations*. He wrote too early to be able to use the second
forgery, as featured in the work of Tritheim, who in 1515 published

a chronicle supposedly based on a *History of the Franks* written by a Frankish historian, Hunibald. This covered the period from the fall of Troy to the death of Clovis, thus filling in a large gap in the Trojan legend.[59]

In the early part of the sixteenth century variations on the Trojan myth were used by several local historians to dignify the origins of their region or patron. Gradually, however, the myth was discredited. It is attacked by more and more writers in the second half of the century, and notably by Pasquier. But such rejection of the Trojan-Frankish myth was often accompanied by an acceptance of the Gallic ones drawn from the pseudo-Berosus.[60] Lemaire had drawn freely on the material derived from Annius, and he is an important source for later writers. Asher shows that from 1521 the *Cronica Cronicarum abregé* was rearranged to use the material, and Corrozet used it, drawing particularly on its etymologies for the names of towns. Many provincial historians follow suit. There is also, however, at the same time, a steady current of doubt about the veracity of Berosus. Champier, while using information from Annius, expresses some doubts in 1515. Outside France, Vives questioned the authenticity of Annius' texts in 1522. Ramus was to use the material while simultaneously expressing doubt in 1559. Pasquier rejected it.

In the *Annales* Bouchet traces the history of his province, in the *Anciennes et modernes généalogies* that of the kings of France. Thus all of this material was potentially interesting to him. He had Lemaire before him as a weighty authority for the strands of the Trojan-Frankish legend as inherited from the Middle Ages and for the Gallic material from Annius. By the time he was writing Tritheim too had published his chronicles, which supplemented the Trojan-Frankish material.

Certainly Lemaire and Tritheim are the two writers whom Bouchet acknowledges as being the major sources for early history:

> [Jehan le Maire et Tritemius] sont deux historiographes modernes, lesquelz ont esté plus curieux et laborieux de s'enquerir de l'antique extraction des François que tous les aultres de ce pays de France.[61]

Bouchet begins the *Annales* with the conventional division of Gaul into three parts, 'Belgique', 'Celtique' and 'Aquitaine'. In describing these three Gauls he cites classical works—Caesar's *Commentaries*, Ptolemy's *Geographia* and Strabo's *Geographia*—and works by Christian writers, the *Historiae* of Orosius and the *Etymologies* of Isidore. He also uses Gaguin. Berosus is first referred to in connection with the naming of 'Gaule Belgique':

> A laquelle partie de Gaule Belgius quatorziesme roy des Gaules bailla premierement le nom, par la description de Berose, autheur Babylonien, lequel je croyrois volontiers, si c'estoit celuy dont parle Pline: car aucuns historiens ont escript et main-

tiennent que c'est ung Berose supposé, non voulans adjouxter
foy à son livre, duquel maistre Jehan le Maire a prins le fondement de son traicté des Illustrations des Gaules.[62]

Similarly he refers to the etymology provided by the pseudo-
Berosus for 'Gaule Celtique':

Et print le nom de Celtique de Jupiter Celte, filz du Roy Lucus,
selon ledict Berose.[63]

And on Aquitaine:

Ce pais fut ainsi appelé par Galateus xi Roy des Gaules, à la
difference des aultres deux parties à cause des eaues, fontaines,
rivieres et ruisseaulx, dont il y a grant quantité, selon le jugement de maistre Jehan le Maire en ses Illustrations, où il s'ayde
dudict Berose: qui n'est autheur approuvé de tous, comme j'ay
dit dessus.[64]

He is thus extremely cautious in his use of material derived from
Annius.

After these primarily geographical descriptions he turns his attention to the origins of the Poitevins. Here he seems genuinely to be
trying to compile a continuous narrative by drawing fragments
from various sources. He thinks that the Poitevins were probably
descended from the Scythians, so his first concern is to trace the
history of Scythia. The account he gives proves clearly that he does
not accept Lemaire's account of the re-peopling of the world derived
from the pseudo-Berosus. Instead he uses material from the summary by Justinus of the *History* of Trogus Pompeius, as amplified in
the *Enneades* of Coccius. He recounts that after the Flood the sur-
vivors lived in caves without rulers, but eventually kings were set
up (the most virtuous men being elected to this office). Greed soon
led to wars, Vexores of Egypt and Thanays of Scythia being the first
to make war on each other. The Scythians won a battle against the
Egyptians, but being unable to conquer Egypt turned towards Asia
and conquered a vast empire.[65] Obviously this account is totally at
variance with Lemaire's account of the re-peopling of the world by
Noah and his descendents after the Flood.[66]

The basis for the connection between the Scythians and the Poitevins is to be found in a quite different account of the Trojan legend,
Geoffrey of Monmouth's *Historia Regum Britanniae*, which Bouchet
now goes on to cite in the first version of the *Annales*.[67] He says that
some Scythians set out to conquer new lands in about 1000 BC, and
it is from these that the Poitevins—or Picts—are probably descended, because Geoffrey of Monmouth tells us that in the time of
Vespasian Scythians or Picts invaded Britain and conquered Albion
but subsequently moved to Hibernia and were called Scots.[68]

Geoffrey of Monmouth also provides evidence that Scythians
called Picts had come to Aquitaine and to Poitou itself 1,000 years
earlier, soon after the destruction of Troy, for Brutus on his travels

came to Aquitaine, and 'Regnabat tunc in aquitania Goffarus pictus eiusdem patriae rex'.[69] On the basis of this evidence Bouchet assumes that Poitiers was built by these people or their successors, and he claims that the correct etymology of *Pictavis* is *picta vis*, that is *force peinte*, the Scythians being called Picts because their faces were red with the blood that they were accustomed to drink.[70]

Having thus accepted the Scythian origin of the people of Aquitaine he now considers the line of kings. Here again there is a reference to Berosus:

> Je n'ay trouvé par histoires certaines et tesmoignage vallable qui fut le premier Roy de la Gaule d'Acquitaine, fors Galatheus, duquel nous avons dessus parlé, si l'autheur qu'on appelle Berose est veritable, ne quelz Roys vindrent après luy.[71]

So in practice Bouchet prefers to begin with the 'Groffarius' attested by Geoffrey of Monmouth and others:

> On dict temps Groffarius Pictus, duquel nous avons parlé cy dessus, estoit Roy d'Aquitaine, et faisoit sa principalle demourance à Poictiers, comme tesmoigne ledict Monumetensis, et semblablement la Grand Mer des Historiens et ung autheur incogneu en une cronique que j'ay veue en la librairie de S. Denis commençant *In Primordio*.[72]

He proceeds to resume the story of the war between the Trojans under Brutus and the Picts as it is recounted by Geoffrey of Monmouth, and then says firmly that nothing more is known of the history of the province until 60 BC and the Roman conquest under Publius Crassus.

There is no evidence at all that Bouchet had any first-hand knowledge of the work of Annius; nearly all his references also cite Lemaire and all could be derived from the *Illustrations*. Lemaire has in fact far more to say about 'Gaule celtique' and 'Gaule Belgique' than Aquitaine, which is no doubt a contributory factor in Bouchet's lack of enthusiasm for the Gallic legends. Geoffrey of Monmouth, on the other hand, provides more specifically local information and so is preferred.

In a later edition Bouchet added to his account of the Scythians and the Picts. From 1532 he has a much more exciting tale to tell, and one which involves Hercules, but not the Libyan Hercules of the pseudo-Berosus and Lemaire.[73] From Herodotus he takes the story that in Scythia Hercules had three sons by a maiden, half-woman, half-snake; their names were Scythes, Gelonus and Agathyrsus.[74] It is from this last that was descended the branch of Scythians that settled in Aquitaine. Bouchet mentions Raphael of Volaterra's description of the Agathyrsi, and it may be that the *Commentarii Urbani* gave the idea for this interesting origin of the Poitevins, for Volaterra stresses that they painted their faces and are called 'picti Agathyrsi' by Virgil.[75] Bouchet completes the interpolation with an epigram by

Nicolas Petit on the Herculean origins of the Poitevins. We have met Petit before as a classicising influence on Bouchet's poetry, and it seems likely that he suggested this ancestry to Bouchet. Certainly the authorities for this part of the Hercules myth are more respectable than the pseudo-Berosus, but no doubt the attraction of a more specifically local connection in the form of Picts makes Bouchet the readier to accept this myth. Certainly the idea that the people of Poitiers were descended from the Agathyrsi proved popular, and it was exploited in the decorations for the entry of Charles v in Poitiers in 1539.[76]

Bouchet is still less interested in the Gallic history provided by the pseudo-Berosus in his *Anciennes et modernes généalogies des roys de France*. The Trojan origin of the Franks alone interests him. So much so that he does in fact cite (again via Lemaire) one sentence from the work of Annius, a sentence not from Berosus but from the pseudo-Manetho:

> que Francus filz d'Hector vint en Pannonnie avec grand compaignie de Troyens et qu'il espousa la fille de Rhemus lors roy de la Gaule Celtique.[77]

This is a sentence that, as Asher shows, was often conveniently forgotten by those writers who dismissed the Trojan story but accepted the Gallic myths. But this is the only part of the Annius forgeries that Bouchet accepts without question.

Asher describes Bouchet's account in the *Généalogies* as 'even more in the mediaeval tradition than Lemaire's version'.[78] No doubt Bouchet was troubled both by the lack of corroboration of Berosus in older chronicles, and by those modern scholars who had questioned the authenticity of the chronicle. The authority of the 'modern' Lemaire is never enough to convince him by itself. But perhaps his lack of interest and expressed doubts about Berosus are helped on by the lack of information about Aquitaine to be gleaned from this source—and the indisputable fact that for tracing the lineage of the French kings the Franks are more important than the Gauls.[79]

When we turn to his treatment of Tritheim the picture is very differerent. The *Chronicles* provide him with the material to fill some of the gaps between the end of the Francus legend and the beginning of the line of Frankish kings, which traditionally began with Pharamond. Tritheim purports to base the first part of his chronicle on a *History of the Franks* from the fall of Troy to the death of Clovis composed by a Frankish historian Hunibald. He can thus give a list of forty-two kings before Pharamond, beginning with Marcomir, son of Anthenor, in 440 B C.

Bouchet in his *Anciennes et modernes généalogies* gives epitaphs and effigies for all the kings of France from Pharamond onwards. But he begins the work with a long introduction tracing the descent of the French kings from Francus right the way down to Pharamond. To

provide this list he draws heavily on Tritheim. Asher calls his
account 'part translation, part paraphrase and part summary' of
Tritheim's chronicle:

> Bouchet, in fact, was one of the few writers to draw from this in
> detail, instead of using it merely as an extra piece of evidence
> for the validity of older generalities of the legend. He was not at
> the same time wholly dependent on Tritheim, whose list of
> Kings, as has been shown, was incomplete in its early parts.
> Where he began his list of names of Franco-Trojan Kings in 440
> BC with Anthenor (not of course the Anthenor of classical
> legend), Bouchet went back to Hector and named six genera-
> tions of his descendants—names given by Jean Lemaire and
> repeated by Gilles Corrozet. Having thus given a good begin-
> ning to his genealogy, Bouchet from then on ignored Lemaire's
> list and repeated exactly the succession traced by Tritheim.[80]

Bouchet seems to have had no doubts at all about Tritheim's veracity. At certain points he remarks that Hunibald's account seems
more fabulous than true, but each time he is merely following the
comment of Tritheim himself.[81] It is interesting to note that after
telling from Tritheim the story of the Frankish King Basan who puts
his own son to death in accordance with the law, Bouchet himself
adds that this followed the example of Manlius Torquatus who
thirty years before had done the same thing[82]—probably the same
story was in the mind of the compiler of Hunibald's *History*.

In the *Annales* the Franks do not appear until Book Two when
Bouchet is dealing with the Germanic invasions. At this point he
says of them (in a passage which demonstrates the simultaneous
composition of the *Annales* and the *Généalogies*):

> On dict an trois cens quatre vingts et six Marcomirus estoit roy
> des François qui encores se tenoient en Germanie dela le Rhin,
> et le quarantiesme roy ainsi que tesmoigne Tritemius. Et sur se
> convient noter que les croniques de France commencent le
> regne des François à Pharamond parce que les croniqueurs
> n'ont eu congnoissance des roys precedents qui regnerent sur
> les François en Germanie par plus de quatre cens ans avant
> ledit Pharamond, ainsi qu'il est au long contenu par mes Gene-
> alogies et Epitaphes des roys de France.[83]

It will be noticed that even the Trojan legend of the French Kings
is not expounded in the *Annales*; it is merely referred to obliquely,
because it reveals nothing about the early history of Aquitaine. The
Brutus strand of the legend as found in Geoffrey of Monmouth is of
more local interest.

Once the Franks enter the history of the province of Aquitaine,
Bouchet uses Tritheim in the *Annales* for information on their King
Marcomir and then for the kings from Pharamond to Clovis. How-
ever, once he arrives at Pharamond he has other sources, notably

Sigebert of Gembloux. For the mythical Kings Pharamond, Clodion, Walia and Meronée he gives the number of years of their reigns from both Sigebert and Tritheim; in each case there is a disagreement, but Bouchet merely gives the two different numbers without comment.

Thus we can see that in the *Annales* the use made of the various mythical histories, which were so to capture the imagination of some of his compatriots, is extremely limited. This would seem to be partly because these histories were not particularly enlightening about his own province, partly, at least in the case of the pseudo-Berosus, because he had his doubts about their truthfulness. In the *Anciennes et modernes généalogies* his subject matter is more compatible with these histories and the genre, mixed prose and verse with an obviously eulogistic intention, seems to invite the most glorious antiquity possible. Here he does elaborate on the myth that has the long and respectable pedigree, the Trojan descent of the French Kings, together with Tritheim's modern masquerade, which confirmed and strengthened it. He has opted, in short, for the Renaissance forgery that best confirms the medieval myth.

3
Hagiography

It seems clear that the lives of saints, and especially local saints, were particularly interesting to Bouchet. His project of writing a life of St Radegonde goes back to the reign of Charles VIII when the King instructed him to translate her legend. 'En visitant les anciennes histoires' he found his work defective, and so ultimately produced the well-researched life, which he published in 1518. Similarly the introduction to the *Annales* points out their hagiographical content, which reflects to the credit of his own city which he wishes to celebrate:

> Pour la decoration de la Cité, Eglise et Université de Poictiers, qui est l'une des plus anciennes cités de toutes les Gaules, j'ay adjousté son origine, combien et quels Evesques il y a eu, et aussi de sainctes personnes. Et entre autres mis au long la louable vie de sainct Hilaire, la lumière de l'Eglise Gallicane, et celle de sainct Guillaume duc d'Aquitaine.[84]

The life of St Hilary is particularly developed in the *Annales*,[85] and in fact he tells us that in writing this life he was fulfilling a vow that he had made. Thus hagiography is clearly a pious duty.

But the study of hagiography is also invaluable to the historian of the Roman occupation and the Dark Ages. Lives of local saints provided Bouchet with a high proportion of the material for the first two parts of the *Annales* (up to 852 AD); in particular they provided him with nearly all his specifically local material. The works that were published as the *Annales* and the *Anciennes et modernes géné-*

alogies are already mentioned in the *Histoire de Clotaire*; clearly all three works are the result of the same period of intensive historical reading and research. In all these works his main sources for the history of France in the Christian era before Charlemagne are Eusebius, Isidore, Sigebert of Gembloux, Gregory of Tours, Vincent of Beauvais, Hugh of Fleury, and among more recent writers Antoninus of Florence and Gaguin. If he had had to rely on these alone he would have had little indeed to say specifically about Aquitaine and Poitiers. But saints' lives are a rich source of local information; moreover he was able to supplement narrative sources with documents drawn from local ecclesiastical archives. So he amplifies his account of the Roman period with details from legends of St Valery and St Martial, which name rulers of Aquitaine and which explain the conversion of the area.[86] For example, while St Martial was preaching in Poitiers a voice from heaven told him that on that very day St Peter had been crucified in Rome and that he must found a church in his memory. This explains the foundation of Poitiers cathedral.[87] The foundation of the church of Saint-Pierre-le-Puellier is explained by reference to the story of St Loubette, supposed to have been one of St Helena's servants and to have been given a piece of the True Cross.[88] The naming of Notre-Dame-la-Grande is traced to a miracle by which a young man was saved from fornication.[89]

The study of local history is thus immeasurably enriched by hagiography. But, by the same token, as a writer of hagiography Bouchet gives a very much better account than that to be found in most contemporary vernacular saints' lives because of his historical studies. Both St Radegonde and St Hilary are placed firmly and clearly in their historical setting. We have already noted that the *Histoire de Clotaire* combines chronicle and saint's life. The life of St Hilary is incorporated into the *Annales*, but is conceived as an entity, filling chapters 6 to 15 in Book 1. A large part of another chapter in Book 2 is devoted to the translation of St Hilary's body. Bouchet's main source is the life by Fortunatus and, for the translation, a narrative that he believed also to be by Fortunatus.[90] But his usual historical sources are also drawn on: Hilary's life is given 'tant par sa legende, que croniques approuvées'.[91] In particular Bouchet gives an account of the progress of the Arian heresy, using the *Ecclesiastical Histories* of Eusebius and Rufinus and, among later writers, Antoninus of Florence and Platina.

He also used more than one edition of the works of St Hilary. A passage in praise of Hilary's writings is drawn in part from a dedicatory letter introducing an edition published in 1510.[92] But he must also have used some other edition of Hilary's works, for this collection does not contain the only texts that Bouchet actually reproduces, a letter in praise of virginity and a morning hymn addressed by St Hilary to his daughter Apra.[93]

Both in using hagiography to compile a history and in his own composition of hagiography, Bouchet demonstrates a conscientious use of a large number of sources. It remains to be seen how critical he was in the use of these sources. Two particularly jagged rocks for him to founder on are first piety, which might lead him to show excessive respect for a saintly subject or a saintly source, or even to indulge in plain dishonesty with the suppression of inconvenient fact or the invention of edifying fiction. The second is the historian's respect for an ancient testimony. This hazard is particularly grave for the eager searcher-out of ancient documents, for not every piece of antique parchment is what it claims to be.

Apart from a hardly surprising disposition to believe in any documented miracle, Bouchet probably comes to grief more often on the second rock than on the first. A good example of the perils of using local documents it to be found in his account of St Helena. The finding of the True Cross is given a great deal of attention, no doubt because several churches near Poitiers claimed to possess portions of it. Chapter 5 of Book 1 is all concerned with Constantine and Helena, and by combining his usual sources with local legends Bouchet weaves together a most cohesive narrative. He accepts the commonly held view that Helena was the daughter of King Coel of England, and he gathered from Geoffrey of Monmouth that she was the grand-daughter of the previous King, Lucius.[94] This piece of information is very useful as it allows him to graft in a story concerning the origin of the cathedral church at Luçon, which he says he found in a hymn entitled *Gauda Lucionium*.[95] He tells us that the second son of Constantius and Helena was called Lucius, 'qui estoyt le nom de son bisayeul Roy d'Angleterre, comme on peut veoir on traicté de Jo. Monumetensis'.[96] Lucius killed his elder brother and was therefore banished from the kingdom and condemned to become a monk by his father. Sent out to sea in a boat laden with riches and relics, he came ashore at the place now called Luçon, where he founded a church and an abbey.

> Desquelles choses noz historiens n'ont rien escrit, mais ont seulement parlé du tiers fils, nommé Constantinus, qui depuis fut Empereur et appellé Constantin le grant.[97]

Having accepted this local legend about 'Lucius' he uses it to justify another one, namely that St Helena brought some of the True Cross to Poitou where it was kept at a hermitage that became the site of the Abbey of St Michel-en-l'Herm. This legend he found in 'ung legendaire fort ancien, estant en l'abbaye sainct Michel en l'her en Poictou'. And he explains why Helena would have landed in Poitou: '. . . voulut veoyr, (comme il est à conjecturer) son filz Lucius, qui estoyt en son monastère de Luçon'.[98]

All his inclinations lead him to accept stories found in such manu-

script sources. The silence of other historians presents no obstacle
to acceptance. A conflicting account in his usual source presents
more of a problem. So for instance in the *Histoire de Clotaire*, after
telling us that St Radegonde had a nun called Agnes made abbess,
he remarks:

> Il est contenu en la legende sainct Pien que ce fut Richilde, mais
> je croy plus l'epistolle de saincte Radegonde qu'elle feit pour la
> confirmation de privileges dudict monastère cy après incor-
> porée que celuy qui a fait ladicte legende sainct Pien. Combien
> qu'il peut estre que Richilde fut abesse après ladicte Agnes.[99]

And later on in the narrative we are told

> Et est à conjecturer que après ladicte saincte Agnes Richilde fut
> abesse, et après ladicte Richilde une bonne et devote religieuse
> nommée Lembouere.[100]

Again the wish to accept the local tradition, if possible, is evident,
although not at the expense of better sources. The letter of St
Radegonde mentioned in the extract above in fact provides an
excellent example of his critical approach. This letter, addressed to
the bishops of Gaul, appears, as Bouchet tells us, in Book 9, chapter
42 of the *Historia Francorum* of Gregory of Tours. But Bouchet had
another text as well which he found 'en une carte en forme auten-
ticque on tressor dudict monastère saincte Croix'.[101]

Sainte-Croix was the convent in Poitiers founded by St Radegonde. The letter appeals to the bishops to maintain the rule of St
Caesarius and the abbacy of Agnes after Radegonde's death, and to
maintain the rights and properties of the convent. Bouchet translates this document and then continues:

> Ladicte espitre fut escripte en une grant peau de parchemin
> et soubsignée par saincte Radegonde qui l'envoia à plusieurs
> evesques et arcevesques de France qui semblablement en
> l'approuvant la soubsignerent. Puis nagueres j'ay veu ladicte
> epistre on monastère de ladicte saincte audict Poictiers en forme
> de carte en une grant peau de parchemin tresbien escripte en
> lectre antique. Et est signée Radegonde; Maroneus evesque de
> Poictiers, ma dame Radegonde presente; Gregorius arcevesque
> de Tours; Medardus evesque de Soissons; Germanus evesque
> de Paris; Elegius evesque de Noyon; Pacencius evesque; Leo-
> donnus archediacre, Austrapius archiprestre et Sanson archi-
> prestre.[102]

The text of the letter is no doubt authentic enough, reproduced as
it is by Gregory of Tours, but a modern historian would have to
assume that the actual charter existing in the sixteenth century was
a forgery, perhaps copied originally from Gregory because it related
to the convent's privileges, and signed with an impressive array of
important signatures—unfortunately, though, of men who were
bishops at different times.[103] Now of this discrepancy Bouchet is

well aware, and he draws his readers' attention to the problem:

> Touteffoiz il fault cy noter que ladicte carte ou epistre ne fut
> ainsi signée en ung temps ne en une année. Car lors qu'elle fut
> faicte, Pacencius estoit evesque de Poictiers qui l'a signée, et
> depuis Maroneus l'a signée lors qu'il fut aussi evesque dudict
> Poictiers, qui fut après le trespas de Pacencius. Aussi Gregorius
> n'estoit lors arcevesque de Tours, mais l'estoit Enfronius.[104]

Bouchet does not draw the—to us—obvious conclusion that the
document was a forgery, merely that it was signed at several different times. This example demonstrates the honesty with which he
treats his sources, but it is difficult to believe that even with their
imperfect knowledge of dealing with ancient documents more sceptical sixteenth-century minds than Bouchet's would not have arrived at a more likely explanation, if one less flattering to Sainte-
Croix. Bouchet is quite innocent himself of pious fraud, but he is an
easy mark for those of other people because he assumes that ancient
documents and clerical sources will be truthful.

His attitude of respect for early sources and for saints is every-
where manifest. He is distressed that Lemaire should speak so
disparagingly of the formidable queen and saint Clotilde.[105] In reproducing St Hilary's letter in praise of virginity and the morning
hymn he is accepting two texts that modern scholarship no longer
attributes to St Hilary and that, more significantly, Erasmus, in the
year before Bouchet published the *Annales*, had included in his
edition of the works of St Hilary while saying

> Haec epistola merum est nugamentum hominis ociose indocti,
> hymnus eiusdem est farinae, sed bene habet, quod non plures
> naenias affinxerent sancto Hilario.[106]

It is tempting to wonder if Bouchet was deliberately trying to counter such a judgement. It is quite clear from other works of his that he
read Erasmus, but he hardly ever mentions him by name.

In the light of this respectful attitude to his sources, it is most
interesting to see what circumstances led him to reject an edifying
story. The most notable example is the rejection of the claim that St
Radegonde remained a virgin. A seventeenth-century life argues
for her virginity, but the Bollandists incline to Bouchet's view of the
matter.[107] His reason for rejecting the story is that only modern
writers have made any such claim. Clearly too the story would
offend his views on matrimony and run counter to his aim of setting
up St Radegonde as a model for all women, including married ones.
Another example of his rejection of a tale comes in his account of the
life of St Hilary. He has found, in 'une legende de S. Martin, qui est
en langaige vulgaire, dont je n'ay peu sçavoir l'autheur'.[108] a story
about St Martin visiting St Hilary and recognising in St Hilary's cook
a devil come to ensnare St Hilary. This story Bouchet denies, saying,
truly, that it does not appear in the account by Sulpitius Severus, St

Martin's most important biographer. The story does indeed appear at some length in the *Vie et miracles de monseigneur sainct Martin translatée de Latin en Françoys*.[109] This account contains many miracles not in Sulpitius Severus, and this episode in particular would seem to be designed to show Martin's superiority over a rival local saint. Bouchet, clear-seeing where his own saint is disparaged, will not accept the story as having any place in the life of St Hilary. Yet he still does not completely reject it:

> Et ay leu qu'à la verité, S. Martin estant en Italie, ledict miracle fut faict en la maison d'un Evesque, qui n'est point nommé, lequel estoyt Arien.[110]

Lack of any documentation of a story may be a reason for not recording it:

> J'ay oy parler d'ung puys qui estoit audit lieu de Sees et d'autres petites choses qui sont à la louange de ladicte saincte. Mais parce que je n'en ay veu tesmoignage suffisant, doubtant que ce soit apocriphe, ne l'ay voulu escrire cy dedans.[111]

But an abstention of this sort must have cost him something, for his predisposition to believe such tales is such that of one miracle of St Hilary he says:

> Je n'ay veu ce miracle par escript, mais l'ay sceu par la commune renommée du pais, et encores ladicte pierre est oudict chemin engravée du fer de la mulle. . . . On en croyra ce qu'on voudra, mais souvent advient que telles choses qui se continuent par commune renommée sont plus veritables que celles qu'on trouve par escript, par ce que le papier ou parchemin souffrent tout, et les choses qu'on sçait par commune renommée, est à presumer qui si elles n'estoient veritables la renommée n'en seroit si longue.[112]

By no stretch of charity then can Bouchet be regarded as critical in his approach unless a discrepancy is absolutely apparent, in which case he will seek for a compromise that allows belief in ancient tales to continue. But he is honest. Only in a very few instances can he be found to be embellishing the histories of his favoured saints, and then only in a very mild way. Gregory of Tours tells us that St Clotilde's prayers to St Martin were responsible for a miraculous storm, which prevented her sons joining battle with each other; Bouchet assumes that Radegonde was praying too, and so associates her with the miracle.[113] He also associates her with Bishop Injuriosus in the successful attempt to persuade Clotaire not to exact a third of their revenues from the clergy. Injuriosus achieved this

> par l'aide, support et faveur de saincte Radegonde qui luy feit avoir audience envers le roy (ainsi que a escript assez confusement ledit sainct Fortune).[114]

It is indeed more than difficult to make the words of Fortunatus cover this account, but, as Radegonde was Queen at this time, Bouchet is perhaps justified in assuming that she helped the Bishop gain audience with Clotaire, and also that she backed up what he said.

Our study of Bouchet's use of hagiography thus reveals that he is on the whole honest: his piety does not lead him into pious fraud. But it does lead him into credulity in instances where contemporary scholars were beginning to be much more critical. On miracles he would also seem even for his age to err on the side of credulity, although perhaps we should note in mitigation that he honestly believed his wife to have been miraculously cured as a result of his prayers to St Radegonde. The credulity is not just the result of piety, it is also part of a general attitude towards the authority of ancient sources. And although he ranks as uncritical in comparison with some sharper minds, his saints' lives appear as paragons of scholarship and truthfulness when compared with much of the available vernacular hagiography to which Sorbonne doctors were so eager to confine the latinless laity's reading.[115]

4
Contemporary History

We shall see in the next chapter that in his controversial writing Bouchet is so concerned with the welfare of the Church that he is sometimes less wholehearted in his flattery of the King than other writers writing on the same occasion. This by no means leads him into actual criticism of the King, and indeed the *relative* unease can only be seen in comparison with other polemical writers.

If in the modern part of the *Annales* we look for criticism of royal policy we are almost always disappointed. An examination of his attitude to the King and of his treatment of issues which brought the King into conflict with the Church and with other foreign powers in his own lifetime, soon reveals that the historian's duty of truth in no way suggests to him the necessity for impartiality. Any possibility of impartiality is ruled out by a hierarchy of loyalties that makes him tend to set a local interest before the national one, and which absolutely ensures his supporting the national interest before any alien one, including the more general interest of the international Church.

In order to demonstrate local loyalty we must take instances where there seems to be some hostility to royal policy. There are in fact some indications that Bouchet was not entirely happy with the government of François 1er, but these are concentrated in a small span of time. It has already been said that between 1515 and 1535 Bouchet has no other chronicler to follow but pieces together a narrative amplified by *plaquettes*, etc. Probably he kept notes year by year. The 1524 and 1526 editions do not go beyond 1519, but the edition of 1532 brings events right up to date. Naturally the battle of Pavia and its consequences loom large. He gives long quotations from exchanges between France and the Emperor, the Treaty of Madrid and the *Paix des Dames*. But before that national crisis there are certain entries that betoken disquiet with regard to royal policy. The years before Pavia were a period of considerable discontent in France; war with the Emperor began in 1521, François Ier was making far more financial demands on the country than had his predecessor, the 'père du peuple' Louis XII, and in some areas soldiers were turning themselves into bandits; other chroniclers complain of their depredations.[116] Finally loyalties were to be deeply divided over the affair of the Constable, Charles de Bourbon.

In an entry for 1521, Bouchet records Bonnivet's capture of Fuenterrabía from Spain, but with no great rejoicing: he says that the expedition was 'de grande mise' and that the people of Poitou and surrounding areas suffered considerably because many animals were taken, ostensibly for the benefit of the army:

> dont les Commissaires, ou aucuns d'eux, firent leur particulier profit, à la foule du peuple, et non au profit du Roy, ne de la chose publicque.[117]

Certainly he pushes the blame on to a few individuals and away from the King, but his lack of enthusiasm for the adventure is manifest and contrasts with the entry found in other chroniclers.[118] Another case in which he does not precisely object to the King's actions, but obviously has his doubts about them, is one instance when François raised money from the Church. Bouchet records that in 1522 a variety of new ways of raising money were devised 'pour les affaires du royaume de France, qui commancerent croistre'. In 1522 the clergy were taxed on their temporal holdings. Bouchet seems to be finding excuses for this decree:

> Lesdites lettres estoient fondées en justice, plus au soulagement des gens d'Eglise qu'à leur foulle, s'elles eussent esté executées comme il appartenoit. Mais en plusieurs dioceses le feuble supporta le fort.[119]

Similarly in the following year the lower orders of the clergy were taxed on small temporal holdings. Again, Bouchet seems to try to find excuses as he says 'en cela y avoit quelque apparence de justice' because these clergy held property that laymen should hold, but again he records that there were many cases of abuse and exaction; this time however the King is said to have intervened to see that justice was done.[120]

So in spite of the fact that in his moral works Bouchet is always stressing that kings must not tax churchmen except with the permission of the Pope, in practice he does not condemn François' continual levies on the Church. The disquiet in these two cases seems to be part of a general dissatisfaction with what things were coming to at this period. Poitiers suffered from the undisciplined soldiery and Bouchet records at some length their unsuccessful attempts to enter Poitiers in 1523.[121] His gloom at this period is expressed in a very striking entry for 1520 when he has recorded that war with the Emperor was just beginning and the soldiers were beginning to trouble the country. Here he is clearly writing with hindsight:

> Et lors commença le temps de pleurs et de douleur, pour les injustices, exactions et autres adversités depuis advenues en France et ailleurs, procedans, comme il est à croire, de plusieurs pechés publiques, sçavoir d'heresies, superstitions, divinations, arts magiques, et choses contraires à la Foy catholicque, qui ont eu depuis cours, et aussi que tous estats sont pervertis et desguisés de mœurs, conditions, et qualités: principallement par le vice d'avarice, si tresgrande, qu'aucun n'ay veu, durant ce douleureux temps, tendre fors à son particulier profit: mais chascun estre contant de veoir perir le bien public, pour sa privée richesse.[122]

This demonstrates clearly a feeling that the world has taken a turn for the worse. The King is not specifically blamed, but neither can he be regarded as exempt. Such a view of the times implies dissatisfaction with the government as well as with the increasing sinfulness of more lowly contemporaries. One wonders whether Bouchet viewed as an example of avarice a subject that he treats a page or two later, Louise de Savoie's claim to the inheritance of Suzanne de Bourbon against the Constable Charles. Well after Bourbon's defection and death, Bouchet remains resolutely non-committal on the rights and wrongs of the claim:

> Je ne sçay les moyens de leurs pretendus droicts: parquoy me deporteray d'en escripre, mais parleray seulement de leurs genealogies . . .[123]

And having given the genealogies and shown that Louise should inherit the duchy if a woman may inherit, but that Charles claimed that his marriage treaty and other treaties with the kings of France had barred women, Bouchet concludes: 'quant à moy, je ne sçay qu'il en est'.[124] In fact it is hard to believe that at the time of the lawsuit Bouchet's sympathies were not with Charles. Bouchet's most important patrons were closely related to the Constable, to whom Bouchet himself had dedicated the *Temple*, because it celebrated his cousin. Charles de Bourbon was the nephew of Gabrielle de Bourbon. The loyalty of Louis de La Trémoille came under suspicion because of his connection with the Duke of Bourbon.[125] There is however no suggestion that Bouchet had any sympathy for the Constable's defection; we must take as a comment on those troubled times a passage from the *Epître aux subjectz* written in January 1533 and warning against rebellious talk:

Il n'y a pas neuf ans que vy plusieurs
Maulvaiz françoys, qui voyans noz grans sieurs
Hors d'amitié prestz à guerre se faire,
Disoient tout hault sans crainte de forfaire,
'Ung tel pourra bien estre nostre roy',
En desirant contre leur propre foy
De leur vray roy la ruyne et la perte
Et qu'entre eulx fust (comme advinst) guerre ouverte,
Et n'eust esté l'ordre qu'on y donna
Soudainement, dont on les estonna,
Nous eussions veu tresgrand ruyne en France
Pour ce discord, et intestine oultrance,
Dont neantmoins en avons des douleurs
Longtemps porté par eulx et par les leurs.[126]

Later passages in the *Annales* deplore the Constable's desertion, as do the references in the *Panégyrique*. But the studied neutrality of his account of the lawsuit probably reflects his dissatisfaction with this and other aspects of royal policy in the early 1520s, a dissatisfaction that he probably found too in his patrons. In this period Bouchet's special source of information and local pride are reflected in the special attention given to La Trémoille's military exploits, and this is often accompanied with implied criticism of the King. We are told how La Trémoille took a totally inexperienced and inadequate army to Picardy in 1523 and succeeded in beating off English and Imperial forces.[127] We are also told that before the siege of Pavia La Trémoille advised the King to pursue his enemy and not to lay siege to any town,

par ce qu'il disoit la principalle force des François estre en emotion et fureur, et que le Roy ne les devoit arester à aucun siege. Ce qui ne fut trouvé bon.[128]

And with that devastating conclusion the paragraph ends, leaving us to reflect that the whole disaster of Pavia might have been averted, if only Bouchet's patron had been listened to.

It would seem, then, that Bouchet like many of his contemporaries was somewhat discontented with his young King's government of the country in the period leading up to Pavia. But it must also be admitted that from the *Annales* this appears to have been a transitory state of affairs. François receives more and more praise as his reign goes on, and this is true already in the later parts of the 1532 edition. The praise of Louise de Savoie on the occasion of her death is warm, particularly for her role as Regent.[129] Bouchet would obviously have liked to see peace instead of endless war with the Emperor, but particularly after Pavia he always blames the Emperor for the wars.

In so normally patriotic and pious a writer one would expect the relation between Church and State to be an area in which problems

of sympathies might arise. But whenever his King came into conflict
with his Pope, Bouchet seems to have experienced no qualms at
all—he always supports the King, to such an extent that Popes are
judged according to whether or not they show themselves to be
'bons François'.

An obvious case to begin with is Julius II. Bouchet's narration of
the crisis that had caused him to write his two polemical poems is
dominated by an account of the Council of Tours—the reason being
that Bouchet was actually there himself. He tells us that Louis,
seeing that Julius was bent on making war and trying to deprive him
of Genoa and Milan, sought to find

> les moyens honnestes, sans offencer l'Eglise, de l'empescher et
> le faire vaquer et veiller à la garde de son parc ecclesiastique et
> non de s'occuper à guerre et effusion de sang.

He therefore called the council at Tours in September 1510

> où je me trouvay à l'issue d'une merveilleuse maladie qui ung
> moys auparavant survinst en tout le royaume de France . . .[130]

I take this to mean that Bouchet was actually at Tours, either by
chance because the illness ('la coqueluche') had overtaken him
there, or perhaps after recovering from the illness: he could have
been accompanying La Trémoille. At all events his account of the
Council is unusually full: he gives in detail the eight articles that
were discussed at the council. He is probably summarising a document issued at Tours, and as such offers one of only two existing
accounts of this council.[131]

After the long account of these deliberations, the brevity of what
follows is all the more striking. In one paragraph he resumes the
rest of the crisis up to the death of Julius in 1513. He records that it
was decided that the King would send ambassadors from the Gallican Church to Julius, asking him to desist from his enterprises and
seek peace, 'et à ce faire fut admonnesté par fraternelle correction
evangelicque'. Otherwise he would be asked to summon a council
in accordance with the decrees of the Council of Basle. When the
King sent these ambassadors, the Pope absolutely refused to call a
council, although asked to do so by both Louis and the Emperor.
Therefore the council was called without papal authority at Pisa,
then transported from Pisa to Milan and from Milan to Lyons by the
Gallican Church:

> Où furent faittes plusieurs sessions, et en icelles aucuns beaus
> decrets. Toutesfois n'y eut aucune conclusion prinse, au moyen
> de ce que ledit pape Julius mourut ung an et demy après ou
> environ.[132]

The important point about this narrative is the total lack of reference to the Lateran Council that Julius II himself called and which
opened in April 1512. Not only is the account told from the French
King's point of view, but it is almost exclusively concerned with the

activities of the French. Although this may to a certain extent reflect availability of information, it is quite inconceivable that Bouchet did not know about the existence of the Lateran Council. And it seems most unlikely that it was because he had *new* information that from 1545 he made the following addition:

> Lequel avant son decès en hayne des choses susdittes, ana-
> thematiza Maximilian roy des Romains, et le roy de France,
> Jehan roy de Navarre son allié, et plusieurs Princes, Cardinaux
> et Evesques: Priva lesdits Roys et Princes de leurs royaumes et
> principautés, les Ecclesiastiques de leurs dignités et benefices:
> donna les Royaumes et principautés à qui premier les occu-
> peroit: dont ils appelerent au futur Concile: où tout ce qui
> avoyt esté fait par ledit pape Julius fut declaré nul par le pape
> Leon qui succeda audit Julius.[133]

Bouchet never before 1545 alluded to the fact that the cardinals and bishops participating in the Council of Pisa were pronounced to be schismatics and heretics at the first session of the Lateran Council, nor that France was placed under an Interdict in August 1512. Now that he does so he contrives to make France sound far less isolated than she had actually been: by August 1512 Julius had every hope of winning the Emperor to his side, and the Emperor was not excommunicated in spite of his half-hearted support for the Council of Pisa. Bouchet also gives a false impression with his reference to a Council: the Council in which Leo x was involved was simply a continuation of the Lateran Council called by Julius. He seeks to suggest that Julius' actions were unjustified, unreasonable, not to say demented. In fact it seems likely that, looking back on the events of 1510–13, Bouchet had decided that Julius had not been a true Pope, and this perhaps helps to explain the impression he seeks to give. But that the impression is deliberately falsified is difficult to deny.

Never again except with Julius III[134] was there quite such a bad Pope as Julius II from the French point of view, but this is certainly the point of view from which all are judged by Bouchet. Of the election of Julius II he says, 'Au commancement se monstra bon François', but ultimately 'il fut tresgrandement ingrat'.[135]

He makes comments on the Popes when he records the death of one and the election of another, and nearly always in terms of their attitude to the French. Of Leo x he says 'Il se monstra du commance-ment assés bon François, mais non à la fin'.[136] On the loss of Milan he says

> Le Pape Leon, fort contraire aux François et de petite fidelité en
> fut le moyen, ainsi qu'on dit, mais ne vesquit gueres après . . .
> On fist de luy et de ses meurs plusieurs ignominieux et scan-
> daleux epigrammes, dont je n'estime les autheurs, par l'irre-
> verence Apostolicque.[137]

Bouchet himself reproduces one epigram against a Pope, and in one edition says that those who wrote it did so 'non à tort, j'extime, veu ce qui est dessus escript'.[138] But this is an epigram about Julius ii, and therefore no doubt a special case.

With Adrian vi we discover the qualities that Bouchet admires in a Pope: he is described as a learned Pope and a reformer.[139] And no doubt another reason for Bouchet's approval is that Adrian attempted at least to remain neutral in the struggle between France and the Emperor.

On Clement vii the most interesting entry is the meeting between Pope and King of France at Marseilles in 1533: we are told that the Pope promised to call a council:

> Le Pape et le Roy firent plusieurs bonnes deliberations pour remedier aux scismes et heresies lors et dès longtemps auparavant procedées des Alemaignes, et dont y avoit ja quelque commancement en la ville de Paris. Et fut promis par le Pape au Roy de France de faire bien tost ung concile pour donner ordre esdits scismes et heresies.[140]

So we are given the impression that the King was eager for a council. This is a travesty of the real facts, since Clement's half-hearted steps towards a council were definitively scotched by François, who certainly did not want one. However Bouchet may not have realised this; his remark reflects the current face-saving formula seen in François' letter to the German princes.[141] Bouchet clearly would have liked to see a council held, everything else being equal—that is, national interest allowing.

With Paul iii came another Pope of whom Bouchet thoroughly approved—again probably in part at least because he was no tool in the hands of the Emperor, but this is not explicit:

> Son election fut libere, unanime et necte de symonie et de violence, à laquelle se trouverent les Cardinaux de France, qui tous furent pour luy, au moyen de sa prud'homie et que c'estoit ung homme droict qui tousjours a eu en abhomination les perverses et maulvaises doctrines, et les dissentions d'entre les Princes Chrestiens. Pour lesquelles causes, et qu'il ne fut onc partial, le Roy de France ne voulut pretendre à faire eslire autre Pape de sa nation, ne de son party, ny le procurer, ne briguer aucunement envers les Cardinaux François ny aultres, dont il eust eu grant nombre pour luy s'il eust voulu, mais pourchassa son election, esperant qu'il en procederoit quelque grant bien à toute la Chrestienté.[142]

This last remark rather runs counter to Bouchet's firm insistence in the *Epîtres Morales* that Cardinals should call a halt in a conclave if any king or prince is trying to bribe them.[143] But then perhaps he thought that François would use only moral pressure.

When dealing with relations between Church and State within

France, Bouchet always supports the Crown. On the Concordat for instance he records with severe disapproval the disturbances at the University of Paris to which it gave rise.[144] And he never actually condemns the King for raising money from the Church although we have seen one occasion when he gives the impression of rather wishing that the King had desisted.

Even when we look abroad to less emotive questions Bouchet does not support other Catholic authorities as much as one might expect. Where no contrary national interest arises he is very interested in the Emperor's attempts to hold discussions with the Protestants, and he reports the Augsburg and Ratisbon meetings in great detail. But even on this he supports the French royal line in opposing the call for a council after Ratisbon. His treatment of the English Reformation in the last edition of the *Annales* is particularly surprising from the religious point of view. He does not mention it at all in earlier editions beyond references to the execution of Thomas More and of Anne Boleyn. In 1557 he records briefly Henry VIII's break with Rome.[145] The longest passages concern the disputed succession after the death of Edward VI.[146] He praises Edward warmly as excellently educated and a great hope to his subjects. He praises Lady Jane Grey, recording the piety of her last words. His account of the persecution of various theologians is oddly ambivalent. He records that Hugh Latimer was imprisoned by Henry, freed by Edward 'à cause de sa doctrine'—i.e. learning—but reimprisoned by Mary. Peter Martyr and Bernardino Ochino are both picked out for mention without any apparent disapproval; the former is described as 'homme de grant renom entre les ministres des Protestans',[147] and he is said to have relied on his innocence because he had in no way offended against the statutes of the kingdom and therefore obtained royal permission to depart instead of merely fleeing. He notes that by October 1553 'n'y demoura aulcun des Predicans Protestans en toute Angleterre et furent les premieres coustumes de servir et prier Dieu et ses Saincts reprises, les Lutheriens chassés'.[148] And yet a few pages later he is recording how some rebels against Mary escaped 'et se retirerent au Roy de France, comme le tuteur et protecteur de tous pauvres affligés'.[149] He particularly cites Peter Carew, whom he calls 'homme de grande estime et renom'. Carew had raised a rebellion because of Mary's plans to marry Philip of Spain. This would seem to be the crucial point of Bouchet's account of Mary; Catholic she may be, but she is also regrettably pro-Spanish. He lists all the reforms Mary made—dangerous books to be burnt, married priests to leave their wives, reintroduction of Latin and the Roman use of sacraments, restoration of the Pope to primacy in the Anglican Church. He then mentions that her sister Elizabeth was imprisoned for suspected sedition, and concludes his remarks on Elizabeth with the comment:

Ceste princesse est de grande vertu et sçavoir eminent, à laquelle doit beaucoup l'Angleterre pour la sublimité de sa doctrine.[150]

Not a word of praise for Mary in spite of her impeccably Catholic reforms, and finally a eulogy of the virtue and learning of the sister she had imprisoned. Although there is no actual attack on Mary, Bouchet shows here considerable sympathy for the representatives of the non-Catholic side in England. The explanation must be French hostility to Mary because of the prospect of her marriage with Philip of Spain. Although it is possible that Bouchet was less hostile to the English reformation than to the German one because of its closeness to some Gallican ideas, the most probable explanation of his attitude would seem to be the obvious one, the dictates of national interest.[151]

It would seem then that in most cases the contemporary part of the *Annales* closely reflects royal policy as revealed for public consumption. Bouchet's efforts in this part involved the collection of information but little critical treatment of it. He makes no attempt to transcend local and national prejudice, and in spite of his preoccupations in his other works Christendom comes a pretty poor third in the *Annales d'Aquitaine*.

Nevertheless, from his contemporaries' point of view the account he provides is quite comprehensive, quite well documented and in places very full. If it is partisan, this his readers would have expected and wanted. It is certainly no more so than the other chronicles we have mentioned. His work is much better and fuller than, for instance, the *Mer des croniques* for the same period. It is not surprising that he was often plagiarised. And it was, in short, with some justification that when Paris printers issued editions of the *Annales d'Aquitaine* with their own continuations in 1537 and 1540, Bouchet was furious and disclaimed such additions in 1545 as 'choses triviales, non sentans l'histoire'.[152]

5

Bouchet and Montaigne

As a postscript to this chapter we may note the reactions of one of Bouchet's readers—Montaigne. Montaigne read the *Annales d'Aquitaine*. He also read Bouchet on the period 1483–1519, probably without realising it, in his copy of Nicole Gilles, *Annales et Croniques de France*. Some of his annotations to Gilles relate to this period, none unfortunately commenting on the quality of the account, although he does note that most writers are more critical of Louis XII's reasons for divorcing his first wife, Jeanne.[153] In the *Essais* themselves Bouchet is twice mentioned by name, and on several occasions the *Annales d'Aquitaine* appear to be the source for an example. Montaigne is believed to have read the *Annales* in about

1572; all but one of the references that have been noticed come from
the first book of *Essais*.[154]

It is difficult to resist the impression that Montaigne found Bouchet rather comic, particularly his miracle stories. In *C'est folie de
rapporter le vray et le faux à nostre suffisance*, Montaigne presents
Bouchet as a good example of the recounter of miracles whose
authority may readily be rejected:

> Quand nous lisons, dans Bouchet, les miracles des reliques de
> Saint Hilaire, passe: son credit n'est pas assez grand pour nous
> oster la licence d'y contredire. Mais de condemner d'un train
> toutes pareilles histoires me semble singulière impudence.[155]

Montaigne immediately goes on to cite the opposite case of St
Augustine, whose evidence may not be lightly set aside. Poor Bouchet thus appears virtually as a stumbling-block to the acceptance of
miracles rather than the stalwart supporter he no doubt wished to
be. And Montaigne particularly noticed the miracles in the *Annales*.
More than half his allusions concern miracles and church history.
Half of the short essay *De fuir les voluptez au pris de la vie* is a
thoroughly tongue-in-cheek account of St Hilary's successful prayer,
first for the death of his daughter, and then for that of his wife.[156] In
that *galimafrée* of an essay *Des noms*, he picks out with unerring
sense of the ludicrous Bouchet's story of the naming of the church
of Notre-Dame-la-Grande in Poitiers.[157] In *La Fortune se rencontre
souvent au train de la raison* he tells two miraculous stories of walls of
besieged cities falling down, both from Bouchet. Fortune, Montaigne says, sometimes seems to vie with our miracles; she did just
the opposite in the case where a French captain mined a wall, which
fell down all in one piece, leaving the besieged as securely protected
as they were before.[158] The editors believe that the details of the
death of Arius and the epitaph on Boniface VIII are also from the
Annales although these are both quite well known.[159] It is from
Bouchet that Montaigne learned that William Duke of Aquitaine
wore a hair shirt: the inclusion of the detail in *Que le goust des biens
et des maux depend en bonne partie de l'opinion que nous en avons* firmly
removes it from its context of admiration in the *Annales*.[160]

Montaigne was apparently reading Bouchet at the same period
when he was reading Guicciardini and the memoirs of the Du
Bellays.[161] That he retained so many miracle stories from Bouchet
reflects a bias of interest in the *Annales*, which we have already
noted. That he reacted somewhat sceptically to them is equally
what we might expect. But that he bothered to read Bouchet at
all—and he read him right through, for there are references to all
parts of the *Annales*—demonstrates that Bouchet as a historian could
hold the attention of even the most intelligent of readers.

NOTES
1. The first four books of *De rebus gestis Francorum* appeared in 1517; more gradually came out up to his death in 1529, but the full ten books were made available only posthumously in 1539. Paolo Emilio's chronology was regarded as more reliable than Gaguin's (see for example Robert Ceneau, *Gallica historia*, Paris, 1557, f.125 ro-vo).
2. Symphorien Champier gives an account of the French monarchy in both *Le triumphe du treschrestien Roy de France [Loys] XII de ce nom*, Lyons, 1509 and in *Les grans croniques et vertueux faictz des . . . ducz et princes des pays de Savoye et Piemont*, Paris, 1516. Claude de Seyssel dealt with the monarchy in propaganda pieces for Louis xii (*Histoire de Louis XII; Victoire du roi*) before his major political work, *La grant monarchie de France*, Paris, 1519; see Michael A. Sherman, 'Political Propaganda and Renaissance Culture: French Reactions to the League of Cambrai, 1509-10', *Sixteenth Century Journal*, viii, no.2 (Supplement), 1977, pp.97-128. Lemaire's *Illustrations* trace the origins of the royal houses of France from the Franks and the Gauls.
3. See Sherman, *art. cit.*
4. *Histoire de Clotaire*, aa1 ro.
5. See the bibliography for details. The edition of 1526 corrects and expands the 1524 text without prolonging the narrative, but the editions of 1532, 1535, 1545 and 1557 bring the narrative up to date. They also include occasional alterations to the text covering earlier periods. For convenience all references are to the 1557 edition unless otherwise stated.
6. He refers to his *Annales et epitaphes* in the *Histoire de Clotaire*, A2 ro, but in the last paragraph of the 1524 *Annales* he explains how he has divided the material. When referring to the *Anciennes et modernes généalogies* I shall for convenience quote from the 1545 *Généalogies*.
7. Cicero, *De Oratore*, Book 2, §53.
8. See Michael F. O. Jenkins, *Artful Eloquence. Jean Lemaire de Belges and the Rhetorical Tradition*, Chapel Hill, 1980, particularly pp.88-91, 104-8, for the way Lemaire employs different levels of style in his different types of history. In the topical and polemical *Légende des Vénitiens* Lemaire employs his plainest style; like Bouchet he claims that he should be read not for his form but for his matter—but even here he is using rhetorical persuasiveness of a type alien to the purpose of *annales*.
9. Prologue addressed to La Trémoille, [f.iv] ro. See also liminary poem [f.iii] ro, col.1.
10. f.275 ro.
11. See Sherman, *art. cit.*, pp.118-22, on Seyssel's discussion of the *panegyricus*; also Ruth Morse, 'Medieval Biography: History as a Branch of Literature', *Modern Language Review*, 80, 1985, pp.257-68.
12. Cf. chapter three, p.75. Bouchet's courtly readers did not appreciate the lessons.
13. See the bibliography, part 1, 13, no.16. The title refers to 'Les Effigies, protraictes au vif, ainsi qu'elles sont taillées en pierre,

par ordre en la grant salle du Palais Royal de Paris'. Chasseneuz reproduces his Latin verse and discusses the statues in his *Catalogus Gloriae mundi*; see the edition printed by George Regnault, Lyons, 1546, f.5 ro. Like Bouchet's *Généalogies* this work was originally dedicated to the chancellor Antoine du Prat. Chasseneuz was one of the lawyers whose commentaries on customary laws contributed to the historical study of medieval law. (Donald R. Kelley, *Foundations of Modern Historical Scholarship*, Columbia University Press, 1970, pp.185, 196-9.)

14. See the presidential address of Noël Valois in *Bulletin de la Société de l'histoire de Paris et de l'Ile-de-France*, 30, 1903, pp.87-90.

15. The inscriptions beneath the statues survive in Bonfon's edition of Corrozet's *Antiquitez, histoires, croniques et singularitez . . . de Paris*, Paris 1577, f.97 vo ff. There were 53 up to and including Louis xii (five more were added up to Henri iii). Valois cites an earlier manuscript copy and shows that the list of kings is consistent with the contemporaneous Saint-Denis chronicle by the monk Yves, 1317. Bouchet however makes Louis xii the 57th king. Cf. n.18.

16. Guenée and Lehoux, *Entrées royales*, pp.27-9. In 1498 in Paris nine kings from Saint Louis were represented. It was also common to construct a genealogical 'tree' bearing effigies of some of the King's ancestors (thirteen at Troyes in 1486, see p.286).

17. *Généalogies*, aa6 ro. See Frances A. Yates, *The Art of Memory*, London, 1966. In chapter 4 she shows that medieval treatment of the ancient memory systems often stressed order rather than the imaginary places of the classical system. But images remained central to the art. Bouchet also remarks elsewhere that verse is more memorable than prose; thus his epitaphs also assist the mnemonic process.

18. *L'Entrée de Henri II à Rouen* (Rouen, 1551) facsimile intr. by Margaret M. McGowan, D5 vo. 'Les predecesseurs Roys de France— par ces cinquante sept hommes armez si richement equippez sont entendues les cinquante sept Roys qui par cy devant & depuys Pharamond ont heureusement regné en France.'
     This version of the list of kings, one shorter than that of Bouchet, may well have been based on that of Jean Du Tillet the younger in *De regibus francorum Chronicon*, first published in 1539; this became very popular and was translated into French. He makes Louis xii the 56th king, he rejects Clotaire iv and Louis Fainéant whom Bouchet includes, but accepts Charles le Gros whom Bouchet mentions but does not count.

19. Apart from Chasseneuz's little book see *Epitome gestorum LVIII regum Franciae*, Lyons, B. Arnoullet, 1546. The 58th king is François ier. The earlier portraits copy particularly closely the main features of those in the *Généalogies* and there is some evidence of use throughout. See Brun, *Livre illustré*, p.182, for several other editions of the same collection, in which each picture is accompanied by a brief account of the reign in Latin. The same numbering is used in *Recueil des effigies des roys de France*, Lyon, Raullant de Neufchatel (1567); see Brun, pp.281-2: the pictures however are different. The *Epitome chronicorum regum Galliae*, Paris, 1566 would appear to use the list which is one shorter, see Brun, p.182.

20. See Donald R. Kelley, *Foundations of Modern Historical Scholarship. Language, Law and History in the French Renaissance*, Columbia University Press, 1970.

21. The gradual discrediting of the Trojan and Celtic descents of the French King is a good example of this process; despite the lustre given to these legends by Lemaire doubts were raised from the beginning of the century and by the end neither were seriously believed. See R. E. Asher, *The Attitudes of French writers of the Renaissance to Early French History, with special reference to their treatment of the Trojan Legend and to the Influence of Annius of Viterbo*, PhD thesis, London, 1955; also his article, 'Myth, Legend and History in Renaissance France', *Studi Francesi*, 13, 1969, pp.409-19.

22. liminary [f.3] ro.

23. +1 ro.

24. aa6 ro.

25. aa1 vo.

26. [f.iv] ro; 2 vo.

27. [f.iii] vo.

28. aa1 vo.

29. *Annales*, f.5 vo.

30. Robert Gaguin, *De Origine et gestis Francorum compendium*, Lyon, J. Bade, 1497 (followed by several editions printed in Paris). The *Compendium* was translated and continued by Pierre Desrey, 1515 (see *infra*). Bouchet defends the Chronicle of pseudo-Turpin against Gaguin, f.52 vo. In this he agrees with Coccius, who accepted Turpin, and he quotes the opinion of Coccius (cf. *infra*, n.77). For other occasions on which Bouchet points out Gaguin's errors see for example *Annales*, f.45 vo and *Histoire de Clotaire*, f.iiii ro, on the translation of the body of St Hilary; *Histoire de Clotaire*, f.ix vo, where he casts doubt on Gaguin's account of the death of Hermenfroy.

31. aa1 vo.

32. *Généalogies*, f.3 ro.

33. f.10 vo.

34. *Ibid.*, St Jerome, *Chronicon, PL* 27, col.679.

35. [f.iii] ro, col.1.

36. *De Oratore*, Book 2, §62. Cf. n.8.

37. See Hamon, p.192 n.3 and pp.201-2. See also C. Auber, *Etude sur les historiens du Poitou*, Niort, 1870, pp.82-98.

38. Events in Poitiers include the entry of François Ier into Poitiers, 1520; the reformation of the convents of Sainte-Croix and La Trinité, 1519; attacks by bands of soldiers in 1523; the murder of a priest called Curzay in 1526; the mystery play of 1534. On the information about La Trémoille in the *Panégyrique*, see especially +1 vo. For details of the four nineteenth-century editions (all incomplete), see the bibliography.

39. H. Hauser, 'Etudes critiques sur les sources narratives de l'histoire de France au XVIe siècle. II. Annales et Chroniques', *Revue d'histoire moderne et contemporaine*, 5, 1903-4, pp.471-89.

40. *Ibid.*, p.488.

41. Alain Bouchard's *Grandes Croniques de Bretaigne* were first published Paris, 1514 (BL G.5999). An edition of 1518 gives some

additions relating to Brittany (Hauser, *art. cit.*, p.485). Thereafter
there are two quite different continuations. An edition of Paris,
1531 (BL C.38.i.20) copies Bouchet 1488-1519, then follows another source to 1530. A 1532 edition (BL C.66.c.3) uses Desrey's
account from 1488 onwards, then a much fuller version of probably the same other source up to 1530. The continuation of the
1532 version, printed in 1541 (BL 806.e.12), copies the 1540 edition of Bouchet's *Annales*; the continuation thus consists of Bouchet's continuations 1531-35 and the unauthorised Paris additions up to 1540. (Cf. Hauser, *art. cit.*, p.488: Bouchet's influence
has been recognised but not clearly established.)
  The first edition of the *Annales* of Nicole Gilles which I have
located was printed in Paris in 1525 (BN Rés. L^{35} 37—but cf.
Hauser, *art. cit.*, p.483, also Brunet). It contains Gilles' text,
which ends with the death of Louis xi, together with continuations. The period from the accession of Charles viii to 1519 is
copied verbatim from Bouchet with a few omissions. Hauser
suspected Bouchet's influence but did not realise the extent of
the borrowing (*art. cit.*, p.484). In later editions, for 1520-30 the
account is substantially the same as that of Bouchard 1532, but
briefer. In the 1536 Paris edition (BL 1474.dd.11) a few episodes
are interpolated from Bouchet's 1532 continuations (the murder
of the priest Curzay and the Lutheran incursions into Lorraine);
these are not present in the 1534 edition (BL 9200.i.22). There are
occasional similarities with Bouchet's text in additions covering
the period 1531-45 in the 1536 edition and editions of 1544 and
1549, but borrowing from Bouchet cannot be proved.

42. Sebastien Picotté; his *Cronique du roy François premier de ce nom*,
     was edited by Guiffrey, Paris, 1860. See Hauser, 'Etude critique
     sur "La Cronique . . ."', *Revue de la Renaissance*, 8, 1907, pp.49-63.
     Neither Guiffrey nor Hauser note the extracts copied from Bou-
     chet, which include passages on pp.3-28 and 51-4. These could
     have been copied via other chronicles, but Bouchet is mentioned
     by the author, who calls him 'homme de nostre temps de singu-
     liere erudition et labeur', p.399.

43. For example: f.264 ro, the letters controlling the sale of grain,
     28 October 1531 (4269), the letters concerning the recovery of
     crown lands, 2 November 1531 (4277); f.265 ro, *Ordonnance*
     against those bearing false witness, March 1532 (4494), rules
     governing prices in hostelries, June 1532 (4600). Numbers in
     brackets from *Catalogue des Actes de François Ier*, Paris, 1887-1908,
     10 vols.

44. f.233 ro. There was a published account of this treaty (see J. P.
     Seguin, *L'Information en France de Louis XII à Henri II*, Geneva,
     1961, p.85 no.56), but this sentence suggests that Bouchet may
     have seen a manuscript.

45. For the Spanish treaty, 1516, see Seguin, *Information*, p.78, nos
     14, 17 and 18; the *Paix des Dames*, pp.90-1, nos 80-7. These do not
     necessarily include the texts that Bouchet used.

46. See Seguin, *Information*, pp.22-3, 29-46.

47. Probably Seguin, *Information*, p.101, no.127. The same account is
     found, more or less abbreviated, in *La Mer des Croniques*, 1536, T4
     vo, *Cronique du roy François Ier*, ed. Guiffrey, pp.114-25, *Journal*

d'un bourgeois de Paris, ed. L. Lalanne, Paris, 1854, pp.442-4. See *Annales*, ff.271 ro-272 vo.

48. See chapter 5.

49. Correspondents and informants are mentioned f.213 vo (François du Fou), 256 ro (Germain Colin Bucher), 263 ro (unnamed correspondents). Mihervé is mentioned 277 vo, 281 ro. Examples of military information obviously emanating from La Trémoille and his circle appear 209 ro, 215 ro—this was of course an important source of information for the *Panégyrique*. See *Ep. Fam.* 65-8 (to and from Germain Colin Bucher), 127 (Mihervé).

50. Guillaume Paradin's *Histoire de nostre temps*, first published in French in 1550, J. de Tournes, Lyon, and reprinted with additions in 1556 and 1561. Bouchet's account of the death of Paul III and the election of Julius III seems to be abridged from the 1556 additions. I have used the edition of 1561 (BL 9077.a.12); cf. p.703-6 and *Annales*, f.346 vo.

51. See *infra* on the Council of Tours and Montaigne's notes on Gilles.

52. [f.15] vo-[f.16] ro. He further says that for him Bouchet has turned a labyrinth into an amphitheatre.

53. *Gallica historia*, f.125 vo.

54. *Ibid.*

55. *Foundations*, p.244.

56. See n.152 and the final section of this chapter.

57. The summary that follows is drawn from Asher's thesis, *Early French History*.

58. *Commentaria fratris Joannis Annii Viterbensis . . . super opera diversorum auctorum de Antiquitatibus loquentium*, Rome, 1498, BL IB.19034.

59. *Compendium sive Breviarium primi voluminis annalium sive historiarum de origine regum et gentis Francorum*, Moguntiae, 1515, BL 183.c.1.

60. Asher, *Early French History*, pp.82-5.

61. *Généalogies*, f.4 vo.

62. f.1 ro. The real Berosus, a Chaldean scholar and astronomer of the time of Alexander the Great, is mentioned by Pliny in *Naturalis Historia* Book 7, 160 and 193. On Belgius, cf. Lemaire, *Illustrations*, ed. Stecher, vol.1, pp.86-8.

63. f.1 vo. Cf. Lemaire, *ibid.*, pp.58-60.

64. f.1 vo. Lemaire, *ibid.*, p.85.

65. Justinus, *Historia*, Book 1, chapter 1 and Book 2, chapter 1. Marcus Antonius Coccius Sabellicus is an author to whom Bouchet refers quite often, both to the *Rerum Venetarum Decades* (Venice, 1487, BL IC.21644), which in its opening pages mentions a Trojan origin for the Venetians consonant with the Frankish version, and, as here, to the *Enneades ab orbe condito ad inclinationem Romani Imperii* (Venice, 1498, BL IC.24321), a history combining classical and Jewish antiquity from the Creation to the Goths' capture of Rome. Coccius recounts the Flood and then uses material derived from Trogus Pompeius concerning the solitary state of men, their first rulers and the war between Vexores and Tanais; he describes the Scythians at length, mentioning, like others, that they drink the blood of their captives (f.4 ro).

66. Lemaire, following the pseudo-Berosus, depicts Noah sending out his descendants as kings. See *Illustrations*, Book 1, chapters 2-5, ed. Stecher, vol.1, pp.16-39. Bouchet says rather sarcastically in the *Annales*, f.205 vo, that some people have asked him to trace the origins of local noble families 'comme si c'estoyent choses establies et arrestées dès le temps de Noé et ses premiers enfans'.

67. The *Historia Regum Britanniae* had been used freely by French writers, including of course Alain Bouchard. It was printed by Badius in Paris in 1508 and 1517. For some reason Bouchet refers to its author as *Johannes* Monemutensis instead of Galfridus.

68. *Annales*, 1524, f.iii ro. See Geoffrey of Monmouth, *Historia Regum Britanniae*, ed. A. Griscom and R. E. Jones, London, 1929, p.326.

69. *Ibid.*, p.241; see *Annales*, 1524, f.iii ro.

70. *Annales*, 1524, f.iii vo; 1557, f.4 vo.

71. *Annales*, 1557, f.5 ro.

72. f.5 vo. By the *Mer des Histoires* Bouchet means a translation of Columna's *Rudimentum Noviciorum*, (Paris, 1488, BN Rés. G.216-17; there were several later editions with additions). See Hauser, *art. cit.*, n.29, pp.476-80.

73. See M-R. Jung, *Hercule*, especially p.64.

74. Herodotus, *History*, IV, 8-10. See *Annales*, ff.3 vo-4 vo.

75. Raphael Maffeius Volaterranus, *Commentariorum urbanorum octo et triginta libri*, Paris, J. Petit and J. Bade, 1511, BL 1248.m.5, f.LXXIV vo. See *Aeneid*, Book 4, 146.

76. Jung, *Hercule*, p.64.

77. *Généalogies*, f.3 vo. Bouchet uses this evidence to support Vincent of Beauvais against Pius II and Coccius, who said that it was Priam, nephew of King Priam, who settled in Pannonia. He uses part of the same sentence in a brief account of the Trojan origins of the French monarchy in the *Histoire de Clotaire*, A2 ro. See Lemaire, *Illustrations*, Book 3, ed. Stecher, vol.2, pp.267-8.

78. p.22.

79. He attempts to do justice to the Gauls as well as the Franks in the preface to the *Anciennes et modernes généalogies*: the Gauls and the Franks now form one nation; both have been less famous than the Romans only because they had no writers to praise their deeds—he mentions Celtic victories against the Romans. (*Généalogies*, ff.1 ro-2 ro. Preface addressed to the Dauphin François.)

80. pp.23-4; see also p.11 n.1. Bouchet mentions Francus, Sicamber, Priam, Hector, Trojus and Trogotus, in a passage explaining a prophetic vision accorded to Marcomir. He claims to have succeeded in reconciling the accounts of Lemaire and Tritheim, *Généalogies*, f.4 vo.

81. Cf. Tritheim, *Compendium*, A3 vo, B1 ro and *Généalogies*, ff.5 ro, 6 ro.

82. *Généalogies*, f.6 ro. Titus Manlius Torquatus, who condemned his son to death, is an *exemplum* of stern duty.

83. 1524 ed. f.xxv ro. (Misprint in 1557 ed.)

84. [f.4] ro.

85. It is found copied into a MS collection of saints' lives: see the bibliography.

86. ff.6 vo-9 ro.

87. f.8 ro-vo.

88. ff.11 ro-12 ro.
89. f.13 ro-vo. This story seems to be a local tradition, introduced by Bouchet with 'On dit communement . . .'.
90. He uses a Life of St Fridolin which is associated with Fortunatus' Life of St Hilary in some manuscripts (see M. Koch, *Sankt Fridolin und sein Biograph Balther*, Zurich, 1959, especially p.37 n.41). The two lives appear together in the *Vita beati Hilarii composita a servo suo Fortunato*, (Basle? 1485? BL G.5210); the author of the Life of Fridolin, Baltherus, is not mentioned. Bouchet assumes that Fortunatus was the author: see f.36 vo.
91. f.12 ro.
92. *Opera complura*, J. Bade, Paris, 1510, BL 469.c.7: see preface by Robertus Fortunatus, [f.1] vo. Bouchet makes a loose translation of part of this preface, with some additions—a good example of his way of using his sources (ff.15 vo-16 ro).
93. ff.16 ro-17 vo. See *infra*, n.106.
94. f.9 vo. In fact Geoffrey actually says that Lucius died without heirs (*Historia*, ed. Griscom and Jones, p.331); Coel is merely his successor.
95. f.9 vo.
96. *Ibid.* Cf. *supra*, n.67.
97. f.9 vo.
98. f.10 vo; f.11 ro.
99. f.1 vo. The main sources for the life of St Radegonde are the Life by Fortunatus and the Life by Baudonivia, St Radegonde's servant (*PL* vol.72, cols 651-80), also Gregory of Tours, *Historia Francorum*. St Pien (Pientius) was bishop of Poitiers. He is mentioned by Baudonivia and Gregory of Tours, but little is known about him (*Acta Sanctorum*, 13 March). In referring to his legend Bouchet is once again using a tradition of his local church.
100. f.lxix ro. Agnes was succeeded by Leubovera.
101. f.l vo.
102. f.lii vo.
103. Cf. René Aigrain, *Sainte Radegonde*, Paris, 1918, p.138 n.2: 'Les signatures que certains manuscrits ajoutent au document ne peuvent être d'aucun secours pour le dater, car elles sont contradictoires et d'ailleurs apocryphes'. The text is reproduced among the additional texts in the seventeenth-century edition of the *Annales*, and it is said to be taken from a charter kept in the treasury of Sainte-Croix (pp.36-41).
104. ff.lii vo-liii ro.
105. f.xvi ro; cf. Lemaire, ed. Stecher, vol.2, pp.400-12.
106. *S.D. Divi Hilarii lucubrationes*, Basle, 1523, p.322. See also p.325: 'Hymnus epistolae respondens, hoc est dignum patella operculum'.
107. *Histoire de Clotaire*, f.xxv vo; *Acta sanctorum*, 13 August. Several 15th- and 16th-century writers assume her virginity: Lemaire does so (ed. Stecher, vol.2, p.419), following Foresti, *De plurimis claris sceletisque* [*sic*] *mulieribus*, Ferrara, 1497, f.cxxxviii ro. An English *Life* makes the same assumption (ed. F. Brittain, Cambridge, 1926). A 17th-century Jesuit argues for the tradition: J. Dumonteil, *Histoire de la vie incomparable de saincte Radegonde*, Rodez, 1627.

108. *Annales*, f.23 ro.
109. [Attributed to Mathieu Lateron, Tours, 1496], BL C.22.b.5, e4 vo-e6 vo.
110. f.23 ro.
111. *Histoire de Clotaire*, f.xl ro.
112. *Annales*, f.23 vo.
113. See Gregory of Tours, *Historia francorum*, Book 2, chapter 28; *Histoire de Clotaire*, f.xvii vo.
114. f.xxxiii ro.
115. See chapter 6.
116. E.g. incidents at Meaux are recorded in the *Mer des Croniques*, 1536, f.ccxlvi vo. On François' financial difficulties, see Knecht, *Francis I*, Cambridge, 1982, pp.121-31.
117. f.207 ro.
118. Accounts in Gilles, Bouchard and the *Mer des Croniques* report with joy Daillon's successful defence of Fuenterrabia. In the *Mer des Croniques* Daillon is wrongly reported to have captured the town in the first place, 'en quoy faisant il acquist tresgrant bruict et honneur' (1536, f.ccxlvii ro).
119. f.207 vo.
120. *Ibid.*
121. ff.210 vo-211 ro.
122. ff.206 vo-207 ro. *La Mer des Croniques* also speaks of 'la persecution que nous avons au bon royaulme de France' (1536, f.ccxlii vo), but it wants to put the blame directly onto Luther and his heresy.
123. f.208 vo. Only the Constable's defection is recorded in the other chronicles. See also *Panégyrique*, f.clxxv ro-vo for the defection. See Knecht, *Francis I*, pp.148-59.
124. f.209 ro.
125. In the *Panégyrique*, f.clxxv vo, Bouchet says that the King never had any distrust of La Trémoille in spite of these connections.
126. 2 *Ep. Mor.* 6, f.31 vo, col.1.
127. ff.209 ro-210 ro. Cf. *Panégyrique*, ff.clxxiv ro-clxxvi vo.
128. f.215 ro. Cf. *Panégyrique*, f.clxxvii ro. Here Bouchet defends La Trémoille against charges of 'trop grant promptitude', arguing that he understood the nature of the French.
129. f.264 ro.
130. f.189 ro.
131. The other is a manuscript letter by a delegate to his bishop (BN MS latin 1559). Bouchet's account is known, but only via the continuations to Gilles (it is reproduced from Gilles in Du Boulay, *Historia Universitatis Parisiensis*, vol.6, Paris, 1673, pp.45-6).
132. f.190 ro. The information here comes from Desrey.
133. f.190 ro.
134. Julius III is discussed in the 1557 edition, f.346 vo ff., an account taken verbatim from the introduction to an official publication of an edict forbidding money to be sent to Rome, *Edict du Roy nostre sire, sur la prohibition . . .*, Paris, Jehan Dallier, 1551, BL 1492.dd.15(4).
135. f.187 vo.
136. f.192 ro.
137. f.207 ro. Knecht, *Francis I*, pp.106-8.
138. Only in the 1526 edition, part 4, f.lxix vo.

139. f.207 ro-vo; f.211 vo. Cf. Knecht, *Francis I*, p.114.
140. f.267 ro.
141. A letter dated 1 February 1535, printed both in German and in French with a privilege. (*Des Königs zu Franckreich Schrifft*, BL 3905.g.7; for the French version see Seguin, *Information*, p.101 no.126—see also no.125.) Bouchet paraphrases this letter; see f.273 vo for the call for a council. Knecht, *Francis I*, pp.229-30.
142. f.269 vo. Cf. Knecht, *Francis I*, pp.235-6 for the King's disapproval of Paul III's policies.
143. 1 *Ep. Mor.* 1, f.7 ro, col.2.
144. f.203 ro. Knecht, *Francis I*, pp.55-65.
145. ff.279 ro, 318 vo-319 ro.
146. Intermittently ff.368 ro-374 ro.
147. f.371 ro.
148. f.371 ro.
149. f.373 vo.
150. f.374 ro.
151. There are difficulties in interpreting these passages. Bouchet was very old when the 1557 edition was published (the last pages are somewhat disjointed), and I have been unable to identify his source of information about England. But a poem published in 1545 already revealed the gentleness of his judgement of the English reformation: his epitaph for Sir Thomas More (*Généalogies*, 1545, f.80 ro). Here he says that Henry VIII, fundamentally a good man ('de luy bon') by bad advice, not recognising his mistake ('sans congnoistre qu'il erre') had himself named 'lieutenant de Jesuchrist en terre'. Bouchet may have regarded the English reformation as little more than an over-doing of Gallican principles. See my article in *Moreana*, 1985.
152. f.275 ro. Hauser's assessment remains broadly fair:
      Très crédule, préoccupé surtout de 'moraliser', Bouchet a cependant cherché à se renseigner; il est sincère et peut être cru pour les faits qui se sont passés dans son voisinage ou au sujet desquels il a été informé par la Trémoille. (*Les Sources de l'histoire de France. Deuxième partie: le XVIᵉ siècle*, vol.1, Paris, 1906, p.31)
      In the seventeenth century Jean de La Haye, whose *Mémoires* are printed after the *Annales* in the 1644 edition, accuses Bouchet of concentrating too much on his employers and the clergy:
      Luy, qui estoit procureur à Poictiers, ne parle volontiers que de ceux desquels il avoit les charges, et semble qu'il soit tousjours partie en son livre: neantmoins il a beaucoup travaillé, et a faict à la verité en aucuns endroicts de belles recherches . . . (p.4)
      Il escrivoit sur tout l'histoire des Evesques de Poictiers, et de ceulx desquels il avoit charge des affaires, ce qu'ils vouloient, et de leurs parties adverses n'en eust ozé ou voulu parler. Neantmoins il a bien en beaucoup de choses, longuement travaillé. (p.6)
153. Montaigne, *Œuvres complètes*, ed. A. Armaingaud etc., 12 vols, Paris, 1924-41; vol.12, p.211. The passages from Bouchet appear pp.205-15, also p.217.
154. *Les Essais*, ed. Villey and Saulnier, Paris, 1965, p.11. The editors

note information taken from Bouchet in Book One, chapters 3, 14, 20, 27, 32, 33, 34, 46, 47 and Book Two, chapter 1.

155. Book One, chapter 27, p.181.
156. p.219.
157. p.277. Cf. *supra*, n.89.
158. p.221.
159. pp.216 and 332.
160. p.60.
161. *Les Essais*, ed. Villey and Saulnier, p.11.

Controversies Concerning the Reformation
of the Church

Our study so far has dealt with different types of writing that
Bouchet cultivated. Before proceeding to an examination of the final
category, religious writing, it is worth pausing to examine what he
has to say on a number of controversial subjects concerning religion.
In describing his religious writing it will be necessary to take account
of the differences imposed by the threat of heresy in the 1520s. We
shall therefore adopt a different approach in this chapter and consider what he says in moral and historical works about the spread of
heresy, also what his attitude to the Church and its reformation had
been before the threat of heresy arose. Bouchet contributed two
works to the collection of polemical writings generated by the war
between Louis xii and Pope Julius ii, 1510–13. The writers engaged
in that propaganda campaign regularly dealt with the abuses in the
Church and used a variety of Gallican and conciliarist arguments.
Bouchet was no exception, so his stance on these questions must be
examined. On the other hand, it is also true that the reform of the
Church can be regarded as a literary commonplace with a long
history, and, as such, a subject that Bouchet treated in moral works
throughout his life. Here too we may examine what he has to say in
the light of his general principles in moral writing, to see if any
idiosyncratic viewpoint can be established. The reasons for attempting this analysis is that Bouchet was for many years to be regarded
as a source of vernacular catholic instruction that was safe and
orthodox, and it is therefore interesting to establish just what views
so respectable a figure might express on these controversial subjects. By the same token, it is also interesting to attempt to discover
what view he took of non-schismatic reform movements in France
itself.[1]

1
Before Luther

a) *Criticism of the Clergy in the 'Renards'*
Bouchet's first extensive treatment of clerical abuses comes in the
Renards. Here he denounces the shortcomings of the Church with-
out having to take account of any international crisis, as he will need

to do in his poems of 1512. We have already seen that the *Renards* adopts a tone of prophetic fulmination against all its targets, of which the Church is only one. The chapter on clerical abuse is preceded by one on 'Les violateurs des franchises de l'eglise', in which Bouchet upholds the rights of the clergy whose corruption he will castigate in the next. The two chapters taken together reveal a less fundamentally anti-clerical Bouchet than one would suppose from the chapter on abuse by itself. A further complication is Bouchet's use of material from Chartier's *Livre de l'Espérance*. Chartier's work contains a bitter indictment of the Church as it appeared in the aftermath of the Great Schism and threatened by the Bohemian heresy, and its strictures still resounded powerfully in the early sixteenth century.

Bouchet's chapter on 'La dissolucion des gens d'eglise' begins with a reservation, but soon warms to the subject:

> Et pour y entrer selon ce que dit est dessus (sans vouloir aucunement parler des bons prestres et prelatz, que bien je congnoys qui vivent sainctement et selon leur ordre), Ezechiel, prophete de Dieu, anathematise les prelatz qui pour leur ambition ou volupté laissent devorer aux loups leurs brebis, qui sont leurs dyocesains ou paroissiens.[2]

This reference to Ezekiel 34 is used in the woodcut illustration of foxes, disguised as clerics, dallying with shepherdesses while wolves in the background carry off the sheep. Loosely following Chartier, Bouchet bases a stern development on Malachi 2 v.7, reminding priests that they are responsible for the sins of others, but he provides his own examples of how the clergy fail to carry out specific spiritual duties, such as saying masses for the dead:

> Et quant est du service ordonné estre fait par succession de temps, se delaisse et demeure en reste, en defraudant les fondateurs, les ames desquelz, qui sont en purgatoyre par vostre faulte tourmentées, cryent à Dieu vengeance contre vous.[3]

Here he adopts an attitude of complete acceptance towards an institution based on the doctrine of purgatory, which later reformers would attack, but he uses it as a powerful weapon against the clergy, above all by evoking the vision of souls tormented because of the clergy's failures.

Looking at the origins of the corruption of the Church he paraphrases Chartier. The Church was founded by Christ and built up by the apostles, who, like Christ, were humble. Their virtues were rewarded by temporal gifts to the Church, including the Donation of Constantine:

> En faveur desquelz et de leur saincteté, l'eglise a esté habondamment dotée par Constantin, empereur des Rommains, et par plusieurs autres roys, princes et seigneurs, cuydans que

leurs successeurs les ensuyvissent en saincteté de vie et perse-
verassent tousjours en la digne conversacion du clergié, affin
que necessité de vivre ne induysist et menast à peché les
ministres d'icelle, ou que leur simple povreté ne feust foulée
trop de legier par temporelle puissance, et non pour en user
ainsi follement qu'on fait à present. Constantin ne les autres
dessusditz ne entendirent oncques que les biens qu'ilz donnoient à l'eglise, les ministres d'icelle en guerroyiassent les
princes chrestiens, mais soubz l'esperance qu'ilz vesquissent
simplement, comme saint Pierre et les autres apostres et disciples de nostre seigneur.[4]

The Donation of Constantine is often referred to in contemporary
polemical writing because it could be seen as an early error in the
Church's history that led to corruption.[5] Some writers regret that
Constantine made the Donation because of the avarice that began to
flourish once the Church became rich. Some go further and, like
Dante, say that the Donation was invalid because Constantine had
no right to alienate control of the Empire. Further still went Lorenzo
Valla, who demonstrated conclusively in 1440 that on philological
grounds the Donation must be a forgery.[6] This latter view gained
ground only very slowly. Chartier, writing in 1428, does not of
course question the authenticity of the Donation, but he does raise
the question of whether it should have been made, saying how
much more reason Dante would now have to deplore Constantine's
gift. However, he concludes that the evil results in no way detract
from the excellence of the action, and he offers the justification that
is repeated by Bouchet here: Constantine intended that priests
should not be led into sin by poverty.[7]

It can be seen that Bouchet, who copies Chartier's very words in
most of the passage, nevertheless deviates from Chartier's thought.
He refrains from mentioning that anyone has ever criticised Constantine's action, and in no way does he criticise it or deplore it
himself. He uses it to show how much more iniquitous are those
who misuse the Emperor's gift in his day. Only by its reference to
making war on Christian princes is the passage specifically aimed at
the Pope. Bouchet is less questioning of the Church's institutions
than Chartier, but this makes him all the more bitter about the
ministers of the Church who misuse or fail to conform to those
institutions. He continues with a list of the clergy's misdeeds, compiled by himself without reference to Chartier, showing how
Church goods are now spent on banquets, building and bastards.[8]

Another similar treatment of material from Chartier occurs in his
section on the compulsory celibacy of the clergy:

₵ Du veu de chasteté fait par l'eglise latine.

   Que diray-je plus, fors que le statut fait en l'eglise latine, par
lequel l'ordre de mariage fut separé d'avec l'ordre de prestrise,

soubz couleur de chasteté et mundicité, donna lieu à concubinaige et vie deshonneste et dissolue, et furent les espousailles
laissées pour prendre l'alliance de lubricité et generacion ille-
gitime.[9]

This aggressive opening uses the words of Chartier. But Bouchet
proceeds to depart from Chartier's text and greatly to reduce its
import:

A quoy toutesfois je me (*sic*) vueil insister que la constitucion
ne soit raisonnable et divinement faicte. Mais par la faulte des
superieurs a fait icelle constitucion le peché de luxure si commun entre les hommes et femmes, qu'ilz en ont perdu toute
honte et vergongne. Et au temps qui court l'aage de douze ans
jusques à quatre vingtz n'en est point excepté. Et ce par faulte
d'en estre corrigez par les prestres, qui entretiennent leurs
concubines à pot et à feu notoirement, et tiennent estat de
concubinaige aussi hardyement comme les gens laiz font l'estat
de mariage.

Qui est cause de ces abuz fors les pralatz, qui reçoyvent à
ordre de prestrise cuysiniers, palefreniers, torcheculz de chevaulx, bastardz et gensdarmes, qui à paine sçavent lyre leur
nom?[10]

Celibacy was another subject often raised in polemic concerning
reformation. The clergy were as immoral as they were avaricious;
compulsory celibacy could be viewed as a reversible mistake. It was
known that it had been enforced relatively late in the history of the
Church and many said that the rule should be abandoned.[11] Chartier was of the generation that had seen Cardinal Zabarella declare
at the Council of Constance that priests should be allowed to marry,
and the passage on celibacy in the *Livre de l'Espérance* leaves little
doubt that Chartier too thought that celibacy should cease to be
compulsory.[12] But Bouchet, while using the strongest language to
deplore the immorality of priests, goes out of his way to defend the
institution and blame the evil results on prelates. The answer to the
keeping of concubines should not be to permit marriage but to
improve recruitment to the priesthood—the same blend of respect
for the institution and vituperation against bad administration of
that institution that we saw in the case of the Donation of Constantine.

His concern with abuse is best seen in a long passage quite
independent of Chartier in which he enumerates some of the
simoniacal practices commonly employed in the collation of benefices; this reveals considerable technical knowledge. Abuses that he
describes include a collator 'freely' conferring one benefice on someone who has made over two small ones to him; buying off a competitor for a benefice under the fiction of reimbursing him for the
expenses of his candidature; keeping hold of a benefice that ought

to be filled in order to use it for bargaining in obtaining a bishopric.[13]
Again, however, we see the balancing respect in his final warnings:
the priests' abuses may cause the Church to be persecuted, but this
does not mean that anyone has the right to persecute the Church:
'Telle offense suffiroit à confondre royaulmes et seigneuries'.[14]
Finally, he offers a solution:

> Mais si le seigneur a puissance, se evertue de y procurer si
> bonne reformacion que Dieu s'en contente, et que chascun se
> retire à son pasturaige.[15]

How a reform was to be brought about and who was to effect it was
another very controversial question, and one that was bound up
with conciliarism. Here Bouchet assumes that the temporal lord has
some role to play, but quite what that role is remains unclear. At the
time when Bouchet was writing, the most obvious practical moves
towards reformation were those concerning monasteries. Renaudet
narrates the sometimes very violent attempts to impose reform on
Paris houses at the beginning of the century.[16] Bouchet mentions
these—in a chapter on hypocrisy:

> O reformation encommencée à faire en la principaulte ville de
> France, bien tost tu es rapaisée: que n'as tu perseveré jusques à
> l'amendement de toutes les religions? qui t'a suffoquée ou
> arrestée? Que n'as tu visité tous les conventz, dont les aucuns
> sont tant desordonnez que l'air en put et le ciel en murmure? Je
> croy, puis que tu es si tost precipitée, que ton fondement estoit
> sur ypocrisie et vaine gloire. Si j'en parle si aigrement je suis à
> excuser, car je sçay veritablement que nous ne prouffiterons en
> bien, jusques à ce que tous les estatz soient refformez, depuis le
> plus petit jusques au plus grant.[17]

Like other writers we shall refer to, Bouchet blames the reformers,
but unlike the others he blames them because they failed; for this
reason alone he is disposed to accuse them of hypocrisy.

Disregarding the rhetoric, the forceful vocabulary, the display of
personal emotion that he brings to every topic in the book, this last
passage in particular and the detailed examples of simoniacal practices leave one with the impression that Bouchet is expressing a
serious concern with the need for reformation in the Church, in the
sense of a return to the proper enforcement of existing rules.

b) *The War between Louis XII and Julius II*
We may now move on to the period 1510–13, when France found
herself at war with the Pope. Julius II, having succeeded in quelling
Venice, was now ready to make peace with her and to turn his
attention to driving the French out of Milan and the rest of Italy.

Louis XII was obliged to use theological as well as military
weapons.[18] Ever since the Great Schism and the development of
conciliarism the threat to call a council and perhaps to depose the

Pope was a favourite royal move.[19] Clearly the religious difficulty of taking up arms against the Head of the Church was alleviated if the Pope could be considered subordinate to a General Council, and further reduced if he could be proved unworthy in himself, even liable to be deposed. Conciliarists could look back to the decrees *Haec Sancta* and *Frequens,* promulgated at the Council of Constance and reaffirmed at the Council of Basle. These decrees assert that when in session the General Council takes precedence over the Pope, and that General Councils should be summoned at regular intervals and also for special purposes that particularly require the council's superior powers, namely schism, heresy, and reform of abuse in the Church.[20] This last point helps to explain why the need for reform is a topic that crops up so frequently in the polemic against Julius II; apart from its emotive value in propaganda it is a good conciliarist argument. A writer may call for a council because he wants to see reformation, but he may equally call for reformation because he wants a council. Conciliarism was strong in France, having become a characteristic tenet of Gallicanism,[21] particularly since the promulgation of the Pragmatic Sanction of Bourges by Charles VII in 1438.[22] This consisted of decrees regulating the French Church and limiting the power of the Pope within it. It incorporated the decrees from the Council of Basle declaring the supremacy of councils. Ever since 1438 successive Popes had tried to have the Pragmatic Sanction quashed, but to the Gallican clergy and the University of Paris it represented the embodiment of their liberties.

Louis' first step was to call an assembly of jurists at Lyons, then a Council of the Gallican Church at Tours in 1510. As we have seen, Bouchet was in Tours at the time. The council supported the King's intention to defend his domains, even against the head of the Church. Louis then declared that he would call a General Council to meet at Pisa on 1 September 1511. Julius II, who was not easily scared, declared that he himself was going to call a council to meet at the Lateran Church in Rome at Easter 1512.

Three main types of polemical writing emerged in France at this time, some of it directly instigated by Louis XII. First there was the specifically theological polemic conducted in Latin. Louis demanded that his Faculty of Theology in Paris should refute the anticonciliar work which Cajetan directed against the Council of Pisa; Jacques Almain obliged, developing earlier French ecclesiology into a defence of the French conciliar position.[23] But Louis did not only need to convince the theologians; he also needed to convince his people that war with Rome was legitimate. So a second type of polemic is written in the vernacular, printed, and plainly intended as persuasive propaganda. Lemaire and Gringore are the main exponents in, for example, the *Traité des schismes et des conciles de l'eglise* and the *Chasse du cerf des cerfz*. A third type of writing was indulged in by nearly all the outstanding poets of the period and seems more courtly in intention, designed primarily to ingratiate the author with the King, although it is not so different in kind from the propaganda just mentioned that it could not have served as such if more widely broadcast. This is the body of poems about the war which survive only in manuscript. The work of Jean Marot, Jean d'Auton and some of Lemaire's work comes into this category.[24] Though no doubt widely disseminated among courtiers and very stirring for the soldier-nobles who read them, it is difficult to regard them as propaganda. Because of his provincial setting and fringe connection with the court, Bouchet's two contributions fall somewhere between these last two categories; both his poems were printed, and were therefore more public than court poetry, but there is no indication that they were commissioned as propaganda. Both owe something to the court polemical poems of Jean d'Auton; there can be little doubt that d'Auton encouraged Bouchet to write them and probably Bouchet had hopes of winning royal favour by so doing.

c) *The Response of d'Auton, Lemaire and Gringore*

Bouchet's two poems must be compared with some of the other vernacular writing on the war. For this purpose, we may consider the work of three writers: first of all the courtier Jean d'Auton, whose work certainly influenced Bouchet, secondly the two major polemicists of the war, Lemaire and Gringore. This brief examination of their work will take account of what these writers had to say about reformation when they were not inspired by a war with the Pope.

Jean d'Auton was for a time official court historiographer.[25] His *Chroniques* end in the year 1507, but he continued to write poetry for Louis xii until about 1512. He wrote little that we know of after that date, and seems to have retired to the monastery of Angle-sur-Anglin of which Louis had made him abbot. Neither of the two poems that Bouchet imitates was printed. *L'Epistre du preux Hector*, written probably in August 1511, is primarily concerned with celebrating Louis' victories in Italy, but it contains passages attacking the Pope for taking up arms against Christians, particularly against the Most Christian King who had restored some of his domains to him.[26] *L'Epistre elegiaque par l'Eglise millitante*, composed in about March 1512 has more to say about the Pope, but still something like a quarter of the poem's 498 lines are devoted to praising Louis' victories.[27] Like the previous *épître*, this is addressed to Louis and to him the Church bewails her many sorrows. The two themes developed are the corruption of the clergy and the guilt of the Pope in the present war. To take as an example a motif we have already encountered, d'Auton raises the subject of the Donation of Constantine. Constantine is mentioned among defenders of the Church, and the Donation is praised, although d'Auton adds that someone blamed the Emperor's liberality even in his time, when religion was well observed. What would the critic say now? He would be quite right to complain, given the disorder of the clergy. That critic predicted, truly, that the Donation would prove a poison:

    Dont mes suppos sont ores tous enflez
    En avarice et d'orgueil boussouflez.[28]

Nevertheless, Constantine's intention was good and his soul is now in paradise.

This treatment of the Donation is rather reminiscent of Chartier's and may be inspired by it. The validity and excellence of Constantine's act is accepted, but the prophecy that it would be a poison shows how regrettable was that act; this legend of contemporary prophecy is actually more impressive than the parallel motif used by Chartier, who simply says that Dante described the Donation as a poison.[29] This passage, with its vision of a clergy swollen with pride and avarice, shows how the need for reformation can be used as indirect propaganda for a King who had called a General Council supposedly to reform the Church and perhaps to depose the Pope. D'Auton goes on to hint that Julius had been elected by simony, which could make his election invalid. Throughout the poem, the abuses in the Church are blamed on the prelates and above all the Pope; the King is seen as having the right and power to correct this state of affairs. But beyond this d'Auton does not go; he does not even explicitly refer to the King's Council. He seems to be first and foremost a court poet reproducing some of the propaganda in the air at the court. The poems are intended to please the King. In his other works, he has little to say about reform, although in his *Chroniques* he records some of the monastic reforms in Paris, fairly impartially, but certainly with no great approval: of one reforming episode he says: 'dont est plus cler que lumiere que ce qu'ilz ont faict ne merite nom de correpcion mais de folye et crudelité'.[30] He himself eventually settled down to a very regular and saintly monastic life, if Bouchet is to be believed.[31]

Lemaire de Belges was a far more militant propagandist. He was trying to attach himself to the French court, and certainly rendered the King a striking service with his *Traicté des schismes et des concilles de l'eglise* of May 1511 which sold in large numbers.[32] His answer to d'Auton, *L'Epistre du roy à Hector de Troye* is a more court-centred piece of flattery as are two other manuscript fragments.[33] But the *Traicté* is true propaganda. It sets out to demonstrate historically that schisms have almost always been caused by Popes and healed by councils, particularly Gallican councils. He gives an account of 23 past schisms and quotes prophecies to show that a terrible 24th schism, yet to come, will herald the coming of Antichrist.[34] The book provides numerous examples of thoroughly unworthy Popes; many of Platina's most damaging stories are retold with considerable verve; by contrast the King of France and where possible the Emperor as well are placed in a good light. The book produces its effect by such indirect means rather than by clear assertion of anti-papal or pro-conciliar dogma. He says that Popes hate councils, and mentions that some people debate whether councils are superior to the Pope or the Pope to councils. He does not expound the point further, but merely to raise the question so clearly in a vernacular text is unusual and effective in casting doubt on papal authority. He devotes considerable space to the Donation of Constantine. According to him, it was the downfall of the papacy. Before it there were 33 martyr popes, since then there have been none, and the clergy have been corrupted by it, with the result that Islam has flourished. A powerful indictment indeed. Lemaire shows himself a brilliant propagandist; suggestion is his weapon. He puts the principal blame on the Pope of the time, Silvester; he mentions the view that the Donation was diabolically inspired, telling the story that a devil was heard to say 'Hodie venenum in ecclesia seminavi' (although disclaiming any guarantee that the story was true). At the same time, he mentions the view that the Donation of the city of Rome was invalid and crowns the discussion by saying that Valla had claimed that the Donation was, in any case, a forgery. Lemaire piously claims that he himself does not know the truth of the matter and will abide by 'la plus saine opinion'.[35] But again, simply raising the point in a vernacular work is sufficiently effective. In the same way, he says in the introduction that three things in particular have harmed the Church: ambition, the mother of avarice; failure to hold general councils; the compulsory celibacy of priests of the Latin Church. He himself does not develop the theme of celibacy; instead he quotes the passage from Chartier which Bouchet had used.[36] However, he goes on to show that it is uncertain when celibacy became compulsory, and to quote a scurrilous rhyme about one of the Popes responsible.[37] The question of celibacy is yet another weapon in a thorough assault on the papacy. The layman is led to the conciliar point of view for practical rather than theological reasons.

Lemaire had not previously in his writing shown much interest in clerical abuse. Gringore, on the other hand, had treated the subject at length in the *Folles Entreprises* of 1505, of which the first part deals with the nobility and the second with the Church.[38] Here he deals vigorously with the abuses arising from avarice, dispensations, pluralism and so on, but interestingly he also attacks the recent monastic reforms on the grounds that the reformers are bigots and hypocrites, no better than those whom they seek to reform, and that the reforms were carried out with violence.[39] He attacks what he calls 'bibliennes', women who read the Bible and expound it wrong-ly.[40] Thus, while deploring clerical abuse, he seems suspicious of practical attempts to reform the clergy. He makes no mention at all of sensitive issues like the Donation of Constantine or the compul-sory celibacy of the clergy. This is in line with the theological teach-ing of some of the stories in *Les Fantasies de Mère Sotte* of 1516.[41] It is not surprising to find him among the earliest writers in French to attack Luther.[42]

But a conservative attitude to religious questions is quite compat-ible with Gallicanism—witness the Sorbonne—and so in *Les Abuz du monde* of 1509, there is a section in praise of the Pragmatic Sanction.[43] Once the war with the Pope began, Gringore attacked Julius II in several works, very probably at the instigation of Louis XII. Two poems were printed in 1510 and 1511, and a play was performed in the *Halles* in Paris on Shrove Tuesday 1512.[44] In all these works, Gringore attacks the person of Julius II as distinct from the papacy. In *La Chasse du Cerf des Cerfs*, Julius is made ridiculous as the stag, hunted by the 'francs veneurs', the French. In *L'Espoir de Paix*, Julius is compared unfavourably with earlier virtuous Popes—a rather different approach from that of Lemaire. Gringore presents Louis as not being at war with the Church; instead he is God's chosen instrument for punishing wrong-doers. Finally, in the *sotie* put on for the entertainment of the people of Paris, *Mère Sotte* masquerades as Mother Church; she want to make war on the *Prince des Sotz* in order to obtain temporal as well as spiritual power. The *Prince* is appalled at the thought of going to war with the Church, but his problem is solved when *Mère Sotte* is unmasked. Once again, the propaganda stresses the distinction between the Church and the present, possibly false, Pope. The *Moralité* which accompanies the *sotie* presents Julius as *l'Homme obstiné*, accompanied by *Symonie* and *Ypocrisie*. Gringore's main aim throughout these works is to render Julius II an object of scorn and mockery.

Although in general all of these writers deplore the abuses in the Church and support the King, there are clear differences between them. D'Auton writes as a Court poet seeking to please the King: he has little to say about reform. Lemaire seems more interested in calling for a crusade than for reform, but he has every appearance of being as anti-clerical as he is pro-monarchical. Certainly he raises radical questions about the Church, considering that he is writing in the vernacular. Gringore, on the other hand, is much more conser-vative, respectful to the institution while attacking an individual unworthy Pope and the abuses arising from the failure to observe Canon Law.

d) *Bouchet's 'Déploration de l'Eglise', May 1512,*
   and the 'Epître d'Henri', September 1512

It seemed possible to discern in the *Renards* a real concern for the
reform of the Church. Such a preoccupation is implicit in Bouchet's
choice of form for his first intervention in the propaganda war. We
have already noted its affinities with his other moral works and in
particular its use of authorities quoted in dense marginalia, a device
fairly common in moral works but not used by other writers in the
polemics of 1510–13.

There are many indications that Bouchet's main interest was
internal abuse in the Church. First, because such a large proportion
of the *Déploration* is devoted to the subject in comparison with the
part dealing with the current political situation. The lament itself,
1,092 lines long, does not touch on the war with the Pope before line
742.

Secondly, Bouchet is comparatively late and lukewarm in his
support of Louis XII. The poem appears late in the war; by the time
it was published, both the Council of Pisa and the Lateran Council
had assembled. D'Auton must have played some role in Bouchet's
decision to publish a poem; the *Déploration* imitates the concept of
the *Epître élégiaque*. No doubt they both hoped that Louis would
reward Bouchet's efforts. But if this was Bouchet's intention he
should perhaps have been more at pains to flatter.

In the first part of the poem, the Church complains of the simony,
avarice and ambition of churchmen. Simony is the root cause of her
sorrow. It is the great here who are principally attacked as Bouchet
lists the abuses resulting from simony: the children of the rich are
given benefices, benefices are sold to men of bad character while
learned men are not only unprovided for, but persecuted; secular
powers govern appointments, elections go by the board, the greatest in the Church are governed by avarice. Only the common people
are truly faithful to the Church; clergy, university and nobility all
fail her.

These complaints are not new, but this is not to say that he did not
believe them to be true. When Bouchet speaks with such eloquence
of the sufferings of virtuous men deprived of benefices, he may
have the recent case of a disputed election to the bishopric of
Poitiers in mind:[45]

Las, on souloit querir gens de vertuz	Abstulit omnes magnificos
Sans regarder s'ilz estoient (gens) bien vestuz	meos de medio mei; vocavit
Pour estre chiefz de moy, dolente eglise,	adversum me
S'ilz y vienent à present sont bastuz	tempus: ut
Et par procès durement combatuz	contereret
C'est la façon, la coustume et la guise . . .[46]	electos meos. Tren. i.

The effect of the marginal texts is to sharpen the criticism for those who know Latin:

Pour ung courtault on baille ung benefice,
Pour ung baisier ou aultre malefice
Quelque champis aura ung evesché;
Pour cent escutz quelque meschant novice
Plain de luxure et de tout autre vice
De dignitez sera tout empesché.[47]

Sola promissio
dandi temporale
per spirituali
indicit symoniam.
C. Nobis, C.
veniens de
symo. C. ii de
confes.

The Church now proceeds to remind all ranks of their duties—King, holders of benefices, university men, pluralists, prelates, building up to a crescendo of denunciation of ambition and avarice amongst the highest before abruptly turning to the balancing theme of the dignity of priests.[48] The remarkable point here is that in a poem published at this moment, and referring to the war with the Pope, the King should receive any share of the criticism. The six stanzas addressed to the King early in the poem are in many ways complimentary, but not unequivocally so. Once again, the marginalia sharpen the point.

Mais on m'a dit qu'ung grant tas de flateurs,
Des sainctes loix faulx prevaricateurs,
Par chascun jour vous donnent à entendre
Que les roys sont de mes biens protecteurs,
Et que jadis furent mes fondateurs.
Il est tout vray, je n'y veulx point contendre.
Ilz dient oultre, que par ce povez prendre
Benefices, et les distribuer.
Vous ne debvez ce droit attribuer
(Qui est divin) à puissance mondaine;
Dieu m'a voulu sur vous constituer
Et en son lieu ça bas substituer,
Doubter n'en fault, la chose est bien certaine.[49]

A zelantibus
te absconde
consilium
Eccle.xxviii c
Popule meus
qui te beatum
dicunt, ipsi te
decipiunt
Isaie. 3.c
Ad imperatores
palatia pertinent:
ad sacerdotes
ecclesie xxiii.q
viii.c convenior
Reddite quae
sunt Cesaris
Cesari et Dei Deo
Mathei xxii

Admittedly the King is subsequently told that he may intervene to ensure that Canon Law is enforced and that virtuous men are given benefices. But he must not reward his soldiers with church livings. All in all, given this particular context, Bouchet is surprisingly critical of the King, and one is again led to the conclusion that he was genuinely concerned with abuses and the need for reform.

This conclusion is supported by the rather unusual and outspoken nature of some of his criticisms in the ensuing sections. As well as saying that virtuous men are persecuted within the Church, he claims that critics are called heretics; new 'confrairies' are set up in order to fleece the common people; confessors wheedle endowments out of penitents and even advise them to disinherit their children; the Gospel advises priests to possess nothing:

Mais le vray texte on pretend exceder,
Interpretant de Jesus la parolle.[50]

When at last he arrives at the Church's exterior persecutions, he begins with 10 stanzas addressed to the Pope. There is no satirical invective here, but the same stern and melancholy reminding of duty which dominates the rest of the poem. The main criticism is that the Pope is going to war with Christians whom he ought to regard as his children. His care ought to be the urgent reformation of abuse, not the accumulation of temporal goods. He should unite with the Christian kings and call a council to reform the Church and then launch a crusade against the Infidel. Here too the marginalia add bite to the criticism; Biblical texts like Matthew 23 v.11 ('But he that is greatest among you shall be your servant') and the Antichrist prophecy from Daniel 9 v.27 combine with passages from Canon Law insisting that fighting must be left to temporal powers and reminding the Pope that the papacy was founded and maintained for the purpose of caring for Christ's flock. Certainly the passage is a devastating denunciation of the Pope's warmongering and avarice. But when one considers that he is writing for a French audience which has read Gringore and Lemaire it is mild stuff as polemic. Themes used by other writers are attenuated:

N'acquerez point les reproches infames
D'ambicion, pour mieulx contregarder
Ce que voulut Constantin vous garder
Voire donner, qui est honneur mondain,
Mais seulement vous plaise regarder
Au charge et faix, sans plus y retarder,
Que vous avez du roy tressouverain.[51]

And in telling the Pope to call a council, Bouchet would seem to be suggesting support for the Lateran Council—he is either very out of touch or very doubtful indeed about the continuing justification for the Council of Pisa.

Bouchet then proceeds to address all Christian kings; he tells them to ally themselves with the Emperor, stop fighting, make the Pope call a council to reform the Church, and then launch a crusade. He reminds them of the League of Cambrai of 1508 which had united the Pope and all the kings against Venice. The peace sworn then is in jeopardy, because although the King of France and the Emperor want to abide by it, the devil has undermined the head of the enterprise and pleased the Turk-loving Venetians by spreading the rumour that the Church's lands were being attacked.[52] With this suggestion that the Pope has been misled by the guile of the devil, the patriotism at last seems more rousing, and the poem ends with a panegyric of Louis xii.

When one considers the other polemics which Louis xii's subjects

had been able to read, Bouchet's support for Louis is remarkably
feeble. It is surprising to find even a hint of criticism of the King in a
poem written at this moment and about the war with the Pope.
Such criticism suits the method of the moral writer rather than the
polemicist. It does not seem likely that Bouchet wished to support
the Council of Pisa. Respect for the Church is made abundantly
clear in the poem, and only occasionally does he criticise what
might be regarded as Church use as opposed to abuse. The *Déploration* is only superficially Gallican in sympathy, but it constitutes a
solemn plea for reform of abuse in the Church.

Bouchet's second contribution in September 1512 suggests a certain change of heart. In the *Epître d'Henri* we find praise of Louis XII
and denunciation of Julius II combined in a way much more reminiscent of d'Auton in particular. It may have been pointed out to
Bouchet that he was not going the best way about finding favour at
court. But the change in the political situation in the course of 1512
must have been the decisive factor. The full strength of the Pope's
Holy League against France became apparent. The Swiss attacked
French possessions in Italy with the support of the Emperor, whose
adherence to the League was plainly imminent. In August, France
was placed under an Interdict. And, providing the threat nearest
home, Henry VIII of England had joined the League and an inva-
sion from Calais was expected.

Bouchet's poem is an attack on the English. In the *Epistre envoyée
des Champs Elisées au Roy Henry d'Engleterre à present regnant audit
royaulme*,[53] the late Henry VII writes to his son Henry VIII to tell him
that he must on no account be so ungrateful as to make war on the
King of France, considering that the French had helped Henry VII
to become king. Henry VIII will have the worst of it and may lose
his crown, given the celebrated rebelliousness of the English. Thereafter, most of the poem is taken up with demonstrating the turbu-
lence of the English and with proving that they have no claim to any
land in France. Only at the very end does Bouchet return to the
current war, and as he attacks Julius II, abuses in the Church are
used as a ploy in the polemic.

> Par quel moyen sont baillez benefices?
> Par quel moyen sont prestres ordonnés?
> Par quel moyen sont sacremens donnés?
> Dis moy quelle est d'aulcuns prestres la vie?
> Sans en mentir ne parler par envie
> Dont vient ce mal et terrible meschief,
> For seulement de la coulpe du chief,
> Qui deust donner exemple de bien vivre?[54]

The Pope is compared to Nero, and in the lines:

> Je dis Pape, je ne sçay par quel sort,
> Car il ne fait ce que deust faire ung pape,[55]

there seems to be a thought now that perhaps Julius is no true Pope. Louis' policy is vigorously defended: he wishes to 'faire faire . . . au dict pape, comme il doit, ung concile', and to 'reduire le Pape à charité'.[56] But Julius is scared of a council:

Ledit Pape, qui devoit procurer
Cestuy grand bien, se print à murmurer
Et à penser comme il fut mys au syège
Et que on prend les fins regnards au piège;
Quoy congnoissant, sans plus se informer
Et qu'on pourroit lui-mesmes reformer,
Pour ce empescher . . .[57]

he has claimed that Louis is attacking the Church.

Thus in this poem Bouchet is more like d'Auton and Gringore in his denunciation of the present unworthy incumbent of the Holy See, complete with the hints that his election was invalid. But it should be noted that this denunciation is only a small part of a poem which is largely taken up with anti-English rather than anti-papal propaganda.

The issues raised by the propaganda war of 1510–13 involved conciliarism and Gallicanism as well as the call for reform. These writings do not suggest that Bouchet was an eager conciliarist who wanted to see the council set above the Pope. He says that a council should take place to reform the Church, but even in his most anti-papal passage he says that the Pope should call the council. His most serious attacks on the Pope are in any case eventually combined with a hint that the present holder of the office was no true Pope. Bouchet's references to Julius II in later years tend to suggest that this was indeed his belief.[58]

Nor does he seem to have much sympathy with the clerical Gallicans, the French clergy, particularly represented by the Sorbonne, who invoked the ancient privileges of the French Church to be independent of Pope and King alike. On the only occasion in these works when Bouchet refers to the Pragmatic Sanction he quotes it not on councils but on the provision which gave special privileges to graduates seeking benefices, and then uses this against the University—now, he says, people study with one eye on the resultant advantages.[59] He thus uses the University's favourite text as a stick with which to beat it. Looking forward a little, the Concordat of 1516 was a disaster for clerical Gallicanism, overthrowing the Pragmatic Sanction and dividing the power over the French Church between the King and the Pope. Bouchet showed no sympathy, condemning the resultant disturbance at the University of Paris:

qui fut chose scandaleuse et non tollerable, mesmement en cité si fameuse où est la court de Parlement, à laquelle appartient reprimer telles factions et murmures.[60]

Gallicanism and conciliarism are not a major concern in Bouchet's writing. But he does on the other hand emerge as very eager for reform of the Church, reform from the top down—although admittedly reform in the sense of a return to original rules and standards.

How would a man so critical of the powerful in the Church react to the criticisms of Luther?

2
After 1520

a) *The Spread of Heresy*
It is not surprising that Bouchet should condemn Luther. What is surprising, however, is the terms in which he originally does so. His earliest reference to Luther—a very early one indeed in French[61]—comes in the *Annales* of 1524 in an entry for 1517 when he is speaking of a projected crusade:

> Et pour ce faire, le pape Leon octroia depuis au Roy de France ung pardon general, tel comme le Jubilé, à ceulx qui se croiseroient pour aller en ladicte armée, ou bailleroient certaine somme de deniers pour y frayer, qui fut cause de plusieurs grans abuz commis par aucuns ambicieux et avaricieux prescheurs, qui soubz umbre dudict pardon donnerent occasion à plusieurs laiz de amasser de grans deniers, dont plusieurs Docteurs et autres notables personnages furent treffort scandalisez. Et parce que maistre Martin Luter, du pays de Alemaigne (homme de grant esprit de l'ordre des Augustins) prescha et escripvit quelque opuscule au contraire dudict Pardon, en calumpniant l'auctorité de nostre sainct pere le Pape, fut declairé herese, et excommunié par ledict pape Leon. En hayne de laquelle censure, dont il appella *ad futurum consilium*, le pauvre et imprudent Luter feit ung opuscule intitullé *De captivitate babilonica*, où il y a inseré plusieurs grans erreurs et heresies, que depuis il s'est efforcé soustenir par autres euvres, en voulant confundre l'auctorité et ierarchie de l'eglise militante et la pluspart des sept Sacremens. Esquelles folles oppinions plusieurs personnes latines, qui ont seulement veu et estudié le texte des evangiles et epistres, ont adheré, voires dilaté lesdictes erreurs par blaphemes que je ne ouseroie escripre, contre l'honneur que nous doyvons porter à la vierge Marie, mere de Jesucrist nostre saulveur et redempteur, et les saincts et sainctes, et dont les bons crestiens doyvent avoir aux yeulx les larmes.[62]

This account reveals an initial sympathy, however quickly suppressed. A series of graver and graver disasters are all shown to stem from one evil: the General Pardon. Bouchet's dislike of the sale of pardons is evident elsewhere in his work.[63] We may compare Bouchet's comments on 'le pauvre et imprudent Luther', 'homme de grand esprit' with the entries in the *Mer des Croniques*:

> En ce temps-là le deable, ennemy des povres humains, qui point ne dort, suscita es parties aquilonales au duché de Saxe ung antechrist nommé Lutel, c'est à dire bœux, lequel de sa damnée secte a esmeu et envenimé* presque toute la chrestienté . . .[64]

> En ce temps-là, du Grant Luthel filz de Pluton infernal les disciples et ministres par nombre infiny descendirent des haultes fins des Allemaignes . . .[65]

As well as using more restrained language, Bouchet's accounts give much more information—not only that Luther attacked the sacraments but, more significantly that he did not deny all of them. It is not impossible that Bouchet had read *De Captivitate babylonica*.

Certainly any sympathy which Bouchet may have had initially was destroyed as Luther rapidly went too far. When this account was published, Bouchet was probably just beginning to realise the threat presented by the spread of Lutheran ideas.[66] It is interesting to note that Bouchet also records with disapproval the activities of 'personnes latines' who have only read the text of the Gospels and Epistles and who are opposed to the cult of saints and of the Virgin. Whom does he mean? Although in this form the ideas are a travesty of the aims of Lefèvre or of Erasmus and their followers, it is difficult to see who is being referred to if not the Meaux group or disciples of Erasmus. The combination of learning, concentration on the text of scripture and dislike of the cult of the Virgin and saints seems to point in that direction and the accusation echoes theologians' descriptions of the innovators.[67] Lefèvre's translation of the New Testament had appeared in 1522–23, and Erasmus had already published some of his more flippant colloquies about the cult of saints.[68] At this period, Bouchet was already interested in providing religious instruction for the unlearned, and he had translated one or two snippets from the liturgy of the Mass,[69] but this passage suggests that he did not approve of the aims of the Meaux group, a conclusion supported by later evidence, as we shall see.

All subsequent references to Luther in later editions of the *Annales* and elsewhere are condemnatory, but they also reveal that Bouchet was deeply interested in the heresy. He cannot give free rein to this interest for fear of spreading the heresy; after recording that the Sorbonne had condemned a number of propositions from Luther, he says:

> Je les eusse cy inserées, mais les clercs les entendent, et les simples gens se passeront bien d'en avoir lecture, car plus pourroient avoir de dommage en les oyant lire que de profit.[70]

He does, however, give some account of them in such a way as to render them patently shocking: Luther seeks to destroy the monarchy of the Church and the power of the Pope, to abolish some of the sacraments including auricular confession, to allow all Christian people the power to consecrate, to prohibit prayer to saints, to destroy all those things instituted by Popes and councils such as fasting and monasticism.

In nine stanzas about the heresy in the revised *Déploration* of 1525, he again avoids too much precision about the errors but does give some impression of them. Here in addition to those heresies mentioned above, he refers to the rejection of the doctrine of purgatory and the denial of the efficacy of good works; he also touches on Luther's doctrines of justification by faith and Christian liberty. The heretics are characterised by the vanity with which they attack the Church and claim to interpret the Gospel for themselves, also by their wicked lives—liberty means licence to these heretics, and they are unwilling to perform good works. Once again he mentions people who might be humanist evangelicals—scholars who encourage the heresy, who neglect the 'saincts docteurs' and read only 'les textes', and even these 'au depourveu'.[71]

This mixture of interest in heresy and fear of spreading it is evident in long accounts of the Diet of Augsburg and the Diet of Ratisbon given in the *Annales*. Bouchet reproduces a contemporary pamphlet describing the meeting between the Emperor and the Lutherans in Augsburg in 1530, but he omits the list of thirteen articles drawn from the Augsburg confession on which the Lutherans could not be moved; he says that he does not want to lead the simple astray.[72] A similar long account of the Diet of Ratisbon, 1541, draws on more than one source. Bouchet must, for instance, have referred to a copy of the Ratisbon Book, which was produced by the Catholics with the hope of obtaining Protestant agreement. The evidence suggests that he may have read it in Calvin's edition.[73] Thus it is clear that Bouchet was greatly interested in the negotiations with the Protestants, and that he knew far more about Protestantism than he was prepared to pass on to the less well educated for fear of spreading the poison.

He was all the more wary of the risk of spreading the heresy because he recognised its attractions. This is obvious from many of his comments. After giving his brief summary of the Lutheran heresies condemned by the Sorbonne, he concludes that the heretics are

> tendans par ces moyens fort cautement attraire les simples personnes à vivre à leur volonté et subsecutivement à devier de la Foy, non apparemment, mais soubs couverture de bien.[74]

So, however much he claims that Lutheranism appeals to people who want licence for bad behaviour, he recognises that the initial appeal is to good impulses. Similarly in the 1525 *Déploration* he speaks of 'doulces controverses' and of heretics 'faignant à Jesus les actraire'.[75] After his account of Augsburg he excuses himself for including it in the *Annales d'Acquitaine* by saying that the people of

Aquitaine, who are not as yet stained by Lutheran errors, may pray for God's grace to shun this diabolical sect which preaches evil:

> toutesfois couvertes et succrées de la doulceur Evangelicque, par fauces et controuvées expositions.[76]

It is appealing just because it manipulates the Gospel which cannot but be attractive. Bouchet's recognition of this great danger was one of the factors which led him to compose the *Triomphes de la noble et amoureuse dame* in 1530:

> . . . pour distraire femmes et filles de plus lire la translacion en françoys du vieil et nouveau testament, qui est chose dangereuse à lire en plusieurs passaiges scelon la seulle lectre, et certains petiz traictez d'aucuns Alemans heretiques traduictz de latin en françoys, esquelz soubz la doulceur de la doctrine evangelique sont plusieurs erreurs interposées trop scandaleuses et pernicieuses en la crestienté.[77]

Again, the notion of 'douceur évangélique' which makes the heresy so subtly pernicious. And here again the propaganda of German heretics is lumped together with the productions of French evangelicals. Bouchet is specifically rejecting the aims of Lefèvre and the Meaux group by trying to divert the uneducated from reading unglossed translations of the Bible.

Doubtless as a result of the publication of the *Triomphes*, Bouchet became known as a campaigner against heresy. This is particularly evident in some of the *Epîtres Familières* of the 1530s. The correspondence with Jacques d'Anglure (*Eps* 111, 112, and 113, written *c*.1538) shows that d'Anglure viewed him in this light.[78] It was no doubt partly for this reason that François Sagon approached Bouchet in the hope that he would write against Marot and condemn Germain Colin Bucher for his interventions in the affair.[79] As we know, Bouchet declined to do so, and he dodges the question of Marot's heresy as much as possible in his reply to Sagon (*Ep. Fam.* 110). In an *épître* to Jacques Le Lieur he says:

> Mais (las) Marot, pour cuider hault voller
> Et les secretz d'Evangile accoller
> Et repugner aux preceptz de l'Eglise
> S'est par sa faulte en tresgrant peine mise;
> Il me desplaist le veoir infortuné
> Parce qu'il est un vray Poete né.[80]

In this fascinating set of letters, Bouchet seems torn between boundless admiration for Marot's poetry and the knowledge that Marot has fallen into heresy. In this *épître* he regretfully acknowledges his guilt, although without any of the vituperation which characterised the *Querelle* between Marot and Sagon and their supporters. Much less well known is his epitaph for Marot, *Gén. Ep.* 100, printed in 1545—a year after the writer had died, again in exile because of his religious opinions:

Epitaphe en dialogue de Clement Marot, qui deceda
l'an mil cinq cent quarante quatre.
Il est mort.—Qui?—Un poete françois,
Clement Marot.—Non est, il dort soubz terre.—
On ne l'oyt plus.—Tous les jours tu le voys.—
Et où?—Par tout, soit au large ou en serre.—
Comment?—Lisant ses vers qui suyvent l'erre.—
De qui?—D'amour.—N'eut-il aultre propos?—
Si eut.—Comment?—Son esprit fut dispos
Aux chants divins, dont feit maint vers et metre;
Prions pour luy, l'ame soit en repos.—
Quel?—Où Jesus a promis ses saincts mettre.[81]

This is not an unkind epitaph. For a poet of the older school and a well-known opponent of heresy to have written this epitaph on Marot is remarkable. Bouchet had no need to publish an epitaph on Marot at all, still less did he need to single out his religious poetry for particular praise. It appears that he valued Marot's translations of the psalms, that he was not unduly troubled by Marot's attitude to the Sorbonne and perhaps that he felt the abjuration of 1536 had settled any serious errors.

There is, in any case, some evidence to show that while himself writing in the hope of combatting heresy, he took no pleasure in the sight of individual heretics being pursued. He refrains from naming those burned in the persecutions which followed the *Placards*, partly 'par ce qu'ilz ne le vallent pas', but also 'afin que leurs parens, innocens desdits crimes, n'en soyent diffamés'.[82] He ends an *Ep. Fam.* by dating it as the day when 'un clerc lutherian' had made 'une amende honnorable' and ends, apparently following on from this:

Par cestuy-là qui dit en infortune
Ha bien touché, de tristesse importune.[83]

b) *Conciliarism and the Need for Reform*
After the spread of Lutheranism, the council was often suggested as the proper means for settling the heresy. Bouchet's apparent views on the desirability of holding a council for such a purpose fluctuate with royal policy. In 1535 he records that the King was pressing the Pope to call a council,[84] but after his account of the Diet of Ratisbon, which ended with the Papal Legate promising a council, he remarks that there is no point in calling a council over these disagreements because they were all settled at the Council of Constance.[85] This reflects the constantly repeated Catholic claim that Luther was merely renewing the errors of Wycliffe and Hus, but it is probably also inspired by the French policy of opposition to any council held by the Pope and the Emperor; this policy led ultimately to the refusal to acknowledge the Council of Trent.[86] However, having dismissed the usefulness of a council for settling the heresy, he continues:

> Bien est vray que par les saincts Conciles a esté ordonné et
> determiné que de sept ans en sept ans y auroyt Concile, pour
> reformer les abus et obmissions des choses tant bien ordonnées
> par les saints Canons. Qui est chose tresraisonnable, veu que
> par la fragilité ou ignorance humaine, n'y a estat en la Religion
> Chrestienne qui ne soyt aucunesfois polu et maculé, tant en
> l'Eglise, qu'en la secularité, comme on veoit à l'œil.[87]

So he refers to a conciliarist decree that councils should take place
at regular intervals and continues to see the council as a desirable
instrument for reform. Just how desirable he thought it is revealed
by an argument which he uses in 1 *Ep. Mor.* 1 in the section addressed to the Pope. Respectfully suggesting that the Pope does not
see the abuses in the Church which have been a cause for the spread
of heresy, he develops this idea to the point of suggesting that God
has permitted the growth of heresy:

> Pour l'Eglise exciter
> A corriger le tout par sainct concille.
> Le temps le veult . . .[88]

If he believed that God was using Luther as an instrument to
bring about the holding of a General Council, he must indeed have
believed strongly that a council was necessary. In fact, this passage
offers the best evidence from any of his work that he subscribed to
the conciliarist opinion that the General Council had jurisdiction
over the Pope, but this opinion is only suggested by the marginal
references accompanying the text, and therefore only to the well-
educated.[89] He does not apparently wish to discuss the relative
power of Pope and council in his French verse; the opinion which is
presented unequivocally is that a council is necessary because it
could reform the Church. The question of reform of abuse is the one
which really appears to concern him.

On this question, we have already noted that the *Epîtres morales*,
although different in tone and method from the *Renards*, still denounce terrible clerical abuses, directing the severest criticism at
those placed high in the Church who ought to ensure that only
suitable people are ordained and that they are properly supervised.
He continues to denounce simony, avarice and ambition, although
he says nothing about the Donation of Constantine. The compulsory celibacy of the clergy is argued for on several grounds; his
answer to the priest who cannot be chaste is that he should not be a
priest; far better to be a married layman than an unchaste priest.[90]
In such arguments we see the desire to combat Lutheranism and the
confirmation that Bouchet wants reformation of abuse, not a change
of institutions. The institution of monasticism is defended for the
same reason in 1 *Ep. Mor.* 2, but we may note that in 1 *Ep. Mor.* 3, to
preachers, he singles out for attack those who sell pardons and
teach that the money will open the way to heaven.[91] Quite apart

from their erroneous doctrine, he knew that such preachers had a good deal to answer for.

Certainly Bouchet found almost nothing to alter, either in 1525 or 1545, in the long sections of the *Déploration* which deal with abuse. The sense of the work as a whole is considerably modified in the *Opuscules*: the title is altered to *Deploracion de l'eglise militante sur les persecutions, laquelle deteste guerre et incite les roys et les princes à paix.*[92] It was published soon after the defeat at Pavia. The structure is completely altered; the Church now has three sorrows. The first is heresy, the second astrology and magic, the third simony. In the later part of the work dealing with external problems there is a new passage in praise of peace, the passage at the end in praise of Louis XII disappears and the appeal to the Pope to persuade the Christian kings to stop fighting is shifted to the end of the poem; some of the criticism of the Pope is dropped. The result of these changes is that the Pope gains in dignity but loses importance as a potential protagonist; the poem has become a plea for peace to the Kings of Christendom. The shadow of the defeat at Pavia is seen in a prophecy made by the Church after a new passage on rulers who have protected the Church, among whom the Kings of France are notable examples:

Parquoy s'ilz ont quelque adversité triste
Ne periront: à cela Dieu resiste.
Ces motz jadis me furent revellez.[93]

In keeping with this attempt to cheer a people whose King was captive, the criticism of the King which struck such an odd note in 1512 disappears. In 1512 the King was told he had no right to distribute benefices at all, now he is reminded that he must not give benefices by force to unworthy people. This change no doubt also reflects the provisions of the Concordat which had given the King indisputable rights over many benefices.

The polemical point of the original poem has disappeared; it gains a different sense with the praise of peace and the stanzas against Lutheranism. Peace is a prerequisite for solving all the problems of the Church.

Quant vous aurez entre vous paix parfaicte,
Que des grans clercs soit assemblée faicte
Et des prelatz, pour ouyr les raisons
Des Lutherins, qui ont presque deffaicte
Ma dignité, quoiquessoit contrefaicte
Et denigré mes temples et maisons.
Ilz ont escript que pour les desraisons
De mes prelatz et prebstres l'evangille
Est corumpue. Helas, que à grant vigille
On voye à l'œiul si desordre il y a,
Et qu'on ne soit en l'affaire fragille

> Ne endurcy, mais chescun soit agille
> De corriger juc au per omnia.[94]

In 1525 the council seemed to be the answer to heresy and reform alike. The notion that abuse has engendered heresy is already clear, and is reinforced by the long passages on simony, avarice and abuse which remain unchanged from the first version.

The most striking expression of the idea of heresy and abuse as twin evils besetting the Church appears in *Ep. Fam.* 113, written probably in 1538 and addressed to Jacques d'Anglure, the man who praised Bouchet for his fight against heresy. He entitled it *Response . . . contenant la maniere de vivre des hereticques et des hypocrites, et comment il faut cheminer entre deulx pour avoir salut.* This is already a rather remarkable title. Who are the hypocrites who are as evil in their way as heretics? First d'Anglure is congratulated for believing what the Church believes, and for abhorring

> ung tas de folles sectes
> Dont nous voions maintes ames infectes,
> Voire de gens qui veulent trop sçavoir
> Et par dessus le ciel empire veoir
> Soubz nom de foy, sans les euvres en faire,
> Pensans à Dieu (qu'offencent) satisfaire.[95]

'Faith not works' is the basis of their heretical errors, which he proceeds to outline, concluding that they are 'seducteurs':

> Ilz ont souvent le nom de Jesucrist
> En leur parler, et non en leur esprit,
> Car rien ne font de ce qu'il veult qu'on face
> Et qu'il inspire en eulx souvent par grace.[96]

This denunciation of the heretics is framed by their refusal to perform good works because they rely on faith alone. Now follows the opposite danger:

> D'une aultre part hypocrisie je voy,
> Qui aussi faict à l'eglise derroy,
> Car la pluspart des ministres d'icelle,
> Participans de l'avare estincelle
> Des Sathanicz, difference ne font
> Entre le sainct et non sainct; tout deffont,
> Et ce qu'ilz ont par la grace divine
> Vendent bien cher soubz umbre colombine
> Et tellement pour le dire à motz rondz
> Que du lieu sainct font la fosse à larrons.
> Ilz ont povoir, mais du povoir abusent;
> Ilz ont sçavoir, mais les gens y amusent,
> Car tant ilz sont par leur vice indiscretz
> Qu'ilz laissent là Concilles et decretz;
> Ilz dient assez ce que Dieu nous commande
> Mais chascun d'eulx le contraire demande.

Que dy-je? helas, à moy pas n'appartient
Dire le deuil que mon cueur en soubtient.[97]

The hypocrites turn out to be most of the ministers of the Church.
They are accused of simony. If it seems bold to equate in evilness
Lutheran heretics and irregular clerics, Bouchet first underlines just
how evil simony is—selling the gifts of divine grace—then accuses
the priests of sin equivalent to heresy in these activities. He creates
a neat balance: the priests are falling into the error exactly opposed
to the Lutheran one, because they believe that works without faith
will save them:

Ilz mettent tout leur espoir en ouvrages
Exterieurs, qui sont à Dieu saulvages,
Voire leur semble, et leur est bien advis
Qu'après leur mort ilz seront vis à viz
De Jesuchrist pour avoir faict la mine
Entre les gens, o puante vermine.
    Voyla, monsieur, deux poincts contrarians
A l'evangille, et par trop varians.
    Les hereticz cuident que par seul croire,
Sans bien ouvrer, avoir divine gloire.
    Les faulx semblans cuident que par leurs faictz
Auront sans foy la gloire des parfaictz.[98]

Here he uses the vocabulary of the faith-versus-works controversy, but of course he is not talking about 'trusting in works' at all
in the way that it was understood in that controversy. 'Ouvrages
exterieurs' here means the pretence of holiness by which simoniacal
priests cover up their wickedness, and in the last couplet quoted,
'faictz' means outward hypocritical show. But only the words 'faict
la mine' and 'faulx semblans' prevent this passage from being an
exposition of the perils of trusting in good works. The solution
which Bouchet offers here is in fact the same as his resolution of that
theological controversy in the *Triomphes*:

Prenons, monsieur, l'entredeux, où consiste
Le vray salut, où l'eglise persiste,
C'est croire et faire, et que fidelité
Euvre tousjours par pure charité,
Tant envers Dieu qu'envers le notre proche,
Et nous n'aurons davant Jesus reproche;
J'entends ouvrer par la grace de Dieu,
Justiffiant noz euvres en ce lieu,
Car ceste grace envers Dieu rectiffie
Les nostres faictz, et sans qu'on s'en deffie
Digne les faict d'envers Dieu meriter
(Non pas dè nous) pour es cieulx heriter,
Car de nous seulz ne povons faire chose
Qui sans la foy à salut nous dispose.

Il fault donc croire et faire ensemblement.
Du salut est la foy le fondement,
Et charité est l'entier ediffice
Où esperance a son logis propice.
Ne pensons pas en paradis aller
Sans ces vertuz, il(z) n'en fault point parler.[99]

As we shall see in a later chapter, his conclusion is that the three theological virtues cannot be separated. From living faith proceeds hope and from hope proceeds charity; living faith is *foy formée de charité* and a man who hypocritically performs external good works while nurturing mortal sin merely proves that his faith is a dead faith. This is the explanation of the passage; 'Auront sans foy la gloire des parfaictz' means 'without living faith'.[100] What concerns us here is the use of this terminology with reference to simoniacal priests. It is done very deliberately, perhaps with the intention of pointing out to those priests who were arguing the importance of works in this controversy just how gross a beam in their own eyes they were ignoring, how deficient in faith and charity alike they must be to permit and persevere in simoniacal abuse. It underlines that correct adherence to forms and ceremonies is no proof of living faith formed by charity if these mechanistic good works are accompanied by grave irregularities. Such actions prove that their perpetrators' faith is, in the words of St James, a dead faith.

To accuse the greater part of the clergy—'la pluspart des ministres de l'eglise'—of an error exactly comparable to that of the Lutherans is drastic indeed. Whatever allowances we may have made for the requirements of a bombastic genre in the *Renards* hardly apply in an *épître familière*. Priests apparently represent a real stumbling-block, and this poem proves how seriously Bouchet felt the need for reform. The exasperation born of having said the same thing for over thirty years no doubt helps to explain the extraordinary ferocity of this *épître*.

c) *Evangelical Groups*
Having examined this outspoken *épître* with its odd use of evangelical terminology, we may finally review such evidence as there is concerning Bouchet's views on the different shades of religious opinion in France. There is no doubt at all that he disapproved of German Lutherans, but his attacks on them are, as we have seen, often accompanied by condemnation of people apparently nearer home than Germany, who are characterised by presumption, scholarly pretentions, and refusal to read anything except the bare text of scripture.

He never refers directly to Lefèvre or to the group at Meaux, but his statement that it is dangerous to let uneducated people read unglossed translations of the New Testament proves conclusively that he did not approve of their work. In this he was accepting the decision of the Sorbonne as embodied in decrees of the Paris Parlement.[101]

Bouchet intended to present an orthodox catholic position, and none of his contemporaries suggest that he did not do so.[102] Bearing this in mind, we can see that he shows no particular enthusiasm for the militantly conservative orthodoxy of the Sorbonne, although he reflects their views on both Biblical translations and on the exposition of the Bible. In his comments on Marot, he more or less says that the Sorbonne can look after itself.[103] He recorded the Sorbonne's protest against the Concordat without any sympathy. In our final chapters, we shall see that his views disagree with the opinions of some Sorbonne doctors in the 1520s concerning the religious instruction of the laity and that almost certainly he disliked the way in which they were presenting the relationship between faith, works and grace.

This said, his outlook is nevertheless probably nearer to that of the Sorbonne than many non-schismatic French catholics of the 1520s and 1530s. Many powerful people wanted to see a reform of the institutions of the Church, and improvement in the quality of instruction given to the laity, a greater emphasis on the Bible, a better text of the Bible and scriptural exposition based on the products of humanist scholarship rather than scholastic theology. Many wanted to see less emphasis on matters which they regarded as mere human tradition—the cult of saints for example. Many such people were influenced by Erasmus, whom François Ier tried to attract to Paris.[104]

Such evidence as we have of Bouchet's attitude to *réformisme* is best exemplified in his treatment of Erasmus, of Marguerite de Navarre, and of some of his own friends and acquaintances.

It is at first sight no easy task to discover his reactions to Erasmus, for he hardly ever mentions him by name, and never when he is discussing religion. Once he gently takes him to task for attacking Ciceronians;[105] twice he links him with Budé and praises their 'science . . . trilinguale' (another point of disagreement with the Sorbonne).[106] But at least twice he quotes without acknowledgement from devotional works by Erasmus.[107] On the other hand, probably on one occasion and possibly on another, he seems deliberately to cite texts whose authenticity had been questioned by Erasmus.[108] One would in any case expect Bouchet's opinion of Erasmus to be rather mixed. The tone of high seriousness in which Bouchet attacks the corruption of the clergy suggests that he would feel that the *Praise of Folly* constituted 'irreverence apostolicque',[109] and he could not have approved of the mockery of the cult of saints in the *Colloquies*; while recognising some of the abuses to which it was subject, he remained extremely attached to the cult. On the other hand, Erasmus in another mood, devotional and reverent, obviously appealed to him; when he quotes him, it is from the *Enchiridion* and from a meditation on the Lord's Prayer.

We may also note Bouchet's references to Marguerite de Navarre. In earlier chapters we have had occasion to suggest that perhaps Bouchet's admiration of François Ier and of his mother was only moderate. No such reservations attach to what he says of Marguerite. He is known to have been employed by her in about 1520. He dedicated to her the *Labyrinthe* of 1522 on the grounds that it deals with 'choses contemplatives et celestes' and that Marguerite's mind is wholly devoted to 'choses spirituelles'.[110] *Ep. Fam.* 120 suggests that he regarded her as his patroness.

Marie Holban has argued that Marguerite's *Miroir de l'âme pécheresse* draws some of its inspiration from the verse *épîtres* in the *Triomphes*; they have in common the theme of the soul as the faithless bride.[111] If this is so, Bouchet returned the compliment by imitating Marguerite's manner in some of his later poetry,[112] and when he records her death in the last edition of the *Annales,* he says:

> C'estoit une prudente et sage dame, devote, charitable, sça-
> vante, et de grand esprit et memoire. Durant son vivant elle
> composa en vers françois ung petit traitté intitulé le Miroir de
> l'Ame, et plusieurs autres livres, le tout à l'honneur de Dieu.[113]

Here too he is praising a book that the Sorbonne had notoriously wanted to condemn.[114] In those of her works which he is likely to have read, Marguerite's most obvious deviation from the theology of the Sorbonne would be on the question of what reliance should be placed on good works, and we shall see that the views which he expresses, while not identical, veer in a similar direction. It seems clear that Marguerite's biblically inspired devotional works were to his taste.

Finally, we may cite again Bouchet's treatment of Marot, in particular the epitaph in which he is praised as a religious poet and regarded as having probably attained salvation. In 1545 he retains in the *Epîtres familières* the exchange of *épîtres* with Rabelais who is described as 'mon grand amy'. Certainly Rabelais was famous enough to add lustre to the collection, but he was famous for *Gargantua* which had ridiculed monasticism, the Sorbonne's definition of faith and the cult of saints. Bouchet also retains the correspondence with Germain Colin Bucher, who by 1545 had served a term in prison in Angers for heresy, and with Jean Chaponneau, who had gone over to the Reform and settled in Neuchâtel. There is evidence that Quintin flirted with the Reform and that Trojan went over to it.[115] Thus he does not seem to have wished to suppress correspondence with, or flattering references to, men whose orthodoxy was doubtful.

This evidence is scrappy and inconclusive; it does not tell us to what extent, if at all, Bouchet was affected by the liberal ideas which were influential in some parts of the French Church and in the circle of François Ier before the rise of Calvinism. We have merely seen some sympathy for some liberally minded people. On the basis of our study so far, Bouchet has emerged as a catholic who has every intention of being orthodox but who is eager to see reform of the Church and is exasperated by the failures of churchmen to observe Canon Law. He is interested in the instruction of the laity, but not on the basis of the Bible alone. There is some evidence that he distinguishes between mechanistic good works and true charity, but he defends institutions of the Church which others were to attack or ridicule as unscriptural. He prefers to tell the truth about saints rather than perpetuate pious fraud, but he is not overcritical in trying to arrive at truth; on the other hand, he is readily sceptical of the results of the new scholarship when they overturn accepted ideas.

Certainly then, Bouchet was conservative. But he was highly critical of the Church's failure to be properly conservative in matters of pastoral care. It is therefore in his theological writings for the uneducated that we shall see most clearly in what ways he regarded as unsatisfactory the contemporary Church's presentation of Christianity to the laity.

NOTES

1. These subjects are treated at greater length in my thesis, J. J. Beard, *A Study of the works of Jean Bouchet, with reference to contemporary religious issues*, PhD, University of London, 1972.
2. *Renards*, d4 vo, col.2. On the French Church at this period see P. Imbart de La Tour, *Les Origines de la Réforme*, vol.2, *L'Eglise catholique. La crise et la renaissance*, deuxieme éd. revue . . . par Y. Lanhers, Melun, 1944, pp.179-310.
3. d5 ro, col.1.
4. d5 ro, col.2-d5 vo, col.1. Cf. *Livre de l'Espérance*, ed. Rouy, Prose VIII, pp.56-7.
5. The 8th- or 9th-century forgery which purported to record the Emperor Constantine's gift to the Pope of spiritual primacy over the whole of Christendom and temporal dominion over the West. It was incorporated into Canon Law, *Dec. Grat.*, Prima pars, Dist.96, ch.14.
6. Dante, *De Monarchia*, III, x, 4; see also *Inferno*, XIX, lines 115-17. Lorenzo Valla, *De falso credita et ementita Constantini Donatione Declamatio*, 1440 (translated into French and printed in about 1520 as *Sur la donation de Constantin empereur*, BL 476.a.8).
7. Ed. Rouy, pp.56-7.
8. *Renards*, d5 vo, col.2.
9. d5 vo, col.2. Cf. Ed. Rouy, Prose XVI, lines 135-8, 153-4:
    Or fut il pieça fait ung nouvel statut en l'Eglise latine, qui dessevra l'ordre de saint mariage d'avec la dignité de prestrise soubz couleur de purté et de chasteté sans soulleure.

Maintenant court le statut de concubinage au contraire . . .
yceulx ministres ont laissé les espousalles, maiz ilz ont repris les illegittimes, vaguez et dissoluez luxures.

10. d5 vo, col.2-d6 ro, col.1. 'me' in the first line is doubtless a
misprint for 'ne'.

11. See H. D. Lea, *History of Sacerdotal Celibacy in the Christian Church*,
3rd edition, 2 vols, London, 1907.

12. On Zabarella see Lea, *Sacerdotal Celibacy*, vol.2, p.25. Chartier,
ed. Rouy, Prose xvi, lines 154-6: Je ne vueil plus avant eslargir
ma parole. Car tant ont telles constitutions de lieu comme on y
prent de plaisir.

13. d6 ro, col.2.

14. d6 vo, col.1.

15. *Ibid.*, cols 1-2.

16. A. Renaudet, *Préréforme et humanisme à Paris pendant les premières
guerres d'Italie (1494-1517)*, Paris, deuxième édition, 1953, especially pp.290-365, 437-62, 524-90.

17. c3 ro, cols 1-2.

18. On this war and the political activity, see Renaudet, *Préréforme*,
pp.524-56; J. S. C. Bridge, *A History of France from the death of Louis
XI*, vol.4, *The Reign of Louis XII, 1508-1514*, Oxford, 1929.

19. On conciliarism, see Hubert Jedin, *Geschichte des Konzils von
Trient*, vol.1, zweite Auflage, Freiburg, 1951; Brian Tierney,
Foundations of the Conciliar Theory, Cambridge, 1955; ed. Remigius
Bäumer, *Die Entwicklung des Konziliarismus*, Darmstadt, 1976.

20. 6 April 1415 and 9 October 1417. *Haec sancta* was a means of
establishing the right of the Council of Constance to impose a
solution to the Great Schism, but *Frequens*, by stating that councils should be called at regular intervals, sought to establish the
General Council not simply as an extraordinary remedy for an
extreme situation but as an integral part of the government of the
Church.

21. On Gallicanism see V. Martin, *Les Origines du Gallicanisme*, 2 vols,
Paris, 1939; also Renaudet, *Préréforme*.

22. See Martin, *Gallicanisme*, vol.2, especially pp.303-15 and Renaudet, *Préréforme*, pp.2-8.

23. See Olivier de la Brosse, *Le Pape et le concile*, Paris, 1965.

24. The works of d'Auton and Lemaire will be examined *infra*. Jean
Marot composed an *Epître d'un complaignant l'abusif gouvernement
du pape* which survives only in manuscript (text reproduced by
J-B. Colbert de Beaulieu in *Scriptorium*, iii, 1949, pp.101-9). The
case of Guillaume Cretin is ambiguous; he composed only one
poem about the war with Julius ii, but, unlike most of his poetry,
this was printed, in a collection of poems about the Italian wars,
Les exellentes vaillances, batailles et conquestes du roy dela les mons,
BN Rés. Ye.1383. For this *Invective contre la guerre papalle* see
Œuvres, ed. Chesney, p.58.

25. On d'Auton, see his *Chroniques de Louis XII*, ed. R. de Maulde La
Clavière, 4 vols, Paris, 1889-95, including a *Notice* on the life of
d'Auton, and Bouchet, *Ep. Fam.* 57.

26. BN ancien fonds français 1952, ff.1-15. There is another copy in
Vienna, Österreichische Nationalbibliothek, MS 2579, and another in Leningrad in a ms made for Louis xii and Anne of

Brittany which contains several poems by different authors on the war: see G. Tournoy-Thoen, 'Fausto Andrelini et la cour de France', in *L'Humanisme français au début de la Renaissance*, Colloque international de Tours (xive stage), Paris, 1973, pp.65-79, particularly pp.70-6. On the group of fictional *épîtres* inspired by this poem see my article, J. J. Beard, 'Letters from the Elysian Fields: a group of poems for Louis xii', *BHR*, 31, 1969, pp.27-38.

27.   In the manuscript in the Saltykov-Shchedrin Library, Leningrad, mentioned in n.26. The poem is on twelve leaves and has 498 lines. Internal evidence suggests a date of composition later than 18 February 1512 (recapture of Brescia) but before the death of Gaston de Foix, 11 April 1512.

28.   Lines 185-6.

29.   According to a legend going back to at least the 13th century, on the day that the Donation was made, a voice from Heaven cried out that this day poison had been infused into the Church. See J. J. I. von Döllinger, *Fables respecting the Popes of the Middle Ages*, tr. A. Plummer, London, 1871, pp.167-8. D'Auton attenuates this story by omitting the heavenly origin of the voice; Lemaire embroiders it by making the voice that of a rejoicing devil; see *infra*.

30.   *Chroniques de Louis XII*, vol.2, p.235; see also pp.222-7.

31.   *Ep. Fam.* 57, f.xxxix vo, col.2-f.xl ro, col.1.

32.   Lyons, Estienne Baland, 1511; see *Œuvres*, ed. Stecher, vol.3, pp.231-359. Lemaire speaks of the sales of his books in a letter; see *Œuvres*, vol.4, p.421. On the *Traité*, see P. Jodogne, *Jean Lemaire de Belges, écrivain franco-bourguignon*, Brussels, 1972, pp. 357-86.

33.   *L'Epistre du roy à Hector de Troye*, Paris, G. de Marnef, 1513; *Œuvres*, vol.3, pp.68-86. The poem circulated earlier in ms: it appears in the Leningrad ms referred to *supra*, n.26. Internal evidence suggests that it was written in November 1511. See my 'Letters from the Elysian Fields' and Jodogne, *Lemaire*, pp.395-403. *Le Dyalogue de Vertu militaire et de Jeunesse française* and the piece commencing 'Umbre de mort, symulachre de vie' are reproduced by Kathleen Munn, *A Contribution to the study of Jean Lemaire de Belges*, New York, 1936, pp.160-6, 169-77.

34.   See my 'Jean Lemaire de Belges and prophecy'.

35.   *Œuvres*, vol.3, p.261.

36.   *Ibid.*, pp.355-7.

37.   *Ibid.*, pp.358-9.

38.   *Œuvres complètes*, vol.1, pp.11-144.

39.   *Ibid.*, pp.74-9. See also pp.102-4.

40.   *Ibid.*, pp.79-83, particularly p.80.

41.   See particularly ed. Frautschi, pp.121-5.

42.   In the *Blazon des heretiques*, Paris, P. Le Noir, 1524; *Œuvres complètes*, vol.1, pp.295-336.

43.   B1 ro-B5 ro.

44.   *La Chasse du cerf des cerfz*, Paris, 1510? BN Rés. Ye.1319, *Œuvres*, pp.157-67; *L'Espoir de paix*, Paris, 1511, BN Rés. Ye.1324, *Œuvres*, pp.169-84; *Le Jeu du Prince des sotz et Mere sotte*, Paris, s.d., BN Rés. Ye.1317, *Œuvres*, pp.201-86.

45.   In 1507 there was violent and scandalous conflict between the supporters of Claude de Tonnerre (the King's candidate) and

Florent d'Allemagne. See F. Villard, 'L'Election de Claude de Tonnerre', *BSAO*, 4ᵉ série, vol.10, 1970, pp.469-80. Bouchet records the contested election in the *Annales*, f.188 ro, noting that d'Allemagne was 'homme de saincte vie'. In *Gén. Ep.* 47 Bouchet praises his piety and learning; he claims that d'Allemagne was elected unanimously, and he blames his death in the *coqueluche* epidemic of 1510 on the strain caused by the lawsuit.

46. A6 ro. Lamentations 1 v.15.

47. A5 vo-A6 ro. *Dec. Greg.* Lib.v, Tit. III, *De Simonia*; cap.xix *Veniens* (an abbot and monks asking to be paid for making a priest a monk); cap.xxvii *Nobis* (elections based on promises of money are to be quashed); Lib.II, Tit.xviii *De Confessis*, cap.ii *Cum super electione* (another case involving a promise of money for an election). Bouchet's sentence in Latin summarises the main point.

48. The passage on the dignity of priests appears B8 ro-C1 vo: lines 677-741.

49. A8 vo-B1 ro. Ecclesiasticus 37 (sic) v.7; Isaiah 3 v.12; *Dec. Grat.*, Secunda pars, c.xxiii, q.viii, cap.xxi; Matthew 22 v.21 (a verse used in the chapter of Canon Law just referred to).

50. B7 ro. The outspoken nature of the criticism was pointed out by O. Douen in 'Avant la Réformation. "La Déploration de l'Eglise" par Jean Bouchet, 1512', *Bulletin de la Société de l'Histoire du Protestantisme Français*, année 5, Paris, 1857, pp.266-74.

51. C2 vo.

52. C5 vo-C7 ro.

53. Two different undated copies survive: see the bibliography. The poem is reproduced in *Recueil de poésies françoises des XVᵉ et XVIᵉ siècles*, ed. A. de Montaiglon, vol.3, Paris, 1856, pp.26-71. Bouchet reproduced it with mainly metrical corrections as *Ep. Fam.* 1.

54. *Recueil*, ed. Montaiglon, p.68.

55. *Ibid.*

56. pp.64 and 69.

57. pp.64-5.

58. Cf. the references in the *Annales* quoted *supra*, chapter 4. In the version of the *Epître d'Henri* that forms *Ep. Fam.* 1, he changes 'le pape' to 'Jules . . . soy disant Pape'; there was no metrical consideration to influence this change, although in another case he eliminates a lyric cesura by altering 'Je dis Pape, je ne sçay par quel sort' to 'Si Pape il est . . .' (f.1 ro, col.1; f.vi ro, col.2).

59. *Déploration*, B2 ro-vo.

60. *Annales*, f.203 ro. See Renaudet, *Préréforme*, pp.580-6.

61. Other early references include Gringore's *Blazon des heretiques* (December 1524), Gachy's *Trialogue nouveau* (1524), and works by Nicolas Volcyr (1525 and 1526). See W. G. Moore, *La Réforme allemande et la littérature française*, Strasburg, 1930, pp.241-61.

62. Text of 1524 edition, part 4, f.lxxiiii vo (*c'est); see *Annales*, 1557, f.201 ro-vo.

63. For instance in the *Déploration*, B6 vo; *Annales*, 1557, f.187 ro; 1 *Ep. Mor.* 3, f.14 vo, col.1.

64. Ed. 1525, f.ccxxxi vo. (*envelimé). On the interpretation of Luther's name cf. Moore, *Réforme allemande*, p.109 and p.252.

65. *Ibid.*, ff.ccxxxiv vo-ccxxxv ro.

66. The *Labyrinthe* of 1522 and the *Cantiques et oraisons de l'âme péni-*

tente seem to be written without any fear of the spread of heresy. Apart from this entry in the 1524 *Annales*, his first extensive treatment of the heresy is in the revised *Déploration*, August 1525.

67. On the first two points see for example the passage from Béda's preface to his *Annotationes* against Erasmus and Lefèvre (1526), quoted and discussed by M–M. de La Garanderie, *Christianisme et lettres profanes (1515-1535)*, Lille-Paris, 1976, pp.234-8.

68. The *Colloquies*, which had begun to appear in 1518, had been augmented in 1522 and in later editions: the *Naufragium* and the *Virgo* μισογαμος for example had first appeared in 1523 (*Opera omnia* (Amsterdam) 1, 3, 1972, pp.10-11).

69. In the *Cantiques*; see chapter 6.

70. f.207 ro (first appeared in ed. of 1532).

71. *Opuscules*, 1526, J8 vo.

72. *Annales*, f.259 vo. Bouchet's slightly shortened version of the pamphlet runs from f.258 vo-f.261 ro (first appeared in ed. of 1532). The pamphlet in question is *Pro religione Christiana res geste in Comitiis Auguste Vindelicorum habitis*, Augsburg, 6 November 1530, BL 697.g.34(9). Seguin mentions a pamphlet in French which could be a translation, *Information*, p.91. For the Diet of Augsburg see Jedin, *Geschichte des Konzils von Trient*, vol.1, pp. 197-215.

73. The account of Ratisbon first appears in the ed. of 1545. Bouchet lists the chapters from the Ratisbon book and quotes a sentence from the chapter on free will. There were editions of the book, all including some account of the proceedings at Ratisbon, by Eck, Melanchthon, Bucer, and, anonymously in French, Calvin. Only Bucer's and Calvin's cover all the information given by Bouchet, and even they omit the names of the assessors who were appointed; these Bouchet must have from some other source. Bouchet's narrative and the sentence from the book itself are very close to the words of Calvin's account, *Les Actes de la Journée imperiale tenue en la cité de Regenspourg*, 1541: cf. a4 ro, a4 vo, a7 ro and *Annales*, 1557, ff.276 ro-287 ro. If this is the edition Bouchet used, he must have been well aware that he was reading Protestant literature: Calvin's introduction leaves no doubt as to his sympathies (text in *Calvini Opera*, v, cols 509-684, *Corpus Reformatorum*, xxxiii). See Jedin, *Geschichte des Konzils von Trient*, vol.1, pp.299-315 and Peter Matheson, *Cardinal Contarini at Regensburg*, Oxford, 1972.

74. *Annales*, f.207 ro.

75. *Opuscules*, 1526, J7 vo, J8 vo.

76. *Annales*, f.261 ro.

77. *Triomphes*, 1530, +2 vo.

78. D'Anglure is said to have enjoyed the *Triomphes*; he praises Bouchet for his constant attacks on heresy, *Ep. Fam.* 112, f.lxxv ro, col.1.

79. *Ep. Fam.* 109. But Bouchet had already raised the subject of the Marot-Sagon *Querelle* in 107 to the Rouen poet Baptiste Le Chandelier. Sagon had called on Bouchet and Germain Colin to attack Marot in *Le rabais du caquet de Fripelippes et de Marot dict Rat pelé*. Germain Colin told them both to stop the quarrel in *Epistre envoyée à Clement Marot et Françoys Sagon, tendant à leur paix* (both

texts reproduced in *Querelle de Marot et Sagon*, ed. Picot and Lacombe, Rouen, 1920).

80. *Ep. Fam.* 114, f.lxxvi ro, col.2. In *Ep. Fam.* 111, f.lxxiiii ro, col.2, part of the correspondence with Jacques d'Anglure (which is interpolated into the series concerning Marot), Bouchet denounces, but without actually naming Marot, the 'Laiz, ballades, rondeaulx, dizains fardez' written by

les gens nouveaulx
Eulx appellans à tort Evangelicques
Pour mieulx couvrir leurs passions iniques.

81. *Généalogies*, 1545, f.85 vo, col.2. My punctuation.

82. *Annales*, f.271 ro (first appears in 1535 ed.).

83. *Ep. Fam.* 108, f.lxxiii ro, col.1. The rest of the *épître* has nothing to do with either heresy or melancholy. It is just possible that Bouchet's friend Trojan had something to do with this incident, which took place on 16 September 1537, since he may have been the Franciscan whose preaching had caused trouble in Poitiers in July 1537. See appendix A.

84. *Annales*, f.267 ro (first appears in 1535 ed.).

85. *Annales*, f.287 ro.

86. See Jedin, *Geschichte des Konzils von Trient*, vol.1, pp.242-4, 262, 367-8.

87. *Annales*, f.287 ro-vo. This looks like a reference to *Frequens*, although this decree actually calls for councils at ten year intervals, but with the two councils immediately following Constance to be held after five and then seven years.

88. 1 *Ep. Mor.* 1, f.7 ro, cols 1 and 2.

89. In particular he includes a reference to *Dec. Grat.*, prima pars, Dist.xix, c.9, Anastasius. This is a crucial conciliarist text which suggests that a heretic Pope may be deposed and that the Council is superior to the Pope (see Tierney, *Foundations*, pp.38-9, 50, 251). Bouchet places the reference beside lines which express rather doubtfully the belief that the Pope is guiltless, particularly of avarice and ambition. Taken together, the learned reader could understand this as a veiled threat to depose an unworthy Pope, since some canonists held that notorious vice was tantamount to heresy in the Pope (Tierney, *Foundations*, p.59). Papal supporters denied that the Pope could be deposed for anything except heresy, e.g. Cajetan (see La Brosse, *Le Pape et le Concile*, p.74). In the *Julius Exclusus* Julius reels off to St Peter a whole list of crimes for which the Pope cannot be deposed (*Erasmi opuscula*, ed. Wallace K. Ferguson, The Hague, 1933, pp.92-3, lines 459-502).

90. f.5 ro-f.6 vo.

91. See f.14 vo, col.1.

92. *Opuscules*, 1526, J6 vo-M4 vo.

93. K6 vo.

94. L8 ro-vo. The phrase 'juc au per omnia' means 'to the very end, completely'; it is a reference to the formula 'per omnia saecula saeculorum' marking the end of prayers, particularly in the Mass.

95. f.lxxv vo, col.1.

96. *Ibid*.

97. *Ibid.*, col.2.
98. *Ibid.*
99. *Ibid.*, f.lxxvi ro, col.1.
100. See the discussion of faith and good works *infra* at the end of
     chapter 7, and in particular see *Triomphes,* cvi ro-vo, the end of
     the passage on charity, when, after defending good works
     against the Lutherans he warns against hypocrisy:
     > On se doit garder de ce vice d'ypochrisie, qui est jusner,
     > macerer son corps, dire grant nombre d'oraisons, visiter
     > eglises; faire longs pellerinages, porter vestemens de humi-
     > lité et saincteté, souvent parler de Dieu, blamer les vices,
     > louer les vertuz, baiser la croix et les ymages, et estre lasci-
     > vieux, mensongier, cavilleux, ambicieux, envieux, orguil-
     > leux, avaricieux, arrogant, presumptueux, inobedient, et
     > vivre sans amendement en tous ces pechez et aultres cou-
     > vers de sainctes et devotes cerymonies et de bonnes euvres
     > exteriores. Il est requis pour avoir charité que le cueur soit
     > correspondant et s'accorde avec l'euvre pour la presenter à
     > Dieu.
101. See F. M. Higman, *Censorship and the Sorbonne,* Geneva, 1979,
     pp.26-7.
102. Bouchet himself tells us that one critic accused him of temerity in
     treating predestination in a vernacular book. See *infra,* chapter 6
     at n.56. Rabelais' eighteenth-century editor Le Duchat asserts
     that Bouchet was imprisoned for his religious beliefs and ab-
     jured: this must simply be dismissed as a mistake (*Ducatiana,*
     vol.1, Amsterdam, 1738, p.18; see Hamon, p.158).
103. *Ep. Fam.* 107, f.lxxii ro, col.1.
104. See Higman, *Censorship,* pp.37-45; La Garanderie, *Christianisme
     et Lettres profanes,* pp.153-203.
105. 1 *Ep. Mor.* 13, f.32 ro, col.2.
106. *Ep. Fam.* 65, f.xliv vo, col.1. See also 89, f.lix vo, col.1.
107. See *infra,* chapter 7.
108. See *supra,* chapter 4, p.134 and chapter 3, p.110, n.115.
109. The phrase he uses to reprove the authors of epigrams against
     Leo x.
110. *Labyrinthe,* 1524, liminary A7 ro.
111. 'Le Miroir de l'âme pécheresse' et 'Les Epistres de la Noble et
     Amoureuse Dame', *Mélanges offerts à M. Abel Lefranc,* Paris, 1936,
     pp.142-54.
112. See chapter 2.
113. *Annales,* 342 ro.
114. See Higman, *Censorship,* pp.31-2.
115. See appendix A. Bouchet may not have known of Chaponneau's
     defection but it seems unlikely that he would not have heard
     about Germain Colin Bucher with whom his relations were less
     casual. In the cases of Quintin and Trojan their manifestations
     of reformist sympathy, if indeed they occurred, took place in
     Poitiers.

Bouchet's Religious Writing

1
Religious Writing for the Laity

a) *The Position Before the Spread of Lutheranism*
In the period between the beginnings of printing in France and the
first reactions to Lutheran heresy, books on religion in French
formed a considerable proportion of books printed.[1] They catered
for a very wide market. The products consisted at one extreme of
superbly illustrated books printed on vellum, at the other of single
gatherings which are no more than pamphlets.[2] The clients ranged
from royalty to very simple people; in plainly printed little books
the preface may stress the usefulness of the work 'à tous chrestiens',
'à toutes gens tant clercz que seculiers', 'pour la consolation et
revocation des simples gens'.[3] Such books are not intended only for
the literate; a formula found in prefaces is 'lire ou ouyr lire'.[4]

The content of the books has a similarly wide range. A number of
translations from major writers were available, most commonly in
large and costly books: St Augustine, *Cité de Dieu*; St John Cassian,
Les Colacions des sains peres anciens; Durandus, *Les Racional des divins
offices*; St Bernard, *Méditations*.[5] The Bible appears in the form of
Guyart des Moulins' *Bible Historiée*, a vast two-volume publication
giving a large proportion of the text, but with glosses interpolated.[6]

Probably the largest single category of religious books printed
was the Book of Hours.[7] This was intended for use in lay devotion,
although it was normally for the most part in Latin. Often, however,
it included some prayers in French.[8] Books of Hours in themselves
offer a wide range of quality from the illuminated copies on vellum
to the paper copies with woodcut illustrations.

Manuals of instruction were sometimes weighty works covering
many subjects,[9] but the books concentrating on simpler people tend
to develop two main themes: living well and, more important still,
dying well. Living well requires moral instruction. Dying well
('pour bien mourir et avoir paradis') requires meeting death in faith
(believing what it is necessary to believe) and with no mortal sin
unabsolved. It was particularly necessary to instruct people on the

latter point, for ignorance was no excuse for mortal sin. There are therefore many examples of forms of confession and preparations for confession.[10] Usually they invite the penitent to examine himself by working through one or more sets of concepts: the Ten Commandments, the seven deadly sins, the seven virtues, the seven corporal works of mercy, the seven spiritual works of mercy, the five senses, the twelve articles of faith. These preparations for, or forms of, confession are usually short,[11] but longer treatises on confession and works on the art of living and dying well can be built around consideration of the same sets.[12] It is quite clear from the questions in confessionals that laymen are envisaged, although of course the books could also be used by parish priests to help them to examine their penitents.

Certain crucial texts are regularly found in French in these books and show what ordinary people were expected to know: the Apostles' Creed, which is the basis for the twelve articles of faith, the Ten Commandments and the Commandments of the Church, less frequently the Lord's Prayer and the Ave Maria.[13] There is a significant amount of material concerning the Mass; again the range is wide, from a full-scale treatise on the Mass for laymen to brief meditations in French for the layman to use during the Mass.[14]

Finally we may mention saints' lives, of very differing quality and authenticity, which were regarded as mirrors in which the reader could recognise his or her sins by contrast with the saint's virtues.

This large body of material combines both works written before the invention of printing and new works exploiting the new technique. It is clear firstly that there must have been an excellent market for such books, secondly that many Churchmen wished to encourage the diffusion of simple books on religion. This was already the case before the beginnings of printing. Jean Charlier de Gerson, Chancellor of the University of Paris in the earlier years of the fifteenth century, had been particularly important. Although he had frowned on translations of the Bible, he believed that the moral and historical parts of scripture could be taught to the laity, and he was so convinced of the value of treatises in French for the laity that he composed many himself.[15] He is constantly quoted and referred to in early printed religious books as other writers follow his example;[16] moreover his own treatises were frequently printed. It is not of course only the laity who are envisaged as readers of such books; it was regarded as essential to any reform or renewal of the Church that the laity should receive better instruction, but the primary mode of instruction would be the sermon, provided that the clergy themselves were sufficiently well instructed to preach properly. Gerson's books are aimed at parish clergy and laity alike. A work of his translated as the *Instruction des curez pour instruire le simple peuple* provides a particularly interesting example of how bishops in the early sixteenth century promoted the instruction of their flocks. In 1507 this manual, which covers virtues and vices, the commandments of God and of the Church, the sacraments and the Mass, was recommended by Etienne Poncher for use in the diocese of Paris and a few months later by François de Luxembourg for the diocese of Le Mans.[17] The book ends with the *Livre de Jesus*—French versions of the Lord's Prayer, Ave Maria, Apostles' creed, Ten Commandments and the commandments of the Church, together with a rhymed version of the twelve articles of faith 'pour mieulx les faire gouster aux enfans et simples gens et y exerciter leur memoire et entendement'.[18] By way of a preface there is a letter from the bishop addressed to all in authority under him which gives a good impression of the urgent need felt at the time to improve the instruction of the laity, of how this might be effected, and what sort of instruction was thought necessary:

> Considerans l'honneur de Dieu et ses commandemens et ses sacremens estre non petitement desprisez, et les ames prochaines à perdition, et les peuples à captivité, et les choses publiques à desolation pour l'ignorance de science salutaire, et desirans y obvier pour le devoir de nostre office pastoral . . . avons ordonné et ordonnons, tant pour l'instruction des curez simples et non lettrez et aultres semblables ayans charge d'ames, que aussi pour l'information du simple peuple, qui n'a pas souvent fructueuses predications et salutaires exhortations, publier ou faire publier et diligemment remonstrer par tout nostre dyocese le contenu de nostre foy catholique, les commandemens de Dieu et de son eglise, la maniere d'examiner sa conscience et de soy accuser par confession pour faire digne fruit de penitence, et la science de bien mourir, dont l'ignorance n'excuse ame, et la congnoissance est à tous chrestiens tresnecessaire et moult proufitable, ainsi qu'elle est descripte . . . par . . . maistre Jehan de Gerson. . . . Et nous l'avons pour ceste cause fait correctement imprimer en toutes les deux langues, affin que plus facilement et à vil pris ung chacun le peust avoir promptement et entendre.[19]

Priests and others in authority are ordered to own the book, study and teach it, and a chapter of it shall be read and explained at the morning Mass for servants; the day before the clergy must study it so that they will be able to explain it, and they are to remind people of the indulgences to be gained from listening to it.

> Nous exhortons tout nostre simple peuple voulentiers y assister, et estre attentifz et diligens à ouyr et entendre et à leur povoir retenir l'instruction et discipline de Dieu leur pere, et de l'eglise leur mere. Et la repeter en leurs maisons et bonnes compaignies, et l'enseigner à leurs enfans et serviteurs et aultres, mesmement orphelins et pupilles, et solliciter les

maistres d'escolle que ainsi facent à leurs enfans.[20]
Those who teach it are given forty days of indulgence each time,
and those who hear it, twenty. All priests must possess and study
it, and so must the laity if possible:

> En exhortant peres et meres et tous bons chrestiens qui n'ont
> plus grant congnoissance de leur salut, avoir s'ilz peuent la
> doctrine dessudicte, au moins en françoys et s'ilz scevent lyre.
> Et quant souvent ilz estudieront, bien leur en prendra.[21]

The instruction of the people is seen here as of urgent necessity.
The most important means is to render the clergy capable of instructing them, but providing the laity with books is presented in this
bishop's letter as desirable, useful and economically viable. This is
in fact a missionary programme; other bishops followed Poncher's
example in recommending Gerson's *Instruction* for use in their dio-
ceses.[22]

Everything suggests that the trend towards providing the laity
with books in French on religion was one which was gaining in
strength during the first twenty years of the sixteenth century. It
accompanies the efforts towards reformation of the monastic orders
which were going on at the same time. Indeed, the parallel is worth
pointing out, for the two things often went together. Authors of
religious books in French written at the time often came from reformed houses or were themselves reformers: Olivier Maillard's
books were printed;[23] François Le Roy, author of several devotional
works was 'religieux de la reformation de l'ordre de Fontevrault'.[24]
Both trends were as prevalent among conservatives as among more
radical reformers: Noël Béda for instance made a small contribution
to both movements.[25]

On the whole, as Eugene Rice has pointed out with regard to
Gerson's *Instruction*,[26] those who seek to provide better instruction
for the laity are not presenting an evangelical programme. The
books we have described are not Bible-based, there is nothing innovatory about them and for the most part they are not concerned
with much beyond moral instruction and the most rudimentary
theological knowledge. But they bear witness nonetheless to a missionary zeal for teaching people the basic rules of their religion and
for helping them to understand some of their prayers. Moreover,
there is no apparent hostility to more substantial material appearing
in the vernacular. One excellent example of a non-evangelical publication which nevertheless represents considerable progress in making an important text more accessible to the laity is the complete
translation into French of the Book of Hours published by Jean de
Brie.[27] This must have appeared some time before January 1523. It
offers translations of the prayers and the psalms which are included
in the Hours. It also gave a translation of the passages from the
Gospels which normally appear at the beginning of Books of Hours;

these were translated with built-in glosses in the manner of the *Bible Historiée*.[28]

It could be argued that more radical Reformers, evangelical, Lutheran and ultimately Calvinist, who were to use vernacular writing to devastating effect, found such a ready audience in part because the literature we have been describing had prepared people for reading about their religion. The Reformers, of course, attacked the existing literature. Both Erasmus and Luther condemned the method of preparation for confession commonly advocated in these books.[29] Rabelais makes fun of the titles of such pious treatises in his comic list of the books in the library of St Victor. But it was worth infiltrating this literature, as is shown by the fact that early evangelical and reformist books sometimes adopted the titles of older and orthodox works.[30] This was no doubt one of the reasons why all such literature was for a time viewed unfavourably in some quarters.

b) *Controversy Arising from the Spread of Lutheranism*

The provision of orthodox religious material in French for the laity never itself became the object of condemnation or even very serious controversy, but the controversy which arose concerning the translation of scripture and the liturgy nevertheless had its effect on the attitudes of some theologians towards vernacular religious material in general.

In the 1520s the theologians of the Sorbonne had to consider both specifically Lutheran writing and the unglossed translations from the Vulgate emanating from Meaux. In public pronouncements they condemned, and the *Parlement* forbade, all translation of the Bible or parts of the Bible.[31] They condemned translations of texts too closely associated with the liturgy, notably the Nicene Creed.[32] After discussions on the activities of the Meaux group they concluded that the common people must neither read nor discuss the Bible.[33] The people might however discuss amongst themselves points arising from a sermon;[34] they might also read 'pios tractatus'.[35] Thus in theory the position was unchanged except that scriptural translation was banned.

However, these controversies had wider ramifications. The Sorbonne criticised Erasmus for saying that prayer in Latin not understood by the person praying was useless.[36] Individual Sorbonne theologians in their writings on these subjects show a lack of enthusiasm for instructing the laity by means of books amounting virtually to hostility. Béda asks why the knowledge of Scripture should be thought to render simple people more charitable and praises saintly ignorance and illiteracy.[37] Sutor, saying that the people cannot know the whole Bible, remarks that it is enough for simple people to know the Lord's Prayer, the articles of faith, the

Ten Commandments, the Commandments of the Church and those things which befit their estate. He subsequently seeks to answer the objection that Bible reading is a good occupation for Holy Days. If possible, people should go to hear a sermon; they will learn more by listening to a sermon for an hour than by studying or reading for a whole day. If there is no sermon, they should devote themselves to works of charity. In the unlikely event of there being no pressing works of charity, pious meditations may be indulged in, although some honest recreation to refresh the body is safer than an idleness which begets evil thoughts. Those who like reading could read pious tales ('pie historie'): saints' lives are amazingly valuable for simple people.[38]

Of all the vernacular religious literature available at the time, saints' lives are the most popular in style, have the least serious theological content, pander most to sensationalism, and were under the strongest attack from reformers. For Sutor at least the missionary spirit evident for instance in the bishop's letter introducing Gerson's book in 1507 is very muted. The knowledge which he advocates is along the lines of that offered by many vernacular works, but he conveys no sense of urgency with regard to it. Study, even meditation, is seen as potentially dangerous and to be discouraged.

From the Sorbonne's point of view even books good in themselves might be dangerous if read by the uneducated—'simples gens', 'simpliciens', 'simplex popellus', 'idiotae'. They certainly did not for a long time appreciate the need to combat Lutheran and Evangelical writings with their own wholesome doctrine delivered in French. Jérôme de Hangest is unusual in writing a few brief anti-Lutheran tracts in French at this period. It is interesting to note that he was in charge of a diocese, standing in for a bishop, and therefore perhaps had a sharper sense of what was needed at the pastoral level than some of his fellow theologians.[39] Apart from Hangest, Sorbonne theologians did not exploit the vernacular for counter-propaganda until Pierre Doré began to do so rather apologetically from 1538.[40] Doré was later to deny that the Sorbonne had attempted to 'oster du tout au peuple l'escripture divine, ainsi que aulcuns mesdisans calumnient'.[41] But it is hardly surprising that they should have been accused of doing so, for the terms of their condemnations are not nuanced. The case of Gringore's translation of the Hours of the Virgin is an excellent example of the Sorbonne's embattled attitude at this period. Gringore was, as we know, rather conservative in religious matters, and had already written a poem against Luther. He had produced a work very much in the spirit of the vernacular religious literature which we have described, a translation of the Hours of the Virgin into French verse, including those psalms which are incorporated into the Hours.[42] In August 1525, with the King imprisoned in Spain, the Sorbonne advised the Parlement that printing of the translation should not be allowed; they had concluded that

> neque expediens est, neque utile Reipublicae Christianae, imo visa hujus temporis conditione, prorsus pernitiosum, non solum illam translationem Horarum, sed etiam alias translationes Bibliae, aut partium ejus, prout jam passim fieri videntur, admitti; & quod illae quae jam emissae sunt, supprimi magis deberent, quam tolerari.[43]

It is difficult to imagine a more 'orthodox' work than Gringore's translation. Books of Hours had always been intended for lay use and Jean de Brie had already published a prose translation of the whole book. The Sorbonne were thus going against a well established trend, and their condemnation and even the Parlement's prohibition were utterly unsuccessful in banning Gringore's work. Gringore obtained a royal privilege in October 1525 and had the work printed and sold in Paris and Rouen; the work was frequently reprinted.[44]

This is an issue on which many catholics disagreed with the Sorbonne. The King had no patience with their condemnation of translations of the Bible, let alone opposition to other vernacular religious literature. It is striking that quite a lot of the new vernacular works of this period emanate from circles near the King's entourage—particularly the works of Guillaume Petit and Jean de Gagny.[45] But among many theologians, worried by heretical pamphlets, there was probably a period when almost any book in French on religion appeared suspect, the more so if it were written by a layman. And this no doubt accounts for the criticism of books for the laity which Bouchet records, and also for his own frequent defence of religious writing in French.

c) *Bouchet's Defence of Religious Writing for the Laity*

In the *Déploration* in 1512 Bouchet said of the common people that

> Leur medecine est bon enseignement
> Et d'amer Dieu et son prochain exemple.[46]

As far as the 'enseignement' was concerned, he began to provide it himself, producing over a period of about six years a saint's life, a collection of prayers, and a more learned discussion of questions involving free will, grace and predestination.

In these first three works, although he mentions his intentions, there is as yet no question of defending himself for writing something controversial. The saint's life, that of St Radegonde, as told in the *Histoire de Clotaire*, is presented as useful above all for the example that it offers. In the dedication to Queen Claude he says:

> Et y pourront voz damoiselles prendre exemple et salutaire doctrine, voire par imitation de vie suyvir en plusieurs actes

quant à pudicité virginalle, et fidelité matrimonialle si saincte et
bonne dame.[47]

It would appear that at this period Bouchet believed that moral
instruction should be the main function of literature read by
women. When describing St Radegonde's studies in her youth, he
defends the right of noble women to read instructive books:

> Car il est fort honneste à une princesse ou autre dame qui a bien
> dequoy vivre de veoir les livres moraulx et les histoires an-
> tiques, tant pour y prendre exemple de bien et vertueusement
> vivre, que pour eviter le peril et dangier d'oysiveté. Aussi puis
> que leur estat n'est de faire euvres mecaniques et mercenaires,
> il leur est plus proffitable pour le salut de leurs ames et consola-
> tion de leurs espritz regarder et lire en quelque beau livre, que
> consumer le temps en dances, dissolutions et parlemens lasci-
> vieux et damnables.[48]

At this stage he supports moral works rather than theological
ones:

> Et pour respondre à ceulx qui dient que l'esprit d'une femme
> n'est disposé ne capable pour recevoir et comprendre une
> bonne proposition concernant nostre foy, je ne dy pas aussi
> qu'elles doibvent estudier en la theologie ne se mectre si avant
> en argumentations theologalles, mais en choses moralles et
> instructives de meurs et vertuz.[49]

But even here he goes on to present arguments which might support
more theological studies:

> Combien que qui vouldroit rememorer combien il y a eu de
> femmes fermes en la foy catholicque et qui l'ont soustenue par
> argumentations et martires, comme saincte Catherine et saincte
> Barbe, on trouveroit qu'elles ont triumphé contre les infidelles
> aussi bien que les hommes. Et diray davantaige à leur honneur
> que jamais femme ne fut reprise de heresie et pertinacité, mais
> ont tousjours esté faciles à convertir à nostre foy.[50]

Thus in his first religious work Bouchet is envisaging moral instruction above all, and he also has leisured ladies in mind, rather
than simple people. The *Labyrinthe de Fortune* of 1522 is also aimed at
ladies, but the range goes far beyond moral instruction. When he
expresses his intentions in a letter to the theologian who checked
the work, he claims that his work is first of all to the honour and
glory of the Trinity, secondly for the recreation of his own mind and
to teach him to know himself, thirdly

> à la consolation des dames et autres personnes qui n'entendent
> les lettres latines, lesquelz pourront veoir en briefve substance
> ce qui est en plusieurs volumes de livres confusement con-
> tenu.[51]

The latinless ladies are to benefit from a method which sets out to
disseminate learning by drawing material together, quoting and

indicating sources:

> Non de ce nom seul sers, mais par la reserche et labeur que j'ay
> prins à extraire les ditz, oppinions et sentences d'aucuns nobles
> poetes, eloquens orateurs, philosophes naturelz et moraulx,
> docteurs sainctz et catholicques, loix cyvilles et canonicques,
> coctez en la marge du langaige vulgaire.[52]

The book is presented as vulgarising knowledge, both Christian
and classical, and the errors it corrects are learned rather than
popular ones. This is not then primarily a work of religious instruction for simple people. But it nevertheless makes available in French
a discussion of areas of theology treated only in the most extensive
vernacular manuals, for Bouchet is concerned with the growth of
erroneous beliefs concerning fortune and divine providence, and
he deals with original sin, free will and predestination.

The most remarkable preface accompanies his collection of prayers. Although dedicated as usual to a great lady, a much wider
audience is envisaged:

> Considerant que oraison est une des partie[s] de satisfaction
> que nous doyvons faire à Dieu, laquelle luy est tresplaisante
> lors qu'elle luy est faicte humblement de cueur et de bouche en
> fervente devocion par l'ame penitente, et que bon et utille
> seroit es hommes et femmes de France ignorans les lettres
> latines faire leurs particulieres et generalles oraisons en langage
> vulgaire à ce qu'ilz entendissent ce qu'ilz dient et demandent à
> Dieu comme font les aultres nacions catholicques . . .[53]

One is reminded of one of Lefèvre's arguments in his preface to his
translation of the New Testament in 1523,

> ainsi que pareillement est maintenant faict en diverses regions
> et diversitez de langues par la plus grande partie de Europe
> entre les Chrestiens.[54]

The idea that prayer should be understood was precisely one on
which the Sorbonne was to take issue with Erasmus. Bouchet is
making no overt criticism here of prayer not understood, but clearly
he thinks that it is highly desirable that people should understand
their prayers. The prayers themselves are firmly traditional, as we
shall see later. He also explains his use of verse for the prayers, with
one argument from tradition and one from utility:

> Toutes le[s]quelles choses j'ay mises en vers et metres tant
> parce qu'ilz sont plus faciles à retenir que la prose, et aussi qui
> les peres de l'ancien testament en ont usé en leurs pseaulmes et
> canticques, et aussi les saincts docteurs es hympnes par ses
> versetz et respons qu'on dit on service de l'eglise.[55]

One of the overriding considerations in the composition of this
collection thus appears to be its utility to the latinless. Bouchet seeks
to make the traditional subjects of the Church's prayers more accessible and memorable to the laity.

These three works reveal a growing enthusiasm for instructing latinless people in the Church's traditions. Once Lutheranism presented a threat Bouchet reacted by providing even more instruction. But this was not the reaction of all Catholic theologians, and in subsequent writing Bouchet defends religious writing for the laity in general and his own in particular. When Bouchet had the *Triomphes* printed in 1530, it appeared with two certificates from theologians from Poitiers. The King's privilege also mentions examination in Paris. Approved by the Sorbonne and local theologians, Bouchet was safe from trouble with authority. But he was not safe from private criticism, as he tells us in *Ep. Fam.* 104: a detractor said that he would not dare to preach what Bouchet dealt with in one chapter, the elect and predestination. He is alluding to the final episode of the book in which, the *Ame raisonnable* having fallen into the *Pas de la Mort* and gone to meet her Maker, *Théologie* discusses with the author her possible fate. These chapters are maintained in all subsequent editions of this very popular book, but obviously one at least of Bouchet's critics thought that he was presumptuous in daring to treat such a knotty problem. Bouchet refers to his critic as 'ce bon frère'; this must be a cleric who is criticising an over-enterprising layman. Bouchet's first defence is an uncompromising one. The critic must have misread or misunderstood the whole chapter, for given the difficulty of the problems involved he had simply based himself on the word of St Paul:

Qui est celuy (dit-il) en la machine
Qui ait congneu la pensée divine?
Qui est celuy, tant sache bien veiller
Et contempler, qui l'ayt sceu conseiller?
Tout vient de Dieu . . .[56]

He is paraphrasing here Romans 11 vv.34 and 36, verses which he had referred to in the chapter criticised. There they served as a reason for simply stating the doctrine of predestination without the arguments surrounding it. So here he is quoting the Bible in order to justify himself for dismissing a theologian's criticism. This might seem distinctly 'evangelical' if it were not immediately followed by an appeal to the authority of the three theologians who checked the work and certified that it was free from error; they would hardly have done so, he says, if there were some passage in it contrary to the faith.

This is not the only reference in the *Epîtres Familières* to a layman being criticised for writing on a religious subject. In *Ep. Fam.* 47, written probably *c*.1527, Bouchet praises Jean Mary de Ruffec for a life of St Andrew which he had submitted to Bouchet for advice. Bouchet encourages him to have it printed, saying it will be valuable for combatting Lutheran error on the subject of the saints. He seems to expect his friend to have to meet some opposition, for he advises

him not to be put off by the fear of criticism; the envious will always
speak ill, and one must ignore them and not be deterred from doing
good. One would have thought that Mary would have been safe
enough in writing a saint's life, but in a subsequent letter to Bouchet,
Mary reveals that he has indeed suffered criticism.[57] However the
only point which his detractors found to make was that he should
not write on theology in the vernacular. This charge he dismisses
contemptuously, defending vernacular writing on the grounds that
the Hebrew of the Bible was a 'vernacular', also that God wants
people to know the Law and the Gospel. Mary is more outspoken
than Bouchet—unfortunately his life of St Andrew does not seem to
survive. But as far as one can judge, both men were attacked on the
sole grounds that they, laymen, were writing on religious subjects
in French. The criticism does not seem to have been sufficient to
trouble either of them seriously, but it does show how dubious
some people were at this time about religious books by, and even
for, the laity.

Subsequently Bouchet twice attempts the defence of such literature. In the *Jugement*, in a long prefatory letter to Anne de Laval
written in about 1536, Bouchet defends the right of women to study.
But his argument goes beyond the case of women when he considers religious books. He says that he is amazed that people should
wish to prevent women reading books in French—good and approved books that is—because he has found no prohibition in the
whole of Scripture. He would like to ask these people what difference there is between reading a sermon and hearing it. He agrees
that the bare text of Scripture may be dangerous:

> la lecture en langue vulgaire d'aucuns passages du vieil et
> nouveau Testament est dangereuse aux femmes et simples
> hommes non letrez, pour les causes qui trop longues seroyent
> à reciter.[58]

But it does not follow that they may not read approved moral books,
and such an occupation at home is better than idle conversations in
social gatherings. If Jean Gerson and Robert Ciboule[59] had believed
that the reading of vernacular books was pernicious they would not
have written any themselves.

Throughout this argument Bouchet appears to be combatting the
opinions of a group of people less liberal than himself. The argument he presents is in the tradition of encouraging lay instruction
which we have been considering, stemming from Gerson and referring back to him. The instruction offered by Gerson is by no means
limited to moral works; Bouchet is glossing over the issues when he
advocates moral works rather than translations. But what he says
about translations would accord with Gerson, who believed that
only the historical and moral parts of scripture were suitable for the
laity. Bouchet's coyness about the reasons for the Bible being

dangerous is perhaps due again to his fear of spreading heresy simply by defining it or quoting dangerous examples. He goes on to point out that, although St Paul forbade women to preach in Church, he directed them to instruct their children and servants at home. He also cites St Jerome as a writer of books for women and in praise of women—a nice way of disarming those who would use St Jerome as an anti-feminist authority. All Bouchet's religious writings are designed at least partly for women.

The second defence appeared in 1544, a time when, although persecution of reformists was more firmly established, Catholic theologians like Pierre Doré had moved away from the positions of the 1520s and were beginning to see the importance of counter-propaganda. Bouchet wrote a prefatory letter for a local prior's translation of Bishop Theodoret's history of the early church.[60] Asserting the work's particular usefulness at the present time, he refers to preachers ('concionateurs') who attack books translated or composed in French. He cannot understand their attacks, for they themselves are eager to read such books for the pleasure of reading French in its present polished state. Moreover reading French books is a laudable pastime for those who know no Latin : men and women of all estates can learn how to live virtuously in their allotted estate, always aiming at love of God and neighbour in true charity.

Bouchet's defence thus begins as a defence of French books in general, but it soon focuses on the question of religious books. Once again he refers to translations of the Bible, but this time suggesting a form, paraphrase, which might be acceptable :

> J'entends parler des livres moraulx et historiaulx, composés ou traduicts par gens de savoyr, et non suspects, fors de la traduction de l'ancien et nouveau Testament, et Pseaulmes, que je trouve dangereuse à simples gens, se la lettre n'est paraphrasée d'aulcuns des docteurs de l'Eglise.[61]

He now goes on to assert that reading is actually more profitable than sermons, in a tone which seems decidedly dismissive of sermons :

> On scet assés qu'on a tousjours les concionnateurs à l'oreille, et qu'en la lecture de quelque bon livre, non suspect, on peut apprendre plus de bonnes choses en ung mois qu'on ne feroit à ouyr toutes les contions d'une année.[62]

Similarly one history book gives an account of more experiences than the twenty that men would meet in their lives. If it were pernicious to have books in French, the Kings of France would not have had so many of all kinds translated, and Gerson and Ciboule would not have composed them. He cites the piety of Chartier's *Livre de Foy et d'Esperance*, the moral utility of the *Lunettes des Princes*, the inspiration given by reading the Annals of Martyrs and Confessors.

The substance of this defence is thus very similar to that of the first one, with its reference to Gerson, its stress primarily on moral books and its disapproval of Biblical translations. But he is certainly admitting the validity of the type of translation current before Lefèvre in the *Bible Historiée*, and in saying that books are more use than a sermon he is in disagreement with the views expressed by Sorbonne theologians several years earlier.

Thus it is clear that Bouchet did feel that knowledge of their religion was vital to the laity. He saw this as a matter on which the Church should promote reform analogous to the other reforms which seemed so necessary, and he could not agree with reactionaries who, terrified by the spread of heresy, sought to discourage the provision of vernacular books for the laity.

2

Bouchet's Religious Works
Before the Spread of Lutheranism

a) *The Life of St Radegonde*

Bouchet's first work of religious instruction was the most orthodox of all forms, the saint's life. We have already considered the *Histoire de Clotaire* of 1517 as Bouchet's earliest piece of historical writing. The fact that it can be considered under such a heading demonstrates its great strength in comparison with many vernacular saints' lives available at the time, and one may say that in his concern for historical accuracy and his attempt to set the life of St Radegonde into its proper historical background he anticipates the efforts of counter-reformation writers to set hagiography on a more scholarly foundation.[63]

The book reveals that Bouchet perceived certain defects in the contemporary treatment of saints. Bouchet stresses that

> je n'ay parlé par adulation mendatieuse, ne adjouxté quant au faict de l'histoire aucune chose non veritable ou supersticieuse.[64]

When like most hagiographers he devotes his final section to the saint's miracles, he takes the trouble to defend the practice:

> Et combien que la forme de sa vie soit suffisante pour attirer le peuple à devotion, touteffoiz parce que toutes parsonnes ne sont de semblable condition, et qu'il en y a aucuns qui avant que croire la saincteté d'une parsonne en veulent veoir proceder evidens signes par miracles et prodiges, j'ay bien voulu cy reciter aucuns miracles faiz aux prieres et intercessions d'icelle saincte depuis sondit decès . . .[65]

As we have seen, he is careful to include only miracles which he regards as adequately substantiated, concluding with his own wife's recovery from a sudden paralysis of her leg.

His pursuit of truth, although not always successful, is one of the merits of his hagiography. We have already noted that he rejects the fifteenth-century view that St Radegonde remained a virgin although married to King Clotaire.[66] Such a view must have appeared very appealing, for in many popular saints' lives the saint's heroic efforts are concentrated on the preservation of virginity in the way that early martyrs strove to preserve their unwavering allegiance to their faith. The whole point of the very popular legend of St Margaret in the form that it was read to women in labour in the sixteenth century is that despite all horrible torments she refused to marry the tyrant who desired her—that he was trying to make her abjure her faith seems almost secondary to this.[67] In the life of St Catherine of Siena the saint's sister is represented as having been caused by God to die in childbirth because she was encouraging her sister to prepare for matrimony.[68] In the life of St Bernard God strikes down a woman who will not give her husband permission to take monastic vows.[69] Thus abstinence from sexual intercourse is a particularly saintly and God-protected virtue in the eyes of a hagiographer by this time, almost a *sine qua non* of sanctity, and inevitably it is attributed to saints without any historical foundation, just as any given miracle tends to be attributed to many saints.

Bouchet however stands by the fact that his prime sources, while showing Radegonde's reluctance to marry, give no hint that she was other than an obedient wife. His sources, he says, maintain

> que saincte Radegonde obeit au roy son espoux tout ainsi qu'une prudente femme doit et est tenue faire à son mary. Mais que pour l'amour maritalle n'oublia celle qu'elle avoit à Jesucrist, car son corps ne habandonna tant à son mary charnel qu'elle ne le gardast immaculé à son espoux spirituel.[70]

No doubt he also wished to demonstrate that it was not impossible to avoid carnal sin in marriage, in an attempt to counter the hostility to matrimony so prevalent in hagiographical writers.[71] St Radegonde could thus serve as a model to women of all estates: maidens and wives as well as nuns. In one of the moral elaborations with which he permits himself to embroider his narrative, Bouchet describes St Radegonde's married life. He assures us that by the concordance of his sources he finds that St Radegonde had many excellent virtues while in the state of matrimony. First of all she loved her husband with a well-ordered marital love, neither lubricious nor licentious:

> Car onques à luy ne se soubmist pour delectacion charnelle, mais seulement pour luy complaire et donner remede à l'infirmité de sa sensualité, et affin qu'il ne tumbast en peché.[72]

Should he seek to indulge in the acts of marriage improperly as some incontinent husbands wish to do

> sans rudement y resister sçavoit bien par doulces et gracieuses parolles le divertir de ce maulvaiz propos.[73]

Instead of talking about frivolous things in bed, she would say to him, 'Alas, my lord, this world is a wretched place. Today we are alive, yet we do not know if we shall still be tomorrow: nothing is more certain than death . . .' Thus she sent the King to sleep, whereupon she got up and knelt down by the bed naked to pray, assuring God that she would really rather be a nun. Then she lay down on the floor on a horse-hair cloak where she would be found by her husband in the morning, cold as marble, much to his annoyance.[74]

This is not exactly a panegyric of the marital state; clearly Radegonde is merely paying the debt of marriage and takes no pleasure in it. In 1 *Ep. Mor.* 7 Bouchet was to adopt a far more positive approach to married love. But at this stage and in the context of a saint's life it is remarkable enough that he should feel that his saint's glory was not irredeemably tarnished by a consummated marriage. His rejection of the convenient modern version of the tale shows considerable independence of mind.

It has been noted that from the point of view of instruction Bouchet aims primarily at moral lessons, concentrating on what his readers can learn from St Radegonde's life for the conduct of their own lives. He describes her behaviour in each state and meditates upon it, drawing examples for his own times. As well as his treatment of her married life we may cite another example from the chapter on St Radegonde's abstinences in her youth. After expatiating on her temperance with both food and drink, and explaining that she ate only enough to prevent herself becoming weak, he adds sternly that young girls should take note of this way of life and should reflect that gluttony is the mother of all vices, for excessive eating and drinking lead to lubricity and shame and thus to scandal. There is no worse vice in a young girl, and one may daily see girls who are lost from having been gluttonous. Nor is it laudable in married women, for a drunkard does not know whether she is chaste or not. But with a balance absolutely typical of him he concludes that this does not mean that women may not drink wine as long as they drink in moderation, for in that case 'il rend la personne plus ferme, asseurée, arrestée et de meilleur esprit'.[75]

Such moralising is the only area in which he regularly goes beyond what his sources tell him; he fills in details of Radegonde's exemplary behaviour and invents speeches for her full of edifying sentiment. But he carefully acknowledges that he has done this in his dedication to the Queen:

> En decorant l'histoire pour la doctrine des dames d'aucunes moralles sentences, persuasions et remonstrances, et de plusieurs aultres petites choses curieuses, où vous pourrez aucuneffoiz contanter vostre trescler esprit, et luy donner recreation profitable pour le salut de vostre ame, l'incolumité, pros-

perité et santé de vostre personne.[76]
Overall his saint's life is remarkable for its attempt to be truthful and
for its historical solidity.

b) *Le Labyrinthe de Fortune*
The *Labyrinthe* finds its place in this chapter because after depicting
the labyrinth of life in this world apparently governed by Fortune,
Bouchet goes on in the second half of the book to introduce Faith,
Hope and Charity and explain in theological terms the forces which
really control men's lives. Bouchet was well aware that he was
dealing with difficult material for a layman; this is the first book
which he claims to have had corrected by a theologian—Jacques
Prévost, 'docteur en theologie, regent en l'université de Poictiers'.[77]
There is no suggestion that he submitted it to this inspection because of any new fear of Lutheran heresy. The book was first
published probably at the end of 1522 with the lament for the death
of Artus Gouffier in 1519 as its starting point; nowhere in it does
Bouchet mention the Lutheran heresy and presumably he was not
yet at this time concerned by it. He was, however, apparently
disturbed by a growth of erroneous beliefs concerning fortune and
divine providence. The same worry is shown three years later when
in the revised version of the *Déploration* he adds not only a section
on heresy, but also one on the spread of magic, astrology and
divination.

It is quite clear that Bouchet connects fatalism with the renaissance of classical learning; the classical ideas of *Humaine Discipline*
have to be countered with the Christian theology of *Véritable Doctrine*, and the poem is in itself a learned one dealing with some
particularly difficult religious problems. At the end of the first half
of the book, *Véritable Doctrine* speaks of the power of the First Cause,
God, and the two second causes deriving from the First, free will
and celestial influences. She explains how original sin perverts free
will, and discusses predestination, the effect of celestial influences,
and divine providence.[78] In the second half the *acteur* travels from
the labyrinth to the *Séjour des trois nobles dames* and the theological
virtues are each explained. Particularly in the section on charity,
which is loosely structured on the basis of the Ten Commandments,
there is extensive moral teaching. But in the main the book is
dealing with theological questions, and in a relatively learned way.

The learning in the book is presented, as Bouchet suggested in his
letter to Prévost, mainly by means of marginal reference and quotation. *Humaine Discipline* quotes from Ovid, Virgil, Valerius Maximus, Apuleius, Juvenal, Seneca, Aristotle, Persius, Sophocles,
Boethius; *Véritable Doctrine* counters with the Bible, Augustine,
Aquinas, Lactantius, and also Aristotle and Boethius. But although
Humaine Discipline must be prepared to be corrected, learning itself

properly used is apparently highly desirable and Bouchet parades
his knowledge, classical as well as Christian. It is worth noting that
one of the allegorical figures is called *Congnoissance de soy*; this is
understood in a strictly Christian sense but it does seem that
Bouchet wishes to evoke 'Nosce te ipsum': he uses the idea repeatedly, and in introducing *Congnoissance de soy* he gives as a note
'Se ipsum cognoscens cognoscit omnia', which he attributes to
Dionysius the Areopagite, *De Divinis nominibus*.[79] Another reference
to Dionysius is linked with a sentence attributed to Hermes, which
again suggests an interest in harmonising classical ideas with Christian teaching.[80]

There is an altogether wider spectrum of authorities evident than
in the 1512 *Déploration*, the only earlier work using the technique of
dense annotation. The major addition is of classical and neo-
platonic sources, but although the Bible and Canon Law are still the
best represented more theologians are also quoted, notably Aquinas
and Peter Lombard who do not appear in the *Déploration*.[81] The
technique makes this book one which can indeed be read at two
levels, depending on whether the reader has Latin or not. Certainly
the French often paraphrases the Latin quotation, as when *Foy*
expounds the doctrine of the Trinity, each stanza explaining a sentence from the Athanasian Creed which is quoted in Latin beside
it.[82] But often the quotation in Latin expresses more complex ideas,
or gives extra information—as for example in these two stanzas
from an attack on logic:

Et qui vouldroit par raison naturelle
Prouver que Dieu se soit vray homme faict
Sans euvre humain en Marie pucelle,
Entreprendroit ung [im]possible faict;
Semblablement que par grace et bien faict
A nous se baille en espece de pain,
De vin aussi, là fault le sens humain.
Pour le sçavoir il fault que à la foy sonnes,
Et simplement le croire non en vain,
Aussi qu'il soit ung Dieu en troys personnes.[83]

> Verbum caro factum est
> – que hoc verba loquen-
> tur? fit caro verbum, id
> est, homo deus. Et qui
> homo est in celis est;
> ascendit descendens,
> sed descendit non des-
> cendens. Est qui erat:
> et quod est non erat.
> Currimus per causas et
> ratione defficimur;
> rationem cernimus et
> causas non intelligimus.
> Hec beatus Hylari.
> li.x.de trini.
> Tu autem fide stas,
> noli altum sapere sed
> time. ad roma. xi.

Les argumens subtilz et logicaulx
Peu serviront à ces grans choses croire
Et bien souvent sont causes de grans maulx
De leurs abuz j'ay encores memoyre,
Ung Arrius plain de mondaine gloire
M'en feit jadis oultrage, et à la foy,

> De arriano et pluribus
> hereticis loquitur
> pred. beatus Hylarius
> pictavensis episcopus.
> in. pred. lib. de. trini.
> et aliis suis operibus.
> Vide hec distinct.
> xxxvii.c.omnem vim.

Autres plusieurs que nommer je ne doy
En plusieurs lieux en ont la foy blessée
Et fait injure à la divine loy,
Dont par long temps fuz comme delessée.[84]

Here the quotation from Hilary beside the first stanza actually demonstrates logical difficulties presented by the doctrine of the incarnation, while the French merely states that it is impossible for human reason to prove the doctrine. The note on Arius in the second stanza directs the latinate reader to source material while the French simply says that a wicked man called Arius attacked the faith.

An even better example occurs when Bouchet says in his French verse:

Homme n'y a tant bien se saiche duyre
Lequel sans Dieu, son ayde et secours,
Puisse à vertuz cheminer le droit cours.
Dieu par raison de tout a la puissance,
Car aultrement des hommes foulz et lours
On feroit dieux par grant mescongnoissance[85]

But in the Latin note he adds:

In hunc errorem ceciderunt Pelagiani,
xxiiii q. iii quid. Et damnatur hec heresis,
dist. iiii Placuit iii.[86]

Clearly Bouchet was prepared to say more in Latin than in the vernacular, particularly on heresy. This prefigures the restraint with which later he was to treat information about Lutheranism.

Many of the theological themes treated here will reappear in the *Triomphes*, but in some cases angled rather differently because the threat to the faith which he perceives is a different one. We may note for instance that in the *Labyrinthe*, although his teaching about the nature of faith and its relation to hope and to charity is fundamentally the same as the later teaching of the *Triomphes*, he does not at this stage lay so much stress on the importance of grace as he will in the later work.[87] In the section on prayer he defends prayer in general against heretics who said that all prayer is useless, but he does not bother to defend prayer to the Virgin and to saints in particular, as he will later in the *Triomphes*.[88] It is worth noting that in the revised *Déploration* Bouchet does not mention errors about free will in his attack on the Lutherans. This is no doubt because for him, having composed the *Labyrinthe*, such errors were bound up with wider questions of divine providence and erroneous belief in fatalism which he attacks in another section of the new *Déploration*.

We have noted in our second chapter that Bouchet remarked to his theologian friend that the style of his verse had necessarily been less easy than he would have liked because of the difficulty of treating such material and the risk of falling into error if the correct terms were not used. Not only is the material of the *Labyrinthe* relatively learned, it is also cut off from more popular religious instruction by its form, the elaborate memorial work. In the *Triomphes* Bouchet will use a story-line as in the *Labyrinthe*, but he will treat his theological subjects in prose once the instructional intention becomes all-important.

c) *Les Cantiques et Oraisons*

We have seen that in the prefatory letter addressed to Gouffier's widow Bouchet writes enthusiastically of helping latinless people to understand the prayers they say. The collection has few literary pretentions; the prayers are composed 'en vers et metres plains et vulgaires'.[89] Nor are they intended to be in the least innovatory; he has composed them 'jouxte et au pluspres des oraisons de saincte eglise qui m'a esté possible'.[90] The prayers, to God, the Virgin, angels and saints, are intended to be said 'es heures ordonnées et convenables à prier Dieu, tant à la messe qu'ailleurs, es festes solennelles et aultres'.[91]

The structure of the collection owes something to the Books of Hours. After various sets of hours these books usually include series of extra prayers, notably a series of prayers to saints, and a series for lay people to say as they go about their day's business, during the Mass, and for particular occasions like harvest-time, war, plague, prayer for friends, for the King, etc. Bouchet's collection is divided into four parts. The first contains prayers to be said while getting up and going to Church; the second, prayers to be said at different moments of the Mass; the third, prayers for all the necessities of the world; and the fourth, prayers for feast-days, including saints' days.[92] In each case Bouchet gives many more prayers than those available in the Book of Hours.

The second part, containing prayers to be said during the Mass, is the part which above all demonstrates Bouchet's desire that people should understand some at least of what was being said. It is much fuller than the six prayers in the Books of Hours which are intended to be said at different moments of the Mass. Devotional books sometimes offer meditations for use during the Mass, usually suggesting suitable subjects for prayer and meditation but without reference to what is going on at the altar.[93] Bouchet's prayers are for the most part suggested by the various parts of the liturgy so that the user would not lose contact with the priest's prayers and actions. In his rubrics he explains the significance of what the priest says and does, normally as figures of some aspect of the life of Christ:

> Oraison quant on dit Gloria in excelsis deo, qui nous
> represente la joyeuse nativité de nostre seigneur qui
> fut nuncié aux pasteurs

Jesus qui en humilité
Avez voulu de vierge naistre,
Vostre saincte nativité
Me face si vous plaist renaistre.
J'entendz, mon Dieu, seigneur et maistre,
Que de mon peché me reliefve,
Et que mon pauvre esprit se eslieve
A vous amer, craindre et servir,
Affin que après ma vie briefve
Veuillez mon ame on ciel ravir.[94]

It can be seen that the prayer itself is minimal in content and bears little relation to the *Gloria*; the rubric here and elsewhere is more informative than the verse. But it is worth noting that more than once Bouchet specifies that the prayer should be said after the priest's words, suggesting again that he does not want the worshipper to cut himself off from the activity at the altar. This is particularly marked when he reaches the Gospel:

Ce pendant qu'on dit l'evvangille on ne doit dire aucune chose mais l'escouter devotement par ce que c'est la parolle de Jesucrist, mais icelle dicte on dira ce qui s'ensuit . . .[95]

It would appear that he expects his reader to listen out of respect to the words of the Gospel which he does not understand, for want of Latin. With the latinless reader in mind he translates two parts of the liturgy into French prose, the *Misereatur* and the *Confiteor*. The rubric preceding the translation probably explains his reason for doing so:

Le misereatur et confiteor qu'on dit pour l'absolucion du prestre avant l'introyt de la messe traduit de latin en françois, laquelle absolucion efface le[s] pechez venielz.[96]

Presumably his decision to translate the confession rested on the belief that this at least must be understood if it is to be effective.

His claim to have written prayers 'jouxte et au plusprès des oraisons de saincte eglise' might lead one to expect more translation, or at least paraphrase, of prayers from the liturgy. But apart from these two translations the prayers for use during the Mass bear little relation to the actual text of the liturgy. In the fourth section of the collection, prayers for feast days, there is some evidence that he based his verse on collects or sequences. The collect for Septuagesima Sunday seems to underlie Bouchet's verse for the day:

Pour la septuagesime jusques au quaresme
Nous vous prions, Dieu tout puissant,
Qui vous plaise ouyr les prieres
De vostre peuple languissant
En pechez et tresgrans miseres;
Justement pour noz vituperes
Et crimes summes affligez.

O bon Dieu, noz cueurs erigez
A vous obeir et servir,
Et noz voluntez dirigez
A vertuz jour et nuyt suivir.[97]

Arguably the best poem in the collection is his long prayer for
Corpus Christi in which he paraphrases part of Aquinas' *Lauda Sion
Salvatorem*, the sequence for the festival. The longer poems give him
the opportunity to develop a more challenging subject matter, and
in these he is more concerned with explaining than with being
memorised. So in the prayer for Corpus Christi he treats the mysteries of the sacrament in the wake of Aquinas:

. . . Soubz especes de vin et pain,
Qui sont signes et non pas choses,
Choses passans le sens humain
Gisent et sont dessoubz encloses.
Car, sans y faire aucunes gloses,
On mange la chair, puis on boit
Le sang, et comme croire on doit,
Et croy sans doubte, estes, Jesus,
En chacune espece qu'on veoit
Tout entier, comme ou ciel lassus.

O tressaincte et sacrée hostie,
Où est Jesus reallement,
Si ores vous estes partie,
Dieu est par tout entierement.
Ce sainct et digne sacrement
Diviser aucun ne presume,
Et qui le prend ne le consume,
Autant en prend ung que plusieurs,
Et comme l'eglise resume
Est pris par bons et par pecheurs.

Touteffoiz non egallement,
Car les bons le prenent à bien,
Et les maulvaiz à dannement,
Mieulx leur vauldroit ne prendre rien.
On ne sauroit dire combien
Proffite aux bons, car c'est leur vie;
Et les maulvaiz, il les convie
Et conduict à mort eternelle.
Donnez moy grace que je obvie
A vous prendre en coulpe mortelle.[98]

But such borrowings are not very numerous.

In the section on the Mass, while making each prayer correspond
with some specified part of the Mass, he does not reproduce the
subject matter of the liturgy but directs his readers' attention to

suitable subjects of meditation, usually drawn from the life of Christ. When he reaches the canon, he does not attempt to reflect the subject matter of the priest's prayers, but instead provides a meditation on the origin of the sacrifice of the Mass—the Passion of Christ.[99] He says that the eleven parts of the canon up to the Lord's prayer represent eleven mysteries of the Passion: first the five journeys made before the crucifixion; then come two prayers for the elevation of the host and the chalice in which the priest's actions at the altar and the meditation coincide; finally four on aspects of the crucifixion. His seven prayers for the canonical hours similarly meditate on events from the life of Christ which occurred at that hour, always including the Passion, and conclude with a simple petition. In his prayers for festivals he usually directs his readers' attention to the historical significance of the festival; for instance, at Christmas:

O Jesus nostre Dieu et maistre,
Engendré eternellement,
Qui d'une belle vierge naistre
Volustes temporellement,
Et prendre corps reallement
Pour salut à tous nous donner,
Voire et vostre naistre ordonner
En Bethleem, cité petite,
Donnez-moy grace que je excite
Mon cueur à toute humilité,
Tellement que par le merite
De vostre sainct naistre, je herite
Au lieu plain de felicité.[100]

In his prayers for saints' days he usually gives some account of striking episodes from the saint's life. Thus most of his prayers are informative at a simple level. In the section on saints he includes a prayer which appears to demonstrate his interest in the controversy between Lefèvre and the Sorbonne concerning the Magdalenes:

Aux trois Magdalenes, ou à une seule
    comprenant les trois
Vous qui fustes si tresmundaine,
Que l'on appelle Magdelaine,
A qui Dieu par dilection
Feit de tous pechez grace plaine
De sa bonté tressouveraine,
Impetrez-moy remission.

   Vous, Magdalaine de Syon,
Ou Jherusalem, seur de Marthe,
Qui fustes tousjours humble et macte,
Tresdevote et contemplative,
Soiez de moy consolative.

> Et vous Magdelaine benigne,
> Dont par la puissance divine
> Jesucrist sept diables chassa,
> Faictes que de sa bonté digne
> Me garde de chose maligne,
> Et me enchasse où vous enchassa.[101]

Although he leaves open the question of whether one or three women were involved, the fact that he raises the question in the title and the way that he divides the prayer, treating them as three, suggest that he was not convinced by the arguments of the Sorbonne—or even by their *Determinatio* on the subject, assuming that he was writing after December 1521.[102] Taken with his preface with its statement that French people should understand their prayers as the people of other nations do, which is so close to Lefèvre's words concerning the New Testament, it can be seen that in spite of the traditional nature of its content this is the one work of Bouchet's which suggests that he might have had some sympathy with the aims of the Meaux group—had heresy not intervened.

The collection is so obviously designed to be useful to the latinless that it is surprising to discover that the sole copy surviving is the manuscript presented to Artus Gouffier's widow. Why did Bouchet not have this collection printed?

In fact some of the prayers were printed, although there is no means of knowing whether Bouchet himself authorised the edition. Bound with a Book of Hours printed in Poitiers in 1525 is a gathering which contains the first two sections of the *Cantiques* with no mention of an author.[103] The only variant of any significance is the omission of the translations of the *Misereatur* and *Confiteor* with the accompanying rubric. It is tempting to explain this omission in the light of the Sorbonne's disapproval of translations of the liturgy, and indeed to see Bouchet's failure to have the whole collection printed as being the result of the growth of heresy. When he began writing these prayers, probably in about 1515, there would have been nothing controversial about them, and by about 1520 they would have seemed completely in tune with the times. Jean de Brie was publishing the entire Book of Hours in translation: many Churchmen were striving to improve the religious life of the laity, and not only those whom we view in retrospect as evangelicals. But five years later the climate was very different: the Sorbonne censured Gringore's translation of the *Heures de Nostre Dame* which is far less extensive than de Brie's complete translation. We have seen Bouchet's own distress at the new heresy from 1524 onward. Perhaps in retrospect, with the Sorbonne condemning translations of Bible and liturgy and questioning the need for the laity to understand the words of their prayers, his collection of prayers seemed to have acquired some undesirable associations.

He may have felt this himself, or others may have pointed it out to him. To translate the text of the Hours had been forbidden, and to replace them might also seem presumptuous. As he says in the *Triomphes* in 1530:

> Se fault garder de laisser les oraisons et heures ordonnées et approuvées par l'Eglise pour dire aultres oraisons faictes et composées par gens devotz en leur particulier.[104]

Since it is impossible to date the manuscript of the *Cantiques* with any certainty one can only speculate with regard to his intentions, but it is tempting indeed to assume that the collection was compiled in a spirit of growing enthusiasm for offering instruction to the laity just before the spread of Lutheranism began to give cause for concern, and that it was never printed by Bouchet because of the changes in opinion brought about by the growth of heresy.

Bouchet's first three works of instruction are traditional. They are not at all evangelical in the sense of being Bible-based. But they are very good of their kind in that they provide in each case fuller information for the laity than the average comparable book. From this point of view Bouchet's work ranks with the best vernacular saints' lives and discussions of theology, and if his collection of prayers had been printed *in extenso* they would have constituted one of the fullest available in French at the time. His inclination to give more rather than less instruction to the laity survives the spread of Lutheranism and finds its fullest expression in *Les Triomphes de la noble et amoureuse dame.*

NOTES

1. For example, of the 286 items printed by Vérard listed by Macfarlane, 94 are French works with a religious subject, 59 more are Latin *Horae*. On some aspects of religious instruction for the laity in this period see J-C. Dhotel, *Les Origines du catéchisme moderne d'après les premiers manuels imprimés en France,* Paris, 1967, especially pp.27-38 and Thomas N. Tentler, *Sin and Confession on the Eve of the Reformation,* Princeton, 1977.
2. The BN holds large numbers of Vérard editions printed on vellum. Examples in the BL include *La Fleur des commandemens de Dieu,* [1499], C.22.b.4; J. Castel, *Le Mirouer des pecheurs,* [1505?], C.22.a.7; St Bernard, *Meditations,* [1506?], C.22.a.5. See Macfarlane, *Antoine Vérard,* p.xii. For pamphlets, see for example *infra,* n.11.
3. Columbi, *Confession generale,* [1520?], BL 845.a.30, d2 ro; *Fleur des commandemens,* a1 ro; *Ordinayre des crestiens,* Paris, 1502, BL C.97.c.4, x8 ro.
4. Found for instance in St Jerome, *La Vie des anciens saintz peres hermites,* Paris, 1486, BL IB.39803, a1 vo; Bonaventura, *Traicté qui est dit l'arbre de la croix,* [Paris, 1510?], BL 3832.aa.24, a1 vo. See also *infra,* at n.20.

5. *Cité de Dieu*, tr. Raoul de Presles, Abbeville, 1486-7, BL I C.43805; Cassianus, *Colacions*, tr. Jean Golein, Paris, Vérard, [1504?], BL 3627.dd.11; Durandus, *Racional*, tr. Jean Golein, Paris, Vérard, 1503, BL C.48.g.8. All of these had been translated in the late fourteenth century for Charles v. For St Bernard see *supra*, n.2.

6. Printed for instance by Vérard, BN Vélins 100, 101. See *The Cambridge History of the Bible*, vol.2, ed. G. W. H. Lampe, C.U.P., 1969, pp.436-52 and vol.3, ed. S. L. Greenslade, C.U.P., 1963, p.425 for a summary of the history of the various versions of the Bible in French. See also S. Berger, *La Bible française au moyen âge*, Paris, 1884. Charles v III had commissioned the revision of the version which Vérard was to publish, an example referred to by Lefèvre in the introduction to his own translation; see *Nouveau Testament*, S. de Colines, 1523 (Facsimile edition Paris–La Haye, 1970), Part 2, A2 ro-vo.

7. See P. Lacombe, *Livres d'heures imprimés au XVe et au XVIe siècle conservés dans les bibliothèques publiques de Paris*, Paris, 1907; H. Bohatta, *Bibliographie der Livres d'Heures*, Vienna, 1909.

8. F. Soleil, *Les Heures gothiques et la littérature pieuse aux XVe et XVIe siècles*, Rouen, 1882, reproduces some of the common prayers in French. As the century went on more and more material in French was included; see Lacombe, *Livre d'heures*, especially p.xlii.

9. For example, *L'Ordinayre des crestiens* (*supra*, n.3); this extensive manual was translated into English and published by W. de Worde, *The Ordynarye of Chrystyanyte*, London, 1502. BL G.11739.

10. See Tentler, *Sin and Confession*, pp.28-53.

11. See for example A. Faren, *La pratique de soy bien confesser* [Paris? 1500?], BL I A.41530; *La Confession de maistre Jehan Jarson*, Paris, [1490?], BL I A.40277; J. Quentin, *Examen de conscience pour soy congnoistre à bien se confesser*, [Paris, 1500?], BL I A.40603 (all 8 leaves). *La Grant confession de Pasques*, Paris, [1495?], BL I A.39501 (6 leaves).

12. For example, *L'Examen de conscience du mal et du bien de l'ame*, Rouen, [1489?], C.22.b.11.

13. The articles of faith and the commandments are found in preparations for confession; for the two prayers see *infra* at nn.18, 25 and 27. See Dhotel, *Origines du catéchisme*, pp.34-5.

14. Raoul de Montfiquet provides an extensive treatise for laymen in *Le Livre du sainct sacrement de l'autel*, Paris, Vérard, [1505?], BL C.22.a.9. Columbi gives prayers for taking communion in his *Confession generale*, c7 vo-d1 ro. Meditations for use during a low mass are found in Jean Barril's little book of instruction, Toulouse, 1535 (dedicated to Marguerite de Navarre but written much earlier for Anne de Beaujeu and Suzanne de Bourbon), BL C.125.dd.21, k1 ro; also Le Roy, *Livre de la femme forte*, Paris, [1505?], BL C.36.b.32, k1 ro.

15. On Gerson (1363-1429) see J. Connolly, *John Gerson, Reformer and Mystic*, Louvain, 1928. For his works see *Opera omnia*, Ellies du Pin, 5 vols, Antwerp, 1706 and *Œuvres complètes*, ed. P. Glorieux, Paris, 10 vols, 1960-74. For his views on translations of the Bible, see *Contra curiositatem studentium*, *Opera omnia*, 1, esp. col.105; ed. Glorieux, 3, esp. p.249.

16. For example in Columbi's *Confession Generale*, and Le Roy's *Dialogue de consolation entre l'ame et raison*, Paris, [1505?], BL C.107.c.5. One of the forms of confession mentioned *supra*, n.11, is falsely attributed to 'Jehan Jarson'.

17. The work is an abridged translation of his *Opus tripartitum* (*Opera omnia* 1, 425-50). For the Paris version see BN Rés.D.7848; Le Mans BL 3835.a.69.

18. BL copy, f.lxxviii vo.

19. *Ibid.*, ff.iv vo-v ro.

20. *Ibid.*, ff.v vo-vi ro.

21. *Ibid.*, f.vi vo.

22. Eugene Rice notes that it was recommended in Evreux, Bordeaux, Langres and Chartres and, in 1517, by Denis Briçonnet at St Malo. See *The Pursuit of Holiness*, ed. C. Trinkaus and H. A. Oberman, Leiden, 1974, E. F. Rice Jr, 'The Meanings of "Evangelical"', pp.472-5. See also Dhotel, *Origines du catéchisme*, pp.29-31. Tentler, *Sin and Confession*, pp.45-6.

23. For Maillard see Renaudet, *Préréforme*, especially pp.163-5, and A. J. Krailsheimer, *Rabelais and the Franciscans*, Oxford, 1964, pp.19-79. Famous above all as a popular preacher, his sermons were printed in Latin summaries, but a few French works were also printed, including two forms of confession and an account of the Passion of Christ based on the Mass. See *Œuvres françaises*, ed. A. de La Borderie, Nantes, 1877.

24. See *supra*, nn.14 and 16, also *Le Mirouer de penitence tres devot et salutaire*, Paris, S. Vostre, 2 vols, 1507-11, BL 1360.e.1.

25. Béda was the pupil and successor of Jean Standonck who reformed the Collège de Montaigu. He collaborated in the publication of St Bernardine's *Petite Dyablerie dont Lucifer est le chef*, Paris, BL C.53.h.9(1). This is a tract condemning swearing, but it includes translations of the Lord's Prayer and the Ave Maria (g2 vo).

26. In *The Pursuit of Holiness*, art. cit., pp.473-4.

27. *Les Heures nostre dame à l'usaige de Romme nouvellement translateez de latin en françoys*, [1520?], BL C.30.e.39. Not in Lacombe; Bohatta No.372. Jean de Brie died between July 1522 and January 1523 (Ph. Renouard, *Répertoire des imprimeurs parisiens*, Paris, 1965).

28. For example, in a passage from St Luke:
    > Comment ce fera ce que tu dis, car j'ay voué à Dieu virginité, et ne congnois homme par charnalité (*Heures*, b2 ro).
    Cf. *Bible historiée*, BN Vélins 101, f.ccxxviii ro, col.1:
    > Comment sera ce fait, car je ay proposé et promiz à Dieu, c'est à dire j'ay voué, que je ne congnoistré mie homme, ne auray charnellement compaignie d'omme.
    Other passages are even closer (e.g. the beginning of the Gospel of St John). De Brie's translator was probably using the *Bible historiée*.

29. The Sorbonne condemned Luther for speaking slightingly of the *ars confitendi* (See *Determinatio theologice Facultatis Parisiensis super doctrina Lutheriana*, [Paris, 1521], BL 807.b.14(2), b1 vo). Erasmus condemns this type of preparation in his *Exomologesis; sive modus confitendi*, Basle, 1524, C.64.a.19(1), *Opera Omnia* (Leiden), vol.5,

cols.145-70. For the contemporary French translation of this tract (1524) see E. Droz, *Chemins de l'hérésie*, vol.1, Geneva, 1970; see especially pp.31-2.

30. For example, under the title of *La Fleur des commandements*, we find the large volume of biblical *exempla* published by Vérard (BL C.22.b.4) and others, also *La Fleur des commandementz et declaration des bonnes œuvres* s.d. BL C.83.a.21), which attacks reliance on works instead of faith, pilgrimages, prayers to saints; it advocates reformation of the Church by kings and princes. (The date suggested in the BL catalogue, [1510?], is plainly too early; the short-title catalogue gives [1525?].) See also the list of titles of books censured by the Sorbonne in Higman, *Censorship*, pp.181-9.

31. The Faculty first discussed the matter in 1523; the condemnation was issued in 1525. See Higman, *Censorship*, pp.24-5, 77-8.

32. Delisle, 'Notice sur un régistre des procès-verbaux de la Faculté de théologie de Paris', *Notices et extraits des manuscrits de la Bibliothèque Nationale*, vol.36, Paris, 1899, p.366 §xxxiv; p.368, §xxxviii.

33. See the discussions of 1525 recorded in Du Boulay, *Historia Universitatis Parisiensis*, 6 vols, Paris, 1665-73, vol.6, pp.173-84.

34. See D'Argentré, *Collectio Judiciorum de novis erroribus*, 3 vols, Paris, 1724-36, vol.2, p.61, col.1 (censuring Erasmus on the question of women and the uneducated discussing scripture).

35. Delisle, 'Régistre', p.370, §xliii.

36. D'Argentré, *Collectio*, vol.2, p.45, col.1 and p.61, col.2.

37. Béda, *Annotationes in Jacobum Fabrum Stapulensem*, Paris, 1526, BL L.17.d.14(2), f.clxxv vo.

38. P. Sutor, *De Tralatione Bibliae*, Paris, 1525, BL 699.1.22, ff.xciiii vo, xcviii vo. He does go on to concede that the portions of the epistles and the gospels appointed to be read each Sunday could be translated into the vernacular if accompanied with proper explanations.

39. After the *Affaire des Placards* he published *Contre les tenebrions lumiere evangelicque* (BN Rés. D.80052). But before that he had produced works in French against Lutherans: see M. M. de La Garanderie, *Christianisme et lettres profanes*, p.219. On his work in the diocese of Le Mans, see *ibid.*, pp.215-22.

40. Doré wrote a string of works beginning with *Les Allumettes du feu divin*, Paris, 1538. At the end of the *College de Sapience . . . avec le Dialogue de la Foy*, Paris, 1539, BL 1360.f.8, he says that he has now written enough in French, 'c'est assez long temps nourry de laict l'enfance Chrestienne', n3 vo. However, he went on to compose many more French works.

41. *College de sapience*, f.lxiiii ro.

42. *Heures de Nostre Dame*, printed with a privilege from the King, dated October 1525, Paris, J. Petit, [1525; see Higman, *Censorship*, p.79]. The translations are discussed by M. Jeanneret in *Poésie et tradition biblique au XVIe siècle*, Paris, 1969, pp.35-42.

43. D'Argentré, *Collectio*, vol.2, p.7, col.1. See Oulmont, *Pierre Gringore*, Paris, 1911, pp.25-6, 57-61; Higman, *Censorship*, pp.25, 77-9.

44. For the editions see Oulmont, Higman and Lacombe, *Livres d'Heures*.

45. Guillaume Petit, d.1536 was bishop of Troyes, then of Senlis, and
was confessor to the King. His works in French include *Tresdevotes oraisons à l'honneur de la . . . Vierge Marie*, Paris, S. de Colines,
s.d. BN Rés. p.Ye.297, *La Formation de l'homme*, Paris, 1538, BN
Rés. D.17409(1). Jean de Gagny, d.1549, was 'premier Aulmosnier du Roy': he published *Le Livre contenant devote exposition sur
le cinquantiesme Pseaulme . . .* Paris [1532], BL C.97.aa.14, *Le livre
faisant mention des sept parolles . . .*, Paris, 1528, BL C.97.b.33 and
a translation of *Sermons de Guerricus, Abbé d'Igny*, Paris, S. de
Colines, s.d. BN C.3347: this translation was made at the specific
command of the King. In the preface de Gagny warns readers
against books printed without the name of author or printer, or
printed outside of France (f.lim.[3] vo).
46. *Déploration*, C3 vo. In the *Labyrinthe* he says that simple people
are misled in the confessional by priests too ignorant to know the
difference between mortal and venial sin (1524, P1 ro).
47. aa1 vo.
48. f.x ro.
49. *Ibid.*
50. *Ibid.*
51. *Labyrinthe*, P. Le Noir ed., GG1 ro.
52. *Ibid.*, FF4 vo.
53. *Cantiques*, f.1 ro. See the bibliography. The manuscript was first
described by Plattard in the *Revue du seizième siècle*, vol.ix, 1922,
pp.80-2. See my article, 'Jean Bouchet's prayers in French for the
laity . . .'.
54. *Nouveau Testament*, (Part 1), a2 vo.
55. f.1 vo.
56. *Ep. Fam.* 104, f.lxviii vo, col.2.
57. *Ep. Fam.* 80, f.lv vo, col.2.
58. *Jugement*, bb2 vo.
59. Robert Ciboule, 'doyen d'Evreux', composed among other works
Le Livre de Meditation sur soy mesmes which was printed in Paris,
1510 (BL C.38.h.11). Bouchet borrows from it in the *Triomphes* for
a description of the parts of the body. See André Combes, 'Un
témoin du socratisme chrétien au XVe siècle: Robert Ciboule
(1403-1458)', *Archives d'histoire doctrinale*, vol.8, 1933, pp.93-259.
60. *Histoire de Theodorite, evesque de Cyropolis*, tr. D. M. Mathée, Poitiers, 1544, A6 vo-A7 vo (see the bibliography).
61. A7 ro.
62. *Ibid.*
63. See R. Aigrain, *L'Hagiographie, ses sources, ses méthodes et son
histoire*, Paris, 1953. In *De locis theologicis*, 1563, the Dominican
Melchior Cano complained that Christian hagiographers showed
less preoccupation with truth than Diogenes Laertius or Sue-
tonius in their biographies; he insisted that 'the saints do not
need our lies' (Aigrain, p.329). Many factors had led to untruthfulness, such as stylised forms, the wish to edify, vested interest
and a popular taste calling for the literary creation of saints' lives
just like epics and romances. The obvious untruthfulness of
many saints' lives was both a cause of Protestant and Evangelical
attacks and a weapon in those attacks. The Catholics, partly
because of these attacks but also no doubt as a natural result of

the new, more critical, approach to their sources, began in the sixteenth century to set hagiography on a sounder historical basis, with the work of Surius in the 1570s and then of Rosweydus, which came to fruition in the work of the Bollandists, the *Acta Sanctorum,* whose first volume was published in 1643.

Bouchet is writing well before these more scholarly projects were under way, also before the main attacks on the cult of saints.

64. *Histoire de Clotaire,* aa1 vo.
65. f.lxxix vo (m1 vo).
66. See chapter 4, n.107.
67. There are many versions of this life, often attached to Books of Hours: for example *La Vie sainte Marguerite* [Lyons 1490?], BL I A.42295; *La Vie madame saincte Marguerite* [Paris, 1520?], bound after *Heures à l'usaige de Meaulx,* Paris, J. de Brie [1521?], BL C.46.d.19(1) and (2).
68. *La Vie de ma dame saincte Katherine de Seine,* Paris, 1503, BL C.97.b.12 ff.v ro-vi ro.
69. *La Vie de monsieur saint Bernard,* [Dijon, 1491?], BL I A.44920, a5 vo.
70. f.xxv vo.
71. He says that she reflected 'qu'elle pourroit en l'estat de mariage vivre chastement et acquerir par bonnes euvres paradis', f.xxv ro. The second part of the sentence might have been put differently if he had been writing later: see chapter 7.
72. f.xxvi ro. Cf. Tentler, *Sin and Confession,* pp.170-4.
73. *Ibid.* Cf. Tentler, *ibid.,* pp.186-208.
74. f.xxvi ro-vo.
75. f.xiii ro-vo.
76. aa1 vo.
77. See appendix A.
78. *Labyrinthe,* 1524, G6 vo-J1 vo, J3 ro-K3 ro, chs 26-9, 31-2.
79. M8 vo, Part 2, ch.2. See *Dionysiaca,* Bruges, 1937, vol.1, p.398: Bouchet's quotation deforms the sense of the sentence from *De divinis nominibus,* ch.7, which reads in the translation of Scotus Erigena: 'Semit igitur divina sapientia cognoscens cognoscit omnia'—this is an attribute of God. But Bouchet is about to discuss the creation of the human soul in the image of God.
80. J1 vo. A reference to the mirror described by Dionysius (probably *De divinis nominibus,* ch.4, *Dionysiaca,* vol.1, p.271, or *De caelesti hierarchia,* ch.3, *ibid.,* vol.2, p.788) is accompanied by the note 'Mortale immortali temporale perpetuo corruptibile incorrupto propinquare non potest. Hermes.' I have not been able to trace this sentence.
81. For example St Thomas G1 ro, G1 vo, G8 vo; Peter Lombard G7 ro, G8 ro (also referring to Gabriel Biel's commentary on the Sentences). See *supra,* chapter 3(c) on the authorities in the *Labyrinthe.*
82. This appears in the first section on faith which concerns belief. Bouchet has far more to say about the doctrine of the Trinity here than in the *Triomphes;* cf. chapter 7, n.28.
83. *Labyrinthe,* 1524, F4 ro. References to St Hilary, *De Trinitate,* Book 10; see *PL* vol.x, cols 386-7; Romans 11 v.20.

84. F4 ro. References to St Hilary, *De Trinitate*, etc., and *Dec. Grat.*
     Prima pars, Dist.xxxvii, c.vi:
     > Omnem vim venenorum suorum in dialectica disputatione
     > constituunt haeretici, quae philosophorum sententia; de-
     > finitur non astruendi vim habere, sed studium destruendi.
     > Sed non in dialectica complacuit Deo salvum facere popu-
     > lum suum. Regnum enim Dei in simplicitate fidei est, non in
     > contentione sermonis.
     This sums up the argument used by Bouchet against logic.
85. H1 vo.
86. *Dec. Grat.* Secunda pars, c.xxiv, q.iii, cap.xxxix, Quidam autem;
     Tertia pars, *De consecratione*, Dist.iv, c.clii, Placuit igitur. The first
     reference is to a chapter which lists and describes heretical sects,
     including Pelagians ('they place free will above divine grace,
     saying that will is sufficient for fulfilling divine command-
     ments'); the second is a pronouncement of the Council of Milevis
     against Pelagian error.
87. See *infra* chapter 7, section 6 for the treatment of these subjects in
     the *Triomphes*. When discussing hope of paradise in the *Laby-
     rinthe* he uses the word *grâce* only once in 84 lines and then in the
     phrase 'espoir de pardon et de grace' so that it may mean 'for-
     giveness' (*Labyrinthe*, 1524, P8 vo). Cf. the passages on hope
     from the *Triomphes* quoted *infra* chapter 7, n.115.
88. *Labyrinthe*, 1524, O7 ro-vo: cf. chapter 7, section 5.
89. *Cantiques*, f.1 ro.
90. *Ibid.*, f.1 ro.
91. *Ibid.*, f.1 ro-vo.
92. ff.3 ro-15 vo, 15 vo-28 ro, 28 ro-40 vo, 40 vo-71 vo.
93. Cf. *supra* n.14. For the six prayers in the Book of Hours see for
     example the *Horae* printed by Vérard, Paris, 1503 (BL C.41.b.2),
     C4 ro-C5 vo. The titles are given in French and indicate that the
     prayers are to be said when the priest turns round, at the eleva-
     tion of the host and of the chalice, at the Pax, before and after
     taking communion.
94. f.18 ro.
95. f.20 ro.
96. f.16 ro-vo. The translations are reproduced in my article, 'Jean
     Bouchet's prayers', p.431.
97. f.42 ro-vo. Cf. 'O Lord, we beseech thee favourably to hear the
     prayers of thy people: that we, who are justly punished for our
     offences, may be mercifully delivered by thy goodness, for the
     glory of thy name. . .', in *The Book of Common Prayer*.
98. f.46 ro-vo. Cf. *Lauda Sion Salvatorem*:
     > xiii Sub diversis speciebus / Signis tantum et non rebus /
     > Latent res eximiae. xiv Caro cibus, sanguis potus / Manet
     > tamen Christus totus / Sub ultraque specie. xv A sumente
     > non consisus / Non confractus, non divisus / Integer accipi-
     > tur. xvi Sumit unus, sumunt mille; / Quantum isti, tantum
     > ille: / Nec sumptus consumitur. xvii Sumunt boni, sumunt
     > mali / Sorte tamen inaequali / Vitae, vel interitus. xviii
     > Mors est malis, vita bonis: / Vide paris sumptionis / Quam
     > sit dispar exitus.
99. See 'Jean Bouchet's prayers', p.432.

100.   f.41 ro.
101.   ff.66 vo-67 ro.
102.   See D'Argentré, *Collectio*, vol.2, p.vii.
103.   BN Vélins 1655. See 'Jean Bouchet's prayers', pp.424 and 435.
104.   *Triomphes*, 1530, f.cxiiii ro.

Bouchet's Religious Writing
After the Spread of Lutheranism:
Les Triomphes de la noble et amoureuse dame

1
The Printing History

Internal evidence shows that Bouchet was already composing *Les Triomphes* in 1527.[1] The first edition was printed for the most part in 1530 although it was probably not published until 1531—Bouchet seems to have taken a few months to collect certificates from theologians and a privilege from the King.[2]

When it appeared, the first edition was thoroughly armed with certificates of its orthodoxy. Two theologians from Poitiers had checked the book, and their conclusions are reproduced *in extenso*. The Dean of the Faculty of Theology 'frater Nicolaus Louandi' praises the work highly: 'hic enim tractatus est totus aureus, mira devotione relucens'; he has found no error in it.[3] Antoine d'Asnières, a Franciscan theologian teaching at the University stresses the care which has been taken to avoid any error; he says that he himself has made such emendations as he thought necessary, and that the work is free from error.[4] In addition to the theologians from Poitiers, the privilege granted in Paris records that the book has been read by 'aulcuns docteurs notables de l'université de Paris'.[5] This is supported by Bouchet's reference in *Ep. Fam.* 104 to a Parisian theologian who checked the work.

Although Bouchet had had the *Labyrinthe* and the *Epître de Justice* checked by theologians, such extensive examination and certification reflects the function of the book, which is intended as a manual of religious instruction, and also the workings of the censorship rules in force in 1530 as a result of the fear of heretical books.[6] It also shows that in any meaningful sense the book can be considered as 'orthodox', since it was approved in both Poitiers and Paris by theologians who were looking for error.

Thus approved, the book was reprinted many times. Later editions do not reproduce the text of the theologians' letters, but otherwise the substance is unchanged. The printing history suggests that the book amply fulfilled its function as a manual of instruction. The first Poitiers edition was a gothic in-folio, which was reprinted in 1532 and 1533. Subsequent editions were printed in Paris. A similar folio volume appeared in Paris in 1536 (with some copies printed on vellum). Then in 1538 a gothic in-octavo was shared between several booksellers. This was reprinted in 1539 and 1541–2, and, now in roman type, in 1545. Thereafter its popularity began to wane, and the next and last Paris edition appeared in 1555. It would appear that in the 1530s and the early 1540s the book was a steady seller and a useful title for booksellers who wanted to sell religious literature of unimpeachable orthodoxy. The smaller format suggests a cheaper edition, but at the same time there is evidence that the book was valued as something worth presenting in a more luxurious form; as well as the vellum copies of the 1536 Paris edition there exists one copy of a folio edition printed in Rennes in 1541; this copy is printed on vellum and includes a series of magnificent manuscript illustrations.

Only one further edition appeared, but this is of great interest as being the only one which has any revisions in the text. Printed in Louvain in 1563, it is therefore post-Tridentine. It contains a form of imprimatur in which a theologian attests that

> Liber iste tradit rectam et catholicam rationem proeliandi adversus Diabolum, Mundum et Carnem, et ideo dignus est qui in publicam utilitatem typis excudatur.[7]

The theologian had done his job thoroughly, for certain alterations were made to the text, some of them in areas which had been controversial in 1530 but where the text had nevertheless satisfied the theologians at the time. We shall examine some of these alterations later. Wherever I quote a passage from the 1530 *Triomphes* any significant alterations in the 1563 edition will be noted.

2

Bouchet's Aims in the Triomphes

The first edition of the work was presented to the new Queen Eleanor; it was almost certainly presented to Marguerite de Navarre as well.[8] But the book is not primarily intended for great ladies. Bouchet describes his work as a

> manuel ou brief recueil de la doctrine necessaire pour batailler contre les vices et en avoir la victoire, à ce que puissons finablement aller au port de salut.[9]

This description sets the book in the tradition of instruction on living and dying well outlined in the last chapter. But its scope is far wider than this description suggests. We have already quoted some of Bouchet's stated intentions in this work, notably the wish to distract women and young girls from reading translations of the New Testament and tracts by German heretics. The book is thus intended to combat the spread of heresy, and since he recognises the attractions of heretical writing his own work must by implication

be equally appealing. He also has a more generally instructive aim; he says that he writes for the instruction of his own children and
> de ceulx qui n'entendent les lectres latines, ou n'ont le povoyr d'avoir tous les livres de la saincte escripture ou ne veulent prendre le labeur de les lire pour la multitude d'iceulx.[10]

He is thus offering a synopsis of the fruits of his own reading, and it is not surprising to find him making a careful statement concerning his authorities:
> Et affin que ne mesprisez mon petit euvre, et que soyez curieux de le veoyr, lire et entendre, je proteste qu'il n'y a rien du mien fors l'invencion, et quelques contemplacions en forme de amou-reuses epistolles pour resjouyr l'esprit en Dieu, et l'induyre à charitable amour. Car quant à la matière et substance, je l'ay prinse et extraicte du texte de la saincte bible et des opinions et sentences des docteurs catholiques, et mesmement des quatre docteurs de l'eglise de ce qui concerne les choses spirituelles, et quant aux corporelles et moralles de Platon, Socrates, Aristote, Seneque, Cicero, Averroys, Ypocras, et aultres aucteurs peritz et doctes es sciences humaines et phisicalles.[11]

There is a certain amount of window-dressing involved in this list of authorities, many of whom, as we shall see when we consider his sources, are represented only via intermediaries. But the impression given here is broadly correct. Bouchet's book consists of passages of instruction drawn from good authorities, fitted in to a fictional story line of Bouchet's own invention which has the function of interesting the reader and breaking up the instruction. This story-line, an allegorical account of the Soul's progress through life, is also instructive in its own right at more than one level. It is intended to be attractive for, as Bouchet suggests here, it is a love story:
> Les triumphes de la noble dame, et l'art de honnestement aymer, tout fondé en amour et dilection charitable, parce que je treuve par la saincte escripture que nostre loy crestienne consiste entierement en amour.[12]

We may therefore examine separately the 'story', the sources for the passages of instruction, and his treatment of controversial issues which Bouchet knew to be the subject of heresies.

3
The Story

All the elements of the story of *Les Triomphes* can be found in many earlier religious allegories, but few writers can have combined quite so many different motifs in one story. Bouchet uses the idea of life as a journey, the soul as the bride of Christ, the seduction of the soul, the judgement in heaven and the *psychomachia*. One theme which is omitted, significantly, is the arrival of the soul in heaven.

The narrative is divided into three books. In Book One the *Ame raisonnable incorporée* enters life with her five senses, and is betrothed to Christ at baptism, with the promise of the dowry of Paradise if she remains faithful. Until her twenty-fifth year she remains in the *Terre d'adolescence* in the company of a vast retinue. The most important of these are *Volunté*, mistress of her palace, *Mémoire* her counsellor and *Entendement* her chancellor. *Raison* is her governess and *Sensualité* her chamber-maid. Most of the first book is taken up with her moral education at the hands of the four cardinal virtues (all of whom have several daughters) and an explanation of the nature of the body and how to look after it from *Dame Phisique*.

The story element really comes into its own in Book Two, which recounts the fall and redemption of the Soul. The *Prince de Volupté* sends her repeated messages until at last she agrees to go to the *Palais de Volupté*. There after a while she and all her companions are seduced (except *Raison* whom they have abandoned) and they are left, stained, spotted and crippled, in the Brothel of Obstinacy.

Suddenly, emerging from the very eyes of the Soul, appears a woman in shining white, *Syndérèse*,[13] who bears torches showing the Soul her dreadful state only too clearly. *Désespérance* immediately arrives to tempt her to suicide. The *acteur*, who is watching the progress of the Soul, underlines this moment of pathos and suspense:

> Et si n'avoit personne qui la consolast ne luy administrast chose aucune pour la reconforter, dont la pitié fut si grant que mes yeulx ne se peurent contenir de gecter habondance de piteuses larmes, tant pour le mal que je luy voioys supporter, aussi que je ne luy povois donner alegence ne confort.[14]

But Christ has seen the plight of the Soul, and he sends *Grace Divine* to help her. Soon they are released from the brothel and have set out on the Path of Penitence. The Soul receives a letter from Christ, reminding her of his love, and *Foy* and *Grace Divine* are sent off to heaven to seek letters of remission for the Soul; they take with them letters from the Soul to Christ and to his Mother, and also her request for remission. While the Soul is making her way to the Fountain of Penitence, a council is held in heaven at which it is decided that God should have mercy on the Soul, and her letters of remission are sent to her. *Dame Confession* gives her the means of ratifying these letters and at last she is washed clean in the Fountain and given new white garments. She is now approaching the *Terre de Vieillesse* and *Grace Divine* warns her that they will soon need to do battle against the World, the Flesh and the Devil.

So ends the second book. In the first part, as far as the fall of the Soul, the story is instructive in its own right, but thereafter Bouchet reverts to the manner of the first book and puts long passages of instruction on sin, confession, etc., into the mouths of his characters.

The third book introduces a further type of allegorical commonplace, the *psychomachia*—the Soul and her companions are forced to
fight three great battles against the World, the Flesh and the Devil.
In the first two they are victorious with the help of *Grace Divine*; in
the third, which is a sea battle against the Devil himself, the Soul is
driven by *Malladie* to the *Pas de la Mort*, two great rocks where the
sea rages and which her body cannot pass. The moment of separation has come. *Grace Divine* helps her in her final battle with *Désespérance* and, fortified by the last sacrament, reciting the first verses
of Psalm 31, she passes through the *Pas de la Mort*. The *acteur* is left
behind with *Théologie* discussing whether or not the Soul will be
saved.

The third book is also remarkable for two passages in which the
Soul is visited by Christ:

> Environ la mynuyt de ce jour, (ainsi que l'Ame incorporée
> reposoit sur le lict de contemplacion) nostre seigneur Jesucrist
> arriva et heurta à l'huys de la chambrette qui estoit le cueur de
> l'Ame. Elle demanda qui c'estoit; il respondit, 'C'est moy ma-
> mye, ma blanche columbe et ma chere espouse.' 'Ha, mon
> seigneur, mon bien aymé, ma gloire, mon desir et mon salut,'
> dist l'Ame, 'vous soyez le tresbien venu . . .'[15]

The ensuing conversations are disappointingly pedestrian, but they
develop the theme of the mutual love of Christ and the Soul, which
is also dealt with more successfully in the various verse *épîtres* of
Books Two and Three.[16]

This narrative is both entertaining and instructive, despite being
rather obvious sugar on a pill. One of its attractions is the description of characters as they are introduced, which we have noted as a
feature of all his fictions. The touches of humour which we noted in
his use of mythological fiction are also apparent. Here for example
is the description of *Prudence*, who suitably eschews *décolleté*:

> Prudence se mist davant les aultres, richement vestue d'une
> robe de veloux noir fourrée de fines martres allant à fleur de
> terre, sans superfluité et bien fermée au collet. Sur ses cheveux
> pendans sur les espaules avoit ung lynumple de fine toile de
> holande fymbrie de riche orfaverie. Sa contenance estoit assez
> grave sans orgueuil, son port raciz, et son regard fort arresté.
> En l'une de ses mains tenoit ung compas, et en l'autre ung
> astrallabe de astronomye pour compasser tous ses affaires et
> congnoistre les temps.[17]

Among his main characters who are present throughout the book
Sensualité the chambermaid is the one who offers the most amusing
possibilities. It is she who is made to enquire of Prudence what
exactly is permissible in the marriage bed; she delivers the message
from the *Prince de Volupté* and is most disappointed when it is
rebuffed; she persuades the Soul to visit the Prince's palace, and

when the others are being cunningly seduced in various apartments of the palace she is in the *garderobbe* with *Plaisir charnel*, offering no resistance at all. After the Soul's rehabilitation she has a very bad time; she gets bored with the Soul's new occupations, *Volunté* never ceases to chastise her and during the battles she is regularly taken prisoner and has to be rescued. As in all his prolonged fictions Bouchet keeps a firm hold on the sense of each personification and uses it appropriately throughout.

The story-line is developed with the least interruptions in the chapters on the seduction of the Soul. We are shown how the Soul's resistance is gradually undermined by each successive message from the *Prince de Volupté. Suggestion* has not had time to finish the first message before she is rebuffed:

L'Ame rougist soubdainement par honneste vergongne, et sans longuement songer à sa response leur dist assez rudement, 'Allez, allez, je n'ay que faire de vous ne de vostre prince, je sçay bien qu'il scet faire. Et par ce retirez vous, ou vous aurez du desplaisir'. L'Ame fut très vertueuse en ceste response et merita envers Dieu.[18]

The next time, however, the Soul is not quite so swift to protest when *Délectacion* persudes *Sensualité* to deliver a message:

où l'Ame print quelque legier plaisir, mais non la Volunté. Laquelle par le conseil d'Entendement et Memoire fist chasser Delectacion, au grant regret de Sensualité. Et par ce s'en retourna toute confuse, et ne pecha l'Ame mortellement, mais veniellement seulement, au moien de ce qu'elle avoit prins quelque legier plaisir es persuasions de Delectacion recitées par Sensualité, esquelles n'avoit fait arrest, et n'y avoit la Volunté donné consentement.[19]

When she receives a love-letter from the Prince she has even more trouble in resisting. At last she is persuaded by *Volunté* to write a refusal—but some damage has already been done:

Mieulx eust fait si sans se arrester par plaisir ne autrement à l'espitre du Prince de Volupté, et sans en avoir fait lecture, eust rudement chassé Delectacion . . . car le petit plaisir qu'elle prinst à plusieurs choses contenues en l'epistre la feit pecher veniellement, et se mist en dangier d'y faire offence mortelle, si par Entendement et Memoire la Volunté n'en eust esté reculée.[20]

And this does indeed cause her downfall, for the next message arrives when the Soul and her companions are still talking about the letter—with the exception of *Raison*, who has fallen asleep out of boredom with this conversation. And so they fall prey to temptation:

Jeunesse parla de telle sorte qu'elle estonna Entendement et Memoire, et au regard de Volunté, par sa grant pusillanimité se accorda à Sensualité . . . et par ce moien l'Ame tumba en peché mortel.[21]

Throughout this account Bouchet is using his character *Volunté* in order to make the point that sin is committed when the will assents to evil. Although he comments on his narrative, the instruction is achieved principally by means of the narrative itself. Once the Soul and her companions arrive at the palace, they are soon given up to feasting and dancing and forget their virtuous retinue. Not that they are as yet wholly lost: 'Quant à l'acte et au faict reculloient eux y habandonner, aussi en avoient esté peu assailliz'.[22]

This ironical afterthought sets the tone for the subsequent account of the seduction which Bouchet uses in order to give a moral as well as a theological lesson. *Chair* finds *Volunté* alone, and assures her that he wants nothing against her honour:

En disant ces parolles ou aultres semblables, approcha sa bouche de celle de Volunté, et après l'avoir baisée commença taster son virginal tetin, ce qu'elle permist, luy defendant le demourant, qui estoit follie à elle, car à peine l'un est sans l'autre. Et voylà la forme et manière comment les jeunes mondains deçoyvent plusieurs filles et femmes qui leur prestent les aureilles et donnent lieu à leurs deceptives parolles.[23]

In view of the importance of the Will in determining the significance of the Soul's actions, we are not surprised to find that similar distressing scenes are taking place all over the palace. *Mémoire* is seduced by *Monde*. *Entendement* is overwhelmed by the desire for *Ambicion*, as Bouchet recounts with yet another of those sentences which end in a devastating subordinate clause:

Ambicion retourna, qui le vinst embrasser et baiser, et par ces amoureux actraictz fut par elle gaigné, sans y povoir donner resistence de luy mesme sans l'ayde de Dieu, du quel il ne demandoit le secours.[24]

Once again a moral lesson accompanies the theological allegory:

C'est une chose tres dangereuse que compaignie de jeune femme avec ung homme en lieu suspect, tant vertueux puisse estre, car c'est vouloir marcher à pié nud sur les ardens charbons sans se brusler, qui est presque impossible.[25]

Finally the Prince finds the Soul alone, 'esloignée de toutes bonnes pensées, au moien de quoy, sans grant resistence, feit d'elle ce qu'il voulut et la prostitua'.[26]

Bouchet's daughters were doubtless pleasurably shocked and duly edified by this tale of the heroine's fall. He follows it with the sombre description of the Brothel of Penitence and the arrival of Despair, changing the mood effectively by means of the burst of authorial sympathy quoted earlier in order to prepare for the divine intervention which will save the Soul from her plight.

It was noted above that Bouchet does not depict the Soul's arrival in heaven. He includes a judgement in heaven, but this relates to the Soul's repentance for her mortal sins and subsequent confession and absolution.[27] In this scene the humanity of Jesus presents to the Trinity[28] the Soul's request for letters of remission, and a council is held. *Dame Vérité* states the Soul's crime and *Dame Justice* demands that she be condemned because she has sinned and has performed no good works. But the Virgin and the saints intercede for her, and *Miséricorde* pleads her repentance, her faith and the merits of Christ. *Dame Paix* settles the debate, reminding God of his promise to forgive those who repent, reminding *Dame Justice* that God's vicar on earth can impose a temporal penalty for the Soul's sins, even though Christ has more than satisfied, and pointing out that men and women are not saved by good works without faith.[29] It is decided that all the points of view have been reconciled, and the Soul is sent her letters of remission.

This scene is similar to the sort of scene that one might expect to encounter after the Soul's separation from her body. On this point it is helpful to compare Bouchet's work with that of other writers. Probably the best known religious allegory which Bouchet could look back to was that of Guillaume Deguileville, whose *Pèlerinage de vie humaine* was written in about 1330 and was followed by the *Pèlerinage de l'ame* and the *Pèlerinage de Jesus-Christ*.[30] The work was readily available in the sixteenth century, having been printed by Vérard.[31] Two major differences separate the lessons of Deguileville's story and that of Bouchet's. First of all Deguileville's pilgrim finds a safe vessel for crossing the world in the Ship of Religion; he dies a monk, whereas the Soul in the *Triomphes* is directed to choose a lay life, *le Grant chemin de chrestienne religion*. The second difference is the judgement of the soul. In Deguileville's *Pèlerinage de vie humaine* the Pilgrim is constantly wandering from the proper path and being helped by *Grace Dieu*. In the second book, the *Pèlerinage de l'ame*, the Pilgrim is dead and has been brought to judgement by his guardian angel, who speaks for him, saying that he was baptised and that he never set down the scrip and staff (faith and hope) which *Grace Dieu* had given him. But Satan insists that the Pilgrim had constantly returned to sin. So Justice is to weigh the Pilgrim's actions. The Pilgrim puts his scrip and staff on one side of the balance, but on the other goes the list of his crimes made out by a horrible old woman, *Synderesis*, remorse of conscience—and she gets into the scale-pan too. Letters from St Benedict containing the good and bad done by the pilgrim in his monastic life redress the balance only a little. The Pilgrim would be damned but for *Miséricorde* who delivers a letter from Christ, which is heavy enough to turn the balance. The Pilgrim sets off for Purgatory.[32]

Deguileville depicts a debate between *Raison, Vérité, Justice* and *Miséricorde* before the weighing takes place. The analogies with

Bouchet's scene are clear, but the differences are also marked.

Bouchet seems to wish to avoid any possibly presumptuous ex-
ploration of God's secret council; his scene in heaven relates to one
act of confession, but the last state of the Soul, predestined to
salvation or damnation, is veiled in secrecy. He also seems to wish
to avoid picturesque fantasies about the after-life. Finally he makes
the merits of Christ alone plead for the Soul, who at this stage has
performed no good works; he avoids representing in allegorical
form how good works will help towards salvation; there is no
parallel to Deguileville's merit in monasticism which is shown as
narrowing the distance between the scale-pans although certainly
not redressing the balance.

These differences can be explained firstly by the fact that Bouchet
was writing for a lay audience, secondly that predestination, the
relative role of faith and works, and purgatory, were all doctrines
which he regarded as the subjects of possible error. He therefore
explains them very clearly in passages of straight instruction which
we will examine later. On the question of faith and works in particular he would probably not have approved of the implications of
Deguileville's scene.

On this latter question we may make a second comparison with
another religious allegory. This, by contrast, was a work hardly
known to anybody, but certainly known to Bouchet. His patroness,
Gabrielle de Bourbon, had been in the habit of writing little devotional works which Bouchet sometimes arranged to have bound
and illuminated for her, and whose subjects are reflected in *épîtres*
that he wrote for her.[33] One of her works depicts the journey of the
soul, *Le Voyage spirituel entreprins par l'ame devote*.[34] The Soul sets out
with three companions, *Bon Vouloir*, *Force* and *Espérance*, to find her
husband and a crown. She has a treasure which she carries with
her, consisting of all her good works (a long list, including belief in
the twelve articles of faith). At the beginning of her journey she
visits *Pénitence*, and then they travel for seven days meeting various
enemies and difficulties, all of which are vanquished with the help
of Virtues. On the seventh day she reaches the *Cité de bon repos* in a
ship steered by *Foy*. At the request of *Charité* and *Espérance*, *Divine
Bonté* orders *Miséricorde* to open the gate, and *Justice* to give the Soul
whatever she has deserved, the robe of immortality, the crown of
victory, the palm of virginity.

There are no passages of instruction to explain the allegory in this
little work, which would appear to be the allegorical account of the
life of a saint rather than a commentary on the progress of ordinary
mortals.[35] The depiction of the Soul winning through accompanied
only by Fortitude, Hope, Good Will and her treasure of good works
has just the theological weaknesses which Evangelical and Reformist criticism of contemporary piety might lead one to expect; it

seriously underplays the role of both faith and divine grace. This is precisely what Bouchet clearly wished to avoid, and he certainly did not wish to present his Soul marching triumphantly into heaven with her bundle of good works. These comparisons serve to highlight the extreme care with which Bouchet treats controversial doctrines in his allegory as well as in his instructive passages. They show already that, while presenting a theology intended and accepted as orthodox in the face of Reformist teachings, he is also correcting what he must have perceived as errors of emphasis in the way in which the Church's doctrine had sometimes been presented, and which now laid it open to Reformist attacks.

4
The Sources for the Instruction

Instructive as Bouchet's story is, most of his teaching is conveyed more directly. The Virtues, and other figures like *Confession, Grace Divine, Vérité* and *Théologie,* explain at length to the Soul what she ought to believe and do.

There are throughout the *Triomphes* numerous marginal references. They take the form not of quotations, but of references to an authority; sometimes an author is simply named but often a reference to a particular work is given, complete with chapter number. These references serve as a starting point for a study of his sources. As always, the largest number by far is to the Bible. Some of these are there because another source quotes a biblical text, but Bouchet was also quite capable of finding texts on his own account.

When the frequency with which other authorities appear is examined, the misleading nature of the list of authorities given in his preface becomes apparent:

Gerson, 34	St Ambrose, 4
St Antoninus of Florence, 15	Seneca, 4
St Augustine, 15	Valerius Maximus, 3
St Bernard, 9	Canon Law, 3
St Thomas Aquinas, 9	Petrus de Palude, 3
St Isidore of Seville, 9	St Jerome, 3
Cicero, 7	St John Chrysostom, 3

To these may be added the following authors who are all referred to either once or twice: Origen, Lactantius, Ovid, Fulgentius, Avicenna, Galen, Richard of St Victor, St Raymond of Pennaforte, St Bonaventura, Alvarus, St John Damascene, St Clement, St John Cassian, Platina, Boethius, Periander, Cassiodorus, Aristotle, Raulin, St Gregory.

Merely from these figures it emerges that fifteenth-century authorities are of much greater importance than the preface, with its stress on the four doctors of the Church and prestigious classical sources, would suggest. When one examines the text to discover whether the marginal reference is simply to an authority quoted in passing or to a source which is actually being followed, the importance of more recent authorities is yet more marked. Gerson and St Antoninus stand out way above all other sources.

St Antoninus of Florence (1389–1459), had been canonised in 1523. As well as a *Chronicle* which Bouchet refers to in his histories, he left several works intended to instruct both clergy and laity. His compendium of moral theology, the *Summa theologica*, was frequently printed at the end of the fifteenth century, only gradually losing popularity in the course of the sixteenth. We know that Bouchet himself purchased a copy in 1508, an indication of his strong interest in theology throughout his career.[36] St Antoninus is cited in the margin ten times in Book One, twice in Book Two and three times in Book Three. He is the main source for moral questions and is also referred to on some specifically theological points. Bouchet takes from the *Summa* the subdivisions and explanations of the four cardinal virtues (personified as the daughters of the Virtues). A brief example will illustrate his method:

> 'Madame Temperance', dist Entendement, qui n'avoit encores tenu propos, 'ne me cellez, si vous plaist, pourquoy tenez avec vous Studiosité, car il me semble qu'elle n'est propre à vous, mais mieux à Madame Prudence.' 'Non est,' dist Temperence, 'et pour l'entendre est à presupposer que studiosité est une vertu contraire à curiosité, reffrenant le courage de toute desordonnée affection de congnoistre. Or vous sçavez que mon office est de moderer le mouvement de l'appetit à ce que superfluement il ne tende à la chose laquelle il cauvoite naturellement.[37]

This is the beginning of a passage that draws on the opening remarks of a section from the *Summa*, part 4, tit.4, chapter xi, *De studiositate*:

> [P]onitur etiam pars modestie et per consequens temperantie secundum beatum Thomam ii. ii. q. clxvi. studiositas que virtus est contraria curiositati refrenans animum ab inordinato affectu cognescendi . . . Quod autem sit pars temperantie declarat beatus Thomas ubi supra. Ad temperantiam pertinet moderari motum appetitus ne superfluo tendat in id quod naturaliter concupiscit.[38]

His method consists of translating the text of Antoninus, usually with substantial cuts and some paraphrases, and this is then fitted in to the conversations of his characters. Occasionally he elaborates or modifies what St Antoninus says, particularly when discussing the day-to-day practice of morality as opposed to theory.[39] Sometimes he adds extra illustrations from the Bible.[40]

We have seen that the *Summa* is frequently cited in the margins, but these references do not indicate all the passages in which Bouchet borrowed from it. He uses it for example in Book Two when he introduces *Syndérèse* and explains the term:

> [Synderese] est, comme a escript sainct Augustin, une lumière dedans née, concréé[e] en l'Ame, par laquelle l'ame est dirigée et mennée à faire les choses appartenans à la justificacion de la coulpe et peine et à l'adeption de gloire, que sainct Basille appelle naturel judicatoire. Elle est differente à la conscience, car la conscience peut recepvoir erreur et perturbacion, et non la synderese, combien que la conscience, quant à la part superiore, se reduise à synderese.[41]

This passage is taken from Antoninus, complete with the references to St Augustine and St Basil.[42] The *Summa theologica*, with its clear definitions, was an invaluable source for all aspects of moral theology.

There are even more references to Gerson, fairly equally divided between Books Two and Three in which the theology of salvation is explained. Once again, marginal references in the case of Gerson indicate very substantial borrowings. We have seen that Bouchet later regularly cited Gerson as the prime example of a writer of religious works for the laity, and in the light of the use of his work in the *Triomphes* this is hardly surprising. The main areas of theology dealt with in Books Two and Three are as follows:

1) The nature of sin, ff.70–3
2) The nature of penitence and absolution, ff.85–6
3) Confession and satisfaction: the power of the keys, ff.86–92
4) Mortal and venial sin; the seven deadly sins, ff.93–8
5) The ten commandments, ff.99–101
6) The three theological virtues (including the twelve articles of faith), ff.101–6
7) Divine and human love, ff.109–11
8) The nature of prayer, ff.111–16
9) The monastic and the active life, ff.117–20
10) The nature of death and preparation for death, ff.144–6, 150–1
11) The nature of the after-life, ff.151–4
12) The sacrament of the altar, ff.155–7
13) Making a will, ff.158–9
14) Extreme unction, ff.159–60
15) Predestination, prescience, free-will, astrology, ff.160–6.

Of these, some are taken almost exclusively from Gerson: the nature of mortal and venial sin (4), making a will (13), extreme unction (14). Many of the others are taken partly from Gerson: the ten commandments (5), the three theological virtues (6), the nature of prayer (8), how to prepare for death (10), the eucharist (12), predestination (15). Many times the Soul asks a question and the lesser figures turn to *Grace Divine* or *Théologie* for an answer. Over and over again they answer in the words of Gerson.

The tracts which Bouchet chooses are in some cases those which Gerson intended for the direct instruction of the laity or for the better preparation of parish priests.[43] For (5) and (6) he draws on various parts of the popular *Compendium Theologiae breve et utile*[44] and for (4) on the *Tractatus de differentia peccatorum venialium et mortalium*.[45] Similarly for (10) and (14) he uses *De scientiis mortis* (or *La Medecine de l'ame*)[46] and for (13) *Considerationes pro volentibus condere testamentum*[47] which were intended to help priests in their pastoral work. Much of the section on prayer (8) is drawn from *De mendicitate spirituali*, which Gerson originally composed in French.[48] But Bouchet also uses Gerson's less popular works. For part of the discussion of prayer he drew on the *Sermo de oratione factus in Concilio Constantiensi*,[49] for parts of (12) he used the *Tractatus nonus super Magnificat*[50] and, in particular, in his last chapter, the long discussion of predestination (15) is taken from *De consolatione theologiae*, which, as the title suggests, Gerson intended as an answer to Boethius.[51] In the same chapter the brief references to astrology draw on Gerson's *Trilogium Astrologiae Theologizatae*.[52] This use of Gerson's less popular works demonstrates Bouchet's willingness to treat some theological subjects in greater depth than was usual in vernacular manuals. Gerson's texts are integrated into the narrative in the same way as those of St Antoninus, and they are similarly subject to considerable abridgement, paraphrase, and slight elaboration.

No other authors are used as extensively as these two. But there are other quite important debts which are not clear from the rough guide provided by numbers of marginal references. For example, the one reference to Richard of St Victor refers to a massive debt: Bouchet paraphrases more than half the chapters of the twelfth-century Victorine's *De potestate ligandi atque solvendi*.[53] This forms the section on confession (3), a controversial subject on which Bouchet wished to explain the Church's position. The contrary case arises with the nine references to St Isidore; these refer to the ultimate source of information about parts of the body in Book One which Bouchet actually takes from intermediaries who are not mentioned, Robert Ciboule and Bartholomaeus Anglicus.[54]

Some passages have no cited authority at all. This may be because Bouchet has written a summary drawn from many sources, but it may also be that he used some authorities which he did not acknowledge. I have discovered him doing this in two passages taken from works by Erasmus; there may be many more which I have not recognised.

One of the passages from Erasmus is in a prominent position at the beginning of the book where Bouchet is explaining his use of the concept *âme raisonnable incorporée*. He explains that man undergoes constant temptation in this world, and that most Christians live like animals without considering the difference between the flesh and the spirit. This dichotomy, he says, is fundamental to ancient philosophers and to St Paul, who speaks of the inner and the outer man, the law of reason and the law of the members. This does not just mean body and spirit; with true faith man is all spiritual, but without it he is all carnal.[55]

This passage is paraphrased from the opening chapters of the *Enchiridion militis christiani*. Erasmus is showing that what the philosophers have said about the duality of man is illustrated in the Bible. Erasmus then goes on to a threefold analysis of man—spirit, soul and flesh—drawn from Origen. This is presented as a refinement of the first analysis.[56] Bouchet continues to follow him, complete with the reference to Origen, but then adds further explanation in order to show that the soul is by nature the same as the spirit, but is different in operation. In fact, the soul is torn between body and spirit:

> L'esprit nous eslieve au ciel, la chair nous deprime en enfer, et de ce on n'impute rien à l'âme si elle n'y consent par son libere arbitre. Tout ce qui est charnel est vilain, tout ce qui est spirituel est bon, et tout ce qui est animal est moyen et indifferent.[57]

Cf. Erasmus:

> Spiritus evehit in coelum. Caro deprimit ad inferos. Animae nihil imputatur. Quidquid carnale, turpe est. Quidquid spirituale, perfectum. Quidquid animale, medium et indifferens.[58]

It is most interesting to find this debt to Erasmus at the very outset of the work, and on a subject central to the work's conception. It seems that Bouchet was drawn by the elegant formulation and superior information of Erasmus's *Handbook*—and let us not forget that he refers to his own book as a *manuel*.

The other borrowing comes from another of the little tracts by Erasmus intended for the ordinary man, his Exposition on the Lord's Prayer.[59] Bouchet abridges this exposition for six out of the seven petitions. But the petition *Et dimitte nobis debita nostra* is taken from a little treatise by Gerson devoted solely to this petition—and the source is acknowledged.[60]

This demonstrates again the ambivalence of Bouchet's attitude to Erasmus already noted in an earlier chapter. It is not just a question of Erasmus being too recent an authority to be named; a comparatively recent author like Jean Raulin is named as the source for instruction about marriage.[61] Either Bouchet does not accord Erasmus great authority or, more probably, he does not wish to appear to do so.

In his explanation of the nature of the Soul, Bouchet elaborates a reference to St Augustine which is used by Erasmus.[62] So far in examining his use of sources we have noted long passages paraphrased from sources much more recent than the Fathers. But Bouchet's own theological competence and knowledge should not be underestimated. All of the borrowings noted here are abridged and paraphrased to suit his purpose and welded into the narrative, and by no means all the instruction uses sources in quite so direct a manner. This is especially true of those doctrines which were a matter of controversy in the 1520s. With particular objections and errors to answer Bouchet could not always rely on finding an earlier source which concentrated sufficiently on the points he needed to make. He did not, as far as I have been able to discover, turn to the writings of orthodox opponents of Lutheranism in the universities; instead he seems quite often to have produced his own summary of the orthodox arguments. We shall examine these passages in the next two sections, the first of which deals with controversial questions other than faith and works, which are treated separately in the following section.

5

Controversial Doctrines

In spite of the reference in the preface to the need to distract women from reading Lutheran books, the *Triomphes* does not read like an anti-Lutheran tract. On the contrary, it is primarily intended as a general instruction in the Christian faith for the benefit of the lay Christian. Naturally Bouchet pays special attention to points which were disputed, but he does not always draw attention to the disputes. And the errors which he refutes are not exclusively Lutheran ones.

Some subjects of controversy are set aside altogether—he says very little for instance about the hierarchy and the government of the Church.[63] A subject like monasticism is touched on without any allusion to controversy; he describes the function of monasticism briefly before making the Soul choose the lower road of the laity.[64]

In other cases he lets the Soul ask a series of questions, raising doubts about some doctrine, which are then resolved by the answering instruction. An example of this is his treatment of confession. Without any reference to Lutheran errors he gives a very detailed exposition of the power of the keys taken from the tract by Richard of St Victor. Thus while almost ignoring the question of the power of the Pope and bishops he concentrates on the most crucial point of contact between the laity and the priesthood, the remission of sins. He does not merely defend auricular confession but explains the effects of sin and how it is remitted in some detail, in answer to a series of questions from the Soul which are taken verbatim from his source.[65]

The tract by Richard of St Victor which he chooses to paraphrase is one which others also considered to be good anti-Lutheran material. It is printed later in the century as an appendix to Johann von

Eck's *Enchiridion locorum communium adversus Lutherum*.[66] But it is interesting to note that the 1563 Louvain edition of the *Triomphes* cuts out the whole section. This can only be explained by a reluctance to allow the simple reader to delve into complex questions concerning the power of priests, however orthodox the instruction.

The denial of free will is seen, as it was in the *Labyrinthe*, as an error perpetrated by those who deny God's providence and omnipotence, replacing them with the blind force of Fortune. Bouchet discusses both free will and predestination in this context, combined with attacks on astrology. However, although much of the relevant section is drawn from works by Gerson, the passage on free will is not, and he appears to write it with the Lutheran denial of free will in mind. It is possible that it owes something to the treatise by Erasmus.[67] Although elsewhere, as we shall see, Bouchet denies that good works performed without grace are valueless, here he comes near to presenting man as helplessly sunk in sin as he describes free will, which is unable to perform a meritorious work without the illumination of faith, as being in the toils of the devil and lying in the depths of sin until delivered by grace. When the gift of faith[68] is given, freely by God without any merit on the part of man, man is justified:

> Mais par ce moyen aura salut de vie, si ce qui est commancé par grace se augmente, cooperant avec icelle le franc arbitre, non tant de luy que de la grace et ayde de Dieu, sans laquelle aulcun ne peult proffiter ne demourer en bien. Parquoy les bonnes euvres des crestiens sont plus à attribuer à la grace de Dieu que au franc arbitre. . . .[69]

However, it is wrong to say that God predestines men to behave well or ill; he does not co-operate in man's evil acts, in which free will acts alone, without grace:

> Et à ceste raison celluy erre qui dict que franc arbitre n'est rien en l'homme, et que predestinacion euvre es humains bien ou mal. Car la grace de Dieu ne tollist le franc arbitre, mais le parfaict, revocque et retire d'erreur en la voye de salut, affin que ce qui de sa liberté estoit parvers, par l'euvre de l'esprit de Dieu soit droict.[70]

There is no verbal reminiscence of the *De Libero Arbitrio* of Erasmus, but this short passage is consistent with the arguments expressed in it and touches on its central preoccupations, particularly the idea that after God's initial free gift of grace man's free will co-operates with grace.[71] It would also appear to be consistent with Rabelais' presentation of free will in *Gargantua*, particularly the misguided free will of Picrochole.[72]

The Eucharist is treated late in the third book when the Soul is to take communion in preparation for death. Again the doctrine of the sacrament is not presented as controversial; it is explained, with no

general source cited, and then a passage of meditations on the
sacrament is taken from Gerson.[73] In the course of the explanation
of the doctrine, the words of Christ at the Last Supper are quoted in
French, with the comment:

> Par ces parolles (qui sont prinses des evangilles et repetées par
> sainct Paul) Jhesucrist institua le sainct sacrement de l'autier, et
> en disant les parolles contenues en l'evangille contenans en
> substance ce qui dit est, il muha et transsubstancia le pain en sa
> chair, et le vin en son sang, et donna la puissance de ainsi le
> faire à ses apostres et disciples et à tous prebstres bien ordonnez
> par la vertu des parolles sacramentalles 'Hoc est enim corpus
> meum'. Et de cecy ne vous esbaissez, Ame raisonnable, et n'en
> demandez les raisons naturelles, car impossible seroit à tout
> esprit humain les vous dire ne les entendre, mais le convient
> ainsi croire simplement par ceste foy mesme que Dieu par sa
> puissance, sapience et bonté a fait de rien toutes choses.[74]

Once again, having given this very careful statement of the
Church's doctrine, underlining the excellent scriptural authority,
using the term 'transsubstancier' and referring to the prerogative of
properly ordained priests[75]—he suggests that his simple reader can
believe this without further explanation. But he goes on to list
'douze choses merveilleuses', twelve miraculous properties of the
Eucharist; he thus in fact enters rather further into the doctrine of
transubstantiation. The twelve items appear to derive ultimately
from St Thomas Aquinas' discussion of the Eucharist, *Summa Theologica*, part 3, q.lxxv-lxxvii, but no doubt via intermediary sources.[76]

With Purgatory we come to an example of a doctrine which is
treated as if it needs to be defended, although the source of attacks
upon it is not identified:

> 'Aulcuns maintiennent', dist l'Ame, 'qu'on ne trouve tesmoy-
> gnage de purgatoire par texte de bible, mais seullement par
> docteurs.'[77]

In response to this objection, *Théologie* marshals the texts which
were regularly used to support the doctrine, both in the sixteenth
century and long before in arguments with other groups of heretics.
The crucial text is 2 Maccabees 12, in which Judas Maccabeus sends
money to Jerusalem for prayer for the dead.[78] This text is explained
in the greatest detail, and Bouchet makes no reference to the disputed canonicity of the Book of Maccabees.[79] Other texts are then
mentioned: Zachariah 9 v.11, Matthew 5 v.25, 12 v.32 and 18 v.34,
Luke 12 v.32. The verse from Zachariah is not explained ('I have
sent forth thy prisoners out of the pit wherein there is no water') but
he gives the substance of the others to show that they all refer to a
means of temporal punishment in the after-life. There were other
texts which were often quoted in the argument for Purgatory, but
which required a great deal more complicated exposition if they

were to support the doctrine. Some of these he simply lists, with no explanation: Ephesians 4 vv.8–10, 1 Corinthians 3 vv.13–15, Acts 2 v.24 and Revelation 5 v.33. *Théologie* concludes:

> Vous me direz que en tous ces textes purgatoire n'est nommé. Il est vray, mais vous trouverez par iceulx que en l'autre monde y a lieu pour pugnir les pechez et les purger temporellement, que Origene, sainct Augustin, sainct Gregoire, sainct Ambroise ont nommé de ce nom purgatoire, comme aussi ont tous les plus approuvez docteurs de la divine loy, à la raison de ce que les pechez dont on n'a satifait en ce monde y sont purgez et puriffiez.[80]

It is clear that Bouchet was well-versed in these arguments, but it appears that while wishing to defend the doctrine he did not, in his vernacular manual, want to enter too far into the argument. He cites no authority for this passage although later he refers to Antoninus and Thomas Aquinas on Limbo. Eck had already written a defence of the doctrine against Luther but I can find no obvious source for Bouchet's discussion which is a summary of well established arguments. Having used the Maccabees text he simply states that souls in purgatory are helped by the prayers of the living and by Masses, without further reference to controversy. His treatment is however much fuller than that of Eck in his more popular *Enchiridion*, or of Pierre Doré in *Le Dialogue instructoire des chrestiens*, 1539, who only cites one biblical text, Revelation 5 v.3.[81]

Having therefore offered what are quite full arguments for the doctrine, given that he is writing a vernacular manual, he goes on to describe purgatory. It is notable that he refrains from any picturesque description of the place or its punishments; indeed from the outset he discourages such speculation:

> Or parlons de purgatoire, qui est (comme croit saincte eglise) ung lieu en enfer ou aultre lieu au vouloyr de Dieu.[82]

A slightly earlier manual would not have bothered to defend the doctrine, but it might well have been more definite about the siting of purgatory or dwelt longer on its pains.[83] Bouchet merely states that its fire is the same as that of hell.

The practice of prayer to saints and to the Virgin receives one of the most vigorous and extensive defences, and on this subject he refers to Luther by name, one of only three such references in the whole book. This is a subject on which attacks on the Church's practice were particularly frequent and widespread; we have already noted that Bouchet mentions errors associated with the doctrine in his very earliest reference to Luther, and moreover associates such errors with people who sound like French evangelicals and Erasmians.

The topic arises three times. The most extensive treatment is in the section on prayer, but an *épître* to the Virgin and the saints is described in its title as being

> confutative des opinions erronées et scandaleuses de ceulx qui
> veulent empescher l'honneur et reverence qu'on leur doit
> faire.[84]

The verse itself deals with the arguments for praying to intermediaries. These arguments are also summarised in the section on
hope, in order to refute 'ung tas de heretiques de la farine de
Luther'.[85]

In the section on prayer the Soul raises the crucial objection to the
doctrine:

> Toutesfoiz aucuns veullent dire que le seul mediateur entre
> Dieu et l'homme et le vray advocat des humains est Jesucrist
> quant à son âme et corps glorieux (comme a escript sainct
> Paul), et que à ceste consideracion on ne se doit adroisser à
> aultre pour prier et interceder pour les humains à la deité,
> actendu qu'il n'y a ange, sainct ne saincte en paradis qui le
> vueille plustost ne saiche mieulx faire que luy.[86]

The final point here is reminiscent of Adolph's reasons for praying
direct to God in the *Naufragium*:

> Recta adibam ipsum Patrem, dicens: *Pater noster qui es in coelis.*
> Nemo divorum illo citius audit aut libentius donat, quod
> petitur.[87]

Grace Divine replies that Christ is indeed the only mediator between God and man as regards salvation, but that to the glory and
honour of his deity and humanity He wants the Virgin, the apostles,
the angels and the saints to be addressed by humans. There is no
need to give proof of this beyond citing

> l'ordonnance qui en a esté faicte par l'eglise, qui est la congrega-
> cion des fidelles, laquelle ne peult errer.[88]

Having carefully made the reservation that the authority of the
Church is sufficient in itself without scriptural justification, he proceeds to provide scriptural authority by quoting Old Testament
examples of prayer to angels, and New Testament authority for
praying for other people—it follows, he says, that souls in glory
will continue out of perfect charity to pray for those on earth. He
then continues his argument by drawing on Gerson, *De mendicitate
spirituali*, in which Gerson is actually explaining the necessity for
any sort of prayer: prayer is used by God as a second cause because
such is His will.[89] Bouchet adapts this argument to the more limited
question of the mediation of the saints; Doré was later to use the
same argument.[90] Bouchet completes his discussion with quotation
from another tract by Gerson, *De oratione et eius valore*,[91] but to this
he brings several significant additions. *Grace Divine* complains about
the abuse, encouraged by avaricious priests, of praying to particular
saints to cure particular illnesses rather than to the Virgin or the
Apostles; also the abuse of venerating images and relics of saints

more than the body of Christ who really performs all miracles (although both relics and images may be venerated, providing that the reverence is for the saint represented). Finally he makes an addition which actually goes a long way towards accepting the original objection mentioned by the Soul, that no saint can answer prayer better than God himself:

> Et vous advertiz, Ame incorporée, que si on faict oraison aux anges, la Vierge Marie, saincts et sainctes de paradis, leur doit estre faicte et dirigée, non qu'on actende avoir d'eulx ce qu'on demande, mais de Dieu seul par leurs merites et intercessions. Et premierement par nostre seigneur Jesucrist et par ses tres-dignes merites speciallement et principallement. Car ne devez tant vous confier es anges, saincts et sainctes que nostre seigneur Jesucrist en soit oublié, mais l'avoir tousjours davant voz yeulx.[92]

The 1563 censor could accept this, but he cut out what immediately followed, to the effect that saints have the prerogative of interceding not because of their merits but because of God's grace—for no man or woman ever deserved heavenly bliss by their own actions, but by the grace of God and the merits of Christ:

> Et pourtant ayez le tousjours davant les yeulx, et vostre totalle et principalle fiance en luy, car qui ne l'a en luy, perd son temps.[93]

We shall examine this passage among the others dealing with faith and works, grace and merits. Here the interesting point is that this Christ-centred concept of trust, using very evangelical language, coexists with such a lively defence of prayer to intermediaries. The theologians in 1530 must have approved of this presentation of the doctrine. It is evident from the Life of St Radegonde and the *Cantiques* that Bouchet had no objection at all to the principle of prayer to intermediaries; on the contrary, we have seen that he had a special devotion to St Radegonde. But it is also true that his verse frequently addresses Christ; there is no question of Christ being crowded out in favour of either the Virgin or the saints.[94] Christ is very much more prominent than the Virgin in the story of the *Triomphes*. Throughout this defence of prayer to intermediaries Bouchet is also at pains to point out abuses in the practice which should be avoided, notably superstitious appeals to saints. He would include among the abuses of this practice the neglect of Christ in favour of the saints. This suggests that he took very seriously some of the objections raised by the opponents of such prayers.

6

Faith and Works, Merit and Grace

There are many separate passages in which Bouchet deals with aspects of how man is saved.[95] These are some of the passages

which fell foul of the 1563 censor, although they had been passed by
the theologians in 1530. Such an extensive treatment of the subject
shows Bouchet's concern with this problem above any other. It is
not so much Lutheranism which troubles him, for this he presents
simply as a presumptuous belief that one can be saved by faith alone
without bothering to do good works. What exercises him far more
is the relative role of human merit and of grace in salvation. In his
treatment of this subject it is possible to discern an acknowledgement of the validity of objections made by writers like Erasmus to
the way in which these doctrines were sometimes presented, notably by the Sorbonne.

Throughout the 1520s the Sorbonne theologians were combating
views which to their mind undervalued the importance of good
works and denied the reality of human merit. In order to understand the implications of Bouchet's exposition we must examine
some of the concepts which they used: merit, the role of grace and
the word *fiducia*.

On the question of merit, scholastic theology distinguishes between *meritum de condigno* and *meritum de congruo*. The former refers
to the due and proper reward for any good action. Man can never
be said to merit his initial gift of grace *de condigno* by his own
unaided actions. He may however deserve a small reward and be
rewarded with disproportionate generosity: this is *meritum de congruo*. In this latter sense a man could before the gift of grace perform
acts which 'deserved' as a reward the beginnings of grace.[96] After
the initial gift of grace had been received, man might merit further
gifts of grace. St Thomas said that although no one could merit the
initial gift of grace *de condigno*, with the help of this grace man might
merit *de condigno* augmentation of grace and, eventually, heavenly
glory.[97] This was the view taken in the discussions on the doctrine
at Trent, although the decrees of the Council do not use this terminology, which was too closely associated with scholastic theology.
Other theologians, however, had doubted whether augmentation
of grace could be said to be merited *de condigno*.[98] This distinction is
an important one for understanding Bouchet, for twice he says in
passages of apparently very evangelical tone that no one can merit
grace or merit salvation, but on both occasions he includes the word
condignement. This must be understood as a reference to the distinction outlined above, and it reduces considerably the import of his
statement. The Sorbonne condemned Lefèvre for the following
proposition:

> Mes frères, ne pensez point que les dons de la grace qui sont en
> vous adviennent par voz merites, mais seulement par la grace,
> largesse et infinie bonté de J.C.[99]

This was condemned as Lutheran because 'indicat nulla dona
gratiae dari hominibus per bona opera et meritoria'. As we shall see,

Bouchet was to say something very similar to this proposition, but with the crucial addition of 'condignement'.

In their condemnations of Luther and others in the 1520s, the Sorbonne tend, within this tradition, towards views which accord man the greatest autonomy. Jérôme de Hangest, writing against Luther on the subject of whether or not it is possible to fulfil God's commandments,[100] gives a clear exposition of the relation between merit and grace. God's commandments can be kept with the help of grace. If a man uses this grace he can be said to perform good and meritorious works and even to merit salvation, always with the reservation that grace makes this possible. He claims that Pelagian error is avoided by this reservation, for Pelagius claimed that man could merit on the basis of his free will alone. One may properly say, 'I can perform a work', 'I can perform a good work', 'I can perform a meritorious work', always with the understanding that one is receiving the appropriate degree of grace from God.

With such arguments in mind the Sorbonne condemned another of Lefèvre's propositions:

> Il est dit en un autre lieu que le salut n'est point en nostre puissance mais en la seule bonté de Dieu.[101]

They condemned this because 'designat salutem non esse in potestate nostra'. In the wording of this condemnation, the role of grace is no doubt implicitly understood, but it is certainly not mentioned. Bouchet will hardly ever fail to underline the importance of grace when he speaks of good works and merit.

Thirdly the term *fiducia*, translated as *fiance*, gives rise to confusion. Luther and many evangelicals made trust in God the highest manifestation of faith.[102] For scholastic theologians *fiducia* was a branch of hope, and it is treated as such by the Sorbonne. This difference and its effects can be seen clearly in the Sorbonne's controversy with Erasmus. Erasmus was censured for saying 'It is dangerous to put one's trust in merits' (Periculum est meritis fidere). The Sorbonne theologians argued that God will reward each man according to his works, and that the faithful must be assured that if they persevere in doing good and keeping God's law they will attain eternal life. The faithful are even obliged to trust in merits in this way, because if they did not do so they would fail to hope. This is why it is wrong to assert that it is dangerous to trust in merits. This trust (*fiducia*) does not leave out of consideration God's grace, by which men merit and are saved. Such a trust cannot be called presumption, because all good works will be attributed to God as the principal author, and the reward for merit will be regarded as primarily the product of divine mercy.[103]

In the same way Erasmus was censured for agreeing with Luther that our *fiducia* should be placed not in meritorious works and our own strength but totally in God and in his promises; again the

Sorbonne insisted that men should have 'certam fiduciam' that their labours will not be in vain with God, who has promised eternal life to those who do good.[104]

In his reply Erasmus touches on the problem of how *fiducia* should be defined. He agrees that no pious person would deny the importance of good works to eternal life; without them a mere profession of faith is insufficient, so whoever exhorts Christians to do good works exhorts them piously:

> But whether he teaches rightly who teaches that a man should put his trust (*fiducia*), that is supreme, certain hope, in his own works, in so far as they are the works of a man, I do not know. . . . Especially since in Latin 'fiducia' does not mean just any kind of hope, but the supreme and highest. Hope has fear as a companion, trust excludes fear. Good works nourish hope as evil works beget despair, but not to an equal degree, because we do evil by ourselves, but we do not ourselves do good works so much as the grace of God working in us. If the divine goodness imputes these works to us as merits, then we should ascribe all the glory to God, without whom we are nothing and can do nothing.[105]

Erasmus here suggests that *fiducia* is such a special type of hope that it must be seen as a separate entity. If *fiance* is seen as supreme trust in God, it may indeed appear presumptuous to speak of *in meritis fidere*. This passage from Erasmus sheds some light on Bouchet's treatment of these problems. He speaks of *fiance* in Christ but of *esperance* in good works.

Finally we should note that in defining faith Bouchet makes very prominent use of a concept which is found in Rabelais and writers influenced by Erasmus, but which is a scholastic concept utterly condemned by Luther—*fides caritate formata*.[106] He defines this concept in his section on faith:

> La foye vraye et vifve qu'on appelle foy formée, est quant la personne croit Dieu, à Dieu et en Dieu: c'est à dire que Dieu est, et tous les articles de la foy, et faict ce qu'il a commandé, qui sont les euvres de la foy. La foy morte ou sans forme est croire Dieu et à Dieu, mais non faire ses commandemens. Et aussi peu vault ceste foy que n'en avoir point. Car comme dict saint Paul, 'Si j'avois telle foy que je peusse transferer les montaignes d'ung lieu en l'autre, et je n'ay charité, je ne suis rien'.[107]

He says over and over again that charity proceeds from hope which itself proceeds from faith; thus the three theological virtues are inseparable.[108] Faith understood as 'foi formée de charité' is a means of avoiding the problem of assessing the relative importance of faith and works. As Bouchet says, one cannot have charity without faith; charity makes people perform good works; if one performs no good works this shows that one has no faith.[109] The advantage of the formula as he uses it is that he can encourage people to perform good works, while at the same time stressing the importance of faith in the process of salvation. In using this formula he makes faith belief, but also much more than just belief. Another formula he favours is the one which appears in the passage just quoted, 'croire Dieu, à Dieu et en Dieu'.[110] Rabelais mocked the Sorbonne for a concept of faith as belief based on Hebrews 11 v.1;[111] when Doré defines faith in his *Dialogue*, the section consists of an exposition of the same verse, although he goes on to say at the end that the faith which saves is 'foy vive', 'foy formée de charité'.[112] Bouchet, however, does not use Hebrews 11 v.1 at all.

His treatment of charity includes good works of the sort attacked by reformers; he defends fasting, prayer to the saints, pilgrimages, against the attacks of Lutherans.[113] But above all he concentrates on love: love of God and love of neighbour as expressed in Christ's summary of the Commandments.[114] The mutual love of Christ and the Christian is of course given great prominence by the story of the allegory.

In the debate between the Sorbonne and Erasmus about trusting in one's merits, both sides are concerned with the pastoral effects of the teaching. The Sorbonne are more disturbed by the prospect of discouraging the faithful from performing good works, Erasmus by the risk that the faithful will forget that good works are only possible by the grace of God. Bouchet tries to eradicate both these dangers.

In his presentation of these doctrines it is obvious that Bouchet is continually warning against two beliefs which are dangerous for a Christian to act upon: first that one can be saved *without* good works when one has had the opportunity to perform them, secondly that one may be saved *by* one's good works alone. His doctrine, as put forward in several different passages, can be summarised as follows:

Unaided by grace, a man can perform no good work which merits any gift of grace, although by performing good works unaided he may dispose himself to be called to penitence. Man is saved by the merits of Christ's passion, in which he participates by baptism and by the gift of faith, freely bestowed upon him by God. Living faith is 'foi formée de charité'. The initial gift of grace is increased by God as the man, exercising his free will aided by grace, loves God, keeps His commandments and performs works of charity. The grace can however be lost if a man fails to perform good works or, worse, if he sins, and in this case the man is again dependent on grace to be called to repentance. If a man inherits eternal life, the first cause is the merits of Christ; but because a man participates in these merits by baptism and faith, and because living faith is 'foi formée' which inevitably gives rise to good works if there is any opportunity to perform them, to this extent man can be said to 'merit' eternal life. But this is said always with the proviso that it is the merits of Christ and the gift of grace which make this secondary merit possible.[115]

This summary is on the whole consistent with the various passages in which he discusses these problems, although at some points he comes near to contradicting himself. He is expressing the doctrines of scholastic theology, except on the type of merit which can be achieved by a man in a state of grace. But he does in some passages stress one aspect at the expense of another, either because he is arguing against a particular error, or because he obviously regarded some subjects as more profitable subjects of meditation than others. It is in such passages that he appears different from the Sorbonne, and occasionally incurred the disapproval of his post-tridentine editor.

He takes issue with Luther by name in the section on charity, in which he vigorously defends good works. Luther and his followers wish to exempt themselves from obedience to the Church and

> ne faire aucunes bonnes euvres de leurs corps ne de leurs biens, mais vivre charnellement en liberté de mal faire.[116]

Therefore they strive to abolish good works such as fasting and prayers,

> disans pour leur fondement inique, mendacieux et maulvaiz que ce ne sont euvres de charité, mais supersticions, telles que celles des pharisées.[117]

He goes on to explain the role of all good works in salvation:

> Toutes lesquelles euvres, qui de soy sont bonnes, ne proffitent quant à meriter la grace de Dieu et avoir paradis si elles ne sont faictes à son honneur en foy, en esperance et charité. Neautmoins, en quelque sorte qu'on les face, peuent proffiter quant aux biens corporelz et temporelz, et aussi pour estre appellé de Dieu à penitence et à recongnoissance des pechez qu'on a contre luy faiz et commis.[118]

Here Bouchet has supported the view that by good works done in faith, hope and charity one may merit augmentation of grace and salvation; he also suggests that a man may dispose himself to receive a gift of grace by performing good works of his own free will—this the contrary of the view of Luther that any act performed without faith must be sinful,[119] and also against that of Erasmus, who noted that the Scotists believed that a man can perform morally good works unaided, by which he may *de congruo* merit a gift of grace; Erasmus suggests that this view goes against the words of St Paul.[120] In the passage on hope, Bouchet attacks 'ceulx qui sont repeuz de la farine de Luther', citing Christ's words in the Sermon on the Mount about works of charity, maintaining that St Matthew tells us that Christ recommended fasting, alms-giving and prayer, and particularly stressing the description of the Last Judgement in

Matthew 25—only good and evil works are mentioned there as determining whether a man shall be saved or not:

> Il n'est aucunement parlé de la foy ne de l'observance des commandemens de Dieu, mais seullement de bonnes et maulvaises euvres.[121]

In these passages Bouchet is defending good works and so stresses those aspects of the doctrine of salvation which relate to what a man is able to do. In two other passages, however, he appears to lean towards an evangelical position as he asserts that no one can merit salvation. The first comes in the section on prayer already mentioned, when he discusses the merits of the saints:

> Car c'est par luy [Jesuchrist] que les saincts et sainctes ont ceste prerogative de prier la deité, non par leurs merites de leur vie, mais par sa grant grace, car onc homme ne femme ne meriterent condignement par leurs seulles euvres, tant bonnes qu'on les sçauroit dire, la beatitude eternelle; elle leur a esté donné, et sera à tous les predestinez, par la grant grace et bonté de Dieu et par les merites de Jesucrist. Et pourtant ayez le tousjours davant les yeulx, et vostre totalle et principalle fiance en luy, car qui ne l'a en luy, perd son temps.[122]

This whole passage was cut out in 1563. In an *épître* addressed by the Soul to Christ when she is near to death, she meditates on the merits of Christ:

> | | Car onc n'y eut homme ne femme au monde |
> | | Qui meritast de vostre grace une unde |
> | | Condignement, ne qui par dict ou faict |
> | | Tant soit il bon, tant devot et parfaict, |
> | Que par le | Ayt eu salut, ne qui es cieulx herite, |
> | seul merite | Car le tout vient de vostre seul merite, |
> | de Jesus on | Par voz tourmens, injures et destroiz, |
> | a paradis. | Et par la mort que endurastes en croix. |
> | | Duquel merite avez de vostre grace |
> | | Voulu que ceulx qui vous suyvent par trace |
> | | Et ont la foy et le baptesme aussi, |
> | | Soyent à tousjours participans sans si.[123] |

Again the editor in 1563 did not approve; he cut out the first five lines (leaving 'merite' with no rhyme). The lines could well be interpreted as conflicting with the decisions of the Council of Trent.[124] The passage on prayer left more room for merit because he spoke there of 'leurs *seulles* euvres'. But in both passages the word *condignement* is crucial. If it is understood as translating the theological term *de condigno* already discussed, then Bouchet is still leaving room for a limited merit disproportionately rewarded by God. In the first passage he has just defended prayer to saints, which critics had attacked as diverting worship from its true object; this final paragraph therefore seems intended to meet that objection.

The vocabulary has a very evangelical flavour apart from *seulles* and *condignement*, particularly with its use of *totalle et principalle fiance*. The sentiments of the verse are that of the proposition of Lefèvre condemned by the Sorbonne—except for the word *condignement* which radically alters the sense. Again the context helps to explain the emphasis; the Soul is near to death. As *Vérité* tells the Soul, devils tempt the dying: they tempt those who have done no good works to despair so that they will not have recourse to the faith by which they may be saved; they tempt those who have performed many good works to trust that they will gain salvation by these works alone without faith formed by charity:

> Et à ceste consideracion on doit dire à ceulx qui sont au pas de
> la mort qu'ilz ayent leur entière foy et fiance à nostre seigneur
> Jesucrist et au merite de sa passion . . .[125]

This is the best and surest way to direct one's thoughts. Yet at the same time, as far as the living are concerned, the best advice which can be given to someone who wishes to die well is 'vive bien en foy, en esperance et charité, et face le plus qu'il pourra de bonnes euvres'.[126] The desire neither to undermine nor to overvalue good works is obvious. It would however seem that Bouchet had changed his mind somewhat in the late 1520s and had become persuaded that people should be encouraged to think more of Christ and less of their own actions. We may cite an example from another work. In the *Epître de Justice* in 1525 he speaks of the effects of penitence. The penitent is restored

> Par ce moien tant sainct et tant exquis
> Voire s'il fait tout ce qui est requis.[127]

In the *Epîtres morales* of 1545 these lines are replaced by

> Tout en Jesus et par sa passion;
> De luy seul vient nostre salvation.[128]

Similarly, in 1525 he says, speaking of Noah and his family:

> Desquelz Dieu eut pour leurs vertuz mercy.

But in 1545

> Desquelz eut Dieu par sa grace mercy.[129]

Denying any possibility of meriting grace *de condigno* puts him on the wing of scholastic theology which took less account of human merit; this no doubt is what the 1563 censor objected to, together with the 'evangelical' flavour of some of his comments.[130] Grappling with these questions had apparently sharpened Bouchet's sense of the all-importance of Christ. His approval of the *Miroir de l'Ame pécheresse* can be explained by such a development. The views expressed in the *Triomphes* and the *Miroir* are not identical. Marguerite depicts a soul helplessly sunk in sin and unable in any circumstances to keep the Commandments.[131] She can be interpreted as denying the necessity for penance,[132] and she appears to allow no role for human merit in the final Judgement.[133] But the similarities are more striking than these differences. Marguerite presents faith as a gift of grace, and makes hope and charity proceed from it.[134] She imagines *Paix* satisfying *Justice* at the Last Judgement;[135] above all the powerful image of the unfaithful wife who has prostituted herself but is nevertheless forgiven by her husband unites the two works. Both stress the mutual love of Christ and the soul, both depict a soul who has fallen into grave sin but is redeemed by Christ's merits, both seek to express her wonder and rapture in verse. It does seem very likely indeed that Marguerite drew inspiration from the verse, as Marie Holban suggested, and also from the allegory of Bouchet's work, which can be accused of clumsiness and prolixity but which is certainly not devoid of attractions.[136] Bouchet for his part, though eager to defend good works, dwells on the all-powerful merits of Christ in a manner that suggests that he felt this to be the proper subject for a Christian's meditations, and with an eloquence that suggests that he could only have taken pleasure in reading the *Miroir*—even without the possible flattering knowledge that he had inspired the royal writer.

Finally it is worth remembering that Bouchet began to write the *Triomphes* in the years when the group that met at Fontaine-le-Comte was at its apogee. One at least of these friends actually went over to the Reformation—Trojan, a Franciscan, whose theology Bouchet had relied on in 1525. Others also, like Rabelais who was soon to set aside his monastic habit for ever, were in the process of reassessment and change. Bouchet remained broadly unconvinced and extremely loyal to the Catholic Church. But should we not see the sharpening in Bouchet's perception of the problems involving faith, works, merit and grace as having been achieved in some measure in that intellectual circle? Rabelais, Quintin, Trojan and the others must have discussed Lutheran views, Erasmian views and Sorbonne ripostes as well as the treatment of these questions by the Fathers and the Scholastics. On these topics, as on others treated in the *Triomphes*, like prayer to saints, Bouchet reveals a grasp of arguments which can be opposed to the teaching he is offering, together with a willingness to accept the validity of objections to ways of presenting doctrines which may lead ordinary people to misplace their trust. This looks like the fruit of debate and discussion in that lively intellectual atmosphere, where more than one of the participants was open to profound changes in his beliefs.

NOTES

1. The Soul's letters of remission from the Trinity are dated September 1527 (f.lxxxv ro). In an introductory poem Bouchet says that he has lived in the world for fifty years 'et ung peu plus' (f.l ro); he was fifty in January 1526. In a prose *épître de l'acteur* he says that he is in his fifty-fourth year (+2 ro).

2. See the bibliography.
3. +1 ro. Dated 22 November 1530.
4. *Ibid.* Dated 27 November 1530.
5. a1 vo.
6. See Higman, *Censorship*, pp.15-16 on the authority of the Sorbonne and of provincial faculties of theology to pass theological judgement on books. If they condemned a book, any ensuing practical measures would have to be taken by the bishops and their courts or by the *Parlement* (pp.16-20). Poitiers came under the jurisdiction of the Paris *Parlement*.
7. f.346 vo. This is signed 'Iudocus Tiletanus, S. Theologiae doctor'.
8. In '"Le Miroir de l'âme pécheresse" et "Les Epistres de la Noble et Amoureuse Dame"', Marie Holban established the similarities between the verse in the *Triomphes* and Marguerite's *Miroir*. The *Miroir* was first published in 1531. Although the main part of the *Triomphes* is dated 20 June 1530 in the colophon, the theologians' certificates and the privilege, printed in a separate gathering, are dated November 1530 and 20 February 1530 (o.s.). Holban suggests that Bouchet presented Marguerite with a manuscript copy before the book was printed (p.153). Another possibility is that he presented her with a printed copy of the main text without the liminary material.
9. +2 vo.
10. *Ibid.*
11. +3 ro.
12. +2 vo.
13. See *infra*, at n.41.
14. f.lxix ro.
15. f.cix ro. The theme of Christ visiting the Soul is to be found in Gerson's *Mendicité spirituelle*, one of the many works by Gerson from which Bouchet borrowed in the *Triomphes*; see *infra*, n.48.
16. The *épîtres* were printed separately without Bouchet's approval by D. Janot. See the bibliography, and Holban, *art. cit.*, pp.143-4.
17. f.iv vo.
18. f.lix vo.
19. f.lx ro.
20. f.lxii vo.
21. f.lxvi ro.
22. f.lxvii ro.
23. f.lxvii vo.
24. f.lxvii vo.
25. *Ibid.* The 'presque' is important; Bouchet would not wish to deny that grace can give man the power to avoid sin.
26. f.lxviii ro.
27. ff.lxxxiii ro-lxxxiiii ro.
28. He refers to the Trinity throughout the passage; the Soul explains in an *épître* to the Virgin that she has offended each person of the Trinity (f.lxxx vo). For some reason the 1563 editor disapproved and sometimes replaces *Trinité* by *Dieu le père* or *Dieu*. Bouchet says less about the Trinity in the *Triomphes* than he had in the *Labyrinthe*, which indicates the different readership envisaged. In the *Triomphes* the Trinity is singled out as a doctrine which simple people may believe 'simplement et generallement en la

foy de l'eglise'; bishops and clergy however 'sont tenuz le croire explicitement et en particulier pour en disputer contre les hereticques', f.cii ro. (These remarks are added to a passage in which he was following Gerson.)

29. See *infra*, section 6, especially n.130.

30. Edited by J. J. Stürzinger for the Roxburghe Club, 3 vols, London, 1893, 1895 and 1897. See also Abbé J. Delacotte, *Trois Romanspoèmes du XIVᵉ siècle*, Paris, [1932] (a paraphrase), and Rosemond Tuve, *Allegorical Imagery*, Princeton, 1966.

31. Paris, 1511, BL C.6.b.15.

32. The judgement forms the first 2,596 lines of an 11,000-line poem.

33. See Hamon, pp.57-8. *Ep. Fam.* 9, 10 and 11 are addressed to Gabrielle de Bourbon. *Ep. Fam.* 10 is written as from the Soul to Christ, and so anticipates to some extent the story of the *Triomphes*; it can be compared with Gabrielle's *Voyage spirituel entreprins par l'ame devote*, described below. *Ep. Fam.* 11 is written in the person of the Virgin and deals with the Passion of Christ; another work by Gabrielle is called *Ung petit traicté sur les doulleurs de la passion du doulx Jesus et de sa benoiste mere, pour lesquelles voir et santir le cueur contemplatif amene avecques soy l'ame devote*, (Chartrier de Thouars, I A P 220). This treatise deals first with the life of Christ, then with the life of the Virgin.

34. *Le Voyage spirituel entreprins par l'ame devote pour parvenir en la cité de bon repoux*, Bib. Mazarine, MS 978. This M s contains another little treatise by Gabrielle entitled *Le fort chasteau pour la retraicte de toutes bonnes ames, fait par le commandement du glorieux sainct esperit*.

35. In heaven she is given a ring called *Augmentation de gloire*; she is welcomed into heaven by St Ursula, and the 'story' has parallels with saints' lives—the Soul berates her temptors much as St Margaret scolds the devil and would-be husbands; the espousals in heaven may be compared with St Catherine's vision of her own betrothal to Christ (*Vie de madame saincte Katherine*, f.xv ro-vo).

36. See Pellechet's *Bibliothèque publique de Versailles: Catalogue des Incunables et des livres imprimés de MD à MDXX*, Paris, 1889, p.12. On the second volume of an edition of the *Summa* printed by J. Grüninger, Argentinae, 1496, is written:

> Quam (i.e. secunda pars) Johannes bouchetus In curiis regalibus pictavis procurator cum ceteris partibus ipsius summe a Johanne de Marnef alias (?) duliege (?) librario jurato xixᵃ mensis decembris anni milleᵐⁱ quingentesimi octavi emit, (signé) Bouchet.

37. f.xxvi ro.

38. *Summa*, J. Grüninger, Argentinae, 1496 (the same edition as Bouchet's copy), BL IB.1431-1434, F1 ro, col.1.

39. He renders 'Debent secundo et aliis virtutum prebere exempla' by 'Secondement en doit donner bon exemple à sa femme, à ses enfans, à sa famille et à ses voisins par frequentation de bonnes euvres' (f.vi ro). He adds notes on lying, says it is unwise to beat one's wife, adds instructions for pregnant women, for maidens, etc.

40. For example, references to Ecclesiasticus, f.xxi vo.

41. f.lxviii ro-vo.

42. *Summa*, pars 1, tit.3, cap.9.
43. Gerson wrote a substantial number of works in French; these are to be found in vols 7(1) and (2) of the *Œuvres complètes*, ed. P. Glorieux, Paris, 1960-73. They were mostly translated into Latin; Bouchet definitely used a Latin version of the *Tractatus de differentia peccatorum mortalium et venialium* rather than Gerson's original French, as printed for instance by Trepperel, Paris, 1495, BL I A.40406. He probably used Wimpheling's edition of the *Opera omnia*, published for instance by Regnault, Paris, 1521, BL 472.f.3. For convenience I shall refer to the E. Du Pin edition of the *Opera omnia*, 5 vols, Antwerp, 1706, as well as to the Glorieux edition.
44. Rejected as inauthentic by Glorieux (1, p.41). Du Pin, 1, cols 233-422.
45. In French, Glorieux, 7(1), pp.370-89; in Latin, Du Pin, 2, cols 485-504.
46. Glorieux, 7(1), pp.404-7; Du Pin, 1, cols 447-50 (see 448).
47. Glorieux, 9, pp.644-6; Du Pin, 3, cols 758-60.
48. In French, Glorieux, 7(1), pp.220-80; in Latin, Du Pin, 3, cols 487-540.
49. Glorieux, 5, pp.398-405; Du Pin, 3, cols 269-75.
50. Glorieux, 8, pp.376-455; Du Pin, 4, cols 392-451. Bouchet uses a passage for a meditation on the sacrament (Du Pin, cols 446-51).
51. Glorieux, 9, pp.185-245; Du Pin, 1, cols 125-84.
52. Glorieux, 10, pp.90-109; Du Pin, 1, cols 189-203.
53. *PL* vol.cxcvi, cols 1159-78. Bouchet gives the source wrongly as 'ex magistro *Johann*. de sancto victore' (f.lxxxviii vo).
54. Robert Ciboule (*Livre de Meditation sur soy mesmes*, S. Vostre, Paris, 1510, BL C.38.h.11., f.xxxiv vo, ff.) borrows parts of an account from Bartholomaeus Anglicus, *Liber de proprietatibus rerum* (see for example the French translation printed in Lyons, 1482, BL IB.41688), which in turn draws its information from Isidore, *Etymologies*, Book xi (*PL* vol.lxxxii, cols 397-424). Bouchet uses Ciboule, but where Ciboule stops short or over-abbreviates, Bouchet continues, using Bartholomaeus (ff.xlii vo-xlviii vo).
55. +2 ro.
56. *Enchiridion militis christiani*, first published 1503, *Opera Omnia*, Leiden, vol.5, cols 1-66; see chapters 6 and 7.
57. +2 vo.
58. *Opera Omnia*, Leiden, vol.5, col.19. Bouchet's addition here concerning the soul's need to assent through its free will is consistent with Erasmus' general argument—Bouchet is only taking small extracts from the text of the *Enchiridion*. But we have already seen the stress which he lays on the role of the will.
59. *Precatio Dominica in septem portiones distributa*, Basle, [1523?], BL 700.b.37; *Opera Omnia*, Leiden, vol.5, cols 1217-28. See *Triomphes*, ff.cxiii vo-cxv vo.
60. *Expositio super Dimitte nobis debita nostra*, Glorieux, 8, pp.76-7; Du Pin, 3, col.694. *Triomphes*, f.cxv ro-vo.
61. Book 1, ff.vii vo-ix ro. *Théologie* is called in to instruct on what is permissible in the marriage bed. Bouchet refers to Raulin's third sermon on matrimony; he also uses the eighth (Jean Raulin,

Itinerarium paradisi . . . *cui adjuncti sunt non minus commendandi sermones eiusdem gravissimi patris de matrimonio ac viduitate,* Paris, 1519, BL G.19717; see especially ff.clxii vo and clxxix vo-clxxxii vo). Raulin, d.1515, had been a celebrated preacher in Paris and an important supporter of ecclesiastical reform: see Renaudet, *Préréforme,* especially pp.165-70 and 563 n.3.

62. To *De Fide et symbolo* (*PL* vol.xL, cols 193-4).

63. On the ninth article of the Creed he departs from the passage of Gerson he is using in order to assert that the Pope is the 'vicaire en terre' of Christ:

> et ce qui est ordonné et commandé par ceste eglise militante doit estre fait et acomply comme fait par inspiracion divine, en ensuyvant ce que Jhesucrist dist à ses apostres et disciples, que toutes les foiz qu'ilz se assembleroient en son nom il seroit on millieu d'eux. Qui est contre l'erreur de ceulx qui veulent confondre la iherarchie de l'eglise militante. (f.ci vo).

64. ff.cxvii vo-cxx vo.

65. These questions appear f.lxxxviii vo, and they come from the first chapter of *De potestate.*

66. See the edition printed at Cologne, 1561, BL 4326.aa.49, pp.601-66. *De potestate* had appeared in the *Opera omnia* of Richard of St Victor (e.g. Paris, J. Petit, 1518, BL 472.f.11, ff.cxxv vo-cxxviii vo) and had also been printed separately by S. de Colines, Paris, 1526 and 1534.

67. *De Libero arbitrio,* Basle, Froben, 1524; *Opera Omnia,* Leiden, vol.9, cols 1215-48. See *Library of Christian Classics,* vol.xvii, *Luther and Erasmus: Free Will and Salvation,* London, 1969. Bouchet's presentation of the questions of merit and grace seems to accord with Erasmus' view as expressed in *De libero arbitrio* that it is desirable for a Christian to reflect on God's love and promises rather than on his own good works (e.g. *Luther and Erasmus,* p.86).

68. i.e. 'foy formée de charité': see *infra,* section 6.

69. f.clxiii vo.

70. *Ibid.*

71. Cf. *Luther and Erasmus,* pp.81, 90.

72. Cf. M. A. Screech, *L'Evangélisme de Rabelais,* Geneva, 1959, pp.23-41, 69-71.

73. ff.clvi vo-clvii vo; Gerson, *Tractatus super Magnificat* (see *supra,* n.50).

74. f.clv vo.

75. The words 'à tous prebstres bien ordonnez' suggest the conventional formula 'rite ordonnatus', meaning any priest whose ordination is valid. But in the context the phrase also serves to underline that only a priest has the power to consecrate the sacrament.

76. These *quaestiones* discuss the conversion of the bread and the wine into the body and blood of Christ, the manner in which Christ is present in the sacrament, and the accidents remaining in the consecrated elements. Bouchet's twelve-point list deals only with the bread; it has the appearance of being a ready-made summary of the doctrine devised for laymen, but I have not discovered his immediate source.

77. f.clii vo.
78. On this and other texts used to support the doctrine before the
     Council of Trent, see Jacques Le Goff, *La Naissance du purgatoire*,
     Paris, 1981, pp.64-8.
79. The canonicity is discussed by Johann von Eck in his *De purgatorio
     contra Lutherum*, composed in 1521. (I have used the edition of
     Antwerp, 1545, BL 3906.a.5: see f.33 *et seq.* The verse from
     Maccabees is quoted on the title page.)
80. f.cliii ro. The four Fathers mentioned here all represent signifi-
     cant stages in the development of the doctrine of purgatory. See
     Le Goff, *Naissance du purgatoire*, pp.79-131.
81. *Dialogue*, f.lxvi ro-vo.
82. f.clii vo.
83. The *Ordinayre des crestiens*, s3 ro-s4 vo, states that purgatory is
     part of hell; its description of the pains of purgatory leads to a
     long denunciation of those on earth who fail to alleviate the
     sufferings of their benefactors or loved ones in purgatory.
84. f.lxxvii vo.
85. f.cv ro.
86. f.cxv vo—on the same page as part of the passage taken from the
     Precatio Dominica by Erasmus.
87. Erasmus, *Opera Omnia*, Amsterdam, vol.1(3), 1972, p.329, lines
     129-30.
88. f.cxvi ro.
89. Du Pin, 3, cols 489-90. Gerson is answering the question, 'Why
     pray when God already knows our needs?' The answer embraces
     prayer to God and prayer to saints.
90. He also asserts that there are examples in scripture of prayers
     made to the saints and friends of God, but the examples he cites
     are all of saints praying for other people: *Dialogue*, ff.lxxii ro-
     lxxxv ro.
91. Glorieux, 2, pp.169-91; Du Pin, 3, cols 247-62: see Part 1, col.249.
92. f.cxvi vo.
93. *Ibid.*
94. There is a prayer to the Virgin in the *Amoureux transi*, but of the
     three *Ep. Fam.* addressed to Gabrielle de Bourbon, one is on the
     theme of the mutual love of Christ and the Soul, and one in the
     person of the Virgin concentrates on the Passion of Christ. Christ
     or God the Father are most frequently addressed in the *Cantiques*,
     and the prayers for the Canon of the Mass have Christ's Passion
     as their subject.
95. The most important are the judgement in heaven (ff.lxxiii ro-
     lxxxiiii ro); the sections on faith (especially ff.cii vo-ciii ro), hope
     (the whole section, ff.ciii ro-cv ro) and charity (especially f.cvi
     ro); a passage on good works (ff.cxxxviii ro and cxxxix ro); the
     passage on free will already quoted (f.clxiii vo). There are also
     relevant passages in the section on prayer (f.cxvi vo), the section
     on making a will (f.clix ro-vo), and in several of the *épîtres* addres-
     sed to Christ by the Soul (especially f.lxxvii ro and f.cxlvii vo).
96. Erasmus mentions this view in *De Libero Arbitrio*, attributing it to
     the Scotists; *Opera Omnia*, Leiden, 9, col.1223; *Luther and Eras-
     mus*, p.51—see also Introduction, pp.11 and 25.
97. *Summa*, Prima secundae, q.cxiv, art. viii; see also art. iii.

98. See Vacant, *Dictionnaire de théologie catholique* under *mérite*, particularly cols 689-93. Up to the thirteenth century theologians were cautious about attributing glory in heaven to merit in any real sense. Thereafter the exposition of St Thomas was generally accepted, although St Bonaventura struck a balance between *meritum de condigno* and *de congruo* when speaking of glory in heaven and would only admit a *meritum digni* with regard to augmentation of grace (col.692). A small number of theologians continued to argue the point. St Bonaventura was naturally an important influence on Franciscans, and it will be remembered that Bouchet had many Franciscan friends, including the theologians who certified the *Triomphes*.

99. See Lefèvre, *Epistres & evangiles pour les cinquante & deux semaines de l'an*, ed. M. A. Screech, Geneva, 1964, p.44.

100. *De possibili praeceptorum divinorum impletione in Lutherum*, Paris, 1528, BL 3837.a.31(2).

101. *Epistres & evangiles*, p.44.

102. For many examples of the use of 'fiducia' and 'fiance' see Screech, *L'Evangélisme de Rabelais*, pp.10-22. Luther's treatment of faith is compared with Aquinas' treatment of hope in S. Pfürtner, *Luther and Aquinas—a Conversation*, tr. E. Quinn, London, 1964.

103. Paraphrased from the text which appears in Erasmus, *Declarationes ad censuras Lutetiae vulgatas*, Basle, 1532, BL C.60.e.12, pp.178-9; *Opera Omnia*, Leiden, vol.9, col.888.

104. *Declarationes*, pp.173-4; *Opera Omnia*, cols 886-7.

105. Translated from *Declarationes*, pp.179-81; *Opera Omnia*, cols 887-8:

> Bona opera esse viaticum ad vitam aeternam nemo pius negat: & sine his non sufficere fidei professionem fatemur: & qui Christianos hortatur, ut hic adnitantur quam plurimum bonorum operum colligere, sancte & pie hortatur: sed qui docet, ut homo in suis operibus, quatenus sunt hominis, fiduciam, hoc est, summam ac certam spem, collocet, an recte moneat, nescio. Diversam cantionem canunt sanctissimi quique. Praesertim cum *fiducia* Latinis non sonet qualemcunque spem, sed summam ac praecipuam. Spes comitem ducit metum, fiducia excludit timorem. Alunt utcunque spem bona opera, quemadmodum mala opera gignunt desperationem: tametsi nec hic par est ratio, quod mala per nos agimus, bona non tam nos agimus, quam gratia Dei operatur in nobis: quae si divina bonitas nobis pro meritis imputat, nostrum tamen est illi totam gloriam adscribere, sine qua nihil sumus, nec possumus quicquam.

106. See St Thomas, *Summa*, Secunda Secundae, q.iv, art.iii; Lucien Febvre, *Le Problème de l'incroyance au XVIe siècle*, Paris, revised ed. 1962, pp.303-6; Screech, *L'Évangélisme de Rabelais*, pp.31-4.

107. f.ciii ro.

108. See for example *ibid.*: Et dit la glose sur le premier chapitre saint Mathieu que esperance procede de foy, et charité d'esperance, c'est à dire que esperance parfaicte n'est sans foy, et charité n'est sans foy et esperance, parce que celluy qui a vraye foy formée en charité espere en Dieu et ayme Dieu sur toutes choses, et son prochain come luy mesme pour l'amour de Dieu.

The interlinear gloss on St Matthew (1 v.2, Abraham genuit Isaac) mentioned here had already been quoted in the *Labyrinthe* (1524, P7 vo). The treatment of the three theological virtues in the *Triomphes du roi* will again stress that charity proceeds from hope, and hope from faith.

109. f.cxxxvii[i] ro, explaining why *Foy* is the mistress of the *Territoire de bonnes euvres*.

110. Found for example in one of the works which Bouchet read as Gerson's, the *Tractatus primus de articulum fidei*, Du Pin, 1, col.234. See also the use of the same formula in the *Labyrinthe*, 1524, O2 vo-P5 ro: there 'croire en Dieu' includes respect for the Church and is a pretext for satirising irregular priests (cf. *Ep. Fam.* 113, cited *supra* in chapter 5).

111. *Gargantua*, ch.5; see Screech, *L'Evangélisme de Rabelais*, pp.10-15.

112. *Dialogue*, f.ii vo.

113. f.cvi ro. However, he also warns against performing such acts hypocritically, i.e. performing the exterior acts while inwardly cultivating serious sins: 'Il est requis pour avoir charité que le cueur soit correspondant et s'accorde avec l'euvre pour la presenter à Dieu' (f.cvi vo).

114. See for example *supra*, n.108.

115. The following passages from the section on hope give a clear statement of the relation between grace and good works. They remain unchanged in 1563:

> Toutesfoiz, Ame raisonnable, ne presumez par ceste diffinicion d'esperance que voz bonnes euvres exterieures soient principalement cause de votre salut, car tout ainsi que ce seroit presumption d'esperer salut eternel par grace sans bonnes euvres, aussi seroit ce de l'avoir par bonnes euvres sans grace, car il n'y eut onc pur home ne femme qui peussent d'eulx mesmes meriter paradis sans la grace de Dieu (f.ciii ro).

> 'Il semble à bien entendre toutes ces parolles [i.e. Romans 3 v.10, 2 Corinthians 3 v.5, Philippians 2 v.13] que ne sçaurions faire aucunes bonnes euvres de nous mesmes.' 'Il est vray,' dist Theologie, 'et que toutes bonnes euvres procedent de la grace de Dieu par la foy formée que avons en luy et qu'il nous a donnée, et que la foy formée est le fondement de tout. Qui est celluy qui ousast ou peust veritablement dire qu'il observera tous ces saincts commandemens et fera aultres bonnes euvres sans l'aide specialle de Dieu? . . . La personne crestienne, congnoissant sa fragilité et ignorance, et qu'elle ne peult faire aulcun bien sans l'aide de Dieu et sa saincte inspiracion, se humiliera davant luy, et en vraye foy luy dira: O Dieu eternel, je congnois mon ignorance, fragilité et malice, et que je n'y puis sans vous et votre aide resister ne garder voz commandemens, ne semblablement faire aulcunes bonnes euvres. Je vous supply, mon Dieu, que par votre eternel filz Jesucrist . . . qu'il vous plaise me aider et me donner la grace de garder voz commandemens, de faire toutes bonnes euvres, et resister à la puissance de la chair, du monde et du diable. Si la personne crestienne veult ainsi faire, soiez asseurée, Ame raison-

nable, que sa requeste luy sera octroyée, car nostre seigneur Jesucrist l'a ainsi promis par le nouveau testament, et comme j'ay dict, il ne peult mentir. Et par ce moyen ceste personne, par la grace de Dieu, gardera ses commandemens et fera bonnes euvres par lesquelles pourra avoir esperance certaine d'avoir salut par la grace de Dieu et non autrement. (ciiii ro).

Thus the advice to the Christian is to think of God's help rather than of his own achievements. This idea runs through the *Triomphes*, and is I think intended to provide a corrective to the teaching that Christians should trust in their works. It will be noticed that he speaks of *'esperance* certaine' in this context, not *fiance.*

116. f.cvi ro.
117. *Ibid.*
118. *Ibid.* From 'Neantmoins' to 'commis' was cut out in 1563.
119. Luther was condemned by the Sorbonne for saying that man's will is free only to sin; *Determinatio*, b7 ro.
120. For Erasmus man's only spark of free will was to accept or reject God's freely offered gift of grace.
121. f.ciii vo.
122. f.cxvi vo. Cf. f.cv ro (on hope): Theology says that the Lutherans maintain

qu'on ne doit prier les saincts et sainctes, et qu'i[l] suffist de l'humanité de Jesucrist, seul propiciateur entre Dieu et les hommes, et que avons habondamment de son merite sans les merites et suffrages de saincts et sainctes. Ce que je ne veulx contredire, car Jesucrist a satisfaict pour tout . . . (retained in 1563).

123. f.cxlvii vo. Cf. Holban, *art. cit.*, p.144.
124. In the *Decretum de Justificatione* of the sixth session of the Council of Trent the terms *de congruo* and *de condigno* are not used, and Canon 32 reads:

Si quis dixerit, hominis iustificati bona opera ita esse dona Dei, ut non sint etiam bona ipsius iustificati merita, aut ipsum iustificatum, bonis operibus, quae ab eo per Dei gratiam et Jesu Christi meritum, cuius membrum vivum est, fiunt, *non vere mereri augmentum gratiae*, vitam aeternam et ipsius vitae aeternae, si tamen in gratia decesserit, consecutionem atque etiam gloriae augmentum, Anathema sit.

Terms too closely associated with any particular school of theology were avoided in drawing up the canons. But the terms *de congruo* and *de condigno* were used by speakers in the preceding discussions: see J. Waterworth, *The Canons and Decrees of the sacred and oecumenical Council of Trent*, London, 1888, p.ciii; cf. Jedin, *Geschichte des Konzils von Trient*, vol.2, pp.148-9, 155.

125. f.cxlv ro. He uses Antoninus, *Summa*, pars 4, tit.14, c.8 for the seven dangers of death, but this development is not from Antoninus. In a similar vein the Soul is made to say in her will 'non me fiant en mes bonnes euvres, lesquelles ne sont que ordures davant vous, ne en aucune chose du monde, mais en vous seullement . . .' (f.clix ro-vo).
126. *Ibid.* One of the places in which Bouchet appears to contradict

himself is at the end of Book One in an *épître* to the Soul from
Raison, who tells her that

> Tu es ça bas pour acquerir merites
> A celle fin que lassus tu herites
> Dont vins premier, ce que faire pourras
> Si aymes Dieu sur tout . . . (f.lvii vo).

However, we may take into account here the 'story' element; so
far the Soul has received only the rudiments of faith and a moral
education; *Raison* may be giving the best advice of which she,
unaided, is capable.

127. *Opuscules*, 1526, B3 ro.
128. 2 *Ep. Mor.* 5, f.23 vo, col.1.
129. *Opuscules*, 1526, A3 vo; 2 *Ep. Mor.* 5, f.21 ro, col.1.
130. Cf. n.124. It is not always clear exactly what the 1563 censor
      objected to. In the judgement in heaven he alters the passage in
      which *Paix* settles the conflicting claims of Justice and Mercy:

> Et quant aux bonnes euvres dont vous avez parlé, Dame
> Justice, vous savez assez *que par bonnes euvres onc homme ne
> femme n'ont esté ne seront saulvez sans la foy*, et que la foy avec
> penitence suffist en extremité pour obtenir pardon, *car cuider
> avoir paradis par bonnes euvres simplement sans foy, c'est pre-
> sumption* (f.lxxxiv ro).

In 1563 the passages italicised were omitted; perhaps the censor thought that Bouchet's tone was unnecessarily slighting towards good works.

131. *Miroir*, ed. Allaire, lines 53-4, 1127-30.
132. Lines 374-5, 411, 821-30.
133. Lines 1135-1206.
134. Lines 1413-20.
135. Lines 1188-90.
136. Marie Holban's article deals with the verse from the *Triomphes*; in
      fact there are also several points of contact between the 'story' of
      the *Triomphes* and the *Miroir*.

Conclusion

Bouchet was a successful writer; the number of editions of his works proves it. Among his contemporaries he had an enthusiastic readership. He was not a great writer, and even to his original readers his appeal was unequal across the wide span of his compositions. But his indisputable successs is not perhaps too difficult to explain. It has been the contention of this book that Bouchet's major importance and his popularity derive from his attempts to spread knowledge among non-latinate readers.

His verse, for which he is best known although not greatly appreciated today, was moderately successful in his lifetime. Most popular was his moralising fixed-form verse, which conveyed ideas that pleased his readers in a form they enjoyed. But the really successful works were his big manuals of information, the *Annales*, the *Généalogies*, the *Triomphes*—works which the *Quintil Horatian* could characterise as 'grands et continuels œuvres'.

These works are the ones that best exploit Bouchet's skills as a writer. His undecorated prose style is a more than adequate instrument for clear explanation and good story-telling, both valuable features of history and instructive religious allegory. To both he brings an occasional unexpected leavening of understated humorous or ironical comments. He also brings to this type of writing other personal characteristics which must have favoured success among the particular audience he addressed. Even allowing for the convention of 'clausulae humilitatis', Bouchet must strike the reader as a markedly unpretentious writer. He exhibits none of the artist's pride which allowed both *rhétoriqueurs* and the Pléiade to assert the claims of their art in spite of a dependent position. Moreover his learning sits lightly on him; he addresses his non-latinate reader with a refreshing lack of condescension. He also writes with every appearance of sincerity; he persuades the reader of his own personal piety and his own disgust at abuses in the Church. These are qualities which would impress the reader who was actually reading the *Triomphes* in the hope of finding moral and spiritual guidance. 'Chaste et chrestien scripteur' is a fair assessment of the impression which Bouchet makes on the reader.

But above all, as we have shown, Bouchet's intentions and achievements in these instructive works were both honest and honourable. He succeeded in passing on the knowledge he had acquired from wide reading, and he was willing to tackle topics not often treated in the vernacular, or certainly treated less thoroughly than he was prepared to do. In both historical and religious writing it is interesting to note in how many ways he foreshadows the later vulgarisation of scholarship. Like many later sixteenth-century historians he was a lawyer by profession, Gallican in sympathy, and helped to build up national consciousness by writing in French and in praise of the French monarchy. Like later historians and hagiographers he saw the need to discard appealing but untruthful embroideries of history. Like the post-Tridentine counter-reformers he believed that the laity must be instructed in French, that scandalous abuse must be corrected and that traditional forms of devotion, such as prayer to saints, should be defended, purified and encouraged. In short he saw clearly what was in many cases to prove the way forward in the public enlightenment which printing had made possible.

This enlightened approach to the vulgarisation of knowledge is brought to bear on a body of teaching which is highly traditional and apparently backward-looking. Bouchet sees no break in continuity between his own and earlier ages. Christendom marches on, and of course the Church must be prepared to reaffirm its ancient standards, its hostility to abuse, its evangelisation of the ignorant. In every subject that he treats he assumes a continuum; new discoveries like printing are admirably useful, but nothing can turn his medieval world-picture upside down. With confidence and enthusiasm he preaches traditional theology, morality, political precepts; he is fundamentally untouched by the rebirth of pagan learning. With gusto he uses an allegorical mode of narrative and instruction long after most writers had discarded it. And so it comes about that in many cases Bouchet turns out to be the last competent writer to treat a theme or use a technique in what can be perceived as a thoroughly 'medieval' way. Since he was not writing for the intellectually sophisticated this was no doubt yet another factor in his popularity. Where Bouchet anticipates later developments it is because he is profoundly imbued with traditional values like respect for truth in history, the necessity for holiness in the ministry, the duty of instructing people in the word of God, and, at a time when some less confident conservatives were inclined to resort to obscurantism, he continues to write in determined accordance with those values.

Bouchet's Correspondents, Patrons
and Acquaintances

The list that follows includes: a) Authors and recipients of *épîtres familières*; b) Contemporaries whose epitaphs appear in the *Généalogies*; c) Authors of liminary material in Bouchet's works; d) People to whom Bouchet's works are dedicated; e) Authors in whose works liminary material by Bouchet appears; f) A small number of other contemporaries mentioned by Bouchet.

The main aim of the notes is to establish Bouchet's connections with the person concerned, but particularly in the case of little-known contemporaries some biographical information has also been given. Bibliographical references relating to only one individual are given under the relevant heading. Otherwise information derives from one or more of the following sources, indicated where necessary in abbreviated form:

CA = *Catalogue des actes de François Ier*, ed. P. Marichal, 10 vols, Paris, 1887–1908.

DBF = Balteau, *Dictionnaire de biographie française*, Paris, 1932– .

DHGP = Beauchet-Filleau et Chergé, *Dictionnaire historique et généalogique des familles de Poitou*, 2nd ed., Poitiers, 1891– .

DLF = Grente, *Dictionnaire des lettres françaises: le seizième siècle*, Paris, 1951.

DN = Aubert de la Chenaye-Desbois et Badier, *Dictionnaire de la noblesse*, Paris, 1863–76.

GC = *Gallia Christiana*, Paris, 1715–70.

H = Hamon, *Un Grand rhétoriqueur poitevin, Jean Bouchet*, Paris, 1901.

HP 1514 = The document reproduced by A. Thibaudeau, *Histoire du Poitou*, vol. 2, pp. 263–5, listing those present at the Franciscan convent in Poitiers at the publication of the *coutume* of Poitou in 1514.

LT = *Les La Trémoille pendant cinq siècles*, 5 vols, Nantes, 1890–96.

MP = Ledain, 'Les Maires de Poitiers', *MSAO*, 1897.

P = Guiot, *Les Trois siècles palinodiques*, ed. Tougard, 2 vols, Rouen-Paris, 1898.

VP = Favreau, *La Ville de Poitiers à la fin du moyen âge*, Poitiers, 1978.

These abbreviations are followed by volume and page number

where appropriate. The numbers of *Ep. Fam* given without brackets are those written by Bouchet, those in square brackets are addressed to Bouchet.

Allemagne, Florent d'. *Gén. Ep.* 47, *Annales*, f.188 ro; d. 17 Sept. 1510 aged 61. A Benedictine, doctor of law, 'abbé commendataire de Saint-Savin, prévôt et chanoine de l'église de Poitiers' (1497). He claimed to have been elected bishop of Poitiers after the death of Jean de La Trémoille in 1507, but the election was contested by La Trémoille's nephew, Claude de Tonnerre, and d'Allemagne died without having established his claim. See F. Villard, 'L'élection de Claude de Tonnerre à l'évêché de Poitiers', *BSAO* 4ᵉ série, 10, 1970, pp.469– 80. Bouchet praises his piety and clearly sympathised with him, although Charles de La Trémoille is known to have supported Claude de Tonnerre, his cousin.

Allemagne, Jean d'. *Gén. Ep.* 56; d. Sept. 1529 aged 57. Brother of the former. 'Licencié en droit, prévôt de l'église de Poitiers, prieur commendataire dc Guéret'; by the time of his death 'doyen de l'église de Poitiers'. *GC* 2, 1218—but Bouchet's *épître* is a source.

Anglure, Jacques d'. *Ep. Fam.* 111, [112], 113. Described as 'chevalier, seigneur dudict lieu et premier baron de Champaigne'. In 111 (1538) Bouchet says that d'Anglure's son is his neighbour and has told him that his father admires Bouchet's work, particularly the *Triomphes*. Their correspondence expresses their disapproval of heresy. The genealogy of the d'Anglure family is to be found in Lefèvre de Caumartin, *Recherche de la noblesse de Champagne*, 1673, but it is not clear whch Jacques d'Anglure is concerned. The likeliest candidate, 'Jacques, sire et baron d'Anglure, chevalier, advoué de Therouennes l'an 1519', was dead by 1529 if Caumartin's information is correct [p.1, col.2]. The other possibility is 'Jacques d'Anglure, seigneur de Bonnecourt et de Ravenfontaine', but again the information implies that he was dead before August 1537 [*ibid.*, *infra*].

Anjou, René d'. *Gén. Ep.* 97, *Annales* f.192 vo–193 ro, *Panégyrique*. Marquis de Mézières, 'gentilhomme de la chambre, sénéchal du Maine' (until 1519), 'capitaine de cent lances des ordonnances'. Nephew of Louis de La Trémoille; according to Bouchet he died from illness at Avignon in 1524, aged 44. *CA, DBF, LT* 2.

Anne de Bretagne, Queen of France, 1477–1514. Her epitaph *Annales* f.193 ro and *Gén. Ep.* 15; epigram in *Jugement*, f.lx[x] ro. Through the intermediary of Gabrielle de Bourbon she instructed Bouchet to revise the life of St Radegonde originally undertaken by order of Charles v III (*Histoire de Clotaire*, aa1 ro, m8 ro).

Ardillon, Antoine. *Ep. Fam.* 29, 30, 34, 35, 50, 57, 73, 78, 100; mentioned in 85 and 86. He wrote a liminary epistle in Latin for the *Labyrinthe* 1522, and is addressed in a verse *épître* which introduces the *Annales*, 1524. Abbot of Fontaine-le-Comte between at least 1513 and 1540 (*GC* 2, 1343), may have known Bouchet as early as 1514 (*HP*1514). The circle which met at Fontaine-le-Comte included Rabelais, Quintin, Trojan, Petit; in 100 Mellin de Saint-Gelais is said to be on his way to visit him (1536). Referred to in *Pantagruel*, ch.5.

Asnières, Antoine d'. One of the theologians who certified the orthodoxy of the *Triomphes*; see also *Ep. Fam.* 104. A Franciscan, 'gardien des Cordeliers de Poitiers, docteur en théologie'. In 1520 he is found signing the protest by the abbess and nuns of the convent of the Trinité in Poitiers concerning the reform which had imposed the rule of Fontevrault on the convent (*DHGP* 1, 123; cf. *supra*, chapter 3 at n.25).

Auffroy, Claude. *Annales*, f.13 vo; d. before 1524. 'Chanoine et aulmosnier de l'eglise Notre-Dame la Grant'; showed Bouchet an ancient book concerning the church. On the Affroy family see *VP* 256 n.748.

Auton, Jean d'. *c.*1467–Jan. 1528. *Gén. Ep.* 60, his death reported to Ardillon *Ep. Fam.* 57; liminary *épîtres* by him and to him in *Labyrinthe* and *Panégyrique*; see also 2 *Ep. Mor.* 1 and *Temple*, f.lxiii ro. Chronicler to Louis x II who made him abbot of the Augustinian house at Angle-sur-Anglin in 1511. The *épître* from Bouchet in the *Labyrinthe* suggests that they were acquainted before Bouchet embarked upon his legal career. Bouchet claims that d'Auton instructed him in the art of poetry; his *Déploration* and *Epître d'Henri* imitate poems by d'Auton. See *Notice* by Maulde La Clavière in his edition of d'Auton's *Chroniques*, also chapter in Guy, *Rhétoriqueurs*.

Aymery, see Emery.

Baïf, Lazare de. 1496?–1547. *Généalogies* f.142 vo, a jocular *épître* in which Bouchet protests to Baïf, 'maître des requêtes ordinaire du roi', about his tax assessment. He says he is nearly 69, therefore writes late 1544–30 Jan. 1545. Baïf, 'maître des requêtes' from 1538, was in Poitou in 1544 with responsibility for various taxes. Bouchet praises the great humanist 'qui des Latins et Grecz estes l'honneur, Et des François aussi la perle fine'. Baïf was the cousin of Louis de Ronsard. See L. Pinvert, *Lazare de Baïf*, Paris, 1900.

Barré, Jehan. *Gén. Ep.* 53, d. June 1525, aged 22. Unmarried merchant from Poitiers.

Bastard, Louis. *Ep. Fam.* 68 (on death of Jacques Prèvost, 1530).

'Docteur en théologie, gardien du couvent des frères prê-
cheurs à Partenay'. Son of Jean Bastard, 'bourgeois de
Poitiers'; his brother Jean was mayor in 1517 and died 1542—
Guillaume Le Riche mentions Louis' sermon on that occasion, *Journal*, pp.40–1. *DHGP* 1, 322; *MP* 501–2.

Beaune, Jacques de, seigneur de Semblançay. *Annales* 231 ro–233
ro, *Gén. Ep.* 40. Like Marot and other poets Bouchet composed an epitaph for the *trésorier* hanged at Montfaucon in
1527. Both the epitaph and the account given in the *Annales*
assume that Semblançay was indeed guilty. Cf. Marot,
Œuvres lyriques, ed. Mayer, London, 1964, p.134 n.1.

Bergier, Mery. *Gén. Ep.* 61. A *pâtissier* who died young.

Berthellot, René. *Ep. Fam.* 59, written in the name of his dead wife,
Catherine Prévoste. He is called 'futur maire'; he became
mayor of Poitiers in 1529 and married Jeanne Dausseure in
February of that year; d. before 19 July 1561. *MP* 518–19,
DHGP 1, 490.

Billon. Mentioned *Ep. Fam.* 92 as author of [91] from the 'habitants
d'Issouldun en Berry' concerning the Mystery of the Passion.
H 117 n.2 suggests that he might be the 'maistre Charles
Billon' addressed by François Habert, who came from Issoudun. Habert says that Billon has listened to the reading of
Habert's verses in Berry and has himself addressed Latin
verse to Habert (*La jeunesse du Banny de lyesse*, Paris, 1541, f.47
ro–vo).

Blanchet, Pierre. *Gén. Ep.* 51, mentioned *Temple*, f.lxiii ro and *Ep.
Fam.* [22]. According to Bouchet, who is the main source of
information about him, he died in 1519, having been a priest
for twenty years after becoming one when already over 40.
He was a 'poète satirique' connected with the Basoche; he
wrote plays—farces and presumably *soties*—but none of his
work survives. Bouchet was an executor of his will. *DHGP* 1,
546.

Boiceau de La Borderie, Jean. 1513–91. His *Vol de l'aigle en France*,
Paris, [1540], on the Emperor Charles v's visit to France, is
prefaced by a *dizain* addressed to 'son amy, le Traverseur'
and another by Bouchet in reply. The author of legal and
satirical works, he studied at the Collège de Navarre in Paris
and then became 'avocat au présidial' at Poitiers, where he
met Calvin in 1533. He was later openly Protestant, requesting Catherine de' Medici for a place of worship for the Protestants of Poitou in 1568, but he is said to have abjured subsequently. *DBF*.

Boilesve, Jean, seigneur de la Brosse. *Gén. Ep.* 55; d. 3 Aug. 1531,
aged 39. 'Licencié ès lois, conseiller du roi à Poitiers'. Son of
Yves Boilesve, q.v. *VP* 598, *DHGP* 1, 581.

Boilesve, Yves, seigneur de la Brosse. Death recorded *Ep. Fam.* 2, based on a poem which first appeared in the *Amoureux transi*; d. aged 33 in Aug. 1501. *Echevin* of Poitiers from 1497; in 1490 he married the daughter of the *avocat du roi* in Poitou, who transferred his office to him. Bouchet claims him as a relation (de mon lignage). *VP*; *DHGP* 1, 581.

Bonnyot, Françoise. Bouchet's wife, whose name was discovered by Richard (*Notes*, pp.13–14). She came from a Chauvigny family. Richard suggests that Bouchet married her on becoming a *procureur* in Poitiers (by 1507); the *épître* to d'Auton in the *Labyrinthe* suggests that marriage made it possible for him to settle down. Two of their daughters were already married by 1524 (*H* 31). She was still alive in 1543 (*Ep. Fam.* 127). Bouchet attributes her recovery from an illness to the miraculous intervention of St Radegonde (*Histoire de Clotaire* m7 vo–m8 ro). He speaks of her with affection, see particularly *Ep. Fam.* 67.

Bouchet, Gabriel. *Ep. Fam.* 51. Bouchet's eldest son and heir, perhaps named after Gabrielle de Bourbon, q.v. He was educated at a *collège* and became a *procureur* like his father; he is found dealing with both the La Trémoille family and the Chauvigny chapter in his father's lifetime. He died before 1575 and was survived by at least two children. *H* 165; Richard, *Notes*, p.15.

Bouchet, Joseph. One of Bouchet's younger sons. In *Ep. Fam.* 125 Bouchet records that he had begun to write verse and had composed a lament on the death of a dog. His epitaph for François de La Trémoille appears in the *Généalogies*, f.86 ro. Hubert Sussanneau, q.v., addresses to Joseph an epigram in praise of Bouchet.

Bouchet, Marie. Mentioned *Ep. Fam.* 95, 105, 115, 116 and 126. One of Bouchet's four daughters, the only one not to marry. She is said to have been steadfast for three years in her wish to adopt the religious life, so in 1533 or 1534 she entered the convent of Sainte-Croix in Poitiers. Louis de Ronsard had obtained letters from the King, the Dauphin, Marguerite de Navarre and the Comte de Saint-Pol asking the abbess, Louise de Bourbon, to admit Marie at no cost to her father. About three years later she was ready to make her profession as a Benedictine nun.

Bouchet, Pierre. *Gén. Ep.* 30 (see also 31), *Annales*, f.162 ro, 1 *Ep. Mor.* 14, f.38 vo col.1. Father of Jean, who was the only survivor of Pierre's seven children. Described as 'procureur en court laye' and 'procureur du palais de Poictiers', he died poisoned on 4 June 1480 at the age of 33. Bouchet says that his parents were of good name and from rich families, but left him nothing but their good reputation.

Bourbon, Charles de, Constable of France. 1490–1527. The son of Gilbert, comte de Montpensier, who was the brother of Gabrielle de Bourbon, q.v. He became Duke of Bourbon when the male line of the elder branch died out with Pierre de Bourbon in 1504. Bouchet dedicated to him the *Temple*, written in memory of the Duke's cousin, Charles de La Trémoille. His defection to the Emperor in 1523 is deplored in the *Panégyrique*, the *Annales* and *Gén. Ep.* 38; references to his earlier activities in the *Annales* are guarded and rather ambivalent—197 ro, 202 ro, 208 vo–209 ro.

Bourbon, François de, comte de Saint-Pol. 1491–1545. Brother of Charles, Duke of Vendôme, and of Louise de Bourbon, q.v. Mentioned *Ep. Fam.* 95, 105, 117. He was one of those who wrote a letter to his sister Louise, asking her to admit Marie Bouchet to Sainte-Croix. *CA, DBF* (under Estouteville).

Bourbon, Gabrielle de. Vicomtesse de Thouars; daughter of Louis de Bourbon, comte de Montpensier, m. Louis de La Trémoille 1484, mother of Charles de La Trémoille, Prince de Talmont; d. 1516, *Gén. Ep.* 18, *Ep. Fam.* 9, 10, 11, *Annales* 203 ro, *Panégyrique*, *Jugement* f.lx[x] ro–vo. According to *Histoire de Clotaire* aa1 ro she gave Bouchet an entrée to the Queen, Anne of Brittany. Bouchet acted as *procureur* for her as for other members of her family; one of his letters to her is reproduced in *Inventaire de François de La Trémoille*, p.128. She wrote devotional treatises of which at least three survive in MS. *H*; *LT* 2 x–xi, 29–77, 107 ff.

Bourbon, Louis de. 'Chevalier, Prince de la Roche-sur-Yon', younger son of Jean, Duke of Vendôme, and brother of Renée de Bourbon, q.v. Married Louise de Bourbon, eldest sister of the Constable, Charles; d. c.1520. Bouchet is named as his *procureur HP* 1514.

Bourbon, Louise de. 1495–1575. *Ep. Fam.* 95, 105, see also 115; *Epîtres, élégies* c3 ro. The sister of Charles, Duke of Vendôme, of François, comte de Saint-Pol and of Antoinette, Duchess of Guise. Abbess of Sainte-Croix at Poitiers May 1533–November 1534 (*GC* 2, 1303); on the death of her aunt, Renée de Bourbon, q.v., she became abbess of Fontevrault. She received Marie Bouchet into Sainte-Croix. *DBF*; *GC* 2, 1326–7.

Bourbon, Madeleine de. *Ep. Fam.* 115, 116. Daughter of Charles, Duke of Vendôme, and sister of Antoine, later King of Navarre, and Louis Prince de Condé; niece of Louise de Bourbon whom she succeeded as abbess of Sainte-Croix. Bouchet asks her to allow Marie Bouchet to make her profession. *GC* 2, 1303.

Bourbon, Renée de. 1468–8 Nov. 1534. Bouchet published the
Epîtres, élégies in her memory, some epigrams from which are
reproduced as *Gén. Ep.* 66–75. Praised before her death in
Ep. Fam. 95. Daughter of Jean, Duke of Vendôme; abbess of
Fontevrault. She reformed several convents dependent on
Fontevrault: see L. A. Bosseboeuf, *Fontevrault, son histoire et
ses monuments*, Tours, 1890.

Bourdeilles, Guy de. *Ep. Fam.* 79, on death of André de Vivonne,
q.v. A Franciscan, brother of 'le sieur et baron de Bourdeilles', i.e. of François, vicomte de Bourdeilles, who had
married Anne de Vivonne, André's daughter. Guy was thus
the uncle of Brantôme.

Brèche, Jean. *Ep. Fam.* [119], 120. This exchange is reproduced from
Brèche's *Manuel royal*, Tours, 1542. In the original volume
there is a second *épître* from Brèche to Bouchet complaining
that the first has not yet been answered, but acknowledging
that Enguilbert [de Marnef] has written to tell him that
Bouchet has urgent business. In his reply Bouchet praises
Brèche's treatises and encourages him to present them to
Marguerite de Navarre. However, Brèche carried out his
expressed intention of dedicating both the *Manuel royal* and
his *Premier Livre de l'honneste exercice du Prince* to Jeanne d'Albret. The *Manuel* consists of a prose and a verse treatise,
together with translations from Plutarch and Xenocrates (?),
all for the instruction of princes. Perhaps in imitation of
Bouchet, Brèche uses the anagram HA BIEN CHERE and the
motto ESPOIR EN BIEN. Brèche, born *c.*1514, was an *avocat*
in Tours. He eventually published legal works and translations from Galen and Hippocrates. He had connections
with Claude Cottereau, q.v. *DLF*.

Breton, Jean, seigneur de Villandry. *Ep. Fam.* 97, mentioned 96. *Secrétaire du roi*, then *secrétaire des finances*; from 1532 *secrétaire
et contrôleur général de la guerre*; d. 1542. He prepared the
King's letter to Louise de Bourbon concerning Marie Bouchet; he is asked for a privilege for four of Bouchet's works.
CA.

Bueil, Louis de. *Gén. Ep.* 86. Seigneur de Mermande, d. Jan. 1532,
unmarried, aged below 40. Heir of the cadet branch of the
comtes de Sancerre. *DHGP* 2, 62–3; *CA* 2 5354, 6610.

Chalon, Philibert de, Prince of Orange. 1502–30. Fought for the
Emperor Charles V; captured by the French at sea near Ville-
franche in July 1524. He was imprisoned at Bourges, then at
Lusignan in the care of François Du Fou, q.v.; he was released Jan. 1526. Bouchet addresses him *Ep. Fam.* 27, and in
the *Annales* records having visited him at Lusignan (219 vo,
255 vo). See U. Robert, *Philibert de Chalon, prince d'Orange,*

Paris, 1902.

Chaponneau, Jean. *Ep. Fam.* 101. 'Docteur en theologie de l'ordre des Augustins'; d. 1545. Directed the *Mystère des Apôtres* at Bourges, 1536; later went over to the Reform, settled in Neuchâtel and married. His theology brought him into conflict with Calvin. See Picot, *Notice sur Jean Chaponneau.*

Charles VIII, King of France 1483–98. According to the *Annales*, the *Panégyrique* and the *Histoire de Clotaire*, Bouchet accompanied a delegation from Poitiers to the court of Charles VIII at Lyons in 1496, presented the King with some poems and was recommended to the service of Florimond Robertet. The King also commanded him to translate the legend of St Radegonde into French. Two poems on Charles VIII appear in the *Amoureux transi*; accounts of his reign in the *Annales* and the *Anciennes et modernes.*

Claude de France, Queen. 1499–1524. The *Histoire de Clotaire* is dedicated to her, aa1 ro–2 ro, m8 ro. Her death is the subject of Bouchet's first poem entitled *épigramme* in the *Annales* of 1532, reproduced as *Gén. Ep.* 32; another epigram *Jugement* f.lxxi ro.

Claveurier, Maurice. *Gén. Ep.* 77. 'Lieutenant général en Poitou', d. 1502 aged 33. He is the unnamed subject of the epitaphs on 'ung lieutenant en Poictou qui trespassa durant le procès de son office, l'an mil cinq centz et deux', *Amoureux transi* O4 vo–O6 ro. Mayor of Poitiers 1499–1500, a member of a long-established Poitiers family. *MP* 481; *VP* 492 for the family and 493 n.282 and 535 n.522 for Maurice III.

Colin Bucher, Germain. *Ep. Fam.* [64], 65, [66], 67; 1 *Ep. Mor.* 5, *Annales* 256 ro, mentioned *Ep. Fam.* [109], 110, 120. In 1529 he was in Nice with the fleet of the Knights of St John of Jerusalem; he was the secretary of the Grand Master, Villiers de l'Isle-Adam. He had been given an introduction to Bouchet by Florent Guyvereau, a Knight Commander of the Order. He writes later from Sicily; he supplied Bouchet with information about Malta and the Knights' projects there. He says in 1529 that he has been writing verse for four years; he seems eager to gain an entrée to literary circles, mentioning Marot and Macé among his correspondents. Later he was to intervene in the *Querelle* between Marot and Sagon, committing himself to neither of them. Sagon complains to Bouchet that Colin has defended Marot [109]; Bouchet expresses his surprise, 110. In 1539 Colin was accused of heresy and imprisoned at Angers; in a verse *épître* to the King dated 1545 he begs for his release. See Denais, *Les Poésies de Germain Colin Bucher*, Paris, 1890, and Picot, 'Supplément aux poésies de Germain Colin', *Bulletin du Bibliophile*, 1890, pp.177–87.

Cottereau, Claude. 1499–1550. *Ep. Fam.* 56, 82, [123], 124. Born in
   Tours; studied law in Poitiers, where he met Bouchet. Later
   he spent some time in Paris; he became a priest, and as
   aumônier to Cardinal Jean Du Bellay he was present at Aigues-
   Mortes for the meeting of François 1er and Charles v,
   1538. He was a friend of Etienne Dolet, who dedicated his
   Genethliacum to him. He contributed a liminary verse to the
   1546 ed. of *De legibus connubialibus* by André Tiraqueau, q.v.
   He published *De iure et privilegiis militum libri tres*, Lyons,
   1539, and his translation of Columella's *De re rustica* was
   published posthumously in 1551 under the direction of Jean
   Brèche, q.v. *DBF.*
Crissé, Seigneur de. *Ep. Fam.* 83. Addressed by Bouchet as from a
   boy to his friend in the name of the 'Prince de Mortaigne',
   q.v. Probably a member of the Turpin family: the second
   husband of Isabelle, daughter of Antoinette d'Illiers, q.v.,
   was Jacques Turpin, seigneur de Crissé.
Dausseure, Jacques. *Gén. Ep.* 65, *Annales* 323 vo–324 ro. *Echevin* of
   Poitiers, *avocat*, mayor 1510–11, *lieutenant du sénéchal*, d. October 1520, aged a little over sixty. Member of a prominent
   Poitiers family. *MP* 493–5; *VP* 491 n.268, 498, 529, 600.
Desarpens, Michel. *Ep. Fam.* [69], 70, [71], 72. A young poet with
   connections in Poitiers and in Rouen. He asks Bouchet to
   revise an epitaph on Jacques Prévost, q.v., and in 108 is
   mentioned as being on his way to see Jacques Le Lieur, q.v.;
   he may be the friend of Le Lieur said in 98 to be studying in
   Poitiers. He had contributed Latin verse to the Rouen *Puy*,
   winning a prize for an allegorical piece in 1521; he is the
   author of two Latin epigrams in Pierre Vidoue's *Recueil*, c.
   1525; *P* 1, 62–3. See Picot, *Notice sur Jacques Le Lieur*, p.57 n.1.
Doyneau, François. Praised in *Ep. Fam.* 58 [to André Tiraqueau]
   and mentioned several times in the *Annales*. Mayor of Poitiers
   1509, 'lieutenant général en la sénéchaussée de Poitou', 1527;
   'conseiller lai' at Paris Parlement, d. 1552. *CA; DHGP* 3, 137.
Doyron, Marie. *Gén. Ep.* 45. 'Damoiselle', said to have died in 1527,
   after 26 years of marriage to Jean Boiceau, 'son noble espoux'.
   Perhaps a relative of Jean Boiceau de La Borderie, q.v.
Du Bourg, François. *c.*1515–68. *Ep. Fam.* 118 is addressed to him
   while he was studying in Poitiers during the period when his
   father, Antoine Du Bourg, was Chancellor of France (1535–
   38); he is described as 'abbé de Saint-Georges'. He was also
   from 1537 both *maître des requêtes* and Bishop of Rieux, although the two offices should have been incompatible. *DBF.*
Du Fou, François i. *Gén. Ep.* 87; *Ep. Fam.* 15, 16, 25, mentioned 27,
   35; see *Annales* 213 vo for information which he provided.
   Seigneur de Vigean, d. 8 Sept. 1536 aged about 60. 'Capitaine

des châteaux de Lusignan et de Melle'. He served under
Charles VIII and Louis XII, lost an eye during the Italian
wars; *chambellan* and *panetier ordinaire du roi* under François
1er. He spent little time at court in the last ten years of his life.
The Prince of Orange (q.v. under Chalon) was imprisoned at
Lusignan in his care. *DBF*, *CA*.

Du Fou, François II. *Ep. Fam.* 45. Eldest son of former. He was
married to Louise Robertet, daughter of Florimond, q.v. He
died in 1581, having become a Protestant. *CA* 5, 15427;
DHGP 3, 506; *DBF*.

Duprat, Antoine, 1464–1535. *Gén. Ep.* 64, addressed in dedicatory
letter in *Anciennes et modernes*, 1528 (referred to as 'Du Pré' in
early eds), *Annales*. Archbishop of Sens, Cardinal, Chancellor of France. See Albert Buisson, *Le Chancelier Antoine Duprat*, Paris, 1935.

Eleanor of Austria, Queen of France, 1498–1558. She arrived in
France 1530, married François in July, and after a slow journey North was crowned Queen on 5 March 1531. Bouchet
had the *Triomphes* presented to her when she came past
Poitiers (2 *Ep. Mor.* 11); in the *Annales*, 258 ro, he mentions
the royal party's stay at the Château de Dissay and the Château du Fou (August–September 1530). The dedicatory *épître*
to Eleanor in the *Triomphes* post-dates the printing of the
main part of the book (20 June 1530). Bouchet planned Eleanor's entry into Nantes; see *supra*, chapter 1.

Emery (Aymery), Germain. *Ep. Fam.* [40], 41. Addressed in *Opuscules*, author of Latin prose reply in praise of the work. 'Licencié ès lois, avocat à Poitiers.' He says [40] that he has been
Bouchet's friend for seven and a half years.

Estissac, Geoffroy d'. 1495–1543. Bishop of Maillezais. Mentioned
in *Ep. Fam.* 49 to Rabelais. Bouchet met him at his monastery,
Ligugé, together with Rabelais, who was his secretary. See
Plattard, *L'Adolescence de Rabelais en Poitou*, Paris, 1923, pp.
34–7, 56–64. He presided at an oration given by Quintin
(q.v.) on 24 Dec. 1524 in the church of Saint-Hilaire in
Poitiers, in the course of which Quintin praised Bouchet's
historical writing.

Estissac, Louis d'. Mentioned *Ep. Fam.* 49 and in 73, to Ardillon, in
which he is said to have told Bouchet that he was unpopular
at Court. The *Angoisses*, 1537, contains a dedicatory prose
letter to him. 'Seigneur de Clermont en Perigord, gentilhomme de la chambre du roi' (*CA*). Nephew of Geoffroy,
married Anne de Daillon in 1527. Plattard, *Adolescence*, pp.36,
55.

Formond, Jean. *Gén. Ep.* 52. Sacristan of Notre-Dame-la-Petite at
Poitiers; d. aged 80; a noted actor. Hamon and Clouzot

assume that he took part in the mystery plays directed by Bouchet.

François Ier, King of France 1515–47. A full account of his reign in the *Annales*, some material in the *Panégyrique*. Bouchet in all probability directed his entry into Poitiers, 1520; on at least one occasion he was sent to the court of François Ier on a deputation from Poitiers (*MP* 509; cf. *Annales* 208 ro). He addresses the King only in the *Jugement*, a memorial for Louise de Savoie which Louis de Ronsard presented to the King, some time between 1533 and 1536 (1534?). François wrote to Louise de Bourbon on behalf of Marie Bouchet (see under Breton). The first part of the *Triomphes du roi* gives an account of François' reign through the medium of poetic fictions.

François de Valois, Dauphin. 1518–36. He is addressed in a dedicatory letter in the *Anciennes et modernes*, 1528, and in 2 *Ep. Mor.* 11 Bouchet claims to have presented the book to him at Bonnivet. This must have been either in February 1526 when he and his brother passed near Poitiers on the way to Spain (*Annales* 223 ro) or in 1530 when they were returning from Spain accompanied by Louis de Ronsard. He wrote a letter in support of Marie Bouchet's entry to Sainte-Croix (*Ep. Fam.* 95, 105). *Déploration* in *Généalogies*, f.68–70. See *Annales*, particularly 217 vo, 223 ro, 277 ro. Bouchet devised his entry into Nantes, 1531; see *supra*, chapter 1.

Frétard, Tristan. 'Escuyer, seigneur de Saulves'. Addressed in *carmen elegum* by Nicolas Petit in *Annales*, 1532; *épîtres* to and from him in *Triomphes du roi*. Bouchet says Frétard did him several favours six years previously, i.e. *c*.1543. He also suggests that Frétard seeks to imitate Mellin de Saint-Gelais in his verse. According to *DHGP* 3, 597, Tristan was the younger son of Pierre Frétard, 'seigneur de Primery et de Sauves', and in 1532 is found involved in a lawsuit with his elder brother René.

Ganay, Margarite de. *Gén. Ep.* 44; d. Feb. 1532. Daughter of Pierre de Ganay, bailly de Berry, who was the cousin of Jean de Ganay, chancellor of France 1507–12; wife of 'Seigneur de Rimbault'.

Genlis, see Hangest.

Gervaise, Pierre. *Ep. Fam.* [22], 23. 'Assesseur de l'official de Poitiers'. Eventually *chanoine* of Saint-Pierre-le-Puellier, *procureur général* to the University. Bouchet's friendship with him dated from their schooldays. *DHGP* 4, 102.

Godart, Jacques, *Ep. Fam.* 125. 'Curé et chanoine de La Chastre en Berry'. His affection for Bouchet's children is mentioned.

Gouffier, Anne. Dame de Montreuil. In *Ep. Fam.* 96 addressed as Madame de Montreuil-Bonnin. She was the wife of Raoul Vernon, seigneur de Montreuil-Bonnin, and governess to the royal princesses. It is probably through the La Trémoille family (see *LT* 3, p.216 [*c*.1529]) or some other local connection that Bouchet asks her to support Louis de Ronsard in asking the King's secretary, Villandry, for a privilege for the *Jugement. DHGP* 4, 252; *CA*.

Gouffier, Artus. Seigneur de Boisy, grand-maître de France, d. 10 May 1519. *Gén. Ep.* 33, *Annales* 201–3, commemorated in the *Labyrinthe*. Both the *Labyrinthe* and the *Cantiques* are dedicated to his wife, Hélène de Hangest, q.v. There is no evidence concerning earlier contact with the family, but Gouffier held lands in Poitou, notably his château at Oiron. *DBF*.

Gouffier, Guillaume. *Gén. Ep.* 37. Younger brother of the former; seigneur de Bonnivet, 'chambellan du roi', admiral; d. 1525 at Pavia. *DBF*.

Gron, Denis. *Gén. Ep.* 59. 'Procureur en parlement à Paris', d. May 1535 aged 56. Bouchet praises his expertise.

Guyvereau, Florent. Knight Commander of the Order of the Knights of St John of Jerusalem. 1 *Ep. Mor.* 5 dated 16 Dec. 1529 is addressed to him, and he gave Germain Colin an introduction to Bouchet (*Ep. Fam.* [64], 65). According to Bouchet he came from Poitiers.

Hangest, Hélène de (or de Genlis). Dame de Magny. Daughter of Jacques, seigneur de Genlis et de Magny; married Artus Gouffier, q.v., 1499; d. 23 Jan. 1537. The *Labyrinthe* was supposedly written to comfort her and the *Cantiques* are dedicated to her, but there are no later references. *DHGP* 4, 696.

Henri ii, King of France 1547–59. The early part of his reign is covered in detail in the *Annales*, but the few years before 1557 are dealt with only sketchily. He is addressed in a dedicatory letter in the *Triomphes du roi*, which commemorates his father.

Herbert, Marie. *Gén. Ep.* 48; d. 1532 aged 23. She is said to have been in the service of a lady who was descended from the La Trémoille (i.e. Jacqueline de La Trémoille, niece of Louis ii) and who was married to the Seigneur de Boisy (i.e. Claude Gouffier, who married Jacqueline in 1526).

Illiers, Antoinette d'. *Ep. Fam.* 74 is a version of one first published in *Le Flagice de peste*, 1530, dedicated to her by its author Simon Nerault, q.v. 'Baroness de Clervaulx, du Chesne doré, dame de Baussay, Boullouhere et de Masoncelles'; widow of Robert Chabot, uncle of the admiral Philippe. She had family connections with other noble families who were Bouchet's patrons: her daughter Ysabeau was married first to Charles de Vivonne, son of André de Vivonne, q.v., then in 1532 to Jacques Turpin, seigneur de Crissé. *DHGP* 5, 117–18; *CA*.

Irland (Hirlant), Robert. 1475–1561. *Ep. Fam.* 77 is addressed to him on the death of his son. A Scot who came to France *c*.1496, studied law at the University of Poitiers and became Professor of Law in 1502. He married in 1515 and had several children, including Bonaventure Irland, for whom see *DLF*.

La Fayolle. *Ep. Fam.* 117. Said to be a lieutenant commanding one hundred men under Saint-Pol, q.v.

La Grève, Ponce de. *Ep. Fam.* 37. 'Docteur es droitz, abbé de Valence'. He appears as 'Me Ponce de la Guesle, abbé de Valence', *HP* 1514. Abbot of the Cistercian house at Valence near Couhé until 1526. In *GC* 2, 1360, he figures as 'Pontius I de La Greze, doctor in legibus ac protonotarius apostolicus'. Bouchet speaks of him as a friend and regrets his absence caused by illness. It is possible that, as a Cistercian, he may be the friend alluded to in *Ep.* 34 to Ardillon, 'qui portoit le blanc'. The illness alluded to in *Ep.* 37 may have been his last one, given that he died *c*.1526. He was succeeded as abbot by Ponce de S. Georges, who went over to the Reform, apparently encouraged by Trojan, q.v. *DHGP* 4, 419 under Grèze.

La Mothe au Groing, Marc, vicomte de, seigneur de La Morinière. Before 1485–after 1532. Addressed in *épître* in *Anciennes et modernes*, 1528, in which he is asked to read and check the work before it is presented to the Dauphin; he is praised for his military and diplomatic skills. Mentioned *Annales* 251 ro, 'Gentilhomme de la chambre du roi; prévôt de l'hôtel'; sent on various diplomatic missions, including to the Elector Palatine in 1519 and to the Pope in 1527; d. poisoned in or after 1532. *CA*; *DN* 9, 873; *DHGP* 4, 455 (under Groing).

Langlois, Bertrand. *Ep. Fam.* 17. In the *Table* said to be 'sommelier' to the Dauphin. Bouchet describes him as 'ung gentilhomme son familier amy', and a lover of French verse. Not in *CA*. A Nicolas Langlois is found in 1532 as 'valet de pied des enfants de France' replacing another man who had been promoted to 'sommelier'; this might perhaps be a younger relation (*CA* 2, 5066).

La Rochefoucault, Dame de. Mentioned in *Ep. Fam.* 47 as protectress of Jean Mary de Ruffec. Probably Anne de Polignac, wife of François II, comte de La Rochefoucauld; widowed 1533. *DN* 17, 308 and 349–50; *CA*.

La Trémoille, Charles de, Prince de Talmont. 1485–1515. Only son of Louis II de La Trémoille and Gabrielle de Bourbon; married Louise de Coétivy 1502; d. from wounds suffered at the battle of Marignano, 7 Sept. 1515. According to the *Panégyrique* he presented some of Bouchet's works at court;

perhaps the *Epître de Marie* which he commissioned (*Annales* 194 ro). The *Chapelet* was written for his son, François, and contains a dedicatory letter and a *ballade* addressed to Charles. The *Temple* was written in his memory. See also *Gén. Ep.* 16, 19–29; *Annales* 199 ro; *Panégyrique*. *LT* 3, v–vi, 1–21.

La Trémoille, François de. The *Chapelet* was written for his edification. *Gén. Ep.* 95, *Déploration* in *Généalogies* ff.86–90. Son of Charles, q.v., grandson and heir of Louis ii; d. 7 Jan. 1542. Married Anne de Laval, q.v., in 1522. He was taken prisoner at Pavia and ransomed; thereafter he became *gouverneur de Poitou* and devoted himself to his estates. Considerable correspondence with Bouchet concerning business transactions survives in the Chartrier de Thouars: see *Inventaire de François de La Trémoille et comptes d'Anne de Laval*, Nantes, 1887. He had seven sons and four daughters, including Louis iii who succeeded him and Guy, q.v., who died young. *Annales*, *Panégyrique*; *LT* 3, vii–viii, 23–88.

La Trémoille, Guy de. *Gén. Ep.* 89. Son of François and of Anne de Laval; d. Sept. 1538 aged 9, while at Collège de la Petite Sorbonne in Paris. *LT* 3, viii, 30–1, 216. *Inventaire de François de La Trémoille*, p.176.

La Trémoille, Jean de. *Gén. Ep.* 17; *Annales* 188 ro; *Panégyrique*. Brother of Louis ii; archbishop of Auch, 1490; bishop of Poitiers, 1505; cardinal, 1506; d. 1507. *LT* 2 xiii–xiv, 135–56; François Villard, 'Jean de La Trémoille administrateur du diocèse de Poitiers (1505–1507)', *BSAO* 4ᵉ série, 10, 1969, pp.205–18.

La Trémoille, Louis ii de. 1460–1525. The subject of the *Panégyrique*; *Gén. Ep.* 36; the *Annales* are dedicated to him; see also 1 *Ep. Mor.* 14, *Ep. Fam.* 26. Bouchet's most important patron. He had led Charles viii's army in Brittany and subsequently fought in the Italian Wars. Although he had imprisoned the Duke of Orléans after the battle of Saint-Aubin-du-Cormier, once the Duke became King Louis xii he confirmed La Trémoille in his position of army commander. La Trémoille fought at Agnadello, Novara, Bologna and, under François iᵉʳ, at Marignano. He led the army in Picardy and was eventually killed at Pavia. He married Gabrielle de Boubon, q.v., and Louise de Valentinois, q.v.; father of Charles de La Trémoille, q.v. *LT* 2 ix–xii, 29–134.

Laval, Anne de. 1505–53. Addressed in a prose introduction to the *Jugement*. Daughter of Guy, comte de Laval and Charlotte d'Aragon; married François de La Trémoille, q.v., in 1522; mother of eleven children. See *Inventaire de François de La Trémoille*, *LT* 3.

Le Chandelier, Baptiste. *Ep. Fam.* [106], 107, mentioned in 108.
'Conseiller du Roy en sa cour de parlement en Normandie';
d. 1549. An influential member of the group of Rouen poets.
Magistrate; *Prince du Puy* in 1546; author of two MS works
published by the Société des Bibliophiles Normands: *Eloges
en vers latins des présidents et conseillers du Parlement de Rouen de
1499 à 1543*, intr. by G. A. Prevost, 1905 and *La Parthénie, ou
Banquet des Palinods de Rouen en 1546. Poème latin*, intr. by
F. Bouquet, 1883. *P* 1, 171–4; *CA*; Picot, *Notice sur Jacques Le
Lieur*, p.64 n.2.

Le Lieur, Jacques. *c.*1475–*c.*1550. *Ep. Fam.* 98, [99], 108, 114. A
leading member of the group of Rouen poets in the 1530s and
1540s; Bouchet calls him 'poète sacré', 'grant poète'. He held
the office of 'notaire et secrétaire du roi' and was active in
municipal affairs; he was responsible for a description and
map of the Rouen water-sources (MS *Livre des Fontaines*, 1525,
facsimile ed. V. Sanson, Rouen, 1911). He had several MSS
made, including Books of Hours and a collection of *Puy*
poetry. One of his poems was printed in the Vidoue *Recueil*
and a *Blason de la cuisse* was printed in several collections of
blasons anatomiques (see *Poètes du XVIe siècle*, ed. Schmidt,
Paris, 1953, p.341–3). But most of his verse survives only in
MS; it includes verse prayers in the Books of Hours and other
devotional verse. His *devise* was *Du bien le bien*. *P* 2, 54–7;
E. Picot, *Notice sur Jacques Le Lieur*, Rouen, 1913.

Le Prévost, Thomas. *Ep. Fam.* [88], 89. A poet from Rouen; arranged
the mystery play at Saumur which took place three weeks
after the performance in Poitiers in 1534. He won prizes for
French verses at the Puy in 1522 and 1544. *P* 2, 180–2.

Lommeau, Conrad de. 'Licencié ès droictz, seigneur de Pompierre,
procureur général de l'ordre de Fontevrault'. Author of an
épître to Bouchet and various other verses on the death of
Renée de Bourbon, together with some written for her.
Bouchet published them, together with his own lament on
Renée's death and his *Ep. Mor.* on nuns, in *Epîtres, élégies*.
Lommeau's contributions (B1 ro–C1 vo, F1 vo–H3 ro) can
be identified because in his French verse he does not alternate
masculine and feminine rhymes. The volume is followed by
an extra gathering containing an *épître* from Bouchet to Lommeau in which he says that Lommeau reproved him for
publishing his verse; he defends himself for having doné so
with many compliments to Lommeau.

Lou[h]andi, Nicolaus. Author of one of the theologian's certificates
in the *Triomphes*, +1 ro, dated 22 November 1530. Describes
himself as 'sacre pagine professor' and 'universitatis Picta-
viensis decanus'.

Louis xii, King of France 1498–1515. His reign is recorded in the *Annales*, the *Panégyrique* and the *Anciennes et modernes*. The *Déploration* and the *Epître d'Henri* were written during his war with the Pope, 1511–13. The *Epître de Marie* laments his death. 2 *Ep. Mor.* 1 to kings, is addressed to him and said to have been commissioned by him, according to 2 *Ep. Mor.* 3 shortly before his death when Bouchet had just begun to gain an entrée at court. Bouchet records that when at court with La Trémoille he heard Louis express his approval of the Basoche plays, *Annales* and 2 *Ep. Mor.* 1.

Louise de Savoie. 1476–1531. Her actions as regent are recorded in various passages in the *Annales*; she is praised 253 vo, 264 ro. The *Jugement* was written to commemorate her.

Macé, René. Mentioned *Ep. Fam.* [66], 67 as a friend of Germain Colin but a critic of Bouchet's work. Praised in *Jugement*, xcvi ro. Monk at the abbey of the Trinity at Vendôme, the continuator of Cretin's *Chronique*. *DLF*.

Maignen, Jean. Seigneur des Aleuz. Addressed in 1 *Ep. Mor.* 14 of 1532, when he is said to be 9 years older than Bouchet (i.e. 67) and to have been Bouchet's colleague in the legal estate for 39 years. From local records he is known to have directed the Mystery of the Passion at Poitiers in 1508 with the help of Bouchet. *H*.

Marguerite d'Angoulême, Queen of Navarre. 1492–1549. Bouchet dedicates the *Labyrinthe* to her as well as to Hélène de Hangest. In *Ep. Fam.* 95 she is said to have written a letter to Louise de Bourbon in support of Marie Bouchet's admission to Sainte-Croix. She is praised in the *Jugement*, and the *Triomphes du roi* contains a dedicatory poem to her. She is mentioned several times in the *Annales*, notably in connection with the *Paix des Dames*; her death is recorded 342 ro. Bouchet is known to have done some work for her with respect to an estate at Fontenay *c*.1520 (Jourda, *Répertoire*, p.5). The *Miroir de l'âme pécheresse* appears to have been influenced by the *Triomphes* (Holban *art. cit.*); some of Bouchet's later verse echoes the *Miroir*. In *Ep. Fam.* 120 Bouchet advises Jean Brèche to present his work to her and speaks warmly of her kindness. It seems likely that Bouchet had more contact with her than is demonstrated by this evidence. She might perhaps be the patroness referred to in *Ep. Fam.* 31, but this could also be Jeanne d'Orléans, q.v., or Jeanne's daughter, Louise de Coétivy. See also under Vivonne.

Marillac. Addressed in *Ep. Fam.* 87, an *avocat de parlement* present at the *Grands Jours de Poitou* held in Tours in 1533. 'Monseigneur Baillet' and he are asked to grant Bouchet an interview.

Marot, Clément. 1496–1544. *Gén. Ep.* 100 (quoted *supra*, ch.5); mentioned in *Ep. Fam.* [66], 67 (as a correspondent of Germain Colin in 1529); 107 (not mentioned by name, but Bouchet refers to the quarrel between him and Sagon); [109], 110 (in which Sagon tries to enlist Bouchet's support, particularly against Germain Colin, but Bouchet refuses and insists on remaining neutral); 114 (in which Bouchet comments on Marot and Sagon to Jacques Le Lieur). In 120 he is included in a list of good contemporary writers. His eclogue on the death of Louise de Savoie is mentioned *Jugement* f.xcvi ro.

Mary (Marin), Jean, de Ruffec. *Ep. Fam.* 47, [80], 81. 'Licentier ès droits et avocat à Ruffec'. In 47 Bouchet praises his Life of St Andrew, for which Mary claims to have been criticised [80]. [80] and 81 refer to another work, a verse *Trilogue*. The Dame de La Rochefoucault is said to be his patroness.

Matthée, Martin. There is a prose *épître* to Bouchet and Bouchet's reply in Matthée's translation of Theodoret's *History of the Church*, 1544. He is described as 'prieur claustral de la royalle abbaye de Monstierneuf'—a Cluniac house in Poitiers. Not, according to La Bouralière ('Bibliographie poitevine', p.385), the Martin Matthée who published translations from Dioscorides, Lyons, 1559.

Mihervé, Seigneur de. *Ep. Fam.* 127 (Aug. 1543). Mihervé had visited Bouchet twice and provided him with information for the *Annales* on the wars between 1530 and 1543. Mihervé came from Boulogne; Bouchet asks him for news of Picardy. See *Annales* 277 vo, 281 ro.

Milhac, Pierre de. *Gén. Ep.* 90–3. 'Docteur ès droictz, conseiller en la cour de Parlement de Bordeaux'. Died young, aged less than 30.

Montberon (Momberon), Adrian de, Prince de Mortaigne. *Gén. Ep.* 58, according to which he died 8 June 1535, aged 16, at Beauvaiz near Châtellerault; he had become wealthy before he was ten years old, having inherited the title of Prince de Mortaigne. *Ep. Fam.* 83 is written in the name of the Prince de Mortaigne, 'le petit Momberon', to his young friend, the seigneur de Crissé. Montberon is said to be studying in Poitiers and to be Bouchet's 'disciple'. *Ep. Fam.* 102, to the 'seigneur de Mombrun', may have been addressed to the same young man shortly before his death; it is dated La Rochechouart, 29 April, and contains the *devise* and *blason* of Montberon's *château* ('escu luysant et flamboyant d'or à la croix, de gueulles sans gisarmes'). This Adrian de Montberon is not the baron d'Archiac (*CA, DN* 14); he might possibly be a son of Antoine de Montberon, seigneur de Mortagne-sur-Gironde (see *CA* 7 23328 and 24301).

Montreuil-Bonnin, see Gouffier, Anne.

More, Sir Thomas. 1478–1535. Bouchet records his execution, *Annales* 279 ro and *Gén. Ep.* 62.

Moreilles en Poitou, abbé de. *Ep. Fam.* 53. Bouchet is gratified that the *abbé* has referred to Bouchet as a friend in a letter to his brother. There has been a family connection between them for 20 years—he was perhaps therefore related to Bouchet's wife. Possibly Jean Mareschal, who was abbot of Moreilles between 1520 and at least 1526; *GC* 2, 1397; *DHGP* 3 (under G. d'Estissac).

Moussy, Regnault de. *Gén. Ep.* 84, *Panégyrique*. 'Chevalier, seigneur de Puybouillart et Saint-Martin-l'Ars'; d. 1529. *Gouverneur* of Charles de La Trémoille, later vice-admiral of Guyenne. *LT* 2, 98–9, 132–3 and 3, 4–5.

Nerault, Simon. A Dominican, mentioned *Ep. Fam.* 74 as the *orateur* of Antoinette d'Illiers and the author of *Le Flagice de peste*. This moral treatise was printed Poitiers, 23 March 1530 (o.s.) and contains an earlier version of *Ep. Fam.* 74. Quetif and Echard, *Scriptores Ordinis Praedicatorum* 2, p.81.

Orléans, Jeanne de, duchesse de Valois. *Histoire de Clotaire* aa8, ro, *Jugement* f.lx[x] vo. The sister of Charles d'Angoulême and thus aunt of François Ier, who in 1516 granted her the duchy of Valois (*CA* 1 578). She was the wife of Charles de Coétivy, comte de Taillebourg, and her daughter, Louise de Coétivy, was the wife of Charles de La Trémoille: Bouchet's connections with her are thus explained (for Louise, see *LT* 3). In the epigram devoted to her in the *Jugement* Bouchet mentions her chaste life as a widow at Taillebourg, her love of scholars, her eloquence and her composition of verse. It is thus quite likely that she is the 'dame tresillustre et chaste dame du sang de France' of whom he says in *Ep. Fam.* 31 that she is the hope of him and his family: 'Je n'ay plus fors à elle recours'. Other possibilities are her daughter Louise or even Marguerite d'Angoulême.

Orneau, Jean. *Gén. Ep.* 76. 'Maître des œuvres de maçonnerie pour le Roy à Poitiers'; d. Oct. 1535 aged 33. He had played the part of Christ in the Mystery of the Passion directed by Bouchet in 1534.

Parmentier, Jean. 1494–1529. *Ep. Fam.* 43, [44] form a civil exchange of compliments and verse between the two poets. Parmentier was passing through Poitiers during the period 1526–29, which he spent in France before setting out on his last voyage, March 1529. He died in Sumatra in December, 1529. See his *Œuvres poétiques*, ed. F. Ferrand, Geneva, 1971.

Perreau, Bartholomée. Dean of the faculty of medicine at Poitiers. The first edition of the *Annales* contains a prose letter in Latin by him (*Annales*, 1524, ++6 ro). In *Ep. Fam.* 82 to Cottereau his recent death is mentioned. He was put in charge of measures to combat the plague of 1521 in Poitiers (*MP* 508).

Petit (Parvus), Nicolas, Bellosanensis. *c.*1497–1532. He contributed Latin verse to the *Annales*, eds of 1524 and 1532, the *Panégyrique*, the *Anciennes et modernes*. Addressed *Ep. Fam.* 21, mentioned in 30 to Ardillon as one of the group meeting at Fontaine-le-Comte along with Rabelais and others; 78, also to Ardillon, records his death in Oct. 1532, aged 35. Bouchet says he was from Normandy; Petit describes himself as 'Bellosanensis', and in a liminary epistle addresses his mentor, 'Michaeli Clerico Abbati Bellosanensi'—i.e. he was from Bellozanne in Normandy, site of a Premonstratensian abbey. He studied arts in Paris, where in 1517 he published with Jean Fossier *Elegiae de Redemptione Humana*, a series of poems on the life of Christ. In about 1522 (the date given in a prefatory letter to Béda and Tempête, addressed from the Collège de Montaigu) he published his *Silvae* in Paris. It must have been soon after this that he went to the University of Poitiers to study law; he was to remain there, teaching law. In 1526 he published in Poitiers an edition of Baptista Mantuan's *De sacris diebus*, another collection of Christian neo-Latin verse. He contributed verse to F. Calphurnius, *Epigrammata*, Paris, s.d. (See also under Quintin).

Prévost, Jacques. 'Docteur en theologie, chanoine theologal de l'eglise cathedralle de Poitiers'. The theologian addressed in a prose letter in the *Labyrinthe* and who examined the work. *Ep. Fam.* 68 to Louis Bastard speaks of his death on 8 Dec. 1530. [69] and 70 mention an epitaph for him written by Michel Desarpens. According to Bouchet he held one priory, together with his office in the cathedral where he preached regularly. He is praised as a good preacher, not satirical, the enemy of schismatics. He is said to have suffered from ill-health for his last 10–12 years.

Prévoste, Catherine. Wife of René Berthelot, q.v.; d. before 1528. *Ep. Fam.* 59 is supposedly addressed by her to her former husband from the Elysian fields, encouraging him to remarry.

Puytesson, Jacques de. Chanoine de Ménigoute. *Ep. Fam.* [85], 86. A civil exchange of *épîtres* between a canon of Ménigoute and Bouchet, who is acting for the curé of Chenay in a lawsuit against the Chapter. Puytesson mentions a visit from Ardillon, q.v. A canon from Poitiers had obtained permission from the King in 1527 to found a church and almonry at Ménigoute, *CA* 1 2744.

Quintin (Quintinus Heduus), Jean. 1500–61. The author of a prose letter in Latin praising the *Annales* in 1524, and of some Latin verse in the *Panégyrique*. Mentioned in *Ep. Fam.* 30 to Ardillon as one of the group meeting at Fontaine-le-Comte. In 82 Cottereau is asked if he has seen him in Paris. Quintin was born in Autun. He was teaching at the College de Sainte-Barbe in Paris *c.*1520, but seems to have been settled in Poitiers by 1524. Twice in that year he delivered sermons in which he praised Bouchet's historical writing—the first on 28 April in the cathedral in the presence of the Dean (Jean d'Allemagne, q.v.) and Chapter, making his subject a eulogy of the Church of Poitiers; the second on 24 December in the church of Saint-Hilaire in the presence of the Bishop of Maillezais, Geoffroy d'Estissac, q.v., taking St Hilary as his subject. (These orations were printed and dedicated to Ardillon, q.v., in a letter by one Karolus Lyveneus who praises Bouchet and Nicolas Petit as well as Quintin; see BN Rés. 8° L³K 500, especially [A2] vo, C2 ro, C3 vo. The dedicatory letter is dated Poitiers, 10 April and the dates of the sermons are given; the volume is otherwise s.l., s.d.) In 1531 he went to Malta, where he became a Knight of St John and composed an *Insulae Melitae descriptio*; he was back in Lyons by 1536 and subsequently became a distinguished professor of Canon Law in Paris. He published several works on Canon Law; in particular he wrote in support of elections in the Church. He was the speaker representing the clergy at the *Etats Généraux* of 1560 and drew down upon himself the wrath of Coligny for his speech which denied that the Church could be corrupt and demanded the persecution of Protestants. Protestant historians recounting this episode maintain that it was widely said at the time that earlier in his life Quintin had been of a very different opinion and had actually been turned out of Poitiers for his religious beliefs—notably La Place (*Commentaires*, 1565, 151 vo) and De Thou (*Histoire universelle*, La Haye, 1740, 3, p.12); the *Histoire ecclésiastique* tells the story, attributing Quintin's return to Catholic orthodoxy to the offer of a rich benefice in the Order of Knights of St John (ed. Baum and Cunitz, 1, p.81). It seems reasonable to suppose that at the least Quintin may have been an outspoken critic of clerical abuse while in Poitiers. But there does not seem to be any surviving evidence from Poitiers or from the period *c.* 1530 to confirm the story that he was forced to leave. See J. Quicherat, *Histoire de Sainte-Barbe*, 3 vols, Paris, 1860–64, vol.1, p.119; vol.2, pp.85–9; H. de Fontenay, 'Epigraphie autunoise', *Mémoires de la Société Eduenne*, nouvelle série, 16, 1888, pp.322–4; *DLF*.

Rabelais, François. *Ep. Fam.* [48] (addressed from Ligugé, 6 Sept.),
49 (dated 8 Sept.). In 49 Bouchet praises Geoffroy d'Estissac
and his nephew, from whom Rabelais may expect a benefice.
In 30 to Ardillon he looks forward to meeting Rabelais at
Fontaine-le-Comte; in 120 he includes Rabelais in a list of
good writers of the present reign. It seems that Bouchet and
Rabelais met and became friends in the circle of humanists
which met at Ligugé and Fontaine-le-Comte *c.*1525–27, during Rabelais' time as a Benedictine in the service of d'Estissac. Plattard, *Adolescence*. Rabelais uses Bouchet's pen-name
when he calls Xenomanes 'le grand voyageur et traverseur
des voyes perilleuses', *Tiers Livre* ch.49, *Quart Livre* ch.1—
perhaps a joke at the expense of his stay-at-home friend.

Régnier, Pierre. *Gén. Ep.* 80. 'Docteur ès droitz, lieutenant général
en Poitou'; mayor 1516–17; d. 1527. *MP* 493–4, 500–1; *HP*
1514; *CA*. See G. Jarousseau, 'L'élection du maire de Poitiers,
Pierre Régnier, en 1516', *BSOA* 4ᵉ série, 14, 1978, pp.567–86.

Rivière, Pierre. *Gén. Ep.* 49. Mentioned by Bouchet and Pierre Gervaise, *Ep. Fam.* [22], 23. One of Bouchet's friends from his
schooldays; he was an *avocat* and about to marry when he
died in 1499. According to Bouchet and Gervaise he translated the *Narrenschiff*; on this evidence the *Nef des Fous* in
verse published in Paris in 1497 is attributed to him. See
E. Du Bruck, 'Sebastian Brant in France: A "Ship of Fools" by
Pierre Rivière (1497)', *Revue de littérature comparée*, 48, 1974,
pp.248–56.

Robertet, Florimond. *Secrétaire des finances* from 1495, later *conseiller
du roi* and *trésorier de France*; d. 29 Nov. 1527. Bouchet addresses him in a dedicatory letter in the *Panégyrique*: he there
states that Charles vɪɪɪ had intended him to enter the service
of Robertet.

Rogier. Mentioned *Ep. Fam.* 23 as schooldays companion of Bouchet, Rivière and Gervaise.

Romanèche, Gaspar. *Ep. Fam.* 20. 'Docteur ès droits, seigneur du
Pin'. He had apparently composed a treatise on the flood 'qui
pourra venir . . .', which suggests a work relating to the
astrological predictions for 1524. This book had been criticised by someone in Poitiers. Bouchet tells him that he must
forget the faults of the Poitevins once he is in Dauphiné. He
is therefore probably the 'Solon daulphinois' mentioned in
Ep. Fam. 34 as one of a group enjoying a banquet and theological discussions, and due to reassemble at Fontaine-le-
Comte.

Ronsard (Roussart), Louis de, sieur de la Possonière, 1469–1544.
Gén. Ep. 101, *Ep. Fam.* 126, mentioned 96 and 97; addressed
in *épître* in *Triomphes* a3 ro–a4 vo. The father of the poet

Pierre de Ronsard; served under Charles VIII, Louis XII and François Iᵉʳ; as *maître d'hôtel* of the sons of François he accompanied them to captivity in Spain 1526–30. His wife, Jeanne de Chaudrier (m. 1515) was related to the La Trémoille family, which perhaps explains how it came about that *c*.1515 he invited Bouchet to come to Paris, and instructed him in various metrical matters. This information derives from the *épître* in the *Triomphes*, in which Bouchet recalls this incident of 15 years earlier which had caused him to correct his draft of the *Chapelet*; he asks Ronsard to present the *Triomphes* to the new Queen, Eleanor. From *Ep. Fam.* 96, 97, 126 it appears that Ronsard presented the *Jugement* to the King (quite probably in 1534) and also persuaded the King, the Dauphin, Marguerite de Navarre and the Comte de Saint-Pol to write letters supporting Marie Bouchet's admission to Sainte-Croix. 126 records a brief meeting at Châtellerault (1539–41) when Ronsard gave Bouchet a verse *épître*. According to the *épître* in the *Triomphes* Ronsard composed two treatises while in Spain, one on a military subject and one apparently on government. His career is reviewed in this *épître* as in 126 and *Gén. Ep.* 101. Bouchet addresses him with the respect of a social inferior, but calls him 'seigneur qui m'aymez, et que j'ame'.

Sagon, François. *Ep. Fam.* [109], 110; referred to 107, 114, 120. *Curé* of Beauvais. He appeals to Bouchet to enter the *Querelle* against Marot, particularly to condemn Germain Colin for defending Marot and trying to mediate. He may have been encouraged to address Bouchet by the correspondence with the Rouen poets, particularly 107 to Baptiste Le Chandelier in which Bouchet alludes to the quarrel. But Bouchet, while praising both Sagon and Colin, declines to involve himself in the controversy. *P* 2, 218–19; Picot and Lacombe, *Querelle*.

Saint-Gelais, Mellin de. 1491–1558. In *Ep. Fam.* 100 the poet is said to have visited Bouchet who was lying ill at Saint-Maixent in Oct. 1536, and then gone on to see Ardillon. He is referred to as an outstanding poet in 120, also in *Généalogies* f.68 in the *Déploration* for the Dauphin, and in the *épîtres* to and from Tristan Frétard in the *Triomphes du roi*. His contribution to the *Tombeau* for Louise de Savoie is noted in the *Jugement*, f.xcv vo. H. J. Molinier, *Mellin de Saint-Gelays (1490?–1558)*, Rodez, 1910.

Saint-Pol, see Bourbon, François de.

Seguier, Martin. Author of a *dizain* and two Latin verses in the liminary ff. of the *Epîtres Morales*. He also contributed one item in French to the *Tombeau de Marguerite de Valois*, Paris, 1551: see F. Lachèvre, *Bibliographie des recueils collectifs de poésies du XVIᵉ siècle*, Paris, 1922, pp.232–3.

Sussanneau (Susannée, de Suzanne), Hubert. 1512–after 1550. A neo-Latin poet who wrote an epigram for the *Jugement*, A4 vo, which he reproduced in his *Ludorum libri*, Paris, 1538, f.36 ro, addressing another to Joseph Bouchet, f.42 ro. He was born in Soissons, studied in Soissons and in Paris, taught in many universities including Poitiers (in about 1530); he spent some time in Lyons. See Ph. Renouard, 'Hubertus Sussannaeus—Hubert de Suzanne', *Revue des livres anciens*, 2, 1914–17, pp.146–58 (also p.311).

Thevet, Frère André. A Franciscan, born in Angoulême 1502, travelled in Italy and, between 1549 and 1554, in the Middle East. His *Cosmographie du Levant*, Lyons, 1554, contains p.214 a *dizain* by Bouchet. *DLF*.

Thibault, Florent. *Ep. Fam.* [62], 63. A relation of the following?

Thibault, François. *Ep. Fam.* [60], 61. 'Licentier ès droits, avocat à Poitiers'. He sends Bouchet a prose and verse treatise on love.

Tillart. 'Secretaire, de Rouen'. *Ep. Fam.* 121: Bouchet declines to send a *chant royal* for the Rouen *Puy*. Not in *P*.

Tiraqueau, André. 1488–1558. In *Ep. Fam.* 46 Bouchet says that he is sending him a copy of the *Panégyrique*. 58 is addressed to the 'Lieutenant de Fontenay-le-Comte en Poitou', the office held by Tiraqueau between at least 1524 and 1535. Tiraqueau is mentioned as present *HP* 1514. Already an eminent legal writer by the time of this correspondence; a friend of Rabelais since the days when Rabelais was a Franciscan at Fontenay-le-Comte. See J. Brejon, *André Tiraqueau, 1488–1558*, Paris, 1937.

Tortereau, Julien. *Gén. Ep.* 46. 'Licentié en théologie, maistre régent en l'université de Poictiers au colliege de Puygareau.' Bouchet's teacher. He edited some works by Filelfo. *H* 5, 87 n.2; *VP* 388.

Trojan, Jean. Franciscan at Poitiers; checked the *Epître de Justice* for Bouchet and contributed a Latin prose letter to the *Opuscules*; he is described as a theologian 'plus sçavant que ancien'. Also mentioned in *Ep. Fam.* 30 to Ardillon as one of the group meeting at Fontaine-le-Comte. It seems very likely that he subsequently went over to the Reform. There are four possible identifications: a) a Franciscan 'De Troye', imprisoned for heresy in 1533; b) 'Le docte Detrosa' who dined with Le Riche (*Journal*, p.14) in April 1537, and who preached Advent and Lent at Saint-Maixent; a learned preacher, but one who 'n'a suivi la forme des autres en ses prédications'; c) the Franciscan whose heretical sermons caused an uproar among the students in Poitiers in July 1537; Le Riche (*Journal*, p.15) records news of this event reaching Saint-Maixent; cf. *Ep.*

Fam. 108; d) the Franciscan 'de Troia', who according to the *Histoire ecclésiastique* joined forces in promoting reform with the abbot of Valence (Ponce de S. Georges, successor of Ponce de La Grève, q.v.) who 'nettoya sa maison de l'idolatrie . . .' (ed. Baum and Cunitz, 1, p.81). See Pierre Dez, *Histoire des protestants et des Eglises réformées de Poitou*, La Rochelle, 1936, pp.24–5, 37–8.

Valentinois, Louise de, vicomtesse de Thouars. *Ep. Fam.* 24, 26. Daughter of Cesare Borgia and of Charlotte d'Albret; second wife of Louis II de La Trémoille, m. 1517. There were no children of the marriage; in 1530 she married Philippe de Bourbon, baron de Busset. *Ep. Fam.* 26 had already appeared in the *Panégyrique*; it is written in her name to La Trémoille away fighting in Italy. *LT* 2, xi–xii, 94ff., 130ff.

Valleus, Nicolaus. Author of Latin prose letter in *Panégyrique*; said to be from Paris.

Valois, Duchesse de, see Orléans, Jeanne de.

Vendôme, Louis de, vidame de Chartres. *Gén. Ep.* 54. Chamberlain, *conseiller du roi, grand veneur de France*; d. 2 Aug. 1526, aged 25. Married Hélène Gouffier, eldest daughter of Artus Gouffier, q.v., and Hélène de Hangest, q.v. He was taken prisoner at Pavia and ransomed, but he died soon afterwards (*Annales* 216 vo). *CA.*

Villandry, see Breton, Jean.

Vivonne, André de. *Gén. Ep.* 42, *Ep. Fam.* 28; see also 1 *Ep. Mor.* 14, *Ep. Fam.* 74, 79 (on his death), *Annales* 206 ro, 265 vo. Seigneur de La Chasteigneraie, sénéchal de Poitou; present *HP* 1514; d. 31 July 1532 aged 80. His wife, Louise de Daillon, and his daughter, Anne de Vivonne, were both ladies-inwaiting to Marguerite de Navarre. Anne, who married François, vicomte de Bourdeille, was the mother of Brantôme. *DN* 19, 911; *DHGP* first ed. (1840–54), vol.2, p.815.

The Chronology of the *Epîtres familières*

The *Epîtres familières* consist of 106 pieces by Bouchet and 21 by other authors. Some 21 of Bouchet's are *epîtres artificielles*, but the remainder are in varying degrees presented as personal poetry. They are a useful source of biographical information about Bouchet and his correspondents, particularly if one can establish the date at which they were written.

Bouchet himself provides a date in many cases—particularly of course when the poem functions as an epitaph, but by no means exclusively so. A predilection for giving dates is part of Bouchet's general concern with the true record of historical fact. This interest in chronology is evident in the arrangement of the *epîtres*, which are plainly intended for the most part to be in chronological order. However, useful as this may be as a guide to the date of an individual undated *epître*, it cannot be entirely relied upon. Chronology is not the only factor governing the arrangement of the *epîtres*. The long and prestigious *Epître d'Henri* is placed at the head of the collection; there are instances where a grouping by subject matter appears to override chronology. In some cases the *epîtres* are out of chronological order for no obvious reason—e.g. 100 before 101, 122 before 123 and 124; by 1545 Bouchet himself may have been unsure of the date of some of his undated verse—it is for instance clear from internal evidence that 22 and 23 are placed far too early. It is therefore also necessary to use where possible internal evidence to improve on the approximate date which can be deduced from an undated *epître*'s position in the collection. *Epîtres* may be dated from deaths which they lament, from references to newly published works by Bouchet and from lists of works which Bouchet had so far written—but in the latter cases it must be remembered that the date of printing given in a book does not always constitute a reliable guide to the date when the work became available (see for example Bibliography on the *Triomphes*). Another guide to dating is reference to the length of time which has elapsed since some other event. Here too it should be noted that these statements, while helpful, are not wholly reliable. In 23, 41, 61, 101 and 104 Bouchet says that he has been writing for 30 years. We know he was writing verse from at least 1496, yet 101 can be dated 1536. In 111 the expression 'huit jours' refers to a period of fourteen days.

Bouchet himself occasionally gives indications of date by means of astronomical data. In particular he refers to days on which the sun entered a new sign of the zodiac. I have taken these dates from J. Stoeffler, *Calendarium romanum magnum*, 1518; they are of course some ten days earlier than the dates now usually assigned to them. In two cases he suggests the relative position of the sun and the moon; although his language in each case poses some difficulty of interpretation it seems reasonable to accept that the data was in intention correct—he was writing to Ardillon and to Rabelais, both of whom may be supposed to have taken an intelligent interest in the movements of celestial bodies. Dates in these cases are taken from Herman H. Goldstine, *New and Full Moons 1001 BC to AD 1651*, Philadelphia, 1973.

The table which follows summarises the deductions which can be made from evidence other than the position of the *épître* in the collection. Some very approximate datings are given, but these may at least be useful in confirming the generally chronological order of the *épîtres*. Where no date at all is suggested the *épître*'s position in the collection is the only guide to the date of its composition.

Dates are given in the table in the following form:

Dates in **bold type** are dates actually given in the *épître*.

Dates in [square brackets] can be established with certainty from internal evidence.

Dates neither in bold type nor in square brackets represent a terminus which can be certainly deduced; if only one terminus can be established it is preceded or followed by an arrow →.

Dates in (round brackets) are approximate, based on some internal evidence but not firmly established.

An asterisk * indicates that a date given old style by Bouchet is here given new style.

1. **21 September 1512**
   Henry VII of England to Henry VIII
2. (August 1501)
   To 'ung sien compaignon à Paris' on death of Y. Boilesve
3. →(1507)
   Un jeune seigneur à celle qu'il pensoit epouser
4. →(1507)
   Une fiancée à un fiancé
5. **25 January 1513***
   Une mercière
6. **December** (1511–16)
   To 'son amy demourant aux champs'

7. →(1516)
     Une dame veufve à un gentilhomme
8. →(1516)
     To 'un sien amy Orateur'
9. **Low Sunday** (1510)
     To Gabrielle de Bourbon
10. (1510)–1516
     L'âme à son amy par amours Jesus (for Gabrielle de Bourbon)
11. (1510)–1516
     La Royne des cieulx ma Dame Marie à nature humaine
     (for Gabrielle de Bourbon)
12. (1517–18)
     Une sage dame qui s'adroisse au papier
13. (1517–18)
     Une dame à ung gentilhomme
14. [1515]
     Queen Mary to Henry VIII on death of Louis XII
15. **1 January** 1520–(1523)
     To François du Fou
16. (1520)→
     To François du Fou
17. **15 May**
     To Bertrand Langlois
18.
     To 'une dame de Poitou'
19.
     Un loyal serviteur à sa desloyalle et impudique maistresse
20. (1523–24)
     To Gaspar Romanèche
21. (1522–25)
     To Nicolas Petit
22. [Autumn] 1528–(1531)
     From Pierre Gervaise
23. 1528–(1532)
     To Pierre Gervaise
24. (1520)–1525
     To Louise de Valentinois
25. **October**
     To François du Fou
26. Late 1524–February 1525
     Louise de Valentinois to Louis de La Trémoille
27. **31 May 1525**
     To the Prince of Orange
28. →1532 (→1528)
     To André de Vivonne

29.
> To Ardillon

30. (1525–27)
> To Ardillon

31.
> To 'la dame de chambre d'une dame tresillustre du sang de France'

32.
> Une jeune dame à ung jeune prince

33. (February 1525)→
> On friendship, to a correspondent addressed as 'Monseigneur'

34. **18 July** (1523 or 1524?)
> To Ardillon

35.
> To Ardillon

36. **Sunday 12 November** [1525]
> To 'ung Advocat'

37. →1526
> To Ponce de La Grève

38. *c.***1 November** [1525]
> From 'Huissiers et sergens royaulx de Paris'

39. [Winter 1525–26]
> To 'Huissiers et sergens'

40. **3 November**
> From Germain Emery

41. **13 November**
> To Germain Emery

42. **5 January** (1526–32)
> To 'Roy de la Bazoche de Bordeaulx'

43. 1526–29
> To Jean Parmentier

44. 1526–29
> From Jean Parmentier

45. **May** 1526→
> To eldest son of François du Fou

46. **30 July** 1526→
> To André Tiraqueau

47. (1523)→
> To Jean Mary de Ruffec

48. **6 September** (1526 or 1527)
> From Rabelais

49. **8 September** (1526 or 1527)
> To Rabelais

50.
> To Ardillon

51.
> To Gabriel Bouchet

52.
> On Shrove Tuesday and Lent, to a correspondent addressed as 'treshonnoré seigneur'

53. **January** (1525–30)
> To Abbé de Moreilles

54.
> To 'un sien cousin'

55. **May**
> Un jeune seigneur à une demoiselle

56. **Monday 4 November** (1527)
> To Claude Cottereau

57. **28 January 1528***
> To Ardillon, on death of Jean d'Auton

58. 1527→
> To Lieutenant de Fontenay-le-Comte [André Tiraqueau]

59. 12 June–13 July (1528)–1529
> Catherine Prévoste to René Berthelot

60. 1525→
> From François Thibault

61. 1526→ (1528→)
> To François Thibault

62.
> From Florent Thibault

63. 14 October–12 November
> To Florent Thibault

64. **7 July 1529**
> From Germain Colin

65. September 1529→
> To Germain Colin

66. March 1530→
> From Germain Colin

67. **Autumn** 1530–(1531)
> To Germain Colin

68. 8 December 1530→
> To Louis Bastard, on death of Jacques Prévost

69. 8 December 1530→
> From Michel Desarpens

70. (1531)
> To Michel Desarpens

71. 1531→
> From Michel Desarpens

72. 1531→
> To Michel Desarpens

73. **7 January** 1528→
    To Ardillon
74. **26 December** [1530]
    To Antoinette d'Illiers
75. **September 1531**
    Dames de Paris à messieurs de la court . . .
76. **14 October** [1531]
    Dames de Poitiers à celles de Paris
77. **October** (1531–33)
    To Robert Irland
78. **17 October 1532**
    To Ardillon, on death of Nicolas Petit
79. **10 August 1532**
    To Guy de Bourdeilles, on death of André de Vivonne
80.
    From Jean Mary de Ruffec
81.
    To Jean Mary de Ruffec
82. **10 February** 1528–37
    To Claude Cottereau
83. **May** →1535
    Prince de Mortaigne to Seigneur de Crissé
84. **16 September 1533**
    To 'un Procureur en parlement'
85. 1527→
    From Jacques de Puytesson
86. 1527→
    To Jacques de Puytesson
87. **October** [1533]
    To Marillac
88. →2 May [1534]
    From Thomas Le Prévost
89. **2 May** [1534]
    To Thomas Le Prévost
90. **August 1534**
    To 'ceulx de Poictiers qui ont monstré par parsonnages
    le mistere de la passion'
91. [1534]
    From 'habitants d'Issoudun en Berry'
92. [1534]
    To 'habitants d'Issoudun'
93.
    Une chaste dame à quelque homme d'honneur
94.
    Epistre responsive à ladicte dame

95. **7 September** [1533 or 1534]
    To Louise de Bourbon
96. (September 1533)–November 1536
    To Madame de Montreuil-Bonnin
97. **Late Autumn**, September 1533–November 1536
    To Villandry
98. **January**
    To Jacques Le Lieur
99. **10 February**
    From Jacques Le Lieur
100. **October 1536**
    To Ardillon
101. **15 May** [1536]
    To Jean Chaponneau
102. **29 April** (→1535)
    →To Seigneur de Mombrun
103. **Before Lent**
    To 'Escoliers et Bazochiens de Poitiers'
104. 1531→
    To a correspondent addressed as 'trescher seigneur'
105. **December** [1536 or 1537]
    To Louise de Bourbon
106. [August–September] **1537**
    From Baptiste Le Chandelier
107. [September 1537]
    To Baptiste Le Chandelier
108. **16 September 1537**
    To Jacques Le Lieur
109. 1537–(1538)
    From François Sagon
110. 1537–(1538)
    To François Sagon
111. **15 April** [1538]
    To Jacques d'Anglure
112. (April–July 1538)
    From Jacques d'Anglure
113. **22 July** (1538)
    To Jacques d'Anglure
114. **August** (1538)
    To Jacques Le Lieur
115. 1536→
    To Madeleine de Bourbon
116. 1536→
    To Madeleine de Bourbon
117. **27 June**
    To La Fayolle

118. 1535–38
To François Du Bourg
119. 1538–41
From Jean Brèche
120. 1538–January 1542
To Jean Brèche
121.
To Tillart
122. 9 September–11 November **1541**
To 'la femme de l'avocat du roy en parlement'
123. **6 August** [1538]
From Claude Cottereau
124. **30 August** [1538]
To Claude Cottereau
125. **August**
To Jacques Godart
126. 1539–41
To Louis de Ronsard
127. **August 1543**
To Seigneur de Mihervé

NOTES

1-11 and 14 do not observe alternation of masculine and feminine
rhymes. In the pair 12 and 13 alternation is observed in 12 except
for one couplet, although 13 is less regular. Alternation is observed in all *épîtres* by Bouchet from 15 onwards. In his other
works using decasyllabic couplets Bouchet does not observe
alternation in the *Temple*, composed in 1516, but does observe it
in the *Labyrinthe*, composed after May 1519, and printed 1522.
We may assume that those *épîtres* in which there is no attempt at
alternation were written in the period up to about 1516, and that
those which observe it date from about 1519. We can tentatively
ascribe 12 and 13 to the intermediate period.
2, 3 and 4 are reworkings of poems from the *Amoureux transi* which was
probably printed by 1507 and possibly as early as 1504. 2 refers
to the apparently recent death of Yves Boilesve in August 1501.
6 uses poetic fictions deriving probably from Book One of Lemaire's
Illustrations (May 1511)—e.g. 'hymnides'.
9, 10 and 11 are addressed to Gabrielle de Bourbon (d. 1516). In 9 he
thanks her for enrolling him in her household; it probably dates
therefore from the beginning of his connection with the La Trémoille family, *c*.1510.
12, 13, see 1.
14 was first published in the *Chapelet*, 1517; it recounts the death of
Louis xii (1 Jan. 1515) and was written three months or more
later at the request of Charles de La Trémoille (d. Sept. 1515).
15 refers to a gift of a copy of the *Labyrinthe* 'le jour qu'on donne les
estreines'. If a printed copy this would be after Nov. 1522, but a
ms copy might have been given earlier.

16, also to François du Fou, is more familiar in tone and probably post-dates 15.

20. References to the need to combat Lutheranism suggest a date of 1523 or later; moreover Romanèche is said to have written a book on the flood which may occur because of men's sins—this sounds like a product of the expectations of floods aroused by the conjunctions predicted for 1524-25.

21. Petit probably came to study law in Poitiers at some time between 1522 and 1524, having previously taught in Paris. He was later to teach law in Poitiers. This *épître* must date from early in his friendship with Bouchet since he is described as 'regent de Paris et lors estudiant à Poictiers'.

22 and 23 are out of chronological order. In 22 Gervaise refers to Jean d'Auton (d. Jan. 1528) in the past tense in a list of priest- poets all the rest of whom are dead; he also mentions works by Bouchet up to and including the *Anciennes et modernes* (printed 1528) and the *Panégyrique* (printed 1527). In 23 Bouchet says that he received Gervaise's *épître* in the autumn and implies that there has been some delay in his reply. In 22 Gervaise speaks of a Passion play which Bouchet is to direct; in 23 Bouchet says that the play will be put on in August, although some people are opposed to the production because of the plague in Poitiers and the failure of the harvest. Bouchet describes himself as 'ton amy dès trente ans a' and speaks of their schooldays together. It seems unlikely that these *épîtres* should be dated as late as 1533-34 and taken to refer to the actual performance of the Passion in 1534. Having carefully listed Bouchet's works it is most unlikely that Gervaise would say that the *Panégyrique* was the most recent if he knew the *Triomphes*, which was certainly available by mid-1531 at the latest. Moreover, a particularly bad outbreak of plague began in March 1531 (*Annales*, f.258 ro), but the mayoral year 1533-34 was marked by an improved harvest and the disappearance of the plague (Ledain, 'Maires', p.525). It seems more likely that the objections mentioned here by Bouchet resulted in an earlier project for the Passion between 1529 and 1532 being deferred.

24 and 26. Louise de Valentinois was the second wife of Louis de La Trémoille. Bouchet had business dealings with her during her husband's absences on military campaigns. 26 dates from the time La Trémoille spent in Italy with the army before his death at Pavia; it first appeared in the *Panégyrique*.

28. André de Vivonne died in 1532. As this *épître* refers to his instruction of his children but does not mention the death of his son Charles (1528: *Annales* 250 vo) it should perhaps be dated before that death.

30. The *épîtres* relating to gatherings that include Rabelais must date from the period when Rabelais was a Benedictine and in the service of Geoffroy d'Estissac—here Rabelais, Quintin, Petit and Trojan, a Franciscan, are said to be 'tous divers en vesture'. Rabelais changed his order in 1524 and seems to have left Poitou in 1528. This *épître* can presumably be placed early in the period 1525-27. Cf. 48 and 49; see Lefranc, *Edition critique* of Rabelais' works, vol.1, p.cxxx.

33. Reference to the 'misère soudaine' of the French suggests a date after the battle of Pavia.

34. If the friend 'qui portoit le blanc' is the Cistercian Ponce de La Grève, his death, thought to have occurred in 1526, would give a *terminus ad quem*. An astronomical indication is given in the opening lines:

> Tantost après qu'Apollo le delphicque
> Se fut assis on trosne leonicque
> Pour veoir Lucine aux pictons radiant.

The sun would enter Leo on 14 July and Bouchet writes on 18 July. If the third line means that the moon was in Leo, the year would be 1520 or, more probably, 1523, when the moon was new on 14 and 13 July respectively; 'pictons' would suggest the points of the crescent moon. If however it means that the moon was full and in opposition to the sun (cf. end of 2 *Ep. Mor.* 4), 1524 would be the most likely date, with full moon on 15 July; 'pictons' in this case might suggest stylised rays of light.

36 is dated Sunday, the day after St Martin's day—i.e. 12 November, which fell on a Sunday in 1525. The subject, the disorders of justice and the other estates, suggests that this exchange with a lawyer arose from the publication of Bouchet's *Epître de Justice* in the *Opuscules*, 1525, and it is probable that the words 'ceste saison tant malle' refer to the defeat at Pavia.

37. To Ponce de La Grève, who seems to have died in 1526.

38 is about the *Epître de Justice* and is dated 'l'an merveilleux environ la Toussaincts'—no doubt a reference to the fearful year of Pavia and the King's exile.

39, the answer to 38, is dated 'the fourth day of the coldest month'.

41 is dated as the day the sun entered Sagittarius.

42. Bouchet says here that he was a member of the Basoche in Paris 30 years before. This gives a very approximate date fitting the generally chronological order.

43 and 44. After voyages in the period 1520-26 Parmentier remained in France between 1526 and his last voyage began in March 1529. This exchange suggests that Parmentier passed through or near Poitiers without having time to visit Bouchet. Bouchet calls Parmentier 'historien' and says he has received both prose and verse from him; he is probably referring to a MS or printed copy of Parmentier's translation of Sallust's *Catilina*, printed in September 1528, Parmentier's only surviving prose or historical work. This perhaps indicates a date towards the end of the period 1526-29.

45 and 46 announce that Bouchet is sending the recipients a copy of the *Panégyrique*. If MS copies were sent these *épîtres* could date from 1526, but it is more likely that he was distributing newly printed copies in 1527.

47. References to Lutheranism show that this was written no earlier than 1523.

48 and 49. This exchange with Rabelais must fall within the period when Rabelais was in the service of d'Estissac, *c*.1525-27. The only dates given are 6 and 8 September. There is however an astronomical indication in 49; Bouchet writes

> Lors que Titan se mussoit en sa chambre
> Et que Lucyne ung peu se desbouchet.

If this means that the moon is just visible at sunset, both 1525 and 1528 are ruled out, since in those years the moon was respectively 20 and 24 days old on 8 September and would not therefore have been visible at sunset. In 1526 the moon was 2 days old, which appears to fit in well with 'ung peu se desbouchet'; however the words could also mean that the moon was just rising (cf. end of *Ep.* 53), therefore 1527, when the moon was about 12 days old, is also possible. 1524 is less satisfactory, with the moon 10 days old.

Clouzot (*Etudes rabelaisiennes* 5, p.195) suggests that as Bouchet includes compliments to both Geoffroy and Louis d'Estissac, but makes no reference to the latter's marriage to Anne de Daillon in 1527, this exchange should be dated no later than 1526. Although not indisputable this argument is very reasonable. On the other hand the position of the *épîtres* would tend to suggest 1527 if our assumptions concerning 43-46 are correct.

51 is addressed to his son Gabriel at college. It seems likely that Bouchet's two daughters married by 1524 were his eldest children and that Gabriel, his heir, was born in or after 1510 when Bouchet had entered the service of Gabrielle de Bourbon. Bouchet appears to address a child or young adolescent here rather than a young man. These slight indications are at least consistent with a more or less chronological arrangement of the *épîtres*.

53. Bouchet claims to have been related to the *abbé* for twenty years, which suggests a connection through Bouchet's marriage (*c.* 1507?).

56 is dated Monday 4 Nov., which indicates 1521, 1527, 1532 or 1538, etc.

58 mentions 'Doyneau, qui maintenant a le tiltre tresbeau de lieutenant general Pictonicque'. This appointment was made in 1527, presumably not long before this *épître* was written.

59. Berthelot, here called 'future maire', was mayor 1529-30; he married in Feb. 1529 (o.s.?). The sun in Cancer.

60 refers to the *Annales* and the *Opuscules*.

61 is the reply to 60. Bouchet says that he is over 50 years old (i.e. after Jan. 1526). He is probably writing after Jan. 1528, since he wishes his correspondent the style of Jean d'Auton, a type of formula he most commonly uses with reference to dead poets rather than living ones. D'Auton's death in Jan. 1528 was recorded in 57.

63. The sun in Scorpio.

64-67 form a correspondence with Germain Colin Bucher. The first, 64, is dated 7 July 1529. In 65 Bouchet says that Colin's *épître* arrived in August, but that he could not have the reply ready by September when the bearer returned and he must apologise for the delay. 1 *Ep. Mor.* 5, addressed to Guyvereau, is dated 16 Dec. 1529; this mentions Colin's *épître* and it may well have been despatched along with 65. The references to Malta in Colin's next *épître*, 66, suggest that it was written in 1530 when at last the Emperor had made over Malta and Tripoli to the Knights of St John and the Knights had accepted the charge (March-July 1530). The Knights arrived on Malta in October 1530. In 67 Bouchet

implies that the Knights are now settled on Malta; he dates this
epître the second month of the autumn and this time makes no
apology for lack of promptness in reply. It is thus not impossible
that 67 dates from late 1530 (October?), although it could have
been written in 1531.

68-72. 68 was no doubt written directly after the death of Jacques
Prévost on 8 Dec. 1530. In 69 Desarpens asks Bouchet to read an
epitaph for Prévost which he has written. 70 answers 69, and 71
and 72 continue the correspondence which, as Desarpens was
probably in Poitiers at the time, can no doubt be dated fairly
close together.

73. The unpopularity at court mentioned here could hardly have been
caused by any work earlier than the *Panégyrique*.

74. Bouchet refers to the work in which a version of this *epître* originally
appeared as a preface, Simon Nérault's *Flagice de peste*, printed
with the date 23 March 1530 (o.s.).

76. Dated the day the sun entered Scorpio. A reply to 75.

77 is said to have been written during a bad outbreak of plague,
probably in the period 1531-33 when Bouchet spent much of his
time out of Poitiers.

82 is later than 56 but earlier than 123 and 124; Cottereau was now in
Paris. The day the sun entered Pisces.

83. 'Le jeune prince de Mortaigne', 'le petit Momberon' is presumably
the Adrian de Montberon who died in 1535.

85, 86. The King granted permission in 1527 to a canon from Poitiers to
found a church and almonry at Ménigoute, where Jacques de
Puytesson is said to be a canon.

87, like 84, was written during the *Grands Jours de Poitou* held at Tours,
Sept.-Nov. 1533.

88-92 are all written in the year of the Passion directed at Poitiers by
Bouchet.

95 is one of a series of *epîtres* (95, 96, 97, 105, 115, 116, 126) which refer
to one or more of the following events, all of which took place
between 1531 and 1536 and which one might hope to date more
precisely from evidence in these *epîtres*:

a) On Bouchet's behalf Louis de Ronsard presented to the
King the *Jugement*, which had been composed in memory of
Louise de Savoie.

b) Ronsard obtained from the King, the Dauphin, Marguerite
de Navarre and the comte de Saint-Pol letters requesting the
abbess of Sainte-Croix, Louise de Bourbon, to admit Marie Bouchet to the convent at no expense to her father.

c) Marie Bouchet entered Sainte-Croix.

d) Bouchet requested a privilege from the King for the *Jugement*
and other works.

Comparison of the chronological data in these *epîtres* does
yield some results. To take first Marie Bouchet's admission to
Sainte-Croix, in 95 Bouchet asks Louise de Bourbon to admit his
daughter and refers to the letters which Louise has received
from the King etc. This *epître*, dated September, was written no
later than 1534, for Louise was to leave Sainte-Croix and become
abbess of Fontevrault in place of her aunt Renée who died in
November 1534. It would seem that Bouchet's request was acted

on promptly; in 105 he tells us that it was Louise who admitted Marie to Sainte-Croix while she was abbess there, therefore by November 1534. In 105 Bouchet also says that Marie has now been at Sainte-Croix for three years. This *épître*, dated December, was composed after the death of the Dauphin (d. 10 Aug. 1536). It is therefore very unlikely that 95 was written earlier than Sept. 1533; it cannot have been written later than Sept. 1534; therefore 105 must have been written either in Dec. 1536 or in Dec. 1537.

Louis de Ronsard's presentation of the *Jugement* at court is mentioned in 96; Bouchet tells Madame de Montreuil-Bonnin that the *Jugement*, for which he now wants a privilege, was presented to the King by Ronsard 'puis demy an'. Since Louise de Savoie died in September 1531 and since Bouchet already mentions the epigrams of the *Jugement* in the *Annales* of Jan. 1532, one might expect the presentation to have taken place in 1532, or 1533 at the latest. But in 111, dated 15 April 1538, Bouchet says that he had written the newly-printed *Jugement* 'des ans a plus de quatre, Voire bien cinq', which suggests that he thought of 1533 as the date of composition. One would suppose that the presentation either preceded or accompanied Ronsard's request for letters in support of Marie Bouchet, which had certainly been obtained by September 1534.

However, the earlier the presentation of the *Jugement* is supposed to have taken place, the greater is the problem presented by the dating of those *épîtres* in which Bouchet requests a privilege for the *Jugement*. In 96 Bouchet says that he wants a privilege for the *Jugement* and also for the *Angoisses* and even for the *Epîtres morales*, one of which in the 1545 edition is dated as late as May 1534. He tells Madame de Montreuil-Bonnin that he has written to Villandry, the King's secretary, asking him to ask the King for a privilege, and he begs her to speak to Villandry about the matter. 97 is addressed to Villandry himself. Bouchet thanks him for getting the King to write the letter by means of which Marie was able to enter Sainte-Croix, and he asks for a privilege. Both 96 and 97 appear then to be poems intended to reinforce a formal request for a privilege which had been made twelve days earlier according to 97, which is dated 'the end of autumn'. The privilege that these *épîtres* request was not granted until November 1536. 97, and presumably 96 too, is certainly later than 95, i.e. Sept. 1533 or 1534, because of the reference in 97 to Marie as already established at Sainte-Croix. And yet they are not, according to the phrase 'puis demy an' in 96, to be dated as much more than six months after the presentation of the *Jugement*. It would seem that, as their position in the collection suggests, 96 and 97 were written a little later in the same year as 95, i.e. 1533 or 1534. Bouchet's request for a privilege must thus have been unsuccessful for two or even three years. Unless of course it is admitted that Ronsard might have obtained the letters concerning Marie before presenting the *Jugement*, in which case both the presentation and the request for a privilege could be as late as 1536. But presenting the King with a memorial to his mother five years after her death seems an odd procedure—even early 1534, the later of the two dates suggested by our preferred hypothesis, betokens a rather surprising delay.

As far as the later *epîtres* referring to these events are concerned, 115 and 116 are addressed to Madeleine de Bourbon, Louise de Bourbon's niece and successor at Sainte-Croix. Bouchet asks her to allow Marie to make her profession, a matter which he had already mentioned to Louise in 105 saying that Marie had now been in the convent for three years. 105, as we have seen, can be dated either Dec. 1536 or Dec. 1537, so 115 and 116 probably date from 1537 or 1538. Finally, in 126 Bouchet thanks Ronsard for his good offices in the matter of Marie's admission to Sainte-Croix, and says that these thanks have been due 'des ans a plus de six'. He does not here refer to Ronsard's presentation of the *Jugement* to the King, from which one might perhaps conclude that he has already thanked him for doing so, and that this is a straw of evidence for the assumption that the presentation preceded the request for help concerning Marie. From our deductions so far, 126 should be dated 1539-40 or 1540-41.

It must be admitted that the chronological data which can be gleaned from internal evidence in these *epîtres* is rather disappointing, and certainly no better a guide than the order of the *epîtres*. It is worth noting in conclusion that the position of these *epîtres* suggests fairly consistently the later of the two possible dates for Marie's admission to Sainte-Croix, i.e. 1534. In this case only 105 would be slightly out of order, since if it is dated Dec. 1537 it is later than the three *epîtres* of Sept. 1537 which immediately follow it. It would however have interrupted a carefully arranged sequence if placed later: see notes on 106 etc. Thus the evidence as a whole suggests that 1534 is the most likely date for all the events here dealt with.

101. The mystery of the Passion was produced at Bourges in 1536.
102. If this 'Seigneur de Mombrun' is Adrian, supposed author of 83 and subject of *Gén. Ep.* 58, it dates from before his death in June 1535.
104 refers to criticism of the *Triomphes*.
105. See 95.
106-110 and 114. This series forms the main body of correspondence with the Rouen poets and contains all the references to the quarrel between Marot and Sagon; they appear deliberately arranged to be read together, along with the group 111-13—allusive references to the *Querelle* thus become much clearer. Baptiste Le Chandelier seems to have it in mind as he deplores contemporary scandal-mongering in the first *epître*, dated 1537. Without actually naming them Bouchet makes a clear reference to Marot and Sagon in his reply, 107. In 108, writing to Jacques Le Lieur ostensibly eight days after receipt of Le Chandelier's letter, Bouchet makes no reference to the *Querelle* but, perhaps by contrast, stresses the affection existing between himself and Le Lieur even though they have never met. Moreover he unprecedentedly says of the date of this *epître*, 16 Sept. 1537, that it is the day that a Lutheran clerk had made his 'amende honorable' in Poitiers. 109 and 110 are from and to Sagon himself, referring to Germain Colin's intervention in the *Querelle*; Bouchet declines

to take part, but makes his views known in 114 to Le Lieur, dated
August, probably therefore 1538. Here he praises Marot's poetry
and regrets his errors.

111-13. This group, to and from Jacques d'Anglure, are not without
relevance to the letters about Marot, for they present Bouchet as
an opponent of heresy but also as a critic of abuses in the Church.
111, dated 15 April, refers to the publication eight days earlier of
the *Jugement* (printed 1 April 1538). D'Anglure's reply is undated, Bouchet's second *épître*, 113, is dated the feast of the
Magdalene, i.e. 22 July, presumably 1538.

114, see 106.

115-16, see 95.

118 refers to the recipient's father, Antoine Du Bourg, having been
made Chancellor 'n'y a pas longtemps'. Du Bourg became Chancellor in 1535 and died in 1538.

119-20. In these leters, first published in Brèche's *Manuel royal* in January 1542, Brèche asks Bouchet to read his treatises, and says that
he is contemplating dedicating his work to a 'fille de roy' who
has left the court of her parents for Tours—i.e. Jeanne d'Albret,
who settled at Plessis-les-Tours in 1538. There was obviously
some gap in time between the two *épîtres* for in the *Manuel royal*
is another *épître* by Brèche regretting Bouchet's failure to reply as
yet.

122 was written during the session of the *Grands Jours* in Poitiers, 9
Sept. to 11 Nov. 1541.

123 and 124, dated 6 and 30 Aug., refer to the recent interview between
the King and the Emperor at Aigues-Mortes (July 1538), at which
Cottereau was present.

126, see 95.

Part One : The Works of Bouchet

The bibliography that follows is divided into sections dealing with each of Bouchet's works in chronological order. Each section comprises a) a discussion of the date of composition and of the first edition where this is uncertain; b) a note of any later versions of the work under a different title; c) a list of editions.

The dating of Bouchet's works presents certain difficulties, as some of them were not printed until several years after their composition and may have been first circulated in manuscript. Bouchet lists his works on more than one occasion, but these lists do not wholly agree with each other. The most authoritative statement is in the *Epître aux Imprimeurs*, 2 *Ep. Mor.* 11, dated 1534; he reviews his writing career and lists his works as having been written in the following order: *Renards, Histoire de Clotaire, Déploration, Chapelet, Cantiques, rondeaux* and *ballades, Temple, Labyrinthe, Annales* (although he says that these had been begun ten years previously), *Panégyrique, Anciennes et Modernes, Triomphes*; he adds that as he writes he has a work for the Dauphin in preparation, and he mentions a work called *L'Honneur des princes* and fifteen other 'livretz' already completed. There is another list in *Ep. Fam.* 41 which mentions fewer works but includes the *Epître de Justice*; the order is different but the list is probably not intended to be arranged chronologically. In neither case does he mention the *Amoureux transi*, but this is referred to in *Ep. Fam.* 61 as the one early work that he regrets, and the circumstances of its publication are explained in the preface to the *Angoisses et remedes*.

The major part of Bouchet's work was printed in Poitiers, although his earliest dealings were with Paris printers. Bouchet had cause to sue Vérard, who published his first two works; later in his career he complained about other Paris printers who published unauthorised adaptations and continuations of his work. After his first unfortunate experiences Bouchet continued for a while to publish in Paris, first with Guillaume Eustace and then Galliot du Pré. But in 1518 he switched to Enguilbert de Marnef, who sold books in both Paris and Poitiers, and thus began his long and enduring association with the succeeding generations of de Marnefs and of

Bouchets, who were printers in Poitiers. Thereafter all his first editions were printed in Poitiers; they were sold in Poitiers and sometimes in Paris too. The Poitiers editions produced by the de Marnefs and Bouchets must be regarded as authoritative. Other Paris printers continued to produce editions, but they were copying or modifying the ones from Poitiers.

First editions of Bouchet's works normally appeared with a privilege. In the first part of his career they were granted to his printer, but later they were granted to him personally. He was granted one by the King in November 1536 for four years; this covered the *Angoisses* and the *Jugement*. He was granted another for four years in January 1544 (n.s.). By this time he was apparently concerned to produce definitive editions of earlier works, so in 1545 under this privilege appeared the *Epîtres morales et familières*, a new edition of the *Annales* and the edition of the *Généalogies* which contains many other works and which he claimed was the third of five projected volumes; no others, however, were printed. There is some evidence that the privileges were respected: it is noticeable that the *Triomphes*, which appears to have been extremely popular among Paris printers, was not printed by any of them until the original four-year privilege had expired. The edition of the *Annales* that they copied and expanded was that of 1535, which had appeared without a privilege.

The bibliography of Bouchet's works given by Hamon was a good one, drawing of course upon earlier bibliographers like La Croix du Maine, Du Verdier, Niceron, Lelong, Goujet, Graesse, Panzer and Brunet. The work of Tchemerzine and La Bouralière in some instances adds to or modifies information given by Hamon. The list which follows does not give detailed bibliographical descriptions, and full titles are normally given for the first edition only, but shelf-marks are given for all copies in the Bibliothèque Nationale, the British Library and the Bibliothèque Municipale de Poitiers. Where this provides fewer than two locations I have where possible referred to copies in other libraries taken in the following order: in France, the Arsenal, Mazarine, Sainte-Geneviève, Musée Condé, provincial French libraries; in England the Bodleian, the Adams Catalogue of Cambridge libraries, the John Rylands Library. Copies in these libraries are thus by no means always mentioned here; they, as well as others in Europe and the United States, are for the most part to be found in the *Répertoire bibliographique des livres imprimés en France au seizième siècle*, the *Inventaire chronologique des éditions parisiennes du XVIe siècle* and the *Index Aureliensis*, to which I have given references wherever possible. Where no copy has been located the item is placed in brackets and a reference given to Hamon, La Bouralière or Tchemerzine—their references to earlier bibliographers are not normally repeated. Where Tchemerzine actually reproduces a title-page or colophon the item is given without brackets with a page reference to his work.

Bibliographical reference works are referred to by the name of their author alone, or with a short title to avoid ambiguity; details of these will be found in the bibliography part 2(d). The following abbreviations are used:

Ars. = Bibliothèque de l'Arsenal
Aur. = *Index Aureliensis*
Bib. = Biblióthèque
BL = British Library
BMP = Bibliothèque Municipale de Poitiers
BN = Bibliothèque Nationale
Bod. = Bodleian Library
Camb. Adams = *Catalogue of Books printed on the Continent of Europe, 1501–1600, in Cambridge Libraries,* compiled by H.M. Adams, 2 vols, Cambridge, 1967
cat. = catalogue
col. = colophon
fol. = in-folio
goth. = gothic print
Inv. = B. Moreau, *Inventaire chronologique des éditions parisiennes du XVIe siècle*
JR = John Rylands Library, Manchester
Maz. = Bibliothèque Mazarine
MC = Musée Condé
Rép. = *Répertoire bibliographique des livres imprimés en France au seizième siècle*
Roth. = Collection Rothschild
SG = Bibliothèque Sainte-Geneviève

The editions marked with an asterisk* are those used throughout the present work unless otherwise stated.

1

L'Amoureux transi sans espoir

a) *Date*
In *Ep. Fam.* 61 we read:
           . . . ne sçay chose immonde
Avoir escript, fors en l'an mil cinq cens
Que folle amour avoit surprins mon sens
Qui contraignit ma folle main escrire
L'aymant transy, voulant amour descrire.
Dont (non à tort) me repenty soubdain
Par ung livret faisant d'amour desdain.
Depuis me mis pour au mal satisfaire
A mes regnards et loups ravissans faire . . .

A slightly different version of the circumstances appears in the preface to the *Angoisses et remedes* in which Bouchet republishes some of these early love poems:

> Au departir de mon imberbe et folle jeunesse, appellé d'aulcuns au secours de leurs amoureuses entreprises, les voyant d'amour improbe surmontez et vaincus, et es destroictz de desperée rage, l'un d'iceux Transi sans espoir, l'aultre esloigné sans cause et accusé de follement aymer, et l'aultre pressé d'amour non voulue, feiz à chascun d'eulx, à leurs prieres et requestes, un lay d'amours, et aussi à une jeune damoiselle seduicte par un desloyal cueur. Et depuis, pour les detourner de si violentes et conciables affections, commençay faire un remede contre leur amoureux mal . . . Certain temps après (qui fut l'an mil cinq cens ung), avant qu'avoir prins fin et conclusion en ces petiz labeurs, ne es Regnars traversans et Loups ravissans, aulcuns imprimeurs de Paris, où lors faisois demourance, plus desireux du remplissement de leurs bourses que de leur honneur ne du mien, avoient trouvé moien de retirer partie de mes compositions petites, et les avoient incorrectement imprimées, et à icelles baillé nom et tiltre à leur plaisir, dont depuis y eut procès en la court de Parlement diffini à la confusion d'aulcuns desdictz Imprimeurs. (a2 ro–vo)

In both these accounts only the love poetry from the *Amoureux transi* is considered and ascribed to approximately 1500. Other poems in the collection can be dated earlier than this; in particular the poem on the Italian wars of Charles v iii may well have been one of the poems presented to the King in 1496. The epitaph for Charles v iii presumably dates from 1498 or soon after.

Thus the *Amoureux* undoubtedly contains some of Bouchet's earliest verse. It is however not certain that it was the first of his works to be printed. Bouchet clearly associates the printing of this work with the printing of the *Renards,* both having been brought about by the unscrupulous behaviour of Paris printers. The first edition of the *Renards,* published by Vérard, can, as will be seen, be ascribed with fair certainty to the period between September 1503 and May 1504. The Vérard *Amoureux,* almost certainly the first edition, cannot have been printed earlier than 1502, because of epitaphs for a 'lieutenant de Poitou' who must be Maurice Claveurier, d. 1502. Moreover all the existing editions of the *Amoureux* describe the author as 'procureur à Poitiers'. Bouchet appears still to have spent much of 1503 in Paris. From the address of the Vérard edition, 'à Paris devant la grant eglise nostre dame', Macfarlane (p.xi and no.154) gives the date as after September 1503, and suggests 1507 (accepted by *Inventaire, c.*1507, 33). One might perhaps have expected it to be more nearly contemporary with the *Renards,* but, on the other hand, the other Paris editions copying Vérard's appear to date from well after

1507; the earliest may be as late as 1512.

b) *Later Versions*

Two of the love poems, *L'Amoureux transy* and *L'Enfant banny*, together with the *Monologue de Raison*, are rewritten for the *Angoisses et remedes*. A *Complaincte de la femme sur le sarcueil de son mary* is recast to form *Ep. Fam.* 2, and the *Lectre envoyée par M.D. à une jeune damoiselle* and the *Lettre envoyée à une fiancée* become respectively *Ep. Fam.* 3 and 4. Out of six *Aultres ballades contre les adveuglez mondains* four were also present in the *Renards* and all were rewritten for the additional *rondeaux et ballades* which follow the *Chapelet*. Three major pieces are never reproduced: *Comment ledict amoureux transy sans espoir se complaint des estatz sur le voyage et guerre de Naples*, a prayer to the Virgin and the *Chronique du feu Roy Charles*.

c) *The Editions*

1. **L'amoureux transy sans espoir*. (col.): Cy finissent les faitz de l'amoureux transy (facteur de ce present livre) maistre Jehan bouchet procureur à poictiers Imprimés à paris par honnorable homme Anthoine Verard, marchant libraire, Demorant à Paris devant la grant eglise nostre Dame; s.d. (1507?).
   4°, goth., BL C.34.g.6(1), MC iv, E.79, Aur.122,843, Inv. c.1507, 33. Davies, *Fairfax Murray*, 1, pp.50–2.

2. —, Paris, Veufve feu Jehan Trepperel, 'en la rue neufve nostre dame A l'enseigne de l'escu de France'; s.d.
   4°, goth., Roth.4, 2826, MC iv, E.78, Aur.122.846.

3. —, Paris, Jehan Jehannot, 'Imprimeur et libraire juré de l'université de Paris, Demourant en la rue neufve nostre dame A l'enseigne de L'escu de France'; s.d.
   4°, goth., BN Rés. Ye.365, Rés. Y².930, Aur.122.844.

4. —, Paris, Jehan Janot, 'Imprimeur et Libraire juré de l'université de Paris, demourant à l'enseigne sainct Jehan baptiste en la rue neufve nostre dame près saincte Geneviefve des ardans'; s.d.
   4°, goth., BN Rés. Ye.364, Aur.122.844.
   (These three eds (2–4) probably appeared in the order given above between about 1512 and 1518. According to Renouard, Jean Trepperel died by 1512 at the latest. Jehan Jehannot practised from 1498 to 1522; between 1512 and 1517 he was associated with Trepperel's widow 'à l'enseigne de l'escu de France . . .', he then practised alone 'à l'enseigne Sainct Jehan Baptiste . . .')

5. (—, Lyons, Olivier Arnoullet, 1507? 4°. Hamon.)

2
Les Regnars traversant

a) *Date*

In the passages quoted in the last section Bouchet ascribes the composition of the *Renards* to 1500–01. The manuscript revision also gives an account of the circumstances of composition and publication, and this suggests that the work was first conceived in the light of texts by Brant published in 1497 and 1498:

> . . . Je, Jehan Bouchet de Poictiers, qui en ce livre me nomme le Traverseur des voies perilleuses, après la premiere traduction de latin en françois de la Nef des Folz, où pour resver je occupay mon petit entendement, ennuyé des abuz du monde et mesprisant la façon de vivre des mondains en tous estatz, deliberay en esjouir ma fantasie, et considerant qu'à ce me pourroient grandement servir vingt et huit vers et metres elegamment composez par ce notable docteur messir Sebastian Brand, qui premierement composa en langue theutonique lad. Nef des Foulz, sur iceulx vers et metres . . . je commençay soubz la conduicte et inspiracion divine rediger par escript mes fantasies par ung petit traicté intitullé le Livre des Renars, esperant le parachever, ce qui ne me fut lors possible. Et pource que [vo] je trouvay les loups pevers servir à ma matiere, voulu les y emploier. Si du tout redigeay par escript sept ou huit cayers, lesquelz avoient depuis esté transportez par moiens ne sçay quelz entre les mains d'aucuns libraires qui ont iceulx imprimez et imposé tiltre et acteur à leur plaisir . . . [f.1] ro

However, he seems to have been writing part at least of the work after 30 January 1503 and before 30 January 1504, since he says, 'Jeune suys et n'ay pas des ans trente, non vingt et huyt' (a2 ro). Moreover, in the chapter entitled 'Des signes advenuz puis dix ans en ça . . .' (e6 ro) he mentions the crime of a heretic in Paris which in the *Annales* he dates as 25 August 1503. He also refers to red crosses which appeared at Liège 'depuis trois ans'; these occurred in August 1501. He is therefore probably writing quite shortly before his 28th birthday—towards the end of 1503. Michel Le Noir's edition, which copies the Vérard folio edition, including small, coarse copies of the set of woodcuts depicting foxes, is dated 21 May 1504. The Vérard folio edition can therefore be firmly dated between September 1503 and May 1504, probably early in the year 1504 (the year suggested by Picot). The date of 22 March 1502 [o.s.] given by some catalogues is a date given at n1 ro in the first Vérard edition in the long poem by Jean de Remin revised for this collection—it replaces the date 1366 that appears in the original. Although it cannot be regarded as the date of printing it provides a *terminus a quo* that helps to confirm the conclusion already reached.

On 3 June 1504, at the request of André de La Vigne, the Parlement prohibited Le Noir and any other printer from printing or
selling the *Vergier d'honneur* and the *Renards* for a year. There is one
poem by La Vigne in the Le Noir edition, but his interest is hard to
explain—Lachèvre suggests that he may have compiled the original
edition for Vérard (*Recueil*, p.136).
Vérard later produced a 4° edition in which the woodcuts were
cut down slightly (cf. Davies, *Fairfax Murray*, 1, p.50). Macfarlane,
at nos 149 and 182, wrongly dates the 4° edition as 1500–03, and the
folio edition as 1510?, an error that has caused considerable confusion to bibliographers.

b) *Later Versions*
In his article Picot discusses the authorship of the various works in
the collection. The *Renards* is obviously by Bouchet, and there seems
no reason to doubt that the section in verse on *folles fiances* is also his.
Apart from a number of *ballades* that appear in the *Amoureux* and
that are revised for the *Chapelet* (being reproduced subsequently in
the *Opuscules* and the *Généalogies*) the only revised version prepared
by Bouchet is that contained in the manuscript once owned by
Richard and now in the Bibliothèque Municipale de Poitiers. This is
a radically revised version of the *Renards* alone. The verse is corrected with regard to the cesuras, which indicates revision in or
after 1515, but there is some evidence to suggest that the revision
was undertaken within about ten years of the original edition. The
manuscript itself was probably made in 1531 (see *infra*, section 23).

c) *Editions* ❦
1. **Les regnars traversant les perilleuses voyes des folles fiances du monde
   Composées par Sebastien brand, lequel composa la nef des folz
   derrenierement Imprimée à Paris Et autres plusieurs choses composées par autres facteurs.* (Col.): Cy finist le livre des renars
   traversant les voyes perilleuses des folles fiances du monde:
   imprimé à paris pour anthoine verard. S.d. [between September 1503 and May 1504].
   Fol., goth, BL C.57.f.4, BN Rés. Yh.7, Roth.3, 2583.
   (Macfarlane (182), wrongly dated 1510? See Davies, *Fairfax
   Murray*, 1, pp.47–50. Isaac attributes the actual printing of
   the folio edition to G. Cousteau, 1503?, and the BL copy of
   the 4° edition to Pierre Le Dru, 1505?, dates that accord
   perfectly with the rest of the evidence. The *Index Aureliensis*,
   122.841, does not distinguish between a folio and a 4° edition
   but refers to four or five different editions printed for Vérard.
   The *Inventaire* gives fol. eds at *c*.1503, 17 and *c*.1510, 36; 4° ed.
   at *c*.1504, 19.)

2. —, Paris, Vérard, s.d.
    4°, goth., BL C.97.bb.1(1), BN 8° Z.Don.594(321) (impf.).
    BN Vélins 1103, in which the woodcuts are painted, ap-
    pears to be the same edition. But there were two or three
    different printings; see Mortimer, *Harvard*, 1, pp.142–4.
    (Macfarlane (149)—wrongly dated 1501–03.)
3. —, Paris, Michel Le Noir, 21 May 1504 (probably earlier than
    Vérard 4° ed. described above, 2).
    Fol., goth., BN Rés. Yh.61, Bod. 4° Buchanan d.36,
    Aur.122.842, Inv. 1504, 18.
4. —, Paris, Philippe Le Noir, 1522.
    4°, goth., BL 88.a.23, SG 4° Y.426[25], Aur.122.856.
5. —, Paris, Philippe Le Noir, for Denis Janot, 25 January 1530
    (o.s.?).
    4°, goth., BN Rés. Yh.60, BMP DP.1738; different col. MC
    vi, G.17. Rawles 5, Aur.122.869.

Dutch Translation
6. *De loose vossen der werelt*, Brussels, T. van der Noot, 1517.
    4°, goth. See Nijhoff and Kronenberg, *Nederlandische Biblio-
    graphie van 1500 tet 1540*, Tweede deel, Gravenhage, 1940,
    p.168, §2553. Aur.122.850.

German Translation
7. *Von den losen füchsen dieser welt*, Frankfurt, [1546].
    4°, BL 721.g.23, Aur.122.911.
8. —, Dresden, 1585.
    4°, BL 3905.g.104(1), Aur.122.919.   •

3
La Déploration de l'église

a) *Date*
Both the privilege and the colophon of the first edition are dated 15
May 1512. Bouchet appears to have been imitating d'Auton's *Epître
élégiaque*, which can be dated between 18 Feb. and 11 April 1512. The
Déploration was thus probably printed promptly after its compos-
ition.

b) *Later Versions*
A revised version appears in the *Opuscules,* and this is reproduced
with some slight further revisions in the *Généalogies*, 1545.

c) *The Editions*
1. **La deploration de l'eglise militante sur ses persecutions interiores et
    exteriores et imploration de aide en ses adversitez par elle soustenues
    en l'an mil cinq cens dix : et cinq cens unze : que presidoit en la chaire*

monseigneur sainct pierre Julius Secundus. Composée par le traver-
seur des voies perilleuses. (Col.): . . . imprimée à Paris à la rue
judas pres les carmes. L'an mil cinq cens et douze le quin-
ziesme Jour de may pour Guillaume eustace libraire et relieur
de livres juré de l'université de paris demourant à la rue de la
juifrie à l'enseigne des deux Sagittaires. Et là se vendent ou
au palays a la grant salle au troiziesme pillier.
8°, goth., BN Rés. Ye.1635, Vélins 2242; Roth. 1, 504; JR
13749, Aur.122.845, Inv. *c.*1512, 255.

(This edition has a privilege from the Paris Parlement
dated 15 May 1512 and granted to the printer for two years.
At the end of the volume there is some Latin verse by B. Dar-
danus for J. Oliverius that has no connection with Bouchet's
work; see note in Rothschild Cat.)

2. —, s.l., s.d.
8°, goth., BL C.53.a.10 (impf., without title page),
C.107.k.2(5) (a fragment, quire B, possibly of this edition).
The marginal annotation of the original is lost in this edition.

4
L'Epistre d'Henri VII

a) *Date*
The poem is dated St Matthew's day (21 Sept.) 1512. There are two
apparently early anonymous editions. In the *Chapelet* in a prefatory
letter to Charles de La Trémoille, Bouchet complains that the 'epistre
d'Angleterre' had been printed 'soubdain et faulcement' (f.xxxiiii
ro)—probably a reference to this work rather than to the *Epître de
Marie.*

b) *Later Versions*
Bouchet published a revised version in 1545 as *Ep. Fam.* 1. In 1544
another edition had appeared which, published anonymously, incorporates a) corrections throughout the poem that eliminate epic
and lyric cesuras, b) passages that alter the sense of the poem and
make it apply to François 1er and Charles v instead of Louis xii and
Julius ii; these passages contain epic cesuras. It is clear that this
edition is an unauthorised reworking of Bouchet's own corrected
version of his poem which, if the dates of printing as given here are
to be believed, must have circulated in manuscript before he himself
had it printed as *Ep. Fam.* 1. The *Ep. Fam* has the stylistic corrections
but maintains the original subject of the poem. (This explanation
replaces the one offered p.34 n.1 in my article, 'Letters from the
Elysian fields'.)

c) *The Editions*
1. *Epistre envoyée par feu Henry roy dangleterre à Henry son filz huytiesme*
   de ce nom à Present regnant oudict Royaulme, s.l., s.d.
   8°, goth., BN Rés. Ye.3973.
2. *Epistre envoyée Des champs Elisées au Roy Henry d'engleterre à present*
   regnant Audit royaulme, s.l., s.d.
   8°, goth., BN Rés. Ye.1370.
   (These two editions are described and the poem reproduced in *Montaiglon, Recueil*, vol.3, pp.26–71.)
3. *L'Esprit d'Henry septiesme, jadis roy d'Angleterre, à Henry huitiesme à*
   present regnant, Lyons, Macé Bonhomme, 1544.
   4°, BL C.34.g.13 (catalogued under *Henry VII*), Ars. 8°
   H.15994.

5
Le Temple de Bonne Renommée

a) *Date*
Printed in January 1517, the work commemorates Charles de La
Trémoille, who died from injuries sustained at Marignano in Sep-
tember 1515.

b) *Later Versions*
None apart from unauthorised Paris editions.

c) *The Editions*
1. **Le temple de bonne renommée, et repos des hommes et femmes illustres,*
   trouvé par le Traverseur des voies perilleuses en plorant le tres
   regretté deces du feu prince de Thalemont, unique filz du Chevalier
   et Prince sans reproche. (Col.): . . . Imprimé à Paris pour Galliot
   du pré . . . Et fut achevé de imprimer le second jour de janvier
   mil cinq cens et seize (o.s.).
   4°, goth., BN Rés. Ye.357, Roth.1, 505, Aur.122.849, Inv.
   1516, 1279.
   (The privilege for the printer from the King for two years is
   dated 10 January 1516, 'Et de nostre regne le troisiesme' (i.e.
   1517). Dedicatory letter to Charles, Duke of Bourbon.)
2. —, Paris, Veufve feu Jehan Trepperel et Jehan Jehannot, 'En la
   Rue neufve nostre Dame, A l'enseigne de l'escu de France',
   s.d.
   4°, goth., BN Rés. Ye.289, 355 and 356.
3. —, Paris, [M. or P. Le Noir], 'Imprimé à l'enseigne de la Rose
   blanche couronnée', s.d.
   4°, goth., BL 1073.i.2, Aur.122.852.
4. —, (Lyons), Olivier Arnoullet, 1538.
   8°, Aur.122.893.

5. (—, Paris, Alain Lotrian, s.d. Hamon). Not found by Tchemerzine.

6

Le Chappellet des princes

a) *Date*

The *Chapelet* was written for the son of Charles de La Trémoille and
contains a dedicatory letter to Charles; it was therefore composed
before September 1515. As it contains a discussion of the rule concerning the cesura, which Bouchet apparently learned from Louis
de Ronsard *c*.1515, it cannot have been composed long before his
patron's death. Bouchet complains that part of it had already been
printed without his permission along with the 'Epistre d'Angleterre'
(f.xxxiiii ro), but no such edition appears to survive (although some
of the additional *Ballades* had already appeared in the *Renards* and
the *Amoureux transi*). The first edition known is that of 1517, in a
collection that begins with works by Chastellain and Ghillebert de
Lannoy. The *Chapelet* itself is followed by a collection of *Rondeaulx et
ballades* by Bouchet, and also the *Epistre de la royne Marie*, a letter on
the death of Louis xii (d. 1 Jan. 1515) supposedly sent by Queen
Mary to her brother, Henry viii—this had been commissioned by
Charles de La Trémoille. (Cf. section 23, *Manuscripts*.)

b) *Later Versions*

Bouchet published corrected versions of the *Chapelet* and the *Rondeaux et ballades* in the *Opuscules* and in the 1545 *Généalogies*. The
Epître de Marie reappears in the *Annales* as a sort of extended epitaph
for Louis xii, and again as *Ep. Fam.* 14.

c) *The Editions*

1. **Le temple Jehan Bocace, de la ruyne d'aulcuns nobles malheureux, faict
par George son imitateur. ₵ L'instruction du jeune Prince. ₵ Le
Chappellet des princes, en cinquante rondeaulx, et cinq Ballades
faict et composé par le Traverseur de voyes perilleuses. ₵ L'epistre
de la royne Marie, à son frere Henry roy D'angleterre faict et
composée par le Traverseur de voyes perilleuses.* Imprimé à Paris
pour Galliot du pré marchant libraire demourant sus le pont
nostre Dame, à l'enseigne de la Gallée, ayant sa bouticques
en la grand salle du Pallays, au second pillier. Mil cinq
cens.xvii. April 18th, 1517.
   Fol., goth., BL G.10232, BN Rés. Z.349, Roth. 1, 506,
   Aur.135.873, Inv. 1517, 1571.
     (Privilege for the printer from the King for two years is
   dated 10 January 1516—the same as for the *Temple*. Dedicatory letter to Charles de La Trémoille.)

2. *Le Chappellet des princes* . . . *par Maistre Jehan Bouchet,* Paris, 'en la rue neufve Nostre Dame à l'anseigne Sainct Jehan Baptiste pres Saincte Genefvieve des Ardans', [D. Janot], 1536.
8°, Bib. Versailles, Rés. in-12-E454C (impf.), Rawles 44.
(Taken from the version in the *Opuscules*.)

7

L'Histoire et cronicque de Clotaire

a) *Date*
Bouchet says in the dedicatory letter to the Queen that he began this work under Charles VIII and was encouraged by Anne of Brittany, but that he corrected his early composition in the light of further study. The first edition can only be dated from the privilege, 27 Jan. 1518.

b) *Later Versions*
The work was not revised for later editions.

c) *The Editions*
1. **L'histoire et cronicque de Clotaire Premier de ce nom. vii. roy des Françoys. et monarque des gaules. Et de sa tresillustre espouse: madame saincte Radegonde extraicte au vray de plusieurs cronicques antiques et modernes.* (Col.): Ceste vie a esté imprimée à poictiers par sire Enguilbert de marnef. libraire juré de ladicte université. demourant à l'enseigne du Pellican devant le palis dud. poictiers. Le   jour du moys de   L'an mil cinq cens,   . Et sont à vendre au pellican aud. poictiers et aussi à paris. [1518].
4°, goth., BN Rés. D.67949(1) and Rés. Lb4.4; MC IV, E.95, Aur.122.851; Rép.115, E. de Marnef 3; Inv. *c.*1517, 1552.
(Privilege for the printer from the King for two years is dated Amboise, 27 January 1517, 'et de notre regne le quatriesme', i.e. 1518. As well as a dedicatory letter to Queen Claude there is a *rondeau* to the Duchess of Valois, Jeanne d'Orléans.)
2. —, Poitiers, Enguilbert de Marnef, March 4th 1527, (o.s.).
4° goth., BN Rés. Lb4.4.A and 4A.α, Lb4.4.B (impf., 8ff. with one different woodcut), BMP DP.1142, Aur.122.865, Rép.115, E. de Marnef 16 (and 17?).
(See La Bouralière, *Imp.,* p.69—a simple reprinting of the earlier edition, with no revisions.)
3. —, Poitiers, Jean Blanchet, s.d.
8°, Ars. 8° H.5795.
(See La Bouralière, *Imp.,* pp.238–9.)
4. (—, Poitiers, 1524, 4°—mentioned only by Panzer. See La Bouralière, *Imp.,* p.301.)

8

Le Labirynth de Fortune

a) *Date*

Artus Gouffier, in whose memory the book was written, died in 1519. Liminary letters from and to Ardillon are dated 16 October and 1 November 1522. The privilege that covers the two Poitiers editions, one undated and one dated 1524, is dated 6 November 1522. It is assumed that the undated edition was the first and that it appeared in or soon after November 1522.

b) *Later Versions*

No revised versions.

c) *The Editions*

1. *Le Labirynth de fortune et Sejour des trois nobles dames Composé par l'acteur des Renars traversans, et loups ravissans surnommé le traverseur des voyes perilleuses* . . . Et sont à vendre à Paris en la rue sainct Jacques devant sainct yves et à poictiers devant le pallays au pellican par Enguilbert de marnef Et à l'imprimerie à la celle et devant les cordeliers par Jacques Bouchet Imprimeur. S.d. (1522?).

   4°, goth., Roth.1, 507; BMP DP.119 (impf.—lacks A8, which should have a woodcut vo depicting Icarus and Daedalus flying out of the Labyrinth); MC iv, E.82 presents slight differences. Aur.122.857, Rép.115, J.Bouchet 2, (see also 1 bis, and E. de Marnef 4 bis).

   (Privilege for the printer from the King for three years, dated S. Germain-en-Laye, 6 November 1522. Prefaced by a Latin prose epistle by Ardillon and a reply in French prose by Bouchet; dedicatory letter to Marguerite d'Alençon; at the end of the volume a prose letter to Jacques Prévost and an exchange of *épîtres* with Jean d'Auton.)

2. *—*, Poitiers, Enguilbert de Marnef and Jacques Bouchet (printer) 26 March 1524.

   4°, goth., BL 85.e.30 (impf.), BN Rés. p.Ye.361, BMP DM.9 (impf.), Aur.122.859, Rép.115, J.Bouchet 10.

3. —, Paris, Alain Lotrian, 'demourant à la rue neufve nostre dame à l'enseigne de l'escu de France', s.d.

   4°, goth., BN Rés. Ye.353, MC iii, F.1, Aur. 122.854.

4. —, Paris, Philippe Le Noir, 'demourant en la grant Rue sainct Jacques à l'enseigne de la Roze blanche couronnée. xxxii c', s.d.

   4°, goth., BN Rés. Ye.352, 8° Z.Don.594(26), Bod. Douce BB.507.

5. —, '. . . xxxiii', Paris, Philippe Le Noir, s.d.

   4°, goth., BN Rés. Ye.354, Maz. Rés. 10.832, Aur.122.853.

9
Cantiques et oraisons contemplatives de l'ame penitente

a) *Date*

In 2 *Ep. Mor.* 1 Bouchet places the composition of the *Cantiques* between the *Chapelet* and the other *rondeaux et ballades—c.*1515. In *Ep. Fam.* 41 they appear in a list after the *Labyrinthe* and the *Epître de Justice.* The manuscript in which the collection survives is dedicated to the widow of Gouffier (d. 1519); his widow is also intended as the recipient of the *Labyrinthe*, but is addressed in no other work by Bouchet. It seems likely that the manuscript at least dates from about the same period as the *Labyrinthe.* I have also argued that the tone of the introduction and of some of the prayers suggests that it was written before the threat from Lutheranism was fully recognised.

b) *Later Versions*

The only printed version reproduces the first two groups of prayers alone, and omits from them the translations of the *Miserere* and the *Confiteor.*

c) *The Editions*

(See section 23, *Manuscripts,* for the complete work.)

1. *Heures à l'usaige de Poictiers,* Poitiers, Jehan Coussot for Jacques Bouchet and Nicolas Pelletier. 20 Dec. 1525, BN Vélins 1655. Bound after the Hours are 8ff., A1–8, in a smaller type, which reproduce the prayers from ff.3–28 of the manuscript. They are anonymous. La Bouralière, *Imp.,* p.169, not knowing the author, said that these leaves 'n'ont rien de poitevin'. The binding of the volume is a sixteenth-century one, and like the Hours the prayers are printed on vellum.

2. (La Croix du Maine mentions various devotional works by Bouchet that do not appear to survive: the following may have connections with these prayers, or with the poems in the *Triomphes,* or it may be a separate composition:

   Les Cantiques de la simple et devote Ame amoureuxe et epouse de notre Sauveur Jesus-Christ: Et comme ladite Ame se doit preparer pour avoir l'amour et la grace de sondit Epoux: aussi y sont les Meditations sur les sept jours de la semaine par Jean Bouchet.

   16°, Jean Mousnier, Lyons 1540. Listed by Baudrier 1, 293, Aur.122.900, but no copies are known.)

10
Annales d'Acquitaine

a) *Date*

The first edition of 1524 covers events up to 1519. In the *Histoire de Clotaire* Bouchet already refers his readers to what he calls his *annalles et epitaphes des roys de France*. Work on the *Annales* and what he subsequently published as the *Anciennes et modernes généalogies* presumably went hand in hand, and from the evidence of 2 *Ep. Mor.* 11 was started in about 1514.

b) *Later Versions*

Five later versions include authoritative corrections and additions. That of 1526 is simply corrected, but those of 1532, 1535, 1545 and 1557 are all extended to cover events of the period since the last major edition. Paris editions after 1535 copied the 1535 edition but also contain continuations that are not by Bouchet and that he disclaimed in the edition of 1545.

Some of the verse from the *Annales,* particularly epitaphs, is reproduced in the 1545 *Généalogies*.

c) *The Editions*

The six major editions will be listed first:

1. *Les annalles d'acquitaine faictz et gestes en sommaire des Roys de France et D'angleterre Et des pays de Naples et de Milan* . . . Et sont à vendre à Paris en la rue sainct Jacques devant sainct yves et à Poictiers devant le pallays au Pellican par Enguilbert de Marnef. ₵ Et à l'imprimerie A la celle et devant les cordeliers par Jaques Bouchet Imprimeur. (Col.) . . . imprimées aud. lieu pour maistres Enguilbert de marnef et Jaques Bouchet . . . le jour du mois de l'an mil Cinq cens. vingt et quatre.
   Fol., goth., BL G.6385; BN Rés. Lkl.25α, Rés. Lkl.25.β; BMP BM.72; Aur.122.858, Rép.115, J. Bouchet 9.
   (On the title page: 'Cum privilegio supreme curie parlamenti'. Introduced by a verse *épître* to Ardillon and a dedication to Louis de La Trémoille. Latin verse by N. Petit on title page, Latin prose *épîtres* by J. Quintin and B. Perreau; the latter appears only in this edition.)

2. *Les Annalles d'acquitaine faictz et gestes en sommaire des Roys de France et D'angleterre Et des pays de Naples et de Milan, Nouvellement corrigées avec aucunes addicions de la duché de Bourgongne et comté de Flandres,* Paris and Poitiers, Enguilbert de Marnef and Jacques Bouchet, 3 March 1525 (o.s.).
   Fol., goth., BL 596.h.11, BN Rés. Lkl.25.A, BMP BP.316 and BM.73, Aur.122.860, Rep.115, J. Bouchet 12.
   (On the title page: 'Cum privilegio'.)

3. *Les Corectes et Additionnées Annales D'acquitaine. Faitz et gesles en sommaire des Roys de France et D'angleterre et pays de Naples et de Milan. Nouvellement corrigées et additionnées par L'acteur mesmes jusques à L'an Mil cinq cens Trente et ung*, Poitiers, Jean and Enguilbert de Marnef and Jacques Bouchet, 1 March 1531 (o.s.).

    Fol., goth., BL 596.h.12; BN Rés. Lkl.25.C; BMP BM.76, BP.43 and BP.44; Aur.122.871, Rép.115, J. & E. de Marnef 3.

    (Privilege for three years granted to printers at Bouchet's request at the *Grands Jours* in Poitiers, 22 October 1531. *Carmen elegum* by N. Petit addressed to T. Frétard only in this edition, title page vo.)

4. *Les Annales D'acquitaine. Faictz & gestes en sommaire des Roys de France et D'angleterre & pays de Naples & de Milan. Tiercement reveues et corrigées par L'acteur mesmes jusques en L'an Mil cinq cens Trente & cinq*, Poitiers, Jacques Bouchet (and sold by J. and E. de Marnef), 18 July 1535.

    Fol., BL 596.h.13, BMP BM.77, Aur.122.879, Rép.115, J. Bouchet 12 bis and 30, J. and E. de Marnef 6.

    (No privilege.)

5. *Les Annales d'Aquitaine . . . quartement reveues & corrigées par l'Autheur mesmes: jusques en l'an mil cinq cents quarante cinq*, Poitiers, J. and E. de Marnef (and sold by Jacques Bouchet), 1545.

    Fol., BL 9200.i.20; BN Lkl.25.G; BMP BM.80 and BP.41; Aur.122.908, Rép.115, J. and E. de Marnef 48; Mortimer, *Harvard*, 1, pp.144–5.

    (Privilege granted to Bouchet for four years by the King, dated 3 January 1543 (o.s.).)

6. **Les Annales d'Aquitaine . . . reveues et corrigées par l'Autheur mesmes: jusques en l'an mil cinq cens cinquante & sept*, Poitiers, E. de Marnef, 1557.

    Fol., BL 596.h.15; BN Lkl.25.H, Rés. Lkl.25.H; BMP BP.42, BM.81 and BM.82; also some copies printed by 'les Bouchets frères': BN Lkl.25.I. Aur.122.915, Rép.115, J. and E. de Marnef 101.

    (On the title page: 'Avec privilege du Roy'.)

Other Editions

7. —, s.l., s.d. (Copy of 1526 edition).

    Fol., goth., BL 596.h.10; BN Rés. Lkl.25.B; BMP BM.74 and BM.75; Aur.122.862 and 122.864, Rép.115, J. Bouchet 15.

8. —, . . . *Reveues et corrigées par L'acteur mesmes jusques en l'an Mil cinq cens trente et cinq et de nouvel jusques en l'an Mil cinq cens XXXVI*, Paris, Galliot Du Pré, 1537; printed by Nicolas Couteau, 22 December 1536.

Fol., goth., BN Rés. Lkl.25.D, Ars. 4° H.3913, Bod. Buchanan d.11. (Also 27 December—Tchemerzine.) The same edition for Ambroise Girault, 'en la rue sainct Jacques à l'enseigne du Pellican, devant sainct Yves', Cat. Bib. Muşée Thomas Dobrée, 733.(Aur.122.889).

9. —, . . . *Reveues et corrigées par L'acteur mesmes jusques en l'an Mil cinq cens trente et cinq et de nouvel jusques en l'an Mil cinq cens XXXVII*, Paris, 1 June 1537.

Fol., goth. Found with the addresses of several different booksellers: Richard Du Hamel, 'en la rue sainct Jacques . . . faisant le coing de la rue des Mathurins', BN Rés. Lkl.25.E, BMP BM.78: Jean Macé, 'en la rue sainct Jacques', Camb. Adams B.2580, Ars. 4° H.3915; (Pierre Sergent?), 'a l'enseigne sainct Nicocas (sic)', Ars. 4° H.3914; (Guillaume Lebret—Hamon, La Bouralière, *Bib.*). References to other copies are collected together in notes at the beginning of the BMP copy of the Du Hamel edition: (Jean André, 'en la grant salle du Palais au premier piller', private collection; Jacques Kerver, 'en la rue sainct Jacques à l'enseigne des deux cochets', Cat. Vaugeois (libraire à Niort), février 1906, no.3259; Charles Langelier, 'en la grande salle du Palais au premier pillier', Cat. Durel 238, Nov. 1905 no.3981—also in Hamon, (Cat. Durel no.82); Denys Janot, 'en la rue neufve nostre dame à l'enseigne sainct Jehan baptiste', (Cat. Gougy, Sept. 1896 no.123 and Feb. 1899 no.972). Also mentioned, from Cat. Lemallier, août 1907, no.5007, Antoine Girault, 'en la rue Sainct Jacques à l'enseigne du Pellican devant Sainct-Yves, 1538.) Rawles 61, Aur.122.889.

10. —, . . . *reveues et corrigées par l'acteur mesmes jusques en l'an Mil cinq cens trente sept, et de nouvel jusques en l'an Mil cinq cens quarante*, Paris, 22 May 1540.

Fol., goth. Several booksellers: Ambroise Girault, BL C.74.d.15, BN Lkl.25.F; Nicolas Gilles, 'en la rue sainct Jacques', BMP BM.79; Charles Langelier, 'en la grant salle du palais au premier pillier', Ars. 4° H.3916; Pierre Sergent, 'en la rue neufve nostre Dame . . . à l'enseigne sainct Nicolas', Ars. 4° H.3917 (impf.); (M. de la Porte, Tchemerzine); J. Petit, Cat. Bib. Douai 4° P.1183; F. Regnault, Cat. Bib. Amiens, Hist.3341; G. Du Pré, Cat. Bib. Besançon, Hist.4424; G. Lebret, Cat. Bib. Troyes, Hist.8267. Aur.122.901.

11. (—, Poitiers, 1607, fol.; Hamon, via Brunet. La Bouralière, *Bib.*, p.74, doubts its existence.)

12. —, . . . *Augmentées de plusieurs pièces rares et historiques, extraictes des Bibliothèques, & recueillies par A. Mounin*, Poitiers, A. Mounin, 1644.

Fol. BL 182.f.14; BN Lkl.25.J, Rés. Lkl.25.J, Rés. Lkl.25.J.α, Roth.3, 2342; BMP B(L),848, BM.83, Salle de lecture 184.

13. (*Louange de la ville de Poictiers,* Poitiers, 1528, 4°—Tchemerzine; Rép.115, E. de Marnef 18—perhaps an extract from the *Annales?*)

11
Opuscules

a) *Date*

Apart from the *Epître de Justice,* dated Autumn 1524, the contents are new versions of the *Déploration,* the *Chapelet* and the *Rondeaux et ballades.* Revisions to the *Déploration* include an attack on Lutheranism and a reference to the disaster at Pavia which had occurred earlier in the year the *Opuscules* were printed, 1525.

b) *Later Versions*

The *Epître de Justice* is reproduced as 2 *Ep. Mor.* 5, and the other works reappear in the 1545 *Généalogies.*

c) *The Editions*

1. *Opuscules du traverseur des voyes perilleuses nouvellement par luy reveuz amendez et corrigez. ₡ Epistre de justice a l'instruction et honneur des ministres d'icelles. ₡ Le chappellet des princes. ₡ Ballades morales. ₡ Deploracion de l'eglise excitant les princes à paix.* (Col.): Imprimez à Poictiers par Jaques bouchet A la celle. le xv. jour D'aougst. L'an Mil cinq cens ving cinq.

   4°, goth., M C ɪ v, E.81, Cat. Bib. Arras B.L.1736, Aur.122.861, Rep.115, J. Bouchet 13.

   (On title page: 'Cum privilegio'. The work is prefaced by a Latin prose epistle by Trojan and *épîtres* to and from Germain Emery.)

2. *—, Poitiers, Jacques Bouchet, 9 April 1526.

   4°, goth., BL G.18193, BN Rés. Ye.359, Roth.1, 508, Aur.122.863, Rép.115, J. Bouchet 16.

3. —, s.l., s.d.

   4°, goth., BL 1073.d.33; BN Rés. Ye.358; (Ars. 8° B.L.8747 also s.l., s.d., is not identical.) Aur.122.855.

4. (—, Paris, 'par la veufve de feu Jehan janot tenant et demourant en la rue de Marchepallu à l'enseigne de la corne de cerf', s.d. Hamon, Tchemerzine.)

5. —, Rouen, Jehan Burges, s.d.

   8°, goth., BN Rés. p.Ye.323.

The *rondeaux et ballades* from this collection were sometimes printed separately:

6. *Cy après suyvent XIII rondeaulx differens. Avec XXV Balades differentes composées par Maistre Jehan Bouchet aultrement dict le traverseur des Voyes perilleuses Procureur à Poictiers,* Paris, Denys Janot, 1536.

8°, BN Rés. Ye.1637, Ars. 8° B.L.11644, Aur.122.884. Rawles
46.
7. —, Rouen, Nicolas Le Roux, s.d.
12°. Tchemerzine, p.80.
8. *La Fleur et triumphe de cent et cinq Rondeaulx* . . . *Et adjousté, xiii
Rondeaulx differans Avec xxv Balades differentes Composées par
Maistre Jehan Bouchet* . . ., Lyons, Jehan Mousnier, 1540.
8°, goth. Baudrier; Tchemerzine, p.80; Aur.122.899.

12
Le Panegyric du Chevallier sans reproche

a) *Date*
Louis de La Trémoille died at Pavia in 1525. The dating of the only
sixteenth-century edition of the *Panégyrique*, 28 March 1527, follows
local custom in beginning the year on 25 March. In 2 *Ep. Mor.* 11
Bouchet lists the *Panégyrique* before the *Anciennes et modernes généalogies*, whose first edition is dated 26 Jan. 1527 (o.s.).

b) *Later Versions*
The work was issued without a privilege and was not reprinted or
copied by other printers, apart from some extracts published by
D. Janot (see section 22). An epitaph for La Trémoille becomes *Gén.
Ep.* 36 and an *épître* in the name of his wife becomes *Ep. Fam.* 26.

c) *The Editions*
1. **Le Panegyric du Chevallier sans reproche*. (Col.): Cy finist le Chevalier sans reproche composé par maistre Jehan Bouchet
Procureur es cours royalles de Poictiers. Imprimé par Jaques
Bouchet demourant aud. Poictiers à la Celle. Et se vendent en
la boutique dudit Bouchet au Pellican pres le Palais. Et fut
achevé le xxviii. jour de mars mil cinq cens xxvii.
4°, goth.; BL 674.b.16 (impf.) and C.125.aaa.5 (impf.); BN
Rés. Ln27.11678 and Rés. Ln27.11678α: BMP DP.118;
Aur.122.866, Rép.115, J. Bouchet 19.
    (Dedications to La Trémoille's great-grandchildren and to
Florimond Robertet. Exchange of *épîtres* with Jean d'Auton.
Latin verse by N. Petit, Nicolaus Valleus Parisiensis, 'I.C.'
and (at end) J. Quintin.)
The *Panégyrique* was reproduced in various abridged forms in eight-
eenth- and nineteenth-century collections:
2. *Collection universelle des Mémoires particuliers relatifs à l'histoire de
    France*, vol.14, London and Paris, 1786.
3. Petitot, *Collection complète des mémoires relatifs à l'histoire de France*,
    sér.1, vol.14, Paris, 1820.
4. Buchon, *Panthéon littéraire*, vol.7, Paris, 1836, 1842.

5. Michaud and Poujoulat, *Nouvelle collection des mémoires pour servir à l'histoire de France*, sér.1, vol.4, Paris, 1837.
6. Sandret, L., *Louis II de la Trémoille . . . d'après le Panégyrique de Jean Bouchet*, Paris, 1881.

13
Les Anciennes et modernes genealogies
des Roys de France

a) *Date*

Bouchet often refers to this work as *Les Epitaphes des Roys Françoys*. In the *Histoire de Clotaire* he refers to his *Annales et epitaphes*, but at the end of the 1524 *Annales* he explains that he has divided the material between two works. The *Anciennes et modernes* were thus probably completed some considerable time before they were printed on 26 January 1528. Some copies of the first edition contain a privilege dated 24 April 1528. The book is dedicated to the Dauphin, and Bouchet says in 2 *Ep. Mor.* 11 that he had presented him with a copy at Bonnivet. It is difficult to determine whether this was a manuscript copy presented in 1526 when the Dauphin was on his way to exile in Spain or, more probably, a manuscript or printed copy presented in 1530 when the Dauphin was on his way back from Spain. None of the liminary pieces makes any reference to Pavia or to the Dauphin's exile.

b) *Later Versions*

The book was even more popular than the *Annales* and was frequently reprinted in Poitiers and in Paris, in 4° or in smaller format. Bouchet gave it a definitive and luxurious folio edition in 1545.

c) *The Editions*

1. *Les Anciennes et modernes genealogies des Roys de France et mesment du roy Pharamond avec leurs Epitaphes et Effigies*. Et sont à vendre à Paris en la rue sainct Jacques Et à Poictiers au Pellican. Et à l'imprimerie à la Celle et devant les Cordeliers par Jacques Bouchet . . . (Col.): . . . Imprimez nouvellement à Poictiers par Jacques bouchet Imprimeur le vingt sixiesme jour de Janvier L'an mil cinq cens vingt et sept (o.s.).
4°, goth. BN Rés. L37.2, BMP C R.152, Aur.122.867, Rép.115, J. Bouchet 20.

(On the title page: 'Cum privilegio'; some copies have an extra leaf bearing a privilege from the King dated 24 April 1528, i.e. later than the date of printing given in the colophon. (La Bouralière, *Imp.*, p.21, Davies, *Fairfax Murray*, 1, pp.52–4.) This privilege was also used for the edition of 1529. Cf. *infra* (14), *Les Triomphes*. The work is dedicated to the Dauphin and also has a prose letter addressed to the Chancellor,

Antoine du Prat, a verse *épître* to Marc de la Mothe au Groing, an *Epigramma* and a *Carmen heroicum* by N. Petit.)

2. —, Poitiers, Jacques Bouchet, 27 November 1529 (privilege dated 24 April 1528).
    4°, goth. BMP DP.1781, Maz.35.846, Aur.122.868, Rép.115, J. Bouchet 22.

3. —, Paris, 1530, 8°—Hamon, Tchemerzine, who reproduces the colophon, pp.51–2.

4. —, Poitiers, Jacques Bouchet (and sold by J. and E. de Marnef), 27 November 1531.
    4°, goth. BL 596.b.11, BN Rés. L37.2.A (title page missing in both these copies); Aur.122.872, Rép.115, J. Bouchet 26.

5. (—, Paris, Vincent Sertenas, 1534, 8°—Hamon, from *Bulletin du Bouquiniste*, 1861, no.4448.)

6. (—, Paris, A. and Ch. Les Angeliers, 1534? 8°—Tchemerzine, pp.53–4, but the col. appears to be dated 1529.)

7. —, Poitiers, Jacques Bouchet (and in some copies sold by J. and E. de Marnef), 12 June 1535.
    4°, goth. BN Rés. 8° L37.2.F; BMP DP.1649, DM.843(1); Ars. 4° H.7134; Maz.35.828 (impf.), 35.967; Aur.122.878, Rép.115, J. Bouchet 29.

8. —, Paris, Galyot Du Pré, 1536.
    16°, BN L37.2.B, Rés. L37.2.B; Roth.2, 2092, BMP DM.844, Aur.122.880.

9. (—, Poitiers, J. Bouchet, 1536, 12°—La Bouralière, *Imp.*, p.302, cites this from Panzer.)

10. —, Poitiers, Jacques Bouchet, 16 July 1537.
    8°, goth. BN Rés. L37.2.D, BMP DP.116, Aur.122.892, Rép.115, J. Bouchet 31.

11. —, Paris, 1537.
    8°, goth. Various booksellers: [J. Petit], 'à l'enseigne de la fleur de lys d'or', BL 9917.aaa.11, BMP DM.847; 'au clos bruneau à l'enseigne de la corne de cerf', Maz. Rés.53.124; A. and Ch. Les Angeliers, 'au premier pillier de la grant salle du palais', BMP DM.845; Jean Longis, 'au Palais en la gallerie par où on va à la chancellerie', (BN Rés. L.37.2.C?— impf.), Roth.2.2093, BMP DM.846; (Guillaume Bonnemere—Tchemerzine and La Bouralière, *Bib.*); ([François Regnault]—Tchemerzine, 'en la grant rue Sainct Jacques à l'enseigne de l'elephant'—La Bouralière, *Bib.*) Aur.122.890.

12. —, Paris, 1539.
    8°, goth. Various booksellers: A. and Ch. Les Angeliers 'en la grant salle du palais au premier et second pilliers'. Maz.33.562, Shaaber, *Pennsylvania*, no.638; 'en la rue neufve nostre dame à l'enseigne de l'escu de France', BMP DM.848; D. Janot, Cat. Vienna; (P. Hermier—La Bouralière, *Bib.*,

Tchemerzine); 'au clos bruneau à l'enseigne sainct Claude', Bod. 8° S.231 Art; Rawles 87, Aur.122.898.

13. —, Paris, 1541.

8°, goth. BN Rés. L37.2.E (impf.) has lacerated title page and the last f. is missing. Various booksellers: (F. Regnault, 'à l'enseigne de l'elephant'—Hamon, Tchemerzine); M. de La Porte, 'à l'enseigne Saint Claude', Cat. Bib. Bordeaux Hist. 5034; (G. du Pré—cited by Brunet, who did not himself know it.) Aur.122.903.

14. *Les Genealogies. Effigies & Epitaphes des Roys de France recentement reveues et corrigées, par l'Autheur mesmes; avecq' plusieurs aultres opuscules . . . On les vend à Poictiers, en la Bouticque de Jacques Bouchet, près les Cordeliers, & à l'enseigne du Pelican par Jehan, & Enguilbert de Marnef, frères. MDXLV.
Fol. BL 136.b.8; BN L37.3, Rés. L37.3α and β, Roth.1, 510; BMP BN.227 and BP.40. Aur.122.909, Rép.115, J. Bouchet 41.

(Privilege granted by the King to Bouchet for four years, dated 3 Jan. 1543, o.s. Apart from the Généalogies this collection contains the following works: Deploration de feu Françoys de Valoys, Daulphin de Viennoys (first edition); Epitaphes de plusieurs personnes (some first ed.); Deploration de feu Monseigneur, Monsieur Françoys de La Tremoille (first ed.); Le Chappelet des Princes; Rondeaulx; Ballades; Deploration de l'Eglise; Dizains moraux sur les apophtegmes et subtiles responses de sept sages de Grece (first ed.); Aultres dizains de plusieurs matieres (first ed.); Des angoysses d'amours Premiere Elegie, Seconde Elegie, Tierce Elegie, Quarte Elegie; Remedes d'amour; Quatrains et cinquains d'aulcuns memorables faictz; Patron pour les filles qui veulent apprendre à escripre (first ed.).

15. (—, 'avec le sommaire des gestes de quarante roys et deux ducs qui regnerent en Germanie sur les Françoys avant Pharamond . . ., s.l., s.d., 12°—Hamon, Tchermerzine, both from Brunet.)

Bouchet's Généalogies are also used in:

16. Epitaphes des Roys de France qui, ont regné depuis le Roy Pharamond, jusques au Roy Francoys premier de ce nom. Avec les Effigies, protraictes au vif, ainsi qu'elles sont taillées en pierre, par ordre en la grant salle du Palais Royal de Paris. Augmentees de mectres en latin, composés par scientifique personne maistre Barthelemy Chasseneu, Bordeaux, Jehan Mentele, alias de Vaten, s.d.
8°. BL C.39.a.17, BN L37.4 and Rés. L37.4. Aur.122.902, Rép.24, J. Mentele 2 (and 1?).

14

Les Triumphes de la noble et amoureuse dame

a) *Date*

Dates given in the text suggest a period of composition between 1527 and 1530. The Soul's letters of remission are dated September 1527; in the *Epître de l'acteur* (+ ro) Bouchet says that he is in his fifty-fourth year (Jan. 1529–Jan. 1530).

The dating of the first edition raises difficulties which were pointed out by Marie Holban. The date of printing given in the colophon is 20 June 1530, but the two theologians' certificates are dated 22 and 27 November 1530 and the privilege is dated 20 February 1530 'et de nostre regne le xvii', i.e. 1531.

The date in the colophon doubtless relates to the main body of the book, foliated i–clxvi, gatherings A–Z, A A–E E. This is preceded by two unfoliated gatherings, a^4 and $+^6$, which contain the privilege, the dedicatory letters, theologians' certificates, list of errata, *Epître de l'acteur* and table of contents. Obviously these gatherings were printed later than the rest of the book. The dedicatory letters are addressed to Queen Eleanor and to Louis de Ronsard, the latter being dated by the sign of the Virgin (14 August–13 September); Ronsard is asked to present the book to the Queen. In 2 *Ep. Mor.* 11 Bouchet says that the Queen was presented with the book when she passed near Poitiers. The sons of François Ier, accompanied by Louis de Ronsard, re-entered France on 1 July 1530, together with Eleanor, who was married to the King on 7 July. The royal party travelled slowly through France to Paris, staying at Dissay and the Château Du Fou in late August and early September. It must have been at this point that the book was presented to the Queen, perhaps in a manuscript copy but equally possibly in printed form with perhaps the *épître* presented separately in M S. Thereafter Bouchet presumably delayed publication of the book until he had had it certified by the theologians and obtained a privilege; the terms of the privilege show that Bouchet himself requested it for the benefit of Jacques Bouchet.

Marie Holban (*art. cit.* pp.143 and 153) assumes that the date in the colophon is a mistake for 1531, and that if Marguerite de Navarre was indeed influenced by the *Triomphes* when she composed the *Miroir* she must have been presented with a manuscript copy in 1530. But it seems more likely that the colophon gives the correct date of printing for the body of the book; Marguerite could thus equally well have received a printed copy at any time from June 1530. The great length of the book and the lack of any surviving manuscripts perhaps make this more probable.

b) *Later Versions*

Bouchet himself made no alterations to the text; only the 1563 Louvain edition has revisions. The book seems to have been extremely popular but was printed only three times in Poitiers, and not after 1533. From 1535 (when Jacques Bouchet's privilege would have expired) editions proliferated in Paris and Bouchet seems to have had no objection to them; Brunet saw a copy with an 'envoi' in Bouchet's own hand; see no.9 (1537). None of these editions was illustrated in spite of the potential visual appeal of the story, but a copy printed in Rennes in 1541 contains numerous miniatures.

c) *The Editions*

1. *Les Triumphes de la noble et amoureuse dame, Et l'art de honnestement aymer. Composé par le Traverseur des voyes perilleuses.* Et sont Imprimez et à vendre à Poictiers à l'imprimerie à la celle, et devant les Cordeliers par Jacques Bouchet Imprimeur. (Col.):
. . . Et imprimé à Poictiers par Jacques Bouchet le xx jour du moy de Juing L'an mil cinq cens trente.
Fol., goth. SG Rés. Y fol.141 inv.201; BMP BM 2(impf.); (BN 4° Z Don.205(13) (impf., B1 to FF2 only)—although the card cat. gives date as 1530, it is not the same edition.); Aur.122.870, Rép.115, J. Bouchet 24.
(Privilege from the King granted to Bouchet on behalf of Jacques Bouchet for four years, dated 20 February 1530 (o.s.). *Epîtres* to Queen Eleanor and Louis de Ronsard; theologians' certificates signed Nicolaus Louandi, 22 November 1530, and Antoine d'Asnières, 27 November 1530.)

2. —, Poitiers, Jacques Bouchet, sold by J. and E. de Marnef, 27 March 1532.
Fol., goth. BL C.107.f.1; Aur.122.873; Rép.115, J. Bouchet 27.

3. —, Poitiers, Jacques Bouchet, sold by J. and E. de Marnef, 15 September 1533.
Fol., goth. Ars. 4° B.L.2862; Aur.122.874; Rép.115, J. Bouchet 28.

4. (—, Paris, Denis Janot, 1534, 8°, goth.—Hamon, Tchermerzine, Rawles 20.)

5. —, Paris, Nicolas Couteau, sold by Galliot Du Pré, 5 August 1535.
Fol., goth. BN Vélins 585; sold by Jacques Kerver, Roth.1, 509. Aur.122.875 and 122.876.

6. —, Paris, Ambroise Girault, 20 June 1536.
Fol., goth. BL C.7.b.2, BMP BM.3 (impf.), Ars. 4° B.L.2863 Rés., Aur.122.882.

7. —, Paris, G. de Bossozel, for Pierre Sergent, 1536.
Fol., goth. BN Rés. Y2.187 and 188; Maz.3.681; Aur.122.881 and 122.883.

8. (—, Paris, Charles L'Angelier, 1536—Hamon).

9. —, Paris, 6 October 1537.

8°, goth. Various booksellers: [J. Macé], 'au clos bruneau à l'enseigne de l'escu de bretaigne', BL 1073.c.2, Ars. 8° B.L.8738; Les Angeliers, Maz. Rés. 45.366; Jean Longis, Munich; P. Hermier, BMP DR.514; ('au clos bruneau, à l'enseigne de la corne de Cerf—Hamon, and Brunet, who mentions a copy with 'un envoi écrit de la main de Bouchet', col.1161.). Aur.122.891.

10. —, Paris, Estienne Caveiller, 6 June 1539.

8°, goth. Various booksellers: Guillaume Lebret, BL C.38.b.3; Henry Pacquot, Camb. Adams B.2583; Simon Colinet, 'au palais en la gallerie par où on va à la Chancellerie', Ars. 8° B.L.8739 Rés.; J. André, 'en la grand salle du palais au premier pillier', Bod. Douce B.570, Cat. Bib. Lyons B.L.5613; ('on la grand rue saint Jacques à l'enseigne de l'elephant'—Tchemerzine); (D. Janot, 'en la rue neufve Nostre Dame à l'enseigne S. Jehan Baptiste pres S. Genviesve des Ardens'—Tchemerzine, La Bouralière Bib.); (Les Angeliers, 'en la grande salle du Palais'—Tchemerzine); (V. Sertenas— La Bouralière, Bib.); Rawles 88, Aur.122.897.

11. —, Rennes, Jean Georget, (col.) . . . demeurant en la Rue de la Bandrayerie, en la Maison Olivier, au lyon painctre, 1541.

Fol., goth. The only known copy is BN Vélins 586 (sic), and this is imperfect. The liminary pages, and certain others, are missing, and were originally replaced by sheets of paper M S which now form BN MS N.A.F.22175. In 1773 these were replaced by M S sheets of parchment, copied partly from the old M S and partly from the first edition in the Bibliothèque Sainte-Geneviève. The old M S bears the mark of the library of the Duke of Orléans.

The interest of this copy lies in the fact that it is very fully illustrated with painted miniatures. Van Praet (vol.4, p.199) says that the missing pages were torn out because they contained 'des figures un peu libres', but this seems most unlikely. It is described by A. de La Borderie in *Archives du bibliophile breton*, vol.2, Rennes, 1882, pp.91–100. Georget printed nothing else on this scale; presumably it was intended for some very rich or powerful person, but nothing more is known. Aur.122.905; Rép.124, J. Georget 9.

12. —, Paris, 20 February 1541 (o.s.?).

8°, goth. Various booksellers: Oudin Petit, Ars. 8° B.L.8740; Philippe Le Noir, Ars. 8° B.L.8741; François Regnault 'en la rue Sainct Jacques à l'enseigne de l'elephant', BMP DP.117 and DM.10; Jehan Réal, BN Rés. Y2.2074 and 2075, BMP DM.11. (Hamon notes Graesse's erroneous reference to a

Paris edition, V. Sertenas, 1514; this may be a further address for the 1541 edition.) Aur.122.904; Davies, *Fairfax Murray*, 1, p.54.

13. —, Paris, 1545.
8°. Various booksellers: Jean André, Maz. 21.805; G. Du Pré, Cat. Bib. St Chamond O.777 p.19; Jacques Tyson, BN Rés. Y²2076; Nicolas Du Chemin, Cat. Vienna; (P. Sergent—Tchemerzine), (Jehan Le Noir, 'en la rue Neufve Nostre Dame à l'enseigne de l'escu de France'—Hamon), (Jehan Réal, P. Regnault, V. Sertenas—La Bouralière, *Bib.*). Aur.122.907.

14. —, Paris, 1555.
8°. Various booksellers: Estienne Groulleau, BMP DM.12, Ars. 8° B.L.8742 Rés. (Hamon quotes from Graesse who cites editions by Groulleau in 1539, 1541 and 1545. But according to Renouard, Groulleau practised 1545–63?); Charles L'Angelier, BN Rés. Y2.2077, Maz.21.804; Veuve M. de la Porte, BL 8416.i.20; Aur.122.914.

15. (—, Paris, Lorain, 1563—Hamon.)

16. —, Louvain, J. Bogard, 1563.
8°. BL 8416.i.7; BN Y2.71821, Rés. Y2.3000 and 3001; BMP DP.1741, DM.13; Aur.122.916.

15
Epistres, Elegies, Epigrammes et Epitaphes

a) *Date*
Renée de Bourbon died in November 1534. The book is dated 27 March 1535; Easter fell on 28 March in 1535, but Poitiers printers would begin the year on 25 March. The last two ff. (a and a2) seem to be a late addition; they contain an *épître* from Bouchet to Lommeau, the author of part of the collection (those pieces which do not alternate masculine and feminine rhymes). Lommeau had apparently objected to Bouchet publishing his work without permission.

b) *Later Versions*
Like the *Panégyrique* this book was published without a privilege and was neither reproduced as a whole by Bouchet nor copied by other printers. The epigrams on Renée's death are reproduced as *Gén. Ep.* 66–75 and an *épître* to nuns becomes 1 *Ep. Mor.* 4.

c) *The Editions*
1. **Epitres, Elegies, Epigrammes et Epitaphes, Composez sur, et pour raison du deces de feu tresillustre, et tresreligieuse Dame, Madame Renee de Bourbon, en son vivant Abbesse du Royal monastere et ordre de Fontevrault, avec aultres choses concernans la Saincteté de ladicte Religion. Par le Procureur general dudict ordre, et par le*

Traverseur. MDXXXV. Et sont à vendre à Poictiers davant le
Palays, A l'enseigne du Pelican. (Col.): Imprimeez à Poic-
tiers. Le xxvii de Mars MDXXXV, par Jehan et Enguilbert de
Marnef, Freres . . .
4°, goth., BN Rés. Ln27.2708, MC III, F.51, Aur.122.877,
Rép.115, J. and E. de Marnef 7.

16
Les Angoysses et remedes d'amours

a) *Date*

La Croix du Maine's allusion to a 1501 Paris edition has caused
confusion in the dating of this work, but clearly he was referring to
an edition of the *Amoureux transi*, part of which is reproduced in the
Angoisses. Bouchet already mentioned this revised collection in *Ep.
Fam.* 96 and 97 when he was trying to obtain the privilege which was
to be granted by the King in November 1536.

b) *Later Versions*

This collection was incorporated by Bouchet into the 1545 *Généalogies*. It had a belated popularity in Rouen.

c) *The Editions*

1. **Les angoysses & remedes d'amours. Du Traverseur, en son adolescence.*
   (Col.): Imprimé à Poictiers le huytiesme jour de Janvier
   MDXXXVI par Jehan et Enguilbert de Marnef, freres (o.s.).
   4°, goth.; BL C.97.b.14; BN Rés. Ye.360, 361 and 362; BMP
   DM.8; Aur.122.885, Rép.115, J. and E. de Marnef 14.

   (Privilege from the King granted to Bouchet himself for
   four years, dated 15 November 1536. Dedication to Louis
   d'Estissac.)

2. —, Poitiers, Jehan and Enguilbert de Marnef freres, 19 February
   1537 (o.s.).
   8°, Camb. Adams B.2582, Rép.115, J. and E. de Marnef 19.

3. (—, Paris, 'à l'enseigne de l'elephant', s.d., 16°—Hamon, Tchemerzine)

4. —, Lyons, Jean de Tournes, 1550.
   12°. Maz. Rés. 22.051, Bod. Douce B6, Aur.122.913.

   (Copied from the version in the *Généalogies*. The Bodleian
   copy contains only the *Angoisses* (136 pp.), whereas the Mazarine copy (173 pp.) contains the *Dizains moraux sur les apophthegmes des sept Sages de Grece* from the *Généalogies*.)

5. —, Rouen, A. Cousturier, 1599 (together with *Une plaisante histoire
   d'Euriale et Lucresse redigée en langue latine par Aeneas Sylvius,
   poete excellent, et depuis trad. en vulgaire françois*).
   12°. BMP DM.71.

6. (—, Rouen, A. Cousturier, 1600, 12°—Tchemerzine.)

7. (—, Rouen, A. Cousturier, 1602, 12°—Tchemerzine.)

17

Le Jugement poetic de l'honneur femenin

a) *Date*

This work was written in memory of Louise de Savoie who died in 1531, and Bouchet already mentions the epigrams which form a large part of it in the *Annales* of 1532. In *Ep. Fam.* 96 and 97 he asks for a privilege and says that Louis de Ronsard had already presented the book to the King. When printed in 1538 (n.st., after 25 March) the book carried the same privilege as the first edition of the *Angoisses*, dated November 1536. The long prose preface addressed to Anne de Laval was written rather later than the work itself, since he speaks of

occasion d'adjouxter ceste briefve Apologie au petit livre que j'ay dès long temps a fait et presenté au Roy. (aa2 vo).

See appendix B on *Ep. Fam.* 95, etc., for a discussion of the date at which the *Jugement* was presented to the King.

b) *Later Versions*
None.

c) *The Editions*
1. **Le Jugement poetic de l'honneur femenin & sejour des illustres claires et honnestes Dames, par le Traverseur*. On les vend à Poictiers à l'enseigne du Pelican, davant le Palais. (Col.): Imprimé à Poictiers le premier d'Avril M.D.XXXVIII, par Jehan et Enguilbert de Marnef Freres.
   4°, goth. BL 241.k.26 and C.46.c.9; BN Rés. Ye.363; BMP DP.113; Aur.122.894, Rép.115, J. and E. de Marnef 21.
   (Privilege from the King granted to Bouchet for four years, dated 15 November 1536. The *Jugement* proper is introduced by an *épître* to the King; prefatory letter to Anne de Laval. Epigram by H. Sussanneau.)

18

Forme et ordre de plaidoirie

a) *Date*

In his preface Bouchet says that he had compiled this manual earlier, but had not wished to publish it before the *ordonnances royaulx* of 6 September 1539 (Villers-Cotterets) fixing procedure for lay courts. Thereafter he had revised it, and took the opportunity of the *Grand Jours* held in Poitiers in 1541 to obtain a privilege.

b) *Later Versions*
Bouchet made no further revisions.

c) *The Editions*

1. **Forme et ordre de plaidoirie en toutes les Cours Royalles, et Subalternes de ce Royaulme, regies par Coustumes, Styles et Ordonnances Royaulx. Avec privilege.* On les vend à Poictiers, à l'enseigne du Pelican, et en la bouticque de Jacques Bouchet. MDXLII. (Col.): Imprimée à Poictiers par Jehan et Enguilbert de Marnef freres demourantz à l'enseigne du Pelican devant le Palays. M.D.XLII.

   8°. BMP DM.1402(1), Cat. Bib. des Avocats à la cour d'appel de Paris 2783, Aur.122.906, Rép.115, J. and E. de Marnef 34.

   (The privilege for two years was granted by the Parlement, 'tenans les Grans jours en la ville de Poictiers', 4 November 1541.)

2. —, Paris, A. and Ch. Les Angeliers, 1542.

   8°. Cat. Bib. Troyes, Jurisprudence 2074.

3. —, Lyons, J. and F. Frellon, 1543.

   16°. Cat. Bib. Vesoul 3210.

4. (—, Paris, A. L'Angelier, 1552, 16°—La Bouralière, *Bib.*)

5. (—, Paris, pour Jean Caveiller, 1559, 16°—La Bouralière, *Bib.*)

6. —, Paris, Barbe Regnault, 1561.

   16°, Cat. Bib. Le Mans, Jurisprudence 980.

7. —, Paris, Vincent Sertenas, 1561.

   16°. BMP DP.114.

8. —, Poitiers, J. de Marnef, 1563.

   8°, Bib. Valognes, Rép.115, J. de Marnef 1 bis.

9. Paris, N. Bonfons, 1583.

   16°. BMP DP.115, Cat. Bib. de la Cour de cassation (Paris), vol.2, Jurisprudence, p.311—another edition, 12°, s.l., s.d. is also mentioned.

10. (—, Paris, Jean Ruelle, s.d.—Hamon, from La Croix du Maine and Du Verdier.)

19

Epistres Morales et Familieres

a) *Date*

The dating of the *Ep. Fam.* is dealt with in appendix B. Bouchet refers to the *Ep. Mor.* in *Ep. Fam.* 96 and 97 (before November 1536) when he asks for a privilege. The earliest in date, 2,1 (for Louis XII, *c.*1514) was certainly substantially revised later, since its rhymes alternate masculine and feminine. Otherwise the earliest is 2,5, dated autumn 1524 and first published in the *Opuscules*, 1525. The latest date given is May 1534 in 2,11. Several were written while Bouchet was in the country escaping the plagues that beset Poitiers in the early 1530s. Other dates given are in 1,5 (16 Dec. 1529), 1,8 (Innocents' Day 1528), 1,14 (1532, said to be the third year of plague).

b) *Later Versions*
None.

c) *The Editions*
1. **Epistres Morales & Familieres du Traverseur*. A Poictiers. Chez
   Jacques Bouchet à l'imprimerie à la Celle, & davant les Cordeliers. Et à l'enseigne du Pelican par Jehan et Enguilbert de
   Marnef. 1545.
   Fol. BL 83.h.5; BN Rés. Ye.55 *bis*, Roth.1, 511; BMP BM.1
   (consists of the *Epistres Familières* bound in front of the
   Epistres Morales), BR.147, BP.39; Aur.122.910, Rép.115,
   J. Bouchet 40.
   (Privilege granted by the King to Bouchet himself for four
   years, dated 3 January 1543 (o.s.). This privilege was also
   used for the 1545 *Annales* and *Généalogies*. *Dizain* and Latin
   verses by M. Seguier.)
2. —, reprinted in the series *French Renaissance Classics*, intr. by
   Jennifer Beard, S.R. Publishers Ltd, Johnson Reprint Corpo-
   ration, Mouton, 1969.

20
Triomphes du tres Chrestien Roy de France

a) *Date*
The pretext for this work is the death of François Ier on 31 March
1547. It may incorporate material in preparation before the King's
death, but there is no need·to suppose that the difference between
the first and second part was brought about by his untimely death
while Bouchet was composing a work in his praise (cf. Guy, §611);
the moral and theological point of the structure is clear and deliberate.

b) *Later Versions*
The book was printed only once in Bouchet's lifetime, and according
to La Bouralière, *Imp.*, p.135, the editions of both 1565 and 1574 are
in fact still copies of the 1550 edition, with only the liminary ff.
reprinted.

c) *The Editions*
1. **Triomphes du treschrestien, trespuissant & invictissime, Roy de France,
   François premier de ce nom : contenant la difference des Nobles*. On
   les vend à Poictiers à l'enseigne du Pelican. M.D.L. (Col.):
   Imprimé à Poictiers par Jean et Enguilbert de Marnef freres,
   demourans à l'enseigne du Pelican: et fut achevé le XVII
   d'Aoust, M.D.XLIX.
   Fol. BL 640.1.2; BN Rés. Ye.191, Rés. Ye.55; BMP BM.4;

Aur.122.912, Rép.115, J. and E. de Marnef 73.

(Privilege granted to Jean et Enguilbert de Marnef for five years from 7 March 1547 (o.s.). Dedicated to Henri ii, it also contains a verse addressed to Marguerite de Navarre and an exchange of *épîtres* with Tristan Frétard.)

2. *Le Parc de Noblesse* . . . (the same work), Poitiers, J. de Marnef, 1565.

Fol. BN Rés. Ye.56 and Rés. Y2.158; Ars. Fol. B.L.843; Aur.122.917, Rép.115, J. and E. de Marnef 154.

3. (—, Poitiers, J. and P. de Marnef, 1572—Hamon.)

4. —, Poitiers, J. and P. de Marnef, 1574.

Fol. Ars. Fol. B.L.844, Aur.122.918, Rép.115, J. de Marnef [111] 1.

21
Liminary Poems, etc.

The following works include first editions of poems, etc. by Bouchet:

L'histoire de Theodorite evesque de Cyropolis . . . *Traduicte du Grec en Françoys, par D. M. Mathee*, Poitiers, J. and E. de Marnef, 1544.

8°. BL 4531.aa.9, BN H.7740, BMP DM.1214, Rép.115, J. and E. de Marnef 44 bis.

(Prose letter.)

Le flagice de peste Composé par venerable et religieuse personne frere Symon Nerault docteur en theologie, Poitiers, Jacques Bouchet, 23 March 1530 (o.s.).

8°, goth, BN Rés. D.13721, BMP DP.1163; Rép.115, J. Bouchet 25.

(Verse *épître* to Antoinette d'Illiers—revised as *Ep. Fam.* 74.)

J. Boiceau, *Le Vol de l'Aigle en France*, Paris, J. André [1540].

8°. Roth.4, 2865.

(Dizain.)

J. Brèche, *Manuel Royal ou Opuscules de la doctrine & condition du Prince: tant en Prose, que Rhythme Françoyse*, Tours, Matthieu Chercelé, 12 Jan. 1541 (o.s.).

4°. BN Rés. Ye.345. Rép.153, M. Chercelé 10.

(Verse *épître* to J. Brèche—reproduced as *Ep. Fam.* 120.)

A. Thevet, *Cosmographie de Levant*, Lyons, Jean de Tournes, 1554.

Fol. Roth.2, 1931.

(Dizain).

22
Unauthorised Extracts

In the *Motif et intention du Traverseur* at the beginning of the *Epistres Morales*, Bouchet complains that

Par l'avarice d'aulcuns Imprimeurs on avoit perverty, voire falsifié, aulcuns de mes livres et separé les epistres rimées de la prose des *Triumphes de la noble dame*, et du *Chevalier sans reproche*, et aussi les rondeaulx du *Labirinth de Fortune*, et de ce faictz livres separez, voire adjousté en mes *Annales d'acquitaine* plusieurs choses à moy incogneues, non en rien sentans l'histoire.

The additions to the *Annales* have already been mentioned. The three other publications he complains of are as follows:

Les Exclamations et episres & oraisons de la noble Dame amoureuse dicte L'ame incorporee; Contenant la deploration de sa misere: Composez par le traverseur des voyes perilleuses appellé Maistre Jehan Bouchet . . ., Paris, D. and S. Janot, 1535.

    8°. Bib. Versailles: Goujet 29, Rawles 34.

(—, Paris, V. Sertenas, 1535, 8°—Hamon, from Du Verdier.)

(—, Lyons, Mousnier, 1540, 16°—Hamon, Tchemerzine, from Du Verdier and Niceron.)

S'ensuit les elegantes epistres extraites du panegyrique du chevalier sans reproche, monseigneur Loys de La Tremoille, composees par le traverseur des voies perilleuses, maistre Jehan Bouchet, procureur en la court de Poictiers. Ausquelles sont comprins plusieurs choses advenues au temps dudict La Tremoille. Avecq: les Epitaphes des pays et lieux dont il estoit seigneur et gouverneur, Paris, D. Janot, 1536.

    8°. Rawles 45 (see also Rawles 245).

(*Le Conflit de l'heur et malheur par Dialogue*, Paris, D. Janot—Hamon, Tchemerzine, from Du Verdier and Niceron; Rawles 244.)

    (This is the title of a series of verses—*cinquains*, not *rondeaux*—from the *Labyrinthe*, so may be the publication Bouchet is complaining of.)

It will be noticed that in each case Denis Janot is the culprit. He had published the *Renards* in 1530, in 1536 produced editions of the *Chapelet* and the *Rondeaux et ballades*, and sold the *Annales* in 1537 and the *Anciennes et modernes* and the *Triomphes* in 1539.

23
Manuscripts of Works by Bouchet

a) *Unpublished Works*

1. BM Poitiers, MS.440. Legs Alfred Richard, *Les Renars Traversant*, 176 ff.

    (A thoroughly revised version of the *Renards* proper. The revision may have been made *c*.1515 (see section 2b) but the MS was probably copied in 1531; the colophon reads: 'Cy finit le livre des Renars traversans et loups ravissans au vray, ainsi qu'il a esté composé par Maistre Jehan Bouchet, bourgeois de Poictiers en l'an mil cinq cens et ung.' The words after 'Bouchet' replace words that have been crossed out: 'et l'an mil vc xxx et ung'.

    The MS was owned by Alfred Richard who described it in

his article, 'Notes sur les Bouchet'. In his opinion the hand
was not that of Bouchet himself, except for the corrections.
The MS contains several drawings copied from the original
woodcuts in the printed version, and also one of the author
surrounded by foxes.)
2. BN MS N.A.F.11555, *Les cantiques et oraisons contemplatives de
l'ame penitente traversant les voies perilleuses,* 71 ff.
    (See section 9. Described by Plattard in *Revue du seizième
siècle,* 9,,1922, pp.80–2.)
3. Bodley MS Douce 252, ff.17 ro–19 vo, *Oraison de Notre Dame.*
    (Composed before Bouchet had abandoned lyric cesuras,
i.e. before about 1515. Published by K.Chesney in *Humanisme et Renaissance,* 1, Paris, 1941, pp.199–202.)

b) *Works Copied from Printed Books*
1. *Sotheby Catalogue of the Huth Collection,* London, 1911, Lot 858: *Le
Livre appellé les Regnars Traversans les perilleuses voyes des folles
fiances du monde composé par Sebastian Brand . . .*
    Vellum, 44 leaves, 8 miniatures (see *Sotheby Cat.,* pp.242,
350).
    (The title, incorporating the name of Brant, shows that this
very sumptuous MS is based on the text as printed by Vérard,
not on an original or revised version by Bouchet himself.)
2. BN MS N.A.F.10721, *Recueil de vies de saints:* f.94 vo, *Declaration
de la vie louable et histoire monseigneur saint Hilaire de Poitiers . . .
nagueres traduites en langage françoys par honnorable homme maistre Jehan Bouchet . . .* (from the *Annales*).
3. Arsenal MS.3171, ff.1–169, *Labirinth de fortune* (copied from a
printed book in 1577).
4. BN MS N.A.F.22175. 'Ce cayer servoit anciennement de supplément à l'ouvrage intitulé : les Triumphes de la noble et amoureuse dame, et l'art de honnestement aymer.'—The original
MS replacing the missing pages of the *Triomphes,* Rennes, J,
Georget, 1541, BN Vélins 586: see section 14c.
5. Rothschild 4, 2964, *Recueil de poésies du XVIe siècle, f.120, Ballade,*
'Homme aveuglé des plaisirs de ce monde'. Identified by
Picot. There are doubtless many more examples in other
Recueils, particularly of *rondeaux* and *ballades*—several are lis-
ted by K.Chesney, *Fleurs de rhétorique,* p.108.

In the *Catalogue des livres de feu M. le Duc de La Vallière,* Première
partie, vol.2, Paris, 1783, p.326, a manuscript is mentioned that is
apparently lost and so cannot be classified:
    3007. *Le Chapellet des Princes par ballade de laquelle les deux
premiers bastons contiennent le nom du Prince à qui il est dirigé le
petit euvre & le tiers baston contient le nom de l'acteur,* (dédié à

Charles de La Trémouille, mort en 1515, par Jean Bouchet),
in-4, couv. de velours.
Manuscrit sur vélin du commencement du XVIe siècle, contenant 18 feuillets écrits en *ancienne bâtarde*, et à longues
lignes.

24

Archive Material: Collections of Letters written by Bouchet

Archives de la Vienne G^8 18: correspondence with the Chauvigny
chapter.
Chartrier de Thouars 1AP 615: 39 letters and 8 other documents
signed by Bouchet concerning his work for François de La
Trémoille. Also letters by his son, Gabriel.

Part Two : Other Works Mentioned

(excepting works mentioned only in the appendixes)

a) *Manuscripts*

BN MS Ancien fonds français 1952, Jean d'Auton, *L'Epistre du preux
Hector.*
Vienna, Österreichische Nationalbibliothek MS 2579, Jean d'Auton,
L'Epistre du preux Hector.
Leningrad, Saltykov-Shchedrin Library, MS containing Jean d'Auton, *Epistre elegiaque par l'eglise militante.*
Bibliothèque Mazarine MS 978, Gabrielle de Bourbon, *Le Voyage
spirituel entreprins par l'ame devote pour parvenir en la cité de bon
repoux* and *Le fort chasteau pour la retraicte de toutes bonnes ames.*
Chartrier de Thouars, 1AP 220, Gabrielle de Bourbon, *Ung petit
traicté sur les doulleurs de la passion du doulx Jesus et de sa benoiste
mere, pour lesquelles voir et santir le cueur contemplatif amene
avecques soy l'ame devote.*

b) *Books Printed before 1600*

Amboise, Michel d', *Les Epistres veneriennes de l'esclave fortuné privé de
la court d'amours,* Paris, D. Janot, 1536, BL 241.g.33.
Amboise, Michel d', *Le Penthaire de l'esclave fortuné,* Paris, A. Lotrian
and D. Janot, 1530, BL 1073.e.1.
Annius of Viterbo, *Commentaria fratris Joannis Annii Viterbensis . . .
super opera diversorum auctorum de Antiquitatibus loquentium,*
Rome, E. Silber, 1498, BL IB.19034.
Antoninus, Saint, Archbishop of Florence, *Summa [theologica],* Stras-
burg, J. Grüninger, 1496, BL IB.1431-1434.
Augustine, Saint, *La Cité de Dieu,* tr. Raoul de Presles, Abbeville,
I. Du Pré and Gerard, 1486-7, BL IC.43805.

[Baltherius], *Vita sancti Fridolini*, in Fortunatus, *Vita beati Hilarii*, [Basle, P. Kollicker, 1483?], BL G.5210.

Barril, Jean, [*Enseignemens*], Toulouse, [N. Vieillard?], 1535, BL C.125.dd.21.

Bartholomaeus Anglicus, *Le Proprietaire des choses*, Lyons, M. Hutz, 1482, BL IB.41688.

Beaulieu, Eustorg de, *Les divers rapportz*, Lyons, P. de Saincte Lucie, 1537, BL G.17886.

Beaulieu, Eustorg de, *Les Gestes des solliciteurs*, Bordeaux, J. Guyart, 1529, BL C.40.c.49.

Béda, Noël, *Annotationum . . . in Jacobum Fabrum Stapulensem libri duo*, Paris, J. Bade, 1526, BL L.17.d.14(2).

Bernard, Saint, *Meditations*, Paris, A. Vérard, [1506?], BL C.22.a.5.

Bernardine, Saint, of Siena, *La petite dyablerie dont Lucifer est le chef*, Paris, veuve J. Trepperel and J. Jehannot, [1520?], BL C.53.h.9(1).

La Bible historiée, 2 vols, Paris, A. Vérard, [1498?], BN Vélins 100, 101.

Bonaventura, Saint, *Traicté qui est dit l'arbre de la croix*, Paris, S. Vostre [1510?], BL 3832.aa.24.

Bouchard, Alain, *Les grandes croniques de Bretaigne*, Paris, G. du Pré, 1514, BL G.5999.

Bouchard, Alain, *Les croniques Annalles des pays d'Angleterre et Bretagne*, Paris, A. Cousteau for J. Petit and G. du Pré, 1531, BL C.38.i.20.

Bouchard, Alain, *Les grandes Cronicques de Bretaigne*, [Caen?], 1532, BL C.66.c.3.

Brant, Sebastian, *Stultifera navis*, tr. J. Locher, Basle, Olpe, 1497, BL IA.37941.

Brant, Sebastian, *Varia carmina*, Basle, Olpe, 1498, BL IA.37949.

Brant, Sebastian, *La nef des folz du monde*, [tr. into verse by P. Rivière], Paris, J. Philippes, Manstener and G. de Marnef, 1497, BL IB.40534.

Brant, Sebastian, *La nef des folz du monde*, [tr. into prose], Lyons, G. Balsarin, 1498, BN Rés. fol. Yh2.

Brant, Sebastian, *La grant nef des folz du monde*, [tr. into prose], Paris, G. de Marnef, 1499 (o.s.), BL IB.40230.

Calphurnius, Francisci, Vindocinensis, *Epigrammata*, Paris, J. de Marnef, s.d., BN Rés. 4° mY^c763.

[Calvin, Jean], *Les Actes de la Journée imperiale tenue en la cité de Regespourg aultrement dicte Ratispone*, [Geneva? J. Gerard?], 1541, BL 701.a.7.

Castel, Jean, *Le Mirouer des pecheurs et pecheresses*, Paris, A. Vérard, [1505?], BL C.22.a.7.

Ceneau, Robert, *Gallica Historia*, Paris, G. du Pré, 1557, Bodleian A.2.10 Art. Seld.

Champier, Symphorien, *Les grans croniques des gestes et vertueux faictz des . . . ducz et princes des pays de Savoye et Piemont*, Paris, J. de La Garde, 1516, BL C.38.g.9.

Champier, Symphorien, *Le triumphe du treschrestien Roy de France* [*Loys*] *XII de ce nom*, Lyons, C. d'Avost, 1509, BL C.118.c.17.

Chasseneuz, Barthélemy de, *Catalogus gloriae mundi*, Lyons, G. Regnault, 1546, BL C.81.h.10.

Ciboule, Robert, *Le Livre de meditation sur soy mesmes*, Paris, S. Vostre, 1510, BL C.38.h.11.

Coccius, Sabellicus, Marcus Antonius, *Enneades ab orbe condito ad inclinationem Romani Imperii*, Venice, Bernardinum [de Vitalibus] et Matheum Venetos, 1498, BL IC.24321.

Coccius, Sabellicus, Marcus Antonius, *Rerum Venetarum Decades*, Venice, A. de Torresanis, 1487, BL IC.21644.

Columbi, Jehan, *Confession generale*, [1520?], BL 845.a.30.

Corrozet, Gilles, *Les Antiquitez, histoires, croniques et singularitez . . . de Paris*, Paris, N. Bonfons, 1577, BL 576.a.2.

Deguileville, Guillaume de, *Le pelerinage de l'homme*, Paris, Vérard, 1511 (o.s.), BL C.6.b.15.

Doré, Pierre, *Les Allumettes du feu divin*, Paris, A. Lotrian, 1538, BL 1360.b.7.

Doré, Pierre, *Le College de Sapience . . . avec le Dialogue de la Foy*, Paris, A. Bonnemere, 1539, BL 1360.f.8.

Durandus, Gulielmus, *Le racional des divins offices*, tr. Jean Golein, Paris, A. Vérard, 1503, BL C.48.g.8.

Du Tillet, Jean (the younger), *De regibus francorum chronicon*, in Paulus Aemilius, *De rebus gestis Francorum libri decem*, Paris, M. Vascosan, 1539, 1543, BL 595.i.2 (impf.).

Eck, Johann von, *De purgatorio: contra Lutherum hostesque Ecclesiae libri quatuor*, Antwerp, 1545, BL 3906.a.5.

Eck, Johann von, *Enchiridion locorum communium adversus Lutheranos*, Cologne, Apud heredes A. Birckmanni, 1561, BL 4326.aa.49.

Epitome gestorum LVIII regum Franciae, Lyons, B. Arnoullet, 1546, BL 596.b.17(1) (impf.).

Erasmus, Desiderius, *Declarationes ad censuras Lutetiae vulgatas sub nomine Facultatis Theologiae Parisiensis*, Basle, H. Froben and N. Episcopius, 1532, BL C.60.e.12.

Erasmus, Desiderius, *De libero arbitrio* διατριβη *sive collatio*, Basle, J. Froben, 1524, BL 700.b.1(1).

Erasmus, Desiderius, *Exomologesis: sive Modus confitendi*, Basle, J. Froben, 1524, BL C.64.a.19(1).

Erasmus, Desiderius, *Precatio dominica in septem portiones distributa*, Basle, J. Froben, [1523?], BL 700.b.37.

L'Examen de conscience du mal et du bien de l'ame, Rouen, J. Le Bourgoys pour P. Regnault, [1489?], BL C.22.b.11.

Les exellentes vaillances, batailles et conquestes du roy dela les mons,
    composées par plusieurs orateurs et facteurs et presentez audit sei-
    gneur, (s.l., s.d.), BN Rés. 8° Ye.1383.

Faren, Antoine, *La pratique de soy bien confesser,* [Paris? 1500?], BL
    IA.41530.

La Fleur des commandemens de Dieu, Paris, A. Vérard, [1499], BL
    C.22.b.4.

La Fleur des commandementz et declaration des bonnes oeuvres, s.d., BL
    C.83.a.21.

Foresti, Bergomensis, Jacobus Philippus, *De plurimis claris sceletisque*
    (sic) *mulieribus,* Ferrara, L. de Rubeis, 1497, BL 167.h.17.

Fortunatus, Venantius, *Vita beati Hilarii compòsita a servo suo Fortu-*
    nato, [Basle, P. Kollicker, 1483?], BL G.5210.

François 1er, *Des Königs zu Franckreich Schrift, an die deutschen Chur*
    und Fürsten vom Concilio und ettlich andern Artickeln, 1535, BL
    3905.g.7.

Gagny, Jean de, *Le Livre contenant devote exposition sur le cinquantiesme*
    Pseaulme du Royal Prophete David, commenceant Miserere mei
    deus, Paris, D. Janot, [1532], BL C.97.aa.14.

Gagny, Jean de, *Le livre faisant mention des sept parolles que nostre*
    benoist saulveur et redempteur Jesuchrist dit en l'arbre de la croix,
    Paris, S. du Bois, 1528, BL C.97.b.33.

Gaguin, Robert, *De origine et gestis Francorum perquam utile compen-*
    dium, Lyons, J. Bade, 1497, BL IB.41937.

[Gaguin, Robert], *La Mer des Croniques et miroir historial de France,*
    Paris, Ph. Le Noir, [1525], BL G.6231; Paris, [A. de la Barre],
    1536, BL C.55.h.8.

Gerson, Jean Charlier de, *Opera omnia,* ed. Wimpheling, Paris, F. Re-
    gnault, 1521, BL 472.f.3–4.

Gerson, Jean Charlier de, *Instruction des curez pour instruire le simple*
    peuple, Paris, S. Vostre, 1507, BN Rés. D.7848; (for diocese of
    Le Mans), [Paris? 1508?], BL 3835.a.69.

Gerson, Jean Charlier de, *Le traicté des dix commandemens de la loy,*
    Paris, J. Trepperel, 1495, BL IA.40406.

(Gerson, Jean Charlier de), *La Confession de maistre Jehan Jarson,*
    Paris, D. Mellier, [1490?], BL IA.40277.

Gilles, Nicole, *Les tres elegantes, tres veridiques et copieuses Annales des*
    tres preux, tres nobles, tres chrestiens et tres excellens moderateurs
    des belliqueueses Gaules, Paris, G. du Pré, 1525, BN Rés. fol.
    L^{35}37.

La Grant confession de Pasques, Paris, A. Cayllaut, [1495], BL
    IA.39501.

Gringore, Pierre, *Les Abuz du monde,* Paris, P. le Dru, 1509, BL
    C.124.dd.24.

Gringore, Pierre, *Les Folles Entreprises,* Paris, P. le Dru, 1505, BN
    Rés. 8° Ye.1321.

Gringore, Pierre, *Heures de Nostre Dame translatees en Françoys et mises en rihtme* [*sic*], Paris, J. Petit, [1525], BL C.24.a.26.

Gringore, Pierre, *Les Menus Propos*, Paris, G. Couteau, 1521, BL C.39.b.23.

Guerricus, Abbot of Igny, *Sermons de Guerricus . . . abbé d'Igny*, tr. Jean de Gagny, Paris, S. de Colines pour E. Roffet, s.d., BN 8° C.3347.

Hangest, Jérôme de, *De possibili praeceptorum divinorum impletione in Lutherum*, Paris, J. Petit, 1528, BL 3837.a.31(2).

Hangest, Jérôme de, *Contre les tenebrions lumiere evangelicque*, Paris, J. Petit, [1534], BN Rés. 8° D.80052.

Henri ii, *Edict du Roy nostre sire, sur la prohibition faicte à toutes personnes . . . de n'expedier et envoyer en court de Romme . . .*, Paris, J. Dallier, 1551, BL 1492.dd.15(4).

Les Heures nostre dame à l'usaige de Romme nouvellement translateez de latin en françoys, Paris, J. de Brie, [1520?], BL C.30.e.39.

Heures nouvellement imprimées à l'usaige de Meaulx, Paris, J. de Brie, [1521?], BL C.46.d.19(1).

Hilary, Saint, *Opera complura*, Paris, J. Bade, 1510, BL 469.C.7.

Hilary, Saint, *S. D. Divi Hilarii lucubrationes*, ed. Erasmus, Basle, J. Froben, 1523, BL C.80.d.4.

Hore intemerate virginis Marie secundum usum R[omanum], Paris, A. Vérard, 1503, BL C.41.b.2.

Jerome, Saint, *La Vie des anciens saintz peres hermites*, Paris, J. du Pré, 1486, BL IB.39803.

[John Cassianus, Saint], *Les Colacions des sains peres anciens*, tr. Jean Golein, Paris, A. Vérard, [1504?], BL 3627.dd.11.

Le Roy, François, *Dialogue de consolation entre l'ame et raison*, Paris, S. Vostre, [1505?], BL C.107.c.5.

Le Roy, François, *Le Livre de la femme forte et vertueuse*, Paris, J. Petit, [1505?], BL C.36.b.32.

Le Roy, François, *Le Mirouer de penitence tres devot et salutaire*, 2 vols, Paris, S. Vostre, 1507–11, BL 1360.e.1.

Maffeius, Volaterranus, Raphael, *Commentariorum urbanorum octo et triginta libri*, Paris, J. Petit and J. Bade, 1511, BL 1248.m.5.

La Mer des Hystoires, (tr. of *Rudimentum noviciorum*), Paris, 1488, BN Rés. fol. G.216–17.

Michel de Tours, Guillaume, *La Forest de conscience contenant la chasse des princes spirituelle*, Paris, M. le Noir, 1516, BL 241.g.35.

Montfiquet, Raoul de, *Le Livre du sainct sacrement de l'autel*, Paris, A. Vérard, [1505?], BL C.22.a.9.

Ordinayre des crestiens, Paris, T. du Guernier, 1502, BL C.97.c.4.

The Ordynarye of Chrystyanyte, London, W. de Worde, 1502, BL G.11739.

Paradin, Guillaume, *Histoire de nostre temps*, Paris, L. Breyer, 1561, BL 9077.a.12.

Paris, University of, *Determinatio theologice facultatis Parisiensis super doctrina Lutheriana hactenus per eam visa*, Paris, In officina Ascensiana, [1521], BL 807.b.14(2).

Petit, Guillaume, *La Formation de l'homme et son excellence*, Paris, G. du Pré, 1538, BN Rés. 8° D.17409(1).

Petit, Guillaume, *Tresdevotes oraisons à l'honneur de la . . . Vierge Marie*, Paris, S. de Colines, s.d., BN Rés. 8° p.Ye.297.

Petit, Nicolas and Fossier, Jean, *Elegiae de redemptione humana*, Paris, J. Petit, 1517 (o.s.?), BL C.125.c.19.

Petit, Nicolas, *Sylvae, Arion, Gornais, Barbaromachia cum aliquot hymnis*, Paris, J. de Gourmont, [1522?], BN Rés. 4° m.Yc.822(1).

ed. Petit, Nicolas, *Fratris Baptistae Mantuani . . . opus absolutissimum de sacris diebus mendis quibus passim inspersum erat, omnino emaculatum ope et diligentia Nicolai Parvi Bellosanensis*, Poitiers, J. Bouchet, 1526, BL 1481.aaa.18(1).

Pro religione Christiana res geste in Comitiis Auguste Vindelicorum habitis, Augsburg, [H. Steiner], 1530, BL 697.g.34(9).

Quentin, Jean, *Examen de conscience pour soy congnoistre à bien se confesser*, [Paris, 1500?], BL I A.40603.

Quintinus Heduus, Joannes, *Sacrarum Aedium Petri, et Hilarii apud Pictavos encomium*, s.l., s.d. (Poitiers? 1525?) BN Rés. 8° L³K 500.

Raulin, Jean, *Itinerarium paradisi . . . cui adjuncti sunt . . . sermones . . . de matrimonio ac viduitate*, Paris, J. de Marnef, 1519, BL G.19717.

Richard of St Victor, *Omnia opera in unum volumen congesta*, Paris, J. Petit, 1518, BL 472.f.11.

Saint-Gelais, Octavien de, and La Vigne, André de, *Le Vergier d'honneur*, Paris, Ph. le Noir, [1520?], BL C.107.e.1.

Seneca, Lucius Annaeus, *L. Annaei Senecae . . . lucubrationes omnes additis etiam nonnullis, Erasmi Roterodami . . . cura*, Basle, J. Froben, 1515, BL 524.i.7.

Seyssel, Claude de, *La grant monarchie de France*, Paris, R. Chauldiere, 1519, BL 521.g.26.

La solenne et triomphante entrata de la Cesarea Maesta nella Franza, [Bologna, V. Bonardi et A. M. da Carpi, 1539], BL 1318. c.7(5).

Sussanneau, Hubert, *Ludorum libri nunc recens conditi atque aediti*, Paris, S. de Colines, 1538, BL 1070.d.14.

Sutor, Petrus, *De Tralatione Bibliae, et novarum reprobatione interpretationum*, Paris, P. Vidoue for J. Petit, 1525, BL 699.l.22.

Tritheim, Johann, *Compendium sive Breviarium primi voluminis annalium sive historiarum de origine regum et gentis Francorum*, Mainz, J. Schöffer, 1515, BL 183.c.1.

Valla, Lorenzo, *Sur la donation de Constantin empereur*, [Paris, 1520?], BL 476.a.8.

La Vie de monsieur saint Bernard. [Dijon, P. Metlinger, 1491?], BL
    I A.44920.
La Vie de ma dame saincte Katherine de Seine, Paris, J. Petit, 1503, BL
    C.97.b.12.
La Vie sainte Marguerite, [Lyons, 1490?], BL I A.42295.
La Vie madame saincte Marguerite, [Paris, 1520?], BL C.46.d.19(2).
La Vie et miracles de . . . saint Martin translatée de latin en françoys,
    [Tours, M. Lateran? 1496], BL C.22.b.5.

c) *Modern Editions and Reprints*
Auton, Jean d', *Chroniques de Louis XII,* ed. R. de Maulde La Cla-
    vière, 4 vols, Paris, 1889–95.
Boccaccio, Giovanni, *Genealogie deorum gentilium libri,* ed. V. Roma-
    no, 2 vols, Bari, 1951.
Brant, Sebastian, *Flugblätter des Sebastian Brant,* ed. P. Heitz, Stras-
    burg, 1915.
Calvin, Jean, *Ioannis Calvini Opera quae supersunt omnia,* ed. G. Baum,
    E. Cunitz, E. Reuss, 59 vols, Brunswick–Berlin, 1863–1900
    (*Corpus Reformatorum*).
Chartier, Alain, *Le Livre de l'Espérance,* ed. F. Rouy (Thèse), Brest,
    1967.
Colin Bucher, Germain, *Les Poésies de Germain Colin Bucher,* ed.
    J. Denais, Paris, 1890; Slatkine reprints, Geneva, 1970.
Cretin, Guillaume, *Œuvres poétiques,* ed. K. Chesney, Paris, 1932.
Deguileville, Guillaume de, *Le Pèlerinage de vie humaine, Le Pèlerinage*
    de l'âme, Le Pèlerinage Jhesucrist, ed. J. J. Stürzinger, Roxburghe
    Club, London, 1893, 1895 and 1897.
Dionysius, Saint, called the Areopagite, *Dionysiaca. Recueil donnant*
    l'ensemble des traductions latines des ouvrages attribués au Denys
    de l'Aréopage, 2 vols, Bruges, 1937.
Du Bellay, Joachim, *La Deffence et Illustration de la langue françoyse,* ed.
    H. Chamard, Paris, 1948.
Du Pont, Gratien, *Art et science de rhetoricques metriffiee,* Toulouse,
    1539; Slatkine reprints, Geneva, 1972.
L'Entrée de Henri II à Rouen, Rouen, 1551; facsimile with an introduc-
    tion by Margaret M. McGowan, Amsterdam–New York.
Erasmus, Desiderius, *Opera omnia,* 9 vols, Leiden, 1703–06; Gregg
    reprints.
Erasmus, Desiderius, *Opera omnia,* ed. J. H. Waszink, etc., 5 parts,
    Amsterdam, 1969– .
Erasmus, Desiderius, *Erasmi opuscula,* ed. W. K. Ferguson, The
    Hague, 1933.
Fabri, Pierre, *Le Grand et vrai art de pleine rhétorique,* ed. A. Héron, 3
    vols, Rouen, 1889–90; Slatkine reprints, Geneva, 1969.
Fleurs de rhétorique. From Villon to Marot, ed. K. Chesney, Oxford,
    1950.

François Ier, Œuvres poétiques, ed. J. E. Kane, Geneva, 1984.

Geoffrey of Monmouth, Historia Regum Britanniae, ed. A. Griscom and R. E. Jones, London, 1929.

Gerson, Jean Charlier de, Opera omnia, 5 vols, Ellies du Pin, Antwerp, 1706.

Gerson, Jean Charlier de, Œuvres complètes, ed. P. Glorieux, 10 vols in 11, Paris, 1960–74.

Gregory, Saint, Bishop of Tours, Histoire des Francs, tr. R. Latouche, 2 vols, Paris, 1963–5 (Les Classiques de l'histoire de France au moyen âge, 27–8).

Gringore, Pierre, Œuvres complètes, ed. C. d'Héricault and A. de Montaiglon, 2 vols, Paris, 1858.

Gringore, Pierre, Blazon des heretiques, Paris, 1524; repr. M. Hérisson, Paris, 1832.

Gringore, Pierre, Les Fantasies de Mere Sote, ed. R. L. Frautschi, Chapel Hill, 1962.

Journal d'un Bourgeois de Paris sous le règne de François premier, ed. L. Lalanne, Paris, 1854.

Lefèvre d'Etaples, Jacques, Epistres et évangiles pour les cinquante et deux sepmaines de l'an, facsimilé de la première édition, Simon du Bois [1525?], ed. M. A. Screech, Geneva, 1964.

Lemaire de Belges, Jean, Œuvres, ed. J. Stecher, 4 vols, Louvain, 1882–91; Georg Olms Reprint, 1972.

Lemaire de Belges, Jean, La Concorde des deux langages, ed. J. Frappier, Paris, 1947.

Lemaire de Belges, Jean, Les Epîtres de l'Amant vert, ed. J. Frappier, Lille–Geneva, 1948.

Lemaire de Belges, Jean, Le Temple d'honneur et de vertus, ed. H. Hornik, Geneva–Paris, 1957.

Le Riche, Guillaume and Michel, Journal, ed. A. D. de la Fontenelle de Vaudoré, Saint-Maixent, 1846.

Lyfe of Saynt Radegunde, ed. F. Brittain, Cambridge, 1926.

Maillard, Olivier, Œuvres françaises d'Olivier Maillard. Sermons et poésies, ed. A. de la Borderie, Nantes, 1877.

Marguerite de Navarre, La Coche, ed. R. Marichal, Geneva, 1971.

Marguerite de Navarre, Le Miroir de l'âme pécheresse, ed. J. L. Allaire, Munich, 1972.

Marot, Clément, Les Epîtres, ed. C. A. Mayer, London, 1958.

Marot, Jean, Le Voyage de Gênes, ed. G. Trisolini, Geneva, 1974.

Molinet, Jean, Les Faictz et dictz, ed. N. Dupire, 3 vols, Paris, SATF, 1936–9.

Montaigne, Michel de, Œuvres complètes, ed. A. Armaingaud, etc., 12 vols, Paris, 1924–41.

Montaigne, Michel de, Les Essais, ed. P. Villey and V. Saulnier, Paris, 1965.

Nouveau Testament, tr. J. Lefèvre d'Etaples, S. de Colines, 1523; facsimile edition, intr. by M. A. Screech, 2 vols, Paris La Haye, 1970.

[Picotté, Sebastien], *Cronique du roy Françoys premier de ce nom*, ed. G. Guiffrey, Paris, 1860.

Palinods présentés au Puy de Rouen. Recueil de Pierre Vidoue (1525), ed. E. de Robillard de Beaurepaire, Rouen, 1897.

Querelle de Marot et Sagon, ed. E. Picot and P. Lacombe, Rouen, 1920.

Rabelais, François, *Œuvres de François Rabelais*, édition critique publiée par Abel Lefranc, etc., Paris, 1912– .

Rabelais, François, *Gargantua*, ed. R. Calder, M. A. Screech, V. L. Saulnier, Geneva, 1970.

Recueil d'arts de seconde rhétorique, ed. E. Langlois, Paris, 1902.

Recueil de poésies françoises des 15ᵉ et 16ᵉ siècles, morales, facétieuses, historiques, ed. A. de Montaiglon and J. de Rothschild, 13 vols, Paris, 1855–78.

Robertet, Jean, *Œuvres*, ed. M. Zsuppán, Geneva, 1970.

Ronsard, Pierre de, *Œuvres complètes*, ed. P. Laumonier, 20 vols, Paris, 1914–75.

Saint-Gelais, Octavien de, *Le Séjour d'honneur*, ed. J. A. James, Chapel Hill, 1977.

Sebillet, Thomas, *Art poétique françoys*, ed. F. Gaiffe, Paris, 1932.

d) *Monographs, Articles and Works of Reference*

Aigrain, René. *L'Hagiographie. Ses sources, ses méthodes et son histoire*, Paris, 1953.

Aigrain, René, *Sainte Radegonde, vers 520–587*, Paris, 1918.

Armstrong, Elizabeth, 'Notes on the Works of Guillaume Michel, dit de Tours', *BHR*, 31, 1969, pp.257–81.

Asher, R. E., *The Attitudes of French Writers of the Renaissance to Early French History, with Special Reference to their Treatment of the Trojan Legend and to the Influence of Annius of Viterbo*, PhD thesis, University of London, 1955.

Asher, R. E., 'Myth, Legend and History in Renaissance France', *Studi Francesi*, 13, 1969, pp.409–19.

Auber, C., *Etude sur les historiens du Poitou depuis ses origines connues jusqu'au milieu du XIXᵉ siècle*, Niort, 1870.

Bäumer, R. (ed.), *Die Entwicklung des Konziliarismus*, Darmstadt, 1976.

Beard, J. J., 'Letters from the Elysian Fields: a Group of Poems for Louis XII', *BHR*, 31, 1969, pp.27–38.

Beard, J. J., *A Study of the Works of Jean Bouchet with Reference to Contemporary Religious Issues*, PhD thesis, University of London, 1972.

Beauchet-Filleau, E. H. E. and Chergé, C. de, *Dictionnaire historique et généalogique des familles du Poitou*, second ed., Poitiers, 1891–.

Berger, Samuel, *La Bible française au moyen âge*, Paris, 1884.

Bohatta, Hanns, *Bibliographie der Livres d'Heures (Horae B.M.V) Officia, Hortuli animae. Coronae B.M.V, Rosaria und Cursus B.M.V. des XV and XVI Jahrhunderts*, Vienna, 1909.

Bollandus, Joannes and Henschenius, Godefridus, *Acta Sanctorum*, 58 vols, Antwerp, 1643–1867.

Bridge, J.S.C., *A History of France from the Death of Louis XI*, 5 vols, Oxford, 1921–36.

Britnell, Jennifer, ' "Clore et rentrer": the Decline of the *Rondeau*', *French Studies*, 37, 1983, pp.285–95.

Britnell, Jennifer, 'Jean Bouchet's Epitaphs for Thomas More and John Fisher', *Moreana*, xxii, April 1985, pp.45–55.

Britnell, Jennifer, 'Jean Bouchet's Prayers in French for the Laity, "Les Cantiques et oraisons contemplatives de l'ame pénitente traversant les voies périlleuses"', *BHR*, 38, 1976, pp. 421–36.

Britnell, Jennifer, 'Jean Lemaire de Belges and Prophecy', *Journal of the Warburg and Courtauld Institutes*, 42, 1979, pp.144–66.

Brun, Robert, *Le Livre français illustré de la renaissance: étude suivie du catalogue des principaux livres à figures du 16e siècle*, Paris, 1969.

The Cambridge History of the Bible, 3 vols, ed. P.R.Ackroyd and C.F.Evans, G.W.H.Lampe, S.L.Greenslade, Cambridge, 1970, 1969, 1963.

Camproux, C., 'Langue et métrique: à propos du décasyllabe des "Epîtres" de Marot', *Le français moderne*, 32, 1964, pp.194–205.

Castor, Grahame, *Pléiade Poetics. A Study in Sixteenth-Century Thought and Terminology*, Cambridge, 1964.

Catalogue des Actes de François Ier, ed. P.Marichal, 10 vols, Paris, 1887–1908.

Cave, Terence (ed.), *Ronsard the Poet*, London, 1973.

Chamard, Henri, *Histoire de la Pléiade*, 4 vols, Paris, 1939–40.

Cigada, Sergio, 'La "Genealogia Deorum Gentilium" del Boccaccio e il "Temple de Bonne Renommee" di Jean Bouchet', in *Il Boccaccio nella cultura francese*, a cura di Carlo Pellegrini, Florence, 1971, pp.521–56.

Clark, John E., *Élégie. The Fortunes of a Classical Genre in Sixteenth-Century France*, The Hague–Paris, 1975.

Clouzot, Henri, *L'Ancien Théâtre en Poitou*, Niort, 1901.

Colbert de Beaulieu, J-B., 'L' "Epitre d'un complaignant l'abusif gouvernement du pape", de Jean Marot (1511)', *Scriptorium*, 3, 1949, pp.91–109.

Combes, André, 'Un témoin du socratisme chrétien au XVe siècle: Robert Ciboule (1403–1458)', *Archives d'histoire doctrinale*, 8, 1933, pp.93–259.

Connolly, J.L., *John Gerson, Reformer and Mystic*, Louvain, 1928.

Cotgrave, Randle, *A Dictionarie of the French and English tongues,* London, 1611; reprint intr. by W. S. Woods, Columbia, 1968.

Davies, Hugh Wm., *Catalogue of a Collection of Early French Books in the Library of C. Fairfax Murray,* 2 vols, London, 1961.

Delacotte, J., *Trois romans-poèmes du XIVᵉ siècle,* Paris, 1932.

Delisle, L., 'Notice sur un régistre de procès-verbaux de la Faculté de théologie de Paris pendant les années 1503–1533', *Notices et extraits des manuscrits de la Bibliothèque Nationale,* 36, 1899, pp.315–408.

Dez, Pierre, *Histoire des protestants et des églises réformées du Poitou,* La Rochelle, 1936.

Dhotel, J-C., *Les Origines du catéchisme moderne d'après les premiers manuels imprimés en France,* Paris, 1967.

Dictionnaire de l'Académie françoise, 4 vols, Paris, 1694.

Döllinger, J. J. I. von, *Fables respecting the Popes of the Middle Ages,* tr. A. Plummer, London, 1871.

Douen, O., 'Avant la Réformation. "La Déploration de l'Eglise" par Jean Bouchet. 1512', *Bulletin de la Société de l'Histoire du Protestantisme français,* année 5, Paris, 1857, pp.266–74.

Dreux du Radier, J. F., *Bibliothèque historique et critique de Poitou, contenant les vies des savans de cette province,* 5 vols, Paris, 1754.

Droz, E., *Chemins de l'hérésie. Textes et documents,* 4 vols, Geneva, 1970–76.

Du Bruck, E., 'Sebastian Brant in France: A "Ship of Fools" by Pierre Rivière (1497)', *Revue de littérature comparée,* 48, 1974, pp.248–56.

Dugast-Matifeux, 'Une fête à Nantes au XVIᵉ siècle: Jean Bouchet de Poitiers', *Revue des provinces de l'Ouest,* 3, 1855, pp.537–49.

Du Plessis d'Argentre, Charles, *Collectio Judiciorum de novis erroribus,* 3 vols, Paris, 1724–36.

Dumonteil, Joseph, s.j., *Histoire de la vie incomparable de saincte Radegonde,* Rodez, 1627.

Egasse du Boulay, César, *Histoire Universitatis Parisiensis,* 6 vols, Paris, 1665–73.

Favreau, Robert, 'Aspects de l'université de Poitiers au XVᵉ siècle', *BSAO,* 4ᵉ série, v, années 1959–60, pp.31–71.

Favreau, Robert, *La Ville de Poitiers à la fin du moyen âge. Une capitale régionale,* 2 vols, Poitiers, 1978, (*MSAO,* 4ᵉ série, xiv, années 1977–78; supplément au *BSAO,* 3ᵉ trimestre, 1977).

Febvre, Lucien, *Le Problème de l'incroyance au XVIᵉ siècle: la religion de Rabelais,* Paris, 1947; revised ed. 1962.

Fraenkel, Eduard, *Horace,* Oxford, 1957; reprinted 1980.

Frappier, Jean, 'Sur quelques emprunts de Clément Marot à Jean Lemaire de Belges', *Mélanges de philologie et d'histoire littéraire offerts à E. Huguet,* Paris, 1940, pp.161–76.

Furetière, Antoine, *Dictionnaire universel*, 3 vols, La Haye–Rotterdam, 1690.

Giraud, Yves, [Reply to C. A. Mayer, 'Le Premier Sonnet français . . .'], *RHLF*, 68, 1968, pp.875–8.

Godefroy, F., *Dictionnaire de l'ancienne langue française et de tous ses dialectes, du IXe au XVe siècle*, 10 vols, Paris, 1880–1902.

Goujet, C. P., *Bibliothèque françoise ou Histoire de la littérature françoise*, 18 vols, Paris, 1741–56.

Grève, Marcel de, *L'Interprétation de Rabelais au XVIe siècle*, Geneva, 1961, (*Etudes rabelaisiennes*, vol.3).

Guenée, B., *Tribunaux et gens de justice dans le bailliage de Senlis à la fin du Moyen Age (vers 1380–vers 1550)*, Paris, 1963 (Publications de la Faculté des Lettres de l'Université de Strasbourg, fasc. 144).

Guenée, B. and Lehoux, F., *Les Entrées royales françaises de 1328 à 1515*, Paris, 1968.

Guiot, J-A. *Les Trois Siècles palinodiques ou Histoire générale des Palinods de Rouen, Dieppe etc.*, ed. A. Tougard, 2 vols, Rouen–Paris, 1898.

Guy, Henry, *Histoire de la poésie française au XVIe siècle*, vol.1, *L'Ecole des rhétoriqueurs*, Paris, 1910.

Hamon, Auguste, *Un Grand Rhétoriqueur poitevin, Jean Bouchet, 1476–1557?*, Paris, 1901; Slatkine reprint, Geneva, 1970.

Harvey, H. G., *The Theatre of the Basoche. The Contribution of the Law Societies to French Mediaeval Comedy*, Harvard University Press, 1941.

Hauser, Henri, *Les Sources de l'histoire de France. Deuxième partie: le XVIe siècle (1494–1610)*, 4 vols, Paris, 1906–15.

Hauser, Henri, 'Etude critique sur "La Cronique du roy François premier de ce nom"', *Revue de la Renaissance*, 8, 1907, pp.49–63.

Hauser, Henri, 'Etudes critiques sur les sources narratives de l'histoire de France au XVIe siècle. ii. Annales et Chroniques', *Revue d'histoire moderne et contemporaine*, 5, 1903–04, pp.471–89.

Higman, Francis M., *Censorship and the Sorbonne. A Bibliographical Study of Books in French censured by the Faculty of Theology of the University of Paris, 1520–1551*, Geneva, 1979.

Histoire de l'Université de Poitiers. Passé et présent (1432–1932), ed. P. Boissonnade, Poitiers, 1932.

Holban, M., ' "Le Miroir de l'âme pécheresse" et "Les Epistres de la Noble et Amoureuse Dame"', *Mélanges offerts à M. Abel Lefranc*, Paris, 1936, pp.142–54.

Hulubei, Alice, *L'Eglogue en France au XVIe siècle. Epoque des Valois (1515–1589)*, Paris, 1938.

Hutton, James, *The Greek Anthology in France and in the Latin Writers of the Netherlands to the year 1800*, Ithaca, 1946.

Imbart de la Tour, P., *Les Origines de la Réforme*, 4 vols, Paris, 1905–35; vols 1 and 2, second ed., Melun, 1947 and 1944.

Index Aureliensis. Catalogus librorum sedecimo saeculo impressorum, Aureliae Aquensis, Prima pars, tomus V, (BOS-BVN), 1974.

Inventaire sommaire des archives communales antérieures à 1790: Ville de Nantes, ed. S. de la Nicollière-Teijeiro (vol.3 ed. R. Blanchard), 3 vols, Nantes, 1888, 1899, 1919.

Isaac, F. S., *An Index to Early Printed Books in the British Museum. Part 2, Section IV—France*, part proof, part MS, available in the British Library.

Jeanneret, Michel, *Poésie et tradition biblique au XVIe siècle*, Paris, 1969.

Jedin, Hubert, *Geschichte des Konzils von Trient*, 4 vols, zweite Auflage, Freiburg, 1951–75.

Jedin, Hubert, *A History of the Council of Trent*, vol.1, tr. E. Graf, London, 1957.

Jenkins, Michael F. O., *Artful Eloquence. Jean Lemaire de Belges and the Rhetorical Tradition*, Chapel Hill, 1980.

Jodogne, Pierre, *Jean Lemaire de Belges écrivain franco-bourguignon*, Brussels, 1972.

Joukovsky, F., *La Gloire dans la poésie française et néolatine du XVIe siècle (des rhétoriqueurs à Agrippa d'Aubigné)*, Geneva, 1969.

Joukovsky-Micha, F., *Poésie et mythologie au XVIe siècle. Quelques mythes de l'inspiration chez les poètes de la Renaissance*, Paris, 1969.

Jourda, Pierre, *Répertoire analytique et chronologique de la correspondance de Marguerite d'Angoulême, duchesse d'Alençon, reine de Navarre (1492–1549)*, Paris, 1930.

Jung, M-R., *Hercule dans la littérature française du XVIe siècle*, Geneva, 1966.

Jung, M-R., 'Poetria. Zur Dichtungstheorie des ausgehenden Mittelalters in Frankreich', *Vox Romanica*, 30, 1971, pp.44–64.

Kastner, L. E., *A History of French Versification*, Oxford, 1903.

Kastner, L. E., 'L'Alternance des rimes depuis Octovien de Saint-Gelais jusqu'à Ronsard', *Revue des langues romanes*, 47, 1904, pp.336–47.

Kastner, L. E., 'Les Grands Rhétoriqueurs et l'abolition de la coupe féminine', *Revue des langues romanes*, 45, 1902, pp.289–97.

Kelley, Donald R., *Foundations of Modern Historical Scholarship. Language, Law and History in the French Renaissance*, Columbia University Press, 1970.

Knecht, R. J., *Francis I*, Cambridge University Press, 1982.

Koch, Margrit, *Sankt Fridolin und sein Biograph Balther*, Zürich, 1959.

Krailsheimer, A. J., *Rabelais and the Franciscans*, Oxford, 1964.

La Bouralière, A. de, 'Bibliographie poitevine, ou dictionnaire des auteurs poitevins et des ouvrages publiés sur le Poitou jusqu'à la fin du XVIIIe siècle', *MSAO*, 3e série, 1, 1907, pp.LXXXIX–CXVI, 1–591.

La Bouralière, A. de, *L'Imprimerie et la librairie à Poitiers pendant le XVIe siècle*, Paris, 1900.

La Brosse, Olivier de, *Le Pape et le concile*, Paris, 1965.

Lachèvre, Frédéric, *Bibliographie des recueils collectifs de poésies du XVIe siècle*, Paris, 1922.

Lacombe, Paul, *Livres d'heure imprimés au XVe et au XVIe siècle conservés dans les bibliothèques publiques de Paris. Catalogue*, Paris, 1907.

La Croix du Maine, G. de and Du Verdier, *Les Bibliothèques françoises*, nouvelle édition, 6 vols, Paris, 1772–73.

La Garanderie, Marie-Madeleine de, *Christianisme et lettres profanes (1515–1535). Essai sur les mentalités des milieux intellectuels parisiens et sur la pensée de Guillaume Budé*, Lille–Paris, 1976.

La Trémoille, L. de, *Inventaire de François de La Trémoille, et comptes d'Anne de Laval*, Nantes, 1887.

[La Trémoille, L. de], *Les La Trémoille pendant cinq siècles*, 5 vols, Nantes, 1890–96.

Laurent, P., 'Contribution à l'histoire du lexique français', *Romania*, 65, 1939, pp.164–82.

Lea, H. C., *History of Sacerdotal Celibacy in the Christian Church*, third ed., 2 vols, London, 1907

Lebègue, R., *Le Mystère des Actes des Apôtres. Contribution à l'étude de l'humanisme et du protestantisme français au XVIe siècle*, Paris, 1929.

Lebègue, R., 'Rabelais et les grands rhétoriqueurs', *Les Lettres romanes*, 12, 1958, pp.5–18.

Ledain, B., 'Les Maires de Poitiers', *MSAO*, 2e série, xx, 1897, pp.215–774.

Lefranc, A., 'Un prétendu V^e livre de Rabelais', *Revue des études rabelaisiennes*, 1, 1903, pp.29–54, 122–42.

Lefranc, A., 'Sur quelques amis de Rabelais', *Revue des études rabelaisiennes*, 5, 1907, pp.52–6.

Lefranc, A., 'Rabelais secrétaire de G. d'Estissac', *Revue des études rabelaisiennes*, 7, 1909, pp.411–13.

Le Goff, Jacques, *La Naissance du purgatoire*, Gallimard, 1981.

Luther and Erasmus: Free Will and Salvation, tr. and comm. E. G. Rupp, A. N. Marlow, P. S. Watson, B. Drewery, *Library of Christian Classics*, vol.XVII, London, 1969.

Macfarlane, John, *Antoine Vérard*, London, 1900.

Marcel, Raymond, *Marsile Ficin (1433–1499)*, Paris, 1958.

Martin, V., *Les Origines du gallicanisme*, 2 vols, Paris, 1939.

Matheson, Peter, *Cardinal Contarini at Regensburg*, Oxford, 1972.

Mayer, C. A., 'Le Premier Sonnet français: Marot, Mellin de Saint-Gelais et Jean Bouchet', *RHLF*, 67, 1967, pp.481–93.

Mohl, Ruth, *The Three Estates in Medieval and Renaissance Literature*, New York, 1933.

Moore, W. G., *La Réforme allemande et la littérature française*, Strasburg, 1930.

Moreau, Brigitte, *Inventaire chronologique des éditions parisiennes du XVIᵉ siècle*, Paris, vol.1 (1501–10), 1972; vol.2 (1511–20), 1977.

Morse, Ruth, 'Medieval Biography: History as a Branch of Literature', *Modern Language Review*, 80, 1985, pp.257–68.

Mortimer, Ruth, *Harvard College Library. Department of Printing and Graphic Arts: Catalogue of Books and Manuscripts, Part 1: French 16th Century Books*, 2 vols, Cambridge, Mass., 1964.

Moss, Ann, *Ovid in Renaissance France. A Survey of the Latin Editions of Ovid and Commentaries printed in France before 1600*, The Warburg Institute, London, 1982.

Moss, Ann, *Poetry and Fable. Studies in Mythological Narrative in Sixteenth-Century France*, Cambridge, 1984.

Munn, Kathleen M., *A Contribution to the Study of Jean Lemaire de Belges*, New York, 1936.

Nelson, N. E., 'Cicero's "De Officiis" in Christian Thought 300–1300', *University of Michigan Publications, Language and Literature*, 10, 1933, pp.59–160.

Niceron, J. P., *Mémoires pour servir à l'histoire des hommes illustres dans la République des Lettres*, 43 vols, Paris, 1729–45.

Oulmont, Charles, *La Poésie morale, politique et dramatique à la veille de la Renaissance. Pierre Gringore*, Paris, 1911.

Ouvré, M. H., *Notice sur Jean Bouchet, poète et historien poitevin du XVIᵉ siècle*, Poitiers, 1858; (also in *MSAO*, année 1857, pp.5–50).

Pellechet, Marie, *Bibliothèque publique de Versailles. Catalogue des incunables et des livres imprimés de MD à MDXX*, Paris, 1889.

Pfürtner, Stephanus, *Luther and Aquinas—a Conversation*, tr. E. Quinn, London, 1964.

Picot, E., *Catalogue des livres composant la bibliothèque de feu M. le Baron J. de Rothschild*, 5 vols, Paris, 1884–1920.

Picot, E., *Notice sur Jacques Le Lieur, échevin de Rouen, et sur ses Heures manuscrites*, Rouen, 1913.

Picot, E., *Notice sur Jehan Chaponneau, docteur de l'Eglise réformée, metteur en scène du 'mistere des actes des Apostres' joué à Bourges en 1536*, Paris, 1879.

Picot, E. and Piaget, A., 'Une supercherie d'Antoine Vérard, "Les Regnars traversans" de Jehan Bouchet', *Romania*, 22, 1893, pp.244–60.

Plattard, Jean, 'Une oeuvre inédite et nouvellement découverte du grand rhétoriqueur Jean Bouchet, "Les Cantiques et oraisons contemplatives de l'ame pénitente"', *Revue du seizième siècle*, 9, 1922, pp.80–2.

Plattard, Jean, *L'Adolescence de Rabelais en Poitou*, Paris, 1923.

Plattard, Jean, 'Rabelais réputé poète par quelques écrivains de son temps', *Revue des études rabelaisiennes*, 10, 1912, pp.291–304.

Rawles, Stephen, *Denis Janot, Parisian Printer and Bookseller (fl.1529–1544)*. *A Bibliographical Study*, 2 vols, PhD thesis, University of Warwick, 1976 (available in BN Réserve).

Reeves, Marjorie, *The Influence of Prophecy in the Later Middle Ages, A Study in Joachimism*, Oxford, 1969.

Renaudet, A., *Préréforme et humanisme à Paris pendant les premières guerres d'Italie (1494–1517)*, Paris, deuxième éd., 1953.

Renouard, Philippe, *Répertoire des imprimeurs parisiens, libraires fondeurs de caractères et correcteurs d'imprimerie, depuis l'introduction de l'imprimerie à Paris (1470) jusqu'à la fin du seizième siècle*, Paris, 1965.

Répertoire bibliographique des livres imprimés en France au seizième siècle, Bibliotheca Bibliographica Aureliana, Baden-Baden, 1968–   .

Rey-Flaud, Henri, *Le Cercle magique. Essai sur le théâtre en rond à la fin du moyen age*, Gallimard, 1973.

Richter, '"Von den losen Füchsen dieser Welt", nur eine Übersetzung aus dem Französischen des Jean Bouchet', *Zeitschrift für neufranzösische Sprache und Litteratur*, 9, 1887, pp.326–33.

Rigolot, François, *Poétique et onomastique. L'exemple de la Renaissance*, Geneva, 1977.

Rouy, François, *L'Esthétique du traité moral d'après les œuvres d'Alain Chartier*, Geneva, 1980.

Rutson, E. M., *The Life and Works of Jean Marot*, Thesis deposited at the Bodleian Library, Oxford, 1961.

Schmidt, C., *Histoire littéraire de l'Alsace à la fin du XVe et au commencement du XVIe siècle*, 2 vols, Paris, 1879.

Scollen, Christine M., *The Birth of the Elegy in France 1500–1550*, Geneva, 1967.

Screech, M. A., *L'Evangélisme de Rabelais*, Geneva, 1959, (*Etudes rabelaisiennes*, vol.2).

Screech, M. A., *The Rabelaisian Marriage*, London, 1958.

Seguin, J-P., *L'Information en France de Louis XII à Henri II*, Geneva, 1961.

Shaaber, M. A., *Sixteenth-century Imprints in the Libraries of the University of Pennsylvania*, Pennsylvania, 1976.

Shaw, D. J., 'More about the "Dramatic *Satyre*"', *BHR*, 30, 1968, pp.301–25.

Sherman, Michael A., 'Political Propaganda and Renaissance Culture: French Reactions to the League of Cambrai, 1509–1510', *Sixteenth Century Journal*, VIII(2), 1977, pp.97–128.

Smith, P. M., *The Anti-Courtier Trend in Sixteenth-Century French Literature*, Geneva, 1966.

Smith, P. M. and Mayer, C. A., 'La Première Epigramme française: Clément Marot, Jean Bouchet et Michel d'Amboise. Définition, sources, antériorité', *BHR*, 32, 1970, pp.579–602.

Soleil, F., *Les Heures gothiques et la littérature pieuse aux XVe et XVIe siècles*, Rouen, 1882.

Tchemerzine, A. and Plee, M., *Bibliographie d'éditions originales ou rares des auteurs français des XVe, XVIe, XVIIe et XVIIIe siècles*, Paris, 10 vols, 1927–33.

Tentler, Thomas N., *Sin and Confession on the Eve of the Reformation*, Princeton, 1977.

Thibaudeau, A. R. H., *Histoire du Poitou*, 3 vols, Niort, 1839–40.

Tierney, Brian, *Foundations of the Conciliar Theory*, Cambridge, 1955.

Tournoy-Thoen, G., 'Fausto Andrelini et la cour de France', *L'Humanisme français au début de la Renaissance*, Colloque international de Tours (XIVe stage), Paris, 1973, pp.65–79.

Trinkaus, C. and Obermann, H. A. (eds), *The Pursuit of Holiness in Late Medieval and Renaissance Religion*, Leiden, 1974.

Trisolini, G., *Le Lexique de Jehan Marot dans 'Le Doctrinal des Princesses et nobles Dames'*, Ravenna, 1978.

Trtnik-Rossettini, Olga, *Les Influences anciennes et italiennes sur la satire en France au XVIe siècle*, Florence, 1958.

Tuve, Rosemond, *Allegorical Imagery. Some Mediaeval Books and their Posterity*, Princeton, 1966.

Vacant, J. M. A., Mangenot, E. and Amann, E. (eds), *Dictionnaire de théologie catholique*, 15 vols, Paris, 1899–1950.

Villard, François, 'L'Election de Claude de Tonnerre à l'évêché de Poitiers (19 août–23 septembre 1507)', *BSAO*, 4e série, 10, 1970, pp.469–80.

Waterworth, Rev. James, *The Canons and Decrees of the sacred and œcumenical Council of Trent*, London, 1888.

Yates, Frances A., *The Art of Memory*, London, 1966.

Zumthor, Paul, *Le Masque et la lumière. La poétique des Grands Rhétoriqueurs*, Paris, 1978.

Index of Names